OFFICE OF POPULATION CE  :YS
GENERAL REGISTER OFFIC

D0893227

1991 Census

Communal Establishments

Great Britain

volume 1 of 2

This report has been bound as two separate volumes. For the convenience of the reader, sections 1 to 14 of the text in the report, together with the Annexes, have been reproduced in full in both volumes. The main tables are divided between the volumes, although all titles are listed in section 14 of the text.

Laid before Parliament pursuant to section 4(1)
Census Act 1920

London: HMSO

© *Crown copyright 1993*

First published 1993

ISBN 0 11 691513 7

(this volume is one of two and should not be sold seperately)

Contents

Page

1 Introduction

1.1 This Report gives statistics for communal establishments in Great Britain from the Census which took place on 21 April 1991. It is published and laid before Parliament under the authority of, and to meet the requirements of, section 4(1) of the Census Act 1920.

1.2 The 1991 Census was the nineteenth in a series begun in 1801, and carried out every tenth year except 1941.

1.3 This Report is one of a series of Topic Reports to be published from the 1991 Census. The tables were designed after extensive consultation with census users.

1.4 The text of this Report gives brief background information on the 1991 Census and an introduction to the tables. It also includes a summary of the complete programme of *Census Reports* and other results from the Census (see section 9 and Annex A). There is guidance on how to obtain further information (see sections 11 and 12).

1.5 This Report was made possible by the co-operation of the public in responding to the Census, by the hard work of the temporary Census field staff who were involved in the delivery and collection of the Census forms, and by other help given locally. The Registrars General for England and Wales, and for Scotland are most grateful for all these contributions.

2 The 1991 Census

2.1 The Census asked 19 questions relating to each person and a further five for households. There was an additional individual question asked in Wales, and an additional individual and a housing question asked in Scotland.

2.2 People in communal establishments, such as hospitals, hotels, and prisons, were required to be listed by the manager or person in charge, and were enumerated on individual forms. A copy of the listing form is shown at Annex B. (In households, people were enumerated using a household form which covered up to six persons on the one form.)

2.3 The forms were delivered shortly before Census day by some 118,000 enumerators, each responsible for a precisely defined area, and then collected during the following days[1]. Enumeration went well over Great Britain as a whole, although some households, mainly in inner city areas, proved difficult to contact. The coverage of the population achieved by the Census is discussed in section 7.

2.4 Preparations for the Census began well in advance, and included trials in the field[2,3]. Consultation on the topics to be included took place in 1987-8 and the Government issued its plans in a Parliamentary White Paper in July 1988[4].

Parliament debated and approved plans for the Census at the end of 1989 and they became law shortly afterwards. Consultation on the form of statistical output started after the White Paper was published. Users were consulted about the content of this report in 1990 and 1991.

2.5 The first results of the Census were published in July 1991 in *Preliminary Reports*[5,6] for England and Wales, and for Scotland. These results were derived from summary records made by the field staff. The main processing of the Census began in June 1991, and the coding of answers and computer entry of data was completed in August 1992. Reports for each county in England and Wales, and for each Region in Scotland were completed with summary reports for Great Britain, Wales, and Scotland covering all topics in the Census (see Annex A).

2.6 The 1991 Census Reports to Parliament will be concluded by a *General Report* covering all aspects of the conduct of the Census; more information may also be obtained from the addresses given in paragraph 12.2.

3 Processing the Census

3.1 Census data were processed in two stages. Those questions ('items') which were easy to code, such as sex, age and marital status, were processed for all forms ('100 per cent level'). Those which were more difficult to code were processed later for only a 10 per cent sample of forms.

3.2 For those items processed at the 100 per cent level, including all results in this Report, data were coded and keyed, and were then automatically edited to remove invalid, inconsistent and missing data. An automatic procedure was used to impute values where no answer had been given, or where the answer was invalid or inconsistent with other answers. In essence, imputation was achieved by copying the value of the item to be imputed from the most recently processed person or household with similar characteristics[7].

3.3 For those items processed at the 10 per cent level, no imputation took place. Any invalid, inconsistent or missing data remaining after the edit stage was marked and a 'not stated' code allocated.

---

[1] Clark A. 1991 Census: data collection. *Population Trends* vol 70, pp 22-27. HMSO, 1992. ISBN 0 11 691368 1.

[2] Pearce D, Clark A and Baird G. The 1987 census test. *Population Trends* vol 53, pp 22-26. HMSO, 1988. ISBN 0 11 691220 0.

[3] Pearce D and Thomas F. The 1989 census test. *Population Trends* vol 61, pp 24-30. HMSO, 1990. ISBN 0 11 691280 4.

[4] *1991 Census of Population* (Cm 430). HMSO, 1988. ISBN 0 10 104302 3.

[5] OPCS. *1991 Census Preliminary Report for England and Wales*. HMSO, 1991. ISBN 0 11 691347 9.

[6] GRO(S). *1991 Census Preliminary Report for Scotland*. HMSO, 1991. ISBN 0 11 494180 7.

[7] Mills I and Teague A. Editing and imputing data for the 1991 Census. *Population Trends* vol 64, pp 30-37. HMSO, 1991. ISBN 0 11 691331 2.

4 Definitions

4.1 The 1991 Census enumerated all persons present on Census night in a variety of types of *communal establishment* in addition to those living in households. The term covers all establishments in which some form of communal catering is provided. Such establishments were enumerated using the L form, on which were listed the names of all persons present on Census night, together with individual (I) forms containing the relevant census questions. A copy of the L form for communal establishments is shown in Annex B.

4.2 In 1991, enumerators were instructed to contact the person in charge of the establishment, for example, the proprietor or manager, who then had the responsibility of listing on an L form all those present in the establishment on Census night and all who arrived on Monday, 22 April and who had not been included as present on a census form elsewhere. The names of any non-resident staff who happened to be on duty on the premises on Census night were not required to be listed.

4.3 The person in charge also had the responsibility of issuing I forms to persons present in the establishment on Census night and of collecting the completed forms, or of completing the forms where necessary in the cases, for example, of any persons who were incapable of completing the forms for themselves.

Special types of establishment

4.4 *Small hotels* and *guest houses* containing ten rooms or more were treated as communal establishments. Those that contained fewer than ten rooms were classified as communal establishments if there were present on Census night any resident staff other than the proprietor and his family *or* five or more guests. Otherwise, they were treated as households. *Inns* and *public houses* with no accommodation were treated as partly residential premises and H forms were issued in the usual way.

4.5 *Nurses' homes* and *students' hostels,* etc, with self-catering facilities were enumerated as communal establishments if there was someone in charge to take responsibility for issuing I forms. Otherwise, each person, or group of persons sharing meals or accommodation, was treated as a separate household.

4.6 *Private residences in the grounds of an establishment,* such as a doctor's house, a caretaker's cottage or a porter's lodge, were treated as households, but *flats or suites of rooms, within the main building* were treated as part of the main establishment, and persons living in such accommodation were enumerated on L and I forms.

4.7 *Service families or civilians, living in married quarters* as part of a military establishment were enumerated as households whether the quarters were located within or outside the boundaries of the establishment.

4.8 *Sheltered housing,* that is, accommodation provided for the elderly, handicapped etc, often fell between a communal establishment and a household, in that a main meal could be taken communally though each person had their own separate accommodation with facilities for cooking their own meals. If at least half the people within the sheltered housing complex *possessed* such facilities, they were all treated as separate households, and, if fewer than half, as members of a communal establishment.

4.9 *Annexes to communal establishments* were treated as part of the main establishment if located in the same Enumeration District (ED) *or* if meals were taken at the main establishment even though the annexe was in a different ED. The annexe was treated as a separate establishment if either located in a different ED *and* meals were provided at the annexe (breakfast counting as a meal) or there were facilities for self-catering; in these circumstances, if there was no one in charge to complete the L form and issue/collect I forms, the annexe was enumerated as though it were accommodation occupied by households, but at coding, such households were transcribed onto L and I forms.

4.10 *Itinerant caravan dwellers* (for example, with circuses or fairs) were treated as households.

Classification of establishments

4.11 A communal establishment is accommodation where some form of communal catering is provided. This includes places such as hospitals, hotels, hostels, homes for the elderly, and prisons; persons sleeping rough were also included in this category of enumeration. Respectively a household is defined as 'one person living alone or a group of persons (not necessarily related) living at the same address with common housekeeping - that is, sharing at least one meal a day or sharing a living room or sitting room'.

4.12 The classification of communal establishments shown below comprises 18 major categories used in the standard published output, and 25 sub-categories relating to 'client groups' which can be identified separately in commissioned tables - see section 11.

4.13 The first digit of the following classification represents the major group and the second digit the more detailed client group classification. In the main tables in this Report, only the first digit categories are identified. However, counts for the full classification of persons present in communal establishments on Census night are shown in Table A on page 4.

MEDICAL AND CARE ESTABLISHMENTS

1   NHS HOSPITALS/HOMES - PSYCHIATRIC

2   NHS HOSPITALS/HOMES - OTHER
     2.1   Mentally handicapped
     2.2   Other (including general)

3   NON-NHS HOSPITALS - PSYCHIATRIC

4 NON-NHS HOSPITALS - OTHER
    4.1 Mentally handicapped
    4.2 Other

5 LOCAL AUTHORITY HOMES
    5.1 Mentally ill (including children)
    5.2 Mentally handicapped (including children)
    5.3 Elderly
    5.4 Other

6 HOUSING ASSOCIATION HOMES AND HOSTELS
    6.1 Mentally ill (including children)
    6.2 Mentally handicapped (including children)
    6.3 Elderly
    6.4 Other

7 NURSING HOMES (non-NHS/LA/HA)
    7.1 Mentally ill
    7.2 Mentally handicapped
    7.3 Elderly mentally infirm
    7.4 Elderly
    7.5 Other

8 RESIDENTIAL HOMES (non-NHS/LA/HA)
    8.1 Mentally ill
    8.2 Mentally handicapped
    8.3 Elderly
    8.4 Other

9 CHILDREN'S HOMES
    9.1 Local authority
    9.2 Other

DETENTION, DEFENCE AND EDUCATION ESTABLISHMENTS

10 PRISON SERVICE ESTABLISHMENTS

11 DEFENCE ESTABLISHMENTS

12 EDUCATION ESTABLISHMENTS

OTHER GROUPS

13 HOTELS, BOARDING HOUSES, ETC

14 HOSTELS AND COMMON LODGING HOUSES (non-HA)

15 OTHER MISCELLANEOUS ESTABLISHMENTS
    15.1 Miscellaneous family establishments
    15.2 Others

16 PERSONS SLEEPING ROUGH

17 CAMPERS

18 CIVILIAN SHIPS, BOATS AND BARGES

4.14 *Groups 1 and 2* comprise:

- hospitals and nursing homes which are self-governed or managed by a Hospital Management Committee, a Board of Governors or a Hospital Trust, or directly by the Department of Health;

- nurses' homes and hostels managed by a Hospital Management Committee or a Board of Governors, even when the accommodation is separate from the main hospital premises; and

- rehabilitation centres provided within the NHS.

Homes and hostels for district nurses and private nurses' associations are included in *Group 15.2*. Separate accommodation occupied by, for example, a Medical Superintendent and his family, is treated as a household.

4.15 The 1981 term *psychiatric* has been retained for output from the 1991 Census, although this category consists only of hospitals and homes for the mentally ill. Hospitals in *Group 1* include those classified as such by the Department of Health and the three Special Hospitals (Broadmoor, Rampton and Ashworth - formerly Moss Side).

4.16 *Groups 3 and 4* include hospitals not managed under the NHS or by the Department of Health, and nurses' homes and hostels linked to such hospitals, even when separate from the main premises. *Group 3* includes mental/mental care hospitals, hospitals for the mentally ill and mental after-care units. *Group 4.1* comprises hospitals for the mentally handicapped and *Group 4.2* all other non-NHS hospitals.

4.17 *Group 5* comprises homes managed by local authorities but excludes homes run by voluntary, charitable or private organisations (see paragraph 4.20), and hostels managed by religious institutions, private individuals, commercial or voluntary organisations (included in *Group 14*).

4.18 *Group 6* includes:

- almshouses or Abbeyfield Societies registered with the Housing Corporation and Scottish Homes;

- residential homes registered with a local authority and managed by a housing association; and

- other homes and hostels managed by a housing association (except for housing association children's homes, which are included in *Group 9.2*).

4.19 *Group 7* includes nursing homes, convalescent homes and hospices run by voluntary, charitable or private organisations.

4.20 *Group 8* includes residential homes registered with the local authority, or exempt from registration and managed or funded by a voluntary, charitable or private organisation, such as Cheshire Homes. Residential homes managed by the NHS, a local authority or a housing association are classified to *Groups 1, 2, 5,* or *6* as appropriate.

Table A Persons present in communal establishments

	TOTAL PERSONS	Males	Females
Persons in communal establishments	**1,527,505**	**722,423**	**805,082**
1 - NHS hospitals/homes - psychiatric	47,302	21,588	25,714
2 - NHS hospitals/homes - other	237,326	91,236	146,090
2.1 - Mentally handicapped	23,196	12,585	10,611
2.2 - Other (including general)	214,130	78,651	135,479
3 - Non-NHS hospitals - psychiatric	4,791	2,331	2,460
4 - Non-NHS hospitals - other	14,405	5,595	8,810
4.1 - Mentally handicapped	1,922	996	926
4.2 - Other	12,483	4,599	7,884
5 - Local authority homes	128,684	42,441	86,243
5.1 - Mentally ill (including children)	6,043	3,760	2,283
5.2 - Mentally handicapped (including children)	17,489	9,699	7,790
5.3 - Elderly	97,291	24,458	72,833
5.4 - Other	7,861	4,524	3,337
6 - Housing association homes and hostels	23,635	10,811	12,824
6.1 - Mentally ill (including children)	1,281	726	555
6.2 - Mentally handicapped (including children)	2,149	1,172	977
6.3 - Elderly	9,845	2,230	7,615
6.4 - Other	10,360	6,683	3,677
7 - Nursing homes (non-NHS/LA/HA)	143,617	36,094	107,523
7.1 - Mentally ill	4,700	2,381	2,319
7.2 - Mentally handicapped	2,964	1,478	1,486
7.3 - Elderly mentally infirm	8,800	2,429	6,371
7.4 - Elderly	115,992	26,231	89,761
7.5 - Other	11,161	3,575	7,586
8 - Residential homes (non-NHS/LA/HA)	190,413	50,894	139,519
8.1 - Mentally ill	6,915	4,124	2,791
8.2 - Mentally handicapped	16,455	9,021	7,434
8.3 - Elderly	156,886	32,716	124,170
8.4 - Other	10,157	5,033	5,124
9 - Children's homes	13,140	7,145	5,995
9.1 - Local authority	8,280	4,522	3,758
9.2 - Other	4,860	2,623	2,237
10 - Prison service establishments	43,633	41,776	1,857
11 - Defence establishments	66,489	58,195	8,294
12 - Education establishments	270,013	154,317	115,696
13 - Hotels, boarding houses etc	269,362	153,281	116,081
14 - Hostels and common lodging houses (non-HA)	23,009	15,680	7,329
15 - Other miscellaneous establishments	40,255	21,348	18,907
15.1 - Miscellaneous family establishments	5,749	2,152	3,597
15.2 - Others	34,506	19,196	15,310
16 - Persons sleeping rough	2,827	2,397	430
17 - Campers	1,522	814	708
18 - Civilian ships, boats and barges	7,082	6,480	602

4.21 *Group 9.1* comprises children's homes maintained, controlled or assisted by the local authority, and *Group 9.2* includes children's homes and hostels provided, or maintained, by voluntary organisations, and 'households' with five or more foster children. Residential schools and homes for physically handicapped and disabled children, maintained or assisted by educational authorities, are included in *Group 12* (see paragraph 4.24).

4.22 *Group 10* includes prisons, detention centres and young offender institutions. Excluded are: approved schools, ex-offenders' hostels, and probation and remand homes (included in *Group 5.4*); police stations with a lock-up (included in *Group 15.2*); and Special Hospitals (see paragraph 4.15).

4.23 *Group 11* comprises:

* Army and Air Force camps or establishments, naval shore stations and vessels maintained by service personnel, Fleet Auxiliary vessels and Service hospitals;

* hostels and similar establishments for NAAFI personnel, even if located outside the grounds of the camp; and

* civilians in services establishments including NAAFI staff.

Married quarters for service personnel or civilians are excluded (see paragraph 4.7).

4.24 *Group 12* comprises:

* residential schools, training colleges, theological colleges, and university halls of residence and students' hostels administered by schools, colleges and universities;

* residential schools and homes for physically handicapped and disabled children maintained or assisted by education authorities; and

* religious institutions which are boarding schools or which have living accommodation for teachers.

Training schools provided exclusively for a single employer or for a trade association or government department are classified in *Group 15.2*. Wholly separate accommodation for teachers, caretakers, groundsmen, etc are treated as households.

4.25 *Group 13* includes hotels, boarding houses, apartment houses, inns, public houses with sleeping accommodation, residential clubs, health farms, holiday camps, YHA/YMCA/YWCA hostels, and other similar establishments providing board and accommodation for visitors. Households with 5 or more paying guests and/or resident staff are also included. Establishments described as hotels or inns but with no sleeping accommodation for guests are excluded, along with bed-and-breakfast accommodation for homeless families (included in *Group 15.1*), hotels with less than 10 rooms and less than 5 guests and 5 resident staff

(which are treated as households), and youth hostels managed by a Housing Association (included in *Group 6.4*).

4.26 *Group 14* includes hostels not covered in other groups, such as, common lodging houses and reception centres with resident staff, used by people as their main or only residence and run by religious institutions or voluntary organisations (for example, Salvation Army), or by private individuals, commercial organisations or local authorities. All housing association hostels are coded to *Group 6*.

4.27 *Group 15.1* includes bed-and-breakfast accommodation for homeless families, homes for families, hostels and shelters for women, and mother-and-baby homes. Maternity homes are classified elsewhere according to the management type. *Group 15.2* is a heterogeneous group consisting of fire stations, lighthouses and lightships, and hostels, homes, training centres, camps and institutions not classified elsewhere.

4.28 *Group 16* comprises *persons sleeping rough* at sites identified before the Census by voluntary organisations, local authorities and churches, as well as those persons who were counted by ordinary enumerators. In the tables, figures relate only to those persons sleeping rough in the open air on Census night and do not include persons of no fixed abode who spent Census night in shelters, hostels or squats, etc. *Group 17* includes persons sleeping in a tent or caravan with communal catering, or spending Census night out of doors for recreational purposes (often at a recognised camp site) with a stated permanent address elsewhere (see paragraph 3.6). Travelling people, encampments and circuses are treated as households (see paragraph 4.10).

4.29 *Group 18* includes all civilian boats, barges, ferries and ships with sleeping accommodation, but excludes naval vessels (*Group 11*), and lightships (*Group 15.2*). Houseboats are treated as households.

Changes since 1981

4.30 The number of major categories in the classification of communal establishments (*type of establishment*) analysed in the tables has expanded since 1981 from 12 to 18. The changes are:

* NHS hospitals/homes and non-NHS hospitals/homes become separately categorised, non-NHS homes are allocated to categories for homes;

* nursing and residential homes, covered by the 1984 Registration of Homes Act, excluding those managed by housing associations - see below; in 1981 nursing homes these were included in the *Hospitals and homes - other* category and residential homes in the *Homes for the old and disables* category;

* nursing homes and residential homes, covered by the 1984 Registration of Homes Act, and hostels, managed by housing associations included in a separate housing association category;

- homes managed by local authorities, except for children's homes, are separately categorised; and

- persons sleeping rough *(Group 16)* and campers *(Group 17)* are separately categorised.

Residence classification and status

4.31 The status of persons enumerated in communal establishments is obtained from the information given on *position in establishment* on the I form

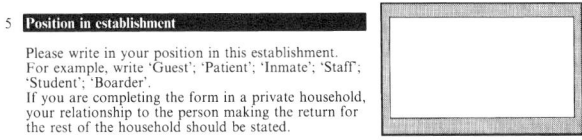

and the response to the *usual address* question. The full range of categories is:

1 Residents (non-staff)

   Visitors/guests
2   Residents in the UK
2a   *of which* Visiting staff/relatives of staff
3   Resident outside the UK
3a   *of which* Visiting staff/relatives of staff

4 Resident staff
5 Resident relatives of staff

4.32 *Residents* are persons stating 'this address' as their usual address; persons with a stated usual address of 'elsewhere' are classified as *visitors*. Visiting relatives of visiting staff are included in (3a). This classification is used in full in Table 8 in the *Communal Establishments* topic report. More generally, however, an abbreviated version of the classification, giving just three categories, is used in output. In terms of the groups shown above these are:

- Residents (non-staff) (1);

- Visitors (2)+(3); and

- Residents (staff) (4)+(5).

4.33 *Residents (non-staff)* comprises resident guests and inmates; *visitors* comprises guests, inmates, staff and relatives of staff with usual address 'elsewhere'; *residents (staff)* includes resident relatives of managers and staff. *Staff* includes managers of establishments.

4.34 Persons in defence establishments, civilian ships, boats and barges, sleeping rough or camping are all allocated to either category (1) or (2) depending on their answer to the usual address question, irrespective of their response to the question on position in establishment.

4.35 Definitions of all the terms used in these tables can be found in *1991 Census Definitions*[8]. Reference may need to be made to the volumes of *Definitions* for previous censuses if comparisons are being made - see also section 8.

---

5 Finding information in the Report

The tables

5.1 This Report contains eight tables. They are *cross-tabulations*, that is, where each element in the population is counted only once in the matrix of table *cells*. Some tables contain more than one cross-tabulation (see paragraph 5.9).

5.2 The answers people give to questions on individual census forms are not always consistent with one another. One of the jobs of the census edit system is to resolve such inconsistencies. Most have been resolved but a very small number of inconsistent records remain on the census data base and these have produced inconsistent results in some of the statistical tables in this volume. Where these occur they have been identified with an appropriate footnote.

5.3 The figure for persons sleeping rough for England and Wales is 21 less than the figure given in the Preliminary report Supplementary Monitor[9] issued in July 1991. The difference is due to minor processing errors, which have caused a shortfall in the figure in this report. The supplementary monitor identified persons sleeping rough at sites identified before the Census. No additional persons sleeping rough were recorded as having been identified by enumerators outside these sites.

5.4 Each table has a short *key word title* which appears at the head of each page and indicates the main feature of the table but not necessarily every aspect that is included. These key word titles are listed in table number order in section 14. The *Topic and key word index* in section 14 shows where particular topics and cross-tabulations of topics are to be found.

Table conventions

5.5 In each table, the figures for Great Britain as a whole are given first, with other area levels following in standard order. The area levels presented for each table are shown in the top right hand corner. They are also listed in the *Full table titles* in section 14. There are also a number of other standard conventions used in the tables.

Margins (row and column headings)

5.6 The *population base* or *bases* for each table (see section 6) are shown in the banner heading over the column headings; when a table contains two or more bases, these are separated by semi-colons.

5.7 Indentation in row headings indicates that counts in that row are *sub-totals* of counts in the previous non-indented rows (equivalent to the sub-divisions of column headings).

---

[8]OPCS/GRO(S). *1991 Census Definitions, Great Britain.* HMSO, 1992. ISBN 0 11 691361 4.
[9]OPCS. *1991 Census, Preliminary report for England and Wales, Supplementary Monitor on People sleeping rough* ISBN 0 90 495269 X.

5.8 Text set in italics signifies either that no counts appear for that row, or that counts in that row are a *sub-set* of a previous row and should not be added to other rows when totalling.

5.9 *Total rows* are indicated by bold type.

Counts

5.10 Counts in this Report are based on processing of all census returns (see paragraphs 6.2 and 6.3). A cell where the count is zero, but where a non-zero count was possible, is shown by a dash.

5.11 Two or more cross-tabulations within tables are separated by *ruled lines*. Where a table has a *total row* or *column* common to a number of cross-tabulations, it is usually shown only for the first cross-tabulation.

6 The population covered in this Report

6.1 The Census counts people in one of two basic ways - those who were *present* in an area on Census night, and those who were *resident* in an area whether or not they were present on Census night. Though the method of counting people present is unchanged from previous censuses, the method of enumerating people resident was revised for the 1991 Census with the inclusion of wholly absent households. Their inclusion provides a more complete count.

6.2 The Census placed a legal obligation on every household in which someone was present on Census night, and on every person present in a communal establishment, to complete a Census form whether they were resident there or a visitor. Additionally in 1991, for the first time in a British census, there was an arrangement to enumerate, on a voluntary basis, households at addresses where *nobody* was present on Census night. Census forms and reply paid envelopes were left for completion on the return of such *wholly absent households*. (This part of the enumeration was on a voluntary basis because members of the absent households would have either fulfilled their legal obligation by filling in forms if they were elsewhere in Great Britain, or, if they were outside Great Britain, had no such obligation.)

6.3 Generally, in cases of wholly absent households, or where no contact was made with a household which appeared to have had someone living there at census time, the census enumerator recorded an estimate of the number of residents, the type of accommodation and an estimate of the number of rooms. Where a wholly absent household did not subsequently return a form or where no contact was made with a household, values for those questions which were fully processed were imputed during computer processing using the basic information returned and data for a similar household living nearby.

6.4 The addition of data from wholly absent households is an improvement compared with the 1981 Census, when people from absent households were only enumerated where they were present on Census night (if in Great Britain). In 1981, people in wholly absent households, although included in the counts of people present if enumerated elsewhere, were excluded from the tables with a base of residents in most reports. An exception was the *1981 Census Usual Residence*[10] report in which people enumerated away from their area of usual residence were transferred back (see also paragraph 8.3).

Population base

6.5 The enumeration of persons in communal establishments comprised only of those persons present on Census night. Absent residents are not included.

6.6 Table 1 analyses all enumerated persons and, for households, identifies those persons present on Census night and resident (residents present); those persons resident but absent on Census night (residents absent); and those persons present on Census night but resident elsewhere (visitors).

6.7 Table 2 analyses enumerated persons present in households and in communal establishments; Tables 3, 4, 5, and 6 analyse persons present in communal establishments; Table 7 analyses the number of communal establishments and Table 8 analyses persons present and the number of rooms in hotels and boarding houses.

7 Evaluation of the Census results

7.1 In an exercise as large and complex as a census it is almost inevitable that some inaccuracies will arise from deficiencies and errors in coverage or response. The main causes are:

(a) failure to identify all residential accommodation;

(b) failure to identify all households and household spaces within accommodation;

(c) failure to enumerate all persons present or resident within households or communal establishments;

(d) errors in the estimates of numbers of persons in wholly absent households or where no contact was made;

(e) mis-classification of accommodation, for example, classifying wholly absent households as vacant, or vice versa;

(f) errors of double counting persons recorded as resident at more than one address;

(g) incorrect information supplied by filling in the forms, including missing responses; and

(h) errors introduced when processing the forms, including the imputation of data.

---

[10]OPCS/GRO(S). *1981 Census Usual Residence Report, Great Britain.* HMSO, 1983. ISBN 0 11 690933 1.

Steps are taken to assess the prevalence of these inaccuracies; but, because of the impracticability of conducting a very large number of one-to-one checks, the results are fairly broad estimates. These provide the basis of allowances for inaccuracies in the Census and provide users with indications of the degree of confidence that may be placed in the results. The figures in Census Reports themselves are **not** adjusted.

Coverage

7.2   At the time of preparation of this Report, the 1991 Census was estimated to have missed 2.2 per cent (or 1.2 million) of the **resident** population of Great Britain. No estimate of the under-coverage of persons present in the 1991 Census will be made but it may be taken to be of a level similar to that of the resident population. No separate estimate on any under-coverage relating to communal establishments has been made.

7.3   The effects of under-enumeration in the 1991 Census are likely to be unimportant for most applications. A coverage of over 98 per cent is very high by most standards - much higher than in most sample surveys. As with comparisons from the 1981 Census, relative differences between groups and areas for most topics included in the 1991 Census will still be valid using unadjusted Census data. There are two circumstances, however, in which the user might find it beneficial to take special action.

7.4   The first is where the user requires population numbers by age and/or by sex, rather than any relationship with other census topics and the requirement is for a local or health authority area, or an aggregate of these. In this case the mid-year population estimates for such areas should be used in preference to the Census resident counts. Mid-1991 population estimates for local authorities and health authorities were published in June 1993[11] and revised for England and Wales, in August 1993[12].

7.5   The second circumstance is where the user is studying census characteristics which are correlated strongly with sex and/or age and where comparisons might be affected by a known sex/age bias in the under-enumerated population. It is estimated that the under-enumeration ranges from zero for people aged 45 to 84, to around nine per cent for men in their twenties. Before considering making any adjustments, users should consider if a deficiency of that order could have a significant effect on the purpose they have in mind. In many cases it will not. If necessary, however, the approximate adjustment factors given in Table B can be applied to the appropriate Census counts, although the characteristics of those missed by the Census are not necessarily the same as for those counted. These adjustment factors are based on the final population estimates for mid-1991[12]. Furthermore, the adjustments may differ slightly between areas in Great Britain; in Scotland, for example there was no evidence of a shortfall in the population over 85.

7.6   Further guidance will be given in a Census User Guide to be published in Autumn 1993 and also in the Census *General Report* to be published in 1994. Information available on the levels of coverage in previous censuses is given in the corresponding *General Reports*[13-16].

Table B   Adjustment factors for estimated under-enumeration

Great Britain

Age	Persons	Males	Females
All ages	**1.02**	**1.03**	**1.01**
0- 4	1.03	1.04	1.03
5- 9	1.03	1.03	1.02
10-14	1.02	1.02	1.01
15-19	1.02	1.03	1.01
20-24	1.06	1.10	1.03
25-29	1.07	1.10	1.03
30-34	1.03	1.05	1.01
35-39	1.01	1.02	1.00
40-44	1.01	1.02	1.01
All age groups			
45-79	1.00	1.00	1.00
80-84	1.02	1.01	1.02
85 and over	1.04	1.01	1.06

8   Comparisons of results with those of earlier censuses

8.1   Comparisons between censuses are affected by changes in: the geographic base; the topics included in the censuses; and the definition of counts presented in the tables. The detail of changes over the long series of censuses is complex, and there is no single guide for users. The *Guide to Census Reports*[17] describes the general changes in censuses up to 1966. The local reports since the 1901 Census have listed intercensal boundary changes - on the lines of Annex A in the 1991 Reports for each county in England and Wales, and for each Region in Scotland. Annex A of *1991 Census Report for Great Britain*[18] gives all boundary changes between 1981 and 1991 in the areas shown in the tables in this Report; all were small changes.

[11]*Final mid-1991 population estimates for England and Wales and constituent local and health authorities based on 1991 Census results*. OPCS Monitor PP1 93/1 (Price £3.20); and *Provisional mid-1991 population estimates, Scotland*. GRO(S)

[12]*Revised final mid-1991 population estimates for England and Wales and constituent local and health authorities based on 1991 Census results*. OPCS Monitor PP1 93/2 (Price £2.00); and *Final mid-1991 population estimates, Scotland*. GRO(S) (to be published).

[13]OPCS/GRO(S). *Census 1981 General Report*. HMSO, 1990. ISBN 0 11 691330 4.

[14]OPCS. *Census 1971 General Report Part 3 Statistical assessment, Coverage checks England and Wales, Quality checks Great Britain*. OPCS, 1983. ISBN 0 904952 11 8.

[15]GRO, London/GRO, Edinburgh. *Census 1961 Great Britain General Report*. HMSO, 1968.

[16]GRO. *Census 1951 England and Wales General Report*. HMSO, 1958.

[17]OPCS/GRO(S). *Guide to Census Reports, Great Britain 1801-1966*. HMSO, 1977. ISBN 0 11 690638 3

[18]OPCS/GRO(S). *1991 Census Report for Great Britain*. HMSO, 1993. ISBN O 11 691536 6

Table C Comparability of classification of communal establishments 1981 and 1991

1981 description/category	1981 code	1991 code	1991 description/category
Hotels and boarding houses, etc	1	13	Hotels, boarding houses, etc
Hospitals/homes - psychiatric	2	1	NHS hospitals/homes - psychiatric
		3	Non-NHS hospitals - psychiatric
Hospitals/homes - other	3	2	NHS hospitals/homes - other
		4	Non-NHS hospitals - other
		7	Nursing homes (non-NHS/LA/HA)
Homes for the old and disabled	4	5	Local authority homes
		6	Housing association homes and hostels
		8	Residential homes (non-NHS/LA/HA)
Children's homes	5	9	Children's homes
Educational establishments	6	12	Educational establishments
Prison department establishments	7	10	Prison services establishments
Defence establishments	8	11	Defence establishments
Civilian ships, boats and barges	9	18	Civilian ships, boats and barges
Hostels and common lodging houses	10	14	Hostels and common lodging houses (non-HA)
Miscellaneous communal establishments	11	15	Other miscellaneous establishments
Campers, persons sleeping rough, etc	12	16	Persons sleeping rough
		17	Campers

8.2 Comparisons between censuses are also affected *in general* by different rates of coverage (see section 7). Users should take these differences into account, where appropriate.

8.3 The main statistical difference between the census reports for 1991, and the corresponding reports for 1981, is the inclusion of residents of wholly absent households in the 1991 resident population base (see section 6). This change does slightly affect comparisons between 1981 and 1991 figures, although not to any large degree.

8.4 The main statistical difference between this Report and the corresponding Report in 1981[19] is that the latter used a less detailed classification of communal establishments. A large degree of comparability however does exist as shown in Table C above.

8.5 There are some inconsistencies in this comparison which need to be noted:

(a) *Nursing homes*
These were coded to 1981 groups 2 or 3 hospitals/homes. In 1991 nursing homes formed a separate group, but nursing homes managed by health authorities, local authorities or housing associations were coded to 1991 groups 1, 2, 5 or 6 respectively. Homes categorised as psychiatric in 1981 would in 1991 have been placed in the appropriate 1991 category 1, 2, 5, 6 or 7, thus losing some comparability.

(b) *Housing association homes*
Homes owned or managed by a housing association in 1991 - whether registered as a 'resident' home or a nursing home - are grouped together in category 6. (A better comparability with 1981 for this group would be achieved by looking at the full classification of 36 categories - see paragraph 4.13.)

(c) *Local authority homes*
In 1981 local authority homes for the old and/or disabled persons etc were categorised to Group 4 and local authority homes and hostels for the mentally disordered (except homes for children) were classified to Group 2. In 1991 both these are categorised to Group 5.

(d) *YHA/YMCA/YWCA hostels*
These were included in Group 13 in 1991. In 1981 YHA hostels were included in Group 11, YMCA/YWCA hostels in Group 10.

8.6 It is probable that in coding establishments some errors have occurred due primarily to insufficient or inaccurate information being provided on the type and management of the establishment. Care therefore needs to be taken in making 1981-91 comparisons. Some confusion in 1991 existed between residential homes and nursing homes and the use of the abbreviation HA either to signify a housing association or a health authority. Some homes registered with a local authority

---

[19]OPCS/GRO(S). *Census 1981 Communal establishments for Great Britain.* HMSO, 1983. ISBN O 11 690935 8.

were confused with local authority homes. It is likely that confusion may also have arisen between private trust and NHS trust hospitals. Where possible reference was made to alternative sources such as *Laings Review of Private Healthcare, Yellow Pages*, telephone books and even telephoning local authorities, in order to achieve the correct categorisation.

8.7 For further information on the coding of establishments in the 1981 and 1991 Censuses please refer to the respective definitions reports. Detailed coding definitions can be obtained for both censuses from Census Customer Services.

9 Further results from the 1991 Census

9.1 The results of the Census are made available in two ways:

(a) in printed reports made to Parliament and sold by HMSO bookshops (or, in some cases, directly from the Census Offices); or

(b) in statistical abstracts available, on request and for a charge, from the Census Offices.

9.2 The results also tend to fall into two broad types: *Local Statistics* which cover a range of census topics for a specified area; and *Topic Statistics* - such as this Report - which focus on a particular census topic or sub-population in more detail, mainly at national and regional levels. There are also other products which provide further information from the Census. All the main results and products are described in *Prospectuses* in the OPCS/GRO(S) *1991 Census User Guide* series, available from the addresses given in paragraph 12.2. A brief guide to sources of results on other census topics and on *Local Statistics*, together with relevant *Prospectuses*, is included at Annex A.

10 Copyright and reproduction of material from this Report

10.1 All text, statistical and other material in this Report and information of any kind derived from the statistics or other material in the Report is CROWN COPYRIGHT and may be reproduced only with the permission of the Office of Population Censuses and Surveys (OPCS), also acting on behalf of the General Register Office (Scotland).

10.2 The Census Offices are prepared to allow extracts of statistics or other material from this Report to be reproduced without a licence, provided that these form part of a larger work not primarily designed to reproduce the extracts *and* provided that any extract of statistics represents only a

limited part of a table or tables *and* provided that Crown Copyright and the source are prominently acknowledged. The Census Offices reserve their rights in all circumstances and should be consulted in any case of uncertainty. Enquiries about the reproduction of material should be directed to OPCS at the address given in paragraph 12.2; reproduction may require a licence and payment of fees.

11 Commissioned tables

11.1 It is possible for users to commission tables to meet needs not met by reports to Parliament. A *1991 Census User Guide* (no.14) is available to assist users in commissioning such output.

11.2 The costs of commissioning a table (under section 4(2) of the Census Act) may be shared by two or more customers, provided that orders are received prior to processing of the request. The following types of commissioned tables are offered:

(a) *Extension tables for standard areas*: these are versions of tables in Topic Reports extended to lower area levels;

(b) *Extension tables - expanded variables*: these are tables in which one or more of the distributions of the standard variables are expanded from those appearing in the Reports;

(c) *New tables - standard variables*: these comprise tables with combinations of standard variables not otherwise cross-analysed in any Report;

(d) *New tables - customised variables*: these are tables with variables not otherwise produced in any of the Topic Reports in combination either with standard variables or with other customer-specified variables; and

(e) *Customer-specified areas*: these are tables (either standard or user-specified) for non-standard areas to be defined by the customer in terms of either wards (in England and Wales), postcode sectors or aggregations of EDs/Scottish Output Areas.

Customers requiring details of commissioned tables for which other users have so far expressed an interest may contact Census Customer Services at the address given in paragraph 12.2.

12 Further information

12.1 Any *queries* about the content of this Report or on the interpretation of the results in the Report should be made to:

> Census Division
> OPCS
> St Catherine's House
> 10 Kingsway
> London WC2B 6JP
>
> *telephone* 071-396 2008

12.2 All *Prospectuses/User Guides* mentioned in this Report may be obtained (by users in England and Wales, or outside Great Britain) from:

> Census Customer Services
> OPCS
> Segensworth Road
> Titchfield
> Fareham
> Hampshire PO15 5RR
>
> *telephone* 0329 813800

or, by users in Scotland, from:

> Census Customer Services
> General Register Office for Scotland
> Ladywell House
> Ladywell Road
> Edinburgh EH12 7TF
>
> *telephone* 031-314 4254

12.3 *Requests to reproduce material* from this Report - see section 9, should be made to Census Customer Services at OPCS. *Reports* published by HMSO may be purchased from the addresses shown on the back cover of this Report.

Census Newsletter

12.4 News on all aspects of the Census, including the availability of results, is provided by the *Census Newsletter* issued several times a year by the Census Offices and distributed without charge. Names may be added to the mailing list by contacting Census Customer Services. It is also possible to register with Census Customer Services as a user of the Census in order to obtain details of relevant products automatically and to ensure inclusion in consultation over future developments.

13 Reference map

13.1 The following map for Great Britain shows the Standard Regions, Counties and Metropolitan Areas of England, the Counties of Wales, and the Regions and Islands Areas of Scotland.

Standard regions and counties of England and Wales, and Regions of Scotland

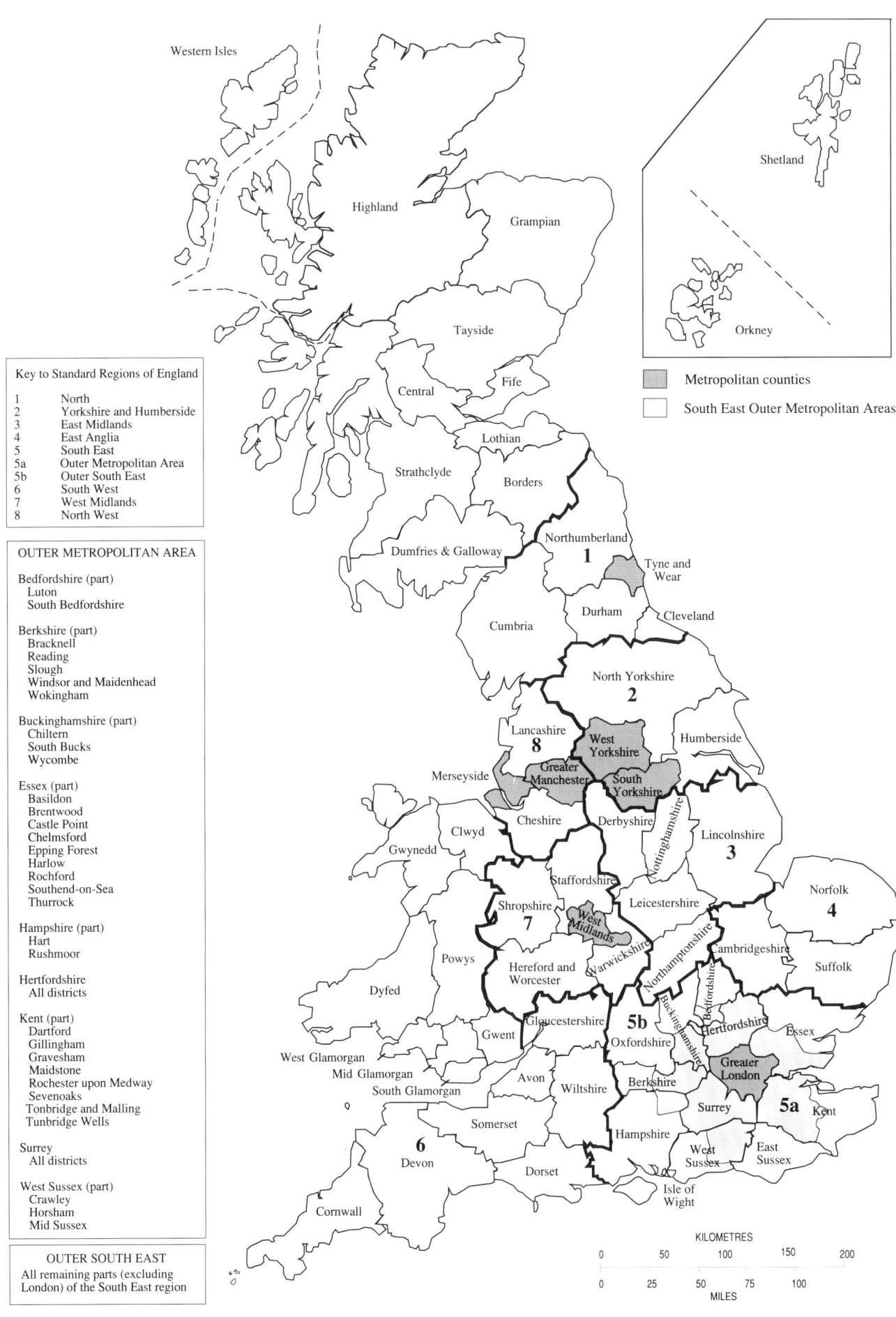

Key to Standard Regions of England

1	North
2	Yorkshire and Humberside
3	East Midlands
4	East Anglia
5	South East
5a	Outer Metropolitan Area
5b	Outer South East
6	South West
7	West Midlands
8	North West

OUTER METROPOLITAN AREA

Bedfordshire (part)
  Luton
  South Bedfordshire

Berkshire (part)
  Bracknell
  Reading
  Slough
  Windsor and Maidenhead
  Wokingham

Buckinghamshire (part)
  Chiltern
  South Bucks
  Wycombe

Essex (part)
  Basildon
  Brentwood
  Castle Point
  Chelmsford
  Epping Forest
  Harlow
  Rochford
  Southend-on-Sea
  Thurrock

Hampshire (part)
  Hart
  Rushmoor

Hertfordshire
  All districts

Kent (part)
  Dartford
  Gillingham
  Gravesham
  Maidstone
  Rochester upon Medway
  Sevenoaks
  Tonbridge and Malling
  Tunbridge Wells

Surrey
  All districts

West Sussex (part)
  Crawley
  Horsham
  Mid Sussex

OUTER SOUTH EAST
All remaining parts (excluding London) of the South East region

Metropolitan counties

South East Outer Metropolitan Areas

KILOMETRES

MILES

14 Indexes and tables

Tables by key word title

Topic and key word index

The numerical references in this index refer to the tables in this Report

Full table titles

Table 1 Present and resident populations

Great Britain, England & Wales, England, regions, metropolitan counties, Inner London, Outer London, regional remainders, Wales, Scotland

Persons present; residents

Sex	TOTAL PERSONS PRESENT	In communal establishments						Present	In households					TOTAL RESIDENTS
		Present	Visitors/guests		Residents		Total residents		Visitors		Residents			
			Resident in UK	Resident outside UK	Non-staff	Staff			Resident in UK	Resident outside UK	Present	Absent	Total	
a	b	c	d	e	f	g	h	i	j	k	l	m	n	o
GREAT BRITAIN														
All persons	**54,156,068**	**1,527,505**	**607,699**	**86,655**	**735,676**	**97,475**	**833,151**	**52,628,563**	**927,106**	**168,795**	**51,532,662**	**2,523,031**	**54,055,693**	**54,888,844**
Males	26,198,162	722,423	327,629	51,836	299,399	43,559	342,958	25,475,739	462,553	81,795	24,931,391	1,300,605	26,231,996	26,574,954
Females	27,957,906	805,082	280,070	34,819	436,277	53,916	490,193	27,152,824	464,553	87,000	26,601,271	1,222,426	27,823,697	28,313,890
ENGLAND & WALES														
All persons	**49,193,916**	**1,372,664**	**537,837**	**79,092**	**667,157**	**88,578**	**755,735**	**47,821,252**	**825,805**	**156,013**	**46,839,434**	**2,295,108**	**49,134,542**	**49,890,277**
Males	23,826,594	647,904	290,237	47,213	270,928	39,526	310,454	23,178,690	412,212	75,063	22,691,415	1,181,124	23,872,539	24,182,993
Females	25,367,322	724,760	247,600	31,879	396,229	49,052	445,281	24,642,562	413,593	80,950	24,148,019	1,113,984	25,262,003	25,707,284
ENGLAND														
All persons	**46,382,051**	**1,300,772**	**506,227**	**76,709**	**633,197**	**84,639**	**717,836**	**45,081,279**	**772,977**	**150,192**	**44,158,110**	**2,179,258**	**46,337,368**	**47,055,204**
Males	22,469,708	616,954	274,584	45,776	258,940	37,654	296,594	21,852,754	386,282	71,890	21,394,582	1,121,713	22,516,295	22,812,889
Females	23,912,343	683,818	231,643	30,933	374,257	46,985	421,242	23,228,525	386,695	78,302	22,763,528	1,057,545	23,821,073	24,242,315
NORTH REGION														
All persons	**3,018,679**	**76,913**	**33,742**	**2,807**	**35,761**	**4,603**	**40,364**	**2,941,766**	**50,317**	**5,757**	**2,885,692**	**100,676**	**2,986,368**	**3,026,732**
Males	1,457,472	36,003	18,464	1,727	13,506	2,306	15,812	1,421,469	26,041	3,357	1,392,071	54,472	1,446,543	1,462,355
Females	1,561,207	40,910	15,278	1,080	22,255	2,297	24,552	1,520,297	24,276	2,400	1,493,621	46,204	1,539,825	1,564,377
Tyne & Wear Metropolitan County														
All persons	**1,089,808**	**22,777**	**9,598**	**839**	**11,758**	**582**	**12,340**	**1,067,031**	**18,828**	**2,429**	**1,045,774**	**37,038**	**1,082,812**	**1,095,152**
Males	521,957	9,953	4,923	505	4,266	259	4,525	512,004	10,021	1,457	500,526	20,187	520,713	525,238
Females	567,851	12,824	4,675	334	7,492	323	7,815	555,027	8,807	972	545,248	16,851	562,099	569,914

Table 1 Present and resident populations – **continued**

Great Britain, England & Wales, England, regions, metropolitan counties, Inner London, Outer London, regional remainders, Wales, Scotland

Persons present; residents

Sex	TOTAL PERSONS PRESENT	In communal establishments								In households					TOTAL RESIDENTS
		Present	Visitors/guests		Residents		Total residents	Present	Visitors		Present	Residents		Total	
			Resident in UK	Resident outside UK	Non-staff	Staff			Resident in UK	Resident outside UK		Absent			
a	b	c	d	e	f	g	h	i	j	k	l	m	n	o
Remainder of North Region														
All persons	1,928,871	54,136	24,144	1,968	24,003	4,021	28,024	1,874,735	31,489	3,328	1,839,918	63,638	1,903,556	1,931,580
Males	935,515	26,050	13,541	1,222	9,240	2,047	11,287	909,465	16,020	1,900	891,545	34,285	925,830	937,117
Females	993,356	28,086	10,603	746	14,763	1,974	16,737	965,270	15,469	1,428	948,373	29,353	977,726	994,463
YORKSHIRE & HUMBERSIDE REGION														
All persons	4,796,562	113,945	44,379	3,466	60,360	5,740	66,100	4,682,617	83,167	9,539	4,589,911	180,513	4,770,424	4,836,524
Males	2,322,506	51,609	23,130	2,193	23,808	2,478	26,286	2,270,897	41,732	4,999	2,224,166	93,677	2,317,843	2,344,129
Females	2,474,056	62,336	21,249	1,273	36,552	3,262	39,814	2,411,720	41,435	4,540	2,365,745	86,836	2,452,581	2,492,395
South Yorkshire Metropolitan County														
All persons	1,253,959	23,750	10,143	402	12,537	668	13,205	1,230,209	19,881	1,788	1,208,540	40,885	1,249,425	1,262,630
Males	610,054	10,691	5,424	234	4,801	232	5,033	599,363	10,342	942	588,079	21,019	609,098	614,131
Females	643,905	13,059	4,719	168	7,736	436	8,172	630,846	9,539	846	620,461	19,866	640,327	648,499
West Yorkshire Metropolitan County														
All persons	1,991,540	40,379	16,400	826	21,406	1,747	23,153	1,951,161	32,248	3,920	1,914,993	75,547	1,990,540	2,013,693
Males	962,073	17,135	8,368	516	7,540	711	8,251	944,938	16,460	2,036	926,442	38,499	964,941	973,192
Females	1,029,467	23,244	8,032	310	13,866	1,036	14,902	1,006,223	15,788	1,884	988,551	37,048	1,025,599	1,040,501
Remainder of Yorkshire & Humberside Region														
All persons	1,551,063	49,816	17,836	2,238	26,417	3,325	29,742	1,501,247	31,038	3,831	1,466,378	64,081	1,530,459	1,560,201
Males	750,379	23,783	9,338	1,443	11,467	1,535	13,002	726,596	14,930	2,021	709,645	34,159	743,804	756,806
Females	800,684	26,033	8,498	795	14,950	1,790	16,740	774,651	16,108	1,810	756,733	29,922	786,655	803,395

Table 1 Present and resident populations – **continued**

Persons present; residents

Sex	TOTAL PERSONS PRESENT	In communal establishments						In households						TOTAL RESIDENTS
		Present	Visitors/guests		Residents			Present	Visitors		Residents			
			Resident in UK	Resident outside UK	Non-staff	Staff	Total residents		Resident in UK	Resident outside UK	Present	Absent	Total	
a	b	c	d	e	f	g	h	i	j	k	l	m	n	o
EAST MIDLANDS REGION														
All persons	3,919,483	91,182	37,812	2,922	46,496	3,952	50,448	3,828,301	58,928	7,443	3,761,930	140,994	3,902,924	3,953,372
Males	1,917,534	43,954	21,496	1,964	18,750	1,744	20,494	1,873,580	29,553	3,826	1,840,201	73,067	1,913,268	1,933,762
Females	2,001,949	47,228	16,316	958	27,746	2,208	29,954	1,954,721	29,375	3,617	1,921,729	67,927	1,989,656	2,019,610
EAST ANGLIA REGION														
All persons	2,018,617	68,263	30,918	3,897	30,191	3,257	33,448	1,950,354	34,701	6,823	1,908,830	84,726	1,993,556	2,027,004
Males	987,989	36,333	17,536	2,453	14,852	1,492	16,344	951,656	16,934	3,274	931,448	44,739	976,187	992,531
Females	1,030,628	31,930	13,382	1,444	15,339	1,765	17,104	998,698	17,767	3,549	977,382	39,987	1,017,369	1,034,473
SOUTH EAST REGION														
All persons	16,793,684	514,062	183,985	48,143	243,361	38,573	281,934	16,279,622	287,278	84,621	15,907,723	1,018,607	16,926,330	17,208,264
Males	8,121,075	250,086	101,987	27,923	103,828	16,348	120,176	7,870,989	142,356	37,939	7,690,694	519,454	8,210,148	8,330,324
Females	8,672,609	263,976	81,998	20,220	139,533	22,225	161,758	8,408,633	144,922	46,682	8,217,029	499,153	8,716,182	8,877,940
Greater London														
All persons	6,393,568	183,034	56,182	27,032	86,326	13,494	99,820	6,210,534	111,434	46,012	6,053,088	526,791	6,579,879	6,679,699
Males	3,064,314	86,291	29,161	15,249	36,990	4,891	41,881	2,978,023	56,184	20,023	2,901,816	261,899	3,163,715	3,205,596
Females	3,329,254	96,743	27,021	11,783	49,336	8,603	57,939	3,232,511	55,250	25,989	3,151,272	264,892	3,416,164	3,474,103
Inner London														
All persons	2,343,133	110,402	33,238	23,631	46,628	6,905	53,533	2,232,731	50,694	25,278	2,156,759	294,159	2,450,918	2,504,451
Males	1,117,125	55,525	17,448	13,219	22,325	2,533	24,858	1,061,600	26,096	11,348	1,024,156	145,828	1,169,984	1,194,842
Females	1,226,008	54,877	15,790	10,412	24,303	4,372	28,675	1,171,131	24,598	13,930	1,132,603	148,331	1,280,934	1,309,609

Table 1 Present and resident populations – **continued**

Great Britain, England & Wales, England, regions, metropolitan counties, Inner London, Outer London, regional remainders, Wales, Scotland

Persons present; residents

Sex	TOTAL PERSONS PRESENT	In communal establishments						Present	In households					TOTAL RESIDENTS
		Visitors/guests			Residents				Visitors		Residents			
		Present	Resident in UK	Resident outside UK	Non-staff	Staff	Total residents		Resident in UK	Resident outside UK	Present	Absent	Total	
a	b	c	d	e	f	g	h	i	j	k	l	m	n	o
Outer London														
All persons	4,050,435	72,632	22,944	3,401	39,698	6,589	46,287	3,977,803	60,740	20,734	3,896,329	232,632	4,128,961	4,175,248
Males	1,947,189	30,766	11,713	2,030	14,665	2,358	17,023	1,916,423	30,088	8,675	1,877,660	116,071	1,993,731	2,010,754
Females	2,103,246	41,866	11,231	1,371	25,033	4,231	29,264	2,061,380	30,652	12,059	2,018,669	116,561	2,135,230	2,164,494
Outer Metropolitan Area														
All persons	5,447,151	142,312	52,260	9,232	67,515	13,305	80,820	5,304,839	81,956	19,497	5,203,386	260,401	5,463,787	5,544,607
Males	2,662,493	69,652	29,907	5,759	28,162	5,824	33,986	2,592,841	39,858	8,773	2,544,210	136,751	2,680,961	2,714,947
Females	2,784,658	72,660	22,353	3,473	39,353	7,481	46,834	2,711,998	42,098	10,724	2,659,176	123,650	2,782,826	2,829,660
Outer South East														
All persons	4,952,965	188,716	75,543	11,879	89,520	11,774	101,294	4,764,249	93,888	19,112	4,651,249	231,415	4,882,664	4,983,958
Males	2,394,268	94,143	42,919	6,915	38,676	5,633	44,309	2,300,125	46,314	9,143	2,244,668	120,804	2,365,472	2,409,781
Females	2,558,697	94,573	32,624	4,964	50,844	6,141	56,985	2,464,124	47,574	9,969	2,406,581	110,611	2,517,192	2,574,177
SOUTH WEST REGION														
All persons	4,599,685	187,250	81,850	8,106	82,621	14,673	97,294	4,412,435	102,850	14,649	4,294,936	217,194	4,512,130	4,609,424
Males	2,218,432	89,974	43,273	4,869	34,542	7,290	41,832	2,128,458	50,176	7,175	2,071,107	112,472	2,183,579	2,225,411
Females	2,381,253	97,276	38,577	3,237	48,079	7,383	55,462	2,283,977	52,674	7,474	2,223,829	104,722	2,328,551	2,384,013
WEST MIDLANDS REGION														
All persons	5,088,565	105,681	42,449	3,719	54,252	5,261	59,513	4,982,884	69,783	9,358	4,903,743	186,931	5,090,674	5,150,187
Males	2,487,399	49,177	23,199	2,283	21,492	2,203	23,695	2,438,222	35,824	4,852	2,397,546	95,402	2,492,948	2,516,643
Females	2,601,166	56,504	19,250	1,436	32,760	3,058	35,818	2,544,662	33,959	4,506	2,506,197	91,529	2,597,726	2,633,544

Table 1　Present and resident populations – continued

Persons present; residents

Sex	TOTAL PERSONS PRESENT	In communal establishments						In households						TOTAL RESIDENTS
		Present	Visitors/guests		Residents		Total residents	Present	Visitors		Residents			
			Resident in UK	Resident outside UK	Non-staff	Staff			Resident in UK	Resident outside UK	Present	Absent	Total	
a	b	c	d	e	f	g	h	i	j	k	l	m	n	o
West Midlands Metropolitan County														
All persons	2,511,007	46,973	18,546	1,623	24,707	2,097	26,804	2,464,034	33,835	4,443	2,425,756	99,111	2,524,867	2,551,671
Males	1,222,308	21,129	9,271	1,005	10,150	703	10,853	1,201,179	17,621	2,274	1,181,284	50,013	1,231,297	1,242,150
Females	1,288,699	25,844	9,275	618	14,557	1,394	15,951	1,262,855	16,214	2,169	1,244,472	49,098	1,293,570	1,309,521
Remainder of West Midlands Region														
All persons	2,577,558	58,708	23,903	2,096	29,545	3,164	32,709	2,518,850	35,948	4,915	2,477,987	87,820	2,565,807	2,598,516
Males	1,265,091	28,048	13,928	1,278	11,342	1,500	12,842	1,237,043	18,203	2,578	1,216,262	45,389	1,261,651	1,274,493
Females	1,312,467	30,660	9,975	818	18,203	1,664	19,867	1,281,807	17,745	2,337	1,261,725	42,431	1,304,156	1,324,023
NORTH WEST REGION														
All persons	6,146,776	143,476	51,092	3,649	80,155	8,580	88,735	6,003,300	85,953	12,002	5,905,345	249,617	6,154,962	6,243,697
Males	2,957,301	59,818	25,499	2,364	28,162	3,793	31,955	2,897,483	43,666	6,468	2,847,349	128,430	2,975,779	3,007,734
Females	3,189,475	83,658	25,593	1,285	51,993	4,787	56,780	3,105,817	42,287	5,534	3,057,996	121,187	3,179,183	3,235,963
Greater Manchester Metropolitan County														
All persons	2,455,093	46,085	17,392	1,403	25,385	1,905	27,290	2,409,008	32,433	4,778	2,371,797	100,354	2,472,151	2,499,441
Males	1,185,536	18,478	8,346	860	8,576	696	9,272	1,167,058	16,913	2,578	1,147,567	51,562	1,199,129	1,208,401
Females	1,269,557	27,607	9,046	543	16,809	1,209	18,018	1,241,950	15,520	2,200	1,224,230	48,792	1,273,022	1,291,040
Merseyside Metropolitan County														
All persons	1,380,465	34,344	11,820	742	20,291	1,491	21,782	1,346,121	19,591	2,474	1,324,056	57,804	1,381,860	1,403,642
Males	654,764	14,229	5,891	528	7,218	592	7,810	640,535	10,073	1,319	629,143	29,413	658,556	666,366
Females	725,701	20,115	5,929	214	13,073	899	13,972	705,586	9,518	1,155	694,913	28,391	723,304	737,276

Table 1   Present and resident populations – **continued**

Great Britain, England & Wales, England, regions,
metropolitan counties, Inner London, Outer London,
regional remainders, Wales, Scotland

Persons present; residents

Sex	TOTAL PERSONS PRESENT	In communal establishments							In households						TOTAL RESIDENTS
		Present	Visitors/guests		Residents		Total residents	Present	Visitors		Residents			
			Resident in UK	Resident outside UK	Non-staff	Staff			Resident in UK	Resident outside UK	Present	Absent	Total	
a	b	c	d	e	f	g	h	i	j	k	l	m	n	o
Remainder of North West Region														
All persons	**2,311,218**	**63,047**	**21,880**	**1,504**	**34,479**	**5,184**	**39,663**	**2,248,171**	**33,929**	**4,750**	**2,209,492**	**91,459**	**2,300,951**	**2,340,614**
Males	1,117,001	27,111	11,262	976	12,368	2,505	14,873	1,089,890	16,680	2,571	1,070,639	47,455	1,118,094	1,132,967
Females	1,194,217	35,936	10,618	528	22,111	2,679	24,790	1,158,281	17,249	2,179	1,138,853	44,004	1,182,857	1,207,647
WALES														
All persons	**2,811,865**	**71,892**	**31,610**	**2,383**	**33,960**	**3,939**	**37,899**	**2,739,973**	**52,828**	**5,821**	**2,681,324**	**115,850**	**2,797,174**	**2,835,073**
Males	1,356,886	30,950	15,653	1,437	11,988	1,872	13,860	1,325,936	25,930	3,173	1,296,833	59,411	1,356,244	1,370,104
Females	1,454,979	40,942	15,957	946	21,972	2,067	24,039	1,414,037	26,898	2,648	1,384,491	56,439	1,440,930	1,464,969
SCOTLAND														
All persons	**4,962,152**	**154,841**	**69,862**	**7,563**	**68,519**	**8,897**	**77,416**	**4,807,311**	**101,301**	**12,782**	**4,693,228**	**227,923**	**4,921,151**	**4,998,567**
Males	2,371,568	74,519	37,392	4,623	28,471	4,033	32,504	2,297,049	50,341	6,732	2,239,976	119,481	2,359,457	2,391,961
Females	2,590,584	80,322	32,470	2,940	40,048	4,864	44,912	2,510,262	50,960	6,050	2,453,252	108,442	2,561,694	2,606,606

Table 2   Age and marital status

Great Britain, England & Wales, England, regions, metropolitan counties, Inner London, Outer London, regional remainders, Wales, Scotland

Persons present

Age	TOTAL PERSONS	Males					Females				
		Total	Single	Married	Widowed	Divorced	Total	Single	Married	Widowed	Divorced
a	b	c	d	e	f	g	h	i	j	k	l

GREAT BRITAIN

Age	TOTAL PERSONS	Total	Single	Married	Widowed	Divorced	Total	Single	Married	Widowed	Divorced
All persons present in communal establishments *	1,527,505	722,423	441,633	178,449	65,203	37,138	805,082	355,292	134,225	291,613	23,952
Aged											
0 - 4	24,684	13,430	13,430				11,254	11,254			
5 - 9	17,466	10,465	10,465				7,001	7,001			
10	8,378	5,167	5,167				3,211	3,211			
11	11,839	7,118	7,118				4,721	4,721			
12 - 14	47,460	29,001	29,001				18,459	18,459			
15	20,862	13,037	13,037				7,825	7,825			
16 - 17	49,952	31,153	31,065	71	5	12	18,799	18,699	88	9	3
18 - 19	115,058	62,745	62,284	387	19	55	52,313	51,691	566	19	37
20 - 24	199,238	112,619	106,732	4,956	80	851	86,619	80,682	5,355	84	498
25 - 29	103,111	64,215	47,757	13,395	116	2,947	38,896	26,342	10,899	114	1,541
30 - 34	67,392	43,823	22,681	17,022	139	3,981	23,569	11,051	10,349	149	2,020
35 - 39	52,501	34,240	13,367	16,292	194	4,387	18,261	7,036	8,861	211	2,153
40 - 44	52,594	33,419	11,481	16,899	263	4,776	19,175	6,461	9,869	322	2,523
45 - 49	46,281	28,332	9,643	14,175	320	4,194	17,949	5,488	9,580	525	2,356
50 - 54	41,489	24,394	7,732	12,676	466	3,520	17,095	4,958	9,200	877	2,060
55 - 59	39,293	21,960	6,991	11,443	671	2,855	17,333	4,840	9,147	1,642	1,704
60 - 64	47,716	24,994	8,711	12,061	1,557	2,665	22,722	6,516	9,939	4,478	1,789
65 - 69	57,951	28,344	9,250	13,120	3,641	2,333	29,607	7,660	10,405	9,761	1,781
70 - 74	67,753	28,341	7,940	12,517	6,135	1,749	39,412	9,107	9,762	19,030	1,513
75 - 79	99,254	33,503	7,444	13,224	11,402	1,433	65,751	12,738	10,552	40,987	1,474
80 - 84	135,334	34,611	5,838	11,440	16,455	878	100,723	17,527	10,111	71,787	1,298
85 - 89	129,783	24,849	3,176	6,503	14,810	360	104,934	18,079	6,550	79,485	820
90 and over	92,116	12,663	1,323	2,268	8,930	142	79,453	13,946	2,992	62,133	382
Visitors/guests	694,354	379,465	230,229	121,231	14,951	13,054	314,889	166,779	86,033	51,581	10,496
Aged											
0 - 4	16,010	8,840	8,840				7,170	7,170			
5 - 9	9,896	6,281	6,281				3,615	3,615			
10	6,632	4,192	4,192				2,440	2,440			
11	9,989	6,083	6,083				3,906	3,906			
12 - 14	40,275	24,929	24,929				15,346	15,346			
15	16,918	10,900	10,900				6,018	6,018			
16 - 17	39,469	24,266	24,204	52	3	7	15,203	15,135	60	7	1
18 - 19	84,153	44,341	44,083	220	13	25	39,812	39,458	323	11	20
20 - 24	108,180	60,331	57,106	2,843	49	333	47,849	44,079	3,515	52	203
25 - 29	47,428	28,944	19,070	8,661	60	1,153	18,484	9,682	7,971	67	764
30 - 34	34,356	21,745	8,073	11,853	67	1,752	12,611	3,763	7,637	89	1,122
35 - 39	27,098	17,537	3,688	11,917	88	1,844	9,561	1,856	6,338	113	1,254
40 - 44	26,856	17,165	2,567	12,559	124	1,915	9,691	1,340	6,779	167	1,405
45 - 49	23,244	14,155	1,905	10,495	154	1,601	9,089	930	6,617	309	1,233
50 - 54	21,234	12,240	1,348	9,450	209	1,233	8,994	796	6,666	538	994
55 - 59	21,051	11,189	1,165	8,754	349	921	9,862	822	7,193	1,048	799
60 - 64	24,407	12,147	1,298	9,427	666	756	12,260	1,085	8,031	2,411	733
65 - 69	28,515	13,830	1,262	10,526	1,447	595	14,685	1,299	8,234	4,479	673
70 - 74	27,566	12,508	1,030	9,036	2,054	388	15,058	1,514	6,429	6,629	486
75 - 79	29,316	12,098	953	7,805	3,043	297	17,218	1,837	5,198	9,814	369
80 - 84	26,523	9,350	762	5,034	3,387	167	17,173	2,127	3,148	11,630	268
85 - 89	17,113	4,770	364	2,074	2,283	49	12,343	1,657	1,405	9,149	132
90 and over	8,125	1,624	126	525	955	18	6,501	904	489	5,068	40

Note: * Includes two male members of staff and three female members of staff incorrectly enumerated as residents.

Table 2   Age and marital status – **continued**

Great Britain, England & Wales, England, regions, metropolitan counties, Inner London, Outer London, regional remainders, Wales, Scotland

Persons present

Age	TOTAL PERSONS	Males					Females				
		Total	Single	Married	Widowed	Divorced	Total	Single	Married	Widowed	Divorced
a	b	c	d	e	f	g	h	i	j	k	l

GREAT BRITAIN – *continued*

Resident - non-staff	735,676	299,399	183,605	44,658	49,962	21,174	436,277	151,015	35,795	238,749	10,718
Aged											
0 - 4	6,872	3,691	3,691				3,181	3,181			
5 - 9	5,395	3,008	3,008				2,387	2,387			
10	1,237	714	714				523	523			
11	1,320	764	764				556	556			
12 - 14	5,551	3,235	3,235				2,316	2,316			
15	3,360	1,820	1,820				1,540	1,540			
16 - 17	8,543	5,958	5,939	13	2	4	2,585	2,560	21	2	2
18 - 19	23,926	15,961	15,779	152	3	27	7,965	7,730	211	8	16
20 - 24	65,223	43,384	41,033	1,857	27	467	21,839	20,223	1,365	30	221
25 - 29	41,420	28,370	22,896	3,886	55	1,533	13,050	10,558	1,896	41	555
30 - 34	25,933	18,122	12,254	3,961	64	1,843	7,811	5,541	1,573	51	646
35 - 39	19,780	13,680	8,514	2,984	97	2,085	6,100	4,301	1,094	79	626
40 - 44	19,259	13,024	8,135	2,362	128	2,399	6,235	4,404	997	111	723
45 - 49	16,626	11,084	7,160	1,617	142	2,165	5,542	3,964	780	130	668
50 - 54	14,414	9,342	5,928	1,312	216	1,886	5,072	3,597	675	206	594
55 - 59	13,579	8,526	5,432	1,147	286	1,661	5,053	3,425	685	402	541
60 - 64	20,715	11,484	7,132	1,728	850	1,774	9,231	5,089	1,351	1,886	905
65 - 69	28,457	14,085	7,854	2,354	2,172	1,705	14,372	6,184	2,003	5,131	1,054
70 - 74	39,619	15,611	6,839	3,370	4,057	1,345	24,008	7,439	3,266	12,289	1,014
75 - 79	69,509	21,277	6,436	5,371	8,335	1,135	48,232	10,770	5,312	31,049	1,101
80 - 84	108,543	25,192	5,049	6,389	13,044	710	83,351	15,326	6,948	60,050	1,027
85 - 89	112,490	20,041	2,800	4,418	12,512	311	92,449	16,382	5,125	70,259	683
90 and over	83,905	11,026	1,193	1,737	7,972	124	72,879	13,019	2,493	57,025	342
Resident - staff	97,475	43,559	27,799	12,560	290	2,910	53,916	37,498	12,397	1,283	2,738
Aged											
0 - 4	1,802	899	899				903	903			
5 - 9	2,175	1,176	1,176				999	999			
10	509	261	261				248	248			
11	530	271	271				259	259			
12 - 14	1,634	837	837				797	797			
15	584	317	317				267	267			
16 - 17	1,940	929	922	6	-	1	1,011	1,004	7	-	-
18 - 19	6,979	2,443	2,422	15	3	3	4,536	4,503	32	-	1
20 - 24	25,835	8,904	8,593	256	4	51	16,931	16,380	475	2	74
25 - 29	14,263	6,901	5,791	848	1	261	7,362	6,102	1,032	6	222
30 - 34	7,103	3,956	2,354	1,208	8	386	3,147	1,747	1,139	9	252
35 - 39	5,623	3,023	1,165	1,391	9	458	2,600	879	1,429	19	273
40 - 44	6,479	3,230	779	1,978	11	462	3,249	717	2,093	44	395
45 - 49	6,411	3,093	578	2,063	24	428	3,318	594	2,183	86	455
50 - 54	5,841	2,812	456	1,914	41	401	3,029	565	1,859	133	472
55 - 59	4,663	2,245	394	1,542	36	273	2,418	593	1,269	192	364
60 - 64	2,594	1,363	281	906	41	135	1,231	342	557	181	151
65 - 69	979	429	134	240	22	33	550	177	168	151	54
70 - 74	568	222	71	111	24	16	346	154	67	112	13
75 - 79	429	128	55	48	24	1	301	131	42	124	4
80 - 84	268	69	27	17	24	1	199	74	15	107	3
85 - 89	180	38	12	11	15	-	142	40	20	77	5
90 and over	86	13	4	6	3	-	73	23	10	40	-

Table 2 Age and marital status – **continued**

Great Britain, England & Wales, England, regions, metropolitan counties, Inner London, Outer London, regional remainders, Wales, Scotland

Persons present

Age	TOTAL PERSONS	Males					Females				
		Total	Single	Married	Widowed	Divorced	Total	Single	Married	Widowed	Divorced
a	b	c	d	e	f	g	h	i	j	k	l

GREAT BRITAIN – continued

All persons present in households	52,628,562	25,475,738	11,374,740	12,307,945	725,140	1,067,913	27,152,824	10,239,818	12,525,091	2,902,475	1,485,440
Aged											
0 - 4	3,562,180	1,822,041	1,822,041				1,740,139	1,740,139			
5 - 9	3,382,516	1,731,957	1,731,957				1,650,559	1,650,559			
10	686,998	350,900	350,900				336,098	336,098			
11	680,952	348,250	348,250				332,702	332,702			
12 - 14	1,851,969	947,854	947,854				904,115	904,115			
15	631,304	322,575	322,575				308,729	308,729			
16 - 17	1,335,300	681,649	679,652	1,649	88	260	653,651	649,577	3,587	238	249
18 - 19	1,413,454	712,881	706,027	6,349	112	393	700,573	675,501	23,937	311	824
20 - 24	3,920,258	1,928,273	1,697,796	220,134	418	9,925	1,991,985	1,496,329	463,777	1,631	30,248
25 - 29	4,173,198	2,039,017	1,081,834	888,325	1,196	67,662	2,134,181	803,565	1,196,515	4,737	129,364
30 - 34	3,846,367	1,892,270	512,692	1,248,817	2,429	128,332	1,954,097	344,637	1,407,779	8,647	193,034
35 - 39	3,525,319	1,738,001	279,114	1,304,545	4,517	149,825	1,787,318	173,991	1,388,180	15,034	210,113
40 - 44	3,892,666	1,924,840	211,255	1,526,652	8,858	178,075	1,967,826	120,181	1,580,652	29,504	237,489
45 - 49	3,258,369	1,618,570	141,405	1,316,030	13,154	147,981	1,639,799	79,410	1,324,750	47,100	188,539
50 - 54	2,896,688	1,438,819	112,716	1,182,357	21,552	122,194	1,457,869	69,027	1,160,799	81,504	146,539
55 - 59	2,739,025	1,352,349	103,820	1,116,531	36,771	95,227	1,386,676	71,983	1,056,762	146,640	111,291
60 - 64	2,711,350	1,303,599	105,156	1,060,903	66,661	70,879	1,407,751	85,715	970,866	264,653	86,517
65 - 69	2,620,301	1,207,519	90,934	958,401	109,650	48,534	1,412,782	95,367	835,544	416,563	65,308
70 - 74	2,103,266	905,460	58,412	695,444	124,968	26,636	1,197,806	87,360	563,930	504,780	41,736
75 - 79	1,701,740	668,983	39,805	472,904	141,860	14,414	1,032,757	88,405	345,544	572,606	26,202
80 - 84	1,079,018	371,797	21,267	229,416	115,411	5,703	707,221	73,191	152,723	468,615	12,692
85 - 89	472,000	136,336	7,598	68,385	58,761	1,592	335,664	39,861	42,481	248,958	4,364
90 and over	144,324	31,798	1,680	11,103	18,734	281	112,526	13,376	7,265	90,954	931

ENGLAND & WALES

All persons present in communal establish-ments *	1,372,664	647,904	399,420	156,891	58,439	33,154	724,760	319,108	119,295	264,443	21,914
Aged											
0 - 4	22,408	12,218	12,218				10,190	10,190			
5 - 9	15,927	9,614	9,614				6,313	6,313			
10	7,800	4,837	4,837				2,963	2,963			
11	11,146	6,718	6,718				4,428	4,428			
12 - 14	44,166	26,992	26,992				17,174	17,174			
15	19,198	12,052	12,052				7,146	7,146			
16 - 17	46,065	28,805	28,726	65	4	10	17,260	17,169	80	8	3
18 - 19	102,404	56,253	55,822	363	16	52	46,151	45,586	517	16	32
20 - 24	181,205	102,180	96,853	4,476	77	774	79,025	73,618	4,866	75	466
25 - 29	92,929	57,605	42,929	11,912	109	2,655	35,324	24,034	9,767	108	1,415
30 - 34	60,204	38,963	20,343	14,950	119	3,551	21,241	9,949	9,332	134	1,826
35 - 39	46,614	30,270	11,991	14,242	162	3,875	16,344	6,322	7,894	195	1,933
40 - 44	46,632	29,522	10,295	14,756	221	4,250	17,110	5,719	8,796	282	2,313
45 - 49	40,993	24,966	8,604	12,349	283	3,730	16,027	4,883	8,527	472	2,145
50 - 54	36,430	21,359	6,839	11,006	399	3,115	15,071	4,408	8,031	765	1,867
55 - 59	34,237	19,096	6,148	9,890	557	2,501	15,141	4,317	7,896	1,382	1,546
60 - 64	41,786	21,939	7,776	10,440	1,356	2,367	19,847	5,729	8,580	3,883	1,655
65 - 69	50,687	24,734	8,134	11,337	3,159	2,104	25,953	6,759	9,022	8,554	1,618
70 - 74	59,928	24,909	6,972	10,997	5,366	1,574	35,019	8,039	8,625	16,959	1,396
75 - 79	88,368	29,694	6,495	11,766	10,126	1,307	58,674	11,223	9,450	36,635	1,366
80 - 84	121,677	31,059	5,170	10,307	14,761	821	90,618	15,239	9,152	65,021	1,206
85 - 89	117,799	22,540	2,739	5,948	13,518	335	95,259	15,796	6,028	72,661	774
90 and over	84,061	11,579	1,153	2,087	8,206	133	72,482	12,104	2,732	57,293	353

Note: * Includes one male member of staff and three female members of staff incorrectly enumerated as residents.

Table 2 Age and marital status – **continued**

Great Britain, England & Wales, England, regions, metropolitan counties, Inner London, Outer London, regional remainders, Wales, Scotland

Persons present

Age	TOTAL PERSONS	Males					Females				
		Total	Single	Married	Widowed	Divorced	Total	Single	Married	Widowed	Divorced
a	b	c	d	e	f	g	h	i	j	k	l

ENGLAND & WALES – *continued*

Visitors/guests	**616,929**	**337,450**	**207,392**	**105,420**	**13,169**	**11,469**	**279,479**	**149,372**	**75,491**	**45,204**	**9,412**
Aged											
0 - 4	14,276	7,937	7,937				6,339	6,339			
5 - 9	9,047	5,808	5,808				3,239	3,239			
10	6,224	3,950	3,950				2,274	2,274			
11	9,436	5,762	5,762				3,674	3,674			
12 - 14	37,697	23,315	23,315				14,382	14,382			
15	15,705	10,153	10,153				5,552	5,552			
16 - 17	36,378	22,367	22,311	48	2	6	14,011	13,948	56	6	1
18 - 19	73,962	39,197	38,959	204	10	24	34,765	34,453	286	8	18
20 - 24	97,099	53,968	51,091	2,531	48	298	43,131	39,760	3,146	43	182
25 - 29	41,824	25,358	16,755	7,541	57	1,005	16,466	8,663	7,052	63	688
30 - 34	30,140	18,903	7,059	10,265	55	1,524	11,237	3,330	6,824	81	1,002
35 - 39	23,728	15,251	3,239	10,339	75	1,598	8,477	1,659	5,602	104	1,112
40 - 44	23,465	14,897	2,235	10,887	107	1,668	8,568	1,180	5,977	140	1,271
45 - 49	20,262	12,246	1,654	9,056	135	1,401	8,016	801	5,834	274	1,107
50 - 54	18,343	10,563	1,172	8,124	177	1,090	7,780	692	5,747	462	879
55 - 59	18,033	9,612	999	7,500	296	817	8,421	692	6,143	871	715
60 - 64	20,934	10,474	1,127	8,116	572	659	10,460	909	6,886	2,009	656
65 - 69	24,483	11,923	1,081	9,061	1,241	540	12,560	1,078	7,101	3,785	596
70 - 74	24,072	10,975	882	7,942	1,800	351	13,097	1,268	5,651	5,735	443
75 - 79	25,791	10,716	823	6,922	2,697	274	15,075	1,536	4,644	8,558	337
80 - 84	23,482	8,352	665	4,527	3,007	153	15,130	1,784	2,822	10,277	247
85 - 89	15,319	4,276	311	1,881	2,039	45	11,043	1,409	1,279	8,231	124
90 and over	7,229	1,447	104	476	851	16	5,782	750	441	4,557	34
Resident - non-staff	**667,157**	**270,928**	**166,800**	**40,101**	**45,007**	**19,020**	**396,229**	**135,627**	**32,552**	**218,097**	**9,953**
Aged											
0 - 4	6,548	3,499	3,499				3,049	3,049			
5 - 9	4,983	2,778	2,778				2,205	2,205			
10	1,129	662	662				467	467			
11	1,228	708	708				520	520			
12 - 14	5,012	2,928	2,928				2,084	2,084			
15	2,969	1,614	1,614				1,355	1,355			
16 - 17	7,972	5,607	5,591	11	2	3	2,365	2,342	19	2	2
18 - 19	22,206	14,858	14,685	145	3	25	7,348	7,125	201	8	14
20 - 24	60,476	40,119	37,944	1,716	25	434	20,357	18,823	1,292	30	212
25 - 29	38,099	25,965	20,902	3,595	51	1,417	12,134	9,784	1,786	39	525
30 - 34	23,592	16,444	11,126	3,584	57	1,677	7,148	5,014	1,497	45	592
35 - 39	17,801	12,298	7,693	2,665	78	1,862	5,503	3,856	999	74	574
40 - 44	17,259	11,686	7,339	2,088	103	2,156	5,573	3,886	913	99	675
45 - 49	14,833	9,882	6,413	1,410	126	1,933	4,951	3,536	686	119	610
50 - 54	12,755	8,241	5,248	1,151	185	1,657	4,514	3,196	596	181	541
55 - 59	11,942	7,425	4,777	992	229	1,427	4,517	3,079	605	339	494
60 - 64	18,468	10,214	6,383	1,503	747	1,581	8,254	4,506	1,180	1,713	855
65 - 69	25,306	12,416	6,923	2,060	1,898	1,535	12,890	5,520	1,766	4,632	972
70 - 74	35,346	13,728	6,021	2,955	3,545	1,207	21,618	6,632	2,914	11,130	942
75 - 79	62,188	18,858	5,622	4,799	7,405	1,032	43,330	9,566	4,772	27,967	1,025
80 - 84	97,952	22,645	4,481	5,766	11,731	667	75,307	13,389	6,315	54,647	956
85 - 89	102,327	18,232	2,417	4,056	11,469	290	84,095	14,355	4,730	64,365	645
90 and over	76,766	10,121	1,046	1,605	7,353	117	66,645	11,338	2,281	52,707	319

Table 2 Age and marital status – **continued**

Great Britain, England & Wales, England, regions, metropolitan counties, Inner London, Outer London, regional remainders, Wales, Scotland

Persons present

Age	TOTAL PERSONS	Males					Females				
		Total	Single	Married	Widowed	Divorced	Total	Single	Married	Widowed	Divorced
a	b	c	d	e	f	g	h	i	j	k	l

ENGLAND & WALES – *continued*

Age	TOTAL PERSONS	Total	Single	Married	Widowed	Divorced	Total	Single	Married	Widowed	Divorced
Resident - staff	88,578	39,526	25,228	11,370	263	2,665	49,052	34,109	11,252	1,142	2,549
Aged											
0 - 4	1,584	782	782				802	802			
5 - 9	1,897	1,028	1,028				869	869			
10	447	225	225				222	222			
11	482	248	248				234	234			
12 - 14	1,457	749	749				708	708			
15	524	285	285				239	239			
16 - 17	1,715	831	824	6	-	1	884	879	5	-	-
18 - 19	6,236	2,198	2,178	14	3	3	4,038	4,008	30	-	-
20 - 24	23,630	8,093	7,818	229	4	42	15,537	15,035	428	2	72
25 - 29	13,006	6,282	5,272	776	1	233	6,724	5,587	929	6	202
30 - 34	6,472	3,616	2,158	1,101	7	350	2,856	1,605	1,011	8	232
35 - 39	5,085	2,721	1,059	1,238	9	415	2,364	807	1,293	17	247
40 - 44	5,908	2,939	721	1,781	11	426	2,969	653	1,906	43	367
45 - 49	5,898	2,838	537	1,883	22	396	3,060	546	2,007	79	428
50 - 54	5,332	2,555	419	1,731	37	368	2,777	520	1,688	122	447
55 - 59	4,262	2,059	372	1,398	32	257	2,203	546	1,148	172	337
60 - 64	2,384	1,251	266	821	37	127	1,133	314	514	161	144
65 - 69	898	395	130	216	20	29	503	161	155	137	50
70 - 74	510	206	69	100	21	16	304	139	60	94	11
75 - 79	389	120	50	45	24	1	269	121	34	110	4
80 - 84	243	62	24	14	23	1	181	66	15	97	3
85 - 89	153	32	11	11	10	-	121	32	19	65	5
90 and over	66	11	3	6	2	-	55	16	10	29	-
All persons present in households	47,821,251	23,178,689	10,340,610	11,197,284	653,072	987,723	24,642,562	9,272,201	11,379,300	2,623,481	1,367,580
Aged											
0 - 4	3,249,432	1,661,828	1,661,828				1,587,604	1,587,604			
5 - 9	3,069,151	1,571,799	1,571,799				1,497,352	1,497,352			
10	621,640	317,374	317,374				304,266	304,266			
11	616,861	315,507	315,507				301,354	301,354			
12 - 14	1,675,437	857,362	857,362				818,075	818,075			
15	569,365	290,847	290,847				278,518	278,518			
16 - 17	1,209,104	617,332	615,556	1,459	80	237	591,772	588,069	3,263	218	222
18 - 19	1,281,154	646,355	640,172	5,720	103	360	634,799	611,945	21,829	276	749
20 - 24	3,554,163	1,748,971	1,542,539	196,950	382	9,100	1,805,192	1,356,835	419,098	1,462	27,797
25 - 29	3,795,478	1,858,073	994,488	800,252	1,074	62,259	1,937,405	734,459	1,080,230	4,224	118,492
30 - 34	3,484,637	1,717,801	470,198	1,127,734	2,165	117,704	1,766,836	312,808	1,270,570	7,649	175,809
35 - 39	3,198,660	1,578,657	255,054	1,181,425	4,044	138,134	1,620,003	157,405	1,256,999	13,308	192,291
40 - 44	3,547,680	1,755,203	192,717	1,389,839	7,900	164,747	1,792,477	108,456	1,438,727	26,289	219,005
45 - 49	2,971,058	1,477,915	128,547	1,200,610	11,601	137,157	1,493,143	71,139	1,205,839	41,815	174,350
50 - 54	2,625,604	1,308,103	101,712	1,074,550	18,919	112,922	1,317,501	60,769	1,049,621	71,967	135,144
55 - 59	2,476,426	1,226,828	93,638	1,012,884	32,208	88,098	1,249,598	62,814	955,068	129,222	102,494
60 - 64	2,456,721	1,184,835	94,846	965,229	58,866	65,894	1,271,886	74,172	882,613	235,018	80,083
65 - 69	2,384,409	1,101,394	81,758	876,466	97,950	45,220	1,283,015	82,214	765,693	374,489	60,619
70 - 74	1,919,815	829,649	52,178	639,961	112,422	25,088	1,090,166	75,748	520,154	455,273	38,991
75 - 79	1,557,569	614,658	35,442	437,166	128,436	13,614	942,911	77,103	320,533	520,688	24,587
80 - 84	989,553	342,482	18,837	212,793	105,429	5,423	647,071	64,151	142,532	428,445	11,943
85 - 89	433,960	126,118	6,714	63,856	54,043	1,505	307,842	35,065	39,707	228,937	4,133
90 and over	133,374	29,598	1,497	10,390	17,450	261	103,776	11,880	6,824	84,201	871

Table 2 Age and marital status – **continued**

Persons present

Age	TOTAL PERSONS	Males					Females				
		Total	Single	Married	Widowed	Divorced	Total	Single	Married	Widowed	Divorced
a	b	c	d	e	f	g	h	i	j	k	l

						ENGLAND					
All persons present in communal establishments *	1,300,772	616,954	381,438	148,974	54,887	31,655	683,818	302,346	112,878	247,787	20,807
Aged											
0 - 4	21,409	11,675	11,675				9,734	9,734			
5 - 9	15,143	9,198	9,198				5,945	5,945			
10	7,022	4,449	4,449				2,573	2,573			
11	9,937	6,062	6,062				3,875	3,875			
12 - 14	42,140	25,841	25,841				16,299	16,299			
15	18,487	11,629	11,629				6,858	6,858			
16 - 17	44,269	27,777	27,706	59	4	8	16,492	16,408	74	7	3
18 - 19	97,015	53,681	53,267	347	16	51	43,334	42,804	487	14	29
20 - 24	173,334	97,885	92,798	4,268	72	747	75,449	70,304	4,649	64	432
25 - 29	89,352	55,381	41,304	11,419	105	2,553	33,971	23,197	9,332	100	1,342
30 - 34	57,961	37,534	19,606	14,395	117	3,416	20,427	9,584	8,993	127	1,723
35 - 39	44,834	29,135	11,548	13,709	156	3,722	15,699	6,077	7,577	187	1,858
40 - 44	44,607	28,336	9,880	14,166	215	4,075	16,271	5,470	8,349	271	2,181
45 - 49	39,043	23,869	8,252	11,769	275	3,573	15,174	4,650	8,036	447	2,041
50 - 54	34,619	20,331	6,512	10,464	384	2,971	14,288	4,170	7,609	727	1,782
55 - 59	32,433	18,118	5,812	9,373	532	2,401	14,315	4,113	7,432	1,295	1,475
60 - 64	39,364	20,752	7,360	9,867	1,283	2,242	18,612	5,373	8,074	3,594	1,571
65 - 69	47,485	23,163	7,592	10,633	2,956	1,982	24,322	6,360	8,439	7,982	1,541
70 - 74	55,885	23,217	6,491	10,234	5,003	1,489	32,668	7,485	8,075	15,789	1,319
75 - 79	82,388	27,693	6,058	11,007	9,400	1,228	54,695	10,512	8,846	34,049	1,288
80 - 84	114,054	29,106	4,797	9,674	13,872	763	84,948	14,274	8,623	60,912	1,139
85 - 89	110,713	21,162	2,537	5,596	12,720	309	89,551	14,846	5,700	68,256	749
90 and over	79,278	10,960	1,064	1,994	7,777	125	68,318	11,435	2,583	53,966	334
Visitors/guests	582,936	320,360	197,112	100,036	12,275	10,937	262,576	140,435	71,319	41,907	8,915
Aged											
0 - 4	13,599	7,574	7,574				6,025	6,025			
5 - 9	8,566	5,551	5,551				3,015	3,015			
10	5,518	3,599	3,599				1,919	1,919			
11	8,317	5,157	5,157				3,160	3,160			
12 - 14	36,042	22,375	22,375				13,667	13,667			
15	15,179	9,834	9,834				5,345	5,345			
16 - 17	34,896	21,522	21,472	43	2	5	13,374	13,316	52	5	1
18 - 19	69,441	37,073	36,845	195	10	23	32,368	32,073	271	7	17
20 - 24	91,886	51,160	48,439	2,387	44	290	40,726	37,545	2,981	36	164
25 - 29	39,932	24,252	16,028	7,212	54	958	15,680	8,278	6,701	56	645
30 - 34	28,980	18,183	6,770	9,903	54	1,456	10,797	3,210	6,564	78	945
35 - 39	22,802	14,681	3,105	9,963	75	1,538	8,121	1,592	5,366	98	1,065
40 - 44	22,398	14,279	2,136	10,455	102	1,586	8,119	1,111	5,675	130	1,203
45 - 49	19,244	11,682	1,575	8,637	130	1,340	7,562	761	5,494	261	1,046
50 - 54	17,394	10,034	1,090	7,739	170	1,035	7,360	659	5,432	435	834
55 - 59	16,984	9,065	917	7,092	281	775	7,919	658	5,771	813	677
60 - 64	19,696	9,901	1,071	7,662	547	621	9,795	832	6,487	1,855	621
65 - 69	22,919	11,175	1,004	8,499	1,156	516	11,744	1,002	6,645	3,526	571
70 - 74	22,337	10,156	805	7,356	1,665	330	12,181	1,173	5,267	5,319	422
75 - 79	23,888	9,962	768	6,452	2,482	260	13,926	1,424	4,336	7,843	323
80 - 84	21,830	7,764	613	4,214	2,790	147	14,066	1,651	2,649	9,537	229
85 - 89	14,300	4,004	285	1,774	1,903	42	10,296	1,318	1,208	7,650	120
90 and over	6,788	1,377	99	453	810	15	5,411	701	420	4,258	32

Note: * Includes one male member of staff and three female members of staff incorrectly enumerated as residents.

Table 2 Age and marital status – **continued**

Great Britain, England & Wales, England, regions, metropolitan counties, Inner London, Outer London, regional remainders, Wales, Scotland

Persons present

Age	TOTAL PERSONS	Males					Females				
		Total	Single	Married	Widowed	Divorced	Total	Single	Married	Widowed	Divorced
a	b	c	d	e	f	g	h	i	j	k	l

ENGLAND – *continued*

Resident - non-staff	**633,197**	**258,940**	**160,269**	**38,135**	**42,364**	**18,172**	**374,257**	**129,154**	**30,851**	**204,790**	**9,462**
Aged											
0 - 4	6,299	3,359	3,359				2,940	2,940			
5 - 9	4,775	2,669	2,669				2,106	2,106			
10	1,080	638	638				442	442			
11	1,159	668	668				491	491			
12 - 14	4,732	2,763	2,763				1,969	1,969			
15	2,817	1,532	1,532				1,285	1,285			
16 - 17	7,743	5,470	5,455	11	2	2	2,273	2,252	17	2	2
18 - 19	21,638	14,523	14,355	140	3	25	7,115	6,909	187	7	12
20 - 24	58,880	39,030	36,930	1,658	25	417	19,850	18,363	1,259	26	202
25 - 29	36,907	25,125	20,236	3,468	50	1,371	11,782	9,507	1,736	38	501
30 - 34	22,777	15,895	10,765	3,446	56	1,628	6,882	4,821	1,462	41	558
35 - 39	17,143	11,850	7,423	2,567	73	1,787	5,293	3,696	973	72	552
40 - 44	16,566	11,250	7,048	2,018	102	2,082	5,316	3,722	860	98	636
45 - 49	14,182	9,484	6,152	1,352	125	1,855	4,698	3,356	647	111	584
50 - 54	12,147	7,874	5,016	1,090	179	1,589	4,273	3,006	569	173	525
55 - 59	11,374	7,084	4,540	945	221	1,378	4,290	2,927	573	315	475
60 - 64	17,406	9,656	6,032	1,424	702	1,498	7,750	4,241	1,108	1,590	811
65 - 69	23,702	11,612	6,463	1,931	1,781	1,437	12,090	5,200	1,644	4,323	923
70 - 74	33,052	12,859	5,618	2,780	3,317	1,144	20,193	6,175	2,751	10,381	886
75 - 79	58,133	17,617	5,242	4,512	6,896	967	40,516	8,973	4,477	26,104	962
80 - 84	91,991	21,282	4,161	5,447	11,059	615	70,709	12,559	5,960	51,283	907
85 - 89	96,266	17,127	2,241	3,811	10,808	267	79,139	13,496	4,474	60,545	624
90 and over	72,428	9,573	963	1,535	6,965	110	62,855	10,718	2,154	49,681	302
Resident - staff	**84,639**	**37,654**	**24,057**	**10,803**	**248**	**2,546**	**46,985**	**32,757**	**10,708**	**1,090**	**2,430**
Aged											
0 - 4	1,511	742	742				769	769			
5 - 9	1,802	978	978				824	824			
10	424	212	212				212	212			
11	461	237	237				224	224			
12 - 14	1,366	703	703				663	663			
15	491	263	263				228	228			
16 - 17	1,630	785	779	5	-	1	845	840	5	-	-
18 - 19	5,936	2,085	2,067	12	3	3	3,851	3,822	29	-	-
20 - 24	22,568	7,695	7,429	223	3	40	14,873	14,396	409	2	66
25 - 29	12,513	6,004	5,040	739	1	224	6,509	5,412	895	6	196
30 - 34	6,204	3,456	2,071	1,046	7	332	2,748	1,553	967	8	220
35 - 39	4,889	2,604	1,020	1,179	8	397	2,285	789	1,238	17	241
40 - 44	5,643	2,807	696	1,693	11	407	2,836	637	1,814	43	342
45 - 49	5,617	2,703	525	1,780	20	378	2,914	533	1,895	75	411
50 - 54	5,078	2,423	406	1,635	35	347	2,655	505	1,608	119	423
55 - 59	4,075	1,969	355	1,336	30	248	2,106	528	1,088	167	323
60 - 64	2,262	1,195	257	781	34	123	1,067	300	479	149	139
65 - 69	864	376	125	203	19	29	488	158	150	133	47
70 - 74	496	202	68	98	21	15	294	137	57	89	11
75 - 79	367	114	48	43	22	1	253	115	33	102	3
80 - 84	233	60	23	13	23	1	173	64	14	92	3
85 - 89	147	31	11	11	9	-	116	32	18	61	5
90 and over	62	10	2	6	2	-	52	16	9	27	-

Table 2   Age and marital status – **continued**

Great Britain, England & Wales, England, regions, metropolitan counties, Inner London, Outer London, regional remainders, Wales, Scotland

Persons present

Age	TOTAL PERSONS	Males					Females				
		Total	Single	Married	Widowed	Divorced	Total	Single	Married	Widowed	Divorced
a	b	c	d	e	f	g	h	i	j	k	l

ENGLAND – continued

All persons present in households	45,081,278	21,852,753	9,762,515	10,546,291	613,178	930,769	23,228,525	8,762,354	10,718,622	2,458,786	1,288,763
Aged											
0 - 4	3,064,723	1,567,337	1,567,337				1,497,386	1,497,386			
5 - 9	2,889,603	1,479,975	1,479,975				1,409,628	1,409,628			
10	585,110	298,789	298,789				286,321	286,321			
11	580,248	296,571	296,571				283,677	283,677			
12 - 14	1,577,531	806,932	806,932				770,599	770,599			
15	535,748	273,526	273,526				262,222	262,222			
16 - 17	1,137,993	580,903	579,229	1,371	77	226	557,090	553,590	3,088	205	207
18 - 19	1,206,979	608,782	602,954	5,396	94	338	598,197	576,766	20,494	249	688
20 - 24	3,361,868	1,653,882	1,460,343	184,793	358	8,388	1,707,986	1,286,713	394,179	1,353	25,741
25 - 29	3,597,924	1,761,290	947,736	754,454	1,017	58,083	1,836,634	702,562	1,019,606	3,959	110,507
30 - 34	3,299,064	1,627,021	448,485	1,065,589	2,038	110,909	1,672,043	299,248	1,200,669	7,195	164,931
35 - 39	3,021,751	1,491,760	242,392	1,115,446	3,789	130,133	1,529,991	150,302	1,186,275	12,592	180,822
40 - 44	3,347,823	1,656,042	182,519	1,310,683	7,452	155,388	1,691,781	103,243	1,357,064	24,735	206,739
45 - 49	2,800,287	1,393,182	121,286	1,131,370	10,903	129,623	1,407,105	67,575	1,135,439	39,323	164,768
50 - 54	2,472,607	1,231,682	95,510	1,011,753	17,744	106,675	1,240,925	57,608	987,715	67,673	127,929
55 - 59	2,329,504	1,154,551	87,704	953,671	30,038	83,138	1,174,953	59,396	897,613	120,918	97,026
60 - 64	2,307,288	1,112,852	88,656	907,049	55,123	62,024	1,194,436	69,993	828,652	220,068	75,723
65 - 69	2,233,232	1,031,149	75,965	821,172	91,492	42,520	1,202,083	77,272	717,591	349,927	57,293
70 - 74	1,798,948	777,662	48,455	600,410	105,159	23,638	1,021,286	70,936	488,455	425,046	36,849
75 - 79	1,465,560	578,442	33,014	411,850	120,734	12,844	887,118	72,591	302,734	488,438	23,355
80 - 84	932,542	323,270	17,500	201,058	99,555	5,157	609,272	60,443	134,949	402,469	11,411
85 - 89	409,081	119,166	6,242	60,360	51,128	1,436	289,915	33,057	37,644	215,268	3,946
90 and over	125,864	27,987	1,395	9,866	16,477	249	97,877	11,226	6,455	79,368	828

NORTH REGION

All persons present in communal establishments	76,913	36,003	21,344	8,829	4,002	1,828	40,910	16,027	6,871	16,855	1,157
Aged											
0 - 4	1,045	586	586				459	459			
5 - 9	761	450	450				311	311			
10	326	193	193				133	133			
11	491	290	290				201	201			
12 - 14	1,753	1,068	1,068				685	685			
15	862	560	560				302	302			
16 - 17	2,305	1,503	1,501	1	1	-	802	798	4	-	-
18 - 19	6,252	3,433	3,412	17	2	2	2,819	2,801	18	-	-
20 - 24	9,226	5,313	5,088	180	4	41	3,913	3,611	276	1	25
25 - 29	4,174	2,661	1,988	550	7	116	1,513	884	550	7	72
30 - 34	2,933	1,948	1,059	704	6	179	985	416	473	5	91
35 - 39	2,376	1,585	670	711	6	198	791	303	381	9	98
40 - 44	2,504	1,609	583	786	12	228	895	266	474	22	133
45 - 49	2,324	1,438	520	709	14	195	886	233	527	23	103
50 - 54	2,177	1,276	406	680	19	171	901	225	508	66	102
55 - 59	2,081	1,162	352	633	43	134	919	232	517	82	88
60 - 64	2,777	1,454	522	686	108	138	1,323	364	605	258	96
65 - 69	3,497	1,747	576	727	267	177	1,750	430	576	640	104
70 - 74	4,095	1,796	519	713	460	104	2,299	467	495	1,253	84
75 - 79	5,799	1,993	432	728	760	73	3,806	660	551	2,534	61
80 - 84	7,617	1,965	334	592	992	47	5,652	803	496	4,304	49
85 - 89	7,066	1,329	179	317	814	19	5,737	854	301	4,542	40
90 and over	4,472	644	56	95	487	6	3,828	589	119	3,109	11

Table 2 Age and marital status – **continued**

Great Britain, England & Wales, England, regions, metropolitan counties, Inner London, Outer London, regional remainders, Wales, Scotland

Persons present

Age	TOTAL PERSONS	Males					Females				
		Total	Single	Married	Widowed	Divorced	Total	Single	Married	Widowed	Divorced
a	b	c	d	e	f	g	h	i	j	k	l

NORTH REGION – *continued*

Age	TOTAL PERSONS	Total	Single	Married	Widowed	Divorced	Total	Single	Married	Widowed	Divorced
Visitors/guests	36,549	20,191	12,296	6,304	861	730	16,358	8,340	4,582	2,895	541
Aged											
0 - 4	742	438	438				304	304			
5 - 9	440	266	266				174	174			
10	247	143	143				104	104			
11	403	241	241				162	162			
12 - 14	1,376	861	861				515	515			
15	627	428	428				199	199			
16 - 17	1,619	952	951	1	-	-	667	664	3	-	-
18 - 19	5,318	2,908	2,895	10	2	1	2,410	2,398	12	-	-
20 - 24	6,518	3,802	3,635	136	3	28	2,716	2,478	225	1	12
25 - 29	2,489	1,581	1,051	459	5	66	908	402	453	4	49
30 - 34	1,679	1,095	435	552	2	106	584	148	370	5	61
35 - 39	1,317	883	215	567	3	98	434	84	284	6	60
40 - 44	1,342	881	140	614	6	121	461	53	319	13	76
45 - 49	1,253	775	134	548	8	85	478	43	370	16	49
50 - 54	1,220	687	81	535	11	60	533	45	387	49	52
55 - 59	1,161	606	53	483	26	44	555	40	417	55	43
60 - 64	1,442	708	66	568	39	35	734	57	512	133	32
65 - 69	1,641	805	76	582	99	48	836	62	453	279	42
70 - 74	1,530	710	62	496	138	14	820	72	322	398	28
75 - 79	1,538	626	48	405	160	13	912	102	240	555	15
80 - 84	1,381	486	42	240	194	10	895	104	140	638	13
85 - 89	859	233	27	94	111	1	626	85	50	484	7
90 and over	407	76	8	14	54	-	331	45	25	259	2
Resident - non-staff	35,761	13,506	7,618	1,796	3,127	965	22,255	6,235	1,608	13,908	504
Aged											
0 - 4	197	106	106				91	91			
5 - 9	200	122	122				78	78			
10	56	39	39				17	17			
11	58	33	33				25	25			
12 - 14	301	170	170				131	131			
15	205	114	114				91	91			
16 - 17	571	496	495	-	1	-	75	75	-	-	-
18 - 19	602	375	370	5	-	-	227	221	6	-	-
20 - 24	1,573	1,028	987	31	1	9	545	513	25	-	7
25 - 29	1,064	743	653	50	2	38	321	265	41	2	13
30 - 34	889	618	497	64	3	54	271	215	40	-	16
35 - 39	787	546	401	64	2	79	241	180	28	3	30
40 - 44	844	561	410	57	5	89	283	196	36	8	43
45 - 49	743	498	365	40	6	87	245	179	31	4	31
50 - 54	683	449	306	43	8	92	234	163	23	11	37
55 - 59	668	419	280	44	15	80	249	178	25	19	27
60 - 64	1,229	686	444	77	67	98	543	303	64	117	59
65 - 69	1,822	928	496	135	168	129	894	366	114	353	61
70 - 74	2,541	1,075	455	209	321	90	1,466	389	170	851	56
75 - 79	4,242	1,364	384	323	597	60	2,878	552	307	1,973	46
80 - 84	6,224	1,472	291	350	795	36	4,752	697	355	3,664	36
85 - 89	6,203	1,096	152	223	703	18	5,107	767	250	4,057	33
90 and over	4,059	568	48	81	433	6	3,491	543	93	2,846	9

Table 2 Age and marital status – **continued**

Great Britain, England & Wales, England, regions, metropolitan counties, Inner London, Outer London, regional remainders, Wales, Scotland

Persons present

Age	TOTAL PERSONS	Males					Females				
		Total	Single	Married	Widowed	Divorced	Total	Single	Married	Widowed	Divorced
a	b	c	d	e	f	g	h	i	j	k	l

NORTH REGION – *continued*

Age	TOTAL PERSONS	Total	Single	Married	Widowed	Divorced	Total	Single	Married	Widowed	Divorced
Resident - staff	**4,603**	**2,306**	**1,430**	**729**	**14**	**133**	**2,297**	**1,452**	**681**	**52**	**112**
Aged											
0 - 4	106	42	42				64	64			
5 - 9	121	62	62				59	59			
10	23	11	11				12	12			
11	30	16	16				14	14			
12 - 14	76	37	37				39	39			
15	30	18	18				12	12			
16 - 17	115	55	55	-	-	-	60	59	1	-	-
18 - 19	332	150	147	2	-	1	182	182	-	-	-
20 - 24	1,135	483	466	13	-	4	652	620	26	-	6
25 - 29	621	337	284	41	-	12	284	217	56	1	10
30 - 34	365	235	127	88	1	19	130	53	63	-	14
35 - 39	272	156	54	80	1	21	116	39	69	-	8
40 - 44	318	167	33	115	1	18	151	17	119	1	14
45 - 49	328	165	21	121	-	23	163	11	126	3	23
50 - 54	274	140	19	102	-	19	134	17	98	6	13
55 - 59	252	137	19	106	2	10	115	14	75	8	18
60 - 64	106	60	12	41	2	5	46	4	29	8	5
65 - 69	34	14	4	10	-	-	20	2	9	8	1
70 - 74	24	11	2	8	1	-	13	6	3	4	-
75 - 79	19	3	-	-	3	-	16	6	4	6	-
80 - 84	12	7	1	2	3	1	5	2	1	2	-
85 - 89	4	-	-	-	-	-	4	2	1	1	-
90 and over	6	-	-	-	-	-	6	1	1	4	-
All persons present in households	**2,941,766**	**1,421,469**	**623,783**	**691,650**	**45,606**	**60,430**	**1,520,297**	**555,219**	**707,982**	**174,519**	**82,577**
Aged											
0 - 4	194,945	99,568	99,568				95,377	95,377			
5 - 9	193,243	99,084	99,084				94,159	94,159			
10	39,288	20,101	20,101				19,187	19,187			
11	39,554	20,118	20,118				19,436	19,436			
12 - 14	105,075	53,806	53,806				51,269	51,269			
15	35,907	18,167	18,167				17,740	17,740			
16 - 17	75,160	38,420	38,334	67	2	17	36,740	36,556	151	15	18
18 - 19	80,467	40,519	40,126	363	5	25	39,948	38,751	1,149	11	37
20 - 24	211,943	103,875	89,982	13,266	17	610	108,068	79,318	26,684	75	1,991
25 - 29	223,035	108,320	51,781	52,023	53	4,463	114,715	38,028	67,981	258	8,448
30 - 34	213,927	104,414	24,589	71,651	150	8,024	109,513	15,981	80,709	541	12,282
35 - 39	196,987	97,132	14,052	74,080	259	8,741	99,855	8,239	78,443	846	12,327
40 - 44	215,283	106,702	11,144	85,382	551	9,625	108,581	5,515	88,691	1,644	12,731
45 - 49	174,363	86,955	7,667	70,928	797	7,563	87,408	3,564	72,053	2,672	9,119
50 - 54	165,652	81,417	6,924	66,486	1,404	6,603	84,235	3,412	68,065	5,072	7,686
55 - 59	161,513	79,423	6,772	64,645	2,615	5,391	82,090	3,659	62,755	9,717	5,959
60 - 64	163,302	78,218	7,210	62,087	4,805	4,116	85,084	4,653	57,791	18,050	4,590
65 - 69	156,301	72,552	6,341	55,460	7,998	2,753	83,749	5,257	47,760	27,264	3,468
70 - 74	120,919	51,830	3,899	38,119	8,369	1,443	69,089	4,744	30,424	31,782	2,139
75 - 79	89,787	34,573	2,412	23,057	8,387	717	55,214	4,422	16,430	33,244	1,118
80 - 84	54,939	18,356	1,205	10,630	6,254	267	36,583	3,533	6,847	25,730	473
85 - 89	23,313	6,407	418	2,962	2,963	64	16,906	1,825	1,747	13,177	157
90 and over	6,863	1,512	83	444	977	8	5,351	594	302	4,421	34

Table 2 Age and marital status – **continued**

Great Britain, England & Wales, England, regions, metropolitan counties, Inner London, Outer London, regional remainders, Wales, Scotland

Persons present

Age	TOTAL PERSONS	Males					Females				
		Total	Single	Married	Widowed	Divorced	Total	Single	Married	Widowed	Divorced
a	b	c	d	e	f	g	h	i	j	k	l

Tyne & Wear Metropolitan County

Age	TOTAL PERSONS	Total	Single	Married	Widowed	Divorced	Total	Single	Married	Widowed	Divorced
All persons present in communal establishments	**22,777**	**9,953**	**5,623**	**2,353**	**1,381**	**596**	**12,824**	**4,855**	**1,753**	**5,882**	**334**
Aged											
0 - 4	368	214	214				154	154			
5 - 9	173	96	96				77	77			
10	46	23	23				23	23			
11	39	22	22				17	17			
12 - 14	184	106	106				78	78			
15	105	50	50				55	55			
16 - 17	376	172	172	-	-	-	204	202	2	-	-
18 - 19	2,487	1,276	1,270	4	1	1	1,211	1,207	4	-	-
20 - 24	2,640	1,421	1,385	29	2	5	1,219	1,134	77	-	8
25 - 29	1,029	636	478	130	3	25	393	222	147	1	23
30 - 34	674	430	231	167	-	32	244	103	113	2	26
35 - 39	586	410	159	191	2	58	176	53	94	1	28
40 - 44	616	406	137	199	4	66	210	60	112	5	33
45 - 49	527	340	102	173	4	61	187	53	103	6	25
50 - 54	528	350	115	161	8	66	178	39	93	18	28
55 - 59	528	313	112	131	14	56	215	56	115	22	22
60 - 64	750	405	164	162	34	45	345	97	127	89	32
65 - 69	1,132	632	212	231	106	83	500	102	151	220	27
70 - 74	1,366	610	189	215	165	41	756	140	122	467	27
75 - 79	1,959	710	166	242	276	26	1,249	207	168	856	18
80 - 84	2,624	678	129	195	333	21	1,946	274	177	1,473	22
85 - 89	2,401	434	67	87	272	8	1,967	277	102	1,577	11
90 and over	1,639	219	24	36	157	2	1,420	225	46	1,145	4
Visitors/guests	**10,437**	**5,428**	**3,232**	**1,706**	**303**	**187**	**5,009**	**2,694**	**1,158**	**1,006**	**151**
Aged											
0 - 4	279	168	168				111	111			
5 - 9	91	46	46				45	45			
10	20	7	7				13	13			
11	14	10	10				4	4			
12 - 14	79	44	44				35	35			
15	40	18	18				22	22			
16 - 17	311	136	136	-	-	-	175	173	2	-	-
18 - 19	2,249	1,144	1,142	1	1	-	1,105	1,103	2	-	-
20 - 24	1,963	1,074	1,051	18	1	4	889	824	61	-	4
25 - 29	630	377	256	110	1	10	253	107	128	-	18
30 - 34	401	253	101	137	-	15	148	38	92	2	16
35 - 39	351	228	51	154	1	22	123	20	83	1	19
40 - 44	356	235	28	177	1	29	121	13	89	4	15
45 - 49	297	190	21	148	2	19	107	10	81	4	12
50 - 54	298	180	19	135	3	23	118	4	82	16	16
55 - 59	284	151	19	110	6	16	133	9	100	15	9
60 - 64	362	185	22	135	14	14	177	14	108	45	10
65 - 69	491	265	29	177	39	20	226	15	110	90	11
70 - 74	458	222	24	147	48	3	236	22	78	127	9
75 - 79	514	216	14	137	59	6	298	34	70	191	3
80 - 84	475	178	13	84	75	6	297	35	47	209	6
85 - 89	314	74	8	32	34	-	240	26	16	195	3
90 and over	160	27	5	4	18	-	133	17	9	107	-

Table 2 Age and marital status – **continued**

Great Britain, England & Wales, England, regions, metropolitan counties, Inner London, Outer London, regional remainders, Wales, Scotland

Persons present

Age	TOTAL PERSONS	Males					Females				
		Total	Single	Married	Widowed	Divorced	Total	Single	Married	Widowed	Divorced
a	b	c	d	e	f	g	h	i	j	k	l

Tyne & Wear Metropolitan County – *continued*

Age	TOTAL PERSONS	Total	Single	Married	Widowed	Divorced	Total	Single	Married	Widowed	Divorced
Resident - non-staff	**11,758**	**4,266**	**2,233**	**565**	**1,073**	**395**	**7,492**	**1,927**	**534**	**4,869**	**162**
Aged											
0 - 4	74	43	43				31	31			
5 - 9	71	42	42				29	29			
10	24	15	15				9	9			
11	22	11	11				11	11			
12 - 14	97	58	58				39	39			
15	64	31	31				33	33			
16 - 17	58	31	31	-	-	-	27	27	-	-	-
18 - 19	210	120	117	3	-	-	90	88	2	-	-
20 - 24	524	311	299	10	1	1	213	195	15	-	3
25 - 29	311	214	184	15	2	13	97	76	16	1	4
30 - 34	213	138	107	15	-	16	75	57	13	-	5
35 - 39	206	166	105	26	1	34	40	27	5	-	8
40 - 44	224	147	98	12	3	34	77	46	14	1	16
45 - 49	188	128	77	10	2	39	60	40	9	1	10
50 - 54	195	152	91	13	5	43	43	30	2	2	9
55 - 59	219	153	92	15	7	39	66	43	8	6	9
60 - 64	371	211	139	22	19	31	160	82	15	42	21
65 - 69	637	366	183	53	67	63	271	86	41	128	16
70 - 74	902	388	165	68	117	38	514	113	44	339	18
75 - 79	1,441	493	152	105	216	20	948	170	98	665	15
80 - 84	2,144	496	115	111	256	14	1,648	238	130	1,264	16
85 - 89	2,085	360	59	55	238	8	1,725	249	86	1,382	8
90 and over	1,478	192	19	32	139	2	1,286	208	36	1,038	4
Resident - staff	**582**	**259**	**158**	**82**	**5**	**14**	**323**	**234**	**61**	**7**	**21**
Aged											
0 - 4	15	3	3				12	12			
5 - 9	11	8	8				3	3			
10	2	1	1				1	1			
11	3	1	1				2	2			
12 - 14	8	4	4				4	4			
15	1	1	1				-	-			
16 - 17	7	5	5	-	-	-	2	2	-	-	-
18 - 19	28	12	11	-	-	1	16	16	-	-	-
20 - 24	153	36	35	1	-	-	117	115	1	-	1
25 - 29	88	45	38	5	-	2	43	39	3	-	1
30 - 34	60	39	23	15	-	1	21	8	8	-	5
35 - 39	29	16	3	11	-	2	13	6	6	-	1
40 - 44	36	24	11	10	-	3	12	1	9	-	2
45 - 49	42	22	4	15	-	3	20	3	13	1	3
50 - 54	35	18	5	13	-	-	17	5	9	-	3
55 - 59	25	9	1	6	1	1	16	4	7	1	4
60 - 64	17	9	3	5	1	-	8	1	4	2	1
65 - 69	4	1	-	1	-	-	3	1	-	2	-
70 - 74	6	-	-	-	-	-	6	5	-	1	-
75 - 79	4	1	-	-	1	-	3	3	-	-	-
80 - 84	5	4	1	-	2	1	1	1	-	-	-
85 - 89	2	-	-	-	-	-	2	2	-	-	-
90 and over	1	-	-	-	-	-	1	-	1	-	-

Persons present

Age	TOTAL PERSONS	Males					Females				
		Total	Single	Married	Widowed	Divorced	Total	Single	Married	Widowed	Divorced
a	b	c	d	e	f	g	h	i	j	k	l

Tyne & Wear Metropolitan County – *continued*

All persons present in households	1,067,031	512,004	232,952	239,239	17,010	22,803	555,027	209,886	246,540	66,617	31,984
Aged											
0 - 4	70,930	36,319	36,319				34,611	34,611			
5 - 9	69,085	35,337	35,337				33,748	33,748			
10	14,037	7,227	7,227				6,810	6,810			
11	14,252	7,278	7,278				6,974	6,974			
12 - 14	36,798	18,731	18,731				18,067	18,067			
15	12,699	6,364	6,364				6,335	6,335			
16 - 17	26,324	13,421	13,392	25	-	4	12,903	12,829	57	9	8
18 - 19	30,205	15,059	14,926	121	2	10	15,146	14,772	360	5	9
20 - 24	82,935	40,550	35,946	4,402	8	194	42,385	32,832	8,857	21	675
25 - 29	83,395	40,293	20,689	18,015	19	1,570	43,102	16,133	23,826	84	3,059
30 - 34	78,917	38,438	9,878	25,515	64	2,981	40,479	6,878	28,606	198	4,797
35 - 39	70,532	34,754	5,527	25,843	93	3,291	35,778	3,332	27,283	323	4,840
40 - 44	74,490	36,879	4,350	28,720	192	3,617	37,611	2,226	29,815	609	4,961
45 - 49	58,800	29,015	2,980	22,978	279	2,778	29,785	1,438	23,942	930	3,475
50 - 54	58,181	28,363	2,757	22,604	526	2,476	29,818	1,353	23,602	1,901	2,962
55 - 59	58,416	28,513	2,722	22,652	1,022	2,117	29,903	1,452	22,326	3,758	2,367
60 - 64	59,879	28,353	2,903	21,946	1,849	1,655	31,526	1,834	20,778	7,012	1,902
65 - 69	57,594	26,559	2,576	19,775	3,071	1,137	31,035	2,178	16,982	10,521	1,354
70 - 74	44,878	18,814	1,535	13,495	3,214	570	26,064	1,976	10,948	12,259	881
75 - 79	32,959	12,398	885	8,155	3,093	265	20,561	1,734	5,841	12,538	448
80 - 84	20,361	6,578	456	3,767	2,244	111	13,783	1,379	2,568	9,664	172
85 - 89	8,719	2,236	147	1,080	987	22	6,483	754	636	5,037	56
90 and over	2,645	525	27	146	347	5	2,120	241	113	1,748	18

Remainder of North Region

All persons present in communal establishments	54,136	26,050	15,721	6,476	2,621	1,232	28,086	11,172	5,118	10,973	823
Aged											
0 - 4	677	372	372				305	305			
5 - 9	588	354	354				234	234			
10	280	170	170				110	110			
11	452	268	268				184	184			
12 - 14	1,569	962	962				607	607			
15	757	510	510				247	247			
16 - 17	1,929	1,331	1,329	1	1	-	598	596	2	-	-
18 - 19	3,765	2,157	2,142	13	1	1	1,608	1,594	14	-	-
20 - 24	6,586	3,892	3,703	151	2	36	2,694	2,477	199	1	17
25 - 29	3,145	2,025	1,510	420	4	91	1,120	662	403	6	49
30 - 34	2,259	1,518	828	537	6	147	741	313	360	3	65
35 - 39	1,790	1,175	511	520	4	140	615	250	287	8	70
40 - 44	1,888	1,203	446	587	8	162	685	206	362	17	100
45 - 49	1,797	1,098	418	536	10	134	699	180	424	17	78
50 - 54	1,649	926	291	519	11	105	723	186	415	48	74
55 - 59	1,553	849	240	502	29	78	704	176	402	60	66
60 - 64	2,027	1,049	358	524	74	93	978	267	478	169	64
65 - 69	2,365	1,115	364	496	161	94	1,250	328	425	420	77
70 - 74	2,729	1,186	330	498	295	63	1,543	327	373	786	57
75 - 79	3,840	1,283	266	486	484	47	2,557	453	383	1,678	43
80 - 84	4,993	1,287	205	397	659	26	3,706	529	319	2,831	27
85 - 89	4,665	895	112	230	542	11	3,770	577	199	2,965	29
90 and over	2,833	425	32	59	330	4	2,408	364	73	1,964	7

Table 2 Age and marital status – **continued**

Great Britain, England & Wales, England, regions, metropolitan counties, Inner London, Outer London, regional remainders, Wales, Scotland

Persons present

Age	TOTAL PERSONS	Males					Females				
		Total	Single	Married	Widowed	Divorced	Total	Single	Married	Widowed	Divorced
a	b	c	d	e	f	g	h	i	j	k	l

Remainder of North Region – *continued*

Visitors/guests	26,112	14,763	9,064	4,598	558	543	11,349	5,646	3,424	1,889	390
Aged											
0 - 4	463	270	270				193	193			
5 - 9	349	220	220				129	129			
10	227	136	136				91	91			
11	389	231	231				158	158			
12 - 14	1,297	817	817				480	480			
15	587	410	410				177	177			
16 - 17	1,308	816	815	1	-	-	492	491	1	-	-
18 - 19	3,069	1,764	1,753	9	1	1	1,305	1,295	10	-	-
20 - 24	4,555	2,728	2,584	118	2	24	1,827	1,654	164	1	8
25 - 29	1,859	1,204	795	349	4	56	655	295	325	4	31
30 - 34	1,278	842	334	415	2	91	436	110	278	3	45
35 - 39	966	655	164	413	2	76	311	64	201	5	41
40 - 44	986	646	112	437	5	92	340	40	230	9	61
45 - 49	956	585	113	400	6	66	371	33	289	12	37
50 - 54	922	507	62	400	8	37	415	41	305	33	36
55 - 59	877	455	34	373	20	28	422	31	317	40	34
60 - 64	1,080	523	44	433	25	21	557	43	404	88	22
65 - 69	1,150	540	47	405	60	28	610	47	343	189	31
70 - 74	1,072	488	38	349	90	11	584	50	244	271	19
75 - 79	1,024	410	34	268	101	7	614	68	170	364	12
80 - 84	906	308	29	156	119	4	598	69	93	429	7
85 - 89	545	159	19	62	77	1	386	59	34	289	4
90 and over	247	49	3	10	36	-	198	28	16	152	2
Resident - non-staff	24,003	9,240	5,385	1,231	2,054	570	14,763	4,308	1,074	9,039	342
Aged											
0 - 4	123	63	63				60	60			
5 - 9	129	80	80				49	49			
10	32	24	24				8	8			
11	36	22	22				14	14			
12 - 14	204	112	112				92	92			
15	141	83	83				58	58			
16 - 17	513	465	464	-	1	-	48	48	-	-	-
18 - 19	392	255	253	2	-	-	137	133	4	-	-
20 - 24	1,049	717	688	21	-	8	332	318	10	-	4
25 - 29	753	529	469	35	-	25	224	189	25	1	9
30 - 34	676	480	390	49	3	38	196	158	27	-	11
35 - 39	581	380	296	38	1	45	201	153	23	3	22
40 - 44	620	414	312	45	2	55	206	150	22	7	27
45 - 49	555	370	288	30	4	48	185	139	22	3	21
50 - 54	488	297	215	30	3	49	191	133	21	9	28
55 - 59	449	266	188	29	8	41	183	135	17	13	18
60 - 64	858	475	305	55	48	67	383	221	49	75	38
65 - 69	1,185	562	313	82	101	66	623	280	73	225	45
70 - 74	1,639	687	290	141	204	52	952	276	126	512	38
75 - 79	2,801	871	232	218	381	40	1,930	382	209	1,308	31
80 - 84	4,080	976	176	239	539	22	3,104	459	225	2,400	20
85 - 89	4,118	736	93	168	465	10	3,382	518	164	2,675	25
90 and over	2,581	376	29	49	294	4	2,205	335	57	1,808	5

Table 2 Age and marital status – **continued**

Great Britain, England & Wales, England, regions, metropolitan counties, Inner London, Outer London, regional remainders, Wales, Scotland

Persons present

Age	TOTAL PERSONS	Males					Females				
		Total	Single	Married	Widowed	Divorced	Total	Single	Married	Widowed	Divorced
a	b	c	d	e	f	g	h	i	j	k	l

Remainder of North Region – *continued*

Resident - staff	4,021	2,047	1,272	647	9	119	1,974	1,218	620	45	91
Aged											
0 - 4	91	39	39				52	52			
5 - 9	110	54	54				56	56			
10	21	10	10				11	11			
11	27	15	15				12	12			
12 - 14	68	33	33				35	35			
15	29	17	17				12	12			
16 - 17	108	50	50	-	-	-	58	57	1	-	-
18 - 19	304	138	136	2	-	-	166	166	-	-	-
20 - 24	982	447	431	12	-	4	535	505	25	-	5
25 - 29	533	292	246	36	-	10	241	178	53	1	9
30 - 34	305	196	104	73	1	18	109	45	55	-	9
35 - 39	243	140	51	69	1	19	103	33	63	-	7
40 - 44	282	143	22	105	1	15	139	16	110	1	12
45 - 49	286	143	17	106	-	20	143	8	113	2	20
50 - 54	239	122	14	89	-	19	117	12	89	6	10
55 - 59	227	128	18	100	1	9	99	10	68	7	14
60 - 64	89	51	9	36	1	5	38	3	25	6	4
65 - 69	30	13	4	9	-	-	17	1	9	6	1
70 - 74	18	11	2	8	1	-	7	1	3	3	-
75 - 79	15	2	-	-	2	-	13	3	4	6	-
80 - 84	7	3	-	2	1	-	4	1	1	2	-
85 - 89	2	-	-	-	-	-	2	-	1	1	-
90 and over	5	-	-	-	-	-	5	1	-	4	-
All persons present in households	1,874,735	909,465	390,831	452,411	28,596	37,627	965,270	345,333	461,442	107,902	50,593
Aged											
0 - 4	124,015	63,249	63,249				60,766	60,766			
5 - 9	124,158	63,747	63,747				60,411	60,411			
10	25,251	12,874	12,874				12,377	12,377			
11	25,302	12,840	12,840				12,462	12,462			
12 - 14	68,277	35,075	35,075				33,202	33,202			
15	23,208	11,803	11,803				11,405	11,405			
16 - 17	48,836	24,999	24,942	42	2	13	23,837	23,727	94	6	10
18 - 19	50,262	25,460	25,200	242	3	15	24,802	23,979	789	6	28
20 - 24	129,008	63,325	54,036	8,864	9	416	65,683	46,486	17,827	54	1,316
25 - 29	139,640	68,027	31,092	34,008	34	2,893	71,613	21,895	44,155	174	5,389
30 - 34	135,010	65,976	14,711	46,136	86	5,043	69,034	9,103	52,103	343	7,485
35 - 39	126,455	62,378	8,525	48,237	166	5,450	64,077	4,907	51,160	523	7,487
40 - 44	140,793	69,823	6,794	56,662	359	6,008	70,970	3,289	58,876	1,035	7,770
45 - 49	115,563	57,940	4,687	47,950	518	4,785	57,623	2,126	48,111	1,742	5,644
50 - 54	107,471	53,054	4,167	43,882	878	4,127	54,417	2,059	44,463	3,171	4,724
55 - 59	103,097	50,910	4,050	41,993	1,593	3,274	52,187	2,207	40,429	5,959	3,592
60 - 64	103,423	49,865	4,307	40,141	2,956	2,461	53,558	2,819	37,013	11,038	2,688
65 - 69	98,707	45,993	3,765	35,685	4,927	1,616	52,714	3,079	30,778	16,743	2,114
70 - 74	76,041	33,016	2,364	24,624	5,155	873	43,025	2,768	19,476	19,523	1,258
75 - 79	56,828	22,175	1,527	14,902	5,294	452	34,653	2,688	10,589	20,706	670
80 - 84	34,578	11,778	749	6,863	4,010	156	22,800	2,154	4,279	16,066	301
85 - 89	14,594	4,171	271	1,882	1,976	42	10,423	1,071	1,111	8,140	101
90 and over	4,218	987	56	298	630	3	3,231	353	189	2,673	16

Table 2   Age and marital status – **continued**

Great Britain, England & Wales, England, regions, metropolitan counties, Inner London, Outer London, regional remainders, Wales, Scotland

Persons present

Age	TOTAL PERSONS	Males					Females				
		Total	Single	Married	Widowed	Divorced	Total	Single	Married	Widowed	Divorced
a	b	c	d	e	f	g	h	i	j	k	l

YORKSHIRE & HUMBERSIDE REGION

Age	TOTAL PERSONS	Total	Single	Married	Widowed	Divorced	Total	Single	Married	Widowed	Divorced
All persons present in communal establishments	113,945	51,609	30,366	12,144	6,136	2,963	62,336	23,845	9,697	27,025	1,769
Aged											
0 - 4	1,832	976	976				856	856			
5 - 9	1,103	667	667				436	436			
10	524	326	326				198	198			
11	614	364	364				250	250			
12 - 14	2,384	1,387	1,387				997	997			
15	1,015	573	573				442	442			
16 - 17	3,042	2,042	2,038	4	-	-	1,000	985	13	1	1
18 - 19	9,836	5,561	5,517	36	2	6	4,275	4,232	40	1	2
20 - 24	13,344	7,904	7,427	382	7	88	5,440	4,978	413	6	43
25 - 29	6,458	4,187	2,982	918	8	279	2,271	1,474	670	7	120
30 - 34	4,105	2,623	1,329	966	10	318	1,482	645	671	10	156
35 - 39	3,391	2,114	853	920	16	325	1,277	494	618	20	145
40 - 44	3,409	2,103	768	968	19	348	1,306	437	664	30	175
45 - 49	3,069	1,833	641	846	34	312	1,236	378	666	37	155
50 - 54	2,752	1,605	507	825	39	234	1,147	335	608	49	155
55 - 59	2,624	1,481	454	759	54	214	1,143	300	622	119	102
60 - 64	3,520	1,856	691	799	142	224	1,664	459	679	387	139
65 - 69	4,479	2,183	738	900	359	186	2,296	558	744	831	163
70 - 74	5,604	2,321	628	938	597	158	3,283	710	737	1,729	107
75 - 79	8,678	2,963	642	1,101	1,084	136	5,715	923	909	3,782	101
80 - 84	12,320	3,175	490	996	1,605	84	9,145	1,365	885	6,786	109
85 - 89	11,642	2,254	257	580	1,383	34	9,388	1,356	551	7,418	63
90 and over	8,200	1,111	111	206	777	17	7,089	1,037	207	5,812	33
Visitors/guests	47,845	25,323	15,004	7,888	1,381	1,050	22,522	11,108	6,105	4,523	786
Aged											
0 - 4	1,250	658	658				592	592			
5 - 9	514	341	341				173	173			
10	376	235	235				141	141			
11	480	286	286				194	194			
12 - 14	1,817	1,040	1,040				777	777			
15	704	395	395				309	309			
16 - 17	1,875	1,137	1,134	3	-	-	738	726	11	1	-
18 - 19	7,355	3,938	3,910	22	2	4	3,417	3,381	33	1	2
20 - 24	7,672	4,423	4,160	224	5	34	3,249	2,909	319	3	18
25 - 29	3,199	1,973	1,248	603	3	119	1,226	610	551	6	59
30 - 34	2,162	1,346	489	701	3	153	816	196	521	7	92
35 - 39	1,716	1,040	233	668	7	132	676	112	459	13	92
40 - 44	1,632	983	157	687	6	133	649	71	467	15	96
45 - 49	1,499	867	110	623	16	118	632	57	459	20	96
50 - 54	1,379	781	83	597	21	80	598	46	448	25	79
55 - 59	1,411	738	72	568	27	71	673	53	485	79	56
60 - 64	1,658	831	102	605	65	59	827	78	507	187	55
65 - 69	2,016	982	89	697	140	56	1,034	90	544	343	57
70 - 74	2,106	967	86	639	205	37	1,139	108	446	555	30
75 - 79	2,429	1,005	77	624	275	29	1,424	130	417	851	26
80 - 84	2,324	790	59	398	314	19	1,534	170	286	1,060	18
85 - 89	1,558	432	28	180	220	4	1,126	128	118	873	7
90 and over	713	135	12	49	72	2	578	57	34	484	3

Table 2 Age and marital status – **continued**

Great Britain, England & Wales, England, regions, metropolitan counties, Inner London, Outer London, regional remainders, Wales, Scotland

Persons present

Age	TOTAL PERSONS	Males					Females				
		Total	Single	Married	Widowed	Divorced	Total	Single	Married	Widowed	Divorced
a	b	c	d	e	f	g	h	i	j	k	l

YORKSHIRE & HUMBERSIDE REGION – *continued*

Age	TOTAL PERSONS	Total	Single	Married	Widowed	Divorced	Total	Single	Married	Widowed	Divorced
Resident - non-staff	**60,360**	**23,808**	**13,891**	**3,424**	**4,733**	**1,760**	**36,552**	**10,466**	**2,807**	**22,432**	**847**
Aged											
0 - 4	473	267	267				206	206			
5 - 9	431	243	243				188	188			
10	107	69	69				38	38			
11	94	58	58				36	36			
12 - 14	449	279	279				170	170			
15	268	149	149				119	119			
16 - 17	1,041	847	846	1	-	-	194	191	2	-	1
18 - 19	1,998	1,486	1,471	13	-	2	512	507	5	-	-
20 - 24	4,149	3,057	2,856	147	2	52	1,092	995	76	2	19
25 - 29	2,573	1,857	1,440	271	5	141	716	582	83	-	51
30 - 34	1,602	1,080	720	205	7	148	522	380	89	2	51
35 - 39	1,348	913	572	155	9	177	435	344	47	6	38
40 - 44	1,335	896	569	125	11	191	439	327	50	10	52
45 - 49	1,165	766	498	86	14	168	399	291	55	13	40
50 - 54	1,015	644	401	91	18	134	371	264	39	18	50
55 - 59	953	604	368	86	26	124	349	230	53	31	35
60 - 64	1,716	947	583	134	73	157	769	367	136	191	75
65 - 69	2,424	1,185	646	191	219	129	1,239	458	192	483	106
70 - 74	3,461	1,336	538	290	388	120	2,125	591	289	1,168	77
75 - 79	6,223	1,950	562	475	806	107	4,273	785	490	2,923	75
80 - 84	9,977	2,379	429	597	1,288	65	7,598	1,191	598	5,718	91
85 - 89	10,076	1,821	228	400	1,163	30	8,255	1,226	431	6,542	56
90 and over	7,482	975	99	157	704	15	6,507	980	172	5,325	30
Resident - staff	**5,740**	**2,478**	**1,471**	**832**	**22**	**153**	**3,262**	**2,271**	**785**	**70**	**136**
Aged											
0 - 4	109	51	51				58	58			
5 - 9	158	83	83				75	75			
10	41	22	22				19	19			
11	40	20	20				20	20			
12 - 14	118	68	68				50	50			
15	43	29	29				14	14			
16 - 17	126	58	58	-	-	-	68	68	-	-	-
18 - 19	483	137	136	1	-	-	346	344	2	-	-
20 - 24	1,523	424	411	11	-	2	1,099	1,074	18	1	6
25 - 29	686	357	294	44	-	19	329	282	36	1	10
30 - 34	341	197	120	60	-	17	144	69	61	1	13
35 - 39	327	161	48	97	-	16	166	38	112	1	15
40 - 44	442	224	42	156	2	24	218	39	147	5	27
45 - 49	405	200	33	137	4	26	205	30	152	4	19
50 - 54	358	180	23	137	-	20	178	25	121	6	26
55 - 59	260	139	14	105	1	19	121	17	84	9	11
60 - 64	146	78	6	60	4	8	68	14	36	9	9
65 - 69	39	16	3	12	-	1	23	10	8	5	-
70 - 74	37	18	4	9	4	1	19	11	2	6	-
75 - 79	26	8	3	2	3	-	18	8	2	8	-
80 - 84	19	6	2	1	3	-	13	4	1	8	-
85 - 89	8	1	1	-	-	-	7	2	2	3	-
90 and over	5	1	-	-	1	-	4	-	1	3	-

Table 2 Age and marital status – **continued**

Great Britain, England & Wales, England, regions, metropolitan counties, Inner London, Outer London, regional remainders, Wales, Scotland

Persons present

Age	TOTAL PERSONS	Males					Females				
		Total	Single	Married	Widowed	Divorced	Total	Single	Married	Widowed	Divorced
a	b	c	d	e	f	g	h	i	j	k	l

YORKSHIRE & HUMBERSIDE REGION – *continued*

All persons present in households	4,682,617	2,270,897	997,842	1,104,317	66,993	101,745	2,411,720	889,903	1,120,672	265,035	136,110
Aged											
0 - 4	321,940	164,317	164,317				157,623	157,623			
5 - 9	304,694	156,180	156,180				148,514	148,514			
10	61,536	31,480	31,480				30,056	30,056			
11	60,863	31,109	31,109				29,754	29,754			
12 - 14	165,449	85,000	85,000				80,449	80,449			
15	57,284	29,494	29,494				27,790	27,790			
16 - 17	120,938	61,749	61,542	177	9	21	59,189	58,756	398	14	21
18 - 19	133,082	66,950	66,149	754	8	39	66,132	63,301	2,715	23	93
20 - 24	361,214	178,298	154,303	22,773	27	1,195	182,916	133,647	45,600	144	3,525
25 - 29	360,717	176,896	85,995	83,325	103	7,473	183,821	61,425	108,632	389	13,375
30 - 34	335,317	165,182	39,199	112,709	197	13,077	170,135	25,506	125,165	725	18,739
35 - 39	308,231	153,510	21,811	116,648	416	14,635	154,721	12,360	121,645	1,248	19,468
40 - 44	344,198	171,086	16,856	136,461	754	17,015	173,112	8,431	140,313	2,618	21,750
45 - 49	283,004	141,206	11,216	115,662	1,173	13,155	141,798	5,629	115,804	4,142	16,223
50 - 54	258,213	128,045	9,011	105,758	2,007	11,269	130,168	5,019	104,723	7,452	12,974
55 - 59	244,298	120,067	8,244	99,854	3,345	8,624	124,231	5,227	95,699	13,565	9,740
60 - 64	240,975	115,303	8,447	94,028	6,238	6,590	125,672	6,252	87,104	24,616	7,700
65 - 69	236,322	109,967	7,413	87,524	10,572	4,458	126,355	7,052	74,918	38,727	5,658
70 - 74	187,229	80,771	4,606	62,012	11,788	2,365	106,458	6,434	50,058	46,592	3,374
75 - 79	150,760	58,613	3,156	40,875	13,346	1,236	92,147	6,738	30,651	52,634	2,124
80 - 84	93,775	31,747	1,641	19,265	10,389	452	62,028	5,670	13,032	42,349	977
85 - 89	40,760	11,454	555	5,624	5,148	127	29,306	3,172	3,655	22,172	307
90 and over	11,818	2,473	118	868	1,473	14	9,345	1,098	560	7,625	62

South Yorkshire Metropolitan County

All persons present in communal establishments	23,750	10,691	6,244	2,303	1,469	675	13,059	4,578	1,926	6,161	394
Aged											
0 - 4	433	237	237				196	196			
5 - 9	223	129	129				94	94			
10	59	38	38				21	21			
11	42	24	24				18	18			
12 - 14	231	155	155				76	76			
15	97	54	54				43	43			
16 - 17	271	157	157	-	-	-	114	112	2	-	-
18 - 19	2,279	1,293	1,283	8	-	2	986	975	11	-	-
20 - 24	3,031	1,862	1,761	78	1	22	1,169	1,073	85	1	10
25 - 29	1,389	912	670	174	1	67	477	315	128	2	32
30 - 34	817	526	298	160	1	67	291	135	112	1	43
35 - 39	633	394	191	129	7	67	239	80	119	7	33
40 - 44	610	367	133	141	4	89	243	95	102	8	38
45 - 49	614	343	138	128	8	69	271	84	142	7	38
50 - 54	537	329	122	140	9	58	208	66	99	9	34
55 - 59	485	298	101	146	10	41	187	52	100	21	14
60 - 64	734	386	153	146	31	56	348	103	129	82	34
65 - 69	1,062	524	182	205	93	44	538	144	174	190	30
70 - 74	1,339	544	125	229	149	41	795	144	171	455	25
75 - 79	2,006	700	151	251	274	24	1,306	172	201	908	25
80 - 84	2,742	685	88	207	375	15	2,057	251	201	1,588	17
85 - 89	2,441	486	34	116	326	10	1,955	196	115	1,628	16
90 and over	1,675	248	20	45	180	3	1,427	133	35	1,254	5

Table 2 Age and marital status – **continued**

Great Britain, England & Wales, England, regions, metropolitan counties, Inner London, Outer London, regional remainders, Wales, Scotland

Persons present

Age	TOTAL PERSONS	Males					Females				
		Total	Single	Married	Widowed	Divorced	Total	Single	Married	Widowed	Divorced
a	b	c	d	e	f	g	h	i	j	k	l

South Yorkshire Metropolitan County – *continued*

Age	TOTAL PERSONS	Males Total	Single	Married	Widowed	Divorced	Females Total	Single	Married	Widowed	Divorced
Visitors/guests	10,545	5,658	3,455	1,575	379	249	4,887	2,140	1,285	1,278	184
Aged											
0 - 4	309	180	180				129	129			
5 - 9	84	56	56				28	28			
10	22	16	16				6	6			
11	18	12	12				6	6			
12 - 14	116	94	94				22	22			
15	33	26	26				7	7			
16 - 17	146	92	92	-	-	-	54	52	2	-	-
18 - 19	1,939	1,094	1,089	4	-	1	845	835	10	-	-
20 - 24	1,946	1,229	1,159	58	1	11	717	643	69	1	4
25 - 29	752	495	331	129	-	35	257	128	110	2	17
30 - 34	411	267	124	112	-	31	144	31	88	1	24
35 - 39	331	176	54	95	3	24	155	18	106	6	25
40 - 44	289	167	31	101	1	34	122	13	81	5	23
45 - 49	310	152	25	99	2	26	158	12	117	5	24
50 - 54	284	167	22	116	6	23	117	10	86	4	17
55 - 59	275	159	19	127	4	9	116	9	86	14	7
60 - 64	324	157	27	105	11	14	167	18	99	37	13
65 - 69	487	239	40	155	29	15	248	29	125	82	12
70 - 74	568	273	22	165	69	17	295	29	98	158	10
75 - 79	638	265	15	159	88	3	373	25	98	246	4
80 - 84	615	192	8	99	82	3	423	49	72	301	1
85 - 89	461	114	10	37	65	2	347	31	30	283	3
90 and over	187	36	3	14	18	1	151	10	8	133	-
Resident - non-staff	12,537	4,801	2,634	663	1,088	416	7,736	2,069	595	4,880	192
Aged											
0 - 4	116	55	55				61	61			
5 - 9	135	71	71				64	64			
10	35	21	21				14	14			
11	24	12	12				12	12			
12 - 14	111	59	59				52	52			
15	62	27	27				35	35			
16 - 17	121	63	63	-	-	-	58	58	-	-	-
18 - 19	300	193	188	4	-	1	107	107	-	-	-
20 - 24	810	586	557	18	-	11	224	207	12	-	5
25 - 29	515	357	287	37	1	32	158	132	16	-	10
30 - 34	345	221	149	38	1	33	124	85	22	-	17
35 - 39	273	199	128	26	4	41	74	59	7	1	7
40 - 44	282	181	97	29	2	53	101	74	12	3	12
45 - 49	277	178	111	19	6	42	99	69	17	1	12
50 - 54	234	155	99	19	3	34	79	50	9	5	15
55 - 59	202	135	82	16	6	31	67	43	11	7	6
60 - 64	395	223	126	35	20	42	172	84	23	45	20
65 - 69	572	283	142	48	64	29	289	114	49	108	18
70 - 74	768	270	103	64	79	24	498	114	73	296	15
75 - 79	1,366	435	136	92	186	21	931	146	103	661	21
80 - 84	2,127	493	80	108	293	12	1,634	202	129	1,287	16
85 - 89	1,979	372	24	79	261	8	1,607	164	85	1,345	13
90 and over	1,488	212	17	31	162	2	1,276	123	27	1,121	5

Table 2 Age and marital status – **continued**

Great Britain, England & Wales, England, regions, metropolitan counties, Inner London, Outer London, regional remainders, Wales, Scotland

Persons present

Age	TOTAL PERSONS	Males					Females				
		Total	Single	Married	Widowed	Divorced	Total	Single	Married	Widowed	Divorced
a	b	c	d	e	f	g	h	i	j	k	l

South Yorkshire Metropolitan County – *continued*

Resident - staff	668	232	155	65	2	10	436	369	46	3	18
Aged											
0 - 4	8	2	2				6	6			
5 - 9	4	2	2				2	2			
10	2	1	1				1	1			
11	-	-	-				-	-			
12 - 14	4	2	2				2	2			
15	2	1	1				1	1			
16 - 17	4	2	2	-	-	-	2	2	-	-	-
18 - 19	40	6	6	-	-	-	34	33	1	-	-
20 - 24	275	47	45	2	-	-	228	223	4	-	1
25 - 29	122	60	52	8	-	-	62	55	2	-	5
30 - 34	61	38	25	10	-	3	23	19	2	-	2
35 - 39	29	19	9	8	-	2	10	3	6	-	1
40 - 44	39	19	5	11	1	2	20	8	9	-	3
45 - 49	27	13	2	10	-	1	14	3	8	1	2
50 - 54	19	7	1	5	-	1	12	6	4	-	2
55 - 59	8	4	-	3	-	1	4	-	3	-	1
60 - 64	15	6	-	6	-	-	9	1	7	-	1
65 - 69	3	2	-	2	-	-	1	1	-	-	-
70 - 74	3	1	-	-	1	-	2	1	-	1	-
75 - 79	2	-	-	-	-	-	2	1	-	1	-
80 - 84	-	-	-	-	-	-	-	-	-	-	-
85 - 89	1	-	-	-	-	-	1	1	-	-	-
90 and over	-	-	-	-	-	-	-	-	-	-	-
All persons present in households	1,230,209	599,363	261,454	291,872	18,863	27,174	630,846	228,745	295,417	72,325	34,359
Aged											
0 - 4	82,684	42,176	42,176				40,508	40,508			
5 - 9	77,502	39,865	39,865				37,637	37,637			
10	15,457	7,932	7,932				7,525	7,525			
11	15,292	7,736	7,736				7,556	7,556			
12 - 14	41,245	21,211	21,211				20,034	20,034			
15	14,338	7,390	7,390				6,948	6,948			
16 - 17	30,739	15,757	15,706	40	1	10	14,982	14,896	76	5	5
18 - 19	35,827	18,190	18,018	156	5	11	17,637	16,997	605	4	31
20 - 24	99,412	49,732	43,177	6,205	6	344	49,680	36,608	12,129	35	908
25 - 29	97,417	48,245	23,194	22,959	23	2,069	49,172	16,677	28,792	98	3,605
30 - 34	88,653	43,785	10,409	29,743	49	3,584	44,868	6,819	32,778	174	5,097
35 - 39	79,866	39,974	5,736	30,203	92	3,943	39,892	3,131	31,442	298	5,021
40 - 44	87,440	43,685	4,218	34,818	211	4,438	43,755	2,134	35,601	678	5,342
45 - 49	75,698	38,058	3,002	31,101	334	3,621	37,640	1,378	31,058	1,051	4,153
50 - 54	68,419	33,975	2,377	28,131	556	2,911	34,444	1,197	27,986	1,969	3,292
55 - 59	64,252	31,594	2,205	26,163	976	2,250	32,658	1,173	25,559	3,646	2,280
60 - 64	63,290	30,491	2,287	24,737	1,729	1,738	32,799	1,345	22,976	6,638	1,840
65 - 69	63,510	29,799	2,098	23,410	3,141	1,150	33,711	1,443	20,289	10,653	1,326
70 - 74	51,366	22,208	1,348	16,777	3,434	649	29,158	1,392	13,780	13,240	746
75 - 79	39,903	15,648	809	10,873	3,665	301	24,255	1,419	8,063	14,318	455
80 - 84	24,335	8,317	391	4,974	2,825	127	16,018	1,145	3,252	11,434	187
85 - 89	10,534	2,950	132	1,378	1,416	24	7,584	583	887	6,054	60
90 and over	3,030	645	37	204	400	4	2,385	200	144	2,030	11

Table 2 Age and marital status – **continued**

Great Britain, England & Wales, England, regions, metropolitan counties, Inner London, Outer London, regional remainders, Wales, Scotland

Persons present

Age	TOTAL PERSONS	Males					Females				
		Total	Single	Married	Widowed	Divorced	Total	Single	Married	Widowed	Divorced
a	b	c	d	e	f	g	h	i	j	k	l

West Yorkshire Metropolitan County

Age	TOTAL PERSONS	Total	Single	Married	Widowed	Divorced	Total	Single	Married	Widowed	Divorced
All persons present in communal establishments	**40,379**	**17,135**	**9,776**	**3,917**	**2,263**	**1,179**	**23,244**	**9,162**	**3,277**	**10,178**	**627**
Aged											
0 - 4	737	391	391				346	346			
5 - 9	330	194	194				136	136			
10	102	67	67				35	35			
11	89	53	53				36	36			
12 - 14	594	390	390				204	204			
15	282	182	182				100	100			
16 - 17	524	332	330	2	-	-	192	185	6	-	1
18 - 19	3,979	1,937	1,932	3	2	-	2,042	2,025	16	-	1
20 - 24	4,484	2,341	2,197	102	4	38	2,143	1,973	156	1	13
25 - 29	2,185	1,349	982	267	4	96	836	548	244	1	43
30 - 34	1,517	958	493	320	6	139	559	242	261	3	53
35 - 39	1,246	776	333	296	6	141	470	195	217	6	52
40 - 44	1,151	708	288	269	10	141	443	155	218	10	60
45 - 49	1,023	657	264	251	14	128	366	129	170	18	49
50 - 54	938	560	211	230	18	101	378	133	182	14	49
55 - 59	899	508	181	215	26	86	391	120	179	49	43
60 - 64	1,250	693	267	285	64	77	557	173	195	138	51
65 - 69	1,601	781	270	289	149	73	820	192	245	313	70
70 - 74	2,007	834	237	313	229	55	1,173	260	249	626	38
75 - 79	3,163	1,069	214	406	400	49	2,094	347	343	1,371	33
80 - 84	4,592	1,179	172	367	599	41	3,413	562	289	2,522	40
85 - 89	4,472	804	97	222	476	9	3,668	599	213	2,835	21
90 and over	3,214	372	31	80	256	5	2,842	467	94	2,271	10
Visitors/guests	**17,226**	**8,884**	**5,276**	**2,551**	**574**	**483**	**8,342**	**4,204**	**2,100**	**1,731**	**307**
Aged											
0 - 4	527	269	269				258	258			
5 - 9	103	63	63				40	40			
10	47	28	28				19	19			
11	39	25	25				14	14			
12 - 14	362	241	241				121	121			
15	147	103	103				44	44			
16 - 17	359	240	238	2	-	-	119	114	5	-	-
18 - 19	3,416	1,704	1,699	3	2	-	1,712	1,697	14	-	1
20 - 24	2,950	1,628	1,544	67	2	15	1,322	1,184	132	-	6
25 - 29	1,164	696	473	176	1	46	468	236	210	-	22
30 - 34	792	466	169	222	2	73	326	70	211	3	42
35 - 39	623	383	96	216	2	69	240	41	165	3	31
40 - 44	539	313	47	201	4	61	226	21	167	5	33
45 - 49	490	308	52	195	7	54	182	17	122	8	35
50 - 54	454	251	33	172	7	39	203	16	150	7	30
55 - 59	455	236	28	159	13	36	219	17	144	31	27
60 - 64	557	321	43	221	33	24	236	29	128	58	21
65 - 69	719	352	25	228	72	27	367	27	178	135	27
70 - 74	720	317	38	196	70	13	403	38	143	214	8
75 - 79	892	369	26	231	101	11	523	45	166	302	10
80 - 84	935	330	20	155	142	13	605	70	100	426	9
85 - 89	620	184	10	83	90	1	436	55	46	332	3
90 and over	316	57	6	24	26	1	259	31	19	207	2

Table 2 Age and marital status – **continued**

Great Britain, England & Wales, England, regions, metropolitan counties, Inner London, Outer London, regional remainders, Wales, Scotland

Persons present

Age	TOTAL PERSONS	Males					Females				
		Total	Single	Married	Widowed	Divorced	Total	Single	Married	Widowed	Divorced
a	b	c	d	e	f	g	h	i	j	k	l

West Yorkshire Metropolitan County – *continued*

Age	b	c	d	e	f	g	h	i	j	k	l
Resident - non-staff	21,406	7,540	4,022	1,177	1,684	657	13,866	4,140	1,012	8,430	284
Aged											
0 - 4	197	116	116				81	81			
5 - 9	189	108	108				81	81			
10	45	32	32				13	13			
11	40	24	24				16	16			
12 - 14	202	128	128				74	74			
15	128	75	75				53	53			
16 - 17	134	81	81	-	-	-	53	51	1	-	1
18 - 19	373	193	193	-	-	-	180	179	1	-	-
20 - 24	955	552	495	33	2	22	403	374	22	1	6
25 - 29	784	530	402	81	3	44	254	209	27	-	18
30 - 34	631	433	286	79	4	64	198	153	37	-	8
35 - 39	536	349	221	54	4	70	187	143	25	3	16
40 - 44	506	343	230	35	6	72	163	126	14	4	19
45 - 49	459	316	208	32	6	70	143	101	22	9	11
50 - 54	411	268	171	33	11	53	143	109	13	7	14
55 - 59	380	235	145	33	12	45	145	99	22	12	12
60 - 64	639	346	221	43	30	52	293	138	53	76	26
65 - 69	870	426	243	60	77	46	444	161	62	178	43
70 - 74	1,271	508	195	114	158	41	763	215	106	412	30
75 - 79	2,258	696	185	174	299	38	1,562	295	177	1,067	23
80 - 84	3,650	846	151	211	456	28	2,804	489	189	2,095	31
85 - 89	3,852	620	87	139	386	8	3,232	544	167	2,503	18
90 and over	2,896	315	25	56	230	4	2,581	436	74	2,063	8
Resident - staff	1,747	711	478	189	5	39	1,036	818	165	17	36
Aged											
0 - 4	13	6	6				7	7			
5 - 9	38	23	23				15	15			
10	10	7	7				3	3			
11	10	4	4				6	6			
12 - 14	30	21	21				9	9			
15	7	4	4				3	3			
16 - 17	31	11	11	-	-	-	20	20	-	-	-
18 - 19	190	40	40	-	-	-	150	149	1	-	-
20 - 24	579	161	158	2	-	1	418	415	2	-	1
25 - 29	237	123	107	10	-	6	114	103	7	1	3
30 - 34	94	59	38	19	-	2	35	19	13	-	3
35 - 39	87	44	16	26	-	2	43	11	27	-	5
40 - 44	106	52	11	33	-	8	54	8	37	1	8
45 - 49	74	33	4	24	1	4	41	11	26	1	3
50 - 54	73	41	7	25	-	9	32	8	19	-	5
55 - 59	64	37	8	23	1	5	27	4	13	6	4
60 - 64	54	26	3	21	1	1	28	6	14	4	4
65 - 69	12	3	2	1	-	-	9	4	5	-	-
70 - 74	16	9	4	3	1	1	7	7	-	-	-
75 - 79	13	4	3	1	-	-	9	7	-	2	-
80 - 84	7	3	1	1	1	-	4	3	-	1	-
85 - 89	-	-	-	-	-	-	-	-	-	-	-
90 and over	2	-	-	-	-	-	2	-	1	1	-

Table 2 Age and marital status – **continued**

Great Britain, England & Wales, England, regions, metropolitan counties, Inner London, Outer London, regional remainders, Wales, Scotland

Persons present

Age	TOTAL PERSONS	Males					Females				
		Total	Single	Married	Widowed	Divorced	Total	Single	Married	Widowed	Divorced
a	b	c	d	e	f	g	h	i	j	k	l

West Yorkshire Metropolitan County – *continued*

Age	TOTAL PERSONS	Total	Single	Married	Widowed	Divorced	Total	Single	Married	Widowed	Divorced
All persons present in households	1,951,161	944,938	427,544	446,396	27,204	43,794	1,006,223	385,865	452,368	108,447	59,543
Aged											
0 - 4	139,965	71,247	71,247				68,718	68,718			
5 - 9	132,136	67,523	67,523				64,613	64,613			
10	26,791	13,734	13,734				13,057	13,057			
11	26,396	13,568	13,568				12,828	12,828			
12 - 14	71,108	36,654	36,654				34,454	34,454			
15	24,683	12,764	12,764				11,919	11,919			
16 - 17	51,120	26,064	25,945	104	5	10	25,056	24,785	253	8	10
18 - 19	57,131	28,710	28,230	461	3	16	28,421	26,888	1,482	17	34
20 - 24	156,791	76,806	66,040	10,214	13	539	79,985	58,311	20,082	61	1,531
25 - 29	153,055	74,656	36,859	34,572	62	3,163	78,399	26,975	45,460	166	5,798
30 - 34	141,681	69,617	16,627	47,290	100	5,600	72,064	11,301	52,309	320	8,134
35 - 39	129,463	64,832	9,265	49,075	194	6,298	64,631	5,511	49,999	585	8,536
40 - 44	142,123	70,607	7,296	55,709	323	7,279	71,516	3,690	57,103	1,147	9,576
45 - 49	113,707	56,800	4,688	46,029	495	5,588	56,907	2,461	45,677	1,783	6,986
50 - 54	104,305	51,915	3,741	42,295	874	5,005	52,390	2,145	41,380	3,135	5,730
55 - 59	98,087	48,206	3,334	39,808	1,341	3,723	49,881	2,249	37,557	5,689	4,386
60 - 64	96,266	45,780	3,291	37,043	2,599	2,847	50,486	2,651	34,194	10,278	3,363
65 - 69	93,763	43,480	2,881	34,365	4,241	1,993	50,283	3,015	29,001	15,765	2,502
70 - 74	73,405	31,301	1,743	23,898	4,671	989	42,104	2,804	19,177	18,692	1,431
75 - 79	60,064	22,932	1,197	15,746	5,478	511	37,132	2,937	11,922	21,341	932
80 - 84	37,653	12,261	640	7,281	4,164	176	25,392	2,575	5,099	17,284	434
85 - 89	16,623	4,531	236	2,185	2,055	55	12,092	1,470	1,442	9,045	135
90 and over	4,845	950	41	321	586	2	3,895	508	231	3,131	25

Remainder of Yorkshire & Humberside Region

Age	TOTAL PERSONS	Total	Single	Married	Widowed	Divorced	Total	Single	Married	Widowed	Divorced
All persons present in communal establishments	49,816	23,783	14,346	5,924	2,404	1,109	26,033	10,105	4,494	10,686	748
Aged											
0 - 4	662	348	348				314	314			
5 - 9	550	344	344				206	206			
10	363	221	221				142	142			
11	483	287	287				196	196			
12 - 14	1,559	842	842				717	717			
15	636	337	337				299	299			
16 - 17	2,247	1,553	1,551	2	-	-	694	688	5	1	-
18 - 19	3,578	2,331	2,302	25	-	4	1,247	1,232	13	1	1
20 - 24	5,829	3,701	3,469	202	2	28	2,128	1,932	172	4	20
25 - 29	2,884	1,926	1,330	477	3	116	958	611	298	4	45
30 - 34	1,771	1,139	538	486	3	112	632	268	298	6	60
35 - 39	1,512	944	329	495	3	117	568	219	282	7	60
40 - 44	1,648	1,028	347	558	5	118	620	187	344	12	77
45 - 49	1,432	833	239	467	12	115	599	165	354	12	68
50 - 54	1,277	716	174	455	12	75	561	136	327	26	72
55 - 59	1,240	675	172	398	18	87	565	128	343	49	45
60 - 64	1,536	777	271	368	47	91	759	183	355	167	54
65 - 69	1,816	878	286	406	117	69	938	222	325	328	63
70 - 74	2,258	943	266	396	219	62	1,315	306	317	648	44
75 - 79	3,509	1,194	277	444	410	63	2,315	404	365	1,503	43
80 - 84	4,986	1,311	230	422	631	28	3,675	552	395	2,676	52
85 - 89	4,729	964	126	242	581	15	3,765	561	223	2,955	26
90 and over	3,311	491	60	81	341	9	2,820	437	78	2,287	18

Table 2 Age and marital status – **continued**

Persons present

Age	TOTAL PERSONS	Males					Females				
		Total	Single	Married	Widowed	Divorced	Total	Single	Married	Widowed	Divorced
a	b	c	d	e	f	g	h	i	j	k	l

Remainder of Yorkshire & Humberside Region – *continued*

Age	TOTAL PERSONS	Total	Single	Married	Widowed	Divorced	Total	Single	Married	Widowed	Divorced
Visitors/guests	20,074	10,781	6,273	3,762	428	318	9,293	4,764	2,720	1,514	295
Aged											
0 - 4	414	209	209				205	205			
5 - 9	327	222	222				105	105			
10	307	191	191				116	116			
11	423	249	249				174	174			
12 - 14	1,339	705	705				634	634			
15	524	266	266				258	258			
16 - 17	1,370	805	804	1	-	-	565	560	4	1	-
18 - 19	2,000	1,140	1,122	15	-	3	860	849	9	1	1
20 - 24	2,776	1,566	1,457	99	2	8	1,210	1,082	118	2	8
25 - 29	1,283	782	444	298	2	38	501	246	231	4	20
30 - 34	959	613	196	367	1	49	346	95	222	3	26
35 - 39	762	481	83	357	2	39	281	53	188	4	36
40 - 44	804	503	79	385	1	38	301	37	219	5	40
45 - 49	699	407	33	329	7	38	292	28	220	7	37
50 - 54	641	363	28	309	8	18	278	20	212	14	32
55 - 59	681	343	25	282	10	26	338	27	255	34	22
60 - 64	777	353	32	279	21	21	424	31	280	92	21
65 - 69	810	391	24	314	39	14	419	34	241	126	18
70 - 74	818	377	26	278	66	7	441	41	205	183	12
75 - 79	899	371	36	234	86	15	528	60	153	303	12
80 - 84	774	268	31	144	90	3	506	51	114	333	8
85 - 89	477	134	8	60	65	1	343	42	42	258	1
90 and over	210	42	3	11	28	-	168	16	7	144	1
Resident - non-staff	26,417	11,467	7,235	1,584	1,961	687	14,950	4,257	1,200	9,122	371
Aged											
0 - 4	160	96	96				64	64			
5 - 9	107	64	64				43	43			
10	27	16	16				11	11			
11	30	22	22				8	8			
12 - 14	136	92	92				44	44			
15	78	47	47				31	31			
16 - 17	786	703	702	1	-	-	83	82	1	-	-
18 - 19	1,325	1,100	1,090	9	-	1	225	221	4	-	-
20 - 24	2,384	1,919	1,804	96	-	19	465	414	42	1	8
25 - 29	1,274	970	751	153	1	65	304	241	40	-	23
30 - 34	626	426	285	88	2	51	200	142	30	2	26
35 - 39	539	365	223	75	1	66	174	142	15	2	15
40 - 44	547	372	242	61	3	66	175	127	24	3	21
45 - 49	429	272	179	35	2	56	157	121	16	3	17
50 - 54	370	221	131	39	4	47	149	105	17	6	21
55 - 59	371	234	141	37	8	48	137	88	20	12	17
60 - 64	682	378	236	56	23	63	304	145	60	70	29
65 - 69	982	476	261	83	78	54	506	183	81	197	45
70 - 74	1,422	558	240	112	151	55	864	262	110	460	32
75 - 79	2,599	819	241	209	321	48	1,780	344	210	1,195	31
80 - 84	4,200	1,040	198	278	539	25	3,160	500	280	2,336	44
85 - 89	4,245	829	117	182	516	14	3,416	518	179	2,694	25
90 and over	3,098	448	57	70	312	9	2,650	421	71	2,141	17

Table 2   Age and marital status – **continued**

Great Britain, England & Wales, England, regions, metropolitan counties, Inner London, Outer London, regional remainders, Wales, Scotland

Persons present

Age	TOTAL PERSONS	Males					Females				
		Total	Single	Married	Widowed	Divorced	Total	Single	Married	Widowed	Divorced
a	b	c	d	e	f	g	h	i	j	k	l

Remainder of Yorkshire & Humberside Region – *continued*

Age	TOTAL PERSONS	Total	Single	Married	Widowed	Divorced	Total	Single	Married	Widowed	Divorced
Resident - staff	3,325	1,535	838	578	15	104	1,790	1,084	574	50	82
Aged											
0 - 4	88	43	43				45	45			
5 - 9	116	58	58				58	58			
10	29	14	14				15	15			
11	30	16	16				14	14			
12 - 14	84	45	45				39	39			
15	34	24	24				10	10			
16 - 17	91	45	45	-	-	-	46	46	-	-	-
18 - 19	253	91	90	1	-	-	162	162	-	-	-
20 - 24	669	216	208	7	-	1	453	436	12	1	4
25 - 29	327	174	135	26	-	13	153	124	27	-	2
30 - 34	186	100	57	31	-	12	86	31	46	1	8
35 - 39	211	98	23	63	-	12	113	24	79	1	9
40 - 44	297	153	26	112	1	14	144	23	101	4	16
45 - 49	304	154	27	103	3	21	150	16	118	2	14
50 - 54	266	132	15	107	-	10	134	11	98	6	19
55 - 59	188	98	6	79	-	13	90	13	68	3	6
60 - 64	77	46	3	33	3	7	31	7	15	5	4
65 - 69	24	11	1	9	-	1	13	5	3	5	-
70 - 74	18	8	-	6	2	-	10	3	2	5	-
75 - 79	11	4	-	1	3	-	7	-	2	5	-
80 - 84	12	3	1	-	2	-	9	1	1	7	-
85 - 89	7	1	1	-	-	-	6	1	2	3	-
90 and over	3	1	-	-	1	-	2	-	-	2	-
All persons present in households	1,501,247	726,596	308,844	366,049	20,926	30,777	774,651	275,293	372,887	84,263	42,208
Aged											
0 - 4	99,291	50,894	50,894				48,397	48,397			
5 - 9	95,056	48,792	48,792				46,264	46,264			
10	19,288	9,814	9,814				9,474	9,474			
11	19,175	9,805	9,805				9,370	9,370			
12 - 14	53,096	27,135	27,135				25,961	25,961			
15	18,263	9,340	9,340				8,923	8,923			
16 - 17	39,079	19,928	19,891	33	3	1	19,151	19,075	69	1	6
18 - 19	40,124	20,050	19,901	137	-	12	20,074	19,416	628	2	28
20 - 24	105,011	51,760	45,086	6,354	8	312	53,251	38,728	13,389	48	1,086
25 - 29	110,245	53,995	25,942	25,794	18	2,241	56,250	17,773	34,380	125	3,972
30 - 34	104,983	51,780	12,163	35,676	48	3,893	53,203	7,386	40,078	231	5,508
35 - 39	98,902	48,704	6,810	37,370	130	4,394	50,198	3,718	40,204	365	5,911
40 - 44	114,635	56,794	5,342	45,934	220	5,298	57,841	2,607	47,609	793	6,832
45 - 49	93,599	46,348	3,526	38,532	344	3,946	47,251	1,790	39,069	1,308	5,084
50 - 54	85,489	42,155	2,893	35,332	577	3,353	43,334	1,677	35,357	2,348	3,952
55 - 59	81,959	40,267	2,705	33,883	1,028	2,651	41,692	1,805	32,583	4,230	3,074
60 - 64	81,419	39,032	2,869	32,248	1,910	2,005	42,387	2,256	29,934	7,700	2,497
65 - 69	79,049	36,688	2,434	29,749	3,190	1,315	42,361	2,594	25,628	12,309	1,830
70 - 74	62,458	27,262	1,515	21,337	3,683	727	35,196	2,238	17,101	14,660	1,197
75 - 79	50,793	20,033	1,150	14,256	4,203	424	30,760	2,382	10,666	16,975	737
80 - 84	31,787	11,169	610	7,010	3,400	149	20,618	1,950	4,681	13,631	356
85 - 89	13,603	3,973	187	2,061	1,677	48	9,630	1,119	1,326	7,073	112
90 and over	3,943	878	40	343	487	8	3,065	390	185	2,464	26

Table 2 Age and marital status – **continued**

Great Britain, England & Wales, England, regions, metropolitan counties, Inner London, Outer London, regional remainders, Wales, Scotland

Persons present

Age	TOTAL PERSONS	Males					Females				
		Total	Single	Married	Widowed	Divorced	Total	Single	Married	Widowed	Divorced
a	b	c	d	e	f	g	h	i	j	k	l

EAST MIDLANDS REGION

All persons present in communal establishments	91,182	43,954	27,330	9,652	4,646	2,326	47,228	18,400	7,562	19,897	1,369

Aged

0 - 4	1,693	924	924				769	769			
5 - 9	1,357	819	819				538	538			
10	516	335	335				181	181			
11	639	421	421				218	218			
12 - 14	2,768	1,923	1,923				845	845			
15	1,259	881	881				378	378			
16 - 17	3,349	2,316	2,309	7	-	-	1,033	1,028	5	-	-
18 - 19	6,641	3,869	3,842	24	1	2	2,772	2,741	27	-	4
20 - 24	10,979	6,623	6,232	326	2	63	4,356	4,030	290	2	34
25 - 29	5,764	3,703	2,770	738	10	185	2,061	1,236	713	5	107
30 - 34	4,122	2,645	1,392	952	8	293	1,477	608	728	8	133
35 - 39	3,092	2,046	835	911	17	283	1,046	375	541	10	120
40 - 44	2,910	1,855	703	830	9	313	1,055	360	515	17	163
45 - 49	2,371	1,499	585	639	16	259	872	283	443	23	123
50 - 54	2,138	1,282	483	570	19	210	856	247	441	59	109
55 - 59	1,958	1,110	409	509	34	158	848	219	444	85	100
60 - 64	2,465	1,374	503	609	97	165	1,091	315	437	251	88
65 - 69	3,109	1,534	530	640	242	122	1,575	402	513	560	100
70 - 74	3,857	1,599	430	682	400	87	2,258	468	511	1,188	91
75 - 79	6,130	2,119	403	832	781	103	4,011	653	655	2,634	69
80 - 84	9,065	2,350	335	779	1,180	56	6,715	869	674	5,104	68
85 - 89	8,707	1,788	194	443	1,130	21	6,919	950	449	5,480	40
90 and over	6,293	939	72	161	700	6	5,354	687	176	4,471	20

Visitors/guests	40,734	23,460	15,340	6,434	892	794	17,274	8,979	4,870	2,810	615

Aged

0 - 4	1,297	723	723				574	574			
5 - 9	962	603	603				359	359			
10	411	276	276				135	135			
11	549	363	363				186	186			
12 - 14	2,388	1,706	1,706				682	682			
15	1,011	747	747				264	264			
16 - 17	2,869	2,028	2,021	7	-	-	841	838	3	-	-
18 - 19	4,998	2,876	2,856	18	1	1	2,122	2,103	16	-	3
20 - 24	6,479	3,833	3,556	244	1	32	2,646	2,409	226	1	10
25 - 29	3,000	1,827	1,198	551	8	70	1,173	515	594	2	62
30 - 34	2,253	1,341	466	725	7	143	912	219	606	5	82
35 - 39	1,667	1,049	199	718	11	121	618	92	453	3	70
40 - 44	1,421	865	114	629	5	117	556	53	402	6	95
45 - 49	1,076	657	96	469	7	85	419	37	310	16	56
50 - 54	1,039	578	71	435	9	63	461	29	343	36	53
55 - 59	998	514	63	397	12	42	484	31	353	56	44
60 - 64	1,129	595	60	458	33	44	534	40	343	118	33
65 - 69	1,355	673	67	495	86	25	682	58	377	209	38
70 - 74	1,288	620	43	437	122	18	668	53	283	305	27
75 - 79	1,471	652	46	406	178	22	819	84	267	455	13
80 - 84	1,547	549	38	291	212	8	998	92	189	700	17
85 - 89	992	267	19	119	126	3	725	76	80	560	9
90 and over	534	118	9	35	74	-	416	50	25	338	3

Table 2 Age and marital status – **continued**

Great Britain, England & Wales, England, regions, metropolitan counties, Inner London, Outer London, regional remainders, Wales, Scotland

Persons present

Age	TOTAL PERSONS	Males					Females				
		Total	Single	Married	Widowed	Divorced	Total	Single	Married	Widowed	Divorced
a	b	c	d	e	f	g	h	i	j	k	l

EAST MIDLANDS REGION – *continued*

Resident - non-staff	46,496	18,750	10,864	2,740	3,742	1,404	27,746	7,865	2,205	17,043	633
Aged											
0 - 4	324	169	169				155	155			
5 - 9	318	178	178				140	140			
10	77	47	47				30	30			
11	72	48	48				24	24			
12 - 14	324	193	193				131	131			
15	234	125	125				109	109			
16 - 17	407	257	257	-	-	-	150	149	1	-	-
18 - 19	1,334	899	892	6	-	1	435	424	10	-	1
20 - 24	3,351	2,422	2,315	75	1	31	929	868	43	1	17
25 - 29	2,166	1,571	1,312	157	2	100	595	491	73	3	28
30 - 34	1,532	1,111	802	169	1	139	421	308	70	3	40
35 - 39	1,230	892	594	149	6	143	338	259	35	5	39
40 - 44	1,241	859	558	124	4	173	382	283	43	11	45
45 - 49	1,049	721	468	87	9	157	328	232	40	5	51
50 - 54	890	604	399	72	8	125	286	206	30	15	35
55 - 59	791	513	337	57	19	100	278	174	38	23	43
60 - 64	1,252	725	436	110	61	118	527	269	76	128	54
65 - 69	1,724	841	458	131	155	97	883	343	131	348	61
70 - 74	2,550	971	385	241	278	67	1,579	415	223	877	64
75 - 79	4,651	1,465	357	425	602	81	3,186	568	388	2,174	56
80 - 84	7,512	1,800	297	488	967	48	5,712	776	484	4,401	51
85 - 89	7,709	1,518	174	323	1,003	18	6,191	874	369	4,917	31
90 and over	5,758	821	63	126	626	6	4,937	637	151	4,132	17
Resident - staff	3,952	1,744	1,126	478	12	128	2,208	1,556	487	44	121
Aged											
0 - 4	72	32	32				40	40			
5 - 9	77	38	38				39	39			
10	28	12	12				16	16			
11	18	10	10				8	8			
12 - 14	56	24	24				32	32			
15	14	9	9				5	5			
16 - 17	73	31	31	-	-	-	42	41	1	-	-
18 - 19	309	94	94	-	-	-	215	214	1	-	-
20 - 24	1,149	368	361	7	-	-	781	753	21	-	7
25 - 29	598	305	260	30	-	15	293	230	46	-	17
30 - 34	337	193	124	58	-	11	144	81	52	-	11
35 - 39	195	105	42	44	-	19	90	24	53	2	11
40 - 44	248	131	31	77	-	23	117	24	70	-	23
45 - 49	246	121	21	83	-	17	125	14	93	2	16
50 - 54	209	100	13	63	2	22	109	12	68	8	21
55 - 59	169	83	9	55	3	16	86	14	53	6	13
60 - 64	84	54	7	41	3	3	30	6	18	5	1
65 - 69	30	20	5	14	1	-	10	1	5	3	1
70 - 74	19	8	2	4	-	2	11	-	5	6	-
75 - 79	8	2	-	1	1	-	6	1	-	5	-
80 - 84	6	1	-	-	1	-	5	1	1	3	-
85 - 89	6	3	1	1	1	-	3	-	-	3	-
90 and over	1	-	-	-	-	-	1	-	-	1	-

Table 2 Age and marital status – **continued**

Great Britain, England & Wales, England, regions, metropolitan counties, Inner London, Outer London, regional remainders, Wales, Scotland

Persons present

Age	TOTAL PERSONS	Males					Females				
		Total	Single	Married	Widowed	Divorced	Total	Single	Married	Widowed	Divorced
a	b	c	d	e	f	g	h	i	j	k	l

EAST MIDLANDS REGION – *continued*

All persons present in households	3,828,301	1,873,580	806,027	936,365	53,236	77,952	1,954,721	707,161	947,557	199,228	100,775
Aged											
0 - 4	257,737	131,917	131,917				125,820	125,820			
5 - 9	245,132	125,687	125,687				119,445	119,445			
10	50,644	25,930	25,930				24,714	24,714			
11	50,008	25,447	25,447				24,561	24,561			
12 - 14	136,407	69,612	69,612				66,795	66,795			
15	46,562	23,776	23,776				22,786	22,786			
16 - 17	99,202	50,567	50,444	100	9	14	48,635	48,342	259	20	14
18 - 19	105,629	53,595	53,122	438	7	28	52,034	50,143	1,814	18	59
20 - 24	283,120	140,171	121,700	17,611	47	813	142,949	102,839	37,558	119	2,433
25 - 29	294,916	145,120	70,442	69,122	93	5,463	149,796	48,660	91,120	321	9,695
30 - 34	274,405	135,888	32,558	93,306	191	9,833	138,517	19,795	104,429	569	13,724
35 - 39	258,937	128,154	17,637	98,782	305	11,430	130,783	9,963	104,992	1,053	14,775
40 - 44	291,756	145,766	13,491	118,458	637	13,180	145,990	6,534	120,973	2,079	16,404
45 - 49	246,940	124,241	9,337	103,076	950	10,878	122,699	4,372	102,162	3,263	12,902
50 - 54	210,039	105,836	7,217	88,557	1,518	8,544	104,203	3,606	85,592	5,533	9,472
55 - 59	197,612	98,706	6,612	83,043	2,502	6,549	98,906	3,746	78,206	9,866	7,088
60 - 64	197,260	95,985	6,916	79,523	4,806	4,740	101,275	4,339	73,374	18,240	5,322
65 - 69	193,518	91,826	5,929	74,455	8,106	3,336	101,692	4,817	63,939	28,964	3,972
70 - 74	152,704	68,102	3,735	53,210	9,407	1,750	84,602	4,461	42,944	34,721	2,476
75 - 79	119,485	48,559	2,556	34,807	10,284	912	70,926	4,643	25,534	39,273	1,476
80 - 84	74,642	26,786	1,375	16,408	8,645	358	47,856	3,962	11,197	32,041	656
85 - 89	32,051	9,707	488	4,775	4,341	103	22,344	2,078	2,965	17,038	263
90 and over	9,595	2,202	99	694	1,388	21	7,393	740	499	6,110	44

EAST ANGLIA REGION

All persons present in communal establishments	68,263	36,333	24,527	7,675	2,398	1,733	31,930	15,713	5,306	10,031	880
Aged											
0 - 4	1,023	545	545				478	478			
5 - 9	920	517	517				403	403			
10	385	239	239				146	146			
11	567	346	346				221	221			
12 - 14	2,610	1,667	1,667				943	943			
15	1,087	693	693				394	394			
16 - 17	2,475	1,480	1,473	6	1	-	995	993	2	-	-
18 - 19	6,348	3,860	3,819	36	1	4	2,488	2,463	25	-	-
20 - 24	13,941	8,894	8,484	311	5	94	5,047	4,738	275	3	31
25 - 29	5,306	3,649	2,713	706	6	224	1,657	1,101	482	7	67
30 - 34	3,133	2,198	1,087	868	14	229	935	385	482	4	64
35 - 39	2,400	1,663	538	873	7	245	737	243	393	13	88
40 - 44	2,138	1,436	435	776	9	216	702	189	404	9	100
45 - 49	1,814	1,137	306	627	12	192	677	175	400	12	90
50 - 54	1,504	941	239	533	26	143	563	139	335	21	68
55 - 59	1,297	738	168	450	23	97	559	125	318	49	67
60 - 64	1,498	784	252	417	33	82	714	179	350	131	54
65 - 69	1,668	799	221	423	83	72	869	196	323	289	61
70 - 74	2,126	876	226	399	195	56	1,250	243	339	608	60
75 - 79	3,211	1,075	212	460	369	34	2,136	389	386	1,317	44
80 - 84	4,527	1,175	159	397	589	30	3,352	496	422	2,390	44
85 - 89	4,763	1,053	134	294	613	12	3,710	600	252	2,827	31
90 and over	3,522	568	54	99	412	3	2,954	474	118	2,351	11

Table 2 Age and marital status – **continued**

Great Britain, England & Wales, England, regions, metropolitan counties, Inner London, Outer London, regional remainders, Wales, Scotland

Persons present

Age	TOTAL PERSONS	Males					Females				
		Total	Single	Married	Widowed	Divorced	Total	Single	Married	Widowed	Divorced
a	b	c	d	e	f	g	h	i	j	k	l

EAST ANGLIA REGION – *continued*

Age	TOTAL PERSONS	Males Total	Single	Married	Widowed	Divorced	Females Total	Single	Married	Widowed	Divorced
Visitors/guests	34,815	19,989	13,676	5,158	532	623	14,826	9,038	3,575	1,812	401
Aged											
0 - 4	762	414	414				348	348			
5 - 9	660	372	372				288	288			
10	332	206	206				126	126			
11	505	313	313				192	192			
12 - 14	2,289	1,482	1,482				807	807			
15	959	622	622				337	337			
16 - 17	2,010	1,181	1,175	5	1	-	829	828	1	-	-
18 - 19	4,501	2,568	2,555	12	1	-	1,933	1,919	14	-	-
20 - 24	8,068	4,792	4,617	142	3	30	3,276	3,072	195	2	7
25 - 29	2,240	1,377	902	423	-	52	863	430	390	5	38
30 - 34	1,647	1,086	373	615	7	91	561	132	396	3	30
35 - 39	1,363	911	185	626	4	96	452	79	310	9	54
40 - 44	1,140	753	110	545	5	93	387	33	294	4	56
45 - 49	971	627	70	475	1	81	344	23	273	5	43
50 - 54	808	505	48	389	13	55	303	23	234	12	34
55 - 59	730	414	36	326	13	39	316	16	244	30	26
60 - 64	860	428	46	336	19	27	432	38	292	74	28
65 - 69	934	457	41	356	37	23	477	45	252	154	26
70 - 74	946	402	30	299	57	16	544	60	236	222	26
75 - 79	1,073	456	36	290	122	8	617	68	207	331	11
80 - 84	993	336	22	188	116	10	657	73	148	427	9
85 - 89	691	210	15	107	88	-	481	67	66	337	11
90 and over	333	77	6	24	45	2	256	34	23	197	2
Resident - non-staff	30,191	14,852	9,922	2,067	1,856	1,007	15,339	5,512	1,291	8,170	366
Aged											
0 - 4	208	104	104				104	104			
5 - 9	178	107	107				71	71			
10	34	22	22				12	12			
11	40	20	20				20	20			
12 - 14	232	135	135				97	97			
15	111	63	63				48	48			
16 - 17	370	252	252	-	-	-	118	117	1	-	-
18 - 19	1,633	1,208	1,181	23	-	4	425	414	11	-	-
20 - 24	5,091	3,841	3,612	163	2	64	1,250	1,157	73	1	19
25 - 29	2,616	2,049	1,614	264	6	165	567	474	69	2	22
30 - 34	1,280	992	626	231	7	128	288	202	59	1	26
35 - 39	875	667	315	213	2	137	208	142	41	3	22
40 - 44	763	554	297	150	4	103	209	144	35	4	26
45 - 49	586	391	219	75	6	91	195	144	26	3	22
50 - 54	479	328	182	66	12	68	151	106	21	5	19
55 - 59	373	229	125	44	10	50	144	94	15	11	24
60 - 64	560	311	198	48	14	51	249	130	44	52	23
65 - 69	699	324	176	56	45	47	375	148	63	129	35
70 - 74	1,158	470	195	98	137	40	688	176	100	380	32
75 - 79	2,128	615	175	168	246	26	1,513	318	179	983	33
80 - 84	3,524	838	137	208	473	20	2,686	422	274	1,956	34
85 - 89	4,066	842	119	186	525	12	3,224	533	185	2,486	20
90 and over	3,187	490	48	74	367	1	2,697	439	95	2,154	9

Table 2   Age and marital status – **continued**

Great Britain, England & Wales, England, regions, metropolitan counties, Inner London, Outer London, regional remainders, Wales, Scotland

Persons present

Age	TOTAL PERSONS	Males					Females				
		Total	Single	Married	Widowed	Divorced	Total	Single	Married	Widowed	Divorced
a	b	c	d	e	f	g	h	i	j	k	l

EAST ANGLIA REGION – *continued*

Resident - staff	3,257	1,492	929	450	10	103	1,765	1,163	440	49	113
Aged											
0 - 4	53	27	27				26	26			
5 - 9	82	38	38				44	44			
10	19	11	11				8	8			
11	22	13	13				9	9			
12 - 14	89	50	50				39	39			
15	17	8	8				9	9			
16 - 17	95	47	46	1	-	-	48	48	-	-	-
18 - 19	214	84	83	1	-	-	130	130	-	-	-
20 - 24	782	261	255	6	-	-	521	509	7	-	5
25 - 29	450	223	197	19	-	7	227	197	23	-	7
30 - 34	206	120	88	22	-	10	86	51	27	-	8
35 - 39	162	85	38	34	1	12	77	22	42	1	12
40 - 44	235	129	28	81	-	20	106	12	75	1	18
45 - 49	257	119	17	77	5	20	138	8	101	4	25
50 - 54	217	108	9	78	1	20	109	10	80	4	15
55 - 59	194	95	7	80	-	8	99	15	59	8	17
60 - 64	78	45	8	33	-	4	33	11	14	5	3
65 - 69	35	18	4	11	1	2	17	3	8	6	-
70 - 74	22	4	1	2	1	-	18	7	3	6	2
75 - 79	10	4	1	2	1	-	6	3	-	3	-
80 - 84	10	1	-	1	-	-	9	1	-	7	1
85 - 89	6	1	-	1	-	-	5	-	1	4	-
90 and over	2	1	-	1	-	-	1	1	-	-	-
All persons present in households	1,950,354	951,656	397,394	488,629	26,116	39,517	998,698	347,826	495,664	102,021	53,187
Aged											
0 - 4	126,970	64,831	64,831				62,139	62,139			
5 - 9	121,538	62,149	62,149				59,389	59,389			
10	25,256	12,930	12,930				12,326	12,326			
11	25,208	12,863	12,863				12,345	12,345			
12 - 14	68,877	35,146	35,146				33,731	33,731			
15	23,475	12,100	12,100				11,375	11,375			
16 - 17	50,178	25,424	25,372	40	2	10	24,754	24,624	113	8	9
18 - 19	51,385	25,901	25,628	258	5	10	25,484	24,369	1,081	7	27
20 - 24	134,692	67,045	57,091	9,567	14	373	67,647	46,308	20,032	53	1,254
25 - 29	145,005	72,193	34,745	34,689	38	2,721	72,812	21,968	45,939	150	4,755
30 - 34	135,520	67,399	16,196	46,388	65	4,750	68,121	8,954	52,298	285	6,584
35 - 39	130,661	63,946	8,871	49,423	143	5,509	66,715	4,765	54,020	464	7,466
40 - 44	150,373	74,237	6,687	60,456	281	6,813	76,136	3,419	62,848	969	8,900
45 - 49	125,026	62,801	4,460	52,279	430	5,632	62,225	2,346	51,657	1,510	6,712
50 - 54	106,036	53,483	3,434	45,052	611	4,386	52,553	1,907	43,316	2,366	4,964
55 - 59	100,253	49,893	3,367	42,193	1,059	3,274	50,360	2,136	40,103	4,400	3,721
60 - 64	102,849	49,696	3,612	41,718	1,922	2,444	53,153	2,615	39,120	8,409	3,009
65 - 69	102,608	48,071	3,139	39,787	3,409	1,736	54,537	3,057	35,357	13,712	2,411
70 - 74	84,635	38,094	2,076	30,625	4,366	1,027	46,541	2,776	24,645	17,471	1,649
75 - 79	69,635	28,943	1,516	21,501	5,393	533	40,692	2,877	15,751	21,029	1,035
80 - 84	44,533	16,660	811	10,746	4,874	229	27,873	2,482	7,045	17,856	490
85 - 89	19,570	6,362	313	3,384	2,603	62	13,208	1,405	1,980	9,664	159
90 and over	6,071	1,489	57	523	901	8	4,582	513	359	3,668	42

Table 2 Age and marital status – **continued**

Great Britain, England & Wales, England, regions, metropolitan counties, Inner London, Outer London, regional remainders, Wales, Scotland

Persons present

Age	TOTAL PERSONS	Males					Females				
		Total	Single	Married	Widowed	Divorced	Total	Single	Married	Widowed	Divorced
a	b	c	d	e	f	g	h	i	j	k	l

SOUTH EAST REGION

All persons present in communal establishments *	514,062	250,086	162,234	58,990	16,900	11,962	263,976	135,213	41,723	78,517	8,523
Aged											
0 - 4	9,305	5,160	5,160				4,145	4,145			
5 - 9	6,350	4,008	4,008				2,342	2,342			
10	2,926	1,969	1,969				957	957			
11	4,489	2,785	2,785				1,704	1,704			
12 - 14	19,657	12,042	12,042				7,615	7,615			
15	8,384	5,252	5,252				3,132	3,132			
16 - 17	19,422	11,938	11,904	28	1	5	7,484	7,452	28	3	1
18 - 19	37,987	20,538	20,376	136	3	23	17,449	17,196	229	9	15
20 - 24	78,057	41,616	39,437	1,875	29	275	36,441	34,209	2,026	29	177
25 - 29	42,665	25,236	18,964	5,295	47	930	17,429	12,659	4,144	41	585
30 - 34	26,883	17,040	8,967	6,730	54	1,289	9,843	5,081	3,948	66	748
35 - 39	19,910	12,865	5,169	6,168	65	1,463	7,045	2,966	3,222	77	780
40 - 44	19,537	12,511	4,318	6,432	100	1,661	7,026	2,657	3,387	108	874
45 - 49	16,557	10,225	3,647	5,083	104	1,391	6,332	2,199	3,058	200	875
50 - 54	14,133	8,354	2,721	4,323	150	1,160	5,779	1,932	2,808	293	746
55 - 59	12,894	7,308	2,524	3,624	179	981	5,586	1,964	2,472	482	668
60 - 64	13,838	7,353	2,758	3,451	390	754	6,485	2,201	2,558	1,122	604
65 - 69	15,728	7,661	2,694	3,439	853	675	8,067	2,482	2,619	2,418	548
70 - 74	18,021	7,560	2,362	3,286	1,400	512	10,461	2,846	2,510	4,618	487
75 - 79	26,321	8,691	2,146	3,439	2,703	403	17,630	4,062	2,824	10,241	503
80 - 84	36,526	9,375	1,764	3,166	4,168	277	27,151	5,332	2,839	18,544	436
85 - 89	36,588	6,888	879	1,841	4,050	118	29,700	5,571	2,041	21,763	325
90 and over	27,884	3,711	388	674	2,604	45	24,173	4,509	1,010	18,503	151
Visitors/guests	232,128	129,910	82,104	39,769	4,007	4,030	102,218	59,344	25,635	13,728	3,511
Aged											
0 - 4	5,251	3,000	3,000				2,251	2,251			
5 - 9	3,567	2,474	2,474				1,093	1,093			
10	2,335	1,648	1,648				687	687			
11	3,829	2,441	2,441				1,388	1,388			
12 - 14	17,379	10,760	10,760				6,619	6,619			
15	7,121	4,575	4,575				2,546	2,546			
16 - 17	15,635	9,515	9,491	20	1	3	6,120	6,101	17	1	1
18 - 19	25,315	13,384	13,294	78	1	11	11,931	11,817	103	4	7
20 - 24	36,928	19,922	18,899	919	14	90	17,006	15,901	1,031	14	60
25 - 29	16,926	10,103	6,801	2,976	23	303	6,823	4,019	2,554	21	229
30 - 34	12,560	7,869	3,022	4,347	26	474	4,691	1,611	2,670	32	378
35 - 39	9,958	6,473	1,380	4,482	30	581	3,485	801	2,229	32	423
40 - 44	9,994	6,569	997	4,913	46	613	3,425	572	2,348	45	460
45 - 49	8,426	5,213	719	3,912	51	531	3,213	400	2,251	110	452
50 - 54	7,087	4,265	454	3,331	65	415	2,822	305	2,007	165	345
55 - 59	6,343	3,592	409	2,771	94	318	2,751	290	1,876	283	302
60 - 64	6,543	3,448	406	2,661	167	214	3,095	305	1,994	566	230
65 - 69	7,214	3,570	361	2,695	343	171	3,644	351	2,024	1,074	195
70 - 74	6,917	3,258	291	2,358	492	117	3,659	393	1,557	1,558	151
75 - 79	7,804	3,244	290	2,074	776	104	4,560	529	1,445	2,462	124
80 - 84	7,403	2,701	254	1,466	923	58	4,702	574	883	3,157	88
85 - 89	4,997	1,382	102	598	663	19	3,615	516	467	2,580	52
90 and over	2,596	504	36	168	292	8	2,092	275	179	1,624	14

Note: * Includes a female member of staff incorrectly enumerated as a resident.

Table 2 Age and marital status – **continued**

Great Britain, England & Wales, England, regions, metropolitan counties, Inner London, Outer London, regional remainders, Wales, Scotland

Persons present

Age	TOTAL PERSONS	Males					Females				
		Total	Single	Married	Widowed	Divorced	Total	Single	Married	Widowed	Divorced
a	b	c	d	e	f	g	h	i	j	k	l
SOUTH EAST REGION – *continued*											
Resident - non-staff	243,361	103,828	68,679	15,596	12,800	6,753	139,533	58,847	12,455	64,360	3,871
Aged											
0 - 4	3,557	1,904	1,904				1,653	1,653			
5 - 9	2,281	1,253	1,253				1,028	1,028			
10	486	268	268				218	218			
11	532	278	278				254	254			
12 - 14	1,935	1,096	1,096				839	839			
15	1,139	613	613				526	526			
16 - 17	3,286	2,199	2,191	7	-	1	1,087	1,076	9	2	-
18 - 19	10,032	6,260	6,194	54	1	11	3,772	3,652	107	5	8
20 - 24	29,314	17,753	16,744	831	13	165	11,561	10,677	781	15	88
25 - 29	18,932	12,019	9,508	1,955	23	533	6,913	5,493	1,148	17	255
30 - 34	11,217	7,550	4,925	1,953	23	649	3,667	2,472	905	29	261
35 - 39	7,710	5,193	3,217	1,261	32	683	2,517	1,662	566	37	252
40 - 44	7,328	4,868	2,967	990	52	859	2,460	1,662	482	43	273
45 - 49	6,105	4,040	2,638	661	46	695	2,065	1,445	298	62	260
50 - 54	5,112	3,231	2,043	517	71	600	1,881	1,305	304	74	198
55 - 59	4,904	2,980	1,908	453	72	547	1,924	1,322	274	127	201
60 - 64	6,318	3,441	2,198	557	210	476	2,877	1,701	397	490	289
65 - 69	8,112	3,924	2,259	672	498	495	4,188	2,036	540	1,289	323
70 - 74	10,884	4,212	2,027	896	904	385	6,672	2,377	929	3,035	331
75 - 79	18,356	5,401	1,829	1,349	1,924	299	12,955	3,464	1,368	7,746	377
80 - 84	29,037	6,649	1,496	1,697	3,237	219	22,388	4,727	1,952	15,361	348
85 - 89	31,525	5,493	772	1,240	3,382	99	26,032	5,034	1,567	19,161	270
90 and over	25,259	3,203	351	503	2,312	37	22,056	4,224	828	16,867	137
Resident - staff	38,573	16,348	11,451	3,625	93	1,179	22,225	17,022	3,633	429	1,141
Aged											
0 - 4	497	256	256				241	241			
5 - 9	502	281	281				221	221			
10	105	53	53				52	52			
11	128	66	66				62	62			
12 - 14	343	186	186				157	157			
15	124	64	64				60	60			
16 - 17	501	224	222	1	-	1	277	275	2	-	-
18 - 19	2,640	894	888	4	1	1	1,746	1,727	19	-	-
20 - 24	11,815	3,941	3,794	125	2	20	7,874	7,631	214	-	29
25 - 29	6,807	3,114	2,655	364	1	94	3,693	3,147	442	3	101
30 - 34	3,106	1,621	1,020	430	5	166	1,485	998	373	5	109
35 - 39	2,242	1,199	572	425	3	199	1,043	503	427	8	105
40 - 44	2,215	1,074	354	529	2	189	1,141	423	557	20	141
45 - 49	2,026	972	290	510	7	165	1,054	354	509	28	163
50 - 54	1,934	858	224	475	14	145	1,076	322	497	54	203
55 - 59	1,647	736	207	400	13	116	911	352	322	72	165
60 - 64	977	464	154	233	13	64	513	195	167	66	85
65 - 69	402	167	74	72	12	9	235	95	55	55	30
70 - 74	220	90	44	32	4	10	130	76	24	25	5
75 - 79	161	46	27	16	3	-	115	69	11	33	2
80 - 84	86	25	14	3	8	-	61	31	4	26	-
85 - 89	66	13	5	3	5	-	53	21	7	22	3
90 and over	29	4	1	3	-	-	25	10	3	12	-

Table 2　Age and marital status – **continued**

Persons present

Age	TOTAL PERSONS	Males					Females				
		Total	Single	Married	Widowed	Divorced	Total	Single	Married	Widowed	Divorced
a	b	c	d	e	f	g	h	i	j	k	l

SOUTH EAST REGION – *continued*

All persons present in households	16,279,621	7,870,988	3,637,367	3,701,665	202,117	329,839	8,408,633	3,316,479	3,764,687	850,609	476,858
Aged											
0 - 4	1,111,343	568,018	568,018				543,325	543,325			
5 - 9	1,020,917	522,450	522,450				498,467	498,467			
10	206,987	105,426	105,426				101,561	101,561			
11	203,240	104,138	104,138				99,102	99,102			
12 - 14	555,370	283,487	283,487				271,883	271,883			
15	185,163	94,332	94,332				90,831	90,831			
16 - 17	393,828	200,885	200,240	540	28	77	192,943	191,699	1,107	74	63
18 - 19	415,261	208,373	206,556	1,665	39	113	206,888	199,908	6,667	95	218
20 - 24	1,245,441	607,380	547,231	57,610	122	2,417	638,061	500,393	129,662	503	7,503
25 - 29	1,411,576	690,093	410,526	261,572	380	17,615	721,483	320,461	364,084	1,540	35,398
30 - 34	1,262,891	625,060	198,602	388,659	713	37,086	637,831	140,055	438,692	2,763	56,321
35 - 39	1,119,243	551,966	103,660	401,900	1,361	45,045	567,277	70,109	427,960	4,686	64,522
40 - 44	1,215,535	597,764	74,820	465,143	2,574	55,227	617,771	48,287	484,185	8,722	76,577
45 - 49	1,003,463	494,869	47,417	396,780	3,526	47,146	508,594	30,779	399,878	14,012	63,925
50 - 54	875,226	435,079	36,633	353,652	5,730	39,064	440,147	25,520	341,787	23,318	49,522
55 - 59	818,233	406,463	32,982	333,536	9,521	30,424	411,770	25,355	308,586	40,183	37,646
60 - 64	791,455	382,503	32,404	310,656	16,802	22,641	408,952	28,766	278,758	71,813	29,615
65 - 69	751,434	344,264	27,520	273,296	27,796	15,652	407,170	30,515	239,349	114,776	22,530
70 - 74	618,130	265,683	18,101	205,482	33,087	9,013	352,447	28,146	167,333	141,815	15,153
75 - 79	524,604	206,533	12,804	148,061	40,327	5,341	318,071	28,770	108,696	170,379	10,226
80 - 84	344,210	119,906	6,878	75,693	35,115	2,220	224,304	24,181	50,597	144,189	5,337
85 - 89	155,880	45,233	2,528	23,364	18,714	627	110,647	13,650	14,740	80,379	1,878
90 and over	50,191	11,083	614	4,056	6,282	131	39,108	4,716	2,606	31,362	424

Greater London

All persons present in communal establishments *	183,034	86,291	51,863	24,759	5,081	4,588	96,743	53,299	17,716	22,272	3,456
Aged											
0 - 4	5,505	3,047	3,047				2,458	2,458			
5 - 9	2,313	1,298	1,298				1,015	1,015			
10	457	242	242				215	215			
11	598	325	325				273	273			
12 - 14	2,687	1,510	1,510				1,177	1,177			
15	1,180	713	713				467	467			
16 - 17	2,767	1,495	1,481	14	-	-	1,272	1,252	18	2	-
18 - 19	12,210	5,595	5,522	57	2	14	6,615	6,488	112	5	10
20 - 24	32,337	14,468	13,801	579	16	72	17,869	16,738	1,038	16	77
25 - 29	19,709	10,362	8,016	2,055	27	264	9,347	6,875	2,191	24	257
30 - 34	12,619	7,470	4,007	2,958	25	480	5,149	2,632	2,112	46	359
35 - 39	9,133	5,629	2,179	2,856	24	570	3,504	1,361	1,711	36	396
40 - 44	8,652	5,353	1,616	3,039	49	649	3,299	1,173	1,678	53	395
45 - 49	7,372	4,489	1,346	2,499	47	597	2,883	946	1,458	104	375
50 - 54	6,291	3,820	1,034	2,214	59	513	2,471	797	1,247	112	315
55 - 59	5,495	3,216	1,006	1,756	77	377	2,279	779	1,036	203	261
60 - 64	5,389	3,057	1,016	1,591	149	301	2,332	781	924	392	235
65 - 69	5,496	2,878	952	1,357	308	261	2,618	849	838	747	184
70 - 74	5,900	2,650	839	1,131	481	199	3,250	952	745	1,398	155
75 - 79	8,192	2,932	808	1,111	875	138	5,260	1,310	823	2,966	161
80 - 84	10,573	2,850	650	923	1,186	91	7,723	1,704	810	5,080	129
85 - 89	10,213	1,905	324	451	1,089	41	8,308	1,713	619	5,875	101
90 and over	7,946	987	131	168	667	21	6,959	1,344	356	5,213	46

Note: * Includes a female member of staff incorrectly enumerated as a resident.

Table 2 Age and marital status – **continued**

Great Britain, England & Wales, England, regions, metropolitan counties, Inner London, Outer London, regional remainders, Wales, Scotland

Persons present

Age	TOTAL PERSONS	Males					Females				
		Total	Single	Married	Widowed	Divorced	Total	Single	Married	Widowed	Divorced
a	b	c	d	e	f	g	h	i	j	k	l

Greater London – *continued*

Visitors/guests	**83,214**	**44,410**	**22,985**	**18,000**	**1,580**	**1,845**	**38,804**	**20,504**	**11,433**	**5,192**	**1,675**
Aged											
0 - 4	2,969	1,688	1,688				1,281	1,281			
5 - 9	835	495	495				340	340			
10	194	101	101				93	93			
11	332	183	183				149	149			
12 - 14	1,807	1,030	1,030				777	777			
15	716	478	478				238	238			
16 - 17	1,761	1,050	1,040	10	-	-	711	699	11	1	-
18 - 19	7,925	3,813	3,765	39	1	8	4,112	4,058	47	2	5
20 - 24	14,764	7,055	6,739	277	9	30	7,709	7,210	465	6	28
25 - 29	7,801	4,242	3,005	1,135	14	88	3,559	2,230	1,219	11	99
30 - 34	6,189	3,659	1,518	1,920	14	207	2,530	951	1,363	17	199
35 - 39	5,092	3,182	746	2,163	10	263	1,910	462	1,214	10	224
40 - 44	5,060	3,279	502	2,463	21	293	1,781	276	1,264	23	218
45 - 49	4,329	2,664	333	2,043	29	259	1,665	216	1,167	64	218
50 - 54	3,672	2,275	218	1,818	28	211	1,397	154	992	77	174
55 - 59	3,117	1,890	235	1,459	43	153	1,227	128	836	120	143
60 - 64	2,923	1,710	229	1,281	87	113	1,213	131	755	219	108
65 - 69	2,720	1,486	195	1,068	130	93	1,234	145	661	352	76
70 - 74	2,461	1,238	144	849	192	53	1,223	158	461	548	56
75 - 79	2,815	1,244	153	732	320	39	1,571	209	428	881	53
80 - 84	2,727	983	120	487	355	21	1,744	239	306	1,163	36
85 - 89	1,906	479	50	192	226	11	1,427	225	166	1,002	34
90 and over	1,099	186	18	64	101	3	913	135	78	696	4
Resident - non-staff	**86,326**	**36,990**	**25,291**	**5,773**	**3,473**	**2,453**	**49,336**	**25,648**	**5,294**	**16,949**	**1,445**
Aged											
0 - 4	2,387	1,276	1,276				1,111	1,111			
5 - 9	1,339	717	717				622	622			
10	239	130	130				109	109			
11	244	133	133				111	111			
12 - 14	810	436	436				374	374			
15	445	224	224				221	221			
16 - 17	913	404	400	4	-	-	509	502	6	1	-
18 - 19	3,488	1,573	1,549	17	1	6	1,915	1,846	61	3	5
20 - 24	13,221	6,199	5,888	266	7	38	7,022	6,461	510	10	41
25 - 29	9,292	5,122	4,151	798	12	161	4,170	3,222	813	12	123
30 - 34	5,296	3,280	2,152	893	8	227	2,016	1,242	632	25	117
35 - 39	3,237	2,067	1,238	562	12	255	1,170	646	367	24	133
40 - 44	2,864	1,773	995	445	28	305	1,091	651	274	24	142
45 - 49	2,373	1,555	908	328	18	301	818	507	168	31	112
50 - 54	2,031	1,317	736	279	27	275	714	451	153	19	91
55 - 59	1,847	1,131	697	212	30	192	716	462	120	59	75
60 - 64	2,112	1,201	720	255	59	167	911	533	127	150	101
65 - 69	2,610	1,323	720	266	172	165	1,287	642	161	384	100
70 - 74	3,344	1,376	670	275	287	144	1,968	746	279	846	97
75 - 79	5,304	1,670	640	376	555	99	3,634	1,059	393	2,074	108
80 - 84	7,816	1,860	527	434	829	70	5,956	1,451	503	3,909	93
85 - 89	8,280	1,423	272	259	862	30	6,857	1,476	450	4,866	65
90 and over	6,834	800	112	104	566	18	6,034	1,203	277	4,512	42

Table 2 Age and marital status – **continued**

Great Britain, England & Wales, England, regions, metropolitan counties, Inner London, Outer London, regional remainders, Wales, Scotland

Persons present

Age	TOTAL PERSONS	Males					Females				
		Total	Single	Married	Widowed	Divorced	Total	Single	Married	Widowed	Divorced
a	b	c	d	e	f	g	h	i	j	k	l

Greater London – *continued*

Age	TOTAL PERSONS	Total	Single	Married	Widowed	Divorced	Total	Single	Married	Widowed	Divorced
Resident - staff	13,494	4,891	3,587	986	28	290	8,603	7,147	989	131	336
Aged											
0 - 4	149	83	83				66	66			
5 - 9	139	86	86				53	53			
10	24	11	11				13	13			
11	22	9	9				13	13			
12 - 14	70	44	44				26	26			
15	19	11	11				8	8			
16 - 17	93	41	41	-	-	-	52	51	1	-	-
18 - 19	797	209	208	1	-	-	588	584	4	-	-
20 - 24	4,352	1,214	1,174	36	-	4	3,138	3,067	63	-	8
25 - 29	2,616	998	860	122	1	15	1,618	1,423	159	1	35
30 - 34	1,134	531	337	145	3	46	603	439	117	4	43
35 - 39	804	380	195	131	2	52	424	253	130	2	39
40 - 44	728	301	119	131	-	51	427	246	140	6	35
45 - 49	670	270	105	128	-	37	400	223	123	9	45
50 - 54	588	228	80	117	4	27	360	192	102	16	50
55 - 59	531	195	74	85	4	32	336	189	80	24	43
60 - 64	354	146	67	55	3	21	208	117	42	23	26
65 - 69	166	69	37	23	6	3	97	62	16	11	8
70 - 74	95	36	25	7	2	2	59	48	5	4	2
75 - 79	73	18	15	3	-	-	55	42	2	11	-
80 - 84	30	7	3	2	2	-	23	14	1	8	-
85 - 89	27	3	2	-	1	-	24	12	3	7	2
90 and over	13	1	1	-	-	-	12	6	1	5	-
All persons present in households	6,210,534	2,978,023	1,517,614	1,255,422	77,015	127,972	3,232,511	1,432,308	1,282,256	325,547	192,400
Aged											
0 - 4	435,275	222,029	222,029				213,246	213,246			
5 - 9	385,069	196,722	196,722				188,347	188,347			
10	75,919	38,702	38,702				37,217	37,217			
11	74,258	38,164	38,164				36,094	36,094			
12 - 14	199,892	102,115	102,115				97,777	97,777			
15	65,764	33,578	33,578				32,186	32,186			
16 - 17	138,787	70,692	70,364	275	18	35	68,095	67,431	593	39	32
18 - 19	152,836	75,547	74,740	725	18	64	77,289	74,266	2,882	45	96
20 - 24	533,088	252,549	232,076	19,642	56	775	280,539	232,165	45,721	229	2,424
25 - 29	629,475	302,185	202,851	93,450	170	5,714	327,290	180,736	133,257	704	12,593
30 - 34	523,706	257,003	101,766	141,707	334	13,196	266,703	83,531	159,686	1,292	22,194
35 - 39	427,255	209,932	52,489	140,101	580	16,762	217,323	41,978	147,250	2,154	25,941
40 - 44	427,771	209,020	38,097	149,316	998	20,609	218,751	28,516	156,087	3,890	30,258
45 - 49	349,333	169,506	24,634	125,549	1,353	17,970	179,827	17,881	129,813	6,099	26,034
50 - 54	321,294	158,604	19,670	120,762	2,268	15,904	162,690	14,518	116,509	10,190	21,473
55 - 59	300,607	149,453	17,702	115,077	3,892	12,782	151,154	13,541	104,876	16,541	16,196
60 - 64	288,100	139,782	17,133	106,067	6,800	9,782	148,318	14,389	93,217	28,175	12,537
65 - 69	268,726	123,515	14,322	91,418	10,945	6,830	145,211	14,250	78,491	43,289	9,181
70 - 74	219,124	92,877	9,051	67,198	12,739	3,889	126,247	12,921	54,269	52,987	6,070
75 - 79	190,869	73,452	6,450	49,473	15,202	2,327	117,417	12,758	36,475	63,987	4,197
80 - 84	126,559	42,831	3,436	25,551	12,842	1,002	83,728	10,718	17,079	53,733	2,198
85 - 89	57,816	15,911	1,219	7,799	6,629	264	41,905	5,821	5,105	30,202	777
90 and over	19,011	3,854	304	1,312	2,171	67	15,157	2,021	946	11,991	199

Table 2 Age and marital status – **continued**

Great Britain, England & Wales, England, regions, metropolitan counties, Inner London, Outer London, regional remainders, Wales, Scotland

Persons present

Age	TOTAL PERSONS	Males					Females				
		Total	Single	Married	Widowed	Divorced	Total	Single	Married	Widowed	Divorced
a	b	c	d	e	f	g	h	i	j	k	l

Inner London

All persons present in communal establishments *	110,402	55,525	33,154	17,034	2,196	3,141	54,877	33,990	11,269	7,508	2,110
Aged											
0 - 4	3,602	2,006	2,006				1,596	1,596			
5 - 9	1,399	782	782				617	617			
10	286	157	157				129	129			
11	364	214	214				150	150			
12 - 14	1,501	783	783				718	718			
15	463	256	256				207	207			
16 - 17	1,299	561	549	12	-	-	738	724	13	1	-
18 - 19	7,705	3,255	3,207	34	2	12	4,450	4,371	71	1	7
20 - 24	22,517	9,837	9,406	370	13	48	12,680	11,967	660	9	44
25 - 29	13,508	7,092	5,452	1,438	20	182	6,416	4,812	1,437	16	151
30 - 34	8,717	5,211	2,733	2,137	13	328	3,506	1,803	1,443	26	234
35 - 39	6,458	4,011	1,484	2,102	17	408	2,447	874	1,271	32	270
40 - 44	6,116	3,851	1,065	2,288	36	462	2,265	751	1,219	36	259
45 - 49	5,265	3,286	920	1,902	39	425	1,979	567	1,085	67	260
50 - 54	4,476	2,796	697	1,706	33	360	1,680	472	916	78	214
55 - 59	3,797	2,285	673	1,306	57	249	1,512	464	739	139	170
60 - 64	3,460	2,066	635	1,140	89	202	1,394	418	613	219	144
65 - 69	3,238	1,831	597	879	175	180	1,407	436	509	365	97
70 - 74	2,969	1,489	499	621	241	128	1,480	452	362	603	63
75 - 79	3,525	1,462	454	532	398	78	2,063	584	349	1,058	72
80 - 84	3,801	1,201	342	353	455	51	2,600	700	256	1,588	56
85 - 89	3,435	760	169	160	415	16	2,675	683	209	1,735	48
90 and over	2,501	333	74	54	193	12	2,168	495	117	1,535	21
Visitors/guests	56,869	30,667	15,593	12,959	750	1,365	26,202	14,692	7,975	2,360	1,175
Aged											
0 - 4	2,122	1,227	1,227				895	895			
5 - 9	550	333	333				217	217			
10	132	66	66				66	66			
11	202	122	122				80	80			
12 - 14	1,026	523	523				503	503			
15	255	147	147				108	108			
16 - 17	734	323	315	8	-	-	411	401	10	-	-
18 - 19	5,158	2,349	2,316	26	1	6	2,809	2,776	28	-	5
20 - 24	11,075	5,172	4,952	189	7	24	5,903	5,583	297	3	20
25 - 29	5,736	3,187	2,266	836	11	74	2,549	1,680	795	9	65
30 - 34	4,624	2,755	1,165	1,426	7	157	1,869	742	971	11	145
35 - 39	3,903	2,441	594	1,636	9	202	1,462	353	938	9	162
40 - 44	3,906	2,533	397	1,896	15	225	1,373	223	980	18	152
45 - 49	3,364	2,073	257	1,599	24	193	1,291	165	920	42	164
50 - 54	2,852	1,781	173	1,437	15	156	1,071	114	769	58	130
55 - 59	2,349	1,436	174	1,122	32	108	913	85	628	91	109
60 - 64	2,058	1,226	148	944	56	78	832	84	542	133	73
65 - 69	1,772	999	130	724	77	68	773	90	426	205	52
70 - 74	1,378	699	92	489	85	33	679	102	260	290	27
75 - 79	1,364	605	89	351	144	21	759	125	201	406	27
80 - 84	1,144	415	71	189	142	13	729	125	112	472	20
85 - 89	737	187	25	62	94	6	550	116	62	351	21
90 and over	428	68	11	25	31	1	360	59	36	262	3

Note: * Includes a female member of staff incorrectly enumerated as a resident.

Persons present

Age	TOTAL PERSONS	Males					Females				
		Total	Single	Married	Widowed	Divorced	Total	Single	Married	Widowed	Divorced
a	b	c	d	e	f	g	h	i	j	k	l

Inner London – *continued*

Age	TOTAL PERSONS	Total	Single	Married	Widowed	Divorced	Total	Single	Married	Widowed	Divorced
Resident - non-staff	**46,628**	**22,325**	**15,689**	**3,580**	**1,431**	**1,625**	**24,303**	**15,628**	**2,815**	**5,088**	**772**
Aged											
0 - 4	1,419	747	747				672	672			
5 - 9	771	398	398				373	373			
10	148	88	88				60	60			
11	152	88	88				64	64			
12 - 14	446	244	244				202	202			
15	200	107	107				93	93			
16 - 17	527	220	216	4	-	-	307	303	3	1	-
18 - 19	2,134	796	781	8	1	6	1,338	1,295	40	1	2
20 - 24	9,344	4,021	3,828	166	6	21	5,323	4,959	338	6	20
25 - 29	6,443	3,416	2,760	548	8	100	3,027	2,388	562	7	70
30 - 34	3,513	2,207	1,413	644	4	146	1,306	814	411	15	66
35 - 39	2,114	1,374	786	394	8	186	740	377	257	21	85
40 - 44	1,800	1,148	602	317	21	208	652	371	176	15	90
45 - 49	1,537	1,061	596	235	15	215	476	266	114	20	76
50 - 54	1,316	904	477	219	15	193	412	238	102	12	60
55 - 59	1,140	737	452	141	23	121	403	251	71	37	44
60 - 64	1,177	744	443	163	31	107	433	258	48	71	56
65 - 69	1,367	787	438	143	95	111	580	306	74	157	43
70 - 74	1,548	773	394	129	155	95	775	327	100	313	35
75 - 79	2,129	846	356	179	254	57	1,283	442	147	649	45
80 - 84	2,643	782	269	163	312	38	1,861	570	144	1,111	36
85 - 89	2,689	572	143	98	321	10	2,117	564	147	1,380	26
90 and over	2,071	265	63	29	162	11	1,806	435	81	1,272	18
Resident - staff	**6,905**	**2,533**	**1,872**	**495**	**15**	**151**	**4,372**	**3,670**	**479**	**60**	**163**
Aged											
0 - 4	61	32	32				29	29			
5 - 9	78	51	51				27	27			
10	6	3	3				3	3			
11	10	4	4				6	6			
12 - 14	29	16	16				13	13			
15	8	2	2				6	6			
16 - 17	38	18	18	-	-	-	20	20	-	-	-
18 - 19	413	110	110	-	-	-	303	300	3	-	-
20 - 24	2,098	644	626	15	-	3	1,454	1,425	25	-	4
25 - 29	1,329	489	426	54	1	8	840	744	80	-	16
30 - 34	580	249	155	67	2	25	331	247	61	-	23
35 - 39	441	196	104	72	-	20	245	144	76	2	23
40 - 44	410	170	66	75	-	29	240	157	63	3	17
45 - 49	364	152	67	68	-	17	212	136	51	5	20
50 - 54	308	111	47	50	3	11	197	120	45	8	24
55 - 59	308	112	47	43	2	20	196	128	40	11	17
60 - 64	225	96	44	33	2	17	129	76	23	15	15
65 - 69	99	45	29	12	3	1	54	40	9	3	2
70 - 74	43	17	13	3	1	-	26	23	2	-	1
75 - 79	32	11	9	2	-	-	21	17	1	3	-
80 - 84	14	4	2	1	1	-	10	5	-	5	-
85 - 89	9	1	1	-	-	-	8	3	-	4	1
90 and over	2	-	-	-	-	-	2	1	-	1	-

Table 2 Age and marital status – **continued**

Great Britain, England & Wales, England, regions, metropolitan counties, Inner London, Outer London, regional remainders, Wales, Scotland

Persons present

Age	TOTAL PERSONS	Males					Females				
		Total	Single	Married	Widowed	Divorced	Total	Single	Married	Widowed	Divorced
a	b	c	d	e	f	g	h	i	j	k	l

Inner London – *continued*

All persons present in households	**2,232,731**	**1,061,600**	**602,148**	**378,901**	**27,194**	**53,357**	**1,171,131**	**588,420**	**390,333**	**111,866**	**80,512**
Aged											
0 - 4	161,569	82,178	82,178				79,391	79,391			
5 - 9	137,342	69,868	69,868				67,474	67,474			
10	26,099	13,235	13,235				12,864	12,864			
11	24,770	12,673	12,673				12,097	12,097			
12 - 14	66,307	33,638	33,638				32,669	32,669			
15	21,626	11,051	11,051				10,575	10,575			
16 - 17	44,888	22,707	22,553	126	8	20	22,181	21,846	296	24	15
18 - 19	51,628	24,645	24,268	332	9	36	26,983	25,517	1,392	19	55
20 - 24	214,354	98,145	90,909	6,902	28	306	116,209	98,936	16,290	100	883
25 - 29	265,236	124,887	92,179	30,523	77	2,108	140,349	90,794	44,418	322	4,815
30 - 34	204,872	99,733	49,095	45,381	150	5,107	105,139	44,324	50,998	605	9,212
35 - 39	151,601	73,905	25,288	41,643	261	6,713	77,696	22,180	43,680	985	10,851
40 - 44	138,718	67,196	17,985	40,626	387	8,198	71,522	14,654	43,252	1,530	12,086
45 - 49	113,354	54,292	11,741	34,720	520	7,311	59,062	9,101	36,949	2,291	10,721
50 - 54	109,595	54,035	9,936	36,429	867	6,803	55,560	7,333	35,019	3,914	9,294
55 - 59	102,597	51,322	8,907	35,274	1,508	5,633	51,275	6,394	31,659	6,052	7,170
60 - 64	100,155	49,186	8,865	33,293	2,608	4,420	50,969	6,744	28,417	10,217	5,591
65 - 69	92,325	43,091	7,310	28,394	4,169	3,218	49,234	6,289	23,946	15,009	3,990
70 - 74	74,131	31,457	4,719	20,339	4,611	1,788	42,674	5,733	16,179	18,136	2,626
75 - 79	63,920	24,397	3,313	14,801	5,206	1,077	39,523	5,539	10,881	21,306	1,797
80 - 84	41,800	13,674	1,717	7,450	4,055	452	28,126	4,570	5,010	17,605	941
85 - 89	19,185	5,016	576	2,263	2,045	132	14,169	2,497	1,608	9,697	367
90 and over	6,659	1,269	144	405	685	35	5,390	899	339	4,054	98

Outer London

All persons present in communal establishments	**72,632**	**30,766**	**18,709**	**7,725**	**2,885**	**1,447**	**41,866**	**19,309**	**6,447**	**14,764**	**1,346**
Aged											
0 - 4	1,903	1,041	1,041				862	862			
5 - 9	914	516	516				398	398			
10	171	85	85				86	86			
11	234	111	111				123	123			
12 - 14	1,186	727	727				459	459			
15	717	457	457				260	260			
16 - 17	1,468	934	932	2	-	-	534	528	5	1	-
18 - 19	4,505	2,340	2,315	23	-	2	2,165	2,117	41	4	3
20 - 24	9,820	4,631	4,395	209	3	24	5,189	4,771	378	7	33
25 - 29	6,201	3,270	2,564	617	7	82	2,931	2,063	754	8	106
30 - 34	3,902	2,259	1,274	821	12	152	1,643	829	669	20	125
35 - 39	2,675	1,618	695	754	7	162	1,057	487	440	4	126
40 - 44	2,536	1,502	551	751	13	187	1,034	422	459	17	136
45 - 49	2,107	1,203	426	597	8	172	904	379	373	37	115
50 - 54	1,815	1,024	337	508	26	153	791	325	331	34	101
55 - 59	1,698	931	333	450	20	128	767	315	297	64	91
60 - 64	1,929	991	381	451	60	99	938	363	311	173	91
65 - 69	2,258	1,047	355	478	133	81	1,211	413	329	382	87
70 - 74	2,931	1,161	340	510	240	71	1,770	500	383	795	92
75 - 79	4,667	1,470	354	579	477	60	3,197	726	474	1,908	89
80 - 84	6,772	1,649	308	570	731	40	5,123	1,004	554	3,492	73
85 - 89	6,778	1,145	155	291	674	25	5,633	1,030	410	4,140	53
90 and over	5,445	654	57	114	474	9	4,791	849	239	3,678	25

Table 2 Age and marital status – **continued**

Great Britain, England & Wales, England, regions, metropolitan counties, Inner London, Outer London, regional remainders, Wales, Scotland

Persons present

Age	TOTAL PERSONS	Males					Females				
		Total	Single	Married	Widowed	Divorced	Total	Single	Married	Widowed	Divorced
a	b	c	d	e	f	g	h	i	j	k	l

Outer London – *continued*

Visitors/guests	**26,345**	**13,743**	**7,392**	**5,041**	**830**	**480**	**12,602**	**5,812**	**3,458**	**2,832**	**500**
Aged											
0 - 4	847	461	461				386	386			
5 - 9	285	162	162				123	123			
10	62	35	35				27	27			
11	130	61	61				69	69			
12 - 14	781	507	507				274	274			
15	461	331	331				130	130			
16 - 17	1,027	727	725	2	-	-	300	298	1	1	-
18 - 19	2,767	1,464	1,449	13	-	2	1,303	1,282	19	2	-
20 - 24	3,689	1,883	1,787	88	2	6	1,806	1,627	168	3	8
25 - 29	2,065	1,055	739	299	3	14	1,010	550	424	2	34
30 - 34	1,565	904	353	494	7	50	661	209	392	6	54
35 - 39	1,189	741	152	527	1	61	448	109	276	1	62
40 - 44	1,154	746	105	567	6	68	408	53	284	5	66
45 - 49	965	591	76	444	5	66	374	51	247	22	54
50 - 54	820	494	45	381	13	55	326	40	223	19	44
55 - 59	768	454	61	337	11	45	314	43	208	29	34
60 - 64	865	484	81	337	31	35	381	47	213	86	35
65 - 69	948	487	65	344	53	25	461	55	235	147	24
70 - 74	1,083	539	52	360	107	20	544	56	201	258	29
75 - 79	1,451	639	64	381	176	18	812	84	227	475	26
80 - 84	1,583	568	49	298	213	8	1,015	114	194	691	16
85 - 89	1,169	292	25	130	132	5	877	109	104	651	13
90 and over	671	118	7	39	70	2	553	76	42	434	1
Resident - non-staff	**39,698**	**14,665**	**9,602**	**2,193**	**2,042**	**828**	**25,033**	**10,020**	**2,479**	**11,861**	**673**
Aged											
0 - 4	968	529	529				439	439			
5 - 9	568	319	319				249	249			
10	91	42	42				49	49			
11	92	45	45				47	47			
12 - 14	364	192	192				172	172			
15	245	117	117				128	128			
16 - 17	386	184	184	-	-	-	202	199	3	-	-
18 - 19	1,354	777	768	9	-	-	577	551	21	2	3
20 - 24	3,877	2,178	2,060	100	1	17	1,699	1,502	172	4	21
25 - 29	2,849	1,706	1,391	250	4	61	1,143	834	251	5	53
30 - 34	1,783	1,073	739	249	4	81	710	428	221	10	51
35 - 39	1,123	693	452	168	4	69	430	269	110	3	48
40 - 44	1,064	625	393	128	7	97	439	280	98	9	52
45 - 49	836	494	312	93	3	86	342	241	54	11	36
50 - 54	715	413	259	60	12	82	302	213	51	7	31
55 - 59	707	394	245	71	7	71	313	211	49	22	31
60 - 64	935	457	277	92	28	60	478	275	79	79	45
65 - 69	1,243	536	282	123	77	54	707	336	87	227	57
70 - 74	1,796	603	276	146	132	49	1,193	419	179	533	62
75 - 79	3,175	824	284	197	301	42	2,351	617	246	1,425	63
80 - 84	5,173	1,078	258	271	517	32	4,095	881	359	2,798	57
85 - 89	5,591	851	129	161	541	20	4,740	912	303	3,486	39
90 and over	4,763	535	49	75	404	7	4,228	768	196	3,240	24

Table 2 Age and marital status – **continued**

Great Britain, England & Wales, England, regions, metropolitan counties, Inner London, Outer London, regional remainders, Wales, Scotland

Persons present

Age	TOTAL PERSONS	Males					Females				
		Total	Single	Married	Widowed	Divorced	Total	Single	Married	Widowed	Divorced
a	b	c	d	e	f	g	h	i	j	k	l

Outer London – *continued*

Resident - staff	6,589	2,358	1,715	491	13	139	4,231	3,477	510	71	173
Aged											
0 - 4	88	51	51				37	37			
5 - 9	61	35	35				26	26			
10	18	8	8				10	10			
11	12	5	5				7	7			
12 - 14	41	28	28				13	13			
15	11	9	9				2	2			
16 - 17	55	23	23	-	-	-	32	31	1	-	-
18 - 19	384	99	98	1	-	-	285	284	1	-	-
20 - 24	2,254	570	548	21	-	1	1,684	1,642	38	-	4
25 - 29	1,287	509	434	68	-	7	778	679	79	1	19
30 - 34	554	282	182	78	1	21	272	192	56	4	20
35 - 39	363	184	91	59	2	32	179	109	54	-	16
40 - 44	318	131	53	56	-	22	187	89	77	3	18
45 - 49	306	118	38	60	-	20	188	87	72	4	25
50 - 54	280	117	33	67	1	16	163	72	57	8	26
55 - 59	223	83	27	42	2	12	140	61	40	13	26
60 - 64	129	50	23	22	1	4	79	41	19	8	11
65 - 69	67	24	8	11	3	2	43	22	7	8	6
70 - 74	52	19	12	4	1	2	33	25	3	4	1
75 - 79	41	7	6	1	-	-	34	25	1	8	-
80 - 84	16	3	1	1	1	-	13	9	1	3	-
85 - 89	18	2	1	-	1	-	16	9	3	3	1
90 and over	11	1	1	-	-	-	10	5	1	4	-
All persons present in households	**3,977,803**	**1,916,423**	**915,466**	**876,521**	**49,821**	**74,615**	**2,061,380**	**843,888**	**891,923**	**213,681**	**111,888**
Aged											
0 - 4	273,706	139,851	139,851				133,855	133,855			
5 - 9	247,727	126,854	126,854				120,873	120,873			
10	49,820	25,467	25,467				24,353	24,353			
11	49,488	25,491	25,491				23,997	23,997			
12 - 14	133,585	68,477	68,477				65,108	65,108			
15	44,138	22,527	22,527				21,611	21,611			
16 - 17	93,899	47,985	47,811	149	10	15	45,914	45,585	297	15	17
18 - 19	101,208	50,902	50,472	393	9	28	50,306	48,749	1,490	26	41
20 - 24	318,734	154,404	141,167	12,740	28	469	164,330	133,229	29,431	129	1,541
25 - 29	364,239	177,298	110,672	62,927	93	3,606	186,941	89,942	88,839	382	7,778
30 - 34	318,834	157,270	52,671	96,326	184	8,089	161,564	39,207	108,688	687	12,982
35 - 39	275,654	136,027	27,201	98,458	319	10,049	139,627	19,798	103,570	1,169	15,090
40 - 44	289,053	141,824	20,112	108,690	611	12,411	147,229	13,862	112,835	2,360	18,172
45 - 49	235,979	115,214	12,893	90,829	833	10,659	120,765	8,780	92,864	3,808	15,313
50 - 54	211,699	104,569	9,734	84,333	1,401	9,101	107,130	7,185	81,490	6,276	12,179
55 - 59	198,010	98,131	8,795	79,803	2,384	7,149	99,879	7,147	73,217	10,489	9,026
60 - 64	187,945	90,596	8,268	72,774	4,192	5,362	97,349	7,645	64,800	17,958	6,946
65 - 69	176,401	80,424	7,012	63,024	6,776	3,612	95,977	7,961	54,545	28,280	5,191
70 - 74	144,993	61,420	4,332	46,859	8,128	2,101	83,573	7,188	38,090	34,851	3,444
75 - 79	126,949	49,055	3,137	34,672	9,996	1,250	77,894	7,219	25,594	42,681	2,400
80 - 84	84,759	29,157	1,719	18,101	8,787	550	55,602	6,148	12,069	36,128	1,257
85 - 89	38,631	10,895	643	5,536	4,584	132	27,736	3,324	3,497	20,505	410
90 and over	12,352	2,585	160	907	1,486	32	9,767	1,122	607	7,937	101

Table 2 Age and marital status – **continued**

Great Britain, England & Wales, England, regions, metropolitan counties, Inner London, Outer London, regional remainders, Wales, Scotland

Persons present

		Males					Females				
Age	TOTAL PERSONS	Total	Single	Married	Widowed	Divorced	Total	Single	Married	Widowed	Divorced
a	b	c	d	e	f	g	h	i	j	k	l

Outer Metropolitan Area

Age	TOTAL PERSONS	Total	Single	Married	Widowed	Divorced	Total	Single	Married	Widowed	Divorced
All persons present in communal establishments	142,312	69,652	48,142	13,912	4,852	2,746	72,660	37,271	9,770	23,437	2,182
Aged											
0 - 4	1,809	1,007	1,007				802	802			
5 - 9	1,713	1,173	1,173				540	540			
10	964	694	694				270	270			
11	1,806	1,157	1,157				649	649			
12 - 14	8,762	5,385	5,385				3,377	3,377			
15	3,878	2,396	2,396				1,482	1,482			
16 - 17	8,417	5,112	5,103	6	-	3	3,305	3,300	5	-	-
18 - 19	9,786	5,653	5,622	27	1	3	4,133	4,071	59	2	1
20 - 24	17,948	9,991	9,311	605	5	70	7,957	7,387	516	7	47
25 - 29	10,674	6,551	4,704	1,606	4	237	4,123	2,923	1,030	8	162
30 - 34	6,673	4,312	2,241	1,755	12	304	2,361	1,301	870	14	176
35 - 39	5,011	3,213	1,455	1,400	16	342	1,798	890	712	24	172
40 - 44	5,089	3,276	1,408	1,483	19	366	1,813	822	743	27	221
45 - 49	4,044	2,450	1,129	1,017	19	285	1,594	691	642	46	215
50 - 54	3,474	1,979	836	850	34	259	1,495	620	610	71	194
55 - 59	3,178	1,725	723	726	36	240	1,453	628	524	109	192
60 - 64	3,245	1,726	827	643	85	171	1,519	604	498	268	149
65 - 69	3,835	1,809	801	661	202	145	2,026	739	531	629	127
70 - 74	4,826	1,956	729	741	372	114	2,870	871	624	1,258	117
75 - 79	7,461	2,316	593	853	767	103	5,145	1,176	764	3,081	124
80 - 84	10,611	2,656	495	824	1,269	68	7,955	1,432	803	5,582	138
85 - 89	10,983	2,048	243	528	1,251	26	8,935	1,487	580	6,772	96
90 and over	8,125	1,067	110	187	760	10	7,058	1,209	259	5,539	51
Visitors/guests	61,492	35,666	25,353	8,438	1,011	864	25,826	16,428	5,393	3,233	772
Aged											
0 - 4	1,056	607	607				449	449			
5 - 9	1,123	842	842				281	281			
10	841	624	624				217	217			
11	1,635	1,072	1,072				563	563			
12 - 14	8,177	5,058	5,058				3,119	3,119			
15	3,491	2,190	2,190				1,301	1,301			
16 - 17	7,164	4,280	4,274	4	-	2	2,884	2,881	3	-	-
18 - 19	6,287	3,638	3,623	15	-	-	2,649	2,619	28	1	1
20 - 24	7,184	4,119	3,823	274	4	18	3,065	2,780	268	4	13
25 - 29	3,979	2,414	1,541	798	-	75	1,565	806	694	5	60
30 - 34	2,745	1,743	601	1,033	5	104	1,002	318	602	10	72
35 - 39	2,124	1,380	244	996	10	130	744	164	475	13	92
40 - 44	2,145	1,435	213	1,084	10	128	710	122	464	7	117
45 - 49	1,624	989	127	750	7	105	635	85	423	21	106
50 - 54	1,361	799	99	614	13	73	562	70	393	34	65
55 - 59	1,153	650	66	489	19	76	503	47	337	50	69
60 - 64	1,128	601	69	460	29	43	527	51	324	104	48
65 - 69	1,260	618	55	461	69	33	642	76	323	209	34
70 - 74	1,381	672	62	460	122	28	709	82	303	289	35
75 - 79	1,816	719	60	442	188	29	1,097	124	343	608	22
80 - 84	1,846	688	68	344	263	13	1,158	123	229	785	21
85 - 89	1,340	393	23	174	192	4	947	97	133	707	10
90 and over	632	135	12	40	80	3	497	53	51	386	7

Table 2 Age and marital status – **continued**

Great Britain, England & Wales, England, regions, metropolitan counties, Inner London, Outer London, regional remainders, Wales, Scotland

Persons present

Age	TOTAL PERSONS	Males					Females				
		Total	Single	Married	Widowed	Divorced	Total	Single	Married	Widowed	Divorced
a	b	c	d	e	f	g	h	i	j	k	l
Outer Metropolitan Area – *continued*											
Resident - non-staff	67,515	28,162	18,612	4,311	3,817	1,422	39,353	15,025	3,228	20,087	1,013
Aged											
0 - 4	619	335	335				284	284			
5 - 9	423	238	238				185	185			
10	93	52	52				41	41			
11	126	63	63				63	63			
12 - 14	483	274	274				209	209			
15	347	189	189				158	158			
16 - 17	1,084	760	757	2	-	1	324	323	1	-	-
18 - 19	2,548	1,709	1,696	11	-	2	839	818	20	1	-
20 - 24	6,384	4,410	4,086	279	1	44	1,974	1,801	149	3	21
25 - 29	4,203	2,901	2,107	672	4	118	1,302	1,066	175	1	60
30 - 34	2,775	1,945	1,241	563	5	136	830	624	135	3	68
35 - 39	2,145	1,404	996	265	5	138	741	574	106	10	51
40 - 44	2,211	1,461	1,061	219	9	172	750	576	108	12	54
45 - 49	1,830	1,153	896	127	9	121	677	525	68	20	64
50 - 54	1,534	905	671	100	15	119	629	473	83	27	46
55 - 59	1,505	825	582	115	13	115	680	487	98	35	60
60 - 64	1,845	982	713	111	52	106	863	517	128	142	76
65 - 69	2,496	1,156	729	185	132	110	1,340	652	199	407	82
70 - 74	3,387	1,261	657	273	249	82	2,126	771	316	957	82
75 - 79	5,612	1,589	528	409	578	74	4,023	1,039	417	2,465	102
80 - 84	8,747	1,964	423	480	1,006	55	6,783	1,300	573	4,793	117
85 - 89	9,629	1,654	220	353	1,059	22	7,975	1,386	445	6,058	86
90 and over	7,489	932	98	147	680	7	6,557	1,153	207	5,153	44
Resident - staff	13,305	5,824	4,177	1,163	24	460	7,481	5,818	1,149	117	397
Aged											
0 - 4	134	65	65				69	69			
5 - 9	167	93	93				74	74			
10	30	18	18				12	12			
11	45	22	22				23	23			
12 - 14	102	53	53				49	49			
15	40	17	17				23	23			
16 - 17	169	72	72	-	-	-	97	96	1	-	-
18 - 19	951	306	303	1	1	1	645	634	11	-	-
20 - 24	4,380	1,462	1,402	52	-	8	2,918	2,806	99	-	13
25 - 29	2,492	1,236	1,056	136	-	44	1,256	1,051	161	2	42
30 - 34	1,153	624	399	159	2	64	529	359	133	1	36
35 - 39	742	429	215	139	1	74	313	152	131	1	29
40 - 44	733	380	134	180	-	66	353	124	171	8	50
45 - 49	590	308	106	140	3	59	282	81	151	5	45
50 - 54	579	275	66	136	6	67	304	77	134	10	83
55 - 59	520	250	75	122	4	49	270	94	89	24	63
60 - 64	272	143	45	72	4	22	129	36	46	22	25
65 - 69	79	35	17	15	1	2	44	11	9	13	11
70 - 74	58	23	10	8	1	4	35	18	5	12	-
75 - 79	33	8	5	2	1	-	25	13	4	8	-
80 - 84	18	4	4	-	-	-	14	9	1	4	-
85 - 89	14	1	-	1	-	-	13	4	2	7	-
90 and over	4	-	-	-	-	-	4	3	1	-	-

Table 2 Age and marital status – **continued**

Great Britain, England & Wales, England, regions, metropolitan counties, Inner London, Outer London, regional remainders, Wales, Scotland

Persons present

Age	TOTAL PERSONS	Males					Females				
		Total	Single	Married	Widowed	Divorced	Total	Single	Married	Widowed	Divorced
a	b	c	d	e	f	g	h	i	j	k	l

Outer Metropolitan Area – *continued*

Age	TOTAL PERSONS	Total	Single	Married	Widowed	Divorced	Total	Single	Married	Widowed	Divorced
All persons present in households	5,304,838	2,592,840	1,137,365	1,291,590	62,088	101,797	2,711,998	1,003,903	1,308,911	257,373	141,811
Aged											
0 - 4	361,109	185,214	185,214				175,895	175,895			
5 - 9	338,534	173,208	173,208				165,326	165,326			
10	70,021	35,723	35,723				34,298	34,298			
11	69,209	35,487	35,487				33,722	33,722			
12 - 14	191,181	97,499	97,499				93,682	93,682			
15	64,356	32,836	32,836				31,520	31,520			
16 - 17	137,663	70,292	70,125	144	4	19	67,371	67,058	278	19	16
18 - 19	140,226	71,101	70,567	493	16	25	69,125	67,181	1,863	28	53
20 - 24	378,412	189,054	169,849	18,427	36	742	189,358	145,260	41,673	124	2,301
25 - 29	425,048	211,380	116,446	88,985	117	5,832	213,668	78,656	123,445	429	11,138
30 - 34	401,613	200,734	53,599	134,716	204	12,215	200,879	31,088	151,715	747	17,329
35 - 39	371,992	184,648	27,507	142,341	413	14,387	187,344	14,842	151,804	1,313	19,385
40 - 44	422,301	208,499	19,171	170,880	803	17,645	213,802	10,245	177,642	2,513	23,402
45 - 49	349,793	173,764	11,458	146,352	1,160	14,794	176,029	6,519	146,112	4,019	19,379
50 - 54	299,136	149,201	8,511	127,024	1,852	11,814	149,935	5,417	123,063	6,990	14,465
55 - 59	279,086	139,497	7,596	119,754	3,079	9,068	139,589	5,778	110,309	12,560	10,942
60 - 64	261,541	128,028	7,216	108,926	5,408	6,478	133,513	6,676	95,855	22,587	8,395
65 - 69	238,245	110,583	6,228	91,451	8,628	4,276	127,662	7,170	78,796	35,376	6,320
70 - 74	189,349	82,531	4,049	66,020	10,088	2,374	106,818	6,702	53,088	43,022	4,006
75 - 79	156,052	62,194	2,836	45,747	12,236	1,375	93,858	6,925	33,166	51,083	2,684
80 - 84	100,677	35,179	1,532	22,489	10,596	562	65,498	5,644	15,104	43,340	1,410
85 - 89	44,981	13,041	564	6,733	5,574	170	31,940	3,177	4,269	24,013	481
90 and over	14,313	3,147	144	1,108	1,874	21	11,166	1,122	729	9,210	105

Outer South East

Age	TOTAL PERSONS	Total	Single	Married	Widowed	Divorced	Total	Single	Married	Widowed	Divorced
All persons present in communal establishments	188,716	94,143	62,229	20,319	6,967	4,628	94,573	44,643	14,237	32,808	2,885
Aged											
0 - 4	1,991	1,106	1,106				885	885			
5 - 9	2,324	1,537	1,537				787	787			
10	1,505	1,033	1,033				472	472			
11	2,085	1,303	1,303				782	782			
12 - 14	8,208	5,147	5,147				3,061	3,061			
15	3,326	2,143	2,143				1,183	1,183			
16 - 17	8,238	5,331	5,320	8	1	2	2,907	2,900	5	1	1
18 - 19	15,991	9,290	9,232	52	-	6	6,701	6,637	58	2	4
20 - 24	27,772	17,157	16,325	691	8	133	10,615	10,084	472	6	53
25 - 29	12,282	8,323	6,244	1,634	16	429	3,959	2,861	923	9	166
30 - 34	7,591	5,258	2,719	2,017	17	505	2,333	1,148	966	6	213
35 - 39	5,766	4,023	1,535	1,912	25	551	1,743	715	799	17	212
40 - 44	5,796	3,882	1,294	1,910	32	646	1,914	662	966	28	258
45 - 49	5,141	3,286	1,172	1,567	38	509	1,855	562	958	50	285
50 - 54	4,368	2,555	851	1,259	57	388	1,813	515	951	110	237
55 - 59	4,221	2,367	795	1,142	66	364	1,854	557	912	170	215
60 - 64	5,204	2,570	915	1,217	156	282	2,634	816	1,136	462	220
65 - 69	6,397	2,974	941	1,421	343	269	3,423	894	1,250	1,042	237
70 - 74	7,295	2,954	794	1,414	547	199	4,341	1,023	1,141	1,962	215
75 - 79	10,668	3,443	745	1,475	1,061	162	7,225	1,576	1,237	4,194	218
80 - 84	15,342	3,869	619	1,419	1,713	118	11,473	2,196	1,226	7,882	169
85 - 89	15,392	2,935	312	862	1,710	51	12,457	2,371	842	9,116	128
90 and over	11,813	1,657	147	319	1,177	14	10,156	1,956	395	7,751	54

Table 2 Age and marital status **– continued**

Persons present

Age	TOTAL PERSONS	Males					Females				
		Total	Single	Married	Widowed	Divorced	Total	Single	Married	Widowed	Divorced
a	b	c	d	e	f	g	h	i	j	k	l

Outer South East – *continued*

Visitors/guests	87,422	49,834	33,766	13,331	1,416	1,321	37,588	22,412	8,809	5,303	1,064
Aged											
0 - 4	1,226	705	705				521	521			
5 - 9	1,609	1,137	1,137				472	472			
10	1,300	923	923				377	377			
11	1,862	1,186	1,186				676	676			
12 - 14	7,395	4,672	4,672				2,723	2,723			
15	2,914	1,907	1,907				1,007	1,007			
16 - 17	6,710	4,185	4,177	6	1	1	2,525	2,521	3	-	1
18 - 19	11,103	5,933	5,906	24	-	3	5,170	5,140	28	1	1
20 - 24	14,980	8,748	8,337	368	1	42	6,232	5,911	298	4	19
25 - 29	5,146	3,447	2,255	1,043	9	140	1,699	983	641	5	70
30 - 34	3,626	2,467	903	1,394	7	163	1,159	342	705	5	107
35 - 39	2,742	1,911	390	1,323	10	188	831	175	540	9	107
40 - 44	2,789	1,855	282	1,366	15	192	934	174	620	15	125
45 - 49	2,473	1,560	259	1,119	15	167	913	99	661	25	128
50 - 54	2,054	1,191	137	899	24	131	863	81	622	54	106
55 - 59	2,073	1,052	108	823	32	89	1,021	115	703	113	90
60 - 64	2,492	1,137	108	920	51	58	1,355	123	915	243	74
65 - 69	3,234	1,466	111	1,166	144	45	1,768	130	1,040	513	85
70 - 74	3,075	1,348	85	1,049	178	36	1,727	153	793	721	60
75 - 79	3,173	1,281	77	900	268	36	1,892	196	674	973	49
80 - 84	2,830	1,030	66	635	305	24	1,800	212	348	1,209	31
85 - 89	1,751	510	29	232	245	4	1,241	194	168	871	8
90 and over	865	183	6	64	111	2	682	87	50	542	3
Resident - non-staff	**89,520**	**38,676**	**24,776**	**5,512**	**5,510**	**2,878**	**50,844**	**18,174**	**3,933**	**27,324**	**1,413**
Aged											
0 - 4	551	293	293				258	258			
5 - 9	519	298	298				221	221			
10	154	86	86				68	68			
11	162	82	82				80	80			
12 - 14	642	386	386				256	256			
15	347	200	200				147	147			
16 - 17	1,289	1,035	1,034	1	-	-	254	251	2	1	-
18 - 19	3,996	2,978	2,949	26	-	3	1,018	988	26	1	3
20 - 24	9,709	7,144	6,770	286	5	83	2,565	2,415	122	2	26
25 - 29	5,437	3,996	3,250	485	7	254	1,441	1,205	160	4	72
30 - 34	3,146	2,325	1,532	497	10	286	821	606	138	1	76
35 - 39	2,328	1,722	983	434	15	290	606	442	93	3	68
40 - 44	2,253	1,634	911	326	15	382	619	435	100	7	77
45 - 49	1,902	1,332	834	206	19	273	570	413	62	11	84
50 - 54	1,547	1,009	636	138	29	206	538	381	68	28	61
55 - 59	1,552	1,024	629	126	29	240	528	373	56	33	66
60 - 64	2,361	1,258	765	191	99	203	1,103	651	142	198	112
65 - 69	3,006	1,445	810	221	194	220	1,561	742	180	498	141
70 - 74	4,153	1,575	700	348	368	159	2,578	860	334	1,232	152
75 - 79	7,440	2,142	661	564	791	126	5,298	1,366	558	3,207	167
80 - 84	12,474	2,825	546	783	1,402	94	9,649	1,976	876	6,659	138
85 - 89	13,616	2,416	280	628	1,461	47	11,200	2,172	672	8,237	119
90 and over	10,936	1,471	141	252	1,066	12	9,465	1,868	344	7,202	51

Table 2 Age and marital status – **continued**

Great Britain, England & Wales, England, regions, metropolitan counties, Inner London, Outer London, regional remainders, Wales, Scotland

Persons present

Age	TOTAL PERSONS	Males					Females				
		Total	Single	Married	Widowed	Divorced	Total	Single	Married	Widowed	Divorced
a	b	c	d	e	f	g	h	i	j	k	l

Outer South East – *continued*

Resident - staff	**11,774**	**5,633**	**3,687**	**1,476**	**41**	**429**	**6,141**	**4,057**	**1,495**	**181**	**408**
Aged											
0 - 4	214	108	108				106	106			
5 - 9	196	102	102				94	94			
10	51	24	24				27	27			
11	61	35	35				26	26			
12 - 14	171	89	89				82	82			
15	65	36	36				29	29			
16 - 17	239	111	109	1	-	1	128	128	-	-	-
18 - 19	892	379	377	2	-	-	513	509	4	-	-
20 - 24	3,083	1,265	1,218	37	2	8	1,818	1,758	52	-	8
25 - 29	1,699	880	739	106	-	35	819	673	122	-	24
30 - 34	819	466	284	126	-	56	353	200	123	-	30
35 - 39	696	390	162	155	-	73	306	98	166	5	37
40 - 44	754	393	101	218	2	72	361	53	246	6	56
45 - 49	766	394	79	242	4	69	372	50	235	14	73
50 - 54	767	355	78	222	4	51	412	53	261	28	70
55 - 59	596	291	58	193	5	35	305	69	153	24	59
60 - 64	351	175	42	106	6	21	176	42	79	21	34
65 - 69	157	63	20	34	5	4	94	22	30	31	11
70 - 74	67	31	9	17	1	4	36	10	14	9	3
75 - 79	55	20	7	11	2	-	35	14	5	14	2
80 - 84	38	14	7	1	6	-	24	8	2	14	-
85 - 89	25	9	3	2	4	-	16	5	2	8	1
90 and over	12	3	-	3	-	-	9	1	1	7	-
All persons present in households	**4,764,249**	**2,300,125**	**982,388**	**1,154,653**	**63,014**	**100,070**	**2,464,124**	**880,268**	**1,173,520**	**267,689**	**142,647**
Aged											
0 - 4	314,959	160,775	160,775				154,184	154,184			
5 - 9	297,314	152,520	152,520				144,794	144,794			
10	61,047	31,001	31,001				30,046	30,046			
11	59,773	30,487	30,487				29,286	29,286			
12 - 14	164,297	83,873	83,873				80,424	80,424			
15	55,043	27,918	27,918				27,125	27,125			
16 - 17	117,378	59,901	59,751	121	6	23	57,477	57,210	236	16	15
18 - 19	122,199	61,725	61,249	447	5	24	60,474	58,461	1,922	22	69
20 - 24	333,941	165,777	145,306	19,541	30	900	168,164	122,968	42,268	150	2,778
25 - 29	357,053	176,528	91,229	79,137	93	6,069	180,525	61,069	107,382	407	11,667
30 - 34	337,572	167,323	43,237	112,236	175	11,675	170,249	25,436	127,291	724	16,798
35 - 39	319,996	157,386	23,664	119,458	368	13,896	162,610	13,289	128,906	1,219	19,196
40 - 44	365,463	180,245	17,552	144,947	773	16,973	185,218	9,526	150,456	2,319	22,917
45 - 49	304,337	151,599	11,325	124,879	1,013	14,382	152,738	6,379	123,953	3,894	18,512
50 - 54	254,796	127,274	8,452	105,866	1,610	11,346	127,522	5,585	102,215	6,138	13,584
55 - 59	238,540	117,513	7,684	98,705	2,550	8,574	121,027	6,036	93,401	11,082	10,508
60 - 64	241,814	114,693	8,055	95,663	4,594	6,381	127,121	7,701	89,686	21,051	8,683
65 - 69	244,463	110,166	6,970	90,427	8,223	4,546	134,297	9,095	82,062	36,111	7,029
70 - 74	209,657	90,275	5,001	72,264	10,260	2,750	119,382	8,523	59,976	45,806	5,077
75 - 79	177,683	70,887	3,518	52,841	12,889	1,639	106,796	9,087	39,055	55,309	3,345
80 - 84	116,974	41,896	1,910	27,653	11,677	656	75,078	7,819	18,414	47,116	1,729
85 - 89	53,083	16,281	745	8,832	6,511	193	36,802	4,652	5,366	26,164	620
90 and over	16,867	4,082	166	1,636	2,237	43	12,785	1,573	931	10,161	120

Table 2 Age and marital status – **continued**

Great Britain, England & Wales, England, regions, metropolitan counties, Inner London, Outer London, regional remainders, Wales, Scotland

Persons present

Age	TOTAL PERSONS	Males					Females				
		Total	Single	Married	Widowed	Divorced	Total	Single	Married	Widowed	Divorced
a	b	c	d	e	f	g	h	i	j	k	l

SOUTH WEST REGION

Age	TOTAL PERSONS	Total	Single	Married	Widowed	Divorced	Total	Single	Married	Widowed	Divorced
All persons present in communal establishments *	187,250	89,974	52,692	25,386	7,494	4,402	97,276	38,523	20,572	35,117	3,064
Aged											
0 - 4	2,354	1,262	1,262				1,092	1,092			
5 - 9	2,155	1,226	1,226				929	929			
10	1,332	749	749				583	583			
11	1,800	1,000	1,000				800	800			
12 - 14	7,864	4,468	4,468				3,396	3,396			
15	3,461	2,151	2,151				1,310	1,310			
16 - 17	8,387	5,263	5,254	6	1	2	3,124	3,111	11	2	-
18 - 19	13,534	8,188	8,139	40	2	7	5,346	5,280	61	2	3
20 - 24	20,025	12,832	12,107	625	8	92	7,193	6,593	542	10	48
25 - 29	10,426	6,985	5,048	1,550	12	375	3,441	2,182	1,088	12	159
30 - 34	7,218	4,861	2,309	2,032	11	509	2,357	921	1,206	14	216
35 - 39	5,789	3,752	1,309	1,902	17	524	2,037	649	1,131	21	236
40 - 44	6,050	3,775	1,178	2,021	28	548	2,275	530	1,397	33	315
45 - 49	5,621	3,282	920	1,856	33	473	2,339	470	1,487	70	312
50 - 54	5,352	3,005	750	1,758	54	443	2,347	443	1,549	106	249
55 - 59	5,472	2,816	603	1,811	82	320	2,656	470	1,778	208	200
60 - 64	6,964	3,377	838	2,076	152	311	3,587	690	2,058	575	264
65 - 69	8,508	3,929	831	2,507	345	246	4,579	828	2,211	1,299	241
70 - 74	9,247	3,784	760	2,215	600	209	5,463	972	1,841	2,422	228
75 - 79	12,176	4,184	710	2,087	1,201	186	7,992	1,402	1,548	4,806	236
80 - 84	16,236	4,241	605	1,606	1,934	96	11,995	2,016	1,338	8,452	189
85 - 89	15,756	3,118	327	927	1,815	49	12,638	2,120	890	9,508	120
90 and over	11,523	1,726	148	367	1,199	12	9,797	1,736	436	7,577	48
Visitors/guests	89,956	48,142	27,452	17,531	1,723	1,436	41,814	19,813	13,936	6,791	1,274
Aged											
0 - 4	1,418	769	769				649	649			
5 - 9	1,285	747	747				538	538			
10	1,109	631	631				478	478			
11	1,548	850	850				698	698			
12 - 14	7,037	4,013	4,013				3,024	3,024			
15	3,069	1,933	1,933				1,136	1,136			
16 - 17	6,915	4,206	4,203	2	-	1	2,709	2,699	8	2	-
18 - 19	9,120	5,008	4,987	18	-	3	4,112	4,074	36	-	2
20 - 24	9,254	5,402	5,011	360	5	26	3,852	3,451	371	7	23
25 - 29	4,704	3,000	1,828	1,048	9	115	1,704	799	834	5	66
30 - 34	3,710	2,383	777	1,413	3	190	1,327	324	878	12	113
35 - 39	2,873	1,840	363	1,277	8	192	1,033	170	718	14	131
40 - 44	2,981	1,858	274	1,359	17	208	1,123	124	817	17	165
45 - 49	2,760	1,595	203	1,201	18	173	1,165	83	886	45	151
50 - 54	2,850	1,521	151	1,187	26	157	1,329	84	1,075	64	106
55 - 59	3,357	1,606	99	1,347	51	109	1,751	115	1,415	141	80
60 - 64	4,480	2,008	156	1,688	75	89	2,472	169	1,803	375	125
65 - 69	5,643	2,594	135	2,218	168	73	3,049	208	1,973	757	111
70 - 74	5,187	2,233	106	1,823	255	49	2,954	241	1,471	1,158	84
75 - 79	4,453	1,855	100	1,392	336	27	2,598	225	935	1,375	63
80 - 84	3,379	1,288	75	810	386	17	2,091	267	464	1,326	34
85 - 89	1,977	599	33	302	257	7	1,378	168	194	1,000	16
90 and over	847	203	8	86	109	-	644	89	58	493	4

Note: * Includes a female member of staff incorrectly enumerated as a resident.

Table 2   Age and marital status – **continued**

Persons present

Age	TOTAL PERSONS	Males					Females				
		Total	Single	Married	Widowed	Divorced	Total	Single	Married	Widowed	Divorced
a	b	c	d	e	f	g	h	i	j	k	l

SOUTH WEST REGION – *continued*

Resident - non-staff	82,621	34,542	21,151	5,215	5,720	2,456	48,079	14,681	3,987	28,076	1,335
Aged											
0 - 4	534	290	290				244	244			
5 - 9	363	208	208				155	155			
10	104	70	70				34	34			
11	117	84	84				33	33			
12 - 14	425	252	252				173	173			
15	236	145	145				91	91			
16 - 17	1,036	822	818	2	1	1	214	211	3	-	-
18 - 19	3,414	2,721	2,697	20	1	3	693	667	23	2	1
20 - 24	8,020	6,183	5,896	228	3	56	1,837	1,700	111	3	23
25 - 29	4,254	3,202	2,597	387	3	215	1,052	863	114	6	69
30 - 34	2,601	1,951	1,259	432	7	253	650	468	116	1	65
35 - 39	1,994	1,437	822	355	8	252	557	389	108	3	57
40 - 44	1,883	1,351	819	263	10	259	532	359	84	7	82
45 - 49	1,529	1,045	644	163	14	224	484	337	73	7	67
50 - 54	1,341	889	532	123	20	214	452	308	61	22	61
55 - 59	1,237	766	466	108	25	167	471	310	71	32	58
60 - 64	1,993	1,080	652	156	71	201	913	502	125	170	116
65 - 69	2,703	1,264	687	241	174	162	1,439	604	202	512	121
70 - 74	3,966	1,506	649	363	336	158	2,460	723	355	1,241	141
75 - 79	7,651	2,304	605	681	860	158	5,347	1,169	602	3,403	173
80 - 84	12,806	2,938	527	790	1,542	79	9,868	1,746	870	7,098	154
85 - 89	13,744	2,511	292	622	1,555	42	11,233	1,949	693	8,488	103
90 and over	10,670	1,523	140	281	1,090	12	9,147	1,646	376	7,081	44
Resident - staff	14,673	7,290	4,089	2,640	51	510	7,383	4,029	2,649	250	455
Aged											
0 - 4	402	203	203				199	199			
5 - 9	507	271	271				236	236			
10	119	48	48				71	71			
11	135	66	66				69	69			
12 - 14	402	203	203				199	199			
15	156	73	73				83	83			
16 - 17	436	235	233	2	-	-	201	201	-	-	-
18 - 19	1,000	459	455	2	1	1	541	539	2	-	-
20 - 24	2,751	1,247	1,200	37	-	10	1,504	1,442	60	-	2
25 - 29	1,468	783	623	115	-	45	685	520	140	1	24
30 - 34	907	527	273	187	1	66	380	129	212	1	38
35 - 39	922	475	124	270	1	80	447	90	305	4	48
40 - 44	1,186	566	85	399	1	81	620	47	496	9	68
45 - 49	1,332	642	73	492	1	76	690	50	528	18	94
50 - 54	1,161	595	67	448	8	72	566	51	413	20	82
55 - 59	878	444	38	356	6	44	434	45	292	35	62
60 - 64	491	289	30	232	6	21	202	19	130	30	23
65 - 69	162	71	9	48	3	11	91	16	36	30	9
70 - 74	94	45	5	29	9	2	49	8	15	23	3
75 - 79	72	25	5	14	5	1	47	8	11	28	-
80 - 84	51	15	3	6	6	-	36	3	4	28	1
85 - 89	35	8	2	3	3	-	27	3	3	20	1
90 and over	6	-	-	-	-	-	6	1	2	3	-

Table 2 Age and marital status – **continued**

Great Britain, England & Wales, England, regions, metropolitan counties, Inner London, Outer London, regional remainders, Wales, Scotland

Persons present

Age	TOTAL PERSONS	Males					Females				
		Total	Single	Married	Widowed	Divorced	Total	Single	Married	Widowed	Divorced
a	b	c	d	e	f	g	h	i	j	k	l

SOUTH WEST REGION – *continued*

All persons present in households	4,412,435	2,128,458	886,320	1,087,739	60,805	93,594	2,283,977	793,644	1,106,210	254,021	130,102
Aged											
0 - 4	280,644	143,870	143,870				136,774	136,774			
5 - 9	266,277	136,607	136,607				129,670	129,670			
10	54,074	27,654	27,654				26,420	26,420			
11	54,272	27,729	27,729				26,543	26,543			
12 - 14	149,214	76,121	76,121				73,093	73,093			
15	50,895	25,705	25,705				25,190	25,190			
16 - 17	109,092	55,306	55,191	94	3	18	53,786	53,547	195	18	26
18 - 19	111,817	56,597	56,158	395	5	39	55,220	53,404	1,730	21	65
20 - 24	300,790	149,017	130,479	17,712	36	790	151,773	110,161	38,837	120	2,655
25 - 29	318,918	157,428	80,292	71,356	78	5,702	161,490	53,446	97,038	344	10,662
30 - 34	301,178	148,357	37,760	99,585	180	10,832	152,821	23,007	113,524	593	15,697
35 - 39	287,667	140,592	21,127	106,359	315	12,791	147,075	12,335	115,943	1,132	17,665
40 - 44	330,236	162,396	16,027	129,986	664	15,719	167,840	8,851	136,083	2,191	20,715
45 - 49	283,379	141,042	10,846	115,672	1,026	13,498	142,337	5,997	116,041	3,575	16,724
50 - 54	242,328	120,137	8,021	100,242	1,406	10,468	122,191	5,214	98,736	5,941	12,300
55 - 59	233,386	114,431	7,573	96,223	2,478	8,157	118,955	5,615	92,602	10,899	9,839
60 - 64	242,103	115,248	7,711	96,610	4,715	6,212	126,855	7,331	90,920	20,554	8,050
65 - 69	247,412	113,284	6,937	93,675	8,236	4,436	134,128	8,584	83,900	35,165	6,479
70 - 74	204,697	89,255	4,600	71,908	10,098	2,649	115,442	7,804	59,307	43,970	4,361
75 - 79	170,216	69,044	3,204	51,878	12,508	1,454	101,172	8,459	37,978	51,861	2,874
80 - 84	110,055	39,558	1,877	26,180	10,867	634	70,497	7,086	17,635	44,371	1,405
85 - 89	48,537	15,293	669	8,388	6,066	170	33,244	3,825	4,895	24,037	487
90 and over	15,248	3,787	162	1,476	2,124	25	11,461	1,288	846	9,229	98

WEST MIDLANDS REGION

All persons present in communal establish-ments *	105,681	49,177	30,046	11,360	5,222	2,549	56,504	23,369	8,547	23,019	1,569
Aged											
0 - 4	1,720	936	936				784	784			
5 - 9	1,057	670	670				387	387			
10	605	391	391				214	214			
11	875	561	561				314	314			
12 - 14	3,101	2,005	2,005				1,096	1,096			
15	1,422	921	921				501	501			
16 - 17	3,505	2,212	2,209	3	-	-	1,293	1,286	6	-	1
18 - 19	7,753	4,133	4,093	36	2	2	3,620	3,568	50	1	1
20 - 24	12,504	6,857	6,519	295	3	40	5,647	5,241	368	7	31
25 - 29	6,600	4,093	3,067	803	6	217	2,507	1,635	763	12	97
30 - 34	4,225	2,760	1,486	1,017	3	254	1,465	689	641	4	131
35 - 39	3,459	2,259	946	1,026	11	276	1,200	484	524	18	174
40 - 44	3,502	2,199	816	1,066	16	301	1,303	484	634	17	168
45 - 49	3,056	1,929	747	855	27	300	1,127	385	564	32	146
50 - 54	2,681	1,600	587	762	26	225	1,081	367	513	52	149
55 - 59	2,449	1,431	562	660	36	173	1,018	323	500	101	94
60 - 64	3,286	1,899	755	789	139	216	1,387	412	536	320	119
65 - 69	4,044	2,115	834	765	324	192	1,929	538	572	712	107
70 - 74	5,042	2,175	658	834	539	144	2,867	632	661	1,493	81
75 - 79	7,499	2,562	570	954	935	103	4,937	832	777	3,233	95
80 - 84	10,382	2,616	414	842	1,289	71	7,766	1,141	756	5,767	102
85 - 89	10,141	1,918	209	492	1,195	22	8,223	1,197	465	6,513	48
90 and over	6,773	935	90	161	671	13	5,838	859	217	4,737	25

Note: * Includes a female member of staff incorrectly enumerated as a resident.

Table 2 Age and marital status – **continued**

Great Britain, England & Wales, England, regions, metropolitan counties, Inner London, Outer London, regional remainders, Wales, Scotland

Persons present

Age	TOTAL PERSONS	Males					Females				
		Total	Single	Married	Widowed	Divorced	Total	Single	Married	Widowed	Divorced
a	b	c	d	e	f	g	h	i	j	k	l

WEST MIDLANDS REGION – *continued*

Visitors/guests	46,168	25,482	15,682	7,706	1,183	911	20,686	10,955	5,324	3,706	701
Aged											
0 - 4	1,172	655	655				517	517			
5 - 9	614	416	416				198	198			
10	500	329	329				171	171			
11	744	486	486				258	258			
12 - 14	2,609	1,706	1,706				903	903			
15	1,173	782	782				391	391			
16 - 17	2,786	1,780	1,777	3	-	-	1,006	1,001	5	-	-
18 - 19	5,676	2,996	2,971	23	1	1	2,680	2,647	32	1	-
20 - 24	7,116	3,865	3,657	186	2	20	3,251	2,960	270	5	16
25 - 29	3,264	1,957	1,279	566	4	108	1,307	659	585	7	56
30 - 34	2,240	1,409	533	757	-	119	831	273	477	2	79
35 - 39	1,746	1,140	232	763	6	139	606	116	383	11	96
40 - 44	1,793	1,100	143	827	6	124	693	103	472	11	107
45 - 49	1,473	890	109	659	16	106	583	57	424	24	78
50 - 54	1,276	749	85	585	11	68	527	55	375	31	66
55 - 59	1,247	672	71	530	16	55	575	49	409	67	50
60 - 64	1,462	807	100	595	55	57	655	51	409	150	45
65 - 69	1,597	840	105	573	112	50	757	65	405	259	28
70 - 74	1,733	828	83	564	157	24	905	92	380	404	29
75 - 79	2,036	882	77	530	253	22	1,154	90	338	709	17
80 - 84	1,934	678	50	341	273	14	1,256	130	223	879	24
85 - 89	1,398	392	25	171	193	3	1,006	105	104	788	9
90 and over	579	123	11	33	78	1	456	64	33	358	1
Resident - non-staff	**54,252**	**21,492**	**12,919**	**3,049**	**4,017**	**1,507**	**32,760**	**10,158**	**2,617**	**19,266**	**719**
Aged											
0 - 4	474	245	245				229	229			
5 - 9	347	188	188				159	159			
10	77	45	45				32	32			
11	105	57	57				48	48			
12 - 14	413	270	270				143	143			
15	225	127	127				98	98			
16 - 17	627	390	390	-	-	-	237	235	1	-	1
18 - 19	1,549	989	976	12	-	1	560	544	15	-	1
20 - 24	3,810	2,529	2,406	103	-	20	1,281	1,191	76	2	12
25 - 29	2,548	1,776	1,489	192	2	93	772	622	114	5	31
30 - 34	1,633	1,145	830	194	3	118	488	345	104	2	37
35 - 39	1,455	974	651	198	5	120	481	344	74	7	56
40 - 44	1,397	931	628	141	7	155	466	354	64	5	43
45 - 49	1,298	896	613	102	10	171	402	305	51	4	42
50 - 54	1,120	726	488	86	12	140	394	291	39	14	50
55 - 59	986	652	468	58	18	108	334	249	31	27	27
60 - 64	1,707	1,027	641	150	82	154	680	344	102	163	71
65 - 69	2,397	1,248	719	180	211	138	1,149	465	156	450	78
70 - 74	3,285	1,337	572	265	380	120	1,948	533	279	1,084	52
75 - 79	5,440	1,668	490	419	678	81	3,772	738	437	2,519	78
80 - 84	8,435	1,935	363	501	1,014	57	6,500	1,007	531	4,884	78
85 - 89	8,736	1,526	184	321	1,002	19	7,210	1,089	361	5,722	38
90 and over	6,188	811	79	127	593	12	5,377	793	182	4,378	24

Table 2 Age and marital status – **continued**

Great Britain, England & Wales, England, regions, metropolitan counties, Inner London, Outer London, regional remainders, Wales, Scotland

Persons present

Age	TOTAL PERSONS	Males					Females				
		Total	Single	Married	Widowed	Divorced	Total	Single	Married	Widowed	Divorced
a	b	c	d	e	f	g	h	i	j	k	l

WEST MIDLANDS REGION – *continued*

Resident - staff	5,261	2,203	1,445	605	22	131	3,058	2,256	606	47	149
Aged											
0 - 4	74	36	36				38	38			
5 - 9	96	66	66				30	30			
10	28	17	17				11	11			
11	26	18	18				8	8			
12 - 14	79	29	29				50	50			
15	24	12	12				12	12			
16 - 17	92	42	42	-	-	-	50	50	-	-	-
18 - 19	528	148	146	1	1	-	380	377	3	-	-
20 - 24	1,578	463	456	6	1	-	1,115	1,090	22	-	3
25 - 29	788	360	299	45	-	16	428	354	64	-	10
30 - 34	352	206	123	66	-	17	146	71	60	-	15
35 - 39	258	145	63	65	-	17	113	24	67	-	22
40 - 44	312	168	45	98	3	22	144	27	98	1	18
45 - 49	285	143	25	94	1	23	142	23	89	4	26
50 - 54	285	125	14	91	3	17	160	21	99	7	33
55 - 59	216	107	23	72	2	10	109	25	60	7	17
60 - 64	117	65	14	44	2	5	52	17	25	7	3
65 - 69	50	27	10	12	1	4	23	8	11	3	1
70 - 74	24	10	3	5	2	-	14	7	2	5	-
75 - 79	23	12	3	5	4	-	11	4	2	5	-
80 - 84	13	3	1	-	2	-	10	4	2	4	-
85 - 89	7	-	-	-	-	-	7	3	-	3	1
90 and over	6	1	-	1	-	-	5	2	2	1	-
All persons present in households	4,982,884	2,438,222	1,089,463	1,180,378	69,323	99,058	2,544,662	952,709	1,193,674	268,839	129,440
Aged											
0 - 4	345,387	176,889	176,889				168,498	168,498			
5 - 9	329,593	168,949	168,949				160,644	160,644			
10	66,621	34,112	34,112				32,509	32,509			
11	66,109	33,724	33,724				32,385	32,385			
12 - 14	179,450	92,196	92,196				87,254	87,254			
15	61,392	31,441	31,441				29,951	29,951			
16 - 17	131,827	67,732	67,492	200	11	29	64,095	63,591	458	25	21
18 - 19	141,449	72,236	71,344	845	9	38	69,213	66,237	2,859	28	89
20 - 24	378,944	189,307	164,753	23,423	44	1,087	189,637	139,055	47,526	158	2,898
25 - 29	379,532	186,566	95,047	84,935	136	6,448	192,966	67,262	113,329	451	11,924
30 - 34	349,082	172,737	44,306	116,460	233	11,738	176,345	28,115	130,517	804	16,909
35 - 39	328,405	163,440	24,888	124,347	439	13,766	164,965	14,133	130,951	1,422	18,459
40 - 44	362,558	180,984	19,497	144,361	837	16,289	181,574	9,591	148,262	2,862	20,859
45 - 49	320,278	160,814	14,176	131,121	1,344	14,173	159,464	6,589	131,381	4,530	16,964
50 - 54	281,552	142,124	11,037	117,471	2,167	11,449	139,428	5,559	113,058	7,900	12,911
55 - 59	261,152	130,688	10,145	108,003	3,530	9,010	130,464	5,743	101,276	13,926	9,519
60 - 64	260,270	128,014	10,322	104,193	6,920	6,579	132,256	6,701	93,166	25,202	7,187
65 - 69	247,406	115,076	8,463	91,357	10,894	4,362	132,330	7,276	79,529	40,199	5,326
70 - 74	196,693	85,187	5,173	65,194	12,458	2,362	111,506	6,618	53,232	48,350	3,306
75 - 79	152,070	60,502	3,246	42,753	13,336	1,167	91,568	6,393	30,970	52,368	1,837
80 - 84	92,011	31,557	1,586	19,313	10,241	417	60,454	5,068	12,944	41,558	884
85 - 89	39,453	11,366	562	5,532	5,146	126	28,087	2,641	3,629	21,521	296
90 and over	11,650	2,581	115	870	1,578	18	9,069	896	587	7,535	51

Persons present

Age	TOTAL PERSONS	Males					Females				
		Total	Single	Married	Widowed	Divorced	Total	Single	Married	Widowed	Divorced
a	b	c	d	e	f	g	h	i	j	k	l

West Midlands Metropolitan County

All persons present in communal establish-ments *	46,973	21,129	12,576	5,016	2,298	1,239	25,844	11,249	3,717	10,182	696
Aged											
0 - 4	929	520	520				409	409			
5 - 9	404	235	235				169	169			
10	105	67	67				38	38			
11	113	62	62				51	51			
12 - 14	408	238	238				170	170			
15	188	90	90				98	98			
16 - 17	444	208	207	1	-	-	236	232	4	-	-
18 - 19	3,943	1,819	1,804	15	-	-	2,124	2,098	25	1	-
20 - 24	6,672	3,328	3,182	131	-	15	3,344	3,136	190	2	16
25 - 29	3,283	1,894	1,475	337	2	80	1,389	945	390	7	47
30 - 34	2,109	1,371	772	501	-	98	738	357	315	3	63
35 - 39	1,704	1,126	501	485	6	134	578	256	232	10	80
40 - 44	1,660	1,050	455	448	7	140	610	254	278	12	66
45 - 49	1,445	913	405	335	9	164	532	206	240	18	68
50 - 54	1,282	787	338	324	15	110	495	184	216	26	69
55 - 59	1,178	748	336	284	23	105	430	160	179	49	42
60 - 64	1,593	994	454	333	81	126	599	188	206	151	54
65 - 69	1,953	1,075	454	343	171	107	878	252	232	343	51
70 - 74	2,480	1,130	383	412	260	75	1,350	297	294	725	34
75 - 79	3,396	1,179	278	441	413	47	2,217	386	337	1,453	41
80 - 84	4,536	1,163	197	369	571	26	3,373	495	312	2,523	43
85 - 89	4,298	796	91	200	496	9	3,502	510	184	2,794	14
90 and over	2,850	336	32	57	244	3	2,514	358	83	2,065	8
Visitors/guests	20,169	10,276	5,889	3,374	595	418	9,893	5,308	2,392	1,875	318
Aged											
0 - 4	642	365	365				277	277			
5 - 9	182	110	110				72	72			
10	60	36	36				24	24			
11	69	40	40				29	29			
12 - 14	198	110	110				88	88			
15	81	35	35				46	46			
16 - 17	248	116	115	1	-	-	132	129	3	-	-
18 - 19	3,249	1,547	1,538	9	-	-	1,702	1,683	18	1	-
20 - 24	4,306	2,210	2,123	80	-	7	2,096	1,948	141	1	6
25 - 29	1,603	904	624	235	2	43	699	373	291	4	31
30 - 34	1,061	644	255	339	-	50	417	148	223	2	44
35 - 39	779	498	115	322	2	59	281	65	171	6	39
40 - 44	784	478	75	339	2	62	306	47	213	8	38
45 - 49	611	349	40	257	5	47	262	26	185	13	38
50 - 54	545	313	36	245	4	28	232	23	164	18	27
55 - 59	543	308	35	231	12	30	235	25	151	33	26
60 - 64	657	385	62	254	34	35	272	19	153	79	21
65 - 69	739	395	52	257	60	26	344	32	167	132	13
70 - 74	884	434	51	289	80	14	450	49	167	219	15
75 - 79	981	417	35	248	124	10	564	40	155	362	7
80 - 84	983	343	23	174	141	5	640	70	117	444	9
85 - 89	689	190	10	79	99	2	499	58	55	383	3
90 and over	275	49	4	15	30	-	226	37	18	170	1

Note: * Includes a female member of staff incorrectly enumerated as a resident.

Table 2 Age and marital status – **continued**

Great Britain, England & Wales, England, regions, metropolitan counties, Inner London, Outer London, regional remainders, Wales, Scotland

Persons present

Age	TOTAL PERSONS	Males					Females				
		Total	Single	Married	Widowed	Divorced	Total	Single	Married	Widowed	Divorced
a	b	c	d	e	f	g	h	i	j	k	l

West Midlands Metropolitan County – *continued*

Resident - non-staff	**24,707**	**10,150**	**6,235**	**1,443**	**1,695**	**777**	**14,557**	**4,811**	**1,139**	**8,289**	**318**
Aged											
0 - 4	261	142	142				119	119			
5 - 9	197	109	109				88	88			
10	39	27	27				12	12			
11	42	21	21				21	21			
12 - 14	183	118	118				65	65			
15	101	53	53				48	48			
16 - 17	177	86	86	-	-	-	91	90	1	-	-
18 - 19	446	240	234	6	-	-	206	201	5	-	-
20 - 24	1,677	995	937	50	-	8	682	632	42	1	7
25 - 29	1,337	860	742	85	-	33	477	394	67	3	13
30 - 34	908	641	472	127	-	42	267	182	71	1	13
35 - 39	821	566	362	133	4	67	255	180	41	4	30
40 - 44	778	522	363	84	3	72	256	190	41	3	22
45 - 49	738	519	353	53	3	110	219	166	29	4	20
50 - 54	626	419	292	40	10	77	207	151	20	7	29
55 - 59	573	412	292	37	11	72	161	122	14	14	11
60 - 64	895	586	383	70	45	88	309	159	48	70	32
65 - 69	1,195	671	397	84	111	79	524	214	63	210	37
70 - 74	1,584	694	330	123	180	61	890	241	126	504	19
75 - 79	2,405	758	240	193	288	37	1,647	342	182	1,089	34
80 - 84	3,547	818	173	195	429	21	2,729	423	195	2,077	34
85 - 89	3,604	606	81	121	397	7	2,998	451	129	2,408	10
90 and over	2,573	287	28	42	214	3	2,286	320	65	1,894	7
Resident - staff	**2,097**	**703**	**452**	**199**	**8**	**44**	**1,394**	**1,130**	**186**	**18**	**60**
Aged											
0 - 4	26	13	13				13	13			
5 - 9	25	16	16				9	9			
10	6	4	4				2	2			
11	2	1	1				1	1			
12 - 14	27	10	10				17	17			
15	6	2	2				4	4			
16 - 17	19	6	6	-	-	-	13	13	-	-	-
18 - 19	248	32	32	-	-	-	216	214	2	-	-
20 - 24	689	123	122	1	-	-	566	556	7	-	3
25 - 29	343	130	109	17	-	4	213	178	32	-	3
30 - 34	140	86	45	35	-	6	54	27	21	-	6
35 - 39	104	62	24	30	-	8	42	11	20	-	11
40 - 44	98	50	17	25	2	6	48	17	24	1	6
45 - 49	96	45	12	25	1	7	51	14	26	1	10
50 - 54	111	55	10	39	1	5	56	10	32	1	13
55 - 59	62	28	9	16	-	3	34	13	14	2	5
60 - 64	41	23	9	9	2	3	18	10	5	2	1
65 - 69	19	9	5	2	-	2	10	6	2	1	1
70 - 74	12	2	2	-	-	-	10	7	1	2	-
75 - 79	10	4	3	-	1	-	6	4	-	2	-
80 - 84	6	2	1	-	1	-	4	2	-	2	-
85 - 89	5	-	-	-	-	-	5	1	-	3	1
90 and over	2	-	-	-	-	-	2	1	-	1	-

Table 2 Age and marital status – **continued**

Great Britain, England & Wales, England, regions, metropolitan counties, Inner London, Outer London, regional remainders, Wales, Scotland

Persons present

Age	TOTAL PERSONS	Males					Females				
		Total	Single	Married	Widowed	Divorced	Total	Single	Married	Widowed	Divorced
a	b	c	d	e	f	g	h	i	j	k	l

West Midlands Metropolitan County – *continued*

All persons present in households	2,464,034	1,201,179	562,702	554,543	35,852	48,082	1,262,855	497,431	561,946	140,118	63,360
Aged											
0 - 4	178,603	91,320	91,320				87,283	87,283			
5 - 9	168,935	86,311	86,311				82,624	82,624			
10	33,375	17,162	17,162				16,213	16,213			
11	32,896	16,754	16,754				16,142	16,142			
12 - 14	88,856	45,769	45,769				43,087	43,087			
15	30,412	15,599	15,599				14,813	14,813			
16 - 17	64,697	33,312	33,148	141	7	16	31,385	31,036	327	12	10
18 - 19	71,703	36,563	35,970	567	2	24	35,140	33,279	1,806	16	39
20 - 24	200,951	99,366	86,296	12,558	23	489	101,585	75,370	24,752	93	1,370
25 - 29	195,164	94,974	50,297	41,743	76	2,858	100,190	38,873	55,452	240	5,625
30 - 34	172,132	85,254	23,948	55,729	107	5,470	86,878	16,671	61,596	423	8,188
35 - 39	154,266	77,161	13,291	57,347	207	6,316	77,105	8,229	59,319	774	8,783
40 - 44	162,688	81,119	10,548	62,495	433	7,643	81,569	5,369	64,789	1,556	9,855
45 - 49	146,041	73,280	7,944	57,768	682	6,886	72,761	3,623	58,467	2,369	8,302
50 - 54	134,682	67,517	6,213	54,411	1,107	5,786	67,165	3,162	53,109	4,248	6,646
55 - 59	128,974	64,378	5,879	51,908	1,867	4,724	64,596	3,193	48,910	7,504	4,989
60 - 64	129,599	63,909	5,878	50,856	3,724	3,451	65,690	3,561	45,148	13,276	3,705
65 - 69	122,618	56,789	4,681	44,077	5,721	2,310	65,829	3,788	38,486	20,875	2,680
70 - 74	99,453	42,661	2,903	31,831	6,670	1,257	56,792	3,493	26,212	25,417	1,670
75 - 79	76,346	29,862	1,695	20,727	6,837	603	46,484	3,210	15,229	27,160	885
80 - 84	45,931	15,305	778	9,251	5,087	189	30,626	2,623	6,309	21,253	441
85 - 89	19,854	5,573	260	2,713	2,548	52	14,281	1,355	1,763	11,017	146
90 and over	5,858	1,241	58	421	754	8	4,617	434	272	3,885	26

Remainder of West Midlands Region

All persons present in communal establishments	58,708	28,048	17,470	6,344	2,924	1,310	30,660	12,120	4,830	12,837	873
Aged											
0 - 4	791	416	416				375	375			
5 - 9	653	435	435				218	218			
10	500	324	324				176	176			
11	762	499	499				263	263			
12 - 14	2,693	1,767	1,767				926	926			
15	1,234	831	831				403	403			
16 - 17	3,061	2,004	2,002	2	-	-	1,057	1,054	2	-	1
18 - 19	3,810	2,314	2,289	21	2	2	1,496	1,470	25	-	1
20 - 24	5,832	3,529	3,337	164	3	25	2,303	2,105	178	5	15
25 - 29	3,317	2,199	1,592	466	4	137	1,118	690	373	5	50
30 - 34	2,116	1,389	714	516	3	156	727	332	326	1	68
35 - 39	1,755	1,133	445	541	5	142	622	228	292	8	94
40 - 44	1,842	1,149	361	618	9	161	693	230	356	5	102
45 - 49	1,611	1,016	342	520	18	136	595	179	324	14	78
50 - 54	1,399	813	249	438	11	115	586	183	297	26	80
55 - 59	1,271	683	226	376	13	68	588	163	321	52	52
60 - 64	1,693	905	301	456	58	90	788	224	330	169	65
65 - 69	2,091	1,040	380	422	153	85	1,051	286	340	369	56
70 - 74	2,562	1,045	275	422	279	69	1,517	335	367	768	47
75 - 79	4,103	1,383	292	513	522	56	2,720	446	440	1,780	54
80 - 84	5,846	1,453	217	473	718	45	4,393	646	444	3,244	59
85 - 89	5,843	1,122	118	292	699	13	4,721	687	281	3,719	34
90 and over	3,923	599	58	104	427	10	3,324	501	134	2,672	17

Table 2   Age and marital status – **continued**

Persons present

Age	TOTAL PERSONS	Males					Females				
		Total	Single	Married	Widowed	Divorced	Total	Single	Married	Widowed	Divorced
a	b	c	d	e	f	g	h	i	j	k	l

Remainder of West Midlands Region – *continued*

Age	TOTAL PERSONS	Total	Single	Married	Widowed	Divorced	Total	Single	Married	Widowed	Divorced
Visitors/guests	25,999	15,206	9,793	4,332	588	493	10,793	5,647	2,932	1,831	383
Aged											
0 - 4	530	290	290				240	240			
5 - 9	432	306	306				126	126			
10	440	293	293				147	147			
11	675	446	446				229	229			
12 - 14	2,411	1,596	1,596				815	815			
15	1,092	747	747				345	345			
16 - 17	2,538	1,664	1,662	2	-	-	874	872	2	-	-
18 - 19	2,427	1,449	1,433	14	1	1	978	964	14	-	-
20 - 24	2,810	1,655	1,534	106	2	13	1,155	1,012	129	4	10
25 - 29	1,661	1,053	655	331	2	65	608	286	294	3	25
30 - 34	1,179	765	278	418	-	69	414	125	254	-	35
35 - 39	967	642	117	441	4	80	325	51	212	5	57
40 - 44	1,009	622	68	488	4	62	387	56	259	3	69
45 - 49	862	541	69	402	11	59	321	31	239	11	40
50 - 54	731	436	49	340	7	40	295	32	211	13	39
55 - 59	704	364	36	299	4	25	340	24	258	34	24
60 - 64	805	422	38	341	21	22	383	32	256	71	24
65 - 69	858	445	53	316	52	24	413	33	238	127	15
70 - 74	849	394	32	275	77	10	455	43	213	185	14
75 - 79	1,055	465	42	282	129	12	590	50	183	347	10
80 - 84	951	335	27	167	132	9	616	60	106	435	15
85 - 89	709	202	15	92	94	1	507	47	49	405	6
90 and over	304	74	7	18	48	1	230	27	15	188	-
Resident - non-staff	29,545	11,342	6,684	1,606	2,322	730	18,203	5,347	1,478	10,977	401
Aged											
0 - 4	213	103	103				110	110			
5 - 9	150	79	79				71	71			
10	38	18	18				20	20			
11	63	36	36				27	27			
12 - 14	230	152	152				78	78			
15	124	74	74				50	50			
16 - 17	450	304	304	-	-	-	146	145	-	-	1
18 - 19	1,103	749	742	6	-	1	354	343	10	-	1
20 - 24	2,133	1,534	1,469	53	-	12	599	559	34	1	5
25 - 29	1,211	916	747	107	2	60	295	228	47	2	18
30 - 34	725	504	358	67	3	76	221	163	33	1	24
35 - 39	634	408	289	65	1	53	226	164	33	3	26
40 - 44	619	409	265	57	4	83	210	164	23	2	21
45 - 49	560	377	260	49	7	61	183	139	22	-	22
50 - 54	494	307	196	46	2	63	187	140	19	7	21
55 - 59	413	240	176	21	7	36	173	127	17	13	16
60 - 64	812	441	258	80	37	66	371	185	54	93	39
65 - 69	1,202	577	322	96	100	59	625	251	93	240	41
70 - 74	1,701	643	242	142	200	59	1,058	292	153	580	33
75 - 79	3,035	910	250	226	390	44	2,125	396	255	1,430	44
80 - 84	4,888	1,117	190	306	585	36	3,771	584	336	2,807	44
85 - 89	5,132	920	103	200	605	12	4,212	638	232	3,314	28
90 and over	3,615	524	51	85	379	9	3,091	473	117	2,484	17

Table 2   Age and marital status – **continued**

Great Britain, England & Wales, England, regions, metropolitan counties, Inner London, Outer London, regional remainders, Wales, Scotland

Persons present

Age	TOTAL PERSONS	Males					Females				
		Total	Single	Married	Widowed	Divorced	Total	Single	Married	Widowed	Divorced
a	b	c	d	e	f	g	h	i	j	k	l

Remainder of West Midlands Region – *continued*

Age	TOTAL PERSONS	Males Total	Single	Married	Widowed	Divorced	Females Total	Single	Married	Widowed	Divorced
Resident - staff	3,164	1,500	993	406	14	87	1,664	1,126	420	29	89
Aged											
0 - 4	48	23	23				25	25			
5 - 9	71	50	50				21	21			
10	22	13	13				9	9			
11	24	17	17				7	7			
12 - 14	52	19	19				33	33			
15	18	10	10				8	8			
16 - 17	73	36	36	-	-	-	37	37	-	-	-
18 - 19	280	116	114	1	1	-	164	163	1	-	-
20 - 24	889	340	334	5	1	-	549	534	15	-	-
25 - 29	445	230	190	28	-	12	215	176	32	-	7
30 - 34	212	120	78	31	-	11	92	44	39	-	9
35 - 39	154	83	39	35	-	9	71	13	47	-	11
40 - 44	214	118	28	73	1	16	96	10	74	-	12
45 - 49	189	98	13	69	-	16	91	9	63	3	16
50 - 54	174	70	4	52	2	12	104	11	67	6	20
55 - 59	154	79	14	56	2	7	75	12	46	5	12
60 - 64	76	42	5	35	-	2	34	7	20	5	2
65 - 69	31	18	5	10	1	2	13	2	9	2	-
70 - 74	12	8	1	5	2	-	4	-	1	3	-
75 - 79	13	8	-	5	3	-	5	-	2	3	-
80 - 84	7	1	-	-	1	-	6	2	2	2	-
85 - 89	2	-	-	-	-	-	2	2	-	-	-
90 and over	4	1	-	1	-	-	3	1	2	-	-
All persons present in households	2,518,850	1,237,043	526,761	625,835	33,471	50,976	1,281,807	455,278	631,728	128,721	66,080
Aged											
0 - 4	166,784	85,569	85,569				81,215	81,215			
5 - 9	160,658	82,638	82,638				78,020	78,020			
10	33,246	16,950	16,950				16,296	16,296			
11	33,213	16,970	16,970				16,243	16,243			
12 - 14	90,594	46,427	46,427				44,167	44,167			
15	30,980	15,842	15,842				15,138	15,138			
16 - 17	67,130	34,420	34,344	59	4	13	32,710	32,555	131	13	11
18 - 19	69,746	35,673	35,374	278	7	14	34,073	32,958	1,053	12	50
20 - 24	177,993	89,941	78,457	10,865	21	598	88,052	63,685	22,774	65	1,528
25 - 29	184,368	91,592	44,750	43,192	60	3,590	92,776	28,389	57,877	211	6,299
30 - 34	176,950	87,483	20,358	60,731	126	6,268	89,467	11,444	68,921	381	8,721
35 - 39	174,139	86,279	11,597	67,000	232	7,450	87,860	5,904	71,632	648	9,676
40 - 44	199,870	99,865	8,949	81,866	404	8,646	100,005	4,222	83,473	1,306	11,004
45 - 49	174,237	87,534	6,232	73,353	662	7,287	86,703	2,966	72,914	2,161	8,662
50 - 54	146,870	74,607	4,824	63,060	1,060	5,663	72,263	2,397	59,949	3,652	6,265
55 - 59	132,178	66,310	4,266	56,095	1,663	4,286	65,868	2,550	52,366	6,422	4,530
60 - 64	130,671	64,105	4,444	53,337	3,196	3,128	66,566	3,140	48,018	11,926	3,482
65 - 69	124,788	58,287	3,782	47,280	5,173	2,052	66,501	3,488	41,043	19,324	2,646
70 - 74	97,240	42,526	2,270	33,363	5,788	1,105	54,714	3,125	27,020	22,933	1,636
75 - 79	75,724	30,640	1,551	22,026	6,499	564	45,084	3,183	15,741	25,208	952
80 - 84	46,080	16,252	808	10,062	5,154	228	29,828	2,445	6,635	20,305	443
85 - 89	19,599	5,793	302	2,819	2,598	74	13,806	1,286	1,866	10,504	150
90 and over	5,792	1,340	57	449	824	10	4,452	462	315	3,650	25

Table 2 Age and marital status – **continued**

Great Britain, England & Wales, England, regions, metropolitan counties, Inner London, Outer London, regional remainders, Wales, Scotland

Persons present

Age	TOTAL PERSONS	Males					Females				
		Total	Single	Married	Widowed	Divorced	Total	Single	Married	Widowed	Divorced
a	b	c	d	e	f	g	h	i	j	k	l

NORTH WEST REGION

Age	TOTAL PERSONS	Total	Single	Married	Widowed	Divorced	Total	Single	Married	Widowed	Divorced
All persons present in communal establish-ments *	143,476	59,818	32,899	14,938	8,089	3,892	83,658	31,256	12,600	37,326	2,476
Aged											
0 - 4	2,437	1,286	1,286				1,151	1,151			
5 - 9	1,440	841	841				599	599			
10	408	247	247				161	161			
11	462	295	295				167	167			
12 - 14	2,003	1,281	1,281				722	722			
15	997	598	598				399	399			
16 - 17	1,784	1,023	1,018	4	-	1	761	755	5	1	-
18 - 19	8,664	4,099	4,069	22	3	5	4,565	4,523	37	1	4
20 - 24	15,258	7,846	7,504	274	14	54	7,412	6,904	459	6	43
25 - 29	7,959	4,867	3,772	859	9	227	3,092	2,026	922	9	135
30 - 34	5,342	3,459	1,977	1,126	11	345	1,883	839	844	16	184
35 - 39	4,417	2,851	1,228	1,198	17	408	1,566	563	767	19	217
40 - 44	4,557	2,848	1,079	1,287	22	460	1,709	547	874	35	253
45 - 49	4,231	2,526	886	1,154	35	451	1,705	527	891	50	237
50 - 54	3,882	2,268	819	1,013	51	385	1,614	482	847	81	204
55 - 59	3,658	2,072	740	927	81	324	1,586	480	781	169	156
60 - 64	5,016	2,655	1,041	1,040	222	352	2,361	753	851	550	207
65 - 69	6,452	3,195	1,168	1,232	483	312	3,257	926	881	1,233	217
70 - 74	7,893	3,106	908	1,167	812	219	4,787	1,147	981	2,478	181
75 - 79	12,574	4,106	943	1,406	1,567	190	8,468	1,591	1,196	5,502	179
80 - 84	17,381	4,209	696	1,296	2,115	102	13,172	2,252	1,213	9,565	142
85 - 89	16,050	2,814	358	702	1,720	34	13,236	2,198	751	10,205	82
90 and over	10,611	1,326	145	231	927	23	9,285	1,544	300	7,406	35
Visitors/guests	54,741	27,863	15,558	9,246	1,696	1,363	26,878	12,858	7,292	5,642	1,086
Aged											
0 - 4	1,707	917	917				790	790			
5 - 9	524	332	332				192	192			
10	208	131	131				77	77			
11	259	177	177				82	82			
12 - 14	1,147	807	807				340	340			
15	515	352	352				163	163			
16 - 17	1,187	723	720	2	-	1	464	459	4	1	-
18 - 19	7,158	3,395	3,377	14	2	2	3,763	3,734	25	1	3
20 - 24	9,851	5,121	4,904	176	11	30	4,730	4,365	344	3	18
25 - 29	4,110	2,434	1,721	586	2	125	1,676	844	740	6	86
30 - 34	2,729	1,654	675	793	6	180	1,075	307	646	12	110
35 - 39	2,162	1,345	298	862	6	179	817	138	530	10	139
40 - 44	2,095	1,270	201	881	11	177	825	102	556	19	148
45 - 49	1,786	1,058	134	750	13	161	728	61	521	25	121
50 - 54	1,735	948	117	680	14	137	787	72	563	53	99
55 - 59	1,737	923	114	670	42	97	814	64	572	102	76
60 - 64	2,122	1,076	135	751	94	96	1,046	94	627	252	73
65 - 69	2,519	1,254	130	883	171	70	1,265	123	617	451	74
70 - 74	2,630	1,138	104	740	239	55	1,492	154	572	719	47
75 - 79	3,084	1,242	94	731	382	35	1,842	196	487	1,105	54
80 - 84	2,869	936	73	480	372	11	1,933	241	316	1,350	26
85 - 89	1,828	489	36	203	245	5	1,339	173	129	1,028	9
90 and over	779	141	9	44	86	2	638	87	43	505	3

Note: * Includes a male member of staff incorrectly enumerated as a resident.

Table 2 Age and marital status – **continued**

Great Britain, England & Wales, England, regions, metropolitan counties, Inner London, Outer London, regional remainders, Wales, Scotland

Persons present

Age	TOTAL PERSONS	Males					Females				
		Total	Single	Married	Widowed	Divorced	Total	Single	Married	Widowed	Divorced
a	b	c	d	e	f	g	h	i	j	k	l

NORTH WEST REGION – continued

Age	TOTAL PERSONS	Males Total	Single	Married	Widowed	Divorced	Females Total	Single	Married	Widowed	Divorced
Resident - non-staff	**80,155**	**28,162**	**15,225**	**4,248**	**6,369**	**2,320**	**51,993**	**15,390**	**3,881**	**31,535**	**1,187**
Aged											
0 - 4	532	274	274				258	258			
5 - 9	657	370	370				287	287			
10	139	78	78				61	61			
11	141	90	90				51	51			
12 - 14	653	368	368				285	285			
15	399	196	196				203	203			
16 - 17	405	207	206	1	-	-	198	198	-	-	-
18 - 19	1,076	585	574	7	1	3	491	480	10	-	1
20 - 24	3,572	2,217	2,114	80	3	20	1,355	1,262	74	2	17
25 - 29	2,754	1,908	1,623	192	7	86	846	717	94	3	32
30 - 34	2,023	1,448	1,106	198	5	139	575	431	79	3	62
35 - 39	1,744	1,228	851	172	9	196	516	376	74	8	58
40 - 44	1,775	1,230	800	168	9	253	545	397	66	10	72
45 - 49	1,707	1,127	707	138	20	262	580	423	73	13	71
50 - 54	1,507	1,003	665	92	30	216	504	363	52	14	75
55 - 59	1,462	921	588	95	36	202	541	370	66	45	60
60 - 64	2,631	1,439	880	192	124	243	1,192	625	164	279	124
65 - 69	3,821	1,898	1,022	325	311	240	1,923	780	246	759	138
70 - 74	5,207	1,952	797	418	573	164	3,255	971	406	1,745	133
75 - 79	9,442	2,850	840	672	1,183	155	6,592	1,379	706	4,383	124
80 - 84	14,476	3,271	621	816	1,743	91	11,205	1,993	896	8,201	115
85 - 89	14,207	2,320	320	496	1,475	29	11,887	2,024	618	9,172	73
90 and over	9,825	1,182	135	186	840	21	8,643	1,456	257	6,898	32
Resident - staff	**8,580**	**3,793**	**2,116**	**1,444**	**24**	**209**	**4,787**	**3,008**	**1,427**	**149**	**203**
Aged											
0 - 4	198	95	95				103	103			
5 - 9	259	139	139				120	120			
10	61	38	38				23	23			
11	62	28	28				34	34			
12 - 14	203	106	106				97	97			
15	83	50	50				33	33			
16 - 17	192	93	92	1	-	-	99	98	1	-	-
18 - 19	430	119	118	1	-	-	311	309	2	-	-
20 - 24	1,835	508	486	18	-	4	1,327	1,277	41	1	8
25 - 29	1,095	525	428	81	-	16	570	465	88	-	17
30 - 34	590	357	196	135	-	26	233	101	119	1	12
35 - 39	511	278	79	164	2	33	233	49	163	1	20
40 - 44	687	348	78	238	2	30	339	48	252	6	33
45 - 49	738	341	45	266	2	28	397	43	297	12	45
50 - 54	640	317	37	241	7	32	323	47	232	14	30
55 - 59	459	228	38	162	3	25	231	46	143	22	20
60 - 64	263	140	26	97	4	13	123	34	60	19	10
65 - 69	112	43	16	24	1	2	69	23	18	23	5
70 - 74	56	16	7	9	-	-	40	22	3	14	1
75 - 79	48	14	9	3	2	-	34	16	3	14	1
80 - 84	36	2	2	-	-	-	34	18	1	14	1
85 - 89	15	5	2	3	-	-	10	1	4	5	-
90 and over	7	3	1	1	1	-	4	1	-	3	-

Table 2 Age and marital status – **continued**

Great Britain, England & Wales, England, regions, metropolitan counties, Inner London, Outer London, regional remainders, Wales, Scotland

Persons present

Age	TOTAL PERSONS	Males					Females				
		Total	Single	Married	Widowed	Divorced	Total	Single	Married	Widowed	Divorced
a	b	c	d	e	f	g	h	i	j	k	l

NORTH WEST REGION – *continued*

Age	TOTAL PERSONS	Total	Single	Married	Widowed	Divorced	Total	Single	Married	Widowed	Divorced
All persons present in households	6,003,300	2,897,483	1,324,319	1,355,548	88,982	128,634	3,105,817	1,199,413	1,382,176	344,514	179,714
Aged											
0 - 4	425,757	217,927	217,927				207,830	207,830			
5 - 9	408,209	208,869	208,869				199,340	199,340			
10	80,704	41,156	41,156				39,548	39,548			
11	80,994	41,443	41,443				39,551	39,551			
12 - 14	217,689	111,564	111,564				106,125	106,125			
15	75,070	38,511	38,511				36,559	36,559			
16 - 17	157,768	80,820	80,614	153	13	40	76,948	76,475	407	31	35
18 - 19	167,889	84,611	83,871	678	16	46	83,278	80,653	2,479	46	100
20 - 24	445,724	218,789	194,804	22,831	51	1,103	226,935	174,992	48,280	181	3,482
25 - 29	464,225	224,674	118,908	97,432	136	8,198	239,551	91,312	131,483	506	16,250
30 - 34	426,744	207,984	55,275	136,831	309	15,569	218,760	37,835	155,335	915	24,675
35 - 39	391,620	193,020	30,346	143,907	551	18,216	198,600	18,398	152,321	1,741	26,140
40 - 44	437,884	217,107	23,997	170,436	1,154	21,520	220,777	12,615	175,709	3,650	28,803
45 - 49	363,834	181,254	16,167	145,852	1,657	17,578	182,580	8,299	146,463	5,619	22,199
50 - 54	333,561	165,561	13,233	134,535	2,901	14,892	168,000	7,371	132,438	10,091	18,100
55 - 59	313,057	154,880	12,009	126,174	4,988	11,709	158,177	7,915	118,386	18,362	13,514
60 - 64	309,074	147,885	12,034	118,234	8,915	8,702	161,189	9,336	108,419	33,184	10,250
65 - 69	298,231	136,109	10,223	105,618	14,481	5,787	162,122	10,714	92,839	51,120	7,449
70 - 74	233,941	98,740	6,265	73,860	15,586	3,029	135,201	9,953	60,512	60,345	4,391
75 - 79	189,003	71,675	4,120	48,918	17,153	1,484	117,328	10,289	36,724	67,650	2,665
80 - 84	118,377	38,700	2,127	22,823	13,170	580	79,677	8,461	15,652	54,375	1,189
85 - 89	49,517	13,344	709	6,331	6,147	157	36,173	4,461	4,033	27,280	399
90 and over	14,428	2,860	147	935	1,754	24	11,568	1,381	696	9,418	73

Greater Manchester Metropolitan County

Age	TOTAL PERSONS	Total	Single	Married	Widowed	Divorced	Total	Single	Married	Widowed	Divorced
All persons present in communal establishments	46,085	18,478	10,050	4,632	2,686	1,110	27,607	9,857	4,189	12,727	834
Aged											
0 - 4	935	491	491				444	444			
5 - 9	427	241	241				186	186			
10	103	62	62				41	41			
11	100	57	57				43	43			
12 - 14	413	245	245				168	168			
15	252	130	130				122	122			
16 - 17	559	271	268	2	-	1	288	284	3	1	-
18 - 19	2,894	1,481	1,465	13	1	2	1,413	1,395	15	-	3
20 - 24	5,451	2,785	2,697	79	3	6	2,666	2,437	208	1	20
25 - 29	2,574	1,408	1,088	269	3	48	1,166	721	397	3	45
30 - 34	1,606	955	533	338	4	80	651	264	306	5	76
35 - 39	1,316	813	307	406	8	92	503	159	266	4	74
40 - 44	1,231	761	253	367	9	132	470	125	243	9	93
45 - 49	1,073	625	216	275	8	126	448	123	248	12	65
50 - 54	1,079	616	199	280	13	124	463	127	246	24	66
55 - 59	1,083	617	212	278	31	96	466	112	245	56	53
60 - 64	1,534	844	320	325	84	115	690	186	261	180	63
65 - 69	2,001	1,013	344	405	155	109	988	241	272	406	69
70 - 74	2,515	1,017	270	396	283	68	1,498	298	311	831	58
75 - 79	4,190	1,384	284	497	537	66	2,806	494	414	1,839	59
80 - 84	5,822	1,374	212	414	720	28	4,448	684	399	3,317	48
85 - 89	5,331	885	116	225	535	9	4,446	673	252	3,493	28
90 and over	3,596	403	40	63	292	8	3,193	530	103	2,546	14

Table 2 Age and marital status – **continued**

Great Britain, England & Wales, England, regions, metropolitan counties, Inner London, Outer London, regional remainders, Wales, Scotland

Persons present

Age	TOTAL PERSONS	Males					Females				
		Total	Single	Married	Widowed	Divorced	Total	Single	Married	Widowed	Divorced
a	b	c	d	e	f	g	h	i	j	k	l

Greater Manchester Metropolitan County – *continued*

Visitors/guests	18,795	9,206	5,116	3,099	635	356	9,589	4,375	2,719	2,103	392
Aged											
0 - 4	705	377	377				328	328			
5 - 9	176	109	109				67	67			
10	57	31	31				26	26			
11	44	27	27				17	17			
12 - 14	176	109	109				67	67			
15	103	56	56				47	47			
16 - 17	387	193	191	1	-	1	194	190	3	1	-
18 - 19	2,375	1,236	1,224	11	-	1	1,139	1,128	9	-	2
20 - 24	3,548	1,870	1,813	51	2	4	1,678	1,503	165	1	9
25 - 29	1,393	702	486	191	-	25	691	329	329	2	31
30 - 34	903	487	201	251	2	33	416	119	250	4	43
35 - 39	764	441	96	312	2	31	323	56	218	1	48
40 - 44	698	390	51	286	3	50	308	38	203	5	62
45 - 49	571	312	42	227	-	43	259	20	193	9	37
50 - 54	590	313	38	233	2	40	277	23	208	12	34
55 - 59	624	319	44	228	15	32	305	23	216	40	26
60 - 64	714	367	52	246	38	31	347	30	207	84	26
65 - 69	852	430	39	298	66	27	422	45	204	150	23
70 - 74	908	419	47	258	97	17	489	44	179	245	21
75 - 79	1,139	451	37	259	140	15	688	82	160	426	20
80 - 84	1,084	332	29	162	138	3	752	94	114	538	6
85 - 89	690	189	14	75	98	2	501	58	47	393	3
90 and over	294	46	3	10	32	1	248	41	14	192	1
Resident - non-staff	25,385	8,576	4,464	1,346	2,047	719	16,809	4,527	1,290	10,602	390
Aged											
0 - 4	202	102	102				100	100			
5 - 9	216	118	118				98	98			
10	40	27	27				13	13			
11	50	27	27				23	23			
12 - 14	222	127	127				95	95			
15	141	68	68				73	73			
16 - 17	152	74	73	1	-	-	78	78	-	-	-
18 - 19	395	223	219	2	1	1	172	165	6	-	1
20 - 24	1,268	784	758	23	1	2	484	450	27	-	7
25 - 29	819	546	463	57	3	23	273	224	39	1	9
30 - 34	538	362	266	55	2	39	176	112	36	1	27
35 - 39	449	311	191	61	5	54	138	87	29	3	19
40 - 44	438	322	194	46	5	77	116	75	17	2	22
45 - 49	423	282	160	35	8	79	141	89	27	2	23
50 - 54	409	271	155	26	10	80	138	91	14	7	26
55 - 59	388	268	160	34	15	59	120	72	14	13	21
60 - 64	785	464	264	71	46	83	321	146	48	92	35
65 - 69	1,134	578	303	105	89	81	556	191	68	253	44
70 - 74	1,594	597	223	137	186	51	997	245	132	583	37
75 - 79	3,046	931	245	238	397	51	2,115	409	254	1,413	39
80 - 84	4,733	1,041	182	252	582	25	3,692	587	285	2,778	42
85 - 89	4,641	696	102	150	437	7	3,945	615	205	3,100	25
90 and over	3,302	357	37	53	260	7	2,945	489	89	2,354	13

Table 2 Age and marital status – **continued**

Great Britain, England & Wales, England, regions, metropolitan counties, Inner London, Outer London, regional remainders, Wales, Scotland

Persons present

Age	TOTAL PERSONS	Males					Females				
		Total	Single	Married	Widowed	Divorced	Total	Single	Married	Widowed	Divorced
a	b	c	d	e	f	g	h	i	j	k	l

Greater Manchester Metropolitan County – *continued*

Resident - staff	**1,905**	**696**	**470**	**187**	**4**	**35**	**1,209**	**955**	**180**	**22**	**52**
Aged											
0 - 4	28	12	12				16	16			
5 - 9	35	14	14				21	21			
10	6	4	4				2	2			
11	6	3	3				3	3			
12 - 14	15	9	9				6	6			
15	8	6	6				2	2			
16 - 17	20	4	4	-	-	-	16	16	-	-	-
18 - 19	124	22	22	-	-	-	102	102	-	-	-
20 - 24	635	131	126	5	-	-	504	484	16	-	4
25 - 29	362	160	139	21	-	-	202	168	29	-	5
30 - 34	165	106	66	32	-	8	59	33	20	-	6
35 - 39	103	61	20	33	1	7	42	16	19	-	7
40 - 44	95	49	8	35	1	5	46	12	23	2	9
45 - 49	79	31	14	13	-	4	48	14	28	1	5
50 - 54	80	32	6	21	1	4	48	13	24	5	6
55 - 59	71	30	8	16	1	5	41	17	15	3	6
60 - 64	35	13	4	8	-	1	22	10	6	4	2
65 - 69	15	5	2	2	-	1	10	5	-	3	2
70 - 74	13	1	-	1	-	-	12	9	-	3	-
75 - 79	5	2	2	-	-	-	3	3	-	-	-
80 - 84	5	1	1	-	-	-	4	3	-	1	-
85 - 89	-	-	-	-	-	-	-	-	-	-	-
90 and over	-	-	-	-	-	-	-	-	-	-	-
All persons present in households	**2,409,008**	**1,167,058**	**547,076**	**529,850**	**36,106**	**54,026**	**1,241,950**	**490,456**	**539,828**	**138,456**	**73,210**
Aged											
0 - 4	175,812	90,015	90,015				85,797	85,797			
5 - 9	166,302	85,186	85,186				81,116	81,116			
10	32,362	16,513	16,513				15,849	15,849			
11	32,584	16,697	16,697				15,887	15,887			
12 - 14	86,868	44,575	44,575				42,293	42,293			
15	29,639	15,231	15,231				14,408	14,408			
16 - 17	62,567	32,242	32,158	63	4	17	30,325	30,103	193	12	17
18 - 19	67,688	34,083	33,768	293	6	16	33,605	32,421	1,124	24	36
20 - 24	188,568	92,694	82,598	9,604	15	477	95,874	73,995	20,326	80	1,473
25 - 29	194,061	94,302	50,948	39,858	62	3,434	99,759	39,141	53,654	229	6,735
30 - 34	173,445	85,197	23,472	55,159	117	6,449	88,248	16,147	61,676	370	10,055
35 - 39	156,021	77,706	13,011	56,788	229	7,678	78,315	7,629	59,419	722	10,545
40 - 44	174,129	86,993	10,253	67,047	504	9,189	87,136	5,107	68,671	1,550	11,808
45 - 49	143,825	72,064	6,931	57,051	696	7,386	71,761	3,356	57,075	2,281	9,049
50 - 54	131,277	65,607	5,593	52,554	1,204	6,256	65,670	2,961	51,226	4,014	7,469
55 - 59	120,728	60,131	5,104	48,164	1,970	4,893	60,597	2,995	44,744	7,364	5,494
60 - 64	118,098	56,417	5,003	44,297	3,532	3,585	61,681	3,543	40,955	13,092	4,091
65 - 69	116,938	53,688	4,409	40,825	6,008	2,446	63,250	4,090	35,539	20,636	2,985
70 - 74	91,839	38,559	2,616	28,254	6,441	1,248	53,280	3,817	23,324	24,382	1,757
75 - 79	74,401	27,959	1,756	18,687	6,900	616	46,442	4,023	14,155	27,206	1,058
80 - 84	46,717	15,009	901	8,542	5,308	258	31,708	3,428	5,956	21,854	470
85 - 89	19,484	5,080	275	2,309	2,429	67	14,404	1,782	1,542	10,933	147
90 and over	5,655	1,110	63	355	681	11	4,545	568	249	3,707	21

Table 2 Age and marital status – **continued**

Great Britain, England & Wales, England, regions, metropolitan counties, Inner London, Outer London, regional remainders, Wales, Scotland

Persons present

Age	TOTAL PERSONS	Males					Females				
		Total	Single	Married	Widowed	Divorced	Total	Single	Married	Widowed	Divorced
a	b	c	d	e	f	g	h	i	j	k	l

Merseyside Metropolitan County

Age	TOTAL PERSONS	Total	Single	Married	Widowed	Divorced	Total	Single	Married	Widowed	Divorced
All persons present in communal establishments	34,344	14,229	8,025	3,120	2,059	1,025	20,115	8,380	2,381	8,794	560
Aged											
0 - 4	586	316	316				270	270			
5 - 9	282	168	168				114	114			
10	67	40	40				27	27			
11	67	38	38				29	29			
12 - 14	311	162	162				149	149			
15	189	96	96				93	93			
16 - 17	176	97	97	-	-	-	79	77	2	-	-
18 - 19	2,397	1,117	1,109	3	2	3	1,280	1,273	6	-	1
20 - 24	3,507	1,767	1,694	51	7	15	1,740	1,670	60	1	9
25 - 29	1,864	1,183	953	174	1	55	681	517	139	2	23
30 - 34	1,285	864	550	229	1	84	421	207	173	3	38
35 - 39	1,033	704	354	229	3	118	329	154	122	5	48
40 - 44	1,046	691	317	250	5	119	355	160	134	5	56
45 - 49	935	599	252	224	11	112	336	138	134	10	54
50 - 54	852	528	238	184	11	95	324	129	130	26	39
55 - 59	838	485	220	163	20	82	353	153	142	31	27
60 - 64	1,228	649	277	215	59	98	579	238	162	131	48
65 - 69	1,604	800	316	248	151	85	804	304	182	263	55
70 - 74	2,044	821	250	295	217	59	1,223	364	222	587	50
75 - 79	3,194	1,032	249	311	408	64	2,162	501	272	1,338	51
80 - 84	4,231	1,023	179	305	516	23	3,208	687	259	2,233	29
85 - 89	3,951	688	105	172	403	8	3,263	669	171	2,401	22
90 and over	2,657	361	45	67	244	5	2,296	457	71	1,758	10
Visitors/guests	12,562	6,419	3,655	1,958	435	371	6,143	3,293	1,405	1,210	235
Aged											
0 - 4	454	243	243				211	211			
5 - 9	91	54	54				37	37			
10	22	15	15				7	7			
11	29	14	14				15	15			
12 - 14	127	66	66				61	61			
15	73	47	47				26	26			
16 - 17	69	36	36	-	-	-	33	32	1	-	-
18 - 19	2,099	976	971	2	2	1	1,123	1,118	4	-	1
20 - 24	2,335	1,193	1,142	38	6	7	1,142	1,094	45	-	3
25 - 29	974	630	475	120	-	35	344	205	120	2	17
30 - 34	634	386	182	159	-	45	248	78	146	3	21
35 - 39	479	311	84	167	1	59	168	38	95	4	31
40 - 44	471	301	61	195	3	42	170	31	110	4	25
45 - 49	398	253	46	159	6	42	145	14	101	5	25
50 - 54	403	235	39	151	2	43	168	22	106	17	23
55 - 59	368	200	39	128	10	23	168	26	111	19	12
60 - 64	456	252	33	168	24	27	204	22	115	52	15
65 - 69	528	274	38	169	50	17	254	36	120	77	21
70 - 74	626	286	27	180	62	17	340	47	117	168	8
75 - 79	704	288	19	150	109	10	416	46	116	238	16
80 - 84	632	219	14	117	86	2	413	57	59	285	12
85 - 89	402	108	7	43	58	-	294	48	25	217	4
90 and over	188	32	3	12	16	1	156	22	14	119	1

Table 2 Age and marital status – **continued**

Great Britain, England & Wales, England, regions, metropolitan counties, Inner London, Outer London, regional remainders, Wales, Scotland

Persons present

Age	TOTAL PERSONS	Males					Females				
		Total	Single	Married	Widowed	Divorced	Total	Single	Married	Widowed	Divorced
a	b	c	d	e	f	g	h	i	j	k	l

Merseyside Metropolitan County – *continued*

Age	TOTAL PERSONS	Total	Single	Married	Widowed	Divorced	Total	Single	Married	Widowed	Divorced
Resident - non-staff	**20,291**	**7,218**	**3,969**	**1,013**	**1,622**	**614**	**13,073**	**4,361**	**862**	**7,561**	**289**
Aged											
0 - 4	103	55	55				48	48			
5 - 9	167	103	103				64	64			
10	41	22	22				19	19			
11	32	22	22				10	10			
12 - 14	168	86	86				82	82			
15	109	43	43				66	66			
16 - 17	92	54	54	-	-	-	38	38	-	-	-
18 - 19	239	132	129	1	-	2	107	105	2	-	-
20 - 24	753	476	458	11	1	6	277	259	14	-	4
25 - 29	659	446	383	43	1	19	213	193	15	-	5
30 - 34	523	398	326	38	1	33	125	94	16	-	15
35 - 39	477	346	250	45	2	49	131	104	11	1	15
40 - 44	499	347	235	38	1	73	152	112	13	1	26
45 - 49	441	305	197	39	5	64	136	103	8	5	20
50 - 54	373	264	192	16	9	47	109	86	8	4	11
55 - 59	389	254	168	20	9	57	135	102	13	9	11
60 - 64	720	375	231	42	35	67	345	198	41	75	31
65 - 69	1,041	515	271	75	101	68	526	255	60	179	32
70 - 74	1,399	529	217	115	155	42	870	307	104	418	41
75 - 79	2,472	739	225	161	299	54	1,733	445	155	1,099	34
80 - 84	3,583	803	164	188	430	21	2,780	616	200	1,947	17
85 - 89	3,543	576	96	127	345	8	2,967	620	145	2,184	18
90 and over	2,468	328	42	54	228	4	2,140	435	57	1,639	9
Resident - staff	**1,491**	**592**	**401**	**149**	**2**	**40**	**899**	**726**	**114**	**23**	**36**
Aged											
0 - 4	29	18	18				11	11			
5 - 9	24	11	11				13	13			
10	4	3	3				1	1			
11	6	2	2				4	4			
12 - 14	16	10	10				6	6			
15	7	6	6				1	1			
16 - 17	15	7	7	-	-	-	8	7	1	-	-
18 - 19	59	9	9	-	-	-	50	50	-	-	-
20 - 24	419	98	94	2	-	2	321	317	1	1	2
25 - 29	231	107	95	11	-	1	124	119	4	-	1
30 - 34	128	80	42	32	-	6	48	35	11	-	2
35 - 39	77	47	20	17	-	10	30	12	16	-	2
40 - 44	76	43	21	17	1	4	33	17	11	-	5
45 - 49	96	41	9	26	-	6	55	21	25	-	9
50 - 54	76	29	7	17	-	5	47	21	16	5	5
55 - 59	81	31	13	15	1	2	50	25	18	3	4
60 - 64	52	22	13	5	-	4	30	18	6	4	2
65 - 69	35	11	7	4	-	-	24	13	2	7	2
70 - 74	19	6	6	-	-	-	13	10	1	1	1
75 - 79	18	5	5	-	-	-	13	10	1	1	1
80 - 84	16	1	1	-	-	-	15	14	-	1	-
85 - 89	6	4	2	2	-	-	2	1	1	-	-
90 and over	1	1	-	1	-	-	-	-	-	-	-

Table 2 Age and marital status – **continued**

Great Britain, England & Wales, England, regions, metropolitan counties, Inner London, Outer London, regional remainders, Wales, Scotland

Persons present

Age	TOTAL PERSONS	Males					Females				
		Total	Single	Married	Widowed	Divorced	Total	Single	Married	Widowed	Divorced
a	b	c	d	e	f	g	h	i	j	k	l

Merseyside Metropolitan County – *continued*

All persons present in households	1,346,121	640,535	304,629	287,755	20,903	27,248	705,586	286,308	296,327	81,140	41,811
Aged											
0 - 4	95,617	48,908	48,908				46,709	46,709			
5 - 9	92,974	47,596	47,596				45,378	45,378			
10	18,323	9,325	9,325				8,998	8,998			
11	18,362	9,474	9,474				8,888	8,888			
12 - 14	49,308	25,204	25,204				24,104	24,104			
15	17,012	8,742	8,742				8,270	8,270			
16 - 17	35,677	18,165	18,125	31	4	5	17,512	17,443	50	10	9
18 - 19	38,152	19,245	19,122	104	5	14	18,907	18,550	328	10	19
20 - 24	99,474	48,407	44,356	3,836	13	202	51,067	42,156	8,262	31	618
25 - 29	102,654	48,214	27,431	19,218	30	1,535	54,440	24,222	26,754	99	3,365
30 - 34	95,764	45,555	13,424	28,837	76	3,218	50,209	10,576	33,689	197	5,747
35 - 39	86,581	41,556	7,092	30,533	120	3,811	45,025	5,244	33,037	399	6,345
40 - 44	92,219	45,073	5,795	34,687	252	4,339	47,146	3,520	36,291	793	6,542
45 - 49	76,035	37,129	3,985	29,207	364	3,573	38,906	2,297	30,219	1,324	5,066
50 - 54	74,407	36,059	3,435	28,667	702	3,255	38,348	2,055	29,436	2,475	4,382
55 - 59	74,371	36,293	3,246	29,014	1,280	2,753	38,078	2,411	27,638	4,728	3,301
60 - 64	74,007	35,100	3,321	27,412	2,308	2,059	38,907	2,850	25,213	8,314	2,530
65 - 69	68,137	30,516	2,598	23,055	3,560	1,303	37,621	3,186	20,316	12,274	1,845
70 - 74	53,511	22,154	1,675	16,023	3,781	675	31,357	2,906	13,069	14,351	1,031
75 - 79	42,995	15,943	1,022	10,716	3,871	334	27,052	2,898	7,844	15,678	632
80 - 84	26,125	8,404	535	4,870	2,865	134	17,721	2,194	3,192	12,085	250
85 - 89	11,094	2,860	178	1,332	1,317	33	8,234	1,121	839	6,172	102
90 and over	3,322	613	40	213	355	5	2,709	332	150	2,200	27

Remainder of North West Region

All persons present in communal establish-ments *	63,047	27,111	14,824	7,186	3,344	1,757	35,936	13,019	6,030	15,805	1,082
Aged											
0 - 4	916	479	479				437	437			
5 - 9	731	432	432				299	299			
10	238	145	145				93	93			
11	295	200	200				95	95			
12 - 14	1,279	874	874				405	405			
15	556	372	372				184	184			
16 - 17	1,049	655	653	2	-	-	394	394	-	-	-
18 - 19	3,373	1,501	1,495	6	-	-	1,872	1,855	16	1	-
20 - 24	6,300	3,294	3,113	144	4	33	3,006	2,797	191	4	14
25 - 29	3,521	2,276	1,731	416	5	124	1,245	788	386	4	67
30 - 34	2,451	1,640	894	559	6	181	811	368	365	8	70
35 - 39	2,068	1,334	567	563	6	198	734	250	379	10	95
40 - 44	2,280	1,396	509	670	8	209	884	262	497	21	104
45 - 49	2,223	1,302	418	655	16	213	921	266	509	28	118
50 - 54	1,951	1,124	382	549	27	166	827	226	471	31	99
55 - 59	1,737	970	308	486	30	146	767	215	394	82	76
60 - 64	2,254	1,162	444	500	79	139	1,092	329	428	239	96
65 - 69	2,847	1,382	508	579	177	118	1,465	381	427	564	93
70 - 74	3,334	1,268	388	476	312	92	2,066	485	448	1,060	73
75 - 79	5,190	1,690	410	598	622	60	3,500	596	510	2,325	69
80 - 84	7,328	1,812	305	577	879	51	5,516	881	555	4,015	65
85 - 89	6,768	1,241	137	305	782	17	5,527	856	328	4,311	32
90 and over	4,358	562	60	101	391	10	3,796	557	126	3,102	11

Note: * Includes a male member of staff incorrectly enumerated as a resident.

Table 2 Age and marital status – **continued**

Great Britain, England & Wales, England, regions, metropolitan counties, Inner London, Outer London, regional remainders, Wales, Scotland

Persons present

Age	TOTAL PERSONS	Males					Females				
		Total	Single	Married	Widowed	Divorced	Total	Single	Married	Widowed	Divorced
a	b	c	d	e	f	g	h	i	j	k	l

Remainder of North West Region – *continued*

Visitors/guests	23,384	12,238	6,787	4,189	626	636	11,146	5,190	3,168	2,329	459
Aged											
0 - 4	548	297	297				251	251			
5 - 9	257	169	169				88	88			
10	129	85	85				44	44			
11	186	136	136				50	50			
12 - 14	844	632	632				212	212			
15	339	249	249				90	90			
16 - 17	731	494	493	1	-	-	237	237	-	-	-
18 - 19	2,684	1,183	1,182	1	-	-	1,501	1,488	12	1	-
20 - 24	3,968	2,058	1,949	87	3	19	1,910	1,768	134	2	6
25 - 29	1,743	1,102	760	275	2	65	641	310	291	2	38
30 - 34	1,192	781	292	383	4	102	411	110	250	5	46
35 - 39	919	593	118	383	3	89	326	44	217	5	60
40 - 44	926	579	89	400	5	85	347	33	243	10	61
45 - 49	817	493	46	364	7	76	324	27	227	11	59
50 - 54	742	400	40	296	10	54	342	27	249	24	42
55 - 59	745	404	31	314	17	42	341	15	245	43	38
60 - 64	952	457	50	337	32	38	495	42	305	116	32
65 - 69	1,139	550	53	416	55	26	589	42	293	224	30
70 - 74	1,096	433	30	302	80	21	663	63	276	306	18
75 - 79	1,241	503	38	322	133	10	738	68	211	441	18
80 - 84	1,153	385	30	201	148	6	768	90	143	527	8
85 - 89	736	192	15	85	89	3	544	67	57	418	2
90 and over	297	63	3	22	38	-	234	24	15	194	1
Resident - non-staff	**34,479**	**12,368**	**6,792**	**1,889**	**2,700**	**987**	**22,111**	**6,502**	**1,729**	**13,372**	**508**
Aged											
0 - 4	227	117	117				110	110			
5 - 9	274	149	149				125	125			
10	58	29	29				29	29			
11	59	41	41				18	18			
12 - 14	263	155	155				108	108			
15	149	85	85				64	64			
16 - 17	161	79	79	-	-	-	82	82	-	-	-
18 - 19	442	230	226	4	-	-	212	210	2	-	-
20 - 24	1,551	957	898	46	1	12	594	553	33	2	6
25 - 29	1,276	916	777	92	3	44	360	300	40	2	18
30 - 34	962	688	514	105	2	67	274	225	27	2	20
35 - 39	818	571	410	66	2	93	247	185	34	4	24
40 - 44	838	561	371	84	3	103	277	210	36	7	24
45 - 49	843	540	350	64	7	119	303	231	38	6	28
50 - 54	725	468	318	50	11	89	257	186	30	3	38
55 - 59	685	399	260	41	12	86	286	196	39	23	28
60 - 64	1,126	600	385	79	43	93	526	281	75	112	58
65 - 69	1,646	805	448	145	121	91	841	334	118	327	62
70 - 74	2,214	826	357	166	232	71	1,388	419	170	744	55
75 - 79	3,924	1,180	370	273	487	50	2,744	525	297	1,871	51
80 - 84	6,160	1,427	275	376	731	45	4,733	790	411	3,476	56
85 - 89	6,023	1,048	122	219	693	14	4,975	789	268	3,888	30
90 and over	4,055	497	56	79	352	10	3,558	532	111	2,905	10

Table 2 Age and marital status – **continued**

Great Britain, England & Wales, England, regions, metropolitan counties, Inner London, Outer London, regional remainders, Wales, Scotland

Persons present

Age	TOTAL PERSONS	Males					Females				
		Total	Single	Married	Widowed	Divorced	Total	Single	Married	Widowed	Divorced
a	b	c	d	e	f	g	h	i	j	k	l

Remainder of North West Region – *continued*

Age	TOTAL PERSONS	Total	Single	Married	Widowed	Divorced	Total	Single	Married	Widowed	Divorced
Resident - staff	5,184	2,505	1,245	1,108	18	134	2,679	1,327	1,133	104	115
Aged											
0 - 4	141	65	65				76	76			
5 - 9	200	114	114				86	86			
10	51	31	31				20	20			
11	50	23	23				27	27			
12 - 14	172	87	87				85	85			
15	68	38	38				30	30			
16 - 17	157	82	81	1	-	-	75	75	-	-	-
18 - 19	247	88	87	1	-	-	159	157	2	-	-
20 - 24	781	279	266	11	-	2	502	476	24	-	2
25 - 29	502	258	194	49	-	15	244	178	55	-	11
30 - 34	297	171	88	71	-	12	126	33	88	1	4
35 - 39	331	170	39	114	1	16	161	21	128	1	11
40 - 44	516	256	49	186	-	21	260	19	218	4	19
45 - 49	563	269	22	227	2	18	294	8	244	11	31
50 - 54	484	256	24	203	6	23	228	13	192	4	19
55 - 59	307	167	17	131	1	18	140	4	110	16	10
60 - 64	176	105	9	84	4	8	71	6	48	11	6
65 - 69	62	27	7	18	1	1	35	5	16	13	1
70 - 74	24	9	1	8	-	-	15	3	2	10	-
75 - 79	25	7	2	3	2	-	18	3	2	13	-
80 - 84	15	-	-	-	-	-	15	1	1	12	1
85 - 89	9	1	-	1	-	-	8	-	3	5	-
90 and over	6	2	1	-	1	-	4	1	-	3	-
All persons present in households	2,248,171	1,089,890	472,614	537,943	31,973	47,360	1,158,281	422,649	546,021	124,918	64,693
Aged											
0 - 4	154,328	79,004	79,004				75,324	75,324			
5 - 9	148,933	76,087	76,087				72,846	72,846			
10	30,019	15,318	15,318				14,701	14,701			
11	30,048	15,272	15,272				14,776	14,776			
12 - 14	81,513	41,785	41,785				39,728	39,728			
15	28,419	14,538	14,538				13,881	13,881			
16 - 17	59,524	30,413	30,331	59	5	18	29,111	28,929	164	9	9
18 - 19	62,049	31,283	30,981	281	5	16	30,766	29,682	1,027	12	45
20 - 24	157,682	77,688	67,850	9,391	23	424	79,994	58,841	19,692	70	1,391
25 - 29	167,510	82,158	40,529	38,356	44	3,229	85,352	27,949	51,075	178	6,150
30 - 34	157,535	77,232	18,379	52,835	116	5,902	80,303	11,112	59,970	348	8,873
35 - 39	149,018	73,758	10,243	56,586	202	6,727	75,260	5,525	59,865	620	9,250
40 - 44	171,536	85,041	7,949	68,702	398	7,992	86,495	3,988	70,747	1,307	10,453
45 - 49	143,974	72,061	5,251	59,594	597	6,619	71,913	2,646	59,169	2,014	8,084
50 - 54	127,877	63,895	4,205	53,314	995	5,381	63,982	2,355	51,776	3,602	6,249
55 - 59	117,958	58,456	3,659	48,996	1,738	4,063	59,502	2,509	46,004	6,270	4,719
60 - 64	116,969	56,368	3,710	46,525	3,075	3,058	60,601	2,943	42,251	11,778	3,629
65 - 69	113,156	51,905	3,216	41,738	4,913	2,038	61,251	3,438	36,984	18,210	2,619
70 - 74	88,591	38,027	1,974	29,583	5,364	1,106	50,564	3,230	24,119	21,612	1,603
75 - 79	71,607	27,773	1,342	19,515	6,382	534	43,834	3,368	14,725	24,766	975
80 - 84	45,535	15,287	691	9,411	4,997	188	30,248	2,839	6,504	20,436	469
85 - 89	18,939	5,404	256	2,690	2,401	57	13,535	1,558	1,652	10,175	150
90 and over	5,451	1,137	44	367	718	8	4,314	481	297	3,511	25

Table 2 Age and marital status – **continued**

Great Britain, England & Wales, England, regions, metropolitan counties, Inner London, Outer London, regional remainders, Wales, Scotland

Persons present

Age	TOTAL PERSONS	Males					Females				
		Total	Single	Married	Widowed	Divorced	Total	Single	Married	Widowed	Divorced
a	b	c	d	e	f	g	h	i	j	k	l

WALES

Age	TOTAL PERSONS	Males Total	Single	Married	Widowed	Divorced	Females Total	Single	Married	Widowed	Divorced
All persons present in communal establishments	71,892	30,950	17,982	7,917	3,552	1,499	40,942	16,762	6,417	16,656	1,107
Aged											
0 - 4	999	543	543				456	456			
5 - 9	784	416	416				368	368			
10	778	388	388				390	390			
11	1,209	656	656				553	553			
12 - 14	2,026	1,151	1,151				875	875			
15	711	423	423				288	288			
16 - 17	1,796	1,028	1,020	6	-	2	768	761	6	1	-
18 - 19	5,389	2,572	2,555	16	-	1	2,817	2,782	30	2	3
20 - 24	7,871	4,295	4,055	208	5	27	3,576	3,314	217	11	34
25 - 29	3,577	2,224	1,625	493	4	102	1,353	837	435	8	73
30 - 34	2,243	1,429	737	555	2	135	814	365	339	7	103
35 - 39	1,780	1,135	443	533	6	153	645	245	317	8	75
40 - 44	2,025	1,186	415	590	6	175	839	249	447	11	132
45 - 49	1,950	1,097	352	580	8	157	853	233	491	25	104
50 - 54	1,811	1,028	327	542	15	144	783	238	422	38	85
55 - 59	1,804	978	336	517	25	100	826	204	464	87	71
60 - 64	2,422	1,187	416	573	73	125	1,235	356	506	289	84
65 - 69	3,202	1,571	542	704	203	122	1,631	399	583	572	77
70 - 74	4,043	1,692	481	763	363	85	2,351	554	550	1,170	77
75 - 79	5,980	2,001	437	759	726	79	3,979	711	604	2,586	78
80 - 84	7,623	1,953	373	633	889	58	5,670	965	529	4,109	67
85 - 89	7,086	1,378	202	352	798	26	5,708	950	328	4,405	25
90 and over	4,783	619	89	93	429	8	4,164	669	149	3,327	19
Visitors/guests	33,993	17,090	10,280	5,384	894	532	16,903	8,937	4,172	3,297	497
Aged											
0 - 4	677	363	363				314	314			
5 - 9	481	257	257				224	224			
10	706	351	351				355	355			
11	1,119	605	605				514	514			
12 - 14	1,655	940	940				715	715			
15	526	319	319				207	207			
16 - 17	1,482	845	839	5	-	1	637	632	4	1	-
18 - 19	4,521	2,124	2,114	9	-	1	2,397	2,380	15	1	1
20 - 24	5,213	2,808	2,652	144	4	8	2,405	2,215	165	7	18
25 - 29	1,892	1,106	727	329	3	47	786	385	351	7	43
30 - 34	1,160	720	289	362	1	68	440	120	260	3	57
35 - 39	926	570	134	376	-	60	356	67	236	6	47
40 - 44	1,067	618	99	432	5	82	449	69	302	10	68
45 - 49	1,018	564	79	419	5	61	454	40	340	13	61
50 - 54	949	529	82	385	7	55	420	33	315	27	45
55 - 59	1,049	547	82	408	15	42	502	34	372	58	38
60 - 64	1,238	573	56	454	25	38	665	77	399	154	35
65 - 69	1,564	748	77	562	85	24	816	76	456	259	25
70 - 74	1,735	819	77	586	135	21	916	95	384	416	21
75 - 79	1,903	754	55	470	215	14	1,149	112	308	715	14
80 - 84	1,652	588	52	313	217	6	1,064	133	173	740	18
85 - 89	1,019	272	26	107	136	3	747	91	71	581	4
90 and over	441	70	5	23	41	1	371	49	21	299	2

Table 2 Age and marital status – **continued**

Great Britain, England & Wales, England, regions, metropolitan counties, Inner London, Outer London, regional remainders, Wales, Scotland

Persons present

Age	TOTAL PERSONS	Males					Females				
		Total	Single	Married	Widowed	Divorced	Total	Single	Married	Widowed	Divorced
a	b	c	d	e	f	g	h	i	j	k	l

WALES – *continued*

Resident - non-staff	33,960	11,988	6,531	1,966	2,643	848	21,972	6,473	1,701	13,307	491
Aged											
0 - 4	249	140	140				109	109			
5 - 9	208	109	109				99	99			
10	49	24	24				25	25			
11	69	40	40				29	29			
12 - 14	280	165	165				115	115			
15	152	82	82				70	70			
16 - 17	229	137	136	-	-	1	92	90	2	-	-
18 - 19	568	335	330	5	-	-	233	216	14	1	2
20 - 24	1,596	1,089	1,014	58	-	17	507	460	33	4	10
25 - 29	1,192	840	666	127	1	46	352	277	50	1	24
30 - 34	815	549	361	138	1	49	266	193	35	4	34
35 - 39	658	448	270	98	5	75	210	160	26	2	22
40 - 44	693	436	291	70	1	74	257	164	53	1	39
45 - 49	651	398	261	58	1	78	253	180	39	8	26
50 - 54	608	367	232	61	6	68	241	190	27	8	16
55 - 59	568	341	237	47	8	49	227	152	32	24	19
60 - 64	1,062	558	351	79	45	83	504	265	72	123	44
65 - 69	1,604	804	460	129	117	98	800	320	122	309	49
70 - 74	2,294	869	403	175	228	63	1,425	457	163	749	56
75 - 79	4,055	1,241	380	287	509	65	2,814	593	295	1,863	63
80 - 84	5,961	1,363	320	319	672	52	4,598	830	355	3,364	49
85 - 89	6,061	1,105	176	245	661	23	4,956	859	256	3,820	21
90 and over	4,338	548	83	70	388	7	3,790	620	127	3,026	17
Resident - staff	3,939	1,872	1,171	567	15	119	2,067	1,352	544	52	119
Aged											
0 - 4	73	40	40				33	33			
5 - 9	95	50	50				45	45			
10	23	13	13				10	10			
11	21	11	11				10	10			
12 - 14	91	46	46				45	45			
15	33	22	22				11	11			
16 - 17	85	46	45	1	-	-	39	39	-	-	-
18 - 19	300	113	111	2	-	-	187	186	1	-	-
20 - 24	1,062	398	389	6	1	2	664	639	19	-	6
25 - 29	493	278	232	37	-	9	215	175	34	-	6
30 - 34	268	160	87	55	-	18	108	52	44	-	12
35 - 39	196	117	39	59	1	18	79	18	55	-	6
40 - 44	265	132	25	88	-	19	133	16	92	-	25
45 - 49	281	135	12	103	2	18	146	13	112	4	17
50 - 54	254	132	13	96	2	21	122	15	80	3	24
55 - 59	187	90	17	62	2	9	97	18	60	5	14
60 - 64	122	56	9	40	3	4	66	14	35	12	5
65 - 69	34	19	5	13	1	-	15	3	5	4	3
70 - 74	14	4	1	2	-	1	10	2	3	5	-
75 - 79	22	6	2	2	2	-	16	6	1	8	1
80 - 84	10	2	1	1	-	-	8	2	1	5	-
85 - 89	6	1	-	-	1	-	5	-	1	4	-
90 and over	4	1	1	-	-	-	3	-	1	2	-

Table 2 Age and marital status – **continued**

Great Britain, England & Wales, England, regions, metropolitan counties, Inner London, Outer London, regional remainders, Wales, Scotland

Persons present

Age	TOTAL PERSONS	Males					Females				
		Total	Single	Married	Widowed	Divorced	Total	Single	Married	Widowed	Divorced
a	b	c	d	e	f	g	h	i	j	k	l

WALES – *continued*

All persons present in households	2,739,973	1,325,936	578,095	650,993	39,894	56,954	1,414,037	509,847	660,678	164,695	78,817
Aged											
0 - 4	184,709	94,491	94,491				90,218	90,218			
5 - 9	179,548	91,824	91,824				87,724	87,724			
10	36,530	18,585	18,585				17,945	17,945			
11	36,613	18,936	18,936				17,677	17,677			
12 - 14	97,906	50,430	50,430				47,476	47,476			
15	33,617	17,321	17,321				16,296	16,296			
16 - 17	71,111	36,429	36,327	88	3	11	34,682	34,479	175	13	15
18 - 19	74,175	37,573	37,218	324	9	22	36,602	35,179	1,335	27	61
20 - 24	192,295	95,089	82,196	12,157	24	712	97,206	70,122	24,919	109	2,056
25 - 29	197,554	96,783	46,752	45,798	57	4,176	100,771	31,897	60,624	265	7,985
30 - 34	185,573	90,780	21,713	62,145	127	6,795	94,793	13,560	69,901	454	10,878
35 - 39	176,909	86,897	12,662	65,979	255	8,001	90,012	7,103	70,724	716	11,469
40 - 44	199,857	99,161	10,198	79,156	448	9,359	100,696	5,213	81,663	1,554	12,266
45 - 49	170,771	84,733	7,261	69,240	698	7,534	86,038	3,564	70,400	2,492	9,582
50 - 54	152,997	76,421	6,202	62,797	1,175	6,247	76,576	3,161	61,906	4,294	7,215
55 - 59	146,922	72,277	5,934	59,213	2,170	4,960	74,645	3,418	57,455	8,304	5,468
60 - 64	149,433	71,983	6,190	58,180	3,743	3,870	77,450	4,179	53,961	14,950	4,360
65 - 69	151,177	70,245	5,793	55,294	6,458	2,700	80,932	4,942	48,102	24,562	3,326
70 - 74	120,867	51,987	3,723	39,551	7,263	1,450	68,880	4,812	31,699	30,227	2,142
75 - 79	92,009	36,216	2,428	25,316	7,702	770	55,793	4,512	17,799	32,250	1,232
80 - 84	57,011	19,212	1,337	11,735	5,874	266	37,799	3,708	7,583	25,976	532
85 - 89	24,879	6,952	472	3,496	2,915	69	17,927	2,008	2,063	13,669	187
90 and over	7,510	1,611	102	524	973	12	5,899	654	369	4,833	43

SCOTLAND

All persons present in communal establish-ments *	154,841	74,519	42,213	21,558	6,764	3,984	80,322	36,184	14,930	27,170	2,038
Aged											
0 - 4	2,276	1,212	1,212				1,064	1,064			
5 - 9	1,539	851	851				688	688			
10	578	330	330				248	248			
11	693	400	400				293	293			
12 - 14	3,294	2,009	2,009				1,285	1,285			
15	1,664	985	985				679	679			
16 - 17	3,887	2,348	2,339	6	1	2	1,539	1,530	8	1	-
18 - 19	12,654	6,492	6,462	24	3	3	6,162	6,105	49	3	5
20 - 24	18,033	10,439	9,879	480	3	77	7,594	7,064	489	9	32
25 - 29	10,182	6,610	4,828	1,483	7	292	3,572	2,308	1,132	6	126
30 - 34	7,188	4,860	2,338	2,072	20	430	2,328	1,102	1,017	15	194
35 - 39	5,887	3,970	1,376	2,050	32	512	1,917	714	967	16	220
40 - 44	5,962	3,897	1,186	2,143	42	526	2,065	742	1,073	40	210
45 - 49	5,288	3,366	1,039	1,826	37	464	1,922	605	1,053	53	211
50 - 54	5,059	3,035	893	1,670	67	405	2,024	550	1,169	112	193
55 - 59	5,056	2,864	843	1,553	114	354	2,192	523	1,251	260	158
60 - 64	5,930	3,055	935	1,621	201	298	2,875	787	1,359	595	134
65 - 69	7,264	3,610	1,116	1,783	482	229	3,654	901	1,383	1,207	163
70 - 74	7,825	3,432	968	1,520	769	175	4,393	1,068	1,137	2,071	117
75 - 79	10,886	3,809	949	1,458	1,276	126	7,077	1,515	1,102	4,352	108
80 - 84	13,657	3,552	668	1,133	1,694	57	10,105	2,288	959	6,766	92
85 - 89	11,984	2,309	437	555	1,292	25	9,675	2,283	522	6,824	46
90 and over	8,055	1,084	170	181	724	9	6,971	1,842	260	4,840	29

Note: * Includes a male member of staff incorrectly enumerated as a resident.

Table 2 Age and marital status – **continued**

Great Britain, England & Wales, England, regions, metropolitan counties, Inner London, Outer London, regional remainders, Wales, Scotland

Persons present

Age	TOTAL PERSONS	Males					Females				
		Total	Single	Married	Widowed	Divorced	Total	Single	Married	Widowed	Divorced
a	b	c	d	e	f	g	h	i	j	k	l

SCOTLAND – *continued*

Visitors/guests	77,425	42,015	22,837	15,811	1,782	1,585	35,410	17,407	10,542	6,377	1,084
Aged											
0 - 4	1,734	903	903				831	831			
5 - 9	849	473	473				376	376			
10	408	242	242				166	166			
11	553	321	321				232	232			
12 - 14	2,578	1,614	1,614				964	964			
15	1,213	747	747				466	466			
16 - 17	3,091	1,899	1,893	4	1	1	1,192	1,187	4	1	-
18 - 19	10,191	5,144	5,124	16	3	1	5,047	5,005	37	3	2
20 - 24	11,081	6,363	6,015	312	1	35	4,718	4,319	369	9	21
25 - 29	5,604	3,586	2,315	1,120	3	148	2,018	1,019	919	4	76
30 - 34	4,216	2,842	1,014	1,588	12	228	1,374	433	813	8	120
35 - 39	3,370	2,286	449	1,578	13	246	1,084	197	736	9	142
40 - 44	3,391	2,268	332	1,672	17	247	1,123	160	802	27	134
45 - 49	2,982	1,909	251	1,439	19	200	1,073	129	783	35	126
50 - 54	2,891	1,677	176	1,326	32	143	1,214	104	919	76	115
55 - 59	3,018	1,577	166	1,254	53	104	1,441	130	1,050	177	84
60 - 64	3,473	1,673	171	1,311	94	97	1,800	176	1,145	402	77
65 - 69	4,032	1,907	181	1,465	206	55	2,125	221	1,133	694	77
70 - 74	3,494	1,533	148	1,094	254	37	1,961	246	778	894	43
75 - 79	3,525	1,382	130	883	346	23	2,143	301	554	1,256	32
80 - 84	3,041	998	97	507	380	14	2,043	343	326	1,353	21
85 - 89	1,794	494	53	193	244	4	1,300	248	126	918	8
90 and over	896	177	22	49	104	2	719	154	48	511	6
Resident - non-staff	68,519	28,471	16,805	4,557	4,955	2,154	40,048	15,388	3,243	20,652	765
Aged											
0 - 4	324	192	192				132	132			
5 - 9	412	230	230				182	182			
10	108	52	52				56	56			
11	92	56	56				36	36			
12 - 14	539	307	307				232	232			
15	391	206	206				185	185			
16 - 17	571	351	348	2	-	1	220	218	2	-	-
18 - 19	1,720	1,103	1,094	7	-	2	617	605	10	-	2
20 - 24	4,747	3,265	3,089	141	2	33	1,482	1,400	73	-	9
25 - 29	3,321	2,405	1,994	291	4	116	916	774	110	2	30
30 - 34	2,341	1,678	1,128	377	7	166	663	527	76	6	54
35 - 39	1,979	1,382	821	319	19	223	597	445	95	5	52
40 - 44	2,000	1,338	796	274	25	243	662	518	84	12	48
45 - 49	1,793	1,202	747	207	16	232	591	428	94	11	58
50 - 54	1,659	1,101	680	161	31	229	558	401	79	25	53
55 - 59	1,637	1,101	655	155	57	234	536	346	80	63	47
60 - 64	2,247	1,270	749	225	103	193	977	583	171	173	50
65 - 69	3,151	1,669	931	294	274	170	1,482	664	237	499	82
70 - 74	4,273	1,883	818	415	512	138	2,390	807	352	1,159	72
75 - 79	7,321	2,419	814	572	930	103	4,902	1,204	540	3,082	76
80 - 84	10,591	2,547	568	623	1,313	43	8,044	1,937	633	5,403	71
85 - 89	10,163	1,809	383	362	1,043	21	8,354	2,027	395	5,894	38
90 and over	7,139	905	147	132	619	7	6,234	1,681	212	4,318	23

Table 2 Age and marital status – **continued**

Great Britain, England & Wales, England, regions, metropolitan counties, Inner London, Outer London, regional remainders, Wales, Scotland

Persons present

Age	TOTAL PERSONS	Males					Females				
		Total	Single	Married	Widowed	Divorced	Total	Single	Married	Widowed	Divorced
a	b	c	d	e	f	g	h	i	j	k	l

SCOTLAND – continued

Age	TOTAL PERSONS	Total	Single	Married	Widowed	Divorced	Total	Single	Married	Widowed	Divorced
Resident - staff	**8,897**	**4,033**	**2,571**	**1,190**	**27**	**245**	**4,864**	**3,389**	**1,145**	**141**	**189**
Aged											
0 - 4	218	117	117				101	101			
5 - 9	278	148	148				130	130			
10	62	36	36				26	26			
11	48	23	23				25	25			
12 - 14	177	88	88				89	89			
15	60	32	32				28	28			
16 - 17	225	98	98	-	-	-	127	125	2	-	-
18 - 19	743	245	244	1	-	-	498	495	2	-	1
20 - 24	2,205	811	775	27	-	9	1,394	1,345	47	-	2
25 - 29	1,257	619	519	72	-	28	638	515	103	-	20
30 - 34	631	340	196	107	1	36	291	142	128	1	20
35 - 39	538	302	106	153	-	43	236	72	136	2	26
40 - 44	571	291	58	197	-	36	280	64	187	1	28
45 - 49	513	255	41	180	2	32	258	48	176	7	27
50 - 54	509	257	37	183	4	33	252	45	171	11	25
55 - 59	401	186	22	144	4	16	215	47	121	20	27
60 - 64	210	112	15	85	4	8	98	28	43	20	7
65 - 69	81	34	4	24	2	4	47	16	13	14	4
70 - 74	58	16	2	11	3	-	42	15	7	18	2
75 - 79	40	8	5	3	-	-	32	10	8	14	-
80 - 84	25	7	3	3	1	-	18	8	-	10	-
85 - 89	27	6	1	-	5	-	21	8	1	12	-
90 and over	20	2	1	-	1	-	18	7	-	11	-
All persons present in households	**4,807,311**	**2,297,049**	**1,034,130**	**1,110,661**	**72,068**	**80,190**	**2,510,262**	**967,617**	**1,145,791**	**278,994**	**117,860**
Aged											
0 - 4	312,748	160,213	160,213				152,535	152,535			
5 - 9	313,365	160,158	160,158				153,207	153,207			
10	65,358	33,526	33,526				31,832	31,832			
11	64,091	32,743	32,743				31,348	31,348			
12 - 14	176,532	90,492	90,492				86,040	86,040			
15	61,939	31,728	31,728				30,211	30,211			
16 - 17	126,196	64,317	64,096	190	8	23	61,879	61,508	324	20	27
18 - 19	132,300	66,526	65,855	629	9	33	65,774	63,556	2,108	35	75
20 - 24	366,095	179,302	155,257	23,184	36	825	186,793	139,494	44,679	169	2,451
25 - 29	377,720	180,944	87,346	88,073	122	5,403	196,776	69,106	116,285	513	10,872
30 - 34	361,730	174,469	42,494	121,083	264	10,628	187,261	31,829	137,209	998	17,225
35 - 39	326,659	159,344	24,060	123,120	473	11,691	167,315	16,586	131,181	1,726	17,822
40 - 44	344,986	169,637	18,538	136,813	958	13,328	175,349	11,725	141,925	3,215	18,484
45 - 49	287,311	140,655	12,858	115,420	1,553	10,824	146,656	8,271	118,911	5,285	14,189
50 - 54	271,084	130,716	11,004	107,807	2,633	9,272	140,368	8,258	111,178	9,537	11,395
55 - 59	262,599	125,521	10,182	103,647	4,563	7,129	137,078	9,169	101,694	17,418	8,797
60 - 64	254,629	118,764	10,310	95,674	7,795	4,985	135,865	11,543	88,253	29,635	6,434
65 - 69	235,892	106,125	9,176	81,935	11,700	3,314	129,767	13,153	69,851	42,074	4,689
70 - 74	183,451	75,811	6,234	55,483	12,546	1,548	107,640	11,612	43,776	49,507	2,745
75 - 79	144,171	54,325	4,363	35,738	13,424	800	89,846	11,302	25,011	51,918	1,615
80 - 84	89,465	29,315	2,430	16,623	9,982	280	60,150	9,040	10,191	40,170	749
85 - 89	38,040	10,218	884	4,529	4,718	87	27,822	4,796	2,774	20,021	231
90 and over	10,950	2,200	183	713	1,284	20	8,750	1,496	441	6,753	60

Table 3   Type of establishment, migrants and long-term illness

Persons present in communal establishments

Type of establishment and age	PERSONS PRESENT			Visitors/guests			Residents - non-staff			Residents - staff			With limiting long-term illness	Migrants
	TOTAL	Males	Females	Total	Males	Females	Total	Males	Females	Total	Males	Females		
a	b	c	d	e	f	g	h	i	j	k	l	m	n	o
GREAT BRITAIN														
*All establishments ***														
All ages	1,527,505	722,423	805,082	694,354	379,465	314,889	735,676	299,399	436,277	97,475	43,559	53,916	689,605	275,057
0 - 15	130,689	78,218	52,471	99,720	61,225	38,495	23,735	13,232	10,503	7,234	3,761	3,473	10,736	13,395
16 - 17	49,952	31,153	18,799	39,469	24,266	15,203	8,543	5,958	2,585	1,940	929	1,011	3,878	7,182
18 - 29	417,407	239,579	177,828	239,761	133,616	106,145	130,569	87,715	42,854	47,077	18,248	28,829	39,122	94,665
30 - 44	172,487	111,482	61,005	88,310	56,447	31,863	64,972	44,826	20,146	19,205	10,209	8,996	47,165	28,060
45 - 59	127,063	74,686	52,377	65,529	37,584	27,945	44,619	28,952	15,667	16,915	8,150	8,765	51,218	11,701
60 - 64	47,716	24,994	22,722	24,407	12,147	12,260	20,715	11,484	9,231	2,594	1,363	1,231	28,132	4,385
65 - 74	125,704	56,685	69,019	56,081	26,338	29,743	68,076	29,696	38,380	1,547	651	896	91,840	16,836
75 - 84	234,588	68,114	166,474	55,839	21,448	34,391	178,052	46,469	131,583	697	197	500	208,976	51,267
85 and over	221,899	37,512	184,387	25,238	6,394	18,844	196,395	31,067	165,328	266	51	215	208,538	47,566
NHS hospitals/homes - psychiatric														
All ages	47,302	21,588	25,714	13,490	5,866	7,624	30,544	14,281	16,263	3,268	1,441	1,827	39,984	5,260
0 - 15	412	222	190	280	139	141	128	82	46	4	1	3	103	25
16 - 17	156	63	93	126	53	73	24	10	14	6	-	6	78	15
18 - 29	6,760	3,316	3,444	2,304	1,206	1,098	2,125	1,244	881	2,331	866	1,465	2,785	1,676
30 - 44	6,624	4,113	2,511	2,427	1,248	1,179	3,545	2,454	1,091	652	411	241	5,138	751
45 - 59	6,483	3,766	2,717	1,945	872	1,073	4,301	2,759	1,542	237	135	102	5,749	382
60 - 64	2,989	1,625	1,364	703	305	398	2,255	1,296	959	31	24	7	2,822	157
65 - 74	8,014	3,760	4,254	1,972	759	1,213	6,036	2,997	3,039	6	4	2	7,704	622
75 - 84	10,377	3,596	6,781	2,586	966	1,620	7,791	2,630	5,161	-	-	-	10,181	1,110
85 and over	5,487	1,127	4,360	1,147	318	829	4,339	809	3,530	1	-	1	5,424	522

Note: * Includes two male members of staff and three female members of staff incorrectly enumerated as residents.

Table 3 Type of establishment, migrants and long-term illness – **continued**

Great Britain, England & Wales, England, regions, metropolitan counties, Inner London, Outer London, regional remainders, Wales, Scotland

Persons present in communal establishments

Type of establishment and age	PERSONS PRESENT			Visitors/guests			Residents - non-staff			Residents - staff			With limiting long-term illness	Migrants
	TOTAL	Males	Females	Total	Males	Females	Total	Males	Females	Total	Males	Females		
a	b	c	d	e	f	g	h	i	j	k	l	m	n	o
GREAT BRITAIN – continued														
NHS hospitals/homes - other														
All ages	**237,326**	**91,236**	**146,090**	**156,905**	**62,634**	**94,271**	**58,414**	**22,567**	**35,847**	**22,007**	**6,035**	**15,972**	**144,347**	**24,124**
0 - 15	15,021	8,130	6,891	14,252	7,747	6,505	593	295	298	176	88	88	2,814	228
16 - 17	1,329	454	875	1,138	383	755	127	63	64	64	8	56	411	113
18 - 29	52,319	13,686	38,633	23,277	5,885	17,392	11,482	3,952	7,530	17,560	3,849	13,711	8,121	13,200
30 - 44	29,124	13,215	15,909	16,141	5,872	10,269	9,658	5,597	4,061	3,325	1,746	1,579	14,021	2,904
45 - 59	23,385	11,686	11,699	15,787	7,672	8,115	6,850	3,728	3,122	748	286	462	16,706	802
60 - 64	10,607	5,516	5,091	8,427	4,436	3,991	2,097	1,037	1,060	83	43	40	8,483	260
65 - 74	31,758	15,296	16,462	25,408	12,447	12,961	6,331	2,841	3,490	19	8	11	26,499	1,226
75 - 84	46,277	17,284	28,993	35,019	13,779	21,240	11,239	3,500	7,739	19	5	14	41,455	2,924
85 and over	27,506	5,969	21,537	17,456	4,413	13,043	10,037	1,554	8,483	13	2	11	25,837	2,467
Non-NHS hospitals - psychiatric														
All ages	**4,791**	**2,331**	**2,460**	**1,861**	**831**	**1,030**	**2,660**	**1,349**	**1,311**	**270**	**151**	**119**	**3,773**	**602**
0 - 15	132	84	48	106	67	39	25	17	8	1	-	1	29	12
16 - 17	46	21	25	35	16	19	10	5	5	1	-	1	23	6
18 - 29	784	412	372	344	155	189	253	166	87	187	91	96	399	172
30 - 44	859	505	354	357	165	192	455	304	151	47	36	11	639	100
45 - 59	772	425	347	342	159	183	396	242	154	34	24	10	616	58
60 - 64	299	163	136	103	51	52	196	112	84	-	-	-	270	22
65 - 74	732	352	380	236	103	133	496	249	247	-	-	-	682	71
75 - 84	758	268	490	233	83	150	525	185	340	-	-	-	717	102
85 and over	409	101	308	105	32	73	304	69	235	-	-	-	398	59

Table 3 Type of establishment, migrants and long-term illness – **continued**

Great Britain, England & Wales, England, regions, metropolitan counties, Inner London, Outer London, regional remainders, Wales, Scotland

Persons present in communal establishments

Type of establishment and age	PERSONS PRESENT			Visitors/guests			Residents - non-staff			Residents - staff			With limiting long-term illness	Migrants
	TOTAL	Males	Females	Total	Males	Females	Total	Males	Females	Total	Males	Females		
a	b	c	d	e	f	g	h	i	j	k	l	m	n	o
GREAT BRITAIN – continued														
Non-NHS hospitals - other														
All ages	14,405	5,595	8,810	9,065	3,531	5,534	4,485	1,762	2,723	855	302	553	8,511	1,363
0 - 15	620	342	278	571	315	256	38	22	16	11	5	6	153	14
16 - 17	71	26	45	56	20	36	9	5	4	6	1	5	24	11
18 - 29	2,114	721	1,393	1,009	281	728	582	273	309	523	167	356	513	506
30 - 44	2,379	918	1,461	1,512	446	1,066	677	381	296	190	91	99	958	164
45 - 59	2,397	1,064	1,333	1,631	668	963	671	367	304	95	29	66	1,305	76
60 - 64	863	431	432	629	329	300	221	101	120	13	1	12	589	26
65 - 74	1,911	906	1,005	1,402	691	711	498	210	288	11	5	6	1,418	90
75 - 84	2,507	883	1,624	1,584	613	971	919	268	651	4	2	2	2,116	253
85 and over	1,543	304	1,239	671	168	503	870	135	735	2	1	1	1,435	223
Local authority homes														
All ages	128,684	42,441	86,243	13,717	6,552	7,165	113,624	35,336	78,288	1,343	553	790	114,336	24,435
0 - 15	5,063	3,754	1,309	3,559	2,774	785	1,346	892	454	158	88	70	1,603	550
16 - 17	1,396	899	497	704	481	223	671	408	263	21	10	11	643	324
18 - 29	7,563	4,235	3,328	1,622	842	780	5,538	3,246	2,292	403	147	256	5,315	1,761
30 - 44	7,595	4,120	3,475	1,150	436	714	6,123	3,544	2,579	322	140	182	6,162	1,150
45 - 59	6,112	3,090	3,022	865	217	648	4,914	2,751	2,163	333	122	211	5,005	709
60 - 64	2,896	1,465	1,431	263	100	163	2,582	1,339	1,243	51	26	25	2,660	537
65 - 74	13,396	5,775	7,621	945	435	510	12,419	5,326	7,093	32	14	18	12,510	2,742
75 - 84	39,655	11,236	28,419	2,461	789	1,672	37,180	10,442	26,738	14	5	9	37,475	8,567
85 and over	45,008	7,867	37,141	2,148	478	1,670	42,851	7,388	35,463	9	1	8	42,963	8,095

Table 3 Type of establishment, migrants and long-term illness – **continued**

Great Britain, England & Wales, England, regions, metropolitan counties, Inner London, Outer London, regional remainders, Wales, Scotland

Persons present in communal establishments

Type of establishment and age	PERSONS PRESENT			Visitors/guests			Residents - non-staff			Residents - staff			With limiting long-term illness	Migrants
	TOTAL	Males	Females	Total	Males	Females	Total	Males	Females	Total	Males	Females		
a	b	c	d	e	f	g	h	i	j	k	l	m	n	o
Housing association homes and hostels														
All ages	**23,635**	**10,811**	**12,824**	**1,665**	**801**	**864**	**21,141**	**9,706**	**11,435**	**829**	**304**	**525**	**13,672**	**7,911**
0 - 15	428	253	175	52	35	17	299	174	125	77	44	33	60	157
16 - 17	417	196	221	85	37	48	321	156	165	11	3	8	68	268
18 - 29	5,187	2,845	2,342	776	348	428	4,265	2,431	1,834	146	66	80	1,279	2,650
30 - 44	3,149	2,111	1,038	319	196	123	2,668	1,857	811	162	58	104	1,676	1,210
45 - 59	2,689	1,863	826	174	102	72	2,199	1,666	533	316	95	221	1,695	800
60 - 64	888	587	301	41	22	19	780	543	237	67	22	45	612	219
65 - 74	2,097	1,123	974	55	20	35	1,999	1,089	910	43	14	29	1,478	535
75 - 84	4,392	1,173	3,219	101	31	70	4,287	1,141	3,146	4	1	3	3,268	1,153
85 and over	4,388	660	3,728	62	10	52	4,323	649	3,674	3	1	2	3,536	919
Nursing homes (non-NHS/ LA/HA)														
All ages	**143,617**	**36,094**	**107,523**	**7,315**	**2,506**	**4,809**	**133,974**	**32,799**	**101,175**	**2,328**	**789**	**1,539**	**135,537**	**48,326**
0 - 15	456	244	212	99	53	46	148	79	69	209	112	97	121	59
16 - 17	141	55	86	33	13	20	53	21	32	55	21	34	51	34
18 - 29	2,175	974	1,201	512	149	363	1,107	647	460	556	178	378	1,121	615
30 - 44	2,917	1,395	1,522	834	240	594	1,639	995	644	444	160	284	1,806	557
45 - 59	3,395	1,537	1,858	790	246	544	1,921	1,069	852	684	222	462	2,281	587
60 - 64	4,170	1,976	2,194	500	226	274	3,530	1,698	1,832	140	52	88	3,767	1,235
65 - 74	17,418	6,661	10,757	1,483	639	844	15,816	5,991	9,825	119	31	88	16,478	6,163
75 - 84	53,903	13,793	40,110	1,954	660	1,294	51,877	13,126	38,751	72	7	65	52,221	20,214
85 and over	59,042	9,459	49,583	1,110	280	830	57,883	9,173	48,710	49	6	43	57,691	18,862

GREAT BRITAIN – *continued*

Table 3 Type of establishment, migrants and long-term illness – **continued**

Great Britain, England & Wales, England, regions, metropolitan counties, Inner London, Outer London, regional remainders, Wales, Scotland

Persons present in communal establishments

Type of establishment and age	PERSONS PRESENT			Visitors/guests			Residents - non-staff			Residents - staff			With limiting long-term illness	Migrants
	TOTAL	Males	Females	Total	Males	Females	Total	Males	Females	Total	Males	Females		
a	b	c	d	e	f	g	h	i	j	k	l	m	n	o
					GREAT BRITAIN – *continued*									
Residential homes (non-NHS/LA/HA)														
All ages	**190,413**	**50,894**	**139,519**	**6,463**	**2,050**	**4,413**	**175,721**	**45,498**	**130,223**	**8,229**	**3,346**	**4,883**	**165,522**	**42,536**
0 - 15	1,594	893	701	277	210	67	222	141	81	1,095	542	553	331	171
16 - 17	564	320	244	158	90	68	202	125	77	204	105	99	271	132
18 - 29	8,596	4,542	4,054	1,096	424	672	5,800	3,492	2,308	1,700	626	1,074	5,993	1,994
30 - 44	9,846	5,304	4,542	906	272	634	7,152	4,301	2,851	1,788	731	1,057	7,232	1,359
45 - 59	9,757	4,922	4,835	637	156	481	6,537	3,754	2,783	2,583	1,012	1,571	6,699	1,132
60 - 64	5,376	2,651	2,725	228	83	145	4,712	2,370	2,342	436	198	238	4,413	973
65 - 74	18,824	7,288	11,536	609	190	419	17,948	7,000	10,948	267	98	169	16,484	4,372
75 - 84	60,964	13,867	47,097	1,411	384	1,027	59,458	13,460	45,998	95	23	72	55,127	16,308
85 and over	74,892	11,107	63,785	1,141	241	900	73,690	10,855	62,835	61	11	50	68,972	16,095
Children's homes														
All ages	**13,140**	**7,145**	**5,995**	**2,520**	**1,371**	**1,149**	**9,397**	**5,223**	**4,174**	**1,223**	**551**	**672**	**1,326**	**5,013**
0 - 15	11,408	6,467	4,941	1,812	1,132	680	9,397	5,223	4,174	199	112	87	1,111	4,824
16 - 17	75	28	47	2	1	1	-	-	-	73	27	46	7	25
18 - 29	609	264	345	259	94	165	-	-	-	350	170	180	107	100
30 - 44	546	218	328	279	109	170	-	-	-	267	109	158	33	43
45 - 59	410	136	274	148	28	120	-	-	-	262	108	154	44	10
60 - 64	48	19	29	12	7	5	-	-	-	36	12	24	7	4
65 - 74	25	10	15	6	-	6	-	-	-	19	10	9	7	4
75 - 84	15	2	13	1	-	1	-	-	-	14	2	12	7	2
85 and over	4	1	3	1	-	1	-	-	-	3	1	2	3	1

Table 3 Type of establishment, migrants and long-term illness – **continued**

Great Britain, England & Wales, England, regions, metropolitan counties, Inner London, Outer London, regional remainders, Wales, Scotland

Persons present in communal establishments

Type of establishment and age	PERSONS PRESENT			Visitors/guests			Residents - non-staff			Residents - staff			With limiting long-term illness	Migrants
	TOTAL	Males	Females	Total	Males	Females	Total	Males	Females	Total	Males	Females		
a	b	c	d	e	f	g	h	i	j	k	l	m	n	o

GREAT BRITAIN – *continued*

Prison service establishments

	b	c	d	e	f	g	h	i	j	k	l	m	n	o
All ages	**43,633**	**41,776**	**1,857**	**28,234**	**27,037**	**1,197**	**15,315**	**14,666**	**649**	**84**	**73**	**11**	**6,192**	**7,833**
0 - 15	163	156	7	123	116	7	9	9	-	31	31	-	13	30
16 - 17	1,489	1,459	30	1,291	1,274	17	198	185	13	-	-	-	131	136
18 - 29	25,655	24,711	944	18,051	17,392	659	7,591	7,307	284	13	12	1	2,684	4,256
30 - 44	11,907	11,283	624	6,557	6,154	403	5,325	5,109	216	25	20	5	1,958	2,514
45 - 59	3,761	3,584	177	1,925	1,835	90	1,828	1,746	82	8	3	5	1,083	766
60 - 64	360	337	23	161	151	10	197	184	13	2	2	-	168	75
65 - 74	192	173	19	90	84	6	99	86	13	3	3	-	110	29
75 - 84	76	51	25	28	24	4	46	25	21	2	2	-	37	19
85 and over	30	22	8	8	7	1	22	15	7	-	-	-	8	8

Defence establishments

	b	c	d	e	f	g	h	i	j	k	l	m	n	o
All ages	**66,489**	**58,195**	**8,294**	**16,869**	**15,240**	**1,629**	**49,620**	**42,955**	**6,665**				**1,904**	**26,071**
0 - 15	35	29	6	35	29	6	-	-	-				2	-
16 - 17	4,507	4,134	373	1,141	1,033	108	3,366	3,101	265				62	3,021
18 - 29	51,028	43,961	7,067	10,543	9,368	1,175	40,485	34,593	5,892				927	20,689
30 - 44	8,893	8,260	633	4,060	3,847	213	4,833	4,413	420				339	2,111
45 - 59	1,379	1,266	113	847	794	53	532	472	60				152	176
60 - 64	140	119	21	78	61	17	62	58	4				49	12
65 - 74	263	227	36	98	68	30	165	159	6				178	35
75 - 84	179	146	33	56	34	22	123	112	11				138	23
85 and over	65	53	12	11	6	5	54	47	7				57	4

Table 3 Type of establishment, migrants and long-term illness – **continued**

Great Britain, England & Wales, England, regions, metropolitan counties, Inner London, Outer London, regional remainders, Wales, Scotland

Persons present in communal establishments

Type of establishment and age	PERSONS PRESENT			Visitors/guests			Residents - non-staff			Residents - staff			With limiting long-term illness	Migrants
	TOTAL	Males	Females	Total	Males	Females	Total	Males	Females	Total	Males	Females		
a	b	c	d	e	f	g	h	i	j	k	l	m	n	o
GREAT BRITAIN – *continued*														
Educational establishments														
All ages	270,013	154,317	115,696	234,494	133,677	100,817	26,684	16,276	10,408	8,835	4,364	4,471	11,564	18,463
0 - 15	63,996	40,955	23,041	61,741	39,648	22,093	1,530	932	598	725	375	350	3,279	740
16 - 17	32,202	19,447	12,755	31,188	18,874	12,314	882	524	358	132	49	83	1,725	427
18 - 29	153,635	82,335	71,300	132,780	69,809	62,971	17,732	11,091	6,641	3,123	1,435	1,688	4,508	13,460
30 - 44	12,688	8,201	4,487	5,778	3,836	1,942	4,411	2,988	1,423	2,499	1,377	1,122	691	3,175
45 - 59	4,856	2,424	2,432	2,137	1,109	1,028	884	427	457	1,835	888	947	466	526
60 - 64	801	361	440	252	109	143	244	94	150	305	158	147	122	43
65 - 74	853	316	537	301	143	158	402	113	289	150	60	90	238	37
75 - 84	714	206	508	230	106	124	429	80	349	55	20	35	344	33
85 and over	268	72	196	87	43	44	170	27	143	11	2	9	191	22
Hotels, boarding houses etc														
All ages	269,362	153,281	116,081	177,990	99,496	78,494	48,638	31,029	17,609	42,734	22,756	19,978	29,009	39,121
0 - 15	25,607	13,602	12,005	15,673	8,361	7,312	5,669	3,019	2,650	4,265	2,222	2,043	801	3,851
16 - 17	5,321	2,708	2,613	2,697	1,384	1,313	1,350	679	671	1,274	645	629	228	1,493
18 - 29	73,884	40,992	32,892	37,842	21,002	16,840	18,280	10,690	7,590	17,762	9,300	8,462	3,251	22,018
30 - 44	59,725	39,703	20,022	41,031	27,654	13,377	10,305	7,376	2,929	8,389	4,673	3,716	3,839	7,369
45 - 59	50,231	30,759	19,472	34,647	20,692	13,955	6,802	5,309	1,493	8,782	4,758	4,024	6,180	3,127
60 - 64	15,247	7,888	7,359	12,348	5,834	6,514	1,686	1,329	357	1,213	725	488	3,075	388
65 - 74	25,619	12,339	13,280	22,716	10,353	12,363	2,242	1,664	578	661	322	339	6,353	399
75 - 84	11,649	4,678	6,971	9,848	3,843	6,005	1,504	744	760	297	91	206	4,181	303
85 and over	2,079	612	1,467	1,188	373	815	800	219	581	91	20	71	1,101	173

Table 3 Type of establishment, migrants and long-term illness – **continued**

Great Britain, England & Wales, England, regions, metropolitan counties, Inner London, Outer London, regional remainders, Wales, Scotland

Persons present in communal establishments

Type of establishment and age	PERSONS PRESENT			Visitors/guests			Residents - non-staff			Residents - staff			With limiting long-term illness	Migrants
	TOTAL	Males	Females	Total	Males	Females	Total	Males	Females	Total	Males	Females		
a	b	c	d	e	f	g	h	i	j	k	l	m	n	o
GREAT BRITAIN – *continued*														
Hostels and common lodging houses (non-HA)														
All ages	**23,009**	**15,680**	**7,329**	**2,661**	**1,533**	**1,128**	**19,417**	**13,596**	**5,821**	**931**	**551**	**380**	**7,578**	**10,806**
0 - 15	2,026	1,102	924	164	82	82	1,783	979	804	79	41	38	96	1,131
16 - 17	794	363	431	73	35	38	707	321	386	14	7	7	89	622
18 - 29	7,466	4,033	3,433	1,214	608	606	5,963	3,279	2,684	289	146	143	1,241	4,618
30 - 44	4,514	3,364	1,150	529	394	135	3,789	2,839	950	196	131	65	1,786	2,357
45 - 59	4,289	3,644	645	328	242	86	3,683	3,221	462	278	181	97	2,267	1,488
60 - 64	1,254	1,096	158	78	56	22	1,126	1,007	119	50	33	17	710	248
65 - 74	1,815	1,567	248	118	66	52	1,676	1,491	185	21	10	11	879	247
75 - 84	649	450	199	100	39	61	546	409	137	3	2	1	357	67
85 and over	202	61	141	57	11	46	144	50	94	1	-	1	153	28
Other miscellaneous establishments														
All ages	**40,255**	**21,348**	**18,907**	**13,098**	**9,455**	**3,643**	**22,623**	**9,552**	**13,071**	**4,534**	**2,341**	**2,193**	**5,315**	**11,177**
0 - 15	3,506	1,859	1,647	833	441	392	2,470	1,319	1,151	203	99	104	206	1,573
16 - 17	1,326	896	430	674	518	156	573	325	248	79	53	26	62	519
18 - 29	16,569	10,069	6,500	6,275	4,512	1,763	8,161	4,362	3,799	2,133	1,195	938	682	6,161
30 - 44	7,417	4,818	2,599	3,312	2,667	645	3,206	1,625	1,581	899	526	373	638	1,628
45 - 59	4,398	2,089	2,309	1,317	1,010	307	2,363	793	1,570	718	286	432	677	626
60 - 64	1,371	463	908	234	129	105	970	267	703	167	67	100	306	168
65 - 74	2,391	657	1,734	281	129	152	1,915	456	1,459	195	72	123	718	249
75 - 84	2,347	411	1,936	136	41	95	2,093	333	1,760	118	37	81	1,294	178
85 and over	930	86	844	36	8	28	872	72	800	22	6	16	732	75

Table 3 Type of establishment, migrants and long-term illness – **continued**

Great Britain, England & Wales, England, regions, metropolitan counties, Inner London, Outer London, regional remainders, Wales, Scotland

Persons present in communal establishments

Type of establishment and age	PERSONS PRESENT			Visitors/guests			Residents - non-staff			Residents - staff			With limiting long-term illness	Migrants
	TOTAL	Males	Females	Total	Males	Females	Total	Males	Females	Total	Males	Females		
a	b	c	d	e	f	g	h	i	j	k	l	m	n	o
GREAT BRITAIN – *continued*														
Persons sleeping rough														
All ages	2,827	2,397	430	882	760	122	1,940	1,635	305				625	1,465
0 - 15	3	3	-	2	2	-	-	-	-				-	-
16 - 17	36	23	13	12	8	4	24	15	9				4	20
18 - 29	1,052	876	176	319	260	59	732	616	116				157	569
30 - 44	905	771	134	247	214	33	658	557	101				199	489
45 - 59	714	626	88	254	231	23	458	394	64				204	354
60 - 64	61	56	5	26	25	1	35	31	4				28	17
65 - 74	44	37	7	21	19	2	22	18	4				24	13
75 - 84	9	4	5	1	1	-	8	3	5				7	2
85 and over	3	1	2	-	-	-	3	1	2				2	1
Campers														
All ages	1,522	814	708	1,264	687	577	258	127	131				276	97
0 - 15	131	64	67	72	29	43	59	35	24				5	20
16 - 17	17	12	5	9	7	2	8	5	3				1	4
18 - 29	251	139	112	185	101	84	66	38	28				11	26
30 - 44	217	129	88	184	111	73	33	18	15				15	16
45 - 59	299	160	139	273	145	128	26	15	11				51	7
60 - 64	180	87	93	177	87	90	3	-	3				41	1
65 - 74	303	168	135	297	165	132	6	3	3				74	2
75 - 84	89	51	38	65	42	23	24	9	15				44	9
85 and over	35	4	31	2	-	2	33	4	29				34	12

Table 3 Type of establishment, migrants and long-term illness – **continued**

Great Britain, England & Wales, England, regions, metropolitan counties, Inner London, Outer London, regional remainders, Wales, Scotland

Persons present in communal establishments

Type of establishment and age	PERSONS PRESENT			Visitors/guests			Residents - non-staff			Residents - staff			With limiting long-term illness	Migrants
	TOTAL	Males	Females	Total	Males	Females	Total	Males	Females	Total	Males	Females		
a	b	c	d	e	f	g	h	i	j	k	l	m	n	o

GREAT BRITAIN – continued

Civilian ships, boats and barges

All ages	**7,082**	**6,480**	**602**	**5,861**	**5,438**	**423**	**1,221**	**1,042**	**179**				**134**	**454**
0 - 15	88	59	29	69	45	24	19	14	5				9	10
16 - 17	65	49	16	47	39	8	18	10	8				-	12
18 - 29	1,760	1,468	292	1,353	1,180	173	407	288	119				28	194
30 - 44	3,182	3,054	128	2,687	2,586	101	495	468	27				35	163
45 - 59	1,736	1,645	91	1,482	1,406	76	254	239	15				38	75
60 - 64	166	154	12	147	136	11	19	18	1				10	-
65 - 74	49	30	19	43	27	16	6	3	3				6	-
75 - 84	28	15	13	25	13	12	3	2	1				7	-
85 and over	8	6	2	8	6	2	-	-	-				1	-

ENGLAND & WALES

All establishments *

All ages	**1,372,664**	**647,904**	**724,760**	**616,929**	**337,450**	**279,479**	**667,157**	**270,928**	**396,229**	**88,578**	**39,526**	**49,052**	**618,864**	**252,031**
0 - 15	120,645	72,431	48,214	92,385	56,925	35,460	21,869	12,189	9,680	6,391	3,317	3,074	9,923	12,290
16 - 17	46,065	28,805	17,260	36,378	22,367	14,011	7,972	5,607	2,365	1,715	831	884	3,603	6,672
18 - 29	376,538	216,038	160,500	212,885	118,523	94,362	120,781	80,942	39,839	42,872	16,573	26,299	35,456	87,639
30 - 44	153,450	98,755	54,695	77,333	49,051	28,282	58,652	40,428	18,224	17,465	9,276	8,189	42,089	25,779
45 - 59	111,660	65,421	46,239	56,638	32,421	24,217	39,530	25,548	13,982	15,492	7,452	8,040	44,992	10,686
60 - 64	41,786	21,939	19,847	20,934	10,474	10,460	18,468	10,214	8,254	2,384	1,251	1,133	24,720	4,028
65 - 74	110,615	49,643	60,972	48,555	22,898	25,657	60,652	26,144	34,508	1,408	601	807	81,300	15,249
75 - 84	210,045	60,753	149,292	49,273	19,068	30,205	160,140	41,503	118,637	632	182	450	187,147	46,341
85 and over	201,860	34,119	167,741	22,548	5,723	16,825	179,093	28,353	150,740	219	43	176	189,634	43,347

Note: * Includes one male member of staff and three female members of staff incorrectly enumerated as residents.

Table 3 Type of establishment, migrants and long-term illness – **continued**

Persons present in communal establishments

Type of establishment and age	PERSONS PRESENT			Visitors/guests			Residents - non-staff			Residents - staff			With limiting long-term illness	Migrants
	TOTAL	Males	Females	Total	Males	Females	Total	Males	Females	Total	Males	Females		
a	b	c	d	e	f	g	h	i	j	k	l	m	n	o

ENGLAND & WALES – *continued*

NHS hospitals/homes - psychiatric

All ages	**35,862**	**16,682**	**19,180**	**11,333**	**4,946**	**6,387**	**21,535**	**10,421**	**11,114**	**2,994**	**1,315**	**1,679**	**29,455**	**4,079**
0 - 15	293	148	145	235	116	119	56	31	25	2	1	1	75	14
16 - 17	120	48	72	100	43	57	17	5	12	3	-	3	62	11
18 - 29	5,833	2,815	3,018	1,889	991	898	1,820	1,045	775	2,124	779	1,345	2,291	1,523
30 - 44	5,405	3,393	2,012	2,004	1,017	987	2,797	1,996	801	604	380	224	4,086	674
45 - 59	5,002	2,901	2,101	1,647	750	897	3,128	2,022	1,106	227	129	98	4,343	316
60 - 64	2,188	1,209	979	580	254	326	1,580	933	647	28	22	6	2,050	117
65 - 74	5,860	2,707	3,153	1,677	644	1,033	4,177	2,059	2,118	6	4	2	5,593	425
75 - 84	7,355	2,628	4,727	2,214	859	1,355	5,141	1,769	3,372	-	-	-	7,201	674
85 and over	3,806	833	2,973	987	272	715	2,819	561	2,258	-	-	-	3,754	325

NHS hospitals/homes - other

All ages	**204,812**	**79,461**	**125,351**	**138,101**	**55,336**	**82,765**	**46,100**	**18,447**	**27,653**	**20,611**	**5,678**	**14,933**	**121,684**	**20,335**
0 - 15	13,177	7,151	6,026	12,486	6,805	5,681	520	262	258	171	84	87	2,431	217
16 - 17	1,161	398	763	1,007	339	668	99	51	48	55	8	47	357	96
18 - 29	46,703	12,170	34,533	20,346	5,222	15,124	9,961	3,350	6,611	16,396	3,598	12,798	7,045	12,026
30 - 44	25,928	11,734	14,194	14,371	5,213	9,158	8,413	4,866	3,547	3,144	1,655	1,489	12,252	2,682
45 - 59	20,594	10,301	10,293	13,912	6,749	7,163	5,960	3,273	2,687	722	279	443	14,593	735
60 - 64	9,175	4,815	4,360	7,350	3,882	3,468	1,751	893	858	74	40	34	7,312	217
65 - 74	27,326	13,239	14,087	22,348	10,987	11,361	4,960	2,245	2,715	18	7	11	22,688	889
75 - 84	38,655	14,714	23,941	30,853	12,227	18,626	7,784	2,482	5,302	18	5	13	34,387	1,922
85 and over	22,093	4,939	17,154	15,428	3,912	11,516	6,652	1,025	5,627	13	2	11	20,619	1,551

Table 3 Type of establishment, migrants and long-term illness – **continued**

Great Britain, England & Wales, England, regions, metropolitan counties, Inner London, Outer London, regional remainders, Wales, Scotland

Persons present in communal establishments

Type of establishment and age	PERSONS PRESENT			Visitors/guests			Residents - non-staff			Residents - staff			With limiting long-term illness	Migrants
	TOTAL	Males	Females	Total	Males	Females	Total	Males	Females	Total	Males	Females		
a	b	c	d	e	f	g	h	i	j	k	l	m	n	o
ENGLAND & WALES – *continued*														
Non-NHS hospitals - psychiatric														
All ages	**4,477**	**2,189**	**2,288**	**1,784**	**795**	**989**	**2,440**	**1,250**	**1,190**	**253**	**144**	**109**	**3,506**	**562**
0 - 15	129	83	46	103	66	37	25	17	8	1	-	1	28	12
16 - 17	46	21	25	35	16	19	10	5	5	1	-	1	23	6
18 - 29	755	397	358	333	148	185	248	163	85	174	86	88	391	168
30 - 44	838	492	346	346	160	186	447	298	149	45	34	11	628	99
45 - 59	735	403	332	334	155	179	369	224	145	32	24	8	584	58
60 - 64	278	148	130	98	48	50	180	100	80	-	-	-	251	22
65 - 74	669	319	350	219	94	125	450	225	225	-	-	-	623	66
75 - 84	672	241	431	221	80	141	451	161	290	-	-	-	633	86
85 and over	355	85	270	95	28	67	260	57	203	-	-	-	345	45
Non-NHS hospitals - other														
All ages	**13,192**	**5,232**	**7,960**	**8,716**	**3,407**	**5,309**	**3,650**	**1,526**	**2,124**	**826**	**299**	**527**	**7,514**	**1,190**
0 - 15	601	333	268	560	311	249	30	17	13	11	5	6	150	12
16 - 17	69	25	44	56	20	36	7	4	3	6	1	5	22	11
18 - 29	2,016	677	1,339	972	264	708	535	248	287	509	165	344	458	494
30 - 44	2,237	859	1,378	1,438	419	1,019	614	349	265	185	91	94	866	160
45 - 59	2,220	987	1,233	1,568	642	926	562	317	245	90	28	62	1,170	67
60 - 64	795	401	394	601	316	285	182	84	98	12	1	11	532	19
65 - 74	1,774	856	918	1,355	669	686	410	182	228	9	5	4	1,300	68
75 - 84	2,203	820	1,383	1,521	599	922	679	219	460	3	2	1	1,834	185
85 and over	1,277	274	1,003	645	167	478	631	106	525	1	1	-	1,182	174

Table 3 Type of establishment, migrants and long-term illness – **continued**

Persons present in communal establishments

Type of establishment and age	PERSONS PRESENT			Visitors/guests			Residents - non-staff			Residents - staff			With limiting long-term illness	Migrants
	TOTAL	Males	Females	Total	Males	Females	Total	Males	Females	Total	Males	Females		
a	b	c	d	e	f	g	h	i	j	k	l	m	n	o
ENGLAND & WALES – *continued*														
Local authority homes														
All ages	**118,027**	**39,012**	**79,015**	**12,618**	**6,050**	**6,568**	**104,290**	**32,502**	**71,788**	**1,119**	**460**	**659**	**105,140**	**22,324**
0 - 15	4,575	3,419	1,156	3,217	2,528	689	1,268	839	429	90	52	38	1,518	516
16 - 17	1,306	842	464	651	443	208	634	389	245	21	10	11	598	303
18 - 29	7,120	3,999	3,121	1,527	799	728	5,231	3,070	2,161	362	130	232	5,036	1,679
30 - 44	7,074	3,890	3,184	1,059	404	655	5,757	3,369	2,388	258	117	141	5,818	1,095
45 - 59	5,717	2,908	2,809	788	206	582	4,632	2,594	2,038	297	108	189	4,723	681
60 - 64	2,708	1,379	1,329	237	94	143	2,426	1,261	1,165	45	24	21	2,504	496
65 - 74	12,254	5,267	6,987	867	399	468	11,361	4,855	6,506	26	13	13	11,463	2,503
75 - 84	36,090	10,160	25,930	2,292	734	1,558	33,786	9,421	24,365	12	5	7	34,114	7,735
85 and over	41,183	7,148	34,035	1,980	443	1,537	39,195	6,704	32,491	8	1	7	39,366	7,316
Housing association homes and hostels														
All ages	**21,793**	**10,070**	**11,723**	**1,585**	**747**	**838**	**19,477**	**9,045**	**10,432**	**731**	**278**	**453**	**12,522**	**7,420**
0 - 15	398	230	168	50	33	17	283	161	122	65	36	29	55	141
16 - 17	385	182	203	84	36	48	291	143	148	10	3	7	63	242
18 - 29	4,918	2,693	2,225	743	327	416	4,037	2,303	1,734	138	63	75	1,174	2,528
30 - 44	2,886	1,952	934	303	184	119	2,438	1,714	724	145	54	91	1,500	1,120
45 - 59	2,448	1,724	724	157	89	68	2,023	1,550	473	268	85	183	1,541	753
60 - 64	833	549	284	37	19	18	736	509	227	60	21	39	571	210
65 - 74	1,946	1,046	900	51	18	33	1,857	1,014	843	38	14	24	1,381	502
75 - 84	4,026	1,094	2,932	100	31	69	3,922	1,062	2,860	4	1	3	3,022	1,072
85 and over	3,953	600	3,353	60	10	50	3,890	589	3,301	3	1	2	3,215	852

Table 3 Type of establishment, migrants and long-term illness – **continued**

Great Britain, England & Wales, England, regions, metropolitan counties, Inner London, Outer London, regional remainders, Wales, Scotland

Persons present in communal establishments

Type of establishment and age	PERSONS PRESENT			Visitors/guests			Residents - non-staff			Residents - staff			With limiting long-term illness	Migrants
	TOTAL	Males	Females	Total	Males	Females	Total	Males	Females	Total	Males	Females		
a	b	c	d	e	f	g	h	i	j	k	l	m	n	o

ENGLAND & WALES – *continued*

Nursing homes (non-NHS/LA/HA)

All ages	**131,561**	**33,459**	**98,102**	**6,650**	**2,279**	**4,371**	**122,795**	**30,442**	**92,353**	**2,116**	**738**	**1,378**	**124,283**	**44,423**
0 - 15	424	231	193	92	52	40	143	76	67	189	103	86	118	55
16 - 17	131	51	80	32	13	19	45	17	28	54	21	33	48	26
18 - 29	2,019	902	1,117	476	142	334	1,013	590	423	530	170	360	1,056	565
30 - 44	2,645	1,265	1,380	756	216	540	1,473	895	578	416	154	262	1,637	512
45 - 59	3,147	1,432	1,715	719	217	502	1,798	1,007	791	630	208	422	2,123	558
60 - 64	3,832	1,824	2,008	441	198	243	3,264	1,580	1,684	127	46	81	3,470	1,138
65 - 74	16,046	6,202	9,844	1,318	570	748	14,621	5,601	9,020	107	31	76	15,201	5,726
75 - 84	49,225	12,768	36,457	1,800	609	1,191	47,380	12,156	35,224	45	3	42	47,729	18,515
85 and over	54,092	8,784	45,308	1,016	262	754	53,058	8,520	44,538	18	2	16	52,901	17,328

Residential homes (non-NHS/LA/HA)

All ages	**181,946**	**48,490**	**133,456**	**6,200**	**1,978**	**4,222**	**167,790**	**43,277**	**124,513**	**7,956**	**3,235**	**4,721**	**158,272**	**40,691**
0 - 15	1,539	866	673	272	208	64	217	140	77	1,050	518	532	326	161
16 - 17	535	304	231	155	89	66	180	112	68	200	103	97	255	114
18 - 29	8,243	4,361	3,882	1,048	403	645	5,536	3,345	2,191	1,659	613	1,046	5,736	1,885
30 - 44	9,309	5,026	4,283	849	256	593	6,729	4,064	2,665	1,731	706	1,025	6,812	1,300
45 - 59	9,202	4,654	4,548	592	147	445	6,126	3,527	2,599	2,484	980	1,504	6,287	1,069
60 - 64	5,128	2,510	2,618	221	80	141	4,485	2,242	2,243	422	188	234	4,216	935
65 - 74	17,978	6,907	11,071	592	186	406	17,129	6,627	10,502	257	94	163	15,792	4,169
75 - 84	58,148	13,191	44,957	1,367	374	993	56,688	12,795	43,893	93	22	71	52,633	15,582
85 and over	71,864	10,671	61,193	1,104	235	869	70,700	10,425	60,275	60	11	49	66,215	15,476

Table 3 Type of establishment, migrants and long-term illness – **continued**

Great Britain, England & Wales, England, regions, metropolitan counties, Inner London, Outer London, regional remainders, Wales, Scotland

Persons present in communal establishments

Type of establishment and age	PERSONS PRESENT			Visitors/guests			Residents - non-staff			Residents - staff			With limiting long-term illness	Migrants
	TOTAL	Males	Females	Total	Males	Females	Total	Males	Females	Total	Males	Females		
a	b	c	d	e	f	g	h	i	j	k	l	m	n	o
ENGLAND & WALES – *continued*														
Children's homes														
All ages	11,745	6,447	5,298	2,191	1,204	987	8,401	4,719	3,682	1,153	524	629	1,182	4,457
0 - 15	10,130	5,815	4,315	1,543	987	556	8,401	4,719	3,682	186	109	77	986	4,281
16 - 17	67	24	43	2	1	1	-	-	-	65	23	42	7	24
18 - 29	579	253	326	246	90	156	-	-	-	333	163	170	100	95
30 - 44	496	197	299	244	93	151	-	-	-	252	104	148	26	38
45 - 59	384	127	257	137	26	111	-	-	-	247	101	146	39	9
60 - 64	46	19	27	11	7	4	-	-	-	35	12	23	7	4
65 - 74	24	9	15	6	-	6	-	-	-	18	9	9	7	3
75 - 84	15	2	13	1	-	1	-	-	-	14	2	12	7	2
85 and over	4	1	3	1	-	1	-	-	-	3	1	2	3	1
Prison service establishments														
All ages	39,043	37,345	1,698	25,255	24,171	1,084	13,704	13,101	603	84	73	11	5,539	7,249
0 - 15	162	155	7	122	115	7	9	9	-	31	31	-	13	30
16 - 17	1,296	1,270	26	1,126	1,111	15	170	159	11	-	-	-	114	116
18 - 29	22,837	21,990	847	16,039	15,456	583	6,785	6,522	263	13	12	1	2,392	3,947
30 - 44	10,684	10,103	581	5,938	5,561	377	4,721	4,522	199	25	20	5	1,736	2,302
45 - 59	3,439	3,276	163	1,761	1,679	82	1,670	1,594	76	8	3	5	979	727
60 - 64	341	319	22	152	143	9	187	174	13	2	2	-	157	73
65 - 74	182	163	19	83	77	6	96	83	13	3	3	-	103	29
75 - 84	73	48	25	26	22	4	45	24	21	2	2	-	37	18
85 and over	29	21	8	8	7	1	21	14	7	-	-	-	8	7

Table 3 Type of establishment, migrants and long-term illness – **continued**

Great Britain, England & Wales, England, regions, metropolitan counties, Inner London, Outer London, regional remainders, Wales, Scotland

Persons present in communal establishments

Type of establishment and age	PERSONS PRESENT			Visitors/guests			Residents - non-staff			Residents - staff			With limiting long-term illness	Migrants
	TOTAL	Males	Females	Total	Males	Females	Total	Males	Females	Total	Males	Females		
a	b	c	d	e	f	g	h	i	j	k	l	m	n	o

ENGLAND & WALES – *continued*

Defence establishments														
All ages	**60,527**	**52,783**	**7,744**	**14,785**	**13,291**	**1,494**	**45,742**	**39,492**	**6,250**				**1,511**	**24,253**
0 - 15	35	29	6	35	29	6	-	-	-				2	-
16 - 17	4,329	3,977	352	1,075	973	102	3,254	3,004	250				61	2,925
18 - 29	46,936	40,310	6,626	9,391	8,304	1,087	37,545	32,006	5,539				869	19,232
30 - 44	7,728	7,160	568	3,390	3,207	183	4,338	3,953	385				301	1,897
45 - 59	1,122	1,024	98	689	643	46	433	381	52				94	148
60 - 64	102	81	21	64	47	17	38	34	4				23	9
65 - 74	152	120	32	86	59	27	66	61	5				79	27
75 - 84	87	57	30	46	25	21	41	32	9				53	14
85 and over	36	25	11	9	4	5	27	21	6				29	1
Educational establishments														
All ages	**246,742**	**141,335**	**105,407**	**214,102**	**122,418**	**91,684**	**24,489**	**14,855**	**9,634**	**8,151**	**4,062**	**4,089**	**10,878**	**16,963**
0 - 15	60,534	38,815	21,719	58,481	37,624	20,857	1,404	849	555	649	342	307	3,199	654
16 - 17	29,914	18,092	11,822	28,988	17,571	11,417	806	477	329	120	44	76	1,663	388
18 - 29	137,705	73,795	63,910	118,607	62,320	56,287	16,216	10,128	6,088	2,882	1,347	1,535	4,060	12,398
30 - 44	11,545	7,466	4,079	5,218	3,481	1,737	4,024	2,714	1,310	2,303	1,271	1,032	637	2,899
45 - 59	4,515	2,263	2,252	1,984	1,040	944	836	397	439	1,695	826	869	441	493
60 - 64	750	338	412	228	101	127	229	84	145	293	153	140	113	42
65 - 74	821	300	521	287	136	151	387	106	281	147	58	89	234	36
75 - 84	695	196	499	222	102	120	420	75	345	53	19	34	342	32
85 and over	263	70	193	87	43	44	167	25	142	9	2	7	189	21

Table 3 Type of establishment, migrants and long-term illness – **continued**

Great Britain, England & Wales, England, regions, metropolitan counties, Inner London, Outer London, regional remainders, Wales, Scotland

Persons present in communal establishments

Type of establishment and age	PERSONS PRESENT			Visitors/guests			Residents - non-staff			Residents - staff			With limiting long-term illness	Migrants
	TOTAL	Males	Females	Total	Males	Females	Total	Males	Females	Total	Males	Females		
a	b	c	d	e	f	g	h	i	j	k	l	m	n	o

ENGLAND & WALES – *continued*

Hotels, boarding houses etc

All ages	**235,336**	**134,068**	**101,268**	**152,736**	**85,388**	**67,348**	**45,227**	**28,741**	**16,486**	**37,373**	**19,939**	**17,434**	**25,204**	**35,548**
0 - 15	23,228	12,273	10,955	14,151	7,511	6,640	5,385	2,852	2,533	3,692	1,910	1,782	731	3,569
16 - 17	4,718	2,404	2,314	2,402	1,233	1,169	1,225	613	612	1,091	558	533	196	1,315
18 - 29	65,400	36,279	29,121	32,785	18,100	14,685	17,208	10,045	7,163	15,407	8,134	7,273	2,923	19,999
30 - 44	52,346	34,643	17,703	35,433	23,752	11,681	9,588	6,831	2,757	7,325	4,060	3,265	3,461	6,725
45 - 59	43,352	26,631	16,721	29,297	17,566	11,731	6,202	4,818	1,384	7,853	4,247	3,606	5,383	2,823
60 - 64	12,979	6,791	6,188	10,342	4,919	5,423	1,560	1,227	333	1,077	645	432	2,602	360
65 - 74	21,584	10,480	11,104	18,974	8,695	10,279	2,035	1,501	534	575	284	291	5,392	355
75 - 84	9,931	4,045	5,886	8,318	3,293	5,025	1,341	667	674	272	85	187	3,579	265
85 and over	1,798	522	1,276	1,034	319	715	683	187	496	81	16	65	937	137

Hostels and common lodging houses (non-HA)

All ages	**20,258**	**13,499**	**6,759**	**2,445**	**1,397**	**1,048**	**16,940**	**11,587**	**5,353**	**873**	**515**	**358**	**6,317**	**9,870**
0 - 15	1,908	1,023	885	143	74	69	1,691	911	780	74	38	36	76	1,084
16 - 17	719	325	394	60	28	32	647	290	357	12	7	5	72	571
18 - 29	6,945	3,683	3,262	1,113	548	565	5,558	2,996	2,562	274	139	135	1,119	4,319
30 - 44	4,031	2,993	1,038	488	364	124	3,362	2,508	854	181	121	60	1,546	2,130
45 - 59	3,498	2,957	541	303	222	81	2,937	2,569	368	258	166	92	1,821	1,264
60 - 64	1,009	885	124	71	51	20	889	802	87	49	32	17	559	210
65 - 74	1,423	1,221	202	113	61	52	1,289	1,150	139	21	10	11	681	206
75 - 84	536	356	180	99	38	61	434	316	118	3	2	1	299	58
85 and over	189	56	133	55	11	44	133	45	88	1	-	1	144	28

Table 3 Type of establishment, migrants and long-term illness – **continued**

Great Britain, England & Wales, England, regions, metropolitan counties, Inner London, Outer London, regional remainders, Wales, Scotland

Persons present in communal establishments

Type of establishment and age	PERSONS PRESENT			Visitors/guests			Residents - non-staff			Residents - staff			With limiting long-term illness	Migrants
	TOTAL	Males	Females	Total	Males	Females	Total	Males	Females	Total	Males	Females		
a	b	c	d	e	f	g	h	i	j	k	l	m	n	o
ENGLAND & WALES – *continued*														
Other miscellaneous establishments														
All ages	**38,287**	**20,228**	**18,059**	**12,251**	**8,758**	**3,493**	**21,702**	**9,205**	**12,497**	**4,334**	**2,265**	**2,069**	**4,969**	**10,855**
0 - 15	3,365	1,776	1,589	794	410	384	2,391	1,278	1,113	180	88	92	205	1,523
16 - 17	1,187	783	404	565	417	148	545	313	232	77	53	24	57	491
18 - 29	15,980	9,675	6,305	5,909	4,212	1,697	8,001	4,289	3,712	2,070	1,174	896	631	6,046
30 - 44	6,988	4,551	2,437	3,128	2,510	618	3,009	1,532	1,477	851	509	342	570	1,566
45 - 59	4,131	1,941	2,190	1,213	928	285	2,239	746	1,493	679	267	412	631	594
60 - 64	1,295	436	859	221	121	100	914	250	664	160	65	95	285	160
65 - 74	2,228	603	1,625	260	119	141	1,786	415	1,371	182	69	113	672	232
75 - 84	2,235	380	1,855	126	33	93	1,996	313	1,683	113	34	79	1,227	171
85 and over	878	83	795	35	8	27	821	69	752	22	6	16	691	72
Persons sleeping rough														
All ages	**2,682**	**2,273**	**409**	**802**	**691**	**111**	**1,876**	**1,581**	**295**				**555**	**1,419**
0 - 15	2	2	-	2	2	-	-	-	-				-	-
16 - 17	35	23	12	11	8	3	24	15	9				4	20
18 - 29	1,026	854	172	302	244	58	723	610	113				148	561
30 - 44	851	730	121	219	193	26	632	537	95				172	472
45 - 59	662	576	86	224	203	21	436	372	64				178	337
60 - 64	56	51	5	24	23	1	32	28	4				25	15
65 - 74	39	33	6	19	17	2	19	16	3				20	12
75 - 84	8	3	5	1	1	-	7	2	5				6	1
85 and over	3	1	2	-	-	-	3	1	2				2	1

Table 3 Type of establishment, migrants and long-term illness – **continued**

Persons present in communal establishments

Type of establishment and age	PERSONS PRESENT			Visitors/guests			Residents - non-staff			Residents - staff			With limiting long-term illness	Migrants
	TOTAL	Males	Females	Total	Males	Females	Total	Males	Females	Total	Males	Females		
a	b	c	d	e	f	g	h	i	j	k	l	m	n	o
ENGLAND & WALES – *continued*														
Campers														
All ages	**1,107**	**576**	**531**	**948**	**507**	**441**	**159**	**69**	**90**				**229**	**63**
0 - 15	68	33	35	41	19	22	27	14	13				4	11
16 - 17	6	6	-	4	4	-	2	2	-				1	2
18 - 29	168	90	78	127	66	61	41	24	17				7	16
30 - 44	122	72	50	112	66	46	10	6	4				10	7
45 - 59	193	97	96	176	88	88	17	9	8				28	4
60 - 64	156	78	78	154	78	76	2	-	2				36	1
65 - 74	277	150	127	273	148	125	4	2	2				67	1
75 - 84	82	46	36	59	38	21	23	8	15				42	9
85 and over	35	4	31	2	-	2	33	4	29				34	12
Civilian ships, boats and barges														
All ages	**5,267**	**4,755**	**512**	**4,427**	**4,087**	**340**	**840**	**668**	**172**				**104**	**330**
0 - 15	77	49	28	58	35	23	19	14	5				6	10
16 - 17	41	30	11	25	22	3	16	8	8				-	11
18 - 29	1,355	1,095	260	1,032	887	145	323	208	115				20	158
30 - 44	2,337	2,229	108	2,037	1,955	82	300	274	26				31	101
45 - 59	1,299	1,219	80	1,137	1,071	66	162	148	14				34	50
60 - 64	115	106	9	102	93	9	13	13	-				7	-
65 - 74	32	21	11	27	19	8	5	2	3				4	-
75 - 84	9	4	5	7	3	4	2	1	1				2	-
85 and over	2	2	-	2	2	-	-	-	-				-	-

Table 3 Type of establishment, migrants and long-term illness – **continued**

Great Britain, England & Wales, England, regions, metropolitan counties, Inner London, Outer London, regional remainders, Wales, Scotland

Persons present in communal establishments

Type of establishment and age	PERSONS PRESENT			Visitors/guests			Residents - non-staff			Residents - staff			With limiting long-term illness	Migrants
	TOTAL	Males	Females	Total	Males	Females	Total	Males	Females	Total	Males	Females		
a	b	c	d	e	f	g	h	i	j	k	l	m	n	o
ENGLAND														
All establishments *														
All ages	**1,300,772**	**616,954**	**683,818**	**582,936**	**320,360**	**262,576**	**633,197**	**258,940**	**374,257**	**84,639**	**37,654**	**46,985**	**581,326**	**240,664**
0 - 15	114,138	68,854	45,284	87,221	54,090	33,131	20,862	11,629	9,233	6,055	3,135	2,920	9,462	11,756
16 - 17	44,269	27,777	16,492	34,896	21,522	13,374	7,743	5,470	2,273	1,630	785	845	3,455	6,508
18 - 29	359,701	206,947	152,754	201,259	112,485	88,774	117,425	78,678	38,747	41,017	15,784	25,233	33,804	84,881
30 - 44	147,402	95,005	52,397	74,180	47,143	27,037	56,486	38,995	17,491	16,736	8,867	7,869	40,161	24,898
45 - 59	106,095	62,318	43,777	53,622	30,781	22,841	37,703	24,442	13,261	14,770	7,095	7,675	42,516	10,275
60 - 64	39,364	20,752	18,612	19,696	9,901	9,795	17,406	9,656	7,750	2,262	1,195	1,067	23,173	3,799
65 - 74	103,370	46,380	56,990	45,256	21,331	23,925	56,754	24,471	32,283	1,360	578	782	75,683	14,207
75 - 84	196,442	56,799	139,643	45,718	17,726	27,992	150,124	38,899	111,225	600	174	426	174,783	43,457
85 and over	189,991	32,122	157,869	21,088	5,381	15,707	168,694	26,700	141,994	209	41	168	178,289	40,883
NHS hospitals/homes - psychiatric														
All ages	**33,744**	**15,744**	**18,000**	**10,671**	**4,668**	**6,003**	**20,113**	**9,784**	**10,329**	**2,960**	**1,292**	**1,668**	**27,552**	**3,862**
0 - 15	285	146	139	227	114	113	56	31	25	2	1	1	75	14
16 - 17	111	46	65	92	41	51	16	5	11	3	-	3	60	11
18 - 29	5,647	2,721	2,926	1,789	947	842	1,759	1,012	747	2,099	762	1,337	2,196	1,492
30 - 44	5,157	3,258	1,899	1,880	951	929	2,681	1,932	749	596	375	221	3,896	653
45 - 59	4,652	2,708	1,944	1,490	678	812	2,936	1,902	1,034	226	128	98	4,027	296
60 - 64	2,055	1,135	920	549	239	310	1,478	874	604	28	22	6	1,919	108
65 - 74	5,454	2,519	2,935	1,587	615	972	3,861	1,900	1,961	6	4	2	5,198	383
75 - 84	6,844	2,438	4,406	2,106	823	1,283	4,738	1,615	3,123	-	-	-	6,694	612
85 and over	3,539	773	2,766	951	260	691	2,588	513	2,075	-	-	-	3,487	293

Note: * Includes one male member of staff and three female members of staff incorrectly enumerated as residents.

Table 3 Type of establishment, migrants and long-term illness – **continued**

Great Britain, England & Wales, England, regions, metropolitan counties, Inner London, Outer London, regional remainders, Wales, Scotland

Persons present in communal establishments

Type of establishment and age	PERSONS PRESENT			Visitors/guests			Residents - non-staff			Residents - staff			With limiting long-term illness	Migrants
	TOTAL	Males	Females	Total	Males	Females	Total	Males	Females	Total	Males	Females		
a	b	c	d	e	f	g	h	i	j	k	l	m	n	o
ENGLAND – continued														
NHS hospitals/homes - other														
All ages	**191,069**	**74,038**	**117,031**	**128,198**	**51,351**	**76,847**	**43,237**	**17,298**	**25,939**	**19,634**	**5,389**	**14,245**	**112,638**	**19,314**
0 - 15	12,306	6,673	5,633	11,643	6,343	5,300	493	246	247	170	84	86	2,316	211
16 - 17	1,083	372	711	937	315	622	96	49	47	50	8	42	337	90
18 - 29	44,261	11,515	32,746	18,989	4,893	14,096	9,715	3,228	6,487	15,557	3,394	12,163	6,648	11,517
30 - 44	24,446	11,061	13,385	13,516	4,905	8,611	7,896	4,574	3,322	3,034	1,582	1,452	11,443	2,560
45 - 59	19,199	9,592	9,607	12,931	6,267	6,664	5,566	3,057	2,509	702	268	434	13,574	711
60 - 64	8,543	4,499	4,044	6,844	3,626	3,218	1,625	833	792	74	40	34	6,783	206
65 - 74	25,192	12,159	13,033	20,581	10,086	10,495	4,593	2,066	2,527	18	7	11	20,887	823
75 - 84	35,565	13,555	22,010	28,420	11,257	17,163	7,129	2,294	4,835	16	4	12	31,573	1,767
85 and over	20,474	4,612	15,862	14,337	3,659	10,678	6,124	951	5,173	13	2	11	19,077	1,429
Non-NHS hospitals - psychiatric														
All ages	**4,477**	**2,189**	**2,288**	**1,784**	**795**	**989**	**2,440**	**1,250**	**1,190**	**253**	**144**	**109**	**3,506**	**562**
0 - 15	129	83	46	103	66	37	25	17	8	1	-	1	28	12
16 - 17	46	21	25	35	16	19	10	5	5	1	-	1	23	6
18 - 29	755	397	358	333	148	185	248	163	85	174	86	88	391	168
30 - 44	838	492	346	346	160	186	447	298	149	45	34	11	628	99
45 - 59	735	403	332	334	155	179	369	224	145	32	24	8	584	58
60 - 64	278	148	130	98	48	50	180	100	80	-	-	-	251	22
65 - 74	669	319	350	219	94	125	450	225	225	-	-	-	623	66
75 - 84	672	241	431	221	80	141	451	161	290	-	-	-	633	86
85 and over	355	85	270	95	28	67	260	57	203	-	-	-	345	45

Table 3 Type of establishment, migrants and long-term illness – **continued**

Great Britain, England & Wales, England, regions, metropolitan counties, Inner London, Outer London, regional remainders, Wales, Scotland

Persons present in communal establishments

Type of establishment and age	PERSONS PRESENT			Visitors/guests			Residents - non-staff			Residents - staff			With limiting long-term illness	Migrants
	TOTAL	Males	Females	Total	Males	Females	Total	Males	Females	Total	Males	Females		
a	b	c	d	e	f	g	h	i	j	k	l	m	n	o
ENGLAND – *continued*														
Non-NHS hospitals - other														
All ages	**12,868**	**5,121**	**7,747**	**8,511**	**3,328**	**5,183**	**3,533**	**1,496**	**2,037**	**824**	**297**	**527**	**7,284**	**1,160**
0 - 15	593	328	265	553	306	247	29	17	12	11	5	6	149	12
16 - 17	67	25	42	54	20	34	7	4	3	6	1	5	20	11
18 - 29	1,989	662	1,327	954	254	700	527	244	283	508	164	344	444	492
30 - 44	2,185	846	1,339	1,403	413	990	598	343	255	184	90	94	849	160
45 - 59	2,177	970	1,207	1,531	627	904	556	315	241	90	28	62	1,150	66
60 - 64	785	396	389	592	311	281	181	84	97	12	1	11	528	19
65 - 74	1,733	836	897	1,327	653	674	397	178	219	9	5	4	1,260	62
75 - 84	2,123	792	1,331	1,478	581	897	642	209	433	3	2	1	1,762	176
85 and over	1,216	266	950	619	163	456	596	102	494	1	1	-	1,122	162
Local authority homes														
All ages	**110,996**	**36,791**	**74,205**	**12,003**	**5,798**	**6,205**	**97,907**	**30,547**	**67,360**	**1,086**	**446**	**640**	**98,640**	**21,026**
0 - 15	4,428	3,322	1,106	3,159	2,483	676	1,186	791	395	83	48	35	1,484	480
16 - 17	1,251	807	444	635	429	206	595	368	227	21	10	11	569	282
18 - 29	6,851	3,843	3,008	1,449	753	696	5,045	2,962	2,083	357	128	229	4,832	1,614
30 - 44	6,800	3,758	3,042	984	373	611	5,564	3,270	2,294	252	115	137	5,592	1,055
45 - 59	5,486	2,794	2,692	727	185	542	4,471	2,504	1,967	288	105	183	4,538	652
60 - 64	2,539	1,295	1,244	217	90	127	2,281	1,183	1,098	41	22	19	2,345	473
65 - 74	11,382	4,865	6,517	816	378	438	10,542	4,475	6,067	24	12	12	10,633	2,325
75 - 84	33,572	9,423	24,149	2,156	688	1,468	31,404	8,730	22,674	12	5	7	31,704	7,218
85 and over	38,687	6,684	32,003	1,860	419	1,441	36,819	6,264	30,555	8	1	7	36,943	6,927

Table 3 Type of establishment, migrants and long-term illness – **continued**

Great Britain, England & Wales, England, regions, metropolitan counties, Inner London, Outer London, regional remainders, Wales, Scotland

Persons present in communal establishments

Type of establishment and age	PERSONS PRESENT			Visitors/guests			Residents - non-staff			Residents - staff			With limiting long-term illness	Migrants
	TOTAL	Males	Females	Total	Males	Females	Total	Males	Females	Total	Males	Females		
a	b	c	d	e	f	g	h	i	j	k	l	m	n	o
ENGLAND – *continued*														
Housing association homes and hostels														
All ages	**21,045**	**9,735**	**11,310**	**1,534**	**727**	**807**	**18,800**	**8,740**	**10,060**	**711**	**268**	**443**	**12,025**	**7,133**
0 - 15	356	212	144	48	33	15	245	144	101	63	35	28	53	125
16 - 17	365	171	194	84	36	48	272	133	139	9	2	7	61	226
18 - 29	4,798	2,629	2,169	731	321	410	3,931	2,247	1,684	136	61	75	1,127	2,459
30 - 44	2,805	1,903	902	299	182	117	2,368	1,671	697	138	50	88	1,450	1,084
45 - 59	2,367	1,679	688	144	85	59	1,961	1,510	451	262	84	178	1,476	724
60 - 64	799	535	264	34	18	16	707	497	210	58	20	38	540	193
65 - 74	1,864	1,000	864	44	15	29	1,782	971	811	38	14	24	1,311	478
75 - 84	3,831	1,028	2,803	91	28	63	3,736	999	2,737	4	1	3	2,870	1,022
85 and over	3,860	578	3,282	59	9	50	3,798	568	3,230	3	1	2	3,137	822
Nursing homes (non-NHS/ LA/HA)														
All ages	**122,381**	**31,096**	**91,285**	**6,139**	**2,128**	**4,011**	**114,245**	**28,280**	**85,965**	**1,997**	**688**	**1,309**	**115,560**	**41,413**
0 - 15	413	222	191	91	51	40	143	76	67	179	95	84	118	53
16 - 17	127	50	77	30	13	17	44	16	28	53	21	32	47	25
18 - 29	1,896	836	1,060	446	135	311	955	547	408	495	154	341	999	522
30 - 44	2,516	1,203	1,313	716	205	511	1,409	855	554	391	143	248	1,566	484
45 - 59	2,977	1,362	1,615	671	197	474	1,710	968	742	596	197	399	2,013	538
60 - 64	3,546	1,685	1,861	400	184	216	3,023	1,457	1,566	123	44	79	3,207	1,054
65 - 74	14,743	5,689	9,054	1,190	520	670	13,452	5,140	8,312	101	29	72	13,959	5,274
75 - 84	45,763	11,870	33,893	1,639	571	1,068	44,081	11,296	32,785	43	3	40	44,366	17,275
85 and over	50,400	8,179	42,221	956	252	704	49,428	7,925	41,503	16	2	14	49,285	16,188

Table 3 Type of establishment, migrants and long-term illness – **continued**

Great Britain, England & Wales, England, regions, metropolitan counties, Inner London, Outer London, regional remainders, Wales, Scotland

Persons present in communal establishments

Type of establishment and age	PERSONS PRESENT			Visitors/guests			Residents - non-staff			Residents - staff			With limiting long-term illness	Migrants
	TOTAL	Males	Females	Total	Males	Females	Total	Males	Females	Total	Males	Females		
a	b	c	d	e	f	g	h	i	j	k	l	m	n	o
ENGLAND – continued														
Residential homes (non-NHS/LA/HA)														
All ages	**173,040**	**46,264**	**126,776**	**5,897**	**1,888**	**4,009**	**159,555**	**41,290**	**118,265**	**7,588**	**3,086**	**4,502**	**150,332**	**38,688**
0 - 15	1,482	835	647	272	208	64	210	135	75	1,000	492	508	324	154
16 - 17	505	287	218	144	83	61	170	104	66	191	100	91	238	109
18 - 29	7,841	4,124	3,717	975	372	603	5,273	3,166	2,107	1,593	586	1,007	5,442	1,817
30 - 44	8,961	4,841	4,120	805	245	560	6,495	3,920	2,575	1,661	676	985	6,571	1,255
45 - 59	8,759	4,441	4,318	559	135	424	5,849	3,376	2,473	2,351	930	1,421	6,000	1,027
60 - 64	4,849	2,375	2,474	216	80	136	4,237	2,116	2,121	396	179	217	3,979	889
65 - 74	17,053	6,583	10,470	563	177	386	16,240	6,314	9,926	250	92	158	14,930	3,933
75 - 84	55,212	12,580	42,632	1,307	362	945	53,818	12,197	41,621	87	21	66	49,900	14,759
85 and over	68,378	10,198	58,180	1,056	226	830	67,263	9,962	57,301	59	10	49	62,948	14,745
Children's homes														
All ages	**11,148**	**6,127**	**5,021**	**2,070**	**1,139**	**931**	**7,985**	**4,494**	**3,491**	**1,093**	**494**	**599**	**1,116**	**4,241**
0 - 15	9,607	5,523	4,084	1,449	930	519	7,985	4,494	3,491	173	99	74	928	4,072
16 - 17	63	23	40	2	1	1	-	-	-	61	22	39	7	22
18 - 29	558	242	316	239	88	151	-	-	-	319	154	165	98	93
30 - 44	469	188	281	231	89	142	-	-	-	238	99	139	26	37
45 - 59	369	121	248	131	24	107	-	-	-	238	97	141	36	8
60 - 64	42	19	23	11	7	4	-	-	-	31	12	19	6	3
65 - 74	22	8	14	5	-	5	-	-	-	17	8	9	6	3
75 - 84	14	2	12	1	-	1	-	-	-	13	2	11	6	2
85 and over	4	1	3	1	-	1	-	-	-	3	1	2	3	1

Table 3 Type of establishment, migrants and long-term illness – **continued**

Great Britain, England & Wales, England, regions,
metropolitan counties, Inner London, Outer London,
regional remainders, Wales, Scotland

Persons present in communal establishments

Type of establishment and age	PERSONS PRESENT			Visitors/guests			Residents - non-staff			Residents - staff			With limiting long-term illness	Migrants
	TOTAL	Males	Females	Total	Males	Females	Total	Males	Females	Total	Males	Females		
a	b	c	d	e	f	g	h	i	j	k	l	m	n	o
Prison service establishments														
All ages	**38,167**	**36,480**	**1,687**	**24,637**	**23,556**	**1,081**	**13,448**	**12,853**	**595**	**82**	**71**	**11**	**5,374**	**7,097**
0 - 15	162	155	7	122	115	7	9	9	-	31	31	-	13	30
16 - 17	1,243	1,217	26	1,078	1,063	15	165	154	11	-	-	-	106	114
18 - 29	22,282	21,438	844	15,616	15,036	580	6,654	6,391	263	12	11	1	2,316	3,867
30 - 44	10,497	9,917	580	5,830	5,453	377	4,642	4,444	198	25	20	5	1,690	2,252
45 - 59	3,375	3,212	163	1,723	1,641	82	1,645	1,569	76	7	2	5	950	714
60 - 64	339	317	22	151	142	9	186	173	13	2	2	-	157	73
65 - 74	177	158	19	83	77	6	91	78	13	3	3	-	100	27
75 - 84	65	45	20	26	22	4	37	21	16	2	2	-	35	14
85 and over	27	21	6	8	7	1	19	14	5	-	-	-	7	6
Defence establishments														
All ages	**58,646**	**51,085**	**7,561**	**13,946**	**12,505**	**1,441**	**44,700**	**38,580**	**6,120**				**1,481**	**23,636**
0 - 15	35	29	6	35	29	6	-	-	-				2	-
16 - 17	4,242	3,898	344	998	900	98	3,244	2,998	246				61	2,915
18 - 29	45,439	38,980	6,459	8,741	7,703	1,038	36,698	31,277	5,421				854	18,725
30 - 44	7,483	6,921	562	3,301	3,118	183	4,182	3,803	379				291	1,809
45 - 59	1,070	974	96	666	620	46	404	354	50				89	136
60 - 64	102	81	21	64	47	17	38	34	4				23	9
65 - 74	152	120	32	86	59	27	66	61	5				79	27
75 - 84	87	57	30	46	25	21	41	32	9				53	14
85 and over	36	25	11	9	4	5	27	21	6				29	1

ENGLAND – *continued*

117

Table 3 Type of establishment, migrants and long-term illness – **continued**

Great Britain, England & Wales, England, regions, metropolitan counties, Inner London, Outer London, regional remainders, Wales, Scotland

Persons present in communal establishments

Type of establishment and age	PERSONS PRESENT			Visitors/guests			Residents - non-staff			Residents - staff			With limiting long-term illness	Migrants
	TOTAL	Males	Females	Total	Males	Females	Total	Males	Females	Total	Males	Females		
a	b	c	d	e	f	g	h	i	j	k	l	m	n	o
ENGLAND – continued														
Educational establishments														
All ages	234,731	135,056	99,675	203,405	116,923	86,482	23,510	14,253	9,257	7,816	3,880	3,936	10,355	16,380
0 - 15	58,286	37,511	20,775	56,358	36,406	19,952	1,325	789	536	603	316	287	3,049	619
16 - 17	28,791	17,490	11,301	27,919	17,007	10,912	756	440	316	116	43	73	1,610	373
18 - 29	129,920	69,885	60,035	111,551	58,866	52,685	15,607	9,745	5,862	2,762	1,274	1,488	3,816	11,985
30 - 44	11,081	7,166	3,915	4,959	3,316	1,643	3,899	2,621	1,278	2,223	1,229	994	613	2,805
45 - 59	4,292	2,156	2,136	1,849	974	875	803	384	419	1,640	798	842	430	473
60 - 64	700	320	380	203	91	112	221	84	137	276	145	131	109	40
65 - 74	764	269	495	266	121	145	356	92	264	142	56	86	222	35
75 - 84	641	190	451	214	100	114	382	73	309	45	17	28	322	29
85 and over	256	69	187	86	42	44	161	25	136	9	2	7	184	21
Hotels, boarding houses etc														
All ages	223,403	127,419	95,984	144,361	80,923	63,438	43,600	27,649	15,951	35,442	18,847	16,595	23,753	34,258
0 - 15	20,936	11,083	9,853	12,236	6,519	5,717	5,206	2,759	2,447	3,494	1,805	1,689	646	3,466
16 - 17	4,477	2,259	2,218	2,284	1,162	1,122	1,163	579	584	1,030	518	512	187	1,252
18 - 29	62,677	34,697	27,980	31,324	17,281	14,043	16,675	9,709	6,966	14,678	7,707	6,971	2,792	19,254
30 - 44	50,481	33,360	17,121	34,280	22,939	11,341	9,266	6,586	2,680	6,935	3,835	3,100	3,307	6,511
45 - 59	41,271	25,390	15,881	27,954	16,801	11,153	5,905	4,583	1,322	7,412	4,006	3,406	5,065	2,702
60 - 64	12,269	6,447	5,822	9,770	4,665	5,105	1,487	1,171	316	1,012	611	401	2,448	348
65 - 74	20,315	9,892	10,423	17,828	8,187	9,641	1,939	1,436	503	548	269	279	5,078	337
75 - 84	9,285	3,805	5,480	7,727	3,078	4,649	1,299	646	653	259	81	178	3,341	257
85 and over	1,692	486	1,206	958	291	667	660	180	480	74	15	59	889	131

Table 3 Type of establishment, migrants and long-term illness – **continued**

Persons present in communal establishments

Type of establishment and age	PERSONS PRESENT			Visitors/guests			Residents - non-staff			Residents - staff			With limiting long-term illness	Migrants
	TOTAL	Males	Females	Total	Males	Females	Total	Males	Females	Total	Males	Females		
a	b	c	d	e	f	g	h	i	j	k	l	m	n	o
ENGLAND – *continued*														
Hostels and common lodging houses (non-HA)														
All ages	**19,577**	**13,043**	**6,534**	**2,379**	**1,354**	**1,025**	**16,346**	**11,189**	**5,157**	**852**	**500**	**352**	**6,045**	**9,511**
0 - 15	1,793	963	830	129	68	61	1,591	858	733	73	37	36	73	1,022
16 - 17	696	312	384	55	26	29	629	279	350	12	7	5	70	558
18 - 29	6,763	3,588	3,175	1,098	538	560	5,395	2,913	2,482	270	137	133	1,064	4,176
30 - 44	3,878	2,875	1,003	461	343	118	3,246	2,419	827	171	113	58	1,477	2,054
45 - 59	3,381	2,859	522	299	219	80	2,830	2,478	352	252	162	90	1,740	1,218
60 - 64	975	855	120	71	51	20	855	772	83	49	32	17	534	199
65 - 74	1,384	1,186	198	112	60	52	1,251	1,116	135	21	10	11	658	200
75 - 84	522	349	173	99	38	61	420	309	111	3	2	1	289	56
85 and over	185	56	129	55	11	44	129	45	84	1	-	1	140	28
Other miscellaneous establishments														
All ages	**37,059**	**19,746**	**17,313**	**11,683**	**8,413**	**3,270**	**21,079**	**9,082**	**11,997**	**4,297**	**2,251**	**2,046**	**4,791**	**10,619**
0 - 15	3,188	1,692	1,496	701	368	333	2,315	1,237	1,078	172	87	85	195	1,466
16 - 17	1,122	742	380	509	376	133	536	313	223	77	53	24	54	482
18 - 29	15,624	9,477	6,147	5,668	4,041	1,627	7,900	4,270	3,630	2,056	1,166	890	614	5,977
30 - 44	6,786	4,465	2,321	3,020	2,448	572	2,923	1,511	1,412	843	506	337	550	1,519
45 - 59	3,983	1,909	2,074	1,177	908	269	2,134	736	1,398	672	265	407	610	575
60 - 64	1,230	422	808	209	119	90	861	238	623	160	65	95	277	147
65 - 74	2,135	584	1,551	243	112	131	1,710	403	1,307	182	69	113	649	222
75 - 84	2,149	373	1,776	122	33	89	1,914	306	1,608	113	34	79	1,185	160
85 and over	842	82	760	34	8	26	786	68	718	22	6	16	657	71

Table 3 Type of establishment, migrants and long-term illness – **continued**

Great Britain, England & Wales, England, regions,
metropolitan counties, Inner London, Outer London,
regional remainders, Wales, Scotland

Persons present in communal establishments

Type of establishment and age	PERSONS PRESENT			Visitors/guests			Residents - non-staff			Residents - staff			With limiting long-term illness	Migrants
	TOTAL	Males	Females	Total	Males	Females	Total	Males	Females	Total	Males	Females		
a	b	c	d	e	f	g	h	i	j	k	l	m	n	o

ENGLAND – *continued*

Persons sleeping rough

Type of establishment and age	PERSONS PRESENT			Visitors/guests			Residents - non-staff			Residents - staff			With limiting long-term illness	Migrants
All ages	**2,650**	**2,243**	**407**	**787**	**677**	**110**	**1,859**	**1,565**	**294**				**550**	**1,406**
0 - 15	-	-	-	-	-	-	-	-	-				-	-
16 - 17	35	23	12	11	8	3	24	15	9				4	20
18 - 29	1,013	843	170	297	240	57	715	603	112				146	555
30 - 44	842	721	121	214	188	26	628	533	95				172	468
45 - 59	657	571	86	222	201	21	433	369	64				177	335
60 - 64	55	50	5	23	22	1	32	28	4				24	15
65 - 74	37	31	6	19	17	2	17	14	3				19	11
75 - 84	8	3	5	1	1	-	7	2	5				6	1
85 and over	3	1	2	-	-	-	3	1	2				2	1

Campers

Type of establishment and age	PERSONS PRESENT			Visitors/guests			Residents - non-staff			Residents - staff			With limiting long-term illness	Migrants
All ages	**1,074**	**561**	**513**	**916**	**493**	**423**	**158**	**68**	**90**				**229**	**63**
0 - 15	68	33	35	41	19	22	27	14	13				4	11
16 - 17	6	6	-	4	4	-	2	2	-				1	2
18 - 29	154	86	68	113	62	51	41	24	17				7	16
30 - 44	121	71	50	111	65	46	10	6	4				10	7
45 - 59	193	97	96	176	88	88	17	9	8				28	4
60 - 64	151	75	76	149	75	74	2	-	2				36	1
65 - 74	265	144	121	262	143	119	3	1	2				67	1
75 - 84	81	45	36	58	37	21	23	8	15				42	9
85 and over	35	4	31	2	-	2	33	4	29				34	12

Table 3 Type of establishment, migrants and long-term illness – **continued**

Great Britain, England & Wales, England, regions, metropolitan counties, Inner London, Outer London, regional remainders, Wales, Scotland

Persons present in communal establishments

Type of establishment and age	PERSONS PRESENT			Visitors/guests			Residents - non-staff			Residents - staff			With limiting long-term illness	Migrants
	TOTAL	Males	Females	Total	Males	Females	Total	Males	Females	Total	Males	Females		
a	b	c	d	e	f	g	h	i	j	k	l	m	n	o

ENGLAND – *continued*

Civilian ships, boats and barges

All ages	**4,697**	**4,216**	**481**	**4,015**	**3,694**	**321**	**682**	**522**	**160**				**95**	**295**
0 - 15	71	44	27	54	32	22	17	12	5				5	9
16 - 17	39	28	11	25	22	3	14	6	8				-	10
18 - 29	1,233	984	249	946	807	139	287	177	110				18	152
30 - 44	2,056	1,959	97	1,824	1,750	74	232	209	23				30	86
45 - 59	1,152	1,080	72	1,038	976	62	114	104	10				29	38
60 - 64	107	98	9	95	86	9	12	12	-				7	-
65 - 74	29	18	11	25	17	8	4	1	3				4	-
75 - 84	8	3	5	6	2	4	2	1	1				2	-
85 and over	2	2	-	2	2	-	-	-	-				-	-

NORTH REGION

All establishments

All ages	**76,913**	**36,003**	**40,910**	**36,549**	**20,191**	**16,358**	**35,761**	**13,506**	**22,255**	**4,603**	**2,306**	**2,297**	**38,355**	**12,883**
0 - 15	5,238	3,147	2,091	3,835	2,377	1,458	1,017	584	433	386	186	200	410	548
16 - 17	2,305	1,503	802	1,619	952	667	571	496	75	115	55	60	130	571
18 - 29	19,652	11,407	8,245	14,325	8,291	6,034	3,239	2,146	1,093	2,088	970	1,118	1,752	2,833
30 - 44	7,813	5,142	2,671	4,338	2,859	1,479	2,520	1,725	795	955	558	397	2,404	997
45 - 59	6,582	3,876	2,706	3,634	2,068	1,566	2,094	1,366	728	854	442	412	2,711	514
60 - 64	2,777	1,454	1,323	1,442	708	734	1,229	686	543	106	60	46	1,735	275
65 - 74	7,592	3,543	4,049	3,171	1,515	1,656	4,363	2,003	2,360	58	25	33	5,929	1,164
75 - 84	13,416	3,958	9,458	2,919	1,112	1,807	10,466	2,836	7,630	31	10	21	12,318	3,241
85 and over	11,538	1,973	9,565	1,266	309	957	10,262	1,664	8,598	10	-	10	10,966	2,740

Table 3 Type of establishment, migrants and long-term illness – **continued**

Great Britain, England & Wales, England, regions, metropolitan counties, Inner London, Outer London, regional remainders, Wales, Scotland

Persons present in communal establishments

Type of establishment and age	PERSONS PRESENT			Visitors/guests			Residents - non-staff			Residents - staff			With limiting long-term illness	Migrants
	TOTAL	Males	Females	Total	Males	Females	Total	Males	Females	Total	Males	Females		
a	b	c	d	e	f	g	h	i	j	k	l	m	n	o
						NORTH REGION – *continued*								
NHS hospitals/homes - psychiatric														
All ages	**2,333**	**1,068**	**1,265**	**741**	**319**	**422**	**1,462**	**691**	**771**	**130**	**58**	**72**	**1,899**	**206**
0 - 15	18	6	12	17	5	12	1	1	-	-	-	-	1	1
16 - 17	7	4	3	5	4	1	-	-	-	2	-	2	1	2
18 - 29	302	156	146	122	66	56	75	46	29	105	44	61	106	80
30 - 44	284	158	126	140	71	69	127	78	49	17	9	8	215	34
45 - 59	295	165	130	92	31	61	198	130	68	5	4	1	250	8
60 - 64	204	108	96	65	21	44	138	86	52	1	1	-	174	8
65 - 74	506	249	257	144	65	79	362	184	178	-	-	-	453	21
75 - 84	500	178	322	116	44	72	384	134	250	-	-	-	483	37
85 and over	217	44	173	40	12	28	177	32	145	-	-	-	216	15
NHS hospitals/homes - other														
All ages	**13,725**	**5,661**	**8,064**	**9,215**	**3,742**	**5,473**	**3,963**	**1,704**	**2,259**	**547**	**215**	**332**	**9,524**	**967**
0 - 15	850	495	355	814	473	341	33	20	13	3	2	1	132	2
16 - 17	89	30	59	86	28	58	2	2	-	1	-	-	19	1
18 - 29	2,149	619	1,530	1,247	288	959	479	212	267	423	119	304	495	346
30 - 44	1,676	811	865	904	334	570	669	394	275	103	83	20	1,012	106
45 - 59	1,517	786	731	1,021	495	526	482	281	201	14	10	4	1,162	40
60 - 64	737	381	356	532	273	259	204	108	96	1	-	1	626	24
65 - 74	2,245	1,115	1,130	1,698	844	854	547	271	276	-	-	-	1,931	91
75 - 84	2,833	1,090	1,743	1,993	789	1,204	839	300	539	1	1	-	2,594	193
85 and over	1,629	334	1,295	920	218	702	708	116	592	1	-	1	1,553	164

Table 3 Type of establishment, migrants and long-term illness – **continued**

Persons present in communal establishments

NORTH REGION – *continued*

Type of establishment and age	PERSONS PRESENT			Visitors/guests			Residents - non-staff			Residents - staff			With limiting long-term illness	Migrants
	TOTAL	Males	Females	Total	Males	Females	Total	Males	Females	Total	Males	Females		
a	b	c	d	e	f	g	h	i	j	k	l	m	n	o
Non-NHS hospitals - psychiatric														
All ages	**330**	**141**	**189**	**77**	**34**	**43**	**236**	**101**	**135**	**17**	**6**	**11**	**309**	**64**
0 - 15	-	-	-	-	-	-	-	-	-	-	-	-	-	-
16 - 17	-	-	-	-	-	-	-	-	-	-	-	-	-	-
18 - 29	34	15	19	10	6	4	8	4	4	16	5	11	15	16
30 - 44	48	28	20	13	8	5	35	20	15	-	-	-	47	16
45 - 59	52	24	28	20	7	13	31	16	15	1	1	-	51	3
60 - 64	19	12	7	3	2	1	16	10	6	-	-	-	19	3
65 - 74	59	28	31	14	4	10	45	24	21	-	-	-	59	12
75 - 84	66	24	42	11	6	5	55	18	37	-	-	-	66	9
85 and over	52	10	42	6	1	5	46	9	37	-	-	-	52	5
Non-NHS hospitals - other														
All ages	**199**	**59**	**140**	**106**	**29**	**77**	**93**	**30**	**63**	**-**	**-**	**-**	**158**	**45**
0 - 15	4	1	3	4	1	3	-	-	-	-	-	-	-	-
16 - 17	-	-	-	-	-	-	-	-	-	-	-	-	-	-
18 - 29	6	2	4	6	2	4	-	-	-	-	-	-	-	-
30 - 44	17	6	11	16	5	11	1	1	-	-	-	-	5	1
45 - 59	23	8	15	22	7	15	1	1	-	-	-	-	11	1
60 - 64	7	3	4	7	3	4	17	10	7	-	-	-	4	-
65 - 74	32	14	18	15	4	11	35	10	25	-	-	-	30	11
75 - 84	60	16	44	25	6	19	39	8	31	-	-	-	58	16
85 and over	50	9	41	11	1	10	-	-	-	-	-	-	50	16

123

Table 3 Type of establishment, migrants and long-term illness – **continued**

Great Britain, England & Wales, England, regions, metropolitan counties, Inner London, Outer London, regional remainders, Wales, Scotland

Persons present in communal establishments

Type of establishment and age	PERSONS PRESENT			Visitors/guests			Residents - non-staff			Residents - staff			With limiting long-term illness	Migrants
	TOTAL	Males	Females	Total	Males	Females	Total	Males	Females	Total	Males	Females		
a	b	c	d	e	f	g	h	i	j	k	l	m	n	o

NORTH REGION – *continued*

Local authority homes

All ages	**9,034**	**3,038**	**5,996**	**970**	**504**	**466**	**8,024**	**2,518**	**5,506**	**40**	**16**	**24**	**8,164**	**1,832**
0 - 15	391	312	79	341	283	58	46	26	20	4	3	1	68	5
16 - 17	71	48	23	29	22	7	42	26	16	-	-	-	21	19
18 - 29	361	195	166	82	39	43	271	153	118	8	3	5	288	57
30 - 44	416	251	165	65	28	37	342	220	122	9	3	6	348	50
45 - 59	411	209	202	77	17	60	321	188	133	13	4	9	329	51
60 - 64	223	105	118	18	7	11	202	96	106	3	2	1	204	42
65 - 74	1,153	527	626	62	27	35	1,089	499	590	2	1	1	1,111	269
75 - 84	2,980	860	2,120	161	50	111	2,818	810	2,008	1	-	1	2,865	754
85 and over	3,028	531	2,497	135	31	104	2,893	500	2,393	-	-	-	2,930	585

Housing association homes and hostels

All ages	**955**	**391**	**564**	**52**	**39**	**13**	**871**	**338**	**533**	**32**	**14**	**18**	**636**	**332**
0 - 15	30	19	11	2	2	-	23	14	9	5	3	2	2	13
16 - 17	22	12	10	2	1	1	19	11	8	1	-	1	5	14
18 - 29	117	92	25	20	17	3	91	71	20	6	4	2	46	72
30 - 44	64	49	15	13	12	1	46	35	11	5	2	3	30	29
45 - 59	59	39	20	9	4	5	37	30	7	13	5	8	31	15
60 - 64	31	14	17	4	3	1	25	11	14	2	-	2	25	7
65 - 74	110	64	46	1	-	1	109	64	45	-	-	-	80	31
75 - 84	277	69	208	-	-	-	277	69	208	-	-	-	224	87
85 and over	245	33	212	1	-	1	244	33	211	-	-	-	193	64

Table 3 Type of establishment, migrants and long-term illness – **continued**

Great Britain, England & Wales, England, regions, metropolitan counties, Inner London, Outer London, regional remainders, Wales, Scotland

Persons present in communal establishments

Type of establishment and age	PERSONS PRESENT			Visitors/guests			Residents - non-staff			Residents - staff			With limiting long-term illness	Migrants
	TOTAL	Males	Females	Total	Males	Females	Total	Males	Females	Total	Males	Females		
a	b	c	d	e	f	g	h	i	j	k	l	m	n	o

NORTH REGION – *continued*

Nursing homes (non-NHS/LA/HA)														
All ages	**7,347**	**1,949**	**5,398**	**302**	**122**	**180**	**6,961**	**1,796**	**5,165**	**84**	**31**	**53**	**6,946**	**2,859**
0 - 15	44	21	23	19	13	6	15	4	11	10	4	6	1	1
16 - 17	6	3	3	-	-	-	6	3	3	-	-	-	-	5
18 - 29	82	34	48	31	9	22	39	21	18	12	4	8	37	19
30 - 44	92	48	44	37	20	17	36	20	16	19	8	11	41	15
45 - 59	114	43	71	21	7	14	56	24	32	37	12	25	65	20
60 - 64	222	114	108	14	7	7	206	105	101	2	2	-	212	87
65 - 74	1,031	409	622	44	24	20	986	384	602	1	1	-	999	440
75 - 84	3,042	777	2,265	83	25	58	2,957	752	2,205	2	-	2	2,956	1,275
85 and over	2,714	500	2,214	53	17	36	2,660	483	2,177	1	-	1	2,635	997
Residential homes (non-NHS/LA/HA)														
All ages	**9,061**	**2,406**	**6,655**	**463**	**196**	**267**	**8,351**	**2,115**	**6,236**	**247**	**95**	**152**	**8,209**	**2,296**
0 - 15	82	61	21	51	48	3	7	6	1	24	7	17	50	10
16 - 17	43	27	16	35	22	13	3	2	1	5	3	2	26	2
18 - 29	348	183	165	130	65	65	151	94	57	67	24	43	202	84
30 - 44	385	214	171	62	17	45	286	181	105	37	16	21	293	76
45 - 59	418	212	206	41	12	29	297	166	131	80	34	46	320	72
60 - 64	261	136	125	4	1	3	244	127	117	13	8	5	239	64
65 - 74	972	378	594	24	6	18	934	369	565	14	3	11	912	253
75 - 84	3,049	715	2,334	64	15	49	2,981	700	2,281	4	-	4	2,877	847
85 and over	3,503	480	3,023	52	10	42	3,448	470	2,978	3	-	3	3,290	888

Table 3 Type of establishment, migrants and long-term illness – **continued**

Great Britain, England & Wales, England, regions, metropolitan counties, Inner London, Outer London, regional remainders, Wales, Scotland

Persons present in communal establishments

NORTH REGION – *continued*

Type of establishment and age	PERSONS PRESENT			Visitors/guests			Residents - non-staff			Residents - staff			With limiting long-term illness	Migrants
	TOTAL	Males	Females	Total	Males	Females	Total	Males	Females	Total	Males	Females		
a	b	c	d	e	f	g	h	i	j	k	l	m	n	o
Children's homes														
All ages	**944**	**563**	**381**	**242**	**155**	**87**	**654**	**385**	**269**	**48**	**23**	**25**	**80**	**349**
0 - 15	845	519	326	188	134	54	654	385	269	3	-	3	69	345
16 - 17	3	2	1	-	-	-	-	-	-	3	2	1	-	-
18 - 29	37	17	20	17	6	11	-	-	-	20	11	9	5	1
30 - 44	40	20	20	30	15	15	-	-	-	10	5	5	2	2
45 - 59	15	4	11	6	-	6	-	-	-	9	4	5	3	-
60 - 64	3	1	2	-	-	-	-	-	-	3	1	2	1	1
65 - 74	1	-	1	1	-	1	-	-	-	-	-	-	-	-
75 - 84	-	-	-	1	1	-	-	-	-	-	-	-	-	-
85 and over	-	-	-	-	-	-	-	-	-	-	-	-	-	-
Prison service establishments														
All ages	**2,828**	**2,753**	**75**	**2,267**	**2,219**	**48**	**559**	**533**	**26**	**2**	**1**	**1**	**311**	**320**
0 - 15	31	31	-	31	31	-	-	-	-	-	-	-	-	-
16 - 17	163	163	-	151	151	-	12	12	-	-	-	-	11	10
18 - 29	1,834	1,810	24	1,503	1,480	23	331	330	1	-	-	-	157	178
30 - 44	557	529	28	413	397	16	143	132	11	1	-	1	70	85
45 - 59	200	191	9	145	141	4	54	49	5	1	1	-	40	32
60 - 64	13	13	-	9	9	-	4	4	-	-	-	-	8	2
65 - 74	11	8	3	8	6	2	3	2	1	-	-	-	11	2
75 - 84	16	5	11	7	4	3	9	1	8	-	-	-	12	8
85 and over	3	3	-	-	-	-	3	3	-	-	-	-	2	3

Table 3 Type of establishment, migrants and long-term illness – **continued**

Great Britain, England & Wales, England, regions, metropolitan counties, Inner London, Outer London, regional remainders, Wales, Scotland

Persons present in communal establishments

NORTH REGION – *continued*

Type of establishment and age	PERSONS PRESENT			Visitors/guests			Residents - non-staff			Residents - staff			With limiting long-term illness	Migrants
	TOTAL	Males	Females	Total	Males	Females	Total	Males	Females	Total	Males	Females		
a	b	c	d	e	f	g	h	i	j	k	l	m	n	o
Defence establishments														
All ages	633	578	55	39	35	4	594	543	51				12	516
0 - 15	-	-	-	-	-	-	-	-	-				-	-
16 - 17	396	389	7	1	1	-	395	388	7				5	390
18 - 29	170	127	43	13	10	3	157	117	40				3	107
30 - 44	62	57	5	22	21	1	40	36	4				4	19
45 - 59	5	5	-	3	3	-	2	2	-				-	-
60 - 64	-	-	-	-	-	-	-	-	-				-	-
65 - 74	-	-	-	-	-	-	-	-	-				-	-
75 - 84	-	-	-	-	-	-	-	-	-				-	-
85 and over	-	-	-	-	-	-	-	-	-				-	-
Educational establishments														
All ages	12,775	7,221	5,554	11,634	6,491	5,143	892	598	294	249	132	117	292	666
0 - 15	1,642	998	644	1,609	981	628	12	9	3	21	8	13	36	15
16 - 17	1,015	566	449	1,002	557	445	10	8	2	3	1	2	24	10
18 - 29	9,576	5,313	4,263	8,765	4,778	3,987	723	490	233	88	45	43	178	538
30 - 44	370	256	114	186	135	51	107	74	33	77	47	30	29	84
45 - 59	120	64	56	55	30	25	17	10	7	48	24	24	15	16
60 - 64	22	12	10	5	4	1	8	2	6	9	6	3	1	3
65 - 74	16	5	11	7	3	4	7	1	6	2	1	1	4	-
75 - 84	9	6	3	5	3	2	4	3	1	-	-	-	2	-
85 and over	5	1	4	-	-	-	4	1	3	1	-	1	3	-

Table 3 Type of establishment, migrants and long-term illness – **continued**

Great Britain, England & Wales, England, regions, metropolitan counties, Inner London, Outer London, regional remainders, Wales, Scotland

Persons present in communal establishments

NORTH REGION – continued

Type of establishment and age	PERSONS PRESENT			Visitors/guests			Residents - non-staff			Residents - staff			With limiting long-term illness	Migrants
	TOTAL	Males	Females	Total	Males	Females	Total	Males	Females	Total	Males	Females		
a	b	c	d	e	f	g	h	i	j	k	l	m	n	o
Hotels, boarding houses etc														
All ages	**14,053**	**8,245**	**5,808**	**9,209**	**5,260**	**3,949**	**1,811**	**1,362**	**449**	**3,033**	**1,623**	**1,410**	**1,393**	**1,747**
0 - 15	1,131	597	534	715	381	334	104	57	47	312	159	153	41	65
16 - 17	395	209	186	241	131	110	57	31	26	97	47	50	14	91
18 - 29	3,800	2,243	1,557	1,930	1,151	779	609	426	183	1,261	666	595	178	1,059
30 - 44	3,136	2,163	973	2,051	1,434	617	437	361	76	648	368	280	231	341
45 - 59	2,834	1,709	1,125	1,896	1,107	789	342	279	63	596	323	273	314	152
60 - 64	899	459	440	746	350	396	90	73	17	63	36	27	175	15
65 - 74	1,298	650	648	1,137	524	613	127	110	17	34	16	18	273	17
75 - 84	495	191	304	448	165	283	29	18	11	18	8	10	142	4
85 and over	65	24	41	45	17	28	16	7	9	4	-	4	25	3
Hostels and common lodging houses (non-HA)														
All ages	**689**	**524**	**165**	**55**	**36**	**19**	**594**	**462**	**132**	**40**	**26**	**14**	**265**	**330**
0 - 15	76	40	36	15	9	6	60	31	29	1	-	1	3	44
16 - 17	19	11	8	-	-	-	17	9	8	2	2	-	2	18
18 - 29	127	67	60	17	10	7	95	49	46	15	8	7	23	94
30 - 44	127	103	24	12	9	3	108	88	20	7	6	1	55	74
45 - 59	168	154	14	6	5	1	150	140	10	12	9	3	91	71
60 - 64	62	56	6	2	2	-	57	53	4	3	1	2	34	17
65 - 74	83	76	7	2	-	2	81	76	5	-	-	-	42	11
75 - 84	21	15	6	1	1	-	20	14	6	-	-	-	12	1
85 and over	6	2	4	-	-	-	6	2	4	-	-	-	3	-

Table 3 Type of establishment, migrants and long-term illness – **continued**

Great Britain, England & Wales, England, regions, metropolitan counties, Inner London, Outer London, regional remainders, Wales, Scotland

Persons present in communal establishments

Type of establishment and age	PERSONS PRESENT			Visitors/guests			Residents - non-staff			Residents - staff			With limiting long-term illness	Migrants
	TOTAL	Males	Females	Total	Males	Females	Total	Males	Females	Total	Males	Females		
a	b	c	d	e	f	g	h	i	j	k	l	m	n	o

NORTH REGION – continued

Other miscellaneous establishments

All ages	**1,323**	**759**	**564**	**573**	**430**	**143**	**616**	**263**	**353**	**134**	**66**	**68**	**135**	**311**
0 - 15	92	46	46	28	16	12	61	30	31	3	-	3	7	47
16 - 17	71	37	34	67	35	32	3	2	1	1	-	1	2	4
18 - 29	529	362	167	271	207	64	191	118	73	67	37	30	17	170
30 - 44	238	162	76	105	93	12	111	58	53	22	11	11	16	53
45 - 59	178	97	81	67	55	12	86	31	55	25	11	14	19	20
60 - 64	58	26	32	19	14	5	33	9	24	6	3	3	12	2
65 - 74	69	16	53	9	5	4	55	8	47	5	3	2	21	5
75 - 84	68	12	56	5	4	1	58	7	51	5	1	4	27	10
85 and over	20	1	19	2	1	1	18	-	18	-	-	-	14	-

Persons sleeping rough

All ages	**43**	**36**	**7**	**12**	**11**	**1**	**31**	**25**	**6**				**10**	**30**
0 - 15	-	-	-	-	-	-	-	-	-				-	-
16 - 17	3	1	2	-	-	-	3	1	2				-	3
18 - 29	16	14	2	7	7	-	9	7	2				1	8
30 - 44	11	8	3	3	2	1	8	6	2				3	8
45 - 59	12	12	-	2	2	-	10	10	-				5	10
60 - 64	-	-	-	-	-	-	-	-	-				-	-
65 - 74	1	1	-	-	-	-	1	1	-				1	1
75 - 84	-	-	-	-	-	-	-	-	-				-	-
85 and over	-	-	-	-	-	-	-	-	-				-	-

Table 3 Type of establishment, migrants and long-term illness – **continued**

Great Britain, England & Wales, England, regions, metropolitan counties, Inner London, Outer London, regional remainders, Wales, Scotland

Persons present in communal establishments

NORTH REGION – *continued*

Type of establishment and age	PERSONS PRESENT			Visitors/guests			Residents - non-staff			Residents - staff			With limiting long-term illness	Migrants
	TOTAL	Males	Females	Total	Males	Females	Total	Males	Females	Total	Males	Females		
a	b	c	d	e	f	g	h	i	j	k	l	m	n	o
Campers														
All ages	**18**	**8**	**10**	**18**	**8**	**10**	**-**	**-**	**-**				**4**	**-**
0 - 15	1	-	1	1	-	1	-	-	-				-	-
16 - 17	-	-	-	-	-	-	-	-	-				-	-
18 - 29	3	2	1	3	2	1	-	-	-				-	-
30 - 44	2	1	1	2	1	1	-	-	-				-	-
45 - 59	6	2	4	6	2	4	-	-	-				2	-
60 - 64	3	1	2	3	1	2	-	-	-				-	-
65 - 74	3	2	1	3	2	1	-	-	-				2	-
75 - 84	-	-	-	-	-	-	-	-	-				-	-
85 and over	-	-	-	-	-	-	-	-	-				-	-
Civilian ships, boats and barges														
All ages	**623**	**603**	**20**	**574**	**561**	**13**	**49**	**42**	**7**				**8**	**13**
0 - 15	1	1	-	-	-	-	1	1	-				-	-
16 - 17	2	1	1	-	-	-	2	1	1				-	2
18 - 29	161	156	5	151	148	3	10	8	1				1	4
30 - 44	288	278	10	264	257	7	24	21	3				3	4
45 - 59	155	152	3	145	143	2	10	9	1				3	3
60 - 64	13	13	-	11	11	-	2	2	-				1	-
65 - 74	2	1	1	2	1	1	-	-	-				-	-
75 - 84	-	-	-	-	-	-	-	-	-				-	-
85 and over	1	1	-	1	1	-	-	-	-				-	-

Table 3 Type of establishment, migrants and long-term illness – continued

Great Britain, England & Wales, England, regions, metropolitan counties, Inner London, Outer London, regional remainders, Wales, Scotland

Persons present in communal establishments

Type of establishment and age	PERSONS PRESENT			Visitors/guests			Residents - non-staff			Residents - staff			With limiting long-term illness	Migrants
	TOTAL	Males	Females	Total	Males	Females	Total	Males	Females	Total	Males	Females		
a	b	c	d	e	f	g	h	i	j	k	l	m	n	o

Tyne & Wear Metropolitan County

All establishments

All ages	**22,777**	**9,953**	**12,824**	**10,437**	**5,428**	**5,009**	**11,758**	**4,266**	**7,492**	**582**	**259**	**323**	**12,875**	**4,014**
0 - 15	915	511	404	523	293	230	352	200	152	40	18	22	145	162
16 - 17	376	172	204	311	136	175	58	31	27	7	5	2	28	39
18 - 29	6,156	3,333	2,823	4,842	2,595	2,247	1,045	645	400	269	93	176	482	769
30 - 44	1,876	1,246	630	1,108	716	392	643	451	192	125	79	46	638	281
45 - 59	1,583	1,003	580	879	521	358	602	433	169	102	49	53	823	177
60 - 64	750	405	345	362	185	177	371	211	160	17	9	8	553	99
65 - 74	2,498	1,242	1,256	949	487	462	1,539	754	785	10	1	9	2,120	410
75 - 84	4,583	1,388	3,195	989	394	595	3,585	989	2,596	9	5	4	4,236	1,123
85 and over	4,040	653	3,387	474	101	373	3,563	552	3,011	3	-	3	3,850	954

NHS hospitals/homes - psychiatric

All ages	**806**	**336**	**470**	**259**	**108**	**151**	**534**	**224**	**310**	**13**	**4**	**9**	**724**	**68**
0 - 15	15	5	10	14	4	10	1	1	-	-	-	-	1	1
16 - 17	4	3	1	4	3	1	-	-	-	-	-	-	1	-
18 - 29	86	47	39	44	24	20	30	19	11	12	4	8	44	15
30 - 44	107	64	43	48	27	21	58	37	21	1	-	1	93	12
45 - 59	88	40	48	24	6	18	64	34	30	-	-	-	84	4
60 - 64	55	23	32	18	7	11	37	16	21	-	-	-	54	2
65 - 74	163	71	92	44	17	27	119	54	65	-	-	-	161	7
75 - 84	189	70	119	43	17	26	146	53	93	-	-	-	187	18
85 and over	99	13	86	20	3	17	79	10	69	-	-	-	99	9

Table 3 Type of establishment, migrants and long-term illness – **continued**

Great Britain, England & Wales, England, regions, metropolitan counties, Inner London, Outer London, regional remainders, Wales, Scotland

Persons present in communal establishments

Type of establishment and age	PERSONS PRESENT			Visitors/guests			Residents - non-staff			Residents - staff			With limiting long-term illness	Migrants
	TOTAL	Males	Females	Total	Males	Females	Total	Males	Females	Total	Males	Females		
a	b	c	d	e	f	g	h	i	j	k	l	m	n	o
Tyne & Wear Metropolitan County – *continued*														
NHS hospitals/homes - other														
All ages	**4,915**	**1,998**	**2,917**	**3,836**	**1,629**	**2,207**	**881**	**304**	**577**	**198**	**65**	**133**	**3,188**	**392**
0 - 15	378	217	161	356	202	154	22	15	7	-	-	-	75	1
16 - 17	41	12	29	40	12	28	-	-	-	-	-	-	8	1
18 - 29	809	171	638	508	105	403	144	34	110	157	32	125	93	163
30 - 44	445	203	242	365	153	212	44	21	23	36	29	7	181	37
45 - 59	475	252	223	436	222	214	36	27	9	3	3	-	345	8
60 - 64	264	142	122	236	128	108	28	14	14	-	-	-	222	6
65 - 74	854	465	389	734	401	333	120	64	56	-	-	-	741	33
75 - 84	1,059	426	633	792	327	465	266	98	168	1	1	-	957	88
85 and over	590	110	480	369	79	290	221	31	190	-	-	-	566	55
Non-NHS hospitals - psychiatric														
All ages	-	-	-	-	-	-	-	-	-	-	-	-	-	-
0 - 15	-	-	-	-	-	-	-	-	-	-	-	-	-	-
16 - 17	-	-	-	-	-	-	-	-	-	-	-	-	-	-
18 - 29	-	-	-	-	-	-	-	-	-	-	-	-	-	-
30 - 44	-	-	-	-	-	-	-	-	-	-	-	-	-	-
45 - 59	-	-	-	-	-	-	-	-	-	-	-	-	-	-
60 - 64	-	-	-	-	-	-	-	-	-	-	-	-	-	-
65 - 74	-	-	-	-	-	-	-	-	-	-	-	-	-	-
75 - 84	-	-	-	-	-	-	-	-	-	-	-	-	-	-
85 and over	-	-	-	-	-	-	-	-	-	-	-	-	-	-

Table 3 Type of establishment, migrants and long-term illness – continued

Persons present in communal establishments

Type of establishment and age	PERSONS PRESENT			Visitors/guests			Residents - non-staff			Residents - staff			With limiting long-term illness	Migrants
	TOTAL	Males	Females	Total	Males	Females	Total	Males	Females	Total	Males	Females		
a	b	c	d	e	f	g	h	i	j	k	l	m	n	o

Tyne & Wear Metropolitan County – *continued*

Non-NHS hospitals - other

All ages	**67**	**21**	**46**	**32**	**12**	**20**	**35**	**9**	**26**	**-**	**-**	**-**	**46**	**24**
0 - 15	-	-	-	-	-	-	-	-	-	-	-	-	-	-
16 - 17	-	-	-	-	-	-	-	-	-	-	-	-	-	-
18 - 29	2	2	-	2	2	-	-	-	-	-	-	-	-	-
30 - 44	11	4	7	10	3	7	1	1	-	-	-	-	2	1
45 - 59	13	3	10	12	2	10	1	1	-	-	-	-	6	1
60 - 64	3	2	1	3	2	1	-	-	-	-	-	-	1	-
65 - 74	9	6	3	3	2	1	6	4	2	-	-	-	9	5
75 - 84	9	1	8	2	1	1	7	-	7	-	-	-	8	2
85 and over	20	3	17	-	-	-	20	3	17	-	-	-	20	15

Local authority homes

All ages	**3,471**	**1,128**	**2,343**	**253**	**95**	**158**	**3,212**	**1,031**	**2,181**	**6**	**2**	**4**	**3,224**	**713**
0 - 15	56	32	24	30	15	15	25	16	9	1	1	-	41	1
16 - 17	29	18	11	3	3	-	26	15	11	-	-	-	14	11
18 - 29	156	85	71	34	18	16	122	67	55	-	-	-	131	24
30 - 44	156	87	69	31	12	19	121	74	47	4	1	3	123	25
45 - 59	149	86	63	27	8	19	121	78	43	1	-	1	127	29
60 - 64	101	51	50	5	2	3	96	49	47	-	-	-	94	22
65 - 74	497	226	271	24	12	12	473	214	259	-	-	-	475	112
75 - 84	1,129	327	802	49	16	33	1,080	311	769	-	-	-	1,068	275
85 and over	1,198	216	982	50	9	41	1,148	207	941	-	-	-	1,151	214

Table 3 Type of establishment, migrants and long-term illness – **continued**

Persons present in communal establishments

Type of establishment and age	PERSONS PRESENT			Visitors/guests			Residents - non-staff			Residents - staff			With limiting long-term illness	Migrants
	TOTAL	Males	Females	Total	Males	Females	Total	Males	Females	Total	Males	Females		
a	b	c	d	e	f	g	h	i	j	k	l	m	n	o

Tyne & Wear Metropolitan County – *continued*

Housing association homes and hostels

All ages	**321**	**126**	**195**	**22**	**17**	**5**	**287**	**105**	**182**	**12**	**4**	**8**	**209**	**99**
0 - 15	-	-	-	-	-	-	-	-	-	-	-	-	-	-
16 - 17	-	-	-	-	-	-	-	-	-	-	-	-	-	-
18 - 29	41	36	5	14	12	2	25	23	2	2	1	1	24	21
30 - 44	14	11	3	3	3	-	9	7	2	2	1	1	7	9
45 - 59	16	8	8	4	2	2	5	4	1	7	2	5	6	3
60 - 64	9	3	6	-	-	-	8	3	5	1	-	1	8	3
65 - 74	42	26	16	1	-	1	41	26	15	-	-	-	24	12
75 - 84	111	28	83	-	-	-	111	28	83	-	-	-	82	27
85 and over	88	14	74	-	-	-	88	14	74	-	-	-	58	24

Nursing homes (non-NHS/LA/HA)

All ages	**1,920**	**519**	**1,401**	**82**	**47**	**35**	**1,834**	**470**	**1,364**	**4**	**2**	**2**	**1,855**	**857**
0 - 15	-	-	-	-	-	-	-	-	-	-	-	-	-	-
16 - 17	-	-	-	-	-	-	-	-	-	-	-	-	-	-
18 - 29	26	14	12	10	8	2	16	6	10	-	-	-	17	6
30 - 44	32	25	7	22	19	3	9	5	4	1	-	1	12	6
45 - 59	14	9	5	6	5	1	5	3	2	3	1	2	7	4
60 - 64	50	21	29	5	2	3	45	19	26	-	-	-	48	22
65 - 74	300	117	183	6	4	2	294	113	181	-	-	-	294	132
75 - 84	817	217	600	19	5	14	798	212	586	-	-	-	802	387
85 and over	681	116	565	14	4	10	667	112	555	-	-	-	675	300

Table 3 Type of establishment, migrants and long-term illness – continued

Great Britain, England & Wales, England, regions, metropolitan counties, Inner London, Outer London, regional remainders, Wales, Scotland

Persons present in communal establishments

Type of establishment and age	PERSONS PRESENT			Visitors/guests			Residents - non-staff			Residents - staff			With limiting long-term illness	Migrants
	TOTAL	Males	Females	Total	Males	Females	Total	Males	Females	Total	Males	Females		
a	b	c	d	e	f	g	h	i	j	k	l	m	n	o

Tyne & Wear Metropolitan County – continued

a	b	c	d	e	f	g	h	i	j	k	l	m	n	o
Residential homes (non-NHS/LA/HA)														
All ages	**3,223**	**808**	**2,415**	**71**	**6**	**65**	**3,105**	**785**	**2,320**	**47**	**17**	**30**	**2,990**	**810**
0 - 15	1	-	1	1	-	1	-	-	-	-	-	-	-	-
16 - 17	1	1	-	-	-	-	-	-	-	1	1	-	-	-
18 - 29	40	16	24	9	-	9	25	12	13	6	4	2	27	5
30 - 44	105	57	48	13	-	13	89	57	32	3	-	3	91	12
45 - 59	123	71	52	10	2	8	93	60	33	20	9	11	97	18
60 - 64	85	53	32	-	-	-	82	51	31	3	2	1	78	26
65 - 74	369	164	205	4	-	4	357	163	194	8	1	7	340	91
75 - 84	1,160	274	886	19	3	16	1,138	271	867	3	-	3	1,090	321
85 and over	1,339	172	1,167	15	1	14	1,321	171	1,150	3	-	3	1,267	337
Children's homes														
All ages	**322**	**175**	**147**	**84**	**45**	**39**	**228**	**127**	**101**	**10**	**3**	**7**	**13**	**121**
0 - 15	297	167	130	67	40	27	228	127	101	2	-	2	13	120
16 - 17	1	1	-	-	-	-	-	-	-	1	1	-	-	-
18 - 29	5	-	5	3	-	3	-	-	-	2	-	2	-	-
30 - 44	17	6	11	14	5	9	-	-	-	3	1	2	-	-
45 - 59	1	1	-	-	-	-	-	-	-	1	1	-	-	-
60 - 64	1	-	1	-	-	-	-	-	-	1	-	1	-	1
65 - 74	-	-	-	-	-	-	-	-	-	-	-	-	-	-
75 - 84	-	-	-	-	-	-	-	-	-	-	-	-	-	-
85 and over	-	-	-	-	-	-	-	-	-	-	-	-	-	-

Table 3 Type of establishment, migrants and long-term illness – **continued**

Great Britain, England & Wales, England, regions, metropolitan counties, Inner London, Outer London, regional remainders, Wales, Scotland

Persons present in communal establishments

Type of establishment and age	PERSONS PRESENT			Visitors/guests			Residents - non-staff			Residents - staff			With limiting long-term illness	Migrants
	TOTAL	Males	Females	Total	Males	Females	Total	Males	Females	Total	Males	Females		
a	b	c	d	e	f	g	h	i	j	k	l	m	n	o

Tyne & Wear Metropolitan County – *continued*

Prison service establishments

All ages

All ages	-	-	-	-	-	-	-	-	-	-	-	-	-	-
0 - 15	-	-	-	-	-	-	-	-	-	-	-	-	-	-
16 - 17	-	-	-	-	-	-	-	-	-	-	-	-	-	-
18 - 29	-	-	-	-	-	-	-	-	-	-	-	-	-	-
30 - 44	-	-	-	-	-	-	-	-	-	-	-	-	-	-
45 - 59	-	-	-	-	-	-	-	-	-	-	-	-	-	-
60 - 64	-	-	-	-	-	-	-	-	-	-	-	-	-	-
65 - 74	-	-	-	-	-	-	-	-	-	-	-	-	-	-
75 - 84	-	-	-	-	-	-	-	-	-	-	-	-	-	-
85 and over	-	-	-	-	-	-	-	-	-	-	-	-	-	-

Defence establishments

All ages

All ages	-	-	-	-	-	-	-	-	-	-	-	-	-	-
0 - 15	-	-	-	-	-	-	-	-	-	-	-	-	-	-
16 - 17	-	-	-	-	-	-	-	-	-	-	-	-	-	-
18 - 29	-	-	-	-	-	-	-	-	-	-	-	-	-	-
30 - 44	-	-	-	-	-	-	-	-	-	-	-	-	-	-
45 - 59	-	-	-	-	-	-	-	-	-	-	-	-	-	-
60 - 64	-	-	-	-	-	-	-	-	-	-	-	-	-	-
65 - 74	-	-	-	-	-	-	-	-	-	-	-	-	-	-
75 - 84	-	-	-	-	-	-	-	-	-	-	-	-	-	-
85 and over	-	-	-	-	-	-	-	-	-	-	-	-	-	-

Table 3 Type of establishment, migrants and long-term illness – **continued**

Great Britain, England & Wales, England, regions, metropolitan counties, Inner London, Outer London, regional remainders, Wales, Scotland

Persons present in communal establishments

Type of establishment and age	PERSONS PRESENT			Visitors/guests			Residents - non-staff			Residents - staff			With limiting long-term illness	Migrants
	TOTAL	Males	Females	Total	Males	Females	Total	Males	Females	Total	Males	Females		
a	b	c	d	e	f	g	h	i	j	k	l	m	n	o

Tyne & Wear Metropolitan County – *continued*

Educational establishments

	b	c	d	e	f	g	h	i	j	k	l	m	n	o
All ages	**4,574**	**2,622**	**1,952**	**4,131**	**2,307**	**1,824**	**413**	**297**	**116**	**30**	**18**	**12**	**79**	**309**
0 - 15	12	7	5	9	5	4	1	1	-	2	1	1	4	1
16 - 17	255	114	141	250	110	140	5	4	1	-	-	-	3	5
18 - 29	4,178	2,403	1,775	3,796	2,129	1,667	372	267	105	10	7	3	70	280
30 - 44	110	87	23	67	58	9	31	22	9	12	7	5	1	20
45 - 59	13	8	5	7	5	2	3	2	1	3	1	2	-	3
60 - 64	4	2	2	1	-	1	1	-	-	3	2	1	-	-
65 - 74	1	1	-	1	-	1	1	1	-	-	-	-	1	-
75 - 84	1	-	1	1	-	1	-	-	-	-	-	-	-	-
85 and over	-	-	-	-	-	-	-	-	-	-	-	-	-	-

Hotels, boarding houses etc

	b	c	d	e	f	g	h	i	j	k	l	m	n	o
All ages	**2,362**	**1,651**	**711**	**1,434**	**955**	**479**	**724**	**585**	**139**	**204**	**111**	**93**	**338**	**381**
0 - 15	92	50	42	28	18	10	29	16	13	35	16	19	6	9
16 - 17	33	15	18	10	4	6	19	8	11	4	3	1	2	14
18 - 29	625	437	188	338	228	110	237	180	57	50	29	21	57	176
30 - 44	708	563	145	459	362	97	193	168	25	56	33	23	89	102
45 - 59	505	375	130	308	224	84	148	127	21	49	24	25	89	62
60 - 64	125	68	57	90	40	50	29	25	4	6	3	3	30	7
65 - 74	191	105	86	133	51	82	57	54	3	1	-	1	44	10
75 - 84	75	32	43	63	24	39	9	5	4	3	3	-	19	1
85 and over	8	6	2	5	4	1	3	2	1	-	-	-	2	-

Table 3 Type of establishment, migrants and long-term illness – **continued**

Great Britain, England & Wales, England, regions, metropolitan counties, Inner London, Outer London, regional remainders, Wales, Scotland

Persons present in communal establishments

Type of establishment and age	PERSONS PRESENT			Visitors/guests			Residents - non-staff			Residents - staff			With limiting long-term illness	Migrants
	TOTAL	Males	Females	Total	Males	Females	Total	Males	Females	Total	Males	Females		
a	b	c	d	e	f	g	h	i	j	k	l	m	n	o

Tyne & Wear Metropolitan County – *continued*

Hostels and common lodging houses (non-HA)

All ages	**410**	**310**	**100**	**23**	**12**	**11**	**369**	**283**	**86**	**18**	**15**	**3**	**161**	**185**
0 - 15	43	20	23	10	4	6	33	16	17	-	-	-	3	21
16 - 17	7	4	3	-	-	-	7	4	3	-	-	-	-	7
18 - 29	65	31	34	4	1	3	58	28	30	3	2	1	14	56
30 - 44	80	61	19	6	4	2	69	52	17	5	5	-	34	46
45 - 59	104	93	11	3	3	-	92	83	9	9	7	2	56	39
60 - 64	34	32	2	-	-	-	33	31	2	1	1	-	15	9
65 - 74	60	58	2	-	-	-	60	58	2	-	-	-	29	7
75 - 84	11	9	2	-	-	-	11	9	2	-	-	-	7	-
85 and over	6	2	4	-	-	-	6	2	4	-	-	-	3	-

Other miscellaneous establishments

All ages	**223**	**101**	**122**	**70**	**57**	**13**	**113**	**26**	**87**	**40**	**18**	**22**	**39**	**43**
0 - 15	20	12	8	8	5	3	12	7	5	-	-	-	2	8
16 - 17	4	4	-	4	4	-	-	-	-	-	-	-	-	-
18 - 29	75	46	29	37	27	10	11	5	6	27	14	13	4	19
30 - 44	30	17	13	15	15	-	13	1	12	2	1	1	2	9
45 - 59	35	11	24	5	5	-	24	5	19	6	1	5	1	1
60 - 64	15	4	11	-	-	-	13	3	10	2	1	1	3	1
65 - 74	12	3	9	-	-	-	11	3	8	1	1	-	2	1
75 - 84	22	4	18	1	1	-	19	2	17	2	1	1	16	4
85 and over	10	-	10	-	-	-	10	-	10	-	-	-	9	-

Table 3 Type of establishment, migrants and long-term illness – **continued**

Great Britain, England & Wales, England, regions, metropolitan counties, Inner London, Outer London, regional remainders, Wales, Scotland

Persons present in communal establishments

Type of establishment and age	PERSONS PRESENT			Visitors/guests			Residents - non-staff			Residents - staff			With limiting long-term illness	Migrants
	TOTAL	Males	Females	Total	Males	Females	Total	Males	Females	Total	Males	Females		
a	b	c	d	e	f	g	h	i	j	k	l	m	n	o

Tyne & Wear Metropolitan County – *continued*

Persons sleeping rough

All ages	**12**	**12**	**-**	**5**	**5**	**-**	**7**	**7**	**-**				**6**	**7**
0 - 15	-	-	-	-	-	-	-	-	-				-	-
16 - 17	-	-	-	-	-	-	-	-	-				-	-
18 - 29	6	6	-	4	4	-	2	2	-				1	2
30 - 44	2	2	-	1	1	-	1	1	-				2	1
45 - 59	4	4	-	-	-	-	4	4	-				3	4
60 - 64	-	-	-	-	-	-	-	-	-				-	-
65 - 74	-	-	-	-	-	-	-	-	-				-	-
75 - 84	-	-	-	-	-	-	-	-	-				-	-
85 and over	-	-	-	-	-	-	-	-	-				-	-

Campers

All ages	**-**	**-**	**-**	**-**	**-**	**-**	**-**	**-**	**-**				**-**	**-**
0 - 15	-	-	-	-	-	-	-	-	-				-	-
16 - 17	-	-	-	-	-	-	-	-	-				-	-
18 - 29	-	-	-	-	-	-	-	-	-				-	-
30 - 44	-	-	-	-	-	-	-	-	-				-	-
45 - 59	-	-	-	-	-	-	-	-	-				-	-
60 - 64	-	-	-	-	-	-	-	-	-				-	-
65 - 74	-	-	-	-	-	-	-	-	-				-	-
75 - 84	-	-	-	-	-	-	-	-	-				-	-
85 and over	-	-	-	-	-	-	-	-	-				-	-

Table 3 Type of establishment, migrants and long-term illness – **continued**

Great Britain, England & Wales, England, regions, metropolitan counties, Inner London, Outer London, regional remainders, Wales, Scotland

Persons present in communal establishments

Type of establishment and age	PERSONS PRESENT			Visitors/guests			Residents - non-staff			Residents - staff			With limiting long-term illness	Migrants
	TOTAL	Males	Females	Total	Males	Females	Total	Males	Females	Total	Males	Females		
a	b	c	d	e	f	g	h	i	j	k	l	m	n	o

Tyne & Wear Metropolitan County – *continued*

Civilian ships, boats and barges

Type of establishment and age														
All ages	**151**	**146**	**5**	**135**	**133**	**2**	**16**	**13**	**3**				**3**	**5**
0 - 15	1	1	-	-	-	-	1	1	-				-	-
16 - 17	1	-	1	-	-	-	1	-	1				-	1
18 - 29	42	39	3	39	37	2	3	2	1				-	2
30 - 44	59	59	-	54	54	-	5	5	-				1	1
45 - 59	43	42	1	37	37	-	6	5	1				2	1
60 - 64	4	4	-	4	4	-	-	-	-				-	-
65 - 74	-	-	-	-	-	-	-	-	-				-	-
75 - 84	-	-	-	-	-	-	-	-	-				-	-
85 and over	1	1	-	1	1	-	-	-	-				-	-

Remainder of North Region

All establishments

Type of establishment and age														
All ages	**54,136**	**26,050**	**28,086**	**26,112**	**14,763**	**11,349**	**24,003**	**9,240**	**14,763**	**4,021**	**2,047**	**1,974**	**25,480**	**8,869**
0 - 15	4,323	2,636	1,687	3,312	2,084	1,228	665	384	281	346	168	178	265	386
16 - 17	1,929	1,331	598	1,308	816	492	513	465	48	108	50	58	102	532
18 - 29	13,496	8,074	5,422	9,483	5,696	3,787	2,194	1,501	693	1,819	877	942	1,270	2,064
30 - 44	5,937	3,896	2,041	3,230	2,143	1,087	1,877	1,274	603	830	479	351	1,766	716
45 - 59	4,999	2,873	2,126	2,755	1,547	1,208	1,492	933	559	752	393	359	1,888	337
60 - 64	2,027	1,049	978	1,080	523	557	858	475	383	89	51	38	1,182	176
65 - 74	5,094	2,301	2,793	2,222	1,028	1,194	2,824	1,249	1,575	48	24	24	3,809	754
75 - 84	8,833	2,570	6,263	1,930	718	1,212	6,881	1,847	5,034	22	5	17	8,082	2,118
85 and over	7,498	1,320	6,178	792	208	584	6,699	1,112	5,587	7	-	7	7,116	1,786

Great Britain, England & Wales, England, regions, metropolitan counties, Inner London, Outer London, regional remainders, Wales, Scotland

Persons present in communal establishments

Type of establishment and age	PERSONS PRESENT			Visitors/guests			Residents - non-staff			Residents - staff			With limiting long-term illness	Migrants
	TOTAL	Males	Females	Total	Males	Females	Total	Males	Females	Total	Males	Females		
a	b	c	d	e	f	g	h	i	j	k	l	m	n	o
Remainder of North Region – *continued*														
NHS hospitals/homes - psychiatric														
All ages	**1,527**	**732**	**795**	**482**	**211**	**271**	**928**	**467**	**461**	**117**	**54**	**63**	**1,175**	**138**
0 - 15	3	1	2	3	1	2	-	-	-	-	-	-	-	-
16 - 17	3	1	2	1	1	-	-	-	-	2	-	2	-	2
18 - 29	216	109	107	78	42	36	45	27	18	93	40	53	62	65
30 - 44	177	94	83	92	44	48	69	41	28	16	9	7	122	22
45 - 59	207	125	82	68	25	43	134	96	38	5	4	1	166	4
60 - 64	149	85	64	47	14	33	101	70	31	1	1	-	120	6
65 - 74	343	178	165	100	48	52	243	130	113	-	-	-	292	14
75 - 84	311	108	203	73	27	46	238	81	157	-	-	-	296	19
85 and over	118	31	87	20	9	11	98	22	76	-	-	-	117	6
NHS hospitals/homes - other														
All ages	**8,810**	**3,663**	**5,147**	**5,379**	**2,113**	**3,266**	**3,082**	**1,400**	**1,682**	**349**	**150**	**199**	**6,336**	**575**
0 - 15	472	278	194	458	271	187	11	5	6	3	2	1	57	1
16 - 17	48	18	30	46	16	30	2	2	-	-	-	-	11	-
18 - 29	1,340	448	892	739	183	556	335	178	157	266	87	179	402	183
30 - 44	1,231	608	623	539	181	358	625	373	252	67	54	13	831	69
45 - 59	1,042	534	508	585	273	312	446	254	192	11	7	4	817	32
60 - 64	473	239	234	296	145	151	176	94	82	1	-	1	404	18
65 - 74	1,391	650	741	964	443	521	427	207	220	-	-	-	1,190	58
75 - 84	1,774	664	1,110	1,201	462	739	573	202	371	-	-	-	1,637	105
85 and over	1,039	224	815	551	139	412	487	85	402	1	-	-	987	109

Table 3 Type of establishment, migrants and long-term illness – **continued**

Great Britain, England & Wales, England, regions, metropolitan counties, Inner London, Outer London, regional remainders, Wales, Scotland

Persons present in communal establishments

Type of establishment and age	PERSONS PRESENT			Visitors/guests			Residents - non-staff			Residents - staff			With limiting long-term illness	Migrants
	TOTAL	Males	Females	Total	Males	Females	Total	Males	Females	Total	Males	Females		
a	b	c	d	e	f	g	h	i	j	k	l	m	n	o

Remainder of North Region – *continued*

Non-NHS hospitals - psychiatric

All ages	**330**	**141**	**189**	**77**	**34**	**43**	**236**	**101**	**135**	**17**	**6**	**11**	**309**	**64**
0 - 15	-	-	-	-	-	-	-	-	-	-	-	-	-	-
16 - 17	-	-	-	-	-	-	-	-	-	-	-	-	-	-
18 - 29	34	15	19	10	6	4	8	4	4	16	5	11	15	16
30 - 44	48	28	20	13	8	5	35	20	15	-	-	-	47	16
45 - 59	52	24	28	20	7	13	31	16	15	1	1	-	51	3
60 - 64	19	12	7	3	2	1	16	10	6	-	-	-	19	3
65 - 74	59	28	31	14	4	10	45	24	21	-	-	-	59	12
75 - 84	66	24	42	11	6	5	55	18	37	-	-	-	66	9
85 and over	52	10	42	6	1	5	46	9	37	-	-	-	52	5

Non-NHS hospitals - other

All ages	**132**	**38**	**94**	**74**	**17**	**57**	**58**	**21**	**37**	**-**	**-**	**-**	**112**	**21**
0 - 15	4	1	3	4	1	3	-	-	-	-	-	-	-	-
16 - 17	-	-	-	-	-	-	-	-	-	-	-	-	-	-
18 - 29	4	-	4	4	-	4	-	-	-	-	-	-	-	-
30 - 44	6	2	4	6	2	4	-	-	-	-	-	-	3	-
45 - 59	10	5	5	10	5	5	-	-	-	-	-	-	5	-
60 - 64	4	1	3	4	1	3	-	-	-	-	-	-	3	-
65 - 74	23	8	15	12	2	10	11	6	5	-	-	-	21	6
75 - 84	51	15	36	23	5	18	28	10	18	-	-	-	50	14
85 and over	30	6	24	11	1	10	19	5	14	-	-	-	30	1

Table 3 Type of establishment, migrants and long-term illness – **continued**

Great Britain, England & Wales, England, regions, metropolitan counties, Inner London, Outer London, regional remainders, Wales, Scotland

Persons present in communal establishments

Type of establishment and age	PERSONS PRESENT			Visitors/guests			Residents - non-staff			Residents - staff			With limiting long-term illness	Migrants
	TOTAL	Males	Females	Total	Males	Females	Total	Males	Females	Total	Males	Females		
a	b	c	d	e	f	g	h	i	j	k	l	m	n	o

Remainder of North Region – *continued*

Local authority homes

All ages	**5,563**	**1,910**	**3,653**	**717**	**409**	**308**	**4,812**	**1,487**	**3,325**	**34**	**14**	**20**	**4,940**	**1,119**
0 - 15	335	280	55	311	268	43	21	10	11	3	2	1	27	4
16 - 17	42	30	12	26	19	7	16	11	5	-	-	-	7	8
18 - 29	205	110	95	48	21	27	149	86	63	8	3	5	157	33
30 - 44	260	164	96	34	16	18	221	146	75	5	2	3	225	25
45 - 59	262	123	139	50	9	41	200	110	90	12	4	8	202	22
60 - 64	122	54	68	13	5	8	106	47	59	3	2	1	110	20
65 - 74	656	301	355	38	15	23	616	285	331	2	1	1	636	157
75 - 84	1,851	533	1,318	112	34	78	1,738	499	1,239	1	-	1	1,797	479
85 and over	1,830	315	1,515	85	22	63	1,745	293	1,452	-	-	-	1,779	371

Housing association homes and hostels

All ages	**634**	**265**	**369**	**30**	**22**	**8**	**584**	**233**	**351**	**20**	**10**	**10**	**427**	**233**
0 - 15	30	19	11	2	2	-	23	14	9	5	3	2	2	13
16 - 17	22	12	10	2	1	1	19	11	8	1	-	1	5	14
18 - 29	76	56	20	6	5	1	66	48	18	4	3	1	22	51
30 - 44	50	38	12	10	9	1	37	28	9	3	1	2	23	20
45 - 59	43	31	12	5	2	3	32	26	6	6	3	3	25	12
60 - 64	22	11	11	4	3	1	17	8	9	1	1	1	17	4
65 - 74	68	38	30	-	-	-	68	38	30	-	-	-	56	19
75 - 84	166	41	125	-	-	-	166	41	125	-	-	-	142	60
85 and over	157	19	138	1	1	1	156	19	137	-	-	-	135	40

Table 3 Type of establishment, migrants and long-term illness – **continued**

Great Britain, England & Wales, England, regions, metropolitan counties, Inner London, Outer London, regional remainders, Wales, Scotland

Persons present in communal establishments

Type of establishment and age	PERSONS PRESENT			Visitors/guests			Residents - non-staff			Residents - staff			With limiting long-term illness	Migrants
	TOTAL	Males	Females	Total	Males	Females	Total	Males	Females	Total	Males	Females		
a	b	c	d	e	f	g	h	i	j	k	l	m	n	o

Remainder of North Region – *continued*

Type of establishment and age	TOTAL	Males	Females	Total	Males	Females	Total	Males	Females	Total	Males	Females	n	o
Nursing homes (non-NHS/LA/HA)														
All ages	**5,427**	**1,430**	**3,997**	**220**	**75**	**145**	**5,127**	**1,326**	**3,801**	**80**	**29**	**51**	**5,091**	**2,002**
0 - 15	44	21	23	19	13	6	15	4	11	10	4	6	1	1
16 - 17	6	3	3	-	-	-	6	3	3	-	-	-	-	5
18 - 29	56	20	36	21	1	20	23	15	8	12	4	8	20	13
30 - 44	60	23	37	15	1	14	27	15	12	18	7	11	29	9
45 - 59	100	34	66	15	2	13	51	21	30	34	11	23	58	16
60 - 64	172	93	79	9	5	4	161	86	75	2	2	-	164	65
65 - 74	731	292	439	38	20	18	692	271	421	1	1	-	705	308
75 - 84	2,225	560	1,665	64	20	44	2,159	540	1,619	2	-	2	2,154	888
85 and over	2,033	384	1,649	39	13	26	1,993	371	1,622	1	-	1	1,960	697
Residential homes (non-NHS/LA/HA)														
All ages	**5,838**	**1,598**	**4,240**	**392**	**190**	**202**	**5,246**	**1,330**	**3,916**	**200**	**78**	**122**	**5,219**	**1,486**
0 - 15	81	61	20	50	48	2	7	6	1	24	7	17	50	10
16 - 17	42	26	16	35	22	13	3	2	1	4	2	2	26	2
18 - 29	308	167	141	121	65	56	126	82	44	61	20	41	175	79
30 - 44	280	157	123	49	17	32	197	124	73	34	16	18	202	64
45 - 59	295	141	154	31	10	21	204	106	98	60	25	35	223	54
60 - 64	176	83	93	4	1	3	162	76	86	10	6	4	161	38
65 - 74	603	214	389	20	6	14	577	206	371	6	2	4	572	162
75 - 84	1,889	441	1,448	45	12	33	1,843	429	1,414	1	-	1	1,787	526
85 and over	2,164	308	1,856	37	9	28	2,127	299	1,828	-	-	-	2,023	551

Table 3 Type of establishment, migrants and long-term illness – **continued**

Great Britain, England & Wales, England, regions, metropolitan counties, Inner London, Outer London, regional remainders, Wales, Scotland

Persons present in communal establishments

Type of establishment and age	PERSONS PRESENT			Visitors/guests			Residents - non-staff			Residents - staff			With limiting long-term illness	Migrants
	TOTAL	Males	Females	Total	Males	Females	Total	Males	Females	Total	Males	Females		
a	b	c	d	e	f	g	h	i	j	k	l	m	n	o

Remainder of North Region – *continued*

Children's homes

All ages	**622**	**388**	**234**	**158**	**110**	**48**	**426**	**258**	**168**	**38**	**20**	**18**	**67**	**228**
0 - 15	548	352	196	121	94	27	426	258	168	1	-	1	56	225
16 - 17	2	1	1	-	-	-	-	-	-	2	1	1	-	-
18 - 29	32	17	15	14	6	8	-	-	-	18	11	7	5	1
30 - 44	23	14	9	16	10	6	-	-	-	7	4	3	2	2
45 - 59	14	3	11	6	-	6	-	-	-	8	3	5	3	-
60 - 64	2	1	1	-	-	-	-	-	-	2	1	1	1	-
65 - 74	1	-	1	1	-	1	-	-	-	-	-	-	-	-
75 - 84	-	-	-	-	-	-	-	-	-	-	-	-	-	-
85 and over	-	-	-	-	-	-	-	-	-	-	-	-	-	-

Prison service establishments

All ages	**2,828**	**2,753**	**75**	**2,267**	**2,219**	**48**	**559**	**533**	**26**	**2**	**1**	**1**	**311**	**320**
0 - 15	31	31	-	31	31	-	-	-	-	-	-	-	-	-
16 - 17	163	163	-	151	151	-	12	12	-	-	-	-	11	10
18 - 29	1,834	1,810	24	1,503	1,480	23	331	330	1	1	-	1	157	178
30 - 44	557	529	28	413	397	16	143	132	11	1	1	-	70	85
45 - 59	200	191	9	145	141	4	54	49	5	1	1	-	40	32
60 - 64	13	13	-	9	9	-	4	4	-	-	-	-	8	2
65 - 74	11	8	3	8	6	2	3	2	1	-	-	-	11	2
75 - 84	16	5	11	7	4	3	9	1	8	-	-	-	12	8
85 and over	3	3	-	-	-	-	3	3	-	-	-	-	2	3

Table 3 Type of establishment, migrants and long-term illness – **continued**

Great Britain, England & Wales, England, regions, metropolitan counties, Inner London, Outer London, regional remainders, Wales, Scotland

Persons present in communal establishments

Type of establishment and age	PERSONS PRESENT			Visitors/guests			Residents - non-staff			Residents - staff			With limiting long-term illness	Migrants
	TOTAL	Males	Females	Total	Males	Females	Total	Males	Females	Total	Males	Females		
a	b	c	d	e	f	g	h	i	j	k	l	m	n	o

Remainder of North Region – *continued*

Defence establishments

All ages	633	578	55	39	35	4	594	543	51				12	516
0 - 15	-	-	-	-	-	-	-	-	-				-	-
16 - 17	396	389	7	1	1	-	395	388	7				5	390
18 - 29	170	127	43	13	10	3	157	117	40				3	107
30 - 44	62	57	5	22	21	1	40	36	4				4	19
45 - 59	5	5	-	3	3	-	2	2	-				-	-
60 - 64	-	-	-	-	-	-	-	-	-				-	-
65 - 74	-	-	-	-	-	-	-	-	-				-	-
75 - 84	-	-	-	-	-	-	-	-	-				-	-
85 and over	-	-	-	-	-	-	-	-	-				-	-

Educational establishments

All ages	8,201	4,599	3,602	7,503	4,184	3,319	479	301	178	219	114	105	213	357
0 - 15	1,630	991	639	1,600	976	624	11	8	3	19	7	12	32	14
16 - 17	760	452	308	752	447	305	5	4	1	3	1	2	21	5
18 - 29	5,398	2,910	2,488	4,969	2,649	2,320	351	223	128	78	38	40	108	258
30 - 44	260	169	91	119	77	42	76	52	24	65	40	25	28	64
45 - 59	107	56	51	48	25	23	14	8	6	45	23	22	15	13
60 - 64	18	10	8	4	4	-	8	2	6	6	4	2	1	3
65 - 74	15	4	11	7	3	4	6	-	6	2	1	1	3	-
75 - 84	8	6	2	4	3	1	4	3	1	-	-	-	2	-
85 and over	5	1	4	-	-	-	4	1	3	1	-	1	3	-

Table 3 Type of establishment, migrants and long-term illness – **continued**

Great Britain, England & Wales, England, regions, metropolitan counties, Inner London, Outer London, regional remainders, Wales, Scotland

Persons present in communal establishments

Type of establishment and age	PERSONS PRESENT			Visitors/guests			Residents - non-staff			Residents - staff			With limiting long-term illness	Migrants
	TOTAL	Males	Females	Total	Males	Females	Total	Males	Females	Total	Males	Females		
a	b	c	d	e	f	g	h	i	j	k	l	m	n	o

Remainder of North Region – *continued*

Hotels, boarding houses etc

All ages	**11,691**	**6,594**	**5,097**	**7,775**	**4,305**	**3,470**	**1,087**	**777**	**310**	**2,829**	**1,512**	**1,317**	**1,055**	**1,366**
0 - 15	1,039	547	492	687	363	324	75	41	34	277	143	134	35	56
16 - 17	362	194	168	231	127	104	38	23	15	93	44	49	12	77
18 - 29	3,175	1,806	1,369	1,592	923	669	372	246	126	1,211	637	574	121	883
30 - 44	2,428	1,600	828	1,592	1,072	520	244	193	51	592	335	257	142	239
45 - 59	2,329	1,334	995	1,588	883	705	194	152	42	547	299	248	225	90
60 - 64	774	391	383	656	310	346	61	48	13	57	33	24	145	8
65 - 74	1,107	545	562	1,004	473	531	70	56	14	33	16	17	229	7
75 - 84	420	159	261	385	141	244	20	13	7	15	5	10	123	3
85 and over	57	18	39	40	13	27	13	5	8	4	-	4	23	3

Hostels and common lodging houses (non-HA)

All ages	**279**	**214**	**65**	**32**	**24**	**8**	**225**	**179**	**46**	**22**	**11**	**11**	**104**	**145**
0 - 15	33	20	13	5	5	-	27	15	12	1	-	1	-	23
16 - 17	12	7	5	-	-	-	10	5	5	2	2	-	2	11
18 - 29	62	36	26	13	9	4	37	21	16	12	6	6	9	38
30 - 44	47	42	5	6	5	1	39	36	3	2	1	1	21	28
45 - 59	64	61	3	3	2	1	58	57	1	3	2	1	35	32
60 - 64	28	24	4	2	2	-	24	22	2	2	-	2	19	8
65 - 74	23	18	5	2	-	2	21	18	3	-	-	-	13	4
75 - 84	10	6	4	1	1	-	9	5	4	-	-	-	5	1
85 and over	-	-	-	-	-	-	-	-	-	-	-	-	-	-

Table 3 Type of establishment, migrants and long-term illness – **continued**

Great Britain, England & Wales, England, regions, metropolitan counties, Inner London, Outer London, regional remainders, Wales, Scotland

Persons present in communal establishments

Remainder of North Region – *continued*

Type of establishment and age	PERSONS PRESENT			Visitors/guests			Residents - non-staff			Residents - staff			With limiting long-term illness	Migrants
	TOTAL	Males	Females	Total	Males	Females	Total	Males	Females	Total	Males	Females		
a	b	c	d	e	f	g	h	i	j	k	l	m	n	o
Other miscellaneous establishments														
All ages	**1,100**	**658**	**442**	**503**	**373**	**130**	**503**	**237**	**266**	**94**	**48**	**46**	**96**	**268**
0 - 15	72	34	38	20	11	9	49	23	26	3	-	3	5	39
16 - 17	67	33	34	63	31	32	3	2	1	1	-	1	2	4
18 - 29	454	316	138	234	180	54	180	113	67	40	23	17	13	151
30 - 44	208	145	63	90	78	12	98	57	41	20	10	10	14	44
45 - 59	143	86	57	62	50	12	62	26	36	19	10	9	18	19
60 - 64	43	22	21	19	14	5	20	6	14	4	2	2	9	1
65 - 74	57	13	44	9	5	4	44	5	39	4	3	1	19	4
75 - 84	46	8	38	4	3	1	39	5	34	3	-	3	11	6
85 and over	10	1	9	2	1	1	8	-	8	-	-	-	5	-
Persons sleeping rough														
All ages	**31**	**24**	**7**	**7**	**6**	**1**	**24**	**18**	**6**				**4**	**23**
0 - 15	-	-	-	-	-	-	-	-	-				-	-
16 - 17	3	1	2	-	-	-	3	1	2				-	3
18 - 29	10	8	2	3	3	-	7	5	2				-	6
30 - 44	9	6	3	2	1	1	7	5	2				1	7
45 - 59	8	8	-	2	2	-	6	6	-				2	6
60 - 64	-	-	-	-	-	-	-	-	-				-	-
65 - 74	1	1	-	-	-	-	1	1	-				1	1
75 - 84	-	-	-	-	-	-	-	-	-				-	-
85 and over	-	-	-	-	-	-	-	-	-				-	-

Table 3 Type of establishment, migrants and long-term illness – **continued**

Great Britain, England & Wales, England, regions, metropolitan counties, Inner London, Outer London, regional remainders, Wales, Scotland

Persons present in communal establishments

Type of establishment and age	PERSONS PRESENT			Visitors/guests			Residents - non-staff			Residents - staff			With limiting long-term illness	Migrants
	TOTAL	Males	Females	Total	Males	Females	Total	Males	Females	Total	Males	Females		
a	b	c	d	e	f	g	h	i	j	k	l	m	n	o
Remainder of North Region – *continued*														
Campers														
All ages	**18**	**8**	**10**	**18**	**8**	**10**	**-**	**-**	**-**				**4**	**-**
0 - 15	1	-	1	1	-	1	-	-	-				-	-
16 - 17	-	-	-	-	-	-	-	-	-				-	-
18 - 29	3	2	1	3	2	1	-	-	-				-	-
30 - 44	2	1	1	2	1	1	-	-	-				-	-
45 - 59	6	2	4	6	2	4	-	-	-				2	-
60 - 64	3	1	2	3	1	2	-	-	-				-	-
65 - 74	3	2	1	3	2	1	-	-	-				2	-
75 - 84	-	-	-	-	-	-	-	-	-				-	-
85 and over	-	-	-	-	-	-	-	-	-				-	-
Civilian ships, boats and barges														
All ages	**472**	**457**	**15**	**439**	**428**	**11**	**33**	**29**	**4**				**5**	**8**
0 - 15	-	-	-	-	-	-	-	-	-				-	-
16 - 17	1	-	-	-	-	-	1	1	-				-	1
18 - 29	119	117	2	112	111	1	7	6	1				1	2
30 - 44	229	219	10	210	203	7	19	16	3				2	3
45 - 59	112	110	2	108	106	2	4	4	-				1	2
60 - 64	9	9	-	7	7	-	2	2	-				-	-
65 - 74	2	1	1	2	1	1	-	-	-				1	-
75 - 84	-	-	-	-	-	-	-	-	-				-	-
85 and over	-	-	-	-	-	-	-	-	-				-	-

Table 3 Type of establishment, migrants and long-term illness – **continued**

Great Britain, England & Wales, England, regions, metropolitan counties, Inner London, Outer London, regional remainders, Wales, Scotland

Persons present in communal establishments

Type of establishment and age	PERSONS PRESENT			Visitors/guests			Residents - non-staff			Residents - staff			With limiting long-term illness	Migrants
	TOTAL	Males	Females	Total	Males	Females	Total	Males	Females	Total	Males	Females		
a	b	c	d	e	f	g	h	i	j	k	l	m	n	o

YORKSHIRE & HUMBERSIDE REGION

All establishments														
All ages	**113,945**	**51,609**	**62,336**	**47,845**	**25,323**	**22,522**	**60,360**	**23,808**	**36,552**	**5,740**	**2,478**	**3,262**	**60,492**	**22,102**
0 - 15	7,472	4,293	3,179	5,141	2,955	2,186	1,822	1,065	757	509	273	236	755	1,042
16 - 17	3,042	2,042	1,000	1,875	1,137	738	1,041	847	194	126	58	68	332	899
18 - 29	29,638	17,652	11,986	18,226	10,334	7,892	8,720	6,400	2,320	2,692	918	1,774	3,000	6,215
30 - 44	10,905	6,840	4,065	5,510	3,369	2,141	4,285	2,889	1,396	1,110	582	528	3,634	1,672
45 - 59	8,445	4,919	3,526	4,289	2,386	1,903	3,133	2,014	1,119	1,023	519	504	4,063	780
60 - 64	3,520	1,856	1,664	1,658	831	827	1,716	947	769	146	78	68	2,407	433
65 - 74	10,083	4,504	5,579	4,122	1,949	2,173	5,885	2,521	3,364	76	34	42	8,146	1,667
75 - 84	20,998	6,138	14,860	4,753	1,795	2,958	16,200	4,329	11,871	45	14	31	19,262	4,977
85 and over	19,842	3,365	16,477	2,271	567	1,704	17,558	2,796	14,762	13	2	11	18,893	4,417
NHS hospitals/homes - psychiatric														
All ages	**2,922**	**1,133**	**1,789**	**1,212**	**481**	**731**	**1,470**	**602**	**868**	**240**	**50**	**190**	**2,509**	**301**
0 - 15	12	7	5	11	7	4	1	-	1	-	-	-	3	-
16 - 17	7	3	4	5	3	2	2	-	2	-	-	-	4	-
18 - 29	420	143	277	140	74	66	60	34	26	220	35	185	139	108
30 - 44	308	165	143	180	76	104	113	78	35	15	11	4	249	45
45 - 59	317	178	139	133	62	71	179	112	67	5	4	1	293	25
60 - 64	170	87	83	57	27	30	113	60	53	-	-	-	165	12
65 - 74	555	225	330	199	74	125	356	151	205	-	-	-	543	37
75 - 84	733	244	489	322	120	202	411	124	287	-	-	-	716	47
85 and over	400	81	319	165	38	127	235	43	192	-	-	-	397	25

Table 3 Type of establishment, migrants and long-term illness – **continued**

Great Britain, England & Wales, England, regions, metropolitan counties, Inner London, Outer London, regional remainders, Wales, Scotland

Persons present in communal establishments

Type of establishment and age	PERSONS PRESENT			Visitors/guests			Residents - non-staff			Residents - staff			With limiting long-term illness	Migrants
	TOTAL	Males	Females	Total	Males	Females	Total	Males	Females	Total	Males	Females		
a	b	c	d	e	f	g	h	i	j	k	l	m	n	o
YORKSHIRE & HUMBERSIDE REGION – _continued_														
NHS hospitals/homes - other														
All ages	**19,001**	**7,401**	**11,600**	**14,043**	**5,561**	**8,482**	**3,592**	**1,487**	**2,105**	**1,366**	**353**	**1,013**	**11,827**	**1,456**
0 - 15	1,321	715	606	1,276	689	587	43	26	17	2	-	2	267	20
16 - 17	114	40	74	104	37	67	6	3	3	4	-	4	36	8
18 - 29	3,920	1,029	2,891	2,051	506	1,545	690	291	399	1,179	232	947	705	813
30 - 44	2,335	1,018	1,317	1,406	498	908	771	412	359	158	108	50	1,238	167
45 - 59	1,988	953	1,035	1,456	691	765	518	253	265	14	9	5	1,440	71
60 - 64	908	465	443	744	391	353	160	71	89	4	3	1	717	26
65 - 74	2,769	1,313	1,456	2,346	1,140	1,206	421	173	248	2	-	2	2,323	95
75 - 84	3,733	1,408	2,325	3,135	1,215	1,920	598	193	405	-	-	-	3,324	165
85 and over	1,913	460	1,453	1,525	394	1,131	385	65	320	3	1	2	1,777	91
Non-NHS hospitals - psychiatric														
All ages	**375**	**200**	**175**	**155**	**77**	**78**	**183**	**97**	**86**	**37**	**26**	**11**	**301**	**48**
0 - 15	5	4	1	5	4	1	-	-	-	-	-	-	2	-
16 - 17	2	1	1	2	1	1	-	-	-	-	-	-	1	-
18 - 29	57	39	18	18	13	5	9	6	3	30	20	10	19	10
30 - 44	62	44	18	31	22	9	28	20	8	3	2	1	51	6
45 - 59	55	31	24	19	9	10	32	18	14	4	4	-	50	10
60 - 64	27	16	11	7	4	3	20	12	8	-	-	-	27	2
65 - 74	60	26	34	18	5	13	42	21	21	-	-	-	55	7
75 - 84	71	28	43	35	13	22	36	15	21	-	-	-	62	10
85 and over	36	11	25	20	6	14	16	5	11	-	-	-	34	3

Persons present in communal establishments

Table 3 Type of establishment, migrants and long-term illness – **continued**

Type of establishment and age	PERSONS PRESENT			Visitors/guests			Residents - non-staff			Residents - staff			With limiting long-term illness	Migrants
	TOTAL	Males	Females	Total	Males	Females	Total	Males	Females	Total	Males	Females		
a	b	c	d	e	f	g	h	i	j	k	l	m	n	o

YORKSHIRE & HUMBERSIDE REGION – *continued*

Non-NHS hospitals - other

	b	c	d	e	f	g	h	i	j	k	l	m	n	o
All ages	**1,523**	**673**	**850**	**1,386**	**577**	**809**	**107**	**81**	**26**	**30**	**15**	**15**	**935**	**57**
0 - 15	108	50	58	108	50	58	-	-	-	-	-	-	49	-
16 - 17	13	4	9	10	2	8	3	2	1	-	-	-	6	2
18 - 29	189	86	103	134	43	91	41	35	6	14	8	6	76	36
30 - 44	218	81	137	193	61	132	18	15	3	7	5	2	74	11
45 - 59	254	128	126	234	115	119	14	11	3	6	2	4	146	6
60 - 64	111	60	51	101	55	46	8	5	3	2	-	2	86	1
65 - 74	285	140	145	276	133	143	8	7	1	1	-	1	209	-
75 - 84	256	100	156	249	95	154	7	5	2	-	-	-	210	-
85 and over	89	24	65	81	23	58	8	1	7	-	-	-	79	1

Local authority homes

	b	c	d	e	f	g	h	i	j	k	l	m	n	o
All ages	**13,567**	**4,323**	**9,244**	**1,279**	**637**	**642**	**12,255**	**3,674**	**8,581**	**33**	**12**	**21**	**12,296**	**2,472**
0 - 15	390	312	78	280	245	35	108	65	43	2	2	-	110	60
16 - 17	127	86	41	62	41	21	64	44	20	1	1	-	68	38
18 - 29	616	366	250	163	86	77	447	279	168	6	1	5	465	125
30 - 44	686	366	320	113	44	69	565	321	244	8	1	7	572	100
45 - 59	567	299	268	69	15	54	488	279	209	10	5	5	491	49
60 - 64	325	161	164	25	14	11	296	146	150	4	1	3	306	55
65 - 74	1,408	630	778	94	54	40	1,314	576	738	-	-	-	1,327	280
75 - 84	4,370	1,251	3,119	281	88	193	4,088	1,162	2,926	1	1	-	4,112	887
85 and over	5,078	852	4,226	192	50	142	4,885	802	4,083	1	-	1	4,845	878

Table 3 Type of establishment, migrants and long-term illness – **continued**

Great Britain, England & Wales, England, regions, metropolitan counties, Inner London, Outer London, regional remainders, Wales, Scotland

Persons present in communal establishments

Type of establishment and age	PERSONS PRESENT			Visitors/guests			Residents - non-staff			Residents - staff			With limiting long-term illness	Migrants
	TOTAL	Males	Females	Total	Males	Females	Total	Males	Females	Total	Males	Females		
a	b	c	d	e	f	g	h	i	j	k	l	m	n	o
YORKSHIRE & HUMBERSIDE REGION – *continued*														
Housing association homes and hostels														
All ages	**1,745**	**883**	**862**	**114**	**62**	**52**	**1,598**	**807**	**791**	**33**	**14**	**19**	**1,148**	**737**
0 - 15	16	13	3	8	7	1	3	3	-	5	3	2	7	1
16 - 17	30	18	12	-	-	-	29	17	12	1	1	-	3	26
18 - 29	302	197	105	57	29	28	241	166	75	4	2	2	107	146
30 - 44	246	170	76	31	16	15	209	152	57	6	2	4	141	96
45 - 59	190	126	64	3	3	-	174	118	56	13	5	8	134	63
60 - 64	86	58	28	3	2	1	81	55	26	2	1	1	56	31
65 - 74	199	111	88	1	1	-	197	110	87	1	-	1	148	76
75 - 84	359	124	235	6	4	2	352	120	232	1	-	1	286	184
85 and over	317	66	251	5	-	5	312	66	246	-	-	-	266	114
Nursing homes (non-NHS/ LA/HA)														
All ages	**13,244**	**3,357**	**9,887**	**700**	**211**	**489**	**12,437**	**3,107**	**9,330**	**107**	**39**	**68**	**12,794**	**4,901**
0 - 15	34	20	14	4	1	3	18	12	6	12	7	5	8	8
16 - 17	16	7	9	3	2	1	6	2	4	7	3	4	7	4
18 - 29	113	42	71	37	8	29	55	27	28	21	7	14	60	28
30 - 44	214	98	116	66	16	50	125	76	49	23	6	17	142	59
45 - 59	288	141	147	90	20	70	167	112	55	31	9	22	213	61
60 - 64	397	207	190	54	31	23	334	170	164	9	6	3	376	147
65 - 74	1,637	612	1,025	122	40	82	1,512	571	941	3	1	2	1,595	663
75 - 84	5,266	1,426	3,840	206	67	139	5,059	1,359	3,700	1	-	1	5,182	2,102
85 and over	5,279	804	4,475	118	26	92	5,161	778	4,383	-	-	-	5,214	1,829

154

Table 3 Type of establishment, migrants and long-term illness – **continued**

Persons present in communal establishments

Type of establishment and age	PERSONS PRESENT			Visitors/guests			Residents - non-staff			Residents - staff			With limiting long-term illness	Migrants
	TOTAL	Males	Females	Total	Males	Females	Total	Males	Females	Total	Males	Females		
a	b	c	d	e	f	g	h	i	j	k	l	m	n	o
YORKSHIRE & HUMBERSIDE REGION – *continued*														
Residential homes (non-NHS/LA/HA)														
All ages	**16,714**	**4,456**	**12,258**	**547**	**138**	**409**	**15,457**	**4,000**	**11,457**	**710**	**318**	**392**	**14,690**	**3,901**
0 - 15	156	84	72	4	2	2	17	12	5	135	70	65	7	13
16 - 17	37	18	19	9	4	5	6	4	2	22	10	12	10	8
18 - 29	532	264	268	101	33	68	328	186	142	103	45	58	365	112
30 - 44	855	446	409	70	14	56	603	350	253	182	82	100	587	109
45 - 59	812	409	403	46	11	35	563	312	251	203	86	117	573	97
60 - 64	508	241	267	42	9	33	434	218	216	32	14	18	401	112
65 - 74	1,729	685	1,044	66	21	45	1,645	654	991	18	10	8	1,527	447
75 - 84	5,543	1,289	4,254	118	32	86	5,413	1,256	4,157	12	1	11	5,068	1,546
85 and over	6,542	1,020	5,522	91	12	79	6,448	1,008	5,440	3	-	3	6,152	1,457
Children's homes														
All ages	**1,308**	**764**	**544**	**228**	**134**	**94**	**941**	**561**	**380**	**139**	**69**	**70**	**126**	**462**
0 - 15	1,153	705	448	173	122	51	941	561	380	39	22	17	107	461
16 - 17	5	1	4	-	-	-	-	-	-	5	1	4	-	-
18 - 29	47	25	22	19	7	12	-	-	-	28	18	10	11	1
30 - 44	54	12	42	21	3	18	-	-	-	33	9	24	2	-
45 - 59	38	16	22	14	2	12	-	-	-	24	14	10	1	-
60 - 64	6	2	4	-	-	-	-	-	-	6	2	4	3	-
65 - 74	5	3	2	1	-	1	-	-	-	4	3	1	2	-
75 - 84	-	-	-	-	-	-	-	-	-	-	-	-	-	-
85 and over	-	-	-	-	-	-	-	-	-	-	-	-	-	-

Table 3　Type of establishment, migrants and long-term illness – continued

Great Britain, England & Wales, England, regions, metropolitan counties, Inner London, Outer London, regional remainders, Wales, Scotland

Persons present in communal establishments

Type of establishment and age	PERSONS PRESENT			Visitors/guests			Residents - non-staff			Residents - staff			With limiting long-term illness	Migrants
	TOTAL	Males	Females	Total	Males	Females	Total	Males	Females	Total	Males	Females		
a	b	c	d	e	f	g	h	i	j	k	l	m	n	o

YORKSHIRE & HUMBERSIDE REGION – *continued*

Prison service establishments

Type of establishment and age	PERSONS PRESENT			Visitors/guests			Residents - non-staff			Residents - staff			With limiting long-term illness	Migrants
	TOTAL	Males	Females	Total	Males	Females	Total	Males	Females	Total	Males	Females		
All ages	**4,294**	**4,057**	**237**	**2,893**	**2,779**	**114**	**1,391**	**1,270**	**121**	**10**	**8**	**2**	**603**	**602**
0 - 15	30	30	-	24	24	-	6	6	-	-	-	-	2	4
16 - 17	162	157	5	147	144	3	15	13	2	-	-	-	13	10
18 - 29	2,597	2,492	105	1,942	1,880	62	651	609	42	4	3	1	262	332
30 - 44	1,062	987	75	584	545	39	474	438	36	4	4	-	165	186
45 - 59	367	335	32	164	156	8	202	179	23	1	-	1	116	65
60 - 64	35	31	4	18	17	1	17	14	3	-	-	-	23	1
65 - 74	29	21	8	12	11	1	17	10	7	-	-	-	13	4
75 - 84	6	2	4	1	1	-	4	-	4	1	1	-	6	-
85 and over	6	2	4	1	1	-	5	1	4	-	-	-	3	-

Defence establishments

Type of establishment and age	PERSONS PRESENT			Visitors/guests			Residents - non-staff			Residents - staff			With limiting long-term illness	Migrants
	TOTAL	Males	Females	Total	Males	Females	Total	Males	Females	Total	Males	Females		
All ages	**5,806**	**5,249**	**557**	**1,211**	**1,071**	**140**	**4,595**	**4,178**	**417**				**150**	**2,795**
0 - 15	-	-	-	-	-	-	-	-	-				-	-
16 - 17	795	767	28	123	116	7	672	651	21				12	591
18 - 29	4,461	3,975	486	852	732	120	3,609	3,243	366				105	2,068
30 - 44	466	432	34	187	179	8	279	253	26				20	122
45 - 59	74	68	6	47	43	4	27	25	2				10	13
60 - 64	3	3	-	-	-	-	3	3	-				2	-
65 - 74	2	1	1	-	-	-	2	1	1				-	1
75 - 84	3	1	2	2	1	1	1	-	1				1	-
85 and over	2	2	-	-	-	-	2	2	-				-	-

Table 3 Type of establishment, migrants and long-term illness – **continued**

Great Britain, England & Wales, England, regions, metropolitan counties, Inner London, Outer London, regional remainders, Wales, Scotland

Persons present in communal establishments

Type of establishment and age	PERSONS PRESENT			Visitors/guests			Residents - non-staff			Residents - staff			With limiting long-term illness	Migrants
	TOTAL	Males	Females	Total	Males	Females	Total	Males	Females	Total	Males	Females		
a	b	c	d	e	f	g	h	i	j	k	l	m	n	o
YORKSHIRE & HUMBERSIDE REGION – *continued*														
Educational establishments														
All ages	**16,163**	**8,815**	**7,348**	**14,533**	**7,804**	**6,729**	**1,310**	**840**	**470**	**320**	**171**	**149**	**711**	**1,022**
0 - 15	2,711	1,569	1,142	2,656	1,532	1,124	46	30	16	9	7	2	135	19
16 - 17	1,160	645	515	1,139	631	508	16	12	4	5	2	3	139	11
18 - 29	11,337	6,014	5,323	10,295	5,385	4,910	919	573	346	123	56	67	356	764
30 - 44	650	428	222	299	195	104	251	172	79	100	61	39	37	192
45 - 59	227	110	117	120	45	75	38	29	9	69	36	33	17	30
60 - 64	33	21	12	14	9	5	8	5	3	11	7	4	8	2
65 - 74	23	14	9	7	4	3	14	9	5	2	1	1	2	2
75 - 84	12	10	2	2	2	-	10	8	2	-	-	-	8	-
85 and over	10	4	6	1	1	-	8	2	6	1	1	-	9	2
Hotels, boarding houses etc														
All ages	**13,006**	**7,614**	**5,392**	**7,897**	**4,505**	**3,392**	**2,627**	**1,819**	**808**	**2,482**	**1,290**	**1,192**	**1,567**	**1,945**
0 - 15	1,062	542	520	498	243	255	259	137	122	305	162	143	30	182
16 - 17	402	210	192	224	127	97	97	43	54	81	40	41	14	88
18 - 29	3,613	2,119	1,494	1,817	1,076	741	928	594	334	868	449	419	186	1,067
30 - 44	2,784	1,848	936	1,785	1,228	557	476	362	114	523	258	265	212	345
45 - 59	2,645	1,653	992	1,617	974	643	442	362	80	586	317	269	397	184
60 - 64	760	408	352	556	243	313	142	125	17	62	40	22	167	27
65 - 74	1,147	602	545	951	448	503	163	138	25	33	16	17	303	26
75 - 84	477	202	275	382	150	232	74	44	30	21	8	13	185	19
85 and over	116	30	86	67	16	51	46	14	32	3	-	3	73	7

Table 3 Type of establishment, migrants and long-term illness – **continued**

Persons present in communal establishments

Type of establishment and age	PERSONS PRESENT			Visitors/guests			Residents - non-staff			Residents - staff			With limiting long-term illness	Migrants
	TOTAL	Males	Females	Total	Males	Females	Total	Males	Females	Total	Males	Females		
a	b	c	d	e	f	g	h	i	j	k	l	m	n	o

YORKSHIRE & HUMBERSIDE REGION – *continued*

Hostels and common lodging houses (non-HA)

Type of establishment and age	TOTAL	Males	Females	Total	Males	Females	Total	Males	Females	Total	Males	Females	n	o
All ages	**1,387**	**913**	**474**	**177**	**100**	**77**	**1,156**	**775**	**381**	**54**	**38**	**16**	**420**	**741**
0 - 15	150	79	71	15	7	8	135	72	63	-	-	-	10	92
16 - 17	124	58	66	26	13	13	98	45	53	-	-	-	13	88
18 - 29	470	247	223	53	23	30	401	215	186	16	9	7	76	334
30 - 44	230	169	61	32	18	14	187	143	44	11	8	3	91	131
45 - 59	227	191	36	36	25	11	167	147	20	24	19	5	122	67
60 - 64	69	62	7	8	7	1	58	53	5	3	2	1	48	14
65 - 74	88	82	6	7	7	-	81	75	6	-	-	-	47	10
75 - 84	26	23	3	-	-	-	26	23	3	-	-	-	13	3
85 and over	3	2	1	-	-	-	3	2	1	-	-	-	-	2

Other miscellaneous establishments

Type of establishment and age	TOTAL	Males	Females	Total	Males	Females	Total	Males	Females	Total	Males	Females	n	o
All ages	**2,015**	**954**	**1,061**	**744**	**506**	**238**	**1,092**	**373**	**719**	**179**	**75**	**104**	**353**	**622**
0 - 15	322	161	161	78	21	57	244	140	104	-	-	-	21	181
16 - 17	40	19	21	16	11	5	24	8	16	-	-	-	5	21
18 - 29	744	408	336	378	280	98	290	95	195	76	33	43	54	256
30 - 44	351	214	137	184	142	42	130	47	83	37	25	12	34	91
45 - 59	171	70	101	52	38	14	86	23	63	33	9	24	39	29
60 - 64	63	17	46	11	6	5	41	9	32	11	2	9	18	3
65 - 74	132	30	102	8	3	5	112	24	88	12	3	9	49	19
75 - 84	141	28	113	12	5	7	121	20	101	8	3	5	89	84
85 and over	51	7	44	5	-	5	44	7	37	2	-	2	44	8

Table 3 Type of establishment, migrants and long-term illness – **continued**

Great Britain, England & Wales, England, regions, metropolitan counties, Inner London, Outer London, regional remainders, Wales, Scotland

Persons present in communal establishments

YORKSHIRE & HUMBERSIDE REGION – *continued*

Type of establishment and age	PERSONS PRESENT			Visitors/guests			Residents - non-staff			Residents - staff			With limiting long-term illness	Migrants
	TOTAL	Males	Females	Total	Males	Females	Total	Males	Females	Total	Males	Females		
a	b	c	d	e	f	g	h	i	j	k	l	m	n	o
Persons sleeping rough														
All ages	**111**	**103**	**8**	**74**	**69**	**5**	**37**	**34**	**3**				**41**	**17**
0 - 15	-	-	-	-	-	-	-	-	-				-	-
16 - 17	3	3	-	1	1	-	2	2	-				1	2
18 - 29	41	35	6	24	20	4	17	15	2				9	8
30 - 44	27	25	2	20	19	1	7	6	1				13	4
45 - 59	34	34	-	25	25	-	9	9	-				14	3
60 - 64	4	4	-	3	3	-	1	1	-				2	-
65 - 74	2	2	-	1	1	-	1	1	-				2	-
75 - 84	-	-	-	-	-	-	-	-	-				-	-
85 and over	-	-	-	-	-	-	-	-	-				-	-
Campers														
All ages	**45**	**28**	**17**	**45**	**28**	**17**	-	-	-				**3**	-
0 - 15	-	-	-	-	-	-	-	-	-				-	-
16 - 17	-	-	-	-	-	-	-	-	-				-	-
18 - 29	3	3	-	3	3	-	-	-	-				-	-
30 - 44	10	6	4	10	6	4	-	-	-				-	-
45 - 59	13	8	5	13	8	5	-	-	-				1	-
60 - 64	6	4	2	6	4	2	-	-	-				1	-
65 - 74	12	6	6	12	6	6	-	-	-				1	-
75 - 84	1	1	-	1	1	-	-	-	-				-	-
85 and over	-	-	-	-	-	-	-	-	-				-	-

Table 3 Type of establishment, migrants and long-term illness – **continued**

Great Britain, England & Wales, England, regions, metropolitan counties, Inner London, Outer London, regional remainders, Wales, Scotland

Persons present in communal establishments

Type of establishment and age	PERSONS PRESENT			Visitors/guests			Residents - non-staff			Residents - staff			With limiting long-term illness	Migrants
	TOTAL	Males	Females	Total	Males	Females	Total	Males	Females	Total	Males	Females		
a	b	c	d	e	f	g	h	i	j	k	l	m	n	o

YORKSHIRE & HUMBERSIDE REGION – *continued*

Civilian ships, boats and barges

All ages	**719**	**686**	**33**	**607**	**583**	**24**	**112**	**103**	**9**				**18**	**23**
0 - 15	2	2	-	1	1	-	1	1	-				-	1
16 - 17	5	5	-	4	4	-	1	1	-				-	1
18 - 29	176	168	8	142	136	6	34	32	2				5	7
30 - 44	347	331	16	298	287	11	49	44	5				6	8
45 - 59	178	169	9	151	144	7	27	25	2				6	7
60 - 64	9	9	-	9	9	-	-	-	-				1	-
65 - 74	1	1	-	1	1	-	-	-	-				-	-
75 - 84	1	1	-	1	1	-	-	-	-				-	-
85 and over	-	-	-	-	-	-	-	-	-				-	-

South Yorkshire Metropolitan County

All establishments

All ages	**23,750**	**10,691**	**13,059**	**10,545**	**5,658**	**4,887**	**12,537**	**4,801**	**7,736**	**668**	**232**	**436**	**13,963**	**4,577**
0 - 15	1,085	637	448	582	384	198	483	245	238	20	8	12	156	277
16 - 17	271	157	114	146	92	54	121	63	58	4	2	2	111	103
18 - 29	6,699	4,067	2,632	4,637	2,818	1,819	1,625	1,136	489	437	113	324	785	1,154
30 - 44	2,060	1,287	773	1,031	610	421	900	601	299	129	76	53	868	363
45 - 59	1,636	970	666	869	478	391	713	468	245	54	24	30	986	152
60 - 64	734	386	348	324	157	167	395	223	172	15	6	9	569	96
65 - 74	2,401	1,068	1,333	1,055	512	543	1,340	553	787	6	3	3	2,059	377
75 - 84	4,748	1,385	3,363	1,253	457	796	3,493	928	2,565	2	-	2	4,442	1,101
85 and over	4,116	734	3,382	648	150	498	3,467	584	2,883	1	-	1	3,987	954

Table 3 Type of establishment, migrants and long-term illness – **continued**

Great Britain, England & Wales, England, regions, metropolitan counties, Inner London, Outer London, regional remainders, Wales, Scotland

Persons present in communal establishments

Type of establishment and age	PERSONS PRESENT			Visitors/guests			Residents - non-staff			Residents - staff			With limiting long-term illness	Migrants
	TOTAL	Males	Females	Total	Males	Females	Total	Males	Females	Total	Males	Females		
a	b	c	d	e	f	g	h	i	j	k	l	m	n	o
South Yorkshire Metropolitan County – *continued*														
NHS hospitals/homes - psychiatric														
All ages	**965**	**381**	**584**	**415**	**174**	**241**	**550**	**207**	**343**	**-**	**-**	**-**	**930**	**62**
0 - 15	-	-	-	-	-	-	-	-	-				-	-
16 - 17	2	2	-	2	2	-	-	-	-				1	-
18 - 29	47	33	14	27	21	6	20	12	8				42	6
30 - 44	75	44	31	46	23	23	29	21	8				68	8
45 - 59	87	50	37	26	14	12	61	36	25				84	4
60 - 64	64	34	30	22	10	12	42	24	18				63	4
65 - 74	231	89	142	98	43	55	133	46	87				225	14
75 - 84	315	98	217	132	48	84	183	50	133				305	19
85 and over	144	31	113	62	13	49	82	18	64				142	7
NHS hospitals/homes - other														
All ages	**5,760**	**2,319**	**3,441**	**4,299**	**1,796**	**2,503**	**1,050**	**412**	**638**	**411**	**111**	**300**	**3,694**	**449**
0 - 15	394	237	157	366	220	146	26	17	9	2	-	2	70	18
16 - 17	28	14	14	25	12	13	3	2	1	-	-	-	13	2
18 - 29	1,190	331	859	644	189	455	213	82	131	333	60	273	246	215
30 - 44	728	330	398	458	179	279	198	103	95	72	48	24	379	68
45 - 59	664	327	337	516	251	265	145	74	71	3	2	1	493	23
60 - 64	269	126	143	227	111	116	41	14	27	1	1	-	226	6
65 - 74	877	421	456	763	383	380	114	38	76	-	-	-	765	28
75 - 84	1,071	408	663	874	349	525	197	59	138	-	-	-	985	55
85 and over	539	125	414	426	102	324	113	23	90	-	-	-	517	34

Table 3 Type of establishment, migrants and long-term illness – **continued**

Great Britain, England & Wales, England, regions, metropolitan counties, Inner London, Outer London, regional remainders, Wales, Scotland

Persons present in communal establishments

Type of establishment and age	PERSONS PRESENT			Visitors/guests			Residents - non-staff			Residents - staff			With limiting long-term illness	Migrants
	TOTAL	Males	Females	Total	Males	Females	Total	Males	Females	Total	Males	Females		
a	b	c	d	e	f	g	h	i	j	k	l	m	n	o

South Yorkshire Metropolitan County – *continued*

Type of establishment and age	TOTAL	Males	Females	Total	Males	Females	Total	Males	Females	Total	Males	Females	n	o
Non-NHS hospitals - psychiatric														
All ages	-	-	-	-	-	-	-	-	-	-	-	-	-	-
0 - 15	-	-	-	-	-	-	-	-	-	-	-	-	-	-
16 - 17	-	-	-	-	-	-	-	-	-	-	-	-	-	-
18 - 29	-	-	-	-	-	-	-	-	-	-	-	-	-	-
30 - 44	-	-	-	-	-	-	-	-	-	-	-	-	-	-
45 - 59	-	-	-	-	-	-	-	-	-	-	-	-	-	-
60 - 64	-	-	-	-	-	-	-	-	-	-	-	-	-	-
65 - 74	-	-	-	-	-	-	-	-	-	-	-	-	-	-
75 - 84	-	-	-	-	-	-	-	-	-	-	-	-	-	-
85 and over	-	-	-	-	-	-	-	-	-	-	-	-	-	-
Non-NHS hospitals - other														
All ages	**91**	**28**	**63**	**76**	**27**	**49**	**7**	**1**	**6**	**8**	**-**	**8**	**37**	**2**
0 - 15	-	-	-	-	-	-	-	-	-	-	-	-	-	-
16 - 17	-	-	-	-	-	-	-	-	-	-	-	-	-	-
18 - 29	3	-	3	3	-	3	-	-	-	-	-	-	-	-
30 - 44	19	5	14	17	5	12	-	-	-	2	-	2	5	-
45 - 59	29	9	20	24	9	15	1	-	1	4	-	4	7	1
60 - 64	7	3	4	6	3	3	-	-	-	1	-	1	3	1
65 - 74	15	7	8	13	7	6	1	-	1	1	-	1	8	-
75 - 84	15	3	12	12	2	10	3	1	2	-	-	-	11	-
85 and over	3	1	2	1	1	-	2	-	2	-	-	-	3	-

Table 3 Type of establishment, migrants and long-term illness – **continued**

Great Britain, England & Wales, England, regions, metropolitan counties, Inner London, Outer London, regional remainders, Wales, Scotland

Persons present in communal establishments

Type of establishment and age	PERSONS PRESENT			Visitors/guests			Residents - non-staff			Residents - staff			With limiting long-term illness	Migrants
	TOTAL	Males	Females	Total	Males	Females	Total	Males	Females	Total	Males	Females		
a	b	c	d	e	f	g	h	i	j	k	l	m	n	o
South Yorkshire Metropolitan County – *continued*														
Local authority homes														
All ages	**3,643**	**1,108**	**2,535**	**337**	**153**	**184**	**3,306**	**955**	**2,351**	**-**	**-**	**-**	**3,337**	**740**
0 - 15	95	79	16	62	58	4	33	21	12	-	-	-	18	21
16 - 17	29	21	8	15	10	5	14	11	3	-	-	-	17	10
18 - 29	131	83	48	35	16	19	96	67	29	-	-	-	91	39
30 - 44	174	91	83	20	10	10	154	81	73	-	-	-	152	31
45 - 59	139	68	71	23	4	19	116	64	52	-	-	-	118	15
60 - 64	90	41	49	8	4	4	82	37	45	-	-	-	84	17
65 - 74	382	154	228	25	15	10	357	139	218	-	-	-	364	81
75 - 84	1,215	330	885	79	19	60	1,136	311	825	-	-	-	1,155	257
85 and over	1,388	241	1,147	70	17	53	1,318	224	1,094	-	-	-	1,338	269
Housing association homes and hostels														
All ages	**343**	**171**	**172**	**56**	**36**	**20**	**286**	**135**	**151**	**1**	**-**	**1**	**250**	**119**
0 - 15	8	7	1	7	6	1	1	1	-	-	-	-	6	1
16 - 17	3	2	1	-	-	-	3	2	1	-	-	-	-	2
18 - 29	100	65	35	31	19	12	69	46	23	-	-	-	52	33
30 - 44	60	39	21	16	10	6	44	29	15	-	-	-	37	21
45 - 59	32	18	14	1	1	-	30	17	13	1	-	1	25	4
60 - 64	11	7	4	1	-	1	10	7	3	-	-	-	10	2
65 - 74	41	16	25	-	-	-	41	16	25	-	-	-	38	16
75 - 84	56	14	42	-	-	-	56	14	42	-	-	-	52	28
85 and over	32	3	29	-	-	-	32	3	29	-	-	-	30	12

Table 3 Type of establishment, migrants and long-term illness – **continued**

Persons present in communal establishments

Type of establishment and age	PERSONS PRESENT			Visitors/guests			Residents - non-staff			Residents - staff			With limiting long-term illness	Migrants
	TOTAL	Males	Females	Total	Males	Females	Total	Males	Females	Total	Males	Females		
a	b	c	d	e	f	g	h	i	j	k	l	m	n	o

South Yorkshire Metropolitan County – *continued*

Nursing homes (non-NHS/LA/HA)

	b	c	d	e	f	g	h	i	j	k	l	m	n	o
All ages	**2,357**	**600**	**1,757**	**136**	**40**	**96**	**2,214**	**558**	**1,656**	**7**	**2**	**5**	**2,333**	**1,008**
0 - 15	-	-	-	-	-	-	-	-	-	-	-	-	-	-
16 - 17	1	-	1	-	-	-	-	-	-	1	-	1	-	-
18 - 29	3	2	1	1	-	1	1	1	-	1	1	-	2	1
30 - 44	6	2	4	2	-	2	2	2	-	2	-	2	4	1
45 - 59	21	13	8	9	3	6	9	9	-	3	1	2	17	2
60 - 64	56	26	30	1	-	1	55	26	29	-	-	-	56	30
65 - 74	318	129	189	21	10	11	297	119	178	-	-	-	317	144
75 - 84	1,011	269	742	52	15	37	959	254	705	-	-	-	1,004	452
85 and over	941	159	782	50	12	38	891	147	744	-	-	-	933	379

Residential homes (non-NHS/LA/HA)

	b	c	d	e	f	g	h	i	j	k	l	m	n	o
All ages	**2,665**	**699**	**1,966**	**116**	**16**	**100**	**2,522**	**673**	**1,849**	**27**	**10**	**17**	**2,457**	**675**
0 - 15	4	1	3	-	-	-	1	1	-	3	1	2	1	-
16 - 17	2	1	1	-	-	-	1	1	-	1	-	1	-	1
18 - 29	61	29	32	6	1	5	47	25	22	8	3	5	47	15
30 - 44	105	64	41	10	1	9	87	59	28	8	4	4	89	12
45 - 59	99	63	36	9	3	6	87	59	28	3	1	2	87	13
60 - 64	92	43	49	7	1	6	84	42	42	1	1	1	68	24
65 - 74	313	119	194	18	4	14	293	114	179	2	1	1	280	81
75 - 84	951	216	735	36	4	32	914	212	702	1	-	1	884	282
85 and over	1,038	163	875	30	2	28	1,008	161	847	-	-	-	1,001	247

Table 3 Type of establishment, migrants and long-term illness – **continued**

Great Britain, England & Wales, England, regions, metropolitan counties, Inner London, Outer London, regional remainders, Wales, Scotland

Persons present in communal establishments

Type of establishment and age	PERSONS PRESENT			Visitors/guests			Residents - non-staff			Residents - staff			With limiting long-term illness	Migrants
	TOTAL	Males	Females	Total	Males	Females	Total	Males	Females	Total	Males	Females		
a	b	c	d	e	f	g	h	i	j	k	l	m	n	o

South Yorkshire Metropolitan County – *continued*

Children's homes

All ages	**322**	**167**	**155**	**55**	**33**	**22**	**238**	**121**	**117**	**29**	**13**	**16**	**20**	**111**
0 - 15	285	154	131	40	30	10	238	121	117	7	3	4	17	111
16 - 17	-	-	-	-	-	-	-	-	-	-	-	-	-	-
18 - 29	9	5	4	1	1	-	-	-	-	8	4	4	3	-
30 - 44	15	5	10	7	1	6	-	-	-	8	4	4	-	-
45 - 59	11	2	9	7	1	6	-	-	-	4	1	3	-	-
60 - 64	1	-	1	-	-	-	-	-	-	1	-	1	-	-
65 - 74	1	1	-	-	-	-	-	-	-	1	1	-	-	-
75 - 84	-	-	-	-	-	-	-	-	-	-	-	-	-	-
85 and over	-	-	-	-	-	-	-	-	-	-	-	-	-	-

Prison service establishments

All ages	**912**	**911**	**1**	**669**	**669**	**-**	**243**	**242**	**1**	**-**	**-**	**-**	**123**	**130**
0 - 15	-	-	-	-	-	-	-	-	-	-	-	-	-	-
16 - 17	11	11	-	11	11	-	-	-	-	-	-	-	-	-
18 - 29	669	669	-	519	519	-	150	150	-	-	-	-	74	90
30 - 44	174	173	1	108	108	-	66	65	1	-	-	-	26	35
45 - 59	53	53	-	29	29	-	24	24	-	-	-	-	18	5
60 - 64	3	3	-	2	2	-	1	1	-	-	-	-	3	-
65 - 74	2	2	-	-	-	-	2	2	-	-	-	-	2	-
75 - 84	-	-	-	-	-	-	-	-	-	-	-	-	-	-
85 and over	-	-	-	-	-	-	-	-	-	-	-	-	-	-

Table 3 Type of establishment, migrants and long-term illness – **continued**

Great Britain, England & Wales, England, regions, metropolitan counties, Inner London, Outer London, regional remainders, Wales, Scotland

Persons present in communal establishments

Type of establishment and age	PERSONS PRESENT			Visitors/guests			Residents - non-staff			Residents - staff			With limiting long-term illness	Migrants
	TOTAL	Males	Females	Total	Males	Females	Total	Males	Females	Total	Males	Females		
a	b	c	d	e	f	g	h	i	j	k	l	m	n	o

South Yorkshire Metropolitan County – *continued*

Defence establishments

All ages	495	428	67	57	50	7	438	378	60				11	264
0 - 15	-	-	-	-	-	-	-	-	-				-	-
16 - 17	21	13	8	1	-	1	20	13	7				1	19
18 - 29	426	369	57	43	38	5	383	331	52				8	233
30 - 44	40	38	2	11	10	1	29	28	1				-	11
45 - 59	8	8	-	2	2	-	6	6	-				2	1
60 - 64	-	-	-	-	-	-	-	-	-				-	-
65 - 74	-	-	-	-	-	-	-	-	-				-	-
75 - 84	-	-	-	-	-	-	-	-	-				-	-
85 and over	-	-	-	-	-	-	-	-	-				-	-

Educational establishments

All ages	3,599	2,164	1,435	3,252	1,946	1,306	308	195	113	39	23	16	228	221
0 - 15	74	50	24	61	44	17	13	6	7	-	-	-	27	10
16 - 17	81	51	30	78	49	29	2	1	1	1	1	-	70	3
18 - 29	3,260	1,953	1,307	3,017	1,793	1,224	227	152	75	16	8	8	118	168
30 - 44	131	81	50	67	44	23	53	29	24	11	8	3	8	32
45 - 59	41	20	21	24	13	11	10	4	6	7	3	4	4	8
60 - 64	8	5	3	3	1	2	1	1	-	4	3	-	1	-
65 - 74	3	3	-	1	1	-	2	2	-	-	-	-	-	-
75 - 84	-	-	-	-	-	-	-	-	-	-	-	-	-	-
85 and over	1	1	-	1	1	-	-	-	-	-	-	-	-	-

Table 3 Type of establishment, migrants and long-term illness – **continued**

Great Britain, England & Wales, England, regions, metropolitan counties, Inner London, Outer London, regional remainders, Wales, Scotland

Persons present in communal establishments

Type of establishment and age	PERSONS PRESENT			Visitors/guests			Residents - non-staff			Residents - staff			With limiting long-term illness	Migrants
	TOTAL	Males	Females	Total	Males	Females	Total	Males	Females	Total	Males	Females		
a	b	c	d	e	f	g	h	i	j	k	l	m	n	o
South Yorkshire Metropolitan County – *continued*														
Hotels, boarding houses etc														
All ages	**1,812**	**1,223**	**589**	**906**	**594**	**312**	**804**	**570**	**234**	**102**	**59**	**43**	**315**	**444**
0 - 15	135	63	72	26	17	9	101	42	59	8	4	4	10	67
16 - 17	44	16	28	11	6	5	32	9	23	1	1	-	2	24
18 - 29	535	360	175	241	167	74	247	162	85	47	31	16	55	215
30 - 44	400	316	84	233	190	43	150	117	33	17	9	8	51	83
45 - 59	332	256	76	169	125	44	143	120	23	20	11	9	82	37
60 - 64	105	76	29	44	23	21	55	51	4	6	2	4	36	8
65 - 74	167	97	70	109	44	65	56	52	4	2	1	1	43	7
75 - 84	80	33	47	66	20	46	13	13	-	1	-	1	27	3
85 and over	14	6	8	7	2	5	7	4	3	-	-	-	9	-
Hostels and common lodging houses (non-HA)														
All ages	**479**	**345**	**134**	**76**	**47**	**29**	**388**	**287**	**101**	**15**	**11**	**4**	**159**	**256**
0 - 15	49	23	26	14	6	8	35	17	18	-	-	-	3	27
16 - 17	46	23	23	2	1	1	44	22	22	-	-	-	6	40
18 - 29	141	93	48	12	6	6	125	83	42	4	4	-	32	95
30 - 44	90	73	17	19	12	7	67	59	8	4	2	2	43	52
45 - 59	85	70	15	21	15	6	57	50	7	7	5	2	44	33
60 - 64	24	22	2	3	2	1	21	20	1	-	-	-	17	4
65 - 74	31	29	2	5	5	-	26	24	2	-	-	-	11	2
75 - 84	11	11	-	-	-	-	11	11	-	-	-	-	3	2
85 and over	2	1	1	-	-	-	2	1	1	-	-	-	-	1

Table 3 Type of establishment, migrants and long-term illness – **continued**

Great Britain, England & Wales, England, regions, metropolitan counties, Inner London, Outer London, regional remainders, Wales, Scotland

Persons present in communal establishments

Type of establishment and age	PERSONS PRESENT			Visitors/guests			Residents - non-staff			Residents - staff			With limiting long-term illness	Migrants
	TOTAL	Males	Females	Total	Males	Females	Total	Males	Females	Total	Males	Females		
a	b	c	d	e	f	g	h	i	j	k	l	m	n	o

South Yorkshire Metropolitan County – *continued*

Other miscellaneous establishments

Type of establishment and age	b	c	d	e	f	g	h	i	j	k	l	m	n	o
All ages	**273**	**120**	**153**	**81**	**66**	**15**	**163**	**51**	**112**	**29**	**3**	**26**	**59**	**82**
0 - 15	41	23	18	6	3	3	35	20	15	-	-	-	4	22
16 - 17	-	-	-	-	-	-	-	-	-	-	-	-	-	-
18 - 29	104	60	44	46	40	6	38	18	20	20	2	18	8	38
30 - 44	40	23	17	16	16	-	19	6	13	5	1	4	6	8
45 - 59	27	7	20	8	7	1	17	-	17	2	-	2	3	2
60 - 64	4	-	4	-	-	-	3	-	3	1	-	1	2	-
65 - 74	20	1	19	2	-	2	18	1	17	-	-	-	6	4
75 - 84	23	3	20	2	-	2	21	3	18	-	-	-	16	3
85 and over	14	3	11	1	-	1	12	3	9	1	-	1	14	5

Persons sleeping rough

Type of establishment and age	b	c	d	e	f	g	h	i	j	k	l	m	n	o
All ages	**26**	**22**	**4**	**14**	**11**	**3**	**12**	**11**	**1**				**7**	**11**
0 - 15	-	-	-	-	-	-	-	-	-				-	-
16 - 17	3	3	-	1	1	-	2	2	-				-	2
18 - 29	18	14	4	11	8	3	7	6	1				1	6
30 - 44	2	2	-	1	1	-	1	1	-				6	1
45 - 59	3	3	-	1	1	-	2	2	-				-	2
60 - 64	-	-	-	-	-	-	-	-	-				-	-
65 - 74	-	-	-	-	-	-	-	-	-				-	-
75 - 84	-	-	-	-	-	-	-	-	-				-	-
85 and over	-	-	-	-	-	-	-	-	-				-	-

Table 3 Type of establishment, migrants and long-term illness – **continued**

Great Britain, England & Wales, England, regions, metropolitan counties, Inner London, Outer London, regional remainders, Wales, Scotland

Persons present in communal establishments

Type of establishment and age	PERSONS PRESENT			Visitors/guests			Residents - non-staff			Residents - staff			With limiting long-term illness	Migrants
	TOTAL	Males	Females	Total	Males	Females	Total	Males	Females	Total	Males	Females		
a	b	c	d	e	f	g	h	i	j	k	l	m	n	o

South Yorkshire Metropolitan County – *continued*

Campers

All ages	-	-	-	-	-	-	-	-	-				-	-
0 - 15	-	-	-	-	-	-	-	-	-				-	-
16 - 17	-	-	-	-	-	-	-	-	-				-	-
18 - 29	-	-	-	-	-	-	-	-	-				-	-
30 - 44	-	-	-	-	-	-	-	-	-				-	-
45 - 59	-	-	-	-	-	-	-	-	-				-	-
60 - 64	-	-	-	-	-	-	-	-	-				-	-
65 - 74	-	-	-	-	-	-	-	-	-				-	-
75 - 84	-	-	-	-	-	-	-	-	-				-	-
85 and over	-	-	-	-	-	-	-	-	-				-	-

Civilian ships, boats and barges

All ages	8	5	3	-	-	-	8	5	3				3	3
0 - 15	-	-	-	-	-	-	-	-	-				-	-
16 - 17	-	-	-	-	-	-	-	-	-				-	-
18 - 29	2	1	1	-	-	-	2	1	1				1	1
30 - 44	1	1	-	-	-	-	1	1	-				1	-
45 - 59	5	3	2	-	-	-	5	3	2				2	2
60 - 64	-	-	-	-	-	-	-	-	-				-	-
65 - 74	-	-	-	-	-	-	-	-	-				-	-
75 - 84	-	-	-	-	-	-	-	-	-				-	-
85 and over	-	-	-	-	-	-	-	-	-				-	-

Table 3 Type of establishment, migrants and long-term illness – **continued**

Great Britain, England & Wales, England, regions, metropolitan counties, Inner London, Outer London, regional remainders, Wales, Scotland

Persons present in communal establishments

Type of establishment and age	PERSONS PRESENT			Visitors/guests			Residents - non-staff			Residents - staff			With limiting long-term illness	Migrants
	TOTAL	Males	Females	Total	Males	Females	Total	Males	Females	Total	Males	Females		
a	b	c	d	e	f	g	h	i	j	k	l	m	n	o

West Yorkshire Metropolitan County

All establishments

Type of establishment and age	PERSONS PRESENT TOTAL	Males	Females	Visitors Total	Males	Females	Res non-staff Total	Males	Females	Res staff Total	Males	Females	Long-term illness	Migrants
All ages	40,379	17,135	23,244	17,226	8,884	8,342	21,406	7,540	13,866	1,747	711	1,036	23,431	7,535
0 - 15	2,134	1,277	857	1,225	729	496	801	483	318	108	65	43	321	422
16 - 17	524	332	192	359	240	119	134	81	53	31	11	20	98	106
18 - 29	10,648	5,627	5,021	7,530	4,028	3,502	2,112	1,275	837	1,006	324	682	1,148	1,649
30 - 44	3,914	2,442	1,472	1,954	1,162	792	1,673	1,125	548	287	155	132	1,471	656
45 - 59	2,860	1,725	1,135	1,399	795	604	1,250	819	431	211	111	100	1,680	321
60 - 64	1,250	693	557	557	321	236	639	346	293	54	26	28	977	171
65 - 74	3,608	1,615	1,993	1,439	669	770	2,141	934	1,207	28	12	16	3,094	647
75 - 84	7,755	2,248	5,507	1,827	699	1,128	5,908	1,542	4,366	20	7	13	7,255	1,852
85 and over	7,686	1,176	6,510	936	241	695	6,748	935	5,813	2	-	2	7,387	1,711

NHS hospitals/homes - psychiatric

Type of establishment and age	PERSONS PRESENT TOTAL	Males	Females	Visitors Total	Males	Females	Res non-staff Total	Males	Females	Res staff Total	Males	Females	Long-term illness	Migrants
All ages	997	425	572	421	164	257	550	249	301	26	12	14	931	113
0 - 15	-	-	-	-	-	-	-	-	-	-	-	-	-	-
16 - 17	-	-	-	-	-	-	-	-	-	-	-	-	-	-
18 - 29	88	42	46	44	21	23	21	11	10	23	10	13	47	19
30 - 44	119	61	58	63	25	38	54	35	19	2	1	1	106	23
45 - 59	139	84	55	57	30	27	81	53	28	1	1	-	130	13
60 - 64	64	34	30	17	10	7	47	24	23	-	-	-	63	5
65 - 74	201	93	108	54	17	37	147	76	71	-	-	-	199	20
75 - 84	232	82	150	113	43	70	119	39	80	-	-	-	232	21
85 and over	154	29	125	73	18	55	81	11	70	-	-	-	154	12

Table 3 Type of establishment, migrants and long-term illness – continued

Great Britain, England & Wales, England, regions, metropolitan counties, Inner London, Outer London, regional remainders, Wales, Scotland

Persons present in communal establishments

Type of establishment and age	PERSONS PRESENT			Visitors/guests			Residents - non-staff			Residents - staff			With limiting long-term illness	Migrants
	TOTAL	Males	Females	Total	Males	Females	Total	Males	Females	Total	Males	Females		
a	b	c	d	e	f	g	h	i	j	k	l	m	n	o
West Yorkshire Metropolitan County – *continued*														
NHS hospitals/homes - other														
All ages	**8,137**	**3,061**	**5,076**	**5,810**	**2,217**	**3,593**	**1,660**	**678**	**982**	**667**	**166**	**501**	**4,969**	**692**
0 - 15	528	268	260	514	261	253	14	7	7	-	-	-	127	1
16 - 17	50	12	38	45	12	33	1	-	1	4	-	4	12	4
18 - 29	1,833	455	1,378	894	201	693	343	132	211	596	122	474	284	432
30 - 44	990	427	563	576	193	383	354	193	161	60	41	19	529	75
45 - 59	847	411	436	605	285	320	238	123	115	4	3	1	613	38
60 - 64	402	218	184	332	184	148	69	34	35	1	-	1	319	14
65 - 74	1,137	532	605	947	447	500	189	85	104	1	-	1	959	43
75 - 84	1,503	543	960	1,255	469	786	248	74	174	-	-	-	1,334	53
85 and over	847	195	652	642	165	477	204	30	174	1	-	1	792	32
Non-NHS hospitals - psychiatric														
All ages	**351**	**185**	**166**	**154**	**76**	**78**	**163**	**85**	**78**	**34**	**24**	**10**	**279**	**42**
0 - 15	5	4	1	5	4	1	-	-	-	-	-	-	2	-
16 - 17	2	1	1	2	1	1	-	-	-	-	-	-	1	-
18 - 29	54	37	17	17	12	5	7	5	2	30	20	10	16	10
30 - 44	59	43	16	31	22	9	26	19	7	2	2	-	49	5
45 - 59	45	23	22	19	9	10	24	12	12	2	2	-	41	5
60 - 64	26	15	11	7	4	3	19	11	8	-	-	-	26	2
65 - 74	56	25	31	18	5	13	38	20	18	-	-	-	51	7
75 - 84	68	26	42	35	13	22	33	13	20	-	-	-	59	10
85 and over	36	11	25	20	6	14	16	5	11	-	-	-	34	3

Table 3 Type of establishment, migrants and long-term illness – continued

Great Britain, England & Wales, England, regions, metropolitan counties, Inner London, Outer London, regional remainders, Wales, Scotland

Persons present in communal establishments

Type of establishment and age	PERSONS PRESENT			Visitors/guests			Residents - non-staff			Residents - staff			With limiting long-term illness	Migrants
	TOTAL	Males	Females	Total	Males	Females	Total	Males	Females	Total	Males	Females		
a	b	c	d	e	f	g	h	i	j	k	l	m	n	o

West Yorkshire Metropolitan County – *continued*

Non-NHS hospitals - other

Type of establishment and age	TOTAL	Males	Females	Total	Males	Females	Total	Males	Females	Total	Males	Females	n	o
All ages	995	436	559	933	388	545	52	42	10	10	6	4	574	19
0 - 15	106	49	57	106	49	57	-	-	-	-	-	-	49	-
16 - 17	11	3	8	10	2	8	1	1	-	-	-	-	4	1
18 - 29	128	43	85	110	29	81	11	10	1	7	4	3	38	13
30 - 44	153	47	106	145	41	104	8	6	2	2	2	-	44	1
45 - 59	148	81	67	136	71	65	10	8	2	2	2	-	89	3
60 - 64	68	41	27	59	36	23	8	5	3	1	-	1	56	-
65 - 74	172	86	86	165	79	86	7	7	-	-	-	-	124	-
75 - 84	153	67	86	149	63	86	4	4	-	-	-	-	122	-
85 and over	56	19	37	53	18	35	3	1	2	-	-	-	48	1

Local authority homes

Type of establishment and age	TOTAL	Males	Females	Total	Males	Females	Total	Males	Females	Total	Males	Females	n	o
All ages	6,103	1,943	4,160	503	296	207	5,586	1,643	3,943	14	4	10	5,614	1,094
0 - 15	142	120	22	110	103	7	32	17	15	-	-	-	20	15
16 - 17	51	36	15	21	16	5	30	20	10	-	-	-	26	17
18 - 29	333	208	125	76	52	24	255	156	99	2	-	2	260	67
30 - 44	318	183	135	37	18	19	276	164	112	5	1	4	275	46
45 - 59	273	145	128	28	9	19	242	134	108	3	2	1	243	24
60 - 64	173	86	87	11	8	3	159	78	81	3	-	3	165	29
65 - 74	626	285	341	40	26	14	586	259	327	-	-	-	599	118
75 - 84	1,908	535	1,373	114	44	70	1,793	490	1,303	1	1	-	1,827	401
85 and over	2,279	345	1,934	66	20	46	2,213	325	1,888	-	-	-	2,199	377

Table 3 Type of establishment, migrants and long-term illness – **continued**

Persons present in communal establishments

Type of establishment and age	PERSONS PRESENT			Visitors/guests			Residents - non-staff			Residents - staff			With limiting long-term illness	Migrants
	TOTAL	Males	Females	Total	Males	Females	Total	Males	Females	Total	Males	Females		
a	b	c	d	e	f	g	h	i	j	k	l	m	n	o
West Yorkshire Metropolitan County – *continued*														
Housing association homes and hostels														
All ages	**586**	**272**	**314**	**14**	**5**	**9**	**560**	**263**	**297**	**12**	**4**	**8**	**455**	**318**
0 - 15	2	2	-	-	-	-	1	1	-	1	1	-	-	-
16 - 17	5	4	1	-	-	-	5	4	1	-	1	-	2	4
18 - 29	60	45	15	5	3	2	52	41	11	3	1	2	19	44
30 - 44	68	42	26	5	-	5	63	42	21	-	-	-	45	35
45 - 59	73	50	23	1	1	-	65	47	18	7	2	5	62	35
60 - 64	23	13	10	-	-	-	23	13	10	-	-	-	20	13
65 - 74	70	36	34	-	-	-	70	36	34	-	-	-	63	34
75 - 84	158	50	108	2	1	1	155	49	106	1	-	1	132	90
85 and over	127	30	97	1	-	1	126	30	96	-	-	-	112	63
Nursing homes (non-NHS/ LA/HA)														
All ages	**5,096**	**1,275**	**3,821**	**279**	**89**	**190**	**4,786**	**1,174**	**3,612**	**31**	**12**	**19**	**4,874**	**2,028**
0 - 15	24	15	9	4	1	3	15	10	5	5	4	1	3	4
16 - 17	7	3	4	3	2	1	2	-	2	2	1	1	3	2
18 - 29	37	9	28	15	2	13	19	5	14	3	2	1	14	14
30 - 44	94	45	49	27	7	20	59	36	23	8	2	6	65	34
45 - 59	130	63	67	40	8	32	82	53	29	8	2	6	101	41
60 - 64	163	85	78	22	15	7	138	69	69	3	1	2	154	63
65 - 74	616	223	393	49	15	34	565	208	357	2	-	2	590	283
75 - 84	1,992	551	1,441	79	31	48	1,913	520	1,393	-	-	-	1,951	832
85 and over	2,033	281	1,752	40	8	32	1,993	273	1,720	-	-	-	1,993	755

Table 3 Type of establishment, migrants and long-term illness – **continued**

Great Britain, England & Wales, England, regions, metropolitan counties, Inner London, Outer London, regional remainders, Wales, Scotland

Persons present in communal establishments

Type of establishment and age	PERSONS PRESENT			Visitors/guests			Residents - non-staff			Residents - staff			With limiting long-term illness	Migrants
	TOTAL	Males	Females	Total	Males	Females	Total	Males	Females	Total	Males	Females		
a	b	c	d	e	f	g	h	i	j	k	l	m	n	o

West Yorkshire Metropolitan County – *continued*

Residential homes (non-NHS/LA/HA)

	b	c	d	e	f	g	h	i	j	k	l	m	n	o
All ages	**4,793**	**1,092**	**3,701**	**78**	**13**	**65**	**4,545**	**1,009**	**3,536**	**170**	**70**	**100**	**4,383**	**1,122**
0 - 15	25	14	11	1	-	1	6	4	2	18	10	8	1	3
16 - 17	10	7	3	-	-	-	5	3	2	5	4	1	4	4
18 - 29	118	63	55	12	3	9	82	49	33	24	11	13	88	15
30 - 44	203	89	114	16	3	13	140	70	70	47	16	31	138	28
45 - 59	201	107	94	12	3	9	144	85	59	45	19	26	152	23
60 - 64	109	54	55	2	-	2	91	47	44	16	7	9	86	30
65 - 74	443	172	271	5	1	4	430	168	262	8	3	5	400	127
75 - 84	1,594	330	1,264	12	3	9	1,576	327	1,249	6	-	6	1,512	429
85 and over	2,090	256	1,834	18	-	18	2,071	256	1,815	1	-	1	2,002	463

Children's homes

	b	c	d	e	f	g	h	i	j	k	l	m	n	o
All ages	**696**	**420**	**276**	**135**	**78**	**57**	**490**	**307**	**183**	**71**	**35**	**36**	**67**	**228**
0 - 15	612	390	222	99	70	29	490	307	183	23	13	10	60	227
16 - 17	3	-	3	-	-	-	-	-	-	3	-	3	-	-
18 - 29	29	15	14	15	6	9	-	-	-	14	9	5	4	1
30 - 44	26	2	24	13	1	12	-	-	-	13	1	12	1	-
45 - 59	21	12	9	7	1	6	-	-	-	14	11	3	-	-
60 - 64	3	1	2	-	-	-	-	-	-	3	1	2	1	-
65 - 74	2	-	2	1	-	1	-	-	-	1	-	1	1	-
75 - 84	-	-	-	-	-	-	-	-	-	-	-	-	-	-
85 and over	-	-	-	-	-	-	-	-	-	-	-	-	-	-

Table 3 Type of establishment, migrants and long-term illness – **continued**

Great Britain, England & Wales, England, regions, metropolitan counties, Inner London, Outer London, regional remainders, Wales, Scotland

Persons present in communal establishments

Type of establishment and age	PERSONS PRESENT			Visitors/guests			Residents - non-staff			Residents - staff			With limiting long-term illness	Migrants
	TOTAL	Males	Females	Total	Males	Females	Total	Males	Females	Total	Males	Females		
a	b	c	d	e	f	g	h	i	j	k	l	m	n	o
West Yorkshire Metropolitan County – *continued*														
Prison service establishments														
All ages	**2,313**	**2,211**	**102**	**1,478**	**1,420**	**58**	**830**	**786**	**44**	**5**	**5**	**-**	**331**	**334**
0 - 15	30	30	-	24	24	-	6	6	-	-	-	-	2	4
16 - 17	84	79	5	74	71	3	10	8	2	-	-	-	7	6
18 - 29	1,206	1,145	61	874	839	35	330	304	26	2	2	-	115	144
30 - 44	710	680	30	375	357	18	333	321	12	2	2	-	100	132
45 - 59	237	232	5	105	104	1	132	128	4	-	-	-	78	45
60 - 64	26	25	1	14	13	1	12	12	-	-	-	-	18	1
65 - 74	16	16	-	10	10	-	6	6	-	-	-	-	8	2
75 - 84	2	2	-	1	1	-	-	-	-	1	1	-	2	-
85 and over	2	2	-	1	1	-	1	1	-	-	-	-	1	-
Defence establishments														
All ages	**15**	**3**	**12**	**15**	**3**	**12**	**-**	**-**	**-**				**3**	**-**
0 - 15	-	-	-	-	-	-	-	-	-				-	-
16 - 17	-	-	-	-	-	-	-	-	-				-	-
18 - 29	11	3	8	11	3	8	-	-	-				2	-
30 - 44	4	-	4	4	-	4	-	-	-				1	-
45 - 59	-	-	-	-	-	-	-	-	-				-	-
60 - 64	-	-	-	-	-	-	-	-	-				-	-
65 - 74	-	-	-	-	-	-	-	-	-				-	-
75 - 84	-	-	-	-	-	-	-	-	-				-	-
85 and over	-	-	-	-	-	-	-	-	-				-	-

Table 3 Type of establishment, migrants and long-term illness – **continued**

Great Britain, England & Wales, England, regions, metropolitan counties, Inner London, Outer London, regional remainders, Wales, Scotland

Persons present in communal establishments

Type of establishment and age	PERSONS PRESENT			Visitors/guests			Residents - non-staff			Residents - staff			With limiting long-term illness	Migrants
	TOTAL	Males	Females	Total	Males	Females	Total	Males	Females	Total	Males	Females		
a	b	c	d	e	f	g	h	i	j	k	l	m	n	o

West Yorkshire Metropolitan County – *continued*

Educational establishments

All ages	**5,947**	**3,146**	**2,801**	**5,281**	**2,730**	**2,551**	**581**	**365**	**216**	**85**	**51**	**34**	**255**	**457**
0 - 15	269	161	108	251	149	102	16	10	6	2	2	-	39	6
16 - 17	166	100	66	160	95	65	6	5	1	-	-	-	30	3
18 - 29	5,199	2,677	2,522	4,737	2,398	2,339	422	261	161	40	18	22	159	346
30 - 44	246	175	71	107	76	31	111	79	32	28	20	8	13	91
45 - 59	42	26	16	19	9	10	11	8	3	12	9	3	3	9
60 - 64	6	3	3	2	1	1	2	-	2	2	2	-	-	-
65 - 74	8	-	8	3	-	3	4	-	4	1	-	1	2	1
75 - 84	5	4	1	2	2	-	3	2	1	-	-	-	3	-
85 and over	6	-	6	-	-	-	6	-	6	-	-	-	6	1

Hotels, boarding houses etc

All ages	**2,780**	**1,735**	**1,045**	**1,699**	**1,088**	**611**	**588**	**400**	**188**	**493**	**247**	**246**	**373**	**433**
0 - 15	190	114	76	93	57	36	38	22	16	59	35	24	3	31
16 - 17	76	57	19	36	35	1	23	16	7	17	6	11	2	22
18 - 29	927	537	390	490	292	198	224	147	77	213	98	115	49	246
30 - 44	636	457	179	447	340	107	99	73	26	90	44	46	51	71
45 - 59	506	346	160	323	224	99	97	77	20	86	45	41	82	44
60 - 64	125	77	48	81	41	40	27	25	2	17	11	6	32	5
65 - 74	180	98	82	144	66	78	28	26	2	8	6	2	60	2
75 - 84	97	43	54	64	28	36	30	13	17	3	2	1	58	9
85 and over	43	6	37	21	5	16	22	1	21	-	-	-	36	3

Table 3 Type of establishment, migrants and long-term illness – **continued**

Great Britain, England & Wales, England, regions, metropolitan counties, Inner London, Outer London, regional remainders, Wales, Scotland

Persons present in communal establishments

Type of establishment and age	PERSONS PRESENT			Visitors/guests			Residents - non-staff			Residents - staff			With limiting long-term illness	Migrants
	TOTAL	Males	Females	Total	Males	Females	Total	Males	Females	Total	Males	Females		
a	b	c	d	e	f	g	h	i	j	k	l	m	n	o

West Yorkshire Metropolitan County – *continued*

Type of establishment and age	b	c	d	e	f	g	h	i	j	k	l	m	n	o
Hostels and common lodging houses (non-HA)														
All ages	**569**	**395**	**174**	**38**	**25**	**13**	**507**	**352**	**155**	**24**	**18**	**6**	**188**	**302**
0 - 15	40	19	21	1	1	-	39	18	21	-	-	-	1	24
16 - 17	40	21	19	1	1	-	39	20	19	-	-	-	4	34
18 - 29	191	111	80	13	8	5	173	101	72	5	2	3	26	143
30 - 44	104	71	33	9	3	6	88	62	26	7	6	1	33	59
45 - 59	107	94	13	8	6	2	90	80	10	9	8	1	63	28
60 - 64	33	30	3	4	4	-	26	24	2	3	2	1	27	6
65 - 74	45	42	3	2	2	-	43	40	3	-	-	-	27	7
75 - 84	9	7	2	-	-	-	9	7	2	-	-	-	7	1
85 and over	-	-	-	-	-	-	-	-	-	-	-	-	-	-
Other miscellaneous establishments														
All ages	**932**	**470**	**462**	**331**	**237**	**94**	**496**	**176**	**320**	**105**	**57**	**48**	**107**	**348**
0 - 15	161	91	70	17	10	7	144	81	63	-	-	-	14	107
16 - 17	19	9	10	7	5	2	12	4	8	-	-	-	3	9
18 - 29	422	226	196	206	149	57	172	52	120	44	25	19	26	154
30 - 44	163	101	62	81	59	22	59	23	36	23	19	4	10	54
45 - 59	60	20	40	15	11	4	27	4	23	18	5	13	10	11
60 - 64	25	7	18	3	2	1	17	3	14	5	2	3	8	3
65 - 74	35	6	29	-	-	-	28	3	25	7	3	4	10	3
75 - 84	34	8	26	1	1	-	25	4	21	8	3	5	16	6
85 and over	13	2	11	1	-	1	12	2	10	-	-	-	10	1

Table 3 Type of establishment, migrants and long-term illness – **continued**

Great Britain, England & Wales, England, regions, metropolitan counties, Inner London, Outer London, regional remainders, Wales, Scotland

Persons present in communal establishments

Type of establishment and age	PERSONS PRESENT			Visitors/guests			Residents - non-staff			Residents - staff			With limiting long-term illness	Migrants
	TOTAL	Males	Females	Total	Males	Females	Total	Males	Females	Total	Males	Females		
a	b	c	d	e	f	g	h	i	j	k	l	m	n	o

West Yorkshire Metropolitan County – *continued*

Persons sleeping rough

Type of establishment and age	PERSONS PRESENT			Visitors/guests			Residents - non-staff			Residents - staff			With limiting long-term illness	Migrants
All ages	**68**	**65**	**3**	**57**	**55**	**2**	**11**	**10**	**1**				**28**	**4**
0 - 15	-	-	-	-	-	-	-	-	-				-	-
16 - 17	-	-	-	-	-	-	-	-	-				-	-
18 - 29	12	11	1	11	10	1	1	1	1				1	1
30 - 44	21	19	2	18	17	1	3	2	1				11	2
45 - 59	30	30	-	24	24	-	6	6	-				13	1
60 - 64	4	4	-	3	3	-	1	1	-				2	-
65 - 74	1	1	-	1	1	-	-	-	-				1	-
75 - 84	-	-	-	-	-	-	-	-	-				-	-
85 and over	-	-	-	-	-	-	-	-	-				-	-

Campers

Type of establishment and age	PERSONS PRESENT			Visitors/guests			Residents - non-staff			Residents - staff			With limiting long-term illness	Migrants
All ages	-	-	-	-	-	-	-	-	-				-	-
0 - 15	-	-	-	-	-	-	-	-	-				-	-
16 - 17	-	-	-	-	-	-	-	-	-				-	-
18 - 29	-	-	-	-	-	-	-	-	-				-	-
30 - 44	-	-	-	-	-	-	-	-	-				-	-
45 - 59	-	-	-	-	-	-	-	-	-				-	-
60 - 64	-	-	-	-	-	-	-	-	-				-	-
65 - 74	-	-	-	-	-	-	-	-	-				-	-
75 - 84	-	-	-	-	-	-	-	-	-				-	-
85 and over	-	-	-	-	-	-	-	-	-				-	-

Table 3 Type of establishment, migrants and long-term illness – **continued**

Great Britain, England & Wales, England, regions, metropolitan counties, Inner London, Outer London, regional remainders, Wales, Scotland

Persons present in communal establishments

Type of establishment and age	PERSONS PRESENT			Visitors/guests			Residents - non-staff			Residents - staff			With limiting long-term illness	Migrants
	TOTAL	Males	Females	Total	Males	Females	Total	Males	Females	Total	Males	Females		
a	b	c	d	e	f	g	h	i	j	k	l	m	n	o
West Yorkshire Metropolitan County – *continued*														
Civilian ships, boats and barges														
All ages	1	1	-	-	-	-	1	1	-				-	1
0 - 15	-	-	-	-	-	-	-	-	-				-	-
16 - 17	-	-	-	-	-	-	-	-	-				-	-
18 - 29	-	-	-	-	-	-	-	-	-				-	-
30 - 44	-	-	-	-	-	-	-	-	-				-	-
45 - 59	1	1	-	-	-	-	1	1	-				-	1
60 - 64	-	-	-	-	-	-	-	-	-				-	-
65 - 74	-	-	-	-	-	-	-	-	-				-	-
75 - 84	-	-	-	-	-	-	-	-	-				-	-
85 and over	-	-	-	-	-	-	-	-	-				-	-
Remainder of Yorkshire & Humberside Region														
All establishments														
All ages	49,816	23,783	26,033	20,074	10,781	9,293	26,417	11,467	14,950	3,325	1,535	1,790	23,098	9,990
0 - 15	4,253	2,379	1,874	3,334	1,842	1,492	538	337	201	381	200	181	278	343
16 - 17	2,247	1,553	694	1,370	805	565	786	703	83	91	45	46	123	690
18 - 29	12,291	7,958	4,333	6,059	3,488	2,571	4,983	3,989	994	1,249	481	768	1,067	3,412
30 - 44	4,931	3,111	1,820	2,525	1,597	928	1,712	1,163	549	694	351	343	1,295	653
45 - 59	3,949	2,224	1,725	2,021	1,113	908	1,170	727	443	758	384	374	1,397	307
60 - 64	1,536	777	759	777	353	424	682	378	304	77	46	31	861	166
65 - 74	4,074	1,821	2,253	1,628	768	860	2,404	1,034	1,370	42	19	23	2,993	643
75 - 84	8,495	2,505	5,990	1,673	639	1,034	6,799	1,859	4,940	23	7	16	7,565	2,024
85 and over	8,040	1,455	6,585	687	176	511	7,343	1,277	6,066	10	2	8	7,519	1,752

Table 3 Type of establishment, migrants and long-term illness – **continued**

Great Britain, England & Wales, England, regions, metropolitan counties, Inner London, Outer London, regional remainders, Wales, Scotland

Persons present in communal establishments

Type of establishment and age	PERSONS PRESENT			Visitors/guests			Residents - non-staff			Residents - staff			With limiting long-term illness	Migrants
	TOTAL	Males	Females	Total	Males	Females	Total	Males	Females	Total	Males	Females		
a	b	c	d	e	f	g	h	i	j	k	l	m	n	o
Remainder of Yorkshire & Humberside Region – *continued*														
NHS hospitals/homes - psychiatric														
All ages	**960**	**327**	**633**	**376**	**143**	**233**	**370**	**146**	**224**	**214**	**38**	**176**	**648**	**126**
0 - 15	12	7	5	11	7	4	1	-	1	-	-	-	3	-
16 - 17	5	1	4	3	1	2	2	-	2	-	-	-	3	-
18 - 29	285	68	217	69	32	37	19	11	8	197	25	172	50	83
30 - 44	114	60	54	71	28	43	30	22	8	13	10	3	75	14
45 - 59	91	44	47	50	18	32	37	23	14	4	3	1	79	8
60 - 64	42	19	23	18	7	11	24	12	12	-	-	-	39	3
65 - 74	123	43	80	47	14	33	76	29	47	-	-	-	119	3
75 - 84	186	64	122	77	29	48	109	35	74	-	-	-	179	7
85 and over	102	21	81	30	7	23	72	14	58	-	-	-	101	6
NHS hospitals/homes - other														
All ages	**5,104**	**2,021**	**3,083**	**3,934**	**1,548**	**2,386**	**882**	**397**	**485**	**288**	**76**	**212**	**3,164**	**315**
0 - 15	399	210	189	396	208	188	3	2	1	-	-	-	70	1
16 - 17	36	14	22	34	13	21	2	1	1	-	-	-	11	2
18 - 29	897	243	654	513	116	397	134	77	57	250	50	200	175	166
30 - 44	617	261	356	372	126	246	219	116	103	26	19	7	330	24
45 - 59	477	215	262	335	155	180	135	56	79	7	4	3	334	10
60 - 64	237	121	116	185	96	89	50	23	27	2	2	-	172	6
65 - 74	755	360	395	636	310	326	118	50	68	1	-	1	599	24
75 - 84	1,159	457	702	1,006	397	609	153	60	93	-	-	-	1,005	57
85 and over	527	140	387	457	127	330	68	12	56	2	2	-	468	25

Table 3 Type of establishment, migrants and long-term illness – **continued**

Great Britain, England & Wales, England, regions, metropolitan counties, Inner London, Outer London, regional remainders, Wales, Scotland

Persons present in communal establishments

Type of establishment and age	PERSONS PRESENT			Visitors/guests			Residents - non-staff			Residents - staff			With limiting long-term illness	Migrants
	TOTAL	Males	Females	Total	Males	Females	Total	Males	Females	Total	Males	Females		
a	b	c	d	e	f	g	h	i	j	k	l	m	n	o

Remainder of Yorkshire & Humberside Region – *continued*

Non-NHS hospitals - psychiatric

All ages	**24**	**15**	**9**	**1**	**1**	**-**	**20**	**12**	**8**	**3**	**2**	**1**	**22**	**6**
0 - 15	-	-	-	-	-	-	-	-	-	-	-	-	-	-
16 - 17	-	-	-	-	-	-	-	-	-	-	-	-	-	-
18 - 29	3	2	1	1	1	-	2	1	1	-	-	-	3	-
30 - 44	3	1	2	-	-	-	2	1	1	1	-	1	2	1
45 - 59	10	8	2	-	-	-	8	6	2	2	2	-	9	5
60 - 64	1	1	-	-	-	-	1	1	-	-	-	-	1	-
65 - 74	4	1	3	-	-	-	4	1	3	-	-	-	4	-
75 - 84	3	2	1	-	-	-	3	2	1	-	-	-	3	-
85 and over	-	-	-	-	-	-	-	-	-	-	-	-	-	-

Non-NHS hospitals - other

All ages	**437**	**209**	**228**	**377**	**162**	**215**	**48**	**38**	**10**	**12**	**9**	**3**	**324**	**36**
0 - 15	2	1	1	2	1	1	-	-	-	-	-	-	-	-
16 - 17	2	1	1	-	-	-	2	1	1	-	-	-	2	1
18 - 29	58	43	15	21	14	7	30	25	5	7	4	3	38	23
30 - 44	46	29	17	31	15	16	10	9	1	5	5	-	25	10
45 - 59	77	38	39	74	35	39	3	3	-	-	-	-	50	2
60 - 64	36	16	20	36	16	20	-	-	-	-	-	-	27	-
65 - 74	98	47	51	98	47	51	-	-	-	-	-	-	77	-
75 - 84	88	30	58	88	30	58	-	-	-	-	-	-	77	-
85 and over	30	4	26	27	4	23	3	-	3	-	-	-	28	-

Table 3 Type of establishment, migrants and long-term illness – **continued**

Great Britain, England & Wales, England, regions, metropolitan counties, Inner London, Outer London, regional remainders, Wales, Scotland

Persons present in communal establishments

Type of establishment and age	PERSONS PRESENT			Visitors/guests			Residents - non-staff			Residents - staff			With limiting long-term illness	Migrants
	TOTAL	Males	Females	Total	Males	Females	Total	Males	Females	Total	Males	Females		
a	b	c	d	e	f	g	h	i	j	k	l	m	n	o
Remainder of Yorkshire & Humberside Region – *continued*														
Local authority homes														
All ages	**3,821**	**1,272**	**2,549**	**439**	**188**	**251**	**3,363**	**1,076**	**2,287**	**19**	**8**	**11**	**3,345**	**638**
0 - 15	153	113	40	108	84	24	43	27	16	2	2	-	72	24
16 - 17	47	29	18	26	15	11	20	13	7	1	1	-	25	11
18 - 29	152	75	77	52	18	34	96	56	40	4	1	3	114	19
30 - 44	194	92	102	56	16	40	135	76	59	3	-	3	145	23
45 - 59	155	86	69	18	2	16	130	81	49	7	3	4	130	10
60 - 64	62	34	28	6	2	4	55	31	24	1	1	-	57	9
65 - 74	400	191	209	29	13	16	371	178	193	-	-	-	364	81
75 - 84	1,247	386	861	88	25	63	1,159	361	798	-	-	-	1,130	229
85 and over	1,411	266	1,145	56	13	43	1,354	253	1,101	1	-	1	1,308	232
Housing association homes and hostels														
All ages	**816**	**440**	**376**	**44**	**21**	**23**	**752**	**409**	**343**	**20**	**10**	**10**	**443**	**300**
0 - 15	6	4	2	1	1	-	1	1	-	4	2	2	1	-
16 - 17	22	12	10	-	-	-	21	11	10	1	1	-	1	20
18 - 29	142	87	55	21	7	14	120	79	41	1	1	-	36	69
30 - 44	118	89	29	10	6	4	102	81	21	6	2	4	59	40
45 - 59	85	58	27	1	1	-	79	54	25	5	3	2	47	24
60 - 64	52	38	14	2	2	-	48	35	13	2	1	1	26	16
65 - 74	88	59	29	1	1	-	86	58	28	1	-	1	47	26
75 - 84	145	60	85	4	3	1	141	57	84	-	-	-	102	66
85 and over	158	33	125	4	-	4	154	33	121	-	-	-	124	39

Table 3 Type of establishment, migrants and long-term illness – **continued**

Persons present in communal establishments

Type of establishment and age	PERSONS PRESENT			Visitors/guests			Residents - non-staff			Residents - staff			With limiting long-term illness	Migrants
	TOTAL	Males	Females	Total	Males	Females	Total	Males	Females	Total	Males	Females		
a	b	c	d	e	f	g	h	i	j	k	l	m	n	o
Remainder of Yorkshire & Humberside Region – *continued*														
Nursing homes (non-NHS/ LA/HA)														
All ages	**5,791**	**1,482**	**4,309**	**285**	**82**	**203**	**5,437**	**1,375**	**4,062**	**69**	**25**	**44**	**5,587**	**1,865**
0 - 15	10	5	5	-	-	-	3	2	1	7	3	4	2	4
16 - 17	8	4	4	-	-	-	4	2	2	4	2	2	4	2
18 - 29	73	31	42	21	6	15	35	21	14	17	4	13	44	14
30 - 44	114	51	63	37	9	28	64	38	26	13	4	9	73	24
45 - 59	137	65	72	41	9	32	76	50	26	20	6	14	95	18
60 - 64	178	96	82	31	16	15	141	75	66	6	5	1	166	54
65 - 74	703	260	443	52	15	37	650	244	406	1	1	-	688	236
75 - 84	2,263	606	1,657	75	21	54	2,187	585	1,602	1	-	1	2,227	818
85 and over	2,305	364	1,941	28	6	22	2,277	358	1,919	-	-	-	2,288	695
Residential homes (non-NHS/LA/HA)														
All ages	**9,256**	**2,665**	**6,591**	**353**	**109**	**244**	**8,390**	**2,318**	**6,072**	**513**	**238**	**275**	**7,850**	**2,104**
0 - 15	127	69	58	3	2	1	10	8	2	114	59	55	5	10
16 - 17	25	10	15	9	4	5	-	-	-	16	6	10	6	3
18 - 29	353	172	181	83	29	54	199	112	87	71	31	40	230	82
30 - 44	547	293	254	44	10	34	376	221	155	127	62	65	360	69
45 - 59	512	239	273	25	5	20	332	168	164	155	66	89	334	61
60 - 64	307	144	163	33	8	25	259	129	130	15	7	8	247	58
65 - 74	973	394	579	43	16	27	922	372	550	8	6	2	847	239
75 - 84	2,998	743	2,255	70	25	45	2,923	717	2,206	5	1	4	2,672	835
85 and over	3,414	601	2,813	43	10	33	3,369	591	2,778	2	-	2	3,149	747

Table 3 Type of establishment, migrants and long-term illness – **continued**

Persons present in communal establishments

Type of establishment and age	PERSONS PRESENT			Visitors/guests			Residents - non-staff			Residents - staff			With limiting long-term illness	Migrants
	TOTAL	Males	Females	Total	Males	Females	Total	Males	Females	Total	Males	Females		
a	b	c	d	e	f	g	h	i	j	k	l	m	n	o

Remainder of Yorkshire & Humberside Region – *continued*

Children's homes

All ages	**290**	**177**	**113**	**38**	**23**	**15**	**213**	**133**	**80**	**39**	**21**	**18**	**39**	**123**
0 - 15	256	161	95	34	22	12	213	133	80	9	6	3	30	123
16 - 17	2	1	1	-	-	-	-	-	-	2	1	1	-	-
18 - 29	9	5	4	3	-	3	-	-	-	6	5	1	4	-
30 - 44	13	5	8	1	1	-	-	-	-	12	4	8	1	-
45 - 59	6	2	4	-	-	-	-	-	-	6	2	4	1	-
60 - 64	2	1	1	-	-	-	-	-	-	2	1	1	2	-
65 - 74	2	2	-	-	-	-	-	-	-	2	2	-	1	-
75 - 84	-	-	-	-	-	-	-	-	-	-	-	-	-	-
85 and over	-	-	-	-	-	-	-	-	-	-	-	-	-	-

Prison service establishments

All ages	**1,069**	**935**	**134**	**746**	**690**	**56**	**318**	**242**	**76**	**5**	**3**	**2**	**149**	**138**
0 - 15	-	-	-	-	-	-	-	-	-	-	-	-	-	-
16 - 17	67	67	-	62	62	-	5	5	-	-	-	-	6	4
18 - 29	722	678	44	549	522	27	171	155	16	2	1	1	73	98
30 - 44	178	134	44	101	80	21	75	52	23	2	2	-	39	19
45 - 59	77	50	27	30	23	7	46	27	19	1	-	1	20	15
60 - 64	6	3	3	2	2	-	4	4	-	-	-	-	2	2
65 - 74	11	3	8	2	1	1	9	2	7	-	-	-	3	2
75 - 84	4	-	4	-	-	-	4	-	4	-	-	-	4	-
85 and over	4	-	4	-	-	-	4	-	4	-	-	-	2	-

Table 3 Type of establishment, migrants and long-term illness – **continued**

Great Britain, England & Wales, England, regions, metropolitan counties, Inner London, Outer London, regional remainders, Wales, Scotland

Persons present in communal establishments

Type of establishment and age	PERSONS PRESENT			Visitors/guests			Residents - non-staff			Residents - staff			With limiting long-term illness	Migrants
	TOTAL	Males	Females	Total	Males	Females	Total	Males	Females	Total	Males	Females		
a	b	c	d	e	f	g	h	i	j	k	l	m	n	o

Remainder of Yorkshire & Humberside Region – *continued*

Defence establishments

Type of establishment and age	PERSONS PRESENT			Visitors/guests			Residents - non-staff			Residents - staff			With limiting long-term illness	Migrants
All ages	**5,296**	**4,818**	**478**	**1,139**	**1,018**	**121**	**4,157**	**3,800**	**357**				**136**	**2,531**
0 - 15	-	-	-	-	-	-	-	-	-				-	-
16 - 17	774	754	20	122	116	6	652	638	14				11	572
18 - 29	4,024	3,603	421	798	691	107	3,226	2,912	314				95	1,835
30 - 44	422	394	28	172	169	3	250	225	25				19	111
45 - 59	66	60	6	45	41	4	21	19	2				8	12
60 - 64	3	3	-	-	-	-	3	3	-				2	-
65 - 74	2	1	1	-	-	-	2	1	1				-	1
75 - 84	3	1	2	2	1	1	1	-	1				1	-
85 and over	2	2	-	-	-	-	2	2	-				-	-

Educational establishments

Type of establishment and age	PERSONS PRESENT			Visitors/guests			Residents - non-staff			Residents - staff			With limiting long-term illness	Migrants
All ages	**6,617**	**3,505**	**3,112**	**6,000**	**3,128**	**2,872**	**421**	**280**	**141**	**196**	**97**	**99**	**228**	**344**
0 - 15	2,368	1,358	1,010	2,344	1,339	1,005	17	14	3	7	5	2	69	3
16 - 17	913	494	419	901	487	414	8	6	2	4	1	3	39	5
18 - 29	2,878	1,384	1,494	2,541	1,194	1,347	270	160	110	67	30	37	79	250
30 - 44	273	172	101	125	75	50	87	64	23	61	33	28	16	69
45 - 59	144	64	80	77	23	54	17	17	-	50	24	26	10	13
60 - 64	19	13	6	9	7	2	5	4	1	5	2	3	7	2
65 - 74	12	11	1	3	3	-	8	7	1	1	1	-	-	1
75 - 84	7	6	1	-	-	-	7	6	1	1	-	-	5	-
85 and over	3	3	-	-	-	-	2	2	-	1	1	-	3	1

Table 3 Type of establishment, migrants and long-term illness – **continued**

Great Britain, England & Wales, England, regions, metropolitan counties, Inner London, Outer London, regional remainders, Wales, Scotland

Persons present in communal establishments

Type of establishment and age	PERSONS PRESENT			Visitors/guests			Residents - non-staff			Residents - staff			With limiting long-term illness	Migrants
	TOTAL	Males	Females	Total	Males	Females	Total	Males	Females	Total	Males	Females		
a	b	c	d	e	f	g	h	i	j	k	l	m	n	o

Remainder of Yorkshire & Humberside Region – *continued*

Type of establishment and age	PERSONS PRESENT			Visitors/guests			Residents - non-staff			Residents - staff			With limiting long-term illness	Migrants
Hotels, boarding houses etc														
All ages	**8,414**	**4,656**	**3,758**	**5,292**	**2,823**	**2,469**	**1,235**	**849**	**386**	**1,887**	**984**	**903**	**879**	**1,068**
0 - 15	737	365	372	379	169	210	120	73	47	238	123	115	17	84
16 - 17	282	137	145	177	86	91	42	18	24	63	33	30	10	42
18 - 29	2,151	1,222	929	1,086	617	469	457	285	172	608	320	288	82	606
30 - 44	1,748	1,075	673	1,105	698	407	227	172	55	416	205	211	110	191
45 - 59	1,807	1,051	756	1,125	625	500	202	165	37	480	261	219	233	103
60 - 64	530	255	275	431	179	252	60	49	11	39	27	12	99	14
65 - 74	800	407	393	698	338	360	79	60	19	23	9	14	200	17
75 - 84	300	126	174	252	102	150	31	18	13	17	6	11	100	7
85 and over	59	18	41	39	9	30	17	9	8	3	-	3	28	4
Hostels and common lodging houses (non-HA)														
All ages	**339**	**173**	**166**	**63**	**28**	**35**	**261**	**136**	**125**	**15**	**9**	**6**	**73**	**183**
0 - 15	61	37	24	-	-	-	61	37	24	-	-	-	6	41
16 - 17	38	14	24	23	11	12	15	3	12	-	-	-	3	14
18 - 29	138	43	95	28	9	19	103	31	72	7	7	-	18	96
30 - 44	36	25	11	4	3	1	32	22	10	-	-	-	15	20
45 - 59	35	27	8	7	4	3	20	17	3	8	6	2	15	6
60 - 64	12	10	2	1	1	-	11	9	2	-	-	-	4	4
65 - 74	12	11	1	-	-	-	12	11	1	-	-	-	9	1
75 - 84	6	5	1	-	-	-	6	5	1	-	-	-	3	-
85 and over	1	1	-	-	-	-	1	1	-	-	-	-	-	1

Table 3 Type of establishment, migrants and long-term illness – **continued**

Great Britain, England & Wales, England, regions, metropolitan counties, Inner London, Outer London, regional remainders, Wales, Scotland

Persons present in communal establishments

Remainder of Yorkshire & Humberside Region – *continued*

Type of establishment and age	PERSONS PRESENT			Visitors/guests			Residents - non-staff			Residents - staff			With limiting long-term illness	Migrants
	TOTAL	Males	Females	Total	Males	Females	Total	Males	Females	Total	Males	Females		
a	b	c	d	e	f	g	h	i	j	k	l	m	n	o
Other miscellaneous establishments														
All ages	810	364	446	332	203	129	433	146	287	45	15	30	187	192
0 - 15	120	47	73	55	8	47	65	39	26	-	-	-	3	52
16 - 17	21	10	11	9	6	3	12	4	8	-	-	-	2	12
18 - 29	218	122	96	126	91	35	80	25	55	12	6	6	20	64
30 - 44	148	90	58	87	67	20	52	18	34	9	5	4	18	29
45 - 59	84	43	41	29	20	9	42	19	23	13	4	9	26	16
60 - 64	34	10	24	8	4	4	21	6	15	5	-	5	8	-
65 - 74	77	23	54	6	3	3	66	20	46	5	-	5	33	12
75 - 84	84	17	67	9	4	5	75	13	62	-	-	-	57	5
85 and over	24	2	22	3	-	3	20	2	18	1	-	1	20	2
Persons sleeping rough														
All ages	17	16	1	3	3	-	14	13	1	-	-	-	6	2
0 - 15	-	-	-	-	-	-	-	-	-	-	-	-	-	-
16 - 17	-	-	-	-	-	-	-	-	-	-	-	-	-	-
18 - 29	11	10	1	2	2	-	9	8	1	-	-	-	2	1
30 - 44	4	4	-	1	1	-	3	3	-	-	-	-	2	1
45 - 59	1	1	-	-	-	-	1	1	-	-	-	-	1	-
60 - 64	-	-	-	-	-	-	-	-	-	-	-	-	-	-
65 - 74	1	1	-	-	-	-	1	1	-	-	-	-	1	1
75 - 84	-	-	-	-	-	-	-	-	-	-	-	-	-	-
85 and over	-	-	-	-	-	-	-	-	-	-	-	-	-	-

Table 3 Type of establishment, migrants and long-term illness – **continued**

Great Britain, England & Wales, England, regions, metropolitan counties, Inner London, Outer London, regional remainders, Wales, Scotland

Persons present in communal establishments

Type of establishment and age	PERSONS PRESENT			Visitors/guests			Residents - non-staff			Residents - staff			With limiting long-term illness	Migrants
	TOTAL	Males	Females	Total	Males	Females	Total	Males	Females	Total	Males	Females		
a	b	c	d	e	f	g	h	i	j	k	l	m	n	o

Remainder of Yorkshire & Humberside Region – *continued*

Campers

All ages	**45**	**28**	**17**	**45**	**28**	**17**	**-**	**-**	**-**				**3**	**-**
0 - 15	-	-	-	-	-	-	-	-	-				-	-
16 - 17	-	-	-	-	-	-	-	-	-				-	-
18 - 29	3	3	-	3	3	-	-	-	-				-	-
30 - 44	10	6	4	10	6	4	-	-	-				-	-
45 - 59	13	8	5	13	8	5	-	-	-				1	-
60 - 64	6	4	2	6	4	2	-	-	-				1	-
65 - 74	12	6	6	12	6	6	-	-	-				1	-
75 - 84	1	1	-	1	1	-	-	-	-				-	-
85 and over	-	-	-	-	-	-	-	-	-				-	-

Civilian ships, boats and barges

All ages	**710**	**680**	**30**	**607**	**583**	**24**	**103**	**97**	**6**				**15**	**19**
0 - 15	2	2	-	1	1	-	1	1	-				-	1
16 - 17	5	5	-	4	4	-	1	1	-				-	-
18 - 29	174	167	7	142	136	6	32	31	1				4	6
30 - 44	346	330	16	298	287	11	48	43	5				6	8
45 - 59	172	165	7	151	144	7	21	21	-				4	4
60 - 64	9	9	-	9	9	-	-	-	-				1	-
65 - 74	1	1	-	1	1	-	-	-	-				-	-
75 - 84	1	1	-	1	1	-	-	-	-				-	-
85 and over	-	-	-	-	-	-	-	-	-				-	-

Table 3 Type of establishment, migrants and long-term illness – **continued**

Great Britain, England & Wales, England, regions, metropolitan counties, Inner London, Outer London, regional remainders, Wales, Scotland

Persons present in communal establishments

EAST MIDLANDS REGION

Type of establishment and age	PERSONS PRESENT			Visitors/guests			Residents - non-staff			Residents - staff			With limiting long-term illness	Migrants
	TOTAL	Males	Females	Total	Males	Females	Total	Males	Females	Total	Males	Females		
a	b	c	d	e	f	g	h	i	j	k	l	m	n	o
All establishments														
All ages	**91,182**	**43,954**	**47,228**	**40,734**	**23,460**	**17,274**	**46,496**	**18,750**	**27,746**	**3,952**	**1,744**	**2,208**	**45,426**	**16,758**
0 - 15	8,232	5,303	2,929	6,618	4,418	2,200	1,349	760	589	265	125	140	607	744
16 - 17	3,349	2,316	1,033	2,869	2,028	841	407	257	150	73	31	42	255	315
18 - 29	23,384	14,195	9,189	14,477	8,536	5,941	6,851	4,892	1,959	2,056	767	1,289	2,651	4,835
30 - 44	10,124	6,546	3,578	5,341	3,255	2,086	4,003	2,862	1,141	780	429	351	3,200	1,489
45 - 59	6,467	3,891	2,576	3,113	1,749	1,364	2,730	1,838	892	624	304	320	3,084	655
60 - 64	2,465	1,374	1,091	1,129	595	534	1,252	725	527	84	54	30	1,672	277
65 - 74	6,966	3,133	3,833	2,643	1,293	1,350	4,274	1,812	2,462	49	28	21	5,621	1,154
75 - 84	15,195	4,469	10,726	3,018	1,201	1,817	12,163	3,265	8,898	14	3	11	14,060	3,829
85 and over	15,000	2,727	12,273	1,526	385	1,141	13,467	2,339	11,128	7	3	4	14,276	3,460
NHS hospitals/homes - psychiatric														
All ages	**2,403**	**1,300**	**1,103**	**724**	**324**	**400**	**1,568**	**912**	**656**	**111**	**64**	**47**	**2,111**	**251**
0 - 15	18	7	11	15	6	9	3	1	2	-	-	-	1	2
16 - 17	8	3	5	6	3	3	2	-	2	-	-	-	6	2
18 - 29	347	214	133	108	61	47	170	120	50	69	33	36	235	80
30 - 44	610	429	181	153	81	72	422	321	101	35	27	8	528	73
45 - 59	387	228	159	115	46	69	266	179	87	6	3	3	339	26
60 - 64	114	66	48	29	18	11	84	47	37	1	1	-	110	5
65 - 74	328	148	180	116	43	73	212	105	107	-	-	-	312	20
75 - 84	396	158	238	136	53	83	260	105	155	-	-	-	385	30
85 and over	195	47	148	46	13	33	149	34	115	-	-	-	195	13

Persons present in communal establishments

Table 3 Type of establishment, migrants and long-term illness – **continued**

Great Britain, England & Wales, England, regions, metropolitan counties, Inner London, Outer London, regional remainders, Wales, Scotland

Type of establishment and age	PERSONS PRESENT			Visitors/guests			Residents - non-staff			Residents - staff			With limiting long-term illness	Migrants
	TOTAL	Males	Females	Total	Males	Females	Total	Males	Females	Total	Males	Females		
a	b	c	d	e	f	g	h	i	j	k	l	m	n	o
EAST MIDLANDS REGION – *continued*														
NHS hospitals/homes - other														
All ages	**13,556**	**5,414**	**8,142**	**9,783**	**3,943**	**5,840**	**2,548**	**1,128**	**1,420**	**1,225**	**343**	**882**	**8,365**	**1,111**
0 - 15	915	508	407	884	490	394	31	18	13	-	-	-	116	3
16 - 17	99	26	73	85	21	64	12	5	7	2	-	2	26	4
18 - 29	2,750	772	1,978	1,299	320	979	389	207	182	1,062	245	817	486	641
30 - 44	1,609	752	857	931	327	604	535	338	197	143	87	56	818	137
45 - 59	1,318	661	657	938	452	486	362	198	164	18	11	7	969	42
60 - 64	644	329	315	546	288	258	98	41	57	-	-	-	512	19
65 - 74	2,001	931	1,070	1,701	818	883	300	113	187	-	-	-	1,619	62
75 - 84	2,722	1,085	1,637	2,275	945	1,330	447	140	307	-	-	-	2,409	114
85 and over	1,498	350	1,148	1,124	282	842	374	68	306	-	-	-	1,410	89
Non-NHS hospitals - psychiatric														
All ages	**310**	**175**	**135**	**59**	**29**	**30**	**230**	**130**	**100**	**21**	**16**	**5**	**236**	**49**
0 - 15	11	7	4	3	2	1	8	5	3	-	-	-	6	5
16 - 17	11	6	5	5	3	2	6	3	3	-	-	-	5	4
18 - 29	86	55	31	17	6	11	51	36	15	18	13	5	44	24
30 - 44	52	36	16	7	4	3	43	30	13	2	2	1	44	12
45 - 59	42	27	15	21	13	8	20	13	7	1	1	-	32	1
60 - 64	21	12	9	1	-	1	20	12	8	-	-	-	21	1
65 - 74	32	14	18	4	1	3	28	13	15	-	-	-	31	-
75 - 84	34	14	20	1	-	1	33	14	19	-	-	-	33	1
85 and over	21	4	17	-	-	-	21	4	17	-	-	-	20	1

Table 3 Type of establishment, migrants and long-term illness – **continued**

Great Britain, England & Wales, England, regions, metropolitan counties, Inner London, Outer London, regional remainders, Wales, Scotland

Persons present in communal establishments

Type of establishment and age	PERSONS PRESENT			Visitors/guests			Residents - non-staff			Residents - staff			With limiting long-term illness	Migrants
	TOTAL	Males	Females	Total	Males	Females	Total	Males	Females	Total	Males	Females		
a	b	c	d	e	f	g	h	i	j	k	l	m	n	o
EAST MIDLANDS REGION – *continued*														
Non-NHS hospitals - other														
All ages	**225**	**85**	**140**	**170**	**63**	**107**	**53**	**22**	**31**	**2**	**-**	**2**	**90**	**25**
0 - 15	11	6	5	1	-	1	10	6	4	-	-	-	-	3
16 - 17	-	-	-	-	-	-	-	-	-	-	-	-	-	-
18 - 29	14	7	7	9	4	5	5	3	2	-	-	-	2	3
30 - 44	56	17	39	53	16	37	3	1	2	-	-	-	10	2
45 - 59	51	19	32	48	18	30	1	1	-	2	-	2	17	2
60 - 64	13	8	5	13	8	5	-	-	-	-	-	-	6	-
65 - 74	30	14	16	26	12	14	4	2	2	-	-	-	15	1
75 - 84	28	10	18	18	5	13	10	5	5	-	-	-	18	4
85 and over	22	4	18	2	-	2	20	4	16	-	-	-	22	10
Local authority homes														
All ages	**9,144**	**3,050**	**6,094**	**1,110**	**514**	**596**	**7,989**	**2,518**	**5,471**	**45**	**18**	**27**	**8,154**	**1,741**
0 - 15	413	282	131	319	224	95	91	56	35	3	2	1	138	49
16 - 17	95	51	44	53	23	30	42	28	14	-	-	-	24	18
18 - 29	389	244	145	98	58	40	280	182	98	11	4	7	288	76
30 - 44	500	261	239	75	37	38	414	221	193	11	3	8	436	56
45 - 59	439	229	210	62	14	48	361	209	152	16	6	10	373	43
60 - 64	179	95	84	16	6	10	162	88	74	1	1	-	168	40
65 - 74	838	355	483	70	34	36	766	319	447	2	2	-	778	176
75 - 84	2,843	831	2,012	222	68	154	2,620	763	1,857	1	1	-	2,683	627
85 and over	3,448	702	2,746	195	50	145	3,253	652	2,601	-	-	-	3,266	656

Table 3 Type of establishment, migrants and long-term illness – **continued**

Persons present in communal establishments

Type of establishment and age	PERSONS PRESENT			Visitors/guests			Residents - non-staff			Residents - staff			With limiting long-term illness	Migrants
	TOTAL	Males	Females	Total	Males	Females	Total	Males	Females	Total	Males	Females		
a	b	c	d	e	f	g	h	i	j	k	l	m	n	o

EAST MIDLANDS REGION – *continued*

Housing association homes and hostels

All ages	879	409	470	42	17	25	816	381	435	21	11	10	595	311
0 - 15	18	9	9	-	-	-	18	9	9	-	-	-	1	11
16 - 17	32	21	11	4	4	-	28	17	11	-	-	-	8	22
18 - 29	158	109	49	18	7	11	131	95	36	9	7	2	45	81
30 - 44	98	70	28	5	1	4	89	68	21	4	1	3	61	38
45 - 59	112	75	37	8	2	6	97	70	27	7	3	4	87	28
60 - 64	36	24	12	3	3	-	33	21	12	-	-	-	28	12
65 - 74	79	40	39	-	-	-	78	40	38	1	1	1	64	24
75 - 84	150	35	115	3	-	3	147	35	112	-	-	-	130	53
85 and over	196	26	170	1	-	1	195	26	169	-	-	-	171	42

Nursing homes (non-NHS/LA/HA)

All ages	11,958	3,240	8,718	364	109	255	11,490	3,096	8,394	104	35	69	11,513	4,202
0 - 15	20	12	8	-	-	-	8	4	4	12	8	4	2	1
16 - 17	13	5	8	-	-	-	9	3	6	4	2	2	5	4
18 - 29	136	63	73	27	6	21	95	54	41	14	3	11	93	28
30 - 44	246	122	124	59	11	48	163	101	62	24	10	14	174	56
45 - 59	263	130	133	57	18	39	174	106	68	32	6	26	195	54
60 - 64	318	164	154	25	11	14	288	151	137	5	2	3	295	90
65 - 74	1,504	606	898	53	26	27	1,442	577	865	9	3	6	1,453	548
75 - 84	4,686	1,295	3,391	81	23	58	4,604	1,272	3,332	1	-	1	4,601	1,847
85 and over	4,772	843	3,929	62	14	48	4,707	828	3,879	3	1	2	4,695	1,574

Table 3 Type of establishment, migrants and long-term illness – **continued**

Great Britain, England & Wales, England, regions, metropolitan counties, Inner London, Outer London, regional remainders, Wales, Scotland

Persons present in communal establishments

Type of establishment and age	PERSONS PRESENT			Visitors/guests			Residents - non-staff			Residents - staff			With limiting long-term illness	Migrants
	TOTAL	Males	Females	Total	Males	Females	Total	Males	Females	Total	Males	Females		
a	b	c	d	e	f	g	h	i	j	k	l	m	n	o

EAST MIDLANDS REGION – *continued*

Residential homes (non-NHS/LA/HA)

Type of establishment and age	TOTAL	Males	Females	Total	Males	Females	Total	Males	Females	Total	Males	Females	n	o
All ages	**12,128**	**3,387**	**8,741**	**331**	**115**	**216**	**11,360**	**3,089**	**8,271**	**437**	**183**	**254**	**10,792**	**2,874**
0 - 15	82	49	33	19	14	5	15	12	3	48	23	25	25	10
16 - 17	30	15	15	3	2	1	15	9	6	12	4	8	12	8
18 - 29	595	334	261	48	22	26	452	277	175	95	35	60	456	155
30 - 44	700	396	304	51	12	39	533	335	198	116	49	67	524	107
45 - 59	608	330	278	33	4	29	441	272	169	134	54	80	434	79
60 - 64	338	195	143	14	9	5	304	175	129	20	11	9	291	62
65 - 74	1,136	461	675	16	7	9	1,110	447	663	10	7	3	1,030	277
75 - 84	3,918	890	3,028	84	31	53	3,833	859	2,974	1	-	1	3,611	1,122
85 and over	4,721	717	4,004	63	14	49	4,657	703	3,954	1	-	1	4,409	1,054

Children's homes

Type of establishment and age	TOTAL	Males	Females	Total	Males	Females	Total	Males	Females	Total	Males	Females	n	o
All ages	**800**	**442**	**358**	**108**	**62**	**46**	**627**	**351**	**276**	**65**	**29**	**36**	**74**	**333**
0 - 15	709	410	299	71	54	17	627	351	276	11	5	6	61	329
16 - 17	3	2	1	-	-	-	-	-	-	3	2	1	1	-
18 - 29	29	10	19	15	3	12	-	-	-	14	7	7	8	3
30 - 44	30	14	16	13	5	8	-	-	-	17	9	8	1	-
45 - 59	24	5	19	9	-	9	-	-	-	15	5	10	3	-
60 - 64	2	-	2	-	-	-	-	-	-	2	-	2	-	-
65 - 74	1	1	-	-	-	-	-	-	-	1	1	-	-	-
75 - 84	2	-	2	-	-	-	-	-	-	2	-	2	-	1
85 and over	-	-	-	-	-	-	-	-	-	-	-	-	-	-

Table 3 Type of establishment, migrants and long-term illness – **continued**

Persons present in communal establishments

EAST MIDLANDS REGION – *continued*

Type of establishment and age	PERSONS PRESENT			Visitors/guests			Residents - non-staff			Residents - staff			With limiting long-term illness	Migrants
	TOTAL	Males	Females	Total	Males	Females	Total	Males	Females	Total	Males	Females		
a	b	c	d	e	f	g	h	i	j	k	l	m	n	o
Prison service establishments														
All ages	**4,210**	**4,186**	**24**	**2,978**	**2,973**	**5**	**1,228**	**1,210**	**18**	**4**	**3**	**1**	**486**	**674**
0 - 15	21	21	-	21	21	-	-	-	-	-	-	-	-	-
16 - 17	233	233	-	208	208	-	25	25	-	-	-	-	20	18
18 - 29	2,604	2,594	10	1,989	1,986	3	615	608	7	-	-	-	229	361
30 - 44	980	977	3	572	570	2	404	404	-	4	3	1	130	221
45 - 59	310	308	2	167	167	-	143	141	2	-	-	-	75	60
60 - 64	34	31	3	11	11	-	23	20	3	-	-	-	16	10
65 - 74	13	10	3	2	2	-	11	8	3	-	-	-	10	3
75 - 84	11	9	2	7	7	-	4	2	2	-	-	-	6	-
85 and over	4	3	1	1	1	-	3	2	1	-	-	-	-	1
Defence establishments														
All ages	**3,969**	**3,232**	**737**	**1,208**	**1,034**	**174**	**2,761**	**2,198**	**563**				**56**	**1,702**
0 - 15	-	-	-	-	-	-	-	-	-				-	-
16 - 17	176	141	35	82	66	16	94	75	19				1	89
18 - 29	3,269	2,590	679	858	708	150	2,411	1,882	529				41	1,499
30 - 44	439	419	20	217	210	7	222	209	13				11	104
45 - 59	75	72	3	47	46	1	28	26	2				3	7
60 - 64	5	5	-	2	2	-	3	3	-				-	-
65 - 74	2	2	-	1	1	-	1	1	-				-	1
75 - 84	3	3	-	1	1	-	2	2	-				-	2
85 and over	-	-	-	-	-	-	-	-	-				-	-

Table 3 Type of establishment, migrants and long-term illness – **continued**

Great Britain, England & Wales, England, regions, metropolitan counties, Inner London, Outer London, regional remainders, Wales, Scotland

Persons present in communal establishments

Type of establishment and age	PERSONS PRESENT			Visitors/guests			Residents - non-staff			Residents - staff			With limiting long-term illness	Migrants
	TOTAL	Males	Females	Total	Males	Females	Total	Males	Females	Total	Males	Females		
a	b	c	d	e	f	g	h	i	j	k	l	m	n	o

EAST MIDLANDS REGION – *continued*

Educational establishments

All ages	**14,632**	**9,104**	**5,528**	**12,986**	**8,131**	**4,855**	**1,140**	**720**	**420**	**506**	**253**	**253**	**780**	**816**
0 - 15	3,524	2,666	858	3,423	2,617	806	44	26	18	57	23	34	182	32
16 - 17	2,274	1,624	650	2,222	1,594	628	41	25	16	11	5	6	122	24
18 - 29	7,914	4,264	3,650	6,945	3,678	3,267	781	496	285	188	90	98	371	607
30 - 44	645	409	236	282	190	92	215	142	73	148	77	71	57	131
45 - 59	229	119	110	92	43	49	48	27	21	89	49	40	36	21
60 - 64	16	9	7	5	3	2	3	1	2	8	5	3	2	-
65 - 74	17	9	8	9	3	6	4	3	1	4	3	1	7	-
75 - 84	6	1	5	4	1	3	2	-	2	-	-	-	2	-
85 and over	7	3	4	4	2	2	2	-	2	1	1	-	1	1

Hotels, boarding houses etc

All ages	**13,684**	**7,821**	**5,863**	**10,140**	**5,601**	**4,539**	**2,259**	**1,502**	**757**	**1,285**	**718**	**567**	**1,388**	**1,479**
0 - 15	2,102	1,105	997	1,810	962	848	183	91	92	109	52	57	56	116
16 - 17	271	123	148	168	72	96	63	33	30	40	18	22	17	66
18 - 29	4,097	2,284	1,813	2,715	1,435	1,280	854	547	307	528	302	226	207	801
30 - 44	3,453	2,150	1,303	2,739	1,647	1,092	456	352	104	258	151	107	229	289
45 - 59	2,048	1,269	779	1,409	843	566	361	276	85	278	150	128	300	139
60 - 64	587	339	248	451	225	226	95	83	12	41	31	10	157	15
65 - 74	766	425	341	639	341	298	107	74	33	20	10	10	226	17
75 - 84	279	102	177	181	67	114	89	32	57	9	3	6	132	20
85 and over	81	24	57	28	9	19	51	14	37	2	1	1	64	16

Great Britain, England & Wales, England, regions, metropolitan counties, Inner London, Outer London, regional remainders, Wales, Scotland

Persons present in communal establishments

EAST MIDLANDS REGION – *continued*

Type of establishment and age	PERSONS PRESENT			Visitors/guests			Residents - non-staff			Residents - staff			With limiting long-term illness	Migrants
	TOTAL	Males	Females	Total	Males	Females	Total	Males	Females	Total	Males	Females		
a	b	c	d	e	f	g	h	i	j	k	l	m	n	o
Hostels and common lodging houses (non-HA)														
All ages	**1,413**	**1,147**	**266**	**136**	**106**	**30**	**1,232**	**1,013**	**219**	**45**	**28**	**17**	**522**	**692**
0 - 15	85	46	39	7	2	5	69	40	29	9	4	5	2	60
16 - 17	33	18	15	2	2	-	31	16	15	-	-	-	3	29
18 - 29	395	300	95	47	39	8	340	255	85	8	6	2	98	266
30 - 44	336	275	61	41	32	9	285	238	47	10	5	5	130	176
45 - 59	343	309	34	32	25	7	297	274	23	14	10	4	184	125
60 - 64	78	71	7	6	5	1	69	64	5	3	2	1	49	15
65 - 74	110	101	9	1	1	-	108	99	9	1	1	-	44	16
75 - 84	31	26	5	-	-	-	31	26	5	-	-	-	11	4
85 and over	2	1	1	-	-	-	2	1	1	-	-	-	1	1
Other miscellaneous establishments														
All ages	**1,676**	**786**	**890**	**456**	**313**	**143**	**1,139**	**430**	**709**	**81**	**43**	**38**	**215**	**456**
0 - 15	301	174	127	43	25	18	242	141	101	16	8	8	17	123
16 - 17	66	43	23	26	25	1	39	18	21	1	-	1	4	27
18 - 29	555	314	241	253	175	78	262	117	145	40	22	18	37	195
30 - 44	306	160	146	97	69	28	201	86	115	8	5	3	31	74
45 - 59	153	51	102	29	17	12	112	28	84	12	6	6	18	16
60 - 64	71	18	53	1	-	1	67	17	50	3	1	2	15	7
65 - 74	106	13	93	3	2	1	102	10	92	1	1	-	32	8
75 - 84	85	10	75	4	-	4	81	10	71	-	-	-	39	4
85 and over	33	3	30	-	-	-	33	3	30	-	-	-	22	2

Table 3 Type of establishment, migrants and long-term illness – **continued**

Great Britain, England & Wales, England, regions, metropolitan counties, Inner London, Outer London, regional remainders, Wales, Scotland

Persons present in communal establishments

EAST MIDLANDS REGION – *continued*

Type of establishment and age	PERSONS PRESENT			Visitors/guests			Residents - non-staff			Residents - staff			With limiting long-term illness	Migrants
	TOTAL	Males	Females	Total	Males	Females	Total	Males	Females	Total	Males	Females		
a	b	c	d	e	f	g	h	i	j	k	l	m	n	o
Persons sleeping rough														
All ages	**107**	**97**	**10**	**52**	**48**	**4**	**55**	**49**	**6**				**45**	**42**
0 - 15	-	-	-	-	-	-	-	-	-				-	-
16 - 17	1	1	-	1	1	-	-	-	-				-	-
18 - 29	32	28	4	17	15	2	15	13	2				11	15
30 - 44	35	31	4	18	16	2	17	15	2				15	13
45 - 59	33	32	1	14	14	-	19	18	1				17	12
60 - 64	5	4	1	2	2	-	3	2	1				2	1
65 - 74	1	1	-	-	-	-	1	1	-				-	1
75 - 84	-	-	-	-	-	-	-	-	-				-	-
85 and over	-	-	-	-	-	-	-	-	-				-	-
Campers														
All ages	**18**	**12**	**6**	**18**	**12**	**6**	**-**	**-**	**-**				**3**	**-**
0 - 15	2	1	1	2	1	1	-	-	-				-	-
16 - 17	2	2	-	2	2	-	-	-	-				1	-
18 - 29	2	1	1	2	1	1	-	-	-				-	-
30 - 44	6	5	1	6	5	1	-	-	-				1	-
45 - 59	5	2	3	5	2	3	-	-	-				1	-
60 - 64	-	-	-	-	-	-	-	-	-				-	-
65 - 74	1	1	-	1	1	-	-	-	-				-	-
75 - 84	-	-	-	-	-	-	-	-	-				-	-
85 and over	-	-	-	-	-	-	-	-	-				-	-

Table 3 Type of establishment, migrants and long-term illness – **continued**

Great Britain, England & Wales, England, regions, metropolitan counties, Inner London, Outer London, regional remainders, Wales, Scotland

Persons present in communal establishments

Type of establishment and age	PERSONS PRESENT			Visitors/guests			Residents - non-staff			Residents - staff			With limiting long-term illness	Migrants
	TOTAL	Males	Females	Total	Males	Females	Total	Males	Females	Total	Males	Females		
a	b	c	d	e	f	g	h	i	j	k	l	m	n	o
EAST MIDLANDS REGION – *continued*														
Civilian ships, boats and barges														
All ages	70	67	3	69	66	3	1	1	-				1	-
0 - 15	-	-	-	-	-	-	-	-	-				-	-
16 - 17	2	2	-	2	2	-	-	-	-				-	-
18 - 29	12	12	-	12	12	-	-	-	-				-	-
30 - 44	23	23	-	22	22	-	1	1	-				1	-
45 - 59	27	25	2	27	25	2	-	-	-				-	-
60 - 64	4	4	-	4	4	-	-	-	-				-	-
65 - 74	1	1	-	1	1	-	-	-	-				-	-
75 - 84	1	-	1	1	-	1	-	-	1				-	-
85 and over	-	-	-	-	-	-	-	-	-				-	-
EAST ANGLIA REGION														
All establishments														
All ages	68,263	36,333	31,930	34,815	19,989	14,826	30,191	14,852	15,339	3,257	1,492	1,765	23,546	11,906
0 - 15	6,592	4,007	2,585	5,507	3,409	2,098	803	451	352	282	147	135	396	420
16 - 17	2,475	1,480	995	2,010	1,181	829	370	252	118	95	47	48	157	306
18 - 29	25,595	16,403	9,192	14,809	8,737	6,072	9,340	7,098	2,242	1,446	568	878	1,552	5,653
30 - 44	7,671	5,297	2,374	4,150	2,750	1,400	2,918	2,213	705	603	334	269	1,580	1,241
45 - 59	4,615	2,816	1,799	2,509	1,546	963	1,438	948	490	668	322	346	1,568	355
60 - 64	1,498	784	714	860	428	432	560	311	249	78	45	33	799	101
65 - 74	3,794	1,675	2,119	1,880	859	1,021	1,857	794	1,063	57	22	35	2,769	434
75 - 84	7,738	2,250	5,488	2,066	792	1,274	5,652	1,453	4,199	20	5	15	6,923	1,636
85 and over	8,285	1,621	6,664	1,024	287	737	7,253	1,332	5,921	8	2	6	7,802	1,760

Table 3 Type of establishment, migrants and long-term illness – **continued**

Great Britain, England & Wales, England, regions, metropolitan counties, Inner London, Outer London, regional remainders, Wales, Scotland

Persons present in communal establishments

Type of establishment and age	PERSONS PRESENT			Visitors/guests			Residents - non-staff			Residents - staff			With limiting long-term illness	Migrants
	TOTAL	Males	Females	Total	Males	Females	Total	Males	Females	Total	Males	Females		
a	b	c	d	e	f	g	h	i	j	k	l	m	n	o

EAST ANGLIA REGION – *continued*

NHS hospitals/homes - psychiatric

All ages	**1,272**	**548**	**724**	**373**	**150**	**223**	**822**	**361**	**461**	**77**	**37**	**40**	**1,110**	**194**
0 - 15	11	4	7	10	4	6	1	-	1	-	-	-	-	-
16 - 17	4	3	1	4	3	1	-	-	-	-	-	-	2	-
18 - 29	150	69	81	46	19	27	50	27	23	54	23	31	64	55
30 - 44	146	96	50	59	33	26	71	52	19	16	11	5	115	17
45 - 59	153	87	66	40	18	22	108	67	41	5	2	3	140	17
60 - 64	76	40	36	13	3	10	62	36	26	1	1	-	72	8
65 - 74	224	91	133	71	22	49	152	69	83	1	1	1	214	25
75 - 84	338	115	223	99	37	62	239	78	161	-	-	-	334	45
85 and over	170	43	127	31	11	20	139	32	107	-	-	-	169	27

NHS hospitals/homes - other

All ages	**7,386**	**2,710**	**4,676**	**5,073**	**1,983**	**3,090**	**1,684**	**580**	**1,104**	**629**	**147**	**482**	**4,445**	**744**
0 - 15	346	172	174	333	165	168	12	7	5	1	-	1	49	4
16 - 17	52	22	30	39	16	23	7	4	3	6	2	4	15	10
18 - 29	1,662	380	1,282	701	160	541	436	122	314	525	98	427	234	465
30 - 44	854	357	497	503	175	328	272	145	127	79	37	42	374	78
45 - 59	706	356	350	498	253	245	195	96	99	13	7	6	496	15
60 - 64	305	156	149	257	129	128	43	24	19	5	3	2	241	5
65 - 74	982	453	529	863	402	461	119	51	68	-	-	-	803	26
75 - 84	1,530	578	952	1,261	510	751	269	68	201	-	-	-	1,345	63
85 and over	949	236	713	618	173	445	331	63	268	-	-	-	888	78

Table 3 Type of establishment, migrants and long-term illness – **continued**

Persons present in communal establishments

Type of establishment and age	PERSONS PRESENT			Visitors/guests			Residents - non-staff			Residents - staff			With limiting long-term illness	Migrants
	TOTAL	Males	Females	Total	Males	Females	Total	Males	Females	Total	Males	Females		
a	b	c	d	e	f	g	h	i	j	k	l	m	n	o

EAST ANGLIA REGION – *continued*

Non-NHS hospitals - psychiatric

	b	c	d	e	f	g	h	i	j	k	l	m	n	o
All ages	**146**	**116**	**30**	**45**	**37**	**8**	**89**	**69**	**20**	**12**	**10**	**2**	**131**	**36**
0 - 15	-	-	-	-	-	-	-	-	-	-	-	-	-	-
16 - 17	6	4	2	4	3	1	1	1	-	1	-	1	5	2
18 - 29	71	53	18	24	19	5	42	30	12	5	4	1	64	19
30 - 44	57	48	9	13	11	2	40	33	7	4	4	-	52	13
45 - 59	10	9	1	4	4	-	4	3	1	2	2	-	8	2
60 - 64	2	2	-	-	-	-	2	2	-	-	-	-	2	-
65 - 74	-	-	-	-	-	-	-	-	-	-	-	-	-	-
75 - 84	-	-	-	-	-	-	-	-	-	-	-	-	-	-
85 and over	-	-	-	-	-	-	-	-	-	-	-	-	-	-

Non-NHS hospitals - other

	b	c	d	e	f	g	h	i	j	k	l	m	n	o
All ages	**1,382**	**564**	**818**	**955**	**363**	**592**	**325**	**158**	**167**	**102**	**43**	**59**	**828**	**113**
0 - 15	100	62	38	93	59	34	4	2	2	3	1	2	7	-
16 - 17	6	5	1	5	5	-	-	-	-	1	-	1	-	1
18 - 29	221	71	150	109	24	85	33	18	15	79	29	50	39	47
30 - 44	193	98	95	97	30	67	80	57	23	16	11	5	105	11
45 - 59	119	55	64	91	34	57	25	19	6	3	2	1	62	4
60 - 64	65	33	32	56	26	30	9	7	2	-	-	-	47	3
65 - 74	192	96	96	164	81	83	28	15	13	-	-	-	139	5
75 - 84	286	99	187	201	73	128	85	26	59	-	-	-	243	27
85 and over	200	45	155	139	31	108	61	14	47	-	-	-	186	15

Table 3 Type of establishment, migrants and long-term illness – **continued**

Great Britain, England & Wales, England, regions, metropolitan counties, Inner London, Outer London, regional remainders, Wales, Scotland

Persons present in communal establishments

EAST ANGLIA REGION – *continued*

Type of establishment and age	PERSONS PRESENT			Visitors/guests			Residents - non-staff			Residents - staff			With limiting long-term illness	Migrants
	TOTAL	Males	Females	Total	Males	Females	Total	Males	Females	Total	Males	Females		
a	b	c	d	e	f	g	h	i	j	k	l	m	n	o
Local authority homes														
All ages	**4,495**	**1,446**	**3,049**	**542**	**236**	**306**	**3,889**	**1,189**	**2,700**	**64**	**21**	**43**	**4,085**	**836**
0 - 15	172	121	51	115	90	25	54	30	24	3	1	2	85	24
16 - 17	57	27	30	30	13	17	26	14	12	1	-	1	39	7
18 - 29	262	144	118	70	36	34	161	100	61	31	8	23	180	62
30 - 44	199	106	93	49	11	38	142	89	53	8	6	2	152	32
45 - 59	152	59	93	30	4	26	109	52	57	13	3	10	109	15
60 - 64	62	35	27	9	3	6	50	29	21	3	3	-	54	6
65 - 74	372	150	222	28	14	14	340	136	204	4	-	4	355	71
75 - 84	1,366	394	972	104	30	74	1,261	364	897	1	-	1	1,325	291
85 and over	1,853	410	1,443	107	35	72	1,746	375	1,371	-	-	-	1,786	328
Housing association homes and hostels														
All ages	**641**	**355**	**286**	**22**	**12**	**10**	**589**	**331**	**258**	**30**	**12**	**18**	**365**	**252**
0 - 15	19	7	12	1	-	1	15	5	10	3	2	1	2	1
16 - 17	21	14	7	-	-	-	20	13	7	1	1	-	5	13
18 - 29	148	119	29	8	5	3	137	112	25	3	2	1	50	99
30 - 44	105	70	35	7	6	1	93	63	30	5	1	4	50	42
45 - 59	102	69	33	3	1	2	83	63	20	16	5	11	61	28
60 - 64	24	18	6	-	-	-	23	17	6	1	1	-	10	6
65 - 74	48	26	22	-	-	-	47	26	21	1	-	1	35	13
75 - 84	84	19	65	1	-	1	83	19	64	-	-	-	75	27
85 and over	90	13	77	2	-	2	88	13	75	-	-	-	77	23

Table 3　Type of establishment, migrants and long-term illness – **continued**

Great Britain, England & Wales, England, regions, metropolitan counties, Inner London, Outer London, regional remainders, Wales, Scotland

Persons present in communal establishments

Type of establishment and age	PERSONS PRESENT			Visitors/guests			Residents - non-staff			Residents - staff			With limiting long-term illness	Migrants
	TOTAL	Males	Females	Total	Males	Females	Total	Males	Females	Total	Males	Females		
a	b	c	d	e	f	g	h	i	j	k	l	m	n	o
EAST ANGLIA REGION – *continued*														
Nursing homes (non-NHS/LA/HA)														
All ages	**3,520**	**946**	**2,574**	**205**	**71**	**134**	**3,262**	**860**	**2,402**	**53**	**15**	**38**	**3,245**	**1,151**
0 - 15	21	11	10	3	1	2	14	9	5	4	1	3	8	6
16 - 17	14	4	10	2	1	1	10	3	7	2	-	2	6	-
18 - 29	80	38	42	22	7	15	42	27	15	16	4	12	41	13
30 - 44	95	47	48	25	7	18	62	38	24	8	2	6	66	8
45 - 59	119	55	64	19	6	13	83	42	41	17	7	10	88	14
60 - 64	120	49	71	18	8	10	99	40	59	3	1	2	106	21
65 - 74	402	167	235	39	15	24	362	152	210	1	-	1	375	124
75 - 84	1,195	293	902	50	15	35	1,143	278	865	2	-	2	1,130	472
85 and over	1,474	282	1,192	27	11	16	1,447	271	1,176	-	-	-	1,425	493
Residential homes (non-NHS/LA/HA)														
All ages	**8,064**	**2,137**	**5,927**	**280**	**71**	**209**	**7,527**	**1,959**	**5,568**	**257**	**107**	**150**	**7,129**	**1,834**
0 - 15	51	22	29	6	2	4	14	7	7	31	13	18	5	9
16 - 17	18	8	10	2	1	1	10	5	5	6	2	4	8	4
18 - 29	359	194	165	30	7	23	290	171	119	39	16	23	269	91
30 - 44	387	213	174	44	12	32	289	175	114	54	26	28	285	50
45 - 59	409	199	210	36	9	27	274	147	127	99	43	56	277	32
60 - 64	182	84	98	10	4	6	158	75	83	14	5	9	151	25
65 - 74	700	266	434	25	5	20	666	259	407	9	2	7	618	148
75 - 84	2,514	586	1,928	59	14	45	2,451	572	1,879	4	-	4	2,308	691
85 and over	3,444	565	2,879	68	17	51	3,375	548	2,827	1	1	1	3,208	784

Table 3 Type of establishment, migrants and long-term illness – **continued**

Persons present in communal establishments

Type of establishment and age	PERSONS PRESENT			Visitors/guests			Residents - non-staff			Residents - staff			With limiting long-term illness	Migrants
	TOTAL	Males	Females	Total	Males	Females	Total	Males	Females	Total	Males	Females		
a	b	c	d	e	f	g	h	i	j	k	l	m	n	o

EAST ANGLIA REGION – *continued*

Children's homes

All ages	**478**	**304**	**174**	**115**	**92**	**23**	**277**	**171**	**106**	**86**	**41**	**45**	**45**	**130**
0 - 15	399	266	133	105	87	18	277	171	106	17	8	9	42	126
16 - 17	8	3	5	-	-	-	-	-	-	8	3	5	-	-
18 - 29	27	12	15	3	3	3	-	-	-	24	12	12	1	4
30 - 44	18	9	9	5	3	2	-	-	-	13	6	7	1	-
45 - 59	25	14	11	2	2	-	-	-	-	23	12	11	2	-
60 - 64	-	-	-	-	-	-	-	-	-	-	-	-	-	-
65 - 74	1	-	1	-	-	-	-	-	-	1	-	1	-	-
75 - 84	-	-	-	-	-	-	-	-	-	-	-	-	-	-
85 and over	-	-	-	-	-	-	-	-	-	-	-	-	-	-

Prison service establishments

All ages	**2,748**	**2,741**	**7**	**1,331**	**1,328**	**3**	**1,417**	**1,413**	**4**	-	-	-	**392**	**695**
0 - 15	-	-	-	-	-	-	-	-	-	-	-	-	-	-
16 - 17	37	37	-	30	30	-	7	7	-	-	-	-	1	7
18 - 29	1,408	1,405	3	765	764	1	643	641	2	-	-	-	137	386
30 - 44	957	953	4	402	400	2	555	553	2	-	-	-	154	221
45 - 59	297	297	-	119	119	-	178	178	-	-	-	-	79	69
60 - 64	29	29	-	10	10	-	19	19	-	-	-	-	12	6
65 - 74	15	15	-	3	3	-	12	12	-	-	-	-	7	5
75 - 84	3	3	-	1	1	-	2	2	-	-	-	-	2	-
85 and over	2	2	-	1	1	-	1	1	-	-	-	-	-	1

Table 3 Type of establishment, migrants and long-term illness – **continued**

Great Britain, England & Wales, England, regions, metropolitan counties, Inner London, Outer London, regional remainders, Wales, Scotland

Persons present in communal establishments

EAST ANGLIA REGION – *continued*

Type of establishment and age	PERSONS PRESENT			Visitors/guests			Residents - non-staff			Residents - staff			With limiting long-term illness	Migrants
	TOTAL	Males	Females	Total	Males	Females	Total	Males	Females	Total	Males	Females		
a	b	c	d	e	f	g	h	i	j	k	l	m	n	o
Defence establishments														
All ages	**6,902**	**5,918**	**984**	**1,028**	**865**	**163**	**5,874**	**5,053**	**821**				**110**	**3,011**
0 - 15	-	-	-	-	-	-	-	-	-				-	-
16 - 17	164	141	23	29	18	11	135	123	12				2	130
18 - 29	5,744	4,881	863	592	481	111	5,152	4,400	752				70	2,594
30 - 44	858	769	89	310	275	35	548	494	54				32	271
45 - 59	121	114	7	86	81	5	35	33	2				4	12
60 - 64	8	6	2	6	5	1	2	1	1				-	2
65 - 74	4	4	-	3	3	-	1	1	-				-	1
75 - 84	3	3	-	2	2	-	1	1	-				2	1
85 and over	-	-	-	-	-	-	-	-	-				-	-
Educational establishments														
All ages	**18,414**	**11,111**	**7,303**	**16,245**	**9,734**	**6,511**	**1,839**	**1,193**	**646**	**330**	**184**	**146**	**502**	**1,151**
0 - 15	3,856	2,485	1,371	3,760	2,424	1,336	83	53	30	13	8	5	159	34
16 - 17	1,754	1,030	724	1,704	1,001	703	45	29	16	5	-	5	57	30
18 - 29	11,921	7,056	4,865	10,395	6,082	4,313	1,396	901	495	130	73	57	235	897
30 - 44	613	395	218	252	155	97	254	176	78	107	64	43	15	172
45 - 59	193	106	87	103	55	48	28	20	8	62	31	31	13	15
60 - 64	23	14	9	11	7	4	4	3	1	8	4	4	3	1
65 - 74	30	16	14	10	6	4	16	7	9	4	3	1	9	2
75 - 84	19	7	12	10	4	6	8	2	6	1	1	-	8	-
85 and over	5	2	3	-	-	-	5	2	3	-	-	-	3	-

203

Table 3 Type of establishment, migrants and long-term illness – **continued**

Great Britain, England & Wales, England, regions, metropolitan counties, Inner London, Outer London, regional remainders, Wales, Scotland

Persons present in communal establishments

Type of establishment and age	PERSONS PRESENT			Visitors/guests			Residents - non-staff			Residents - staff			With limiting long-term illness	Migrants
	TOTAL	Males	Females	Total	Males	Females	Total	Males	Females	Total	Males	Females		
a	b	c	d	e	f	g	h	i	j	k	l	m	n	o
EAST ANGLIA REGION – *continued*														
Hotels, boarding houses etc														
All ages	**10,277**	**5,739**	**4,538**	**7,345**	**4,060**	**3,285**	**1,427**	**871**	**556**	**1,505**	**808**	**697**	**851**	**1,175**
0 - 15	1,444	770	674	1,054	569	485	190	92	98	200	109	91	31	124
16 - 17	272	148	124	141	74	67	70	38	32	61	36	25	11	70
18 - 29	2,801	1,547	1,254	1,698	898	800	588	369	219	515	280	235	128	682
30 - 44	2,465	1,555	910	1,938	1,233	705	264	177	87	263	145	118	110	196
45 - 59	1,688	983	705	1,171	694	477	135	97	38	382	192	190	149	63
60 - 64	483	242	241	414	193	221	34	25	9	35	24	11	76	8
65 - 74	716	341	375	636	291	345	47	33	14	33	17	16	174	8
75 - 84	329	133	196	263	100	163	57	30	27	9	3	6	123	14
85 and over	79	20	59	30	8	22	42	10	32	7	2	5	49	10
Hostels and common lodging houses (non-HA)														
All ages	**602**	**382**	**220**	**55**	**37**	**18**	**514**	**327**	**187**	**33**	**18**	**15**	**171**	**310**
0 - 15	98	51	47	-	-	-	95	50	45	3	1	2	5	59
16 - 17	28	11	17	-	-	-	26	9	17	2	2	-	3	25
18 - 29	165	87	78	13	10	3	144	71	73	8	6	2	25	124
30 - 44	124	78	46	20	15	5	97	61	36	7	2	5	50	57
45 - 59	109	89	20	12	8	4	87	75	12	10	6	4	55	38
60 - 64	30	26	4	5	4	1	23	22	1	2	-	2	12	3
65 - 74	32	28	4	2	-	2	30	28	2	-	-	-	15	1
75 - 84	13	10	3	2	-	2	10	9	1	1	1	-	4	2
85 and over	3	2	1	1	-	1	2	2	-	-	-	-	2	1

Table 3 Type of establishment, migrants and long-term illness – **continued**

Great Britain, England & Wales, England, regions, metropolitan counties, Inner London, Outer London, regional remainders, Wales, Scotland

Persons present in communal establishments

EAST ANGLIA REGION – *continued*

Type of establishment and age	PERSONS PRESENT			Visitors/guests			Residents - non-staff			Residents - staff			With limiting long-term illness	Migrants
	TOTAL	Males	Females	Total	Males	Females	Total	Males	Females	Total	Males	Females		
a	b	c	d	e	f	g	h	i	j	k	l	m	n	o
Other miscellaneous establishments														
All ages	**1,236**	**779**	**457**	**543**	**452**	**91**	**614**	**278**	**336**	**79**	**49**	**30**	**106**	**252**
0 - 15	54	32	22	7	4	3	43	25	18	4	3	1	1	32
16 - 17	28	18	10	14	11	3	13	6	7	1	1	-	3	7
18 - 29	434	259	175	199	145	54	218	101	117	17	13	4	14	109
30 - 44	320	255	65	165	155	10	132	81	51	23	19	4	14	61
45 - 59	237	179	58	130	122	8	84	47	37	23	10	13	15	29
60 - 64	47	21	26	13	10	3	28	8	20	6	3	3	9	6
65 - 74	52	8	44	12	3	9	37	5	32	3	-	3	19	5
75 - 84	48	6	42	3	2	1	43	4	39	2	-	2	22	3
85 and over	16	1	15	-	-	-	16	1	15	-	-	-	9	-
Persons sleeping rough														
All ages	**14**	**12**	**2**	-	-	-	**14**	**12**	**2**				**4**	**11**
0 - 15	-	-	-	-	-	-	-	-	-				-	-
16 - 17	-	-	-	-	-	-	-	-	-				-	-
18 - 29	5	5	-	-	-	-	5	5	-				-	5
30 - 44	4	4	-	-	-	-	4	4	-				1	4
45 - 59	4	3	1	-	-	-	4	3	1				3	1
60 - 64	1	-	1	-	-	-	1	-	1				-	1
65 - 74	-	-	-	-	-	-	-	-	-				-	-
75 - 84	-	-	-	-	-	-	-	-	-				-	-
85 and over	-	-	-	-	-	-	-	-	-				-	-

Table 3 Type of establishment, migrants and long-term illness – **continued**

Great Britain, England & Wales, England, regions, metropolitan counties, Inner London, Outer London, regional remainders, Wales, Scotland

Persons present in communal establishments

Type of establishment and age	PERSONS PRESENT			Visitors/guests			Residents - non-staff			Residents - staff			With limiting long-term illness	Migrants
	TOTAL	Males	Females	Total	Males	Females	Total	Males	Females	Total	Males	Females		
a	b	c	d	e	f	g	h	i	j	k	l	m	n	o
EAST ANGLIA REGION – *continued*														
Campers														
All ages	**66**	**30**	**36**	**63**	**28**	**35**	**3**	**2**	**1**				**10**	**2**
0 - 15	11	2	9	10	2	8	1	-	1				-	1
16 - 17	-	-	-	-	-	-	-	-	-				-	-
18 - 29	10	5	5	10	5	5	-	-	-				1	-
30 - 44	14	6	8	13	5	8	1	1	-				-	1
45 - 59	8	5	3	7	4	3	1	1	-				2	-
60 - 64	8	4	4	8	4	4	-	-	-				3	-
65 - 74	9	5	4	9	5	4	-	-	-				3	-
75 - 84	6	3	3	6	3	3	-	-	-				1	-
85 and over	-	-	-	-	-	-	-	-	-				-	-
Civilian ships, boats and barges														
All ages	**620**	**495**	**125**	**595**	**470**	**125**	**25**	**25**	**-**				**17**	**9**
0 - 15	10	2	8	10	2	8	-	-	-				2	-
16 - 17	6	5	1	6	5	1	-	-	-				-	-
18 - 29	127	78	49	124	75	49	3	3	-				-	1
30 - 44	262	238	24	248	224	24	14	14	-				5	7
45 - 59	163	137	26	158	132	26	5	5	-				5	1
60 - 64	33	25	8	30	22	8	3	3	-				1	-
65 - 74	15	9	6	15	9	6	-	-	-				3	-
75 - 84	4	1	3	4	1	3	-	-	-				1	-
85 and over	-	-	-	-	-	-	-	-	-				-	-

Table 3 Type of establishment, migrants and long-term illness – **continued**

Great Britain, England & Wales, England, regions, metropolitan counties, Inner London, Outer London, regional remainders, Wales, Scotland

Persons present in communal establishments

Type of establishment and age	PERSONS PRESENT			Visitors/guests			Residents - non-staff			Residents - staff			With limiting long-term illness	Migrants
	TOTAL	Males	Females	Total	Males	Females	Total	Males	Females	Total	Males	Females		
a	b	c	d	e	f	g	h	i	j	k	l	m	n	o
All establishments *														
						SOUTH EAST REGION								
All ages	**514,062**	**250,086**	**263,976**	**232,128**	**129,910**	**102,218**	**243,361**	**103,828**	**139,533**	**38,573**	**16,348**	**22,225**	**198,281**	**100,201**
0 - 15	51,111	31,216	19,895	39,482	24,898	14,584	9,930	5,412	4,518	1,699	906	793	4,479	5,629
16 - 17	19,422	11,938	7,484	15,635	9,515	6,120	3,286	2,199	1,087	501	224	277	1,360	2,714
18 - 29	158,709	87,390	71,319	79,169	43,409	35,760	58,278	36,032	22,246	21,262	7,949	13,313	13,636	43,419
30 - 44	66,330	42,416	23,914	32,512	20,911	11,601	26,255	17,611	8,644	7,563	3,894	3,669	16,036	12,552
45 - 59	43,584	25,887	17,697	21,856	13,070	8,786	16,121	10,251	5,870	5,607	2,566	3,041	16,231	4,733
60 - 64	13,838	7,353	6,485	6,543	3,448	3,095	6,318	3,441	2,877	977	464	513	7,698	1,272
65 - 74	33,749	15,221	18,528	14,131	6,828	7,303	18,996	8,136	10,860	622	257	365	24,075	4,145
75 - 84	62,847	18,066	44,781	15,207	5,945	9,262	47,393	12,050	35,343	247	71	176	54,856	12,617
85 and over	64,472	10,599	53,873	7,593	1,886	5,707	56,784	8,696	48,088	95	17	78	59,910	13,120
NHS hospitals/homes - psychiatric														
All ages	**15,124**	**6,989**	**8,135**	**4,036**	**1,830**	**2,206**	**9,185**	**4,298**	**4,887**	**1,903**	**861**	**1,042**	**11,603**	**1,884**
0 - 15	155	88	67	121	69	52	34	19	15	-	-	-	43	6
16 - 17	38	16	22	31	14	17	6	2	4	1	-	1	23	1
18 - 29	3,098	1,427	1,671	860	464	396	966	469	497	1,272	494	778	984	874
30 - 44	2,336	1,433	903	740	383	357	1,172	800	372	424	250	174	1,627	315
45 - 59	2,164	1,260	904	597	283	314	1,385	878	507	182	99	83	1,816	117
60 - 64	863	510	353	166	76	90	677	420	257	20	14	6	811	46
65 - 74	2,214	1,014	1,200	514	192	322	1,696	818	878	4	4	-	2,128	148
75 - 84	2,794	948	1,846	699	270	429	2,095	678	1,417	-	-	-	2,736	252
85 and over	1,462	293	1,169	308	79	229	1,154	214	940	-	-	-	1,435	125

Note: * Includes a female member of staff incorrectly enumerated as a resident.

Great Britain, England & Wales, England, regions, metropolitan counties, Inner London, Outer London, regional remainders, Wales, Scotland

Table 3 Type of establishment, migrants and long-term illness – **continued**

Persons present in communal establishments

Type of establishment and age	PERSONS PRESENT			Visitors/guests			Residents - non-staff			Residents - staff			With limiting long-term illness	Migrants
	TOTAL	Males	Females	Total	Males	Females	Total	Males	Females	Total	Males	Females		
a	b	c	d	e	f	g	h	i	j	k	l	m	n	o
SOUTH EAST REGION – *continued*														
NHS hospitals/homes - other														
All ages	**74,351**	**27,718**	**46,633**	**44,442**	**17,727**	**26,715**	**19,087**	**7,107**	**11,980**	**10,822**	**2,884**	**7,938**	**40,198**	**9,629**
0 - 15	4,502	2,409	2,093	4,210	2,278	1,932	230	99	131	62	32	30	1,114	102
16 - 17	323	114	209	267	94	173	32	15	17	24	5	19	105	42
18 - 29	20,618	5,133	15,485	6,964	1,829	5,135	5,351	1,470	3,881	8,303	1,834	6,469	2,518	6,160
30 - 44	10,358	4,623	5,735	5,117	1,855	3,262	3,427	1,975	1,452	1,814	793	1,021	4,330	1,291
45 - 59	7,159	3,614	3,545	4,357	2,161	2,196	2,267	1,268	999	535	185	350	4,776	310
60 - 64	2,831	1,526	1,305	2,185	1,194	991	592	303	289	54	29	25	2,215	76
65 - 74	8,179	3,949	4,230	6,389	3,178	3,211	1,778	767	1,011	12	4	8	6,762	287
75 - 84	12,441	4,659	7,782	9,615	3,802	5,813	2,814	855	1,959	12	2	10	11,014	740
85 and over	7,940	1,691	6,249	5,338	1,336	4,002	2,596	355	2,241	6	-	6	7,364	621
Non-NHS hospitals - psychiatric														
All ages	**2,485**	**1,153**	**1,332**	**1,103**	**478**	**625**	**1,238**	**596**	**642**	**144**	**79**	**65**	**1,872**	**269**
0 - 15	94	61	33	89	58	31	5	3	2	-	-	-	12	-
16 - 17	17	4	13	16	4	12	1	-	1	-	-	-	9	-
18 - 29	393	182	211	195	74	121	108	68	40	90	40	50	200	78
30 - 44	489	267	222	205	80	125	251	162	89	33	25	8	340	36
45 - 59	422	231	191	199	97	102	202	120	82	21	14	7	320	31
60 - 64	148	80	68	59	32	27	89	48	41	-	-	-	129	11
65 - 74	372	171	201	143	66	77	229	105	124	-	-	-	340	38
75 - 84	354	109	245	135	49	86	219	60	159	-	-	-	332	44
85 and over	196	48	148	62	18	44	134	30	104	-	-	-	190	31

Table 3 Type of establishment, migrants and long-term illness – **continued**

Great Britain, England & Wales, England, regions, metropolitan counties, Inner London, Outer London, regional remainders, Wales, Scotland

Persons present in communal establishments

Type of establishment and age	PERSONS PRESENT			Visitors/guests			Residents - non-staff			Residents - staff			With limiting long-term illness	Migrants
	TOTAL	Males	Females	Total	Males	Females	Total	Males	Females	Total	Males	Females		
a	b	c	d	e	f	g	h	i	j	k	l	m	n	o
SOUTH EAST REGION – *continued*														
Non-NHS hospitals - other														
All ages	**5,689**	**2,250**	**3,439**	**3,188**	**1,268**	**1,920**	**1,890**	**775**	**1,115**	**611**	**207**	**404**	**2,855**	**659**
0 - 15	135	79	56	117	69	48	11	6	5	7	4	3	40	8
16 - 17	28	10	18	21	8	13	2	1	1	5	1	4	10	6
18 - 29	1,116	356	760	393	118	275	357	126	231	366	112	254	211	355
30 - 44	1,116	423	693	615	180	435	359	184	175	142	59	83	427	110
45 - 59	1,176	502	674	735	289	446	370	190	180	71	23	48	599	41
60 - 64	354	177	177	235	131	104	109	45	64	10	1	9	216	7
65 - 74	652	322	330	452	236	216	193	82	111	7	4	3	450	17
75 - 84	717	288	429	446	189	257	269	97	172	2	2	-	551	59
85 and over	395	93	302	174	48	126	220	44	176	1	1	-	351	56
Local authority homes														
All ages	**35,860**	**11,632**	**24,228**	**3,626**	**1,668**	**1,958**	**31,762**	**9,776**	**21,986**	**472**	**188**	**284**	**31,607**	**7,129**
0 - 15	1,346	975	371	875	664	211	455	302	153	16	9	7	479	173
16 - 17	389	222	167	172	94	78	209	126	83	8	2	6	197	108
18 - 29	2,734	1,473	1,261	476	245	231	2,111	1,166	945	147	62	85	1,839	717
30 - 44	2,585	1,439	1,146	341	124	217	2,110	1,254	856	134	61	73	2,032	425
45 - 59	1,827	959	868	263	86	177	1,432	834	598	132	39	93	1,445	257
60 - 64	718	338	380	70	26	44	632	305	327	16	7	9	646	129
65 - 74	3,272	1,346	1,926	239	113	126	3,024	1,228	1,796	9	5	4	3,068	668
75 - 84	10,299	2,777	7,522	600	196	404	9,693	2,578	7,115	6	3	3	9,747	2,258
85 and over	12,690	2,103	10,587	590	120	470	12,096	1,983	10,113	4	-	4	12,154	2,394

Table 3 Type of establishment, migrants and long-term illness – **continued**

Great Britain, England & Wales, England, regions, metropolitan counties, Inner London, Outer London, regional remainders, Wales, Scotland

Persons present in communal establishments

Type of establishment and age	PERSONS PRESENT			Visitors/guests			Residents - non-staff			Residents - staff			With limiting long-term illness	Migrants
	TOTAL	Males	Females	Total	Males	Females	Total	Males	Females	Total	Males	Females		
a	b	c	d	e	f	g	h	i	j	k	l	m	n	o
SOUTH EAST REGION – *continued*														
Housing association homes and hostels														
All ages	**11,106**	**5,188**	**5,918**	**969**	**441**	**528**	**9,772**	**4,615**	**5,157**	**365**	**132**	**233**	**5,807**	**3,658**
0 - 15	169	102	67	29	20	9	119	73	46	21	9	12	23	60
16 - 17	144	52	92	54	17	37	87	35	52	3	-	3	14	70
18 - 29	3,077	1,512	1,565	511	209	302	2,474	1,266	1,208	92	37	55	558	1,496
30 - 44	1,596	1,077	519	156	96	60	1,357	952	405	83	29	54	810	615
45 - 59	1,265	910	355	80	54	26	1,071	820	251	114	36	78	779	402
60 - 64	396	270	126	20	8	12	349	254	95	27	8	19	272	85
65 - 74	937	502	435	33	12	21	883	478	405	21	12	9	637	219
75 - 84	1,766	500	1,266	53	18	35	1,712	482	1,230	1	-	1	1,278	380
85 and over	1,756	263	1,493	33	7	26	1,720	255	1,465	3	1	2	1,436	331
Nursing homes (non-NHS/ LA/HA)														
All ages	**34,656**	**8,457**	**26,199**	**2,109**	**742**	**1,367**	**31,660**	**7,422**	**24,238**	**887**	**293**	**594**	**31,984**	**10,601**
0 - 15	159	91	68	59	33	26	57	36	21	43	22	21	88	21
16 - 17	45	15	30	17	5	12	8	3	5	20	7	13	21	8
18 - 29	919	400	519	165	62	103	443	245	198	311	93	218	449	292
30 - 44	920	437	483	244	74	170	509	300	209	167	63	104	559	178
45 - 59	1,024	434	590	242	77	165	557	284	273	225	73	152	643	180
60 - 64	921	387	534	125	53	72	744	318	426	52	16	36	803	217
65 - 74	3,726	1,363	2,363	385	155	230	3,293	1,192	2,101	48	16	32	3,431	1,161
75 - 84	11,821	2,996	8,825	566	213	353	11,237	2,780	8,457	18	3	15	11,294	4,006
85 and over	15,121	2,334	12,787	306	70	236	14,812	2,264	12,548	3	-	3	14,696	4,538

Table 3 Type of establishment, migrants and long-term illness – **continued**

Great Britain, England & Wales, England, regions, metropolitan counties, Inner London, Outer London, regional remainders, Wales, Scotland

Persons present in communal establishments

SOUTH EAST REGION – *continued*

Type of establishment and age	PERSONS PRESENT			Visitors/guests			Residents - non-staff			Residents - staff			With limiting long-term illness	Migrants
	TOTAL	Males	Females	Total	Males	Females	Total	Males	Females	Total	Males	Females		
a	b	c	d	e	f	g	h	i	j	k	l	m	n	o
Residential homes (non-NHS/LA/HA)														
All ages	**58,697**	**15,700**	**42,997**	**1,950**	**593**	**1,357**	**54,155**	**14,143**	**40,012**	**2,592**	**964**	**1,628**	**50,346**	**12,641**
0 - 15	444	264	180	104	82	22	101	65	36	239	117	122	131	41
16 - 17	160	86	74	38	16	22	68	40	28	54	30	24	79	38
18 - 29	3,103	1,556	1,547	324	112	212	2,044	1,189	855	735	255	480	2,062	824
30 - 44	3,122	1,676	1,446	269	85	184	2,329	1,392	937	524	199	325	2,359	441
45 - 59	3,182	1,608	1,574	169	40	129	2,267	1,306	961	746	262	484	2,302	372
60 - 64	1,672	794	878	65	21	44	1,461	716	745	146	57	89	1,366	266
65 - 74	5,762	2,244	3,518	188	59	129	5,483	2,158	3,325	91	27	64	4,944	1,184
75 - 84	17,777	4,020	13,757	443	107	336	17,309	3,902	13,407	25	11	14	15,772	4,604
85 and over	23,475	3,452	20,023	350	71	279	23,093	3,375	19,718	32	6	26	21,331	4,871
Children's homes														
All ages	**3,886**	**2,036**	**1,850**	**612**	**307**	**305**	**2,798**	**1,512**	**1,286**	**476**	**217**	**259**	**429**	**1,542**
0 - 15	3,222	1,770	1,452	355	210	145	2,798	1,512	1,286	69	48	21	344	1,430
16 - 17	29	13	16	2	1	1	-	-	-	27	12	15	6	13
18 - 29	266	110	156	122	46	76	-	-	-	144	64	80	43	60
30 - 44	184	85	99	77	40	37	-	-	-	107	45	62	14	28
45 - 59	157	47	110	47	8	39	-	-	-	110	39	71	16	8
60 - 64	14	7	7	5	2	3	-	-	-	9	5	4	-	1
65 - 74	9	4	5	2	-	2	-	-	-	7	4	3	2	2
75 - 84	3	-	3	1	-	1	-	-	-	2	-	2	2	-
85 and over	2	-	2	1	-	1	-	-	-	1	-	1	2	-

Table 3 Type of establishment, migrants and long-term illness – **continued**

Great Britain, England & Wales, England, regions, metropolitan counties, Inner London, Outer London, regional remainders, Wales, Scotland

Persons present in communal establishments

Type of establishment and age	PERSONS PRESENT			Visitors/guests			Residents - non-staff			Residents - staff			With limiting long-term illness	Migrants
	TOTAL	Males	Females	Total	Males	Females	Total	Males	Females	Total	Males	Females		
a	b	c	d	e	f	g	h	i	j	k	l	m	n	o
SOUTH EAST REGION – *continued*														
Prison service establishments														
All ages	**12,234**	**11,397**	**837**	**7,383**	**6,870**	**513**	**4,803**	**4,485**	**318**	**48**	**42**	**6**	**1,882**	**2,707**
0 - 15	56	52	4	29	25	4	3	3	-	24	24	-	10	22
16 - 17	305	293	12	250	247	3	55	46	9	-	-	-	31	36
18 - 29	6,615	6,201	414	4,397	4,134	263	2,212	2,061	151	6	6	-	734	1,341
30 - 44	3,775	3,464	311	1,981	1,792	189	1,780	1,661	119	14	11	3	631	957
45 - 59	1,265	1,186	79	636	591	45	626	595	31	3	-	3	372	300
60 - 64	147	135	12	55	49	6	91	85	6	1	1	-	67	40
65 - 74	53	49	4	30	27	3	23	22	1	-	-	-	30	7
75 - 84	13	12	1	3	3	-	10	9	1	-	-	-	6	3
85 and over	5	5	-	2	2	-	3	3	-	-	-	-	1	1
Defence establishments														
All ages	**24,874**	**21,174**	**3,700**	**6,230**	**5,521**	**709**	**18,644**	**15,653**	**2,991**				**776**	**9,243**
0 - 15	-	-	-	-	-	-	-	-	-				-	-
16 - 17	1,708	1,523	185	463	412	51	1,245	1,111	134				17	1,105
18 - 29	19,109	16,015	3,094	3,885	3,408	477	15,224	12,607	2,617				420	7,335
30 - 44	3,318	3,025	293	1,456	1,356	100	1,862	1,669	193				145	720
45 - 59	471	414	57	284	256	28	187	158	29				42	56
60 - 64	62	44	18	42	27	15	20	17	3				17	3
65 - 74	115	91	24	66	46	20	49	45	4				66	14
75 - 84	57	39	18	25	12	13	32	27	5				40	9
85 and over	34	23	11	9	4	5	25	19	6				29	1

Table 3 Type of establishment, migrants and long-term illness – **continued**

Persons present in communal establishments

Type of establishment and age	PERSONS PRESENT			Visitors/guests			Residents - non-staff			Residents - staff			With limiting long-term illness	Migrants
	TOTAL	Males	Females	Total	Males	Females	Total	Males	Females	Total	Males	Females		
a	b	c	d	e	f	g	h	i	j	k	l	m	n	o

SOUTH EAST REGION – *continued*

Educational establishments

All ages	106,096	61,394	44,702	88,983	51,943	37,040	12,457	7,221	5,236	4,656	2,230	2,426	5,043	8,672
0 - 15	29,313	19,172	10,141	28,331	18,624	9,707	673	385	288	309	163	146	1,768	298
16 - 17	13,643	8,254	5,389	13,207	8,049	5,158	385	190	195	51	15	36	720	159
18 - 29	53,332	28,528	24,804	43,571	22,890	20,681	8,093	4,904	3,189	1,668	734	934	1,482	6,387
30 - 44	5,754	3,650	2,104	2,394	1,598	796	2,086	1,357	729	1,274	695	579	279	1,470
45 - 59	2,500	1,263	1,237	991	562	429	490	216	274	1,019	485	534	251	274
60 - 64	471	208	263	122	52	70	154	60	94	195	96	99	73	25
65 - 74	506	169	337	185	83	102	225	55	170	96	31	65	152	26
75 - 84	429	116	313	135	62	73	256	43	213	38	11	27	211	23
85 and over	148	34	114	47	23	24	95	11	84	6	-	6	107	10

Hotels, boarding houses etc

All ages	94,521	54,763	39,758	58,092	33,763	24,329	23,910	14,272	9,638	12,519	6,728	5,791	8,489	19,110
0 - 15	9,020	4,806	4,214	4,798	2,542	2,256	3,434	1,850	1,584	788	414	374	292	2,239
16 - 17	1,676	762	914	827	348	479	581	286	295	268	128	140	80	591
18 - 29	29,526	15,800	13,726	13,073	6,994	6,079	9,749	5,314	4,435	6,704	3,492	3,212	1,252	10,813
30 - 44	23,620	15,772	7,848	16,305	11,072	5,233	5,111	3,402	1,709	2,204	1,298	906	1,442	3,653
45 - 59	16,546	10,613	5,933	12,006	7,562	4,444	2,607	1,961	646	1,933	1,090	843	1,763	1,269
60 - 64	4,160	2,313	1,847	3,186	1,649	1,537	640	480	160	334	184	150	756	187
65 - 74	6,295	3,237	3,058	5,247	2,525	2,722	854	614	240	194	98	96	1,483	166
75 - 84	3,050	1,281	1,769	2,339	975	1,364	637	287	350	74	19	55	1,100	127
85 and over	628	179	449	311	96	215	297	78	219	20	5	15	321	65

Table 3 Type of establishment, migrants and long-term illness – **continued**

Great Britain, England & Wales, England, regions, metropolitan counties, Inner London, Outer London, regional remainders, Wales, Scotland

Persons present in communal establishments

Type of establishment and age	PERSONS PRESENT			Visitors/guests			Residents - non-staff			Residents - staff			With limiting long-term illness	Migrants
	TOTAL	Males	Females	Total	Males	Females	Total	Males	Females	Total	Males	Females		
a	b	c	d	e	f	g	h	i	j	k	l	m	n	o

SOUTH EAST REGION – continued

Hostels and common lodging houses (non-HA)

All ages	**9,521**	**5,652**	**3,869**	**1,430**	**771**	**659**	**7,657**	**4,649**	**3,008**	**434**	**232**	**202**	**2,532**	**4,551**
0 - 15	959	507	452	73	40	33	859	451	408	27	16	11	29	516
16 - 17	275	109	166	22	10	12	248	98	150	5	1	4	26	210
18 - 29	3,758	1,705	2,053	736	330	406	2,859	1,307	1,552	163	68	95	499	2,111
30 - 44	1,917	1,337	580	253	197	56	1,573	1,080	493	91	60	31	646	1,013
45 - 59	1,362	1,100	262	141	106	35	1,113	927	186	108	67	41	679	514
60 - 64	354	298	56	33	23	10	300	264	36	21	11	10	172	77
65 - 74	524	428	96	52	30	22	456	390	66	16	8	8	235	78
75 - 84	243	136	107	73	27	46	168	108	60	2	1	1	146	17
85 and over	129	32	97	47	8	39	81	24	57	1	-	1	100	15

Other miscellaneous establishments

All ages	**21,395**	**11,623**	**9,772**	**6,150**	**4,388**	**1,762**	**12,602**	**5,944**	**6,658**	**2,643**	**1,291**	**1,352**	**2,480**	**6,684**
0 - 15	1,517	827	690	279	176	103	1,144	603	541	94	48	46	105	711
16 - 17	605	441	164	232	183	49	338	235	103	35	23	12	21	309
18 - 29	9,808	6,047	3,761	2,966	2,078	888	5,581	3,311	2,270	1,261	658	603	303	4,064
30 - 44	3,973	2,568	1,405	1,657	1,321	336	1,764	941	823	552	306	246	299	901
45 - 59	2,237	1,013	1,224	636	462	174	1,194	397	797	407	154	253	326	346
60 - 64	659	206	453	128	64	64	439	107	332	92	35	57	134	94
65 - 74	1,087	305	782	171	84	87	799	177	622	117	44	73	328	124
75 - 84	1,053	173	880	67	17	50	919	137	782	67	19	48	604	87
85 and over	456	43	413	14	3	11	424	36	388	18	4	14	360	48

Table 3 Type of establishment, migrants and long-term illness – **continued**

Great Britain, England & Wales, England, regions, metropolitan counties, Inner London, Outer London, regional remainders, Wales, Scotland

Persons present in communal establishments

SOUTH EAST REGION – *continued*

Type of establishment and age	PERSONS PRESENT			Visitors/guests			Residents - non-staff			Residents - staff			With limiting long-term illness	Migrants
	TOTAL	Males	Females	Total	Males	Females	Total	Males	Females	Total	Males	Females		
a	b	c	d	e	f	g	h	i	j	k	l	m	n	o
Persons sleeping rough														
All ages	**1,787**	**1,511**	**276**	**465**	**396**	**69**	**1,321**	**1,115**	**206**				**276**	**1,001**
0 - 15	-	-	-	-	-	-	-	-	-				-	-
16 - 17	24	16	8	7	6	1	17	10	7				-	14
18 - 29	678	566	112	174	136	38	504	430	74				74	389
30 - 44	592	509	83	125	112	13	467	397	70				91	346
45 - 59	437	372	65	130	116	14	306	256	50				88	238
60 - 64	31	28	3	13	12	1	18	16	2				12	8
65 - 74	23	18	5	15	13	2	8	5	3				10	5
75 - 84	1	1	-	1	1	-	-	-	-				-	-
85 and over	1	1	-	-	-	-	1	1	-				-	1
Campers														
All ages	**202**	**101**	**101**	**122**	**76**	**46**	**80**	**25**	**55**				**77**	**34**
0 - 15	6	4	2	3	2	1	3	2	1				1	1
16 - 17	2	2	-	1	1	-	1	1	-				-	1
18 - 29	42	26	16	30	18	12	12	8	4				1	7
30 - 44	30	18	12	25	16	9	5	2	3				1	4
45 - 59	27	18	9	23	16	7	4	2	2				5	-
60 - 64	15	10	5	15	10	5	-	-	-				6	-
65 - 74	20	9	11	19	9	10	1	-	1				8	1
75 - 84	27	10	17	6	4	2	21	6	15				22	8
85 and over	33	4	29	-	-	-	33	4	29				33	12

Table 3 Type of establishment, migrants and long-term illness – **continued**

Great Britain, England & Wales, England, regions, metropolitan counties, Inner London, Outer London, regional remainders, Wales, Scotland

Persons present in communal establishments

Type of establishment and age	PERSONS PRESENT			Visitors/guests			Residents - non-staff			Residents - staff			With limiting long-term illness	Migrants
	TOTAL	Males	Females	Total	Males	Females	Total	Males	Females	Total	Males	Females		
a	b	c	d	e	f	g	h	i	j	k	l	m	n	o
SOUTH EAST REGION – *continued*														
Civilian ships, boats and barges														
All ages	**1,578**	**1,348**	**230**	**1,238**	**1,128**	**110**	**340**	**220**	**120**				**25**	**187**
0 - 15	14	9	5	10	6	4	4	3	1				-	1
16 - 17	11	6	5	8	6	2	3	-	3				-	3
18 - 29	517	353	164	327	262	65	190	91	99				7	116
30 - 44	645	613	32	552	530	22	93	83	10				4	49
45 - 59	363	343	20	320	304	16	43	39	4				9	18
60 - 64	22	22	-	19	19	-	3	3	-				3	-
65 - 74	3	-	3	1	-	1	2	-	2				1	-
75 - 84	2	1	1	-	-	-	2	1	1				1	-
85 and over	1	1	-	1	1	-	-	-	-				-	-
Greater London														
All establishments *														
All ages	**183,034**	**86,291**	**96,743**	**83,214**	**44,410**	**38,804**	**86,326**	**36,990**	**49,336**	**13,494**	**4,891**	**8,603**	**62,045**	**41,416**
0 - 15	12,740	7,135	5,605	6,853	3,975	2,878	5,464	2,916	2,548	423	244	179	1,266	3,439
16 - 17	2,767	1,495	1,272	1,761	1,050	711	913	404	509	93	41	52	245	757
18 - 29	64,256	30,425	33,831	30,490	15,110	15,380	26,001	12,894	13,107	7,765	2,421	5,344	5,062	19,896
30 - 44	30,404	18,452	11,952	16,341	10,120	6,221	11,397	7,120	4,277	2,666	1,212	1,454	5,843	6,585
45 - 59	19,158	11,525	7,633	11,118	6,829	4,289	6,251	4,003	2,248	1,789	693	1,096	6,056	2,467
60 - 64	5,389	3,057	2,332	2,923	1,710	1,213	2,112	1,201	911	354	146	208	2,700	522
65 - 74	11,396	5,528	5,868	5,181	2,724	2,457	5,954	2,699	3,255	261	105	156	7,773	1,329
75 - 84	18,765	5,782	12,983	5,542	2,227	3,315	13,120	3,530	9,590	103	25	78	16,225	3,158
85 and over	18,159	2,892	15,267	3,005	665	2,340	15,114	2,223	12,891	40	4	36	16,875	3,263

Note: * Includes a female member of staff incorrectly enumerated as a resident.

Table 3 Type of establishment, migrants and long-term illness – **continued**

Persons present in communal establishments

Greater London – *continued*

Type of establishment and age	PERSONS PRESENT			Visitors/guests			Residents - non-staff			Residents - staff			With limiting long-term illness	Migrants
	TOTAL	Males	Females	Total	Males	Females	Total	Males	Females	Total	Males	Females		
a	b	c	d	e	f	g	h	i	j	k	l	m	n	o
NHS hospitals/homes - psychiatric														
All ages	3,924	1,618	2,306	1,545	689	856	2,013	795	1,218	366	134	232	2,727	572
0 - 15	82	49	33	72	43	29	10	6	4	-	-	-	17	1
16 - 17	17	7	10	13	6	7	4	1	3	-	-	-	10	-
18 - 29	1,030	382	648	332	157	175	450	145	305	248	80	168	311	324
30 - 44	574	315	259	270	137	133	224	136	88	80	42	38	369	92
45 - 59	498	252	246	231	112	119	231	129	102	36	11	25	391	37
60 - 64	174	99	75	70	35	35	102	63	39	2	1	1	156	8
65 - 74	502	216	286	206	79	127	296	137	159	-	-	-	464	33
75 - 84	663	223	440	245	98	147	418	125	293	-	-	-	637	56
85 and over	384	75	309	106	22	84	278	53	225	-	-	-	372	21
NHS hospitals/homes - other														
All ages	33,677	11,773	21,904	20,739	8,396	12,343	8,017	2,194	5,823	4,921	1,183	3,738	16,768	5,139
0 - 15	2,100	1,135	965	1,986	1,071	915	90	49	41	24	15	9	705	34
16 - 17	133	43	90	116	38	78	14	4	10	3	1	2	47	13
18 - 29	10,541	2,382	8,159	3,458	931	2,527	3,393	694	2,699	3,690	757	2,933	1,012	3,505
30 - 44	4,428	1,752	2,676	2,602	983	1,619	962	449	513	864	320	544	1,356	679
45 - 59	3,052	1,492	1,560	2,264	1,174	1,090	493	242	251	295	76	219	1,874	148
60 - 64	1,319	714	605	1,124	637	487	167	66	101	28	11	17	1,021	32
65 - 74	3,397	1,677	1,720	2,850	1,448	1,402	539	226	313	8	3	5	2,809	127
75 - 84	5,195	1,894	3,301	4,014	1,587	2,427	1,175	307	868	6	-	6	4,658	320
85 and over	3,512	684	2,828	2,325	527	1,798	1,184	157	1,027	3	-	3	3,286	281

Table 3 Type of establishment, migrants and long-term illness – **continued**

Great Britain, England & Wales, England, regions, metropolitan counties, Inner London, Outer London, regional remainders, Wales, Scotland

Persons present in communal establishments

Greater London – *continued*

Type of establishment and age	PERSONS PRESENT			Visitors/guests			Residents - non-staff			Residents - staff			With limiting long-term illness	Migrants
	TOTAL	Males	Females	Total	Males	Females	Total	Males	Females	Total	Males	Females		
a	b	c	d	e	f	g	h	i	j	k	l	m	n	o
Non-NHS hospitals - psychiatric														
All ages	**1,063**	**492**	**571**	**822**	**371**	**451**	**224**	**115**	**109**	**17**	**6**	**11**	**684**	**82**
0 - 15	85	58	27	82	56	26	3	2	1	-	-	-	10	-
16 - 17	12	3	9	12	3	9	-	-	-	-	-	-	8	-
18 - 29	172	67	105	134	46	88	25	17	8	13	4	9	87	18
30 - 44	196	82	114	145	54	91	49	27	22	2	1	1	109	15
45 - 59	188	108	80	138	75	63	48	32	16	2	1	1	127	21
60 - 64	70	39	31	47	26	21	23	13	10	-	-	-	55	9
65 - 74	158	71	87	111	55	56	47	16	31	-	-	-	130	13
75 - 84	122	48	74	100	42	58	22	6	16	-	-	-	103	2
85 and over	60	16	44	53	14	39	7	2	5	-	-	-	55	4
Non-NHS hospitals - other														
All ages	**2,999**	**1,153**	**1,846**	**1,709**	**698**	**1,011**	**935**	**348**	**587**	**355**	**107**	**248**	**1,439**	**470**
0 - 15	102	58	44	84	48	36	11	6	5	7	4	3	34	8
16 - 17	17	5	12	13	3	10	2	1	1	2	1	1	7	3
18 - 29	698	192	506	263	67	196	243	77	166	192	48	144	121	251
30 - 44	584	224	360	331	116	215	154	70	84	99	38	61	190	82
45 - 59	590	257	333	378	166	212	171	80	91	41	11	30	318	29
60 - 64	180	90	90	132	78	54	40	11	29	8	1	7	103	4
65 - 74	300	156	144	225	124	101	71	30	41	4	2	2	220	10
75 - 84	331	129	202	210	81	129	119	46	73	2	2	-	262	41
85 and over	197	42	155	73	15	58	124	27	97	-	-	-	184	42

Table 3 Type of establishment, migrants and long-term illness – **continued**

Great Britain, England & Wales, England, regions, metropolitan counties, Inner London, Outer London, regional remainders, Wales, Scotland

Persons present in communal establishments

Greater London – *continued*

Type of establishment and age	PERSONS PRESENT			Visitors/guests			Residents - non-staff			Residents - staff			With limiting long-term illness	Migrants
	TOTAL	Males	Females	Total	Males	Females	Total	Males	Females	Total	Males	Females		
a	b	c	d	e	f	g	h	i	j	k	l	m	n	o
Local authority homes														
All ages	**14,021**	**4,501**	**9,520**	**966**	**378**	**588**	**12,863**	**4,050**	**8,813**	**192**	**73**	**119**	**12,280**	**2,801**
0 - 15	182	119	63	83	54	29	93	61	32	6	4	2	79	53
16 - 17	106	52	54	32	14	18	73	38	35	1	-	1	37	52
18 - 29	1,244	657	587	190	94	96	999	541	458	55	22	33	702	401
30 - 44	1,105	642	463	111	43	68	940	576	364	54	23	31	838	233
45 - 59	793	443	350	77	34	43	657	392	265	59	17	42	634	149
60 - 64	329	177	152	30	15	15	291	159	132	8	3	5	294	63
65 - 74	1,441	604	837	72	39	33	1,365	563	802	4	2	2	1,335	275
75 - 84	4,037	1,077	2,960	186	52	134	3,848	1,023	2,825	3	2	1	3,774	775
85 and over	4,784	730	4,054	185	33	152	4,597	697	3,900	2	-	2	4,587	800
Housing association homes and hostels														
All ages	**6,461**	**3,287**	**3,174**	**681**	**321**	**360**	**5,572**	**2,876**	**2,696**	**208**	**90**	**118**	**2,908**	**2,295**
0 - 15	88	46	42	10	4	6	62	36	26	16	6	10	7	33
16 - 17	101	35	66	51	15	36	50	20	30	-	-	-	8	37
18 - 29	2,236	1,055	1,181	398	163	235	1,778	862	916	60	30	30	316	1,054
30 - 44	979	652	327	105	71	34	826	564	262	48	17	31	438	392
45 - 59	755	578	177	62	50	12	638	508	130	55	20	35	428	249
60 - 64	225	167	58	7	3	4	205	158	47	13	6	7	146	55
65 - 74	580	352	228	8	5	3	559	337	222	13	10	3	380	132
75 - 84	797	287	510	24	7	17	773	280	493	-	-	-	595	178
85 and over	700	115	585	16	3	13	681	111	570	3	1	2	590	165

Table 3 Type of establishment, migrants and long-term illness – **continued**

Great Britain, England & Wales, England, regions, metropolitan counties, Inner London, Outer London, regional remainders, Wales, Scotland

Persons present in communal establishments

Type of establishment and age	PERSONS PRESENT			Visitors/guests			Residents - non-staff			Residents - staff			With limiting long-term illness	Migrants
	TOTAL	Males	Females	Total	Males	Females	Total	Males	Females	Total	Males	Females		
a	b	c	d	e	f	g	h	i	j	k	l	m	n	o
Greater London – *continued*														
Nursing homes (non-NHS/LA/HA)														
All ages	7,641	1,829	5,812	380	161	219	7,035	1,619	5,416	226	49	177	6,990	2,262
0 - 15	13	7	6	2	2	-	6	2	4	5	3	2	3	1
16 - 17	2	-	2	-	-	-	1	-	1	1	-	1	1	1
18 - 29	234	102	132	30	16	14	134	72	62	70	14	56	126	89
30 - 44	275	154	121	61	32	29	173	110	63	41	12	29	197	69
45 - 59	274	112	162	50	15	35	168	85	83	56	12	44	184	62
60 - 64	226	96	130	29	15	14	171	76	95	26	5	21	188	57
65 - 74	833	303	530	71	38	33	742	262	480	20	3	17	751	256
75 - 84	2,522	598	1,924	98	33	65	2,419	565	1,854	5	-	5	2,389	812
85 and over	3,262	457	2,805	39	10	29	3,221	447	2,774	2	-	2	3,151	915
Residential homes (non-NHS/LA/HA)														
All ages	12,218	3,369	8,849	395	124	271	11,352	3,097	8,255	471	148	323	10,248	2,641
0 - 15	47	29	18	10	8	2	16	7	9	21	14	7	4	8
16 - 17	22	8	14	9	5	4	7	2	5	6	1	5	8	8
18 - 29	655	327	328	89	35	54	427	241	186	139	51	88	427	183
30 - 44	750	390	360	78	25	53	575	335	240	97	30	67	569	143
45 - 59	670	292	378	44	9	35	484	245	239	142	38	104	488	116
60 - 64	347	164	183	14	6	8	305	152	153	28	6	22	270	67
65 - 74	1,287	522	765	33	8	25	1,231	510	721	23	4	19	1,015	256
75 - 84	3,660	948	2,712	57	17	40	3,595	927	2,668	8	4	4	3,160	876
85 and over	4,780	689	4,091	61	11	50	4,712	678	4,034	7	-	7	4,307	984

Table 3 Type of establishment, migrants and long-term illness – **continued**

Great Britain, England & Wales, England, regions, metropolitan counties, Inner London, Outer London, regional remainders, Wales, Scotland

Persons present in communal establishments

Type of establishment and age	PERSONS PRESENT			Visitors/guests			Residents - non-staff			Residents - staff			With limiting long-term illness	Migrants
	TOTAL	Males	Females	Total	Males	Females	Total	Males	Females	Total	Males	Females		
a	b	c	d	e	f	g	h	i	j	k	l	m	n	o

Greater London – *continued*

Children's homes

All ages	**1,550**	**790**	**760**	**269**	**137**	**132**	**1,151**	**599**	**552**	**130**	**54**	**76**	**134**	**670**
0 - 15	1,334	709	625	162	95	67	1,151	599	552	21	15	6	127	637
16 - 17	12	4	8	-	-	-	-	-	-	12	4	8	-	8
18 - 29	84	26	58	53	18	35	-	-	-	31	8	23	5	13
30 - 44	70	37	33	32	20	12	-	-	-	38	17	21	2	12
45 - 59	45	14	31	17	4	13	-	-	-	28	10	18	-	-
60 - 64	3	-	3	3	-	3	-	-	-	-	-	-	-	-
65 - 74	1	-	1	1	-	1	-	-	-	-	-	-	-	-
75 - 84	1	-	1	1	-	1	-	-	-	-	-	-	-	-
85 and over	-	-	-	-	-	-	-	-	-	-	-	-	-	-

Prison service establishments

All ages	**4,746**	**4,234**	**512**	**3,283**	**2,907**	**376**	**1,439**	**1,304**	**135**	**24**	**23**	**1**	**749**	**912**
0 - 15	52	48	4	28	24	4	3	3	-	21	21	-	10	19
16 - 17	174	167	7	136	133	3	38	34	4	-	-	-	18	23
18 - 29	2,638	2,363	275	1,883	1,679	204	754	683	71	1	1	-	310	485
30 - 44	1,385	1,204	181	932	793	139	452	410	42	1	1	-	252	281
45 - 59	440	401	39	268	245	23	171	156	15	1	-	1	122	96
60 - 64	38	35	3	22	21	1	16	14	2	-	-	-	26	6
65 - 74	15	13	2	11	9	2	4	4	-	-	-	-	9	2
75 - 84	3	2	1	2	2	-	1	-	1	-	-	-	2	-
85 and over	1	1	-	1	1	-	-	-	-	-	-	-	-	-

Table 3 Type of establishment, migrants and long-term illness – **continued**

Persons present in communal establishments

Type of establishment and age	PERSONS PRESENT			Visitors/guests			Residents - non-staff			Residents - staff			With limiting long-term illness	Migrants
	TOTAL	Males	Females	Total	Males	Females	Total	Males	Females	Total	Males	Females		
a	b	c	d	e	f	g	h	i	j	k	l	m	n	o

Greater London – *continued*

Defence establishments

All ages	**2,719**	**1,913**	**806**	**569**	**472**	**97**	**2,150**	**1,441**	**709**				**140**	**898**
0 - 15	-	-	-	-	-	-	-	-	-				-	-
16 - 17	73	64	9	19	19	-	54	45	9				2	45
18 - 29	2,070	1,394	676	288	239	49	1,782	1,155	627				69	736
30 - 44	420	340	80	168	144	24	252	196	56				26	102
45 - 59	105	84	21	63	50	13	42	34	8				13	9
60 - 64	10	7	3	5	3	2	5	4	1				3	1
65 - 74	26	18	8	20	14	6	6	4	2				15	3
75 - 84	11	6	5	6	3	3	5	3	2				8	2
85 and over	4	-	4	-	-	-	4	-	4				4	-

Educational establishments

All ages	**24,008**	**12,543**	**11,465**	**17,464**	**9,180**	**8,284**	**5,639**	**3,009**	**2,630**	**905**	**354**	**551**	**786**	**3,736**
0 - 15	1,629	1,042	587	1,380	931	449	204	90	114	45	21	24	59	92
16 - 17	943	616	327	859	598	261	79	17	62	5	1	4	37	52
18 - 29	18,474	9,361	9,113	14,308	7,201	7,207	3,832	2,135	1,697	334	125	209	418	2,843
30 - 44	1,909	1,132	777	645	406	239	1,022	617	405	242	109	133	85	616
45 - 59	615	283	332	216	119	97	212	92	120	187	72	115	58	93
60 - 64	123	51	72	27	10	17	55	22	33	41	19	22	15	5
65 - 74	155	36	119	18	8	10	104	22	82	33	6	27	29	17
75 - 84	112	18	94	9	6	3	88	11	77	15	1	14	50	11
85 and over	48	4	44	2	1	1	43	3	40	3	-	3	35	7

Table 3 Type of establishment, migrants and long-term illness – **continued**

Great Britain, England & Wales, England, regions, metropolitan counties, Inner London, Outer London, regional remainders, Wales, Scotland

Type of establishment and age	PERSONS PRESENT			Visitors/guests			Residents - non-staff			Residents - staff			With limiting long-term illness	Migrants
	TOTAL	Males	Females	Total	Males	Females	Total	Males	Females	Total	Males	Females		
a	b	c	d	e	f	g	h	i	j	k	l	m	n	o
Greater London – *continued*														
Hotels, boarding houses etc														
All ages	**50,133**	**29,121**	**21,012**	**31,309**	**18,795**	**12,514**	**14,750**	**8,406**	**6,344**	**4,074**	**1,920**	**2,154**	**3,407**	**11,171**
0 - 15	5,429	2,924	2,505	2,726	1,482	1,244	2,478	1,317	1,161	225	125	100	157	1,666
16 - 17	842	371	471	457	190	267	329	153	176	56	28	28	43	289
18 - 29	16,233	8,083	8,150	7,571	3,833	3,738	6,384	3,271	3,113	2,278	979	1,299	725	5,928
30 - 44	14,285	9,336	4,949	10,214	6,829	3,385	3,336	2,114	1,222	735	393	342	832	2,322
45 - 59	8,931	5,823	3,108	6,997	4,543	2,454	1,368	983	385	566	297	269	782	719
60 - 64	1,773	1,104	669	1,324	815	509	322	230	92	127	59	68	242	107
65 - 74	1,812	1,090	722	1,420	815	605	327	240	87	65	35	30	313	94
75 - 84	680	351	329	503	268	235	160	80	80	17	3	14	230	36
85 and over	148	39	109	97	20	77	46	18	28	5	1	4	83	10
Hostels and common lodging houses (non-HA)														
All ages	**6,478**	**3,500**	**2,978**	**966**	**434**	**532**	**5,257**	**2,944**	**2,313**	**255**	**122**	**133**	**1,607**	**3,107**
0 - 15	646	341	305	51	30	21	581	303	278	14	8	6	16	352
16 - 17	148	42	106	11	5	6	137	37	100	-	-	-	9	118
18 - 29	2,598	1,013	1,585	486	165	321	2,006	812	1,194	106	36	70	255	1,447
30 - 44	1,277	816	461	141	99	42	1,081	680	401	55	37	18	393	704
45 - 59	890	694	196	90	63	27	747	603	144	53	28	25	448	351
60 - 64	231	183	48	23	14	9	197	164	33	11	5	6	109	50
65 - 74	384	295	89	46	25	21	324	263	61	14	7	7	162	59
75 - 84	198	95	103	71	25	46	126	69	57	1	1	-	128	15
85 and over	106	21	85	47	8	39	58	13	45	1	-	1	87	11

Persons present in communal establishments

Table 3 Type of establishment, migrants and long-term illness – **continued**

Great Britain, England & Wales, England, regions, metropolitan counties, Inner London, Outer London, regional remainders, Wales, Scotland

Type of establishment and age	PERSONS PRESENT			Visitors/guests			Residents - non-staff			Residents - staff			With limiting long-term illness	Migrants
	TOTAL	Males	Females	Total	Males	Females	Total	Males	Females	Total	Males	Females		
a	b	c	d	e	f	g	h	i	j	k	l	m	n	o

Greater London – *continued*

Other miscellaneous establishments														
All ages	**10,102**	**5,109**	**4,993**	**1,954**	**1,201**	**753**	**6,799**	**3,280**	**3,519**	**1,349**	**628**	**721**	**985**	**3,806**
0 - 15	949	569	380	177	127	50	754	434	320	18	8	10	38	535
16 - 17	144	65	79	28	16	12	109	44	65	7	5	2	9	93
18 - 29	4,883	2,627	2,256	954	521	433	3,381	1,840	1,541	548	266	282	138	2,288
30 - 44	1,747	1,015	732	465	330	135	972	513	459	310	172	138	142	563
45 - 59	1,009	435	574	169	121	48	573	214	359	267	100	167	149	192
60 - 64	323	114	209	61	27	34	200	57	143	62	30	32	65	51
65 - 74	496	169	327	85	53	32	334	83	251	77	33	44	135	48
75 - 84	412	101	311	15	6	9	351	83	268	46	12	34	208	26
85 and over	139	14	125	-	-	-	125	12	113	14	2	12	101	10
Persons sleeping rough														
All ages	**1,197**	**1,019**	**178**	**141**	**127**	**14**	**1,055**	**892**	**163**				**137**	**821**
0 - 15	-	-	-	-	-	-	-	-	-				-	-
16 - 17	19	13	6	5	5	-	14	8	6				1	13
18 - 29	453	385	68	47	40	7	406	345	61				39	324
30 - 44	404	348	56	34	31	3	370	317	53				45	277
45 - 59	295	250	45	47	43	4	247	207	40				40	196
60 - 64	17	16	1	4	4	-	13	12	1				7	7
65 - 74	8	6	2	4	4	-	4	2	2				5	3
75 - 84	-	-	-	-	-	-	-	-	-				-	-
85 and over	1	1	-	-	-	-	1	1	-				-	1

Table 3 Type of establishment, migrants and long-term illness – **continued**

Great Britain, England & Wales, England, regions, metropolitan counties, Inner London, Outer London, regional remainders, Wales, Scotland

Persons present in communal establishments

Type of establishment and age	PERSONS PRESENT			Visitors/guests			Residents - non-staff			Residents - staff			With limiting long-term illness	Migrants
	TOTAL	Males	Females	Total	Males	Females	Total	Males	Females	Total	Males	Females		
a	b	c	d	e	f	g	h	i	j	k	l	m	n	o
Greater London – *continued*														
Campers														
All ages	**68**	**18**	**50**	**5**	**3**	**2**	**63**	**15**	**48**				**56**	**30**
0 - 15	-	-	-	-	-	-	-	-	-				-	-
16 - 17	-	-	-	-	-	-	-	-	-				-	-
18 - 29	10	7	3	4	3	1	6	4	2				1	6
30 - 44	3	2	1	-	-	-	3	2	1				-	3
45 - 59	-	-	-	-	-	-	-	-	-				-	-
60 - 64	-	-	-	-	-	-	-	-	-				-	-
65 - 74	1	-	1	-	-	-	1	-	1				1	-
75 - 84	21	5	16	1	-	1	20	5	15				21	8
85 and over	33	4	29	-	-	-	33	4	29				33	12
Civilian ships, boats and barges														
All ages	**29**	**22**	**7**	**17**	**16**	**1**	**12**	**6**	**6**				**-**	**3**
0 - 15	2	1	1	-	-	-	2	1	1				-	-
16 - 17	2	-	2	-	-	-	2	-	2				-	2
18 - 29	3	2	1	2	2	-	1	-	1				-	1
30 - 44	13	11	2	7	7	-	6	4	2				-	-
45 - 59	8	7	1	7	6	1	1	1	-				-	-
60 - 64	1	1	-	1	1	-	-	-	-				-	-
65 - 74	-	-	-	-	-	-	-	-	-				-	-
75 - 84	-	-	-	-	-	-	-	-	-				-	-
85 and over	-	-	-	-	-	-	-	-	-				-	-

Table 3 Type of establishment, migrants and long-term illness – **continued**

Great Britain, England & Wales, England, regions, metropolitan counties, Inner London, Outer London, regional remainders, Wales, Scotland

Persons present in communal establishments

Type of establishment and age	PERSONS PRESENT			Visitors/guests			Residents - non-staff			Residents - staff			With limiting long-term illness	Migrants
	TOTAL	Males	Females	Total	Males	Females	Total	Males	Females	Total	Males	Females		
a	b	c	d	e	f	g	h	i	j	k	l	m	n	o
All establishments *														
All ages	**110,402**	**55,525**	**54,877**	**56,869**	**30,667**	**26,202**	**46,628**	**22,325**	**24,303**	**6,905**	**2,533**	**4,372**	**27,168**	**25,117**
0 - 15	7,615	4,198	3,417	4,287	2,418	1,869	3,136	1,672	1,464	192	108	84	776	2,014
16 - 17	1,299	561	738	734	323	411	527	220	307	38	18	20	111	448
18 - 29	43,730	20,184	23,546	21,969	10,708	11,261	17,921	8,233	9,688	3,840	1,243	2,597	2,887	13,345
30 - 44	21,291	13,073	8,218	12,433	7,729	4,704	7,427	4,729	2,698	1,431	615	816	3,299	4,524
45 - 59	13,538	8,367	5,171	8,565	5,290	3,275	3,993	2,702	1,291	980	375	605	3,568	1,770
60 - 64	3,460	2,066	1,394	2,058	1,226	832	1,177	744	433	225	96	129	1,453	320
65 - 74	6,207	3,320	2,887	3,150	1,698	1,452	2,915	1,560	1,355	142	62	80	3,640	649
75 - 84	7,326	2,663	4,663	2,508	1,020	1,488	4,772	1,628	3,144	46	15	31	5,977	1,084
85 and over	5,936	1,093	4,843	1,165	255	910	4,760	837	3,923	11	1	10	5,457	963
NHS hospitals/homes - psychiatric														
All ages	**1,950**	**729**	**1,221**	**1,025**	**449**	**576**	**793**	**270**	**523**	**132**	**10**	**122**	**1,101**	**314**
0 - 15	64	38	26	57	34	23	7	4	3	-	-	-	14	-
16 - 17	5	1	4	3	1	2	2	-	2	-	-	-	1	-
18 - 29	661	183	478	212	94	118	352	79	273	97	10	87	131	215
30 - 44	269	134	135	158	81	77	87	53	34	24	-	24	139	32
45 - 59	230	102	128	154	71	83	65	31	34	11	-	11	164	14
60 - 64	73	41	32	47	23	24	26	18	8	-	-	-	57	3
65 - 74	238	101	137	153	65	88	85	36	49	-	-	-	208	18
75 - 84	274	95	179	171	64	107	103	31	72	-	-	-	254	22
85 and over	136	34	102	70	16	54	66	18	48	-	-	-	133	10

Inner London

Note: * Includes a female member of staff incorrectly enumerated as a resident.

Table 3 Type of establishment, migrants and long-term illness – **continued**

Great Britain, England & Wales, England, regions, metropolitan counties, Inner London, Outer London, regional remainders, Wales, Scotland

Persons present in communal establishments

Type of establishment and age	PERSONS PRESENT			Visitors/guests			Residents - non-staff			Residents - staff			With limiting long-term illness	Migrants
	TOTAL	Males	Females	Total	Males	Females	Total	Males	Females	Total	Males	Females		
a	b	c	d	e	f	g	h	i	j	k	l	m	n	o
Inner London – *continued*														
NHS hospitals/homes - other														
All ages	16,120	5,640	10,480	9,850	4,102	5,748	4,627	1,200	3,427	1,643	338	1,305	7,457	2,709
0 - 15	1,116	622	494	1,078	600	478	36	20	16	2	2	-	517	3
16 - 17	72	23	49	65	22	43	6	1	5	1	-	1	34	6
18 - 29	5,738	1,239	4,499	1,918	536	1,382	2,651	495	2,156	1,169	208	961	536	1,967
30 - 44	2,269	892	1,377	1,395	540	855	567	257	310	307	95	212	705	343
45 - 59	1,571	767	804	1,212	643	569	220	96	124	139	28	111	974	64
60 - 64	623	357	266	547	324	223	63	29	34	13	4	9	501	8
65 - 74	1,478	754	724	1,262	649	613	213	104	109	6	1	2	1,229	63
75 - 84	1,992	733	1,259	1,540	605	935	446	128	318	6	-	6	1,782	145
85 and over	1,261	253	1,008	833	183	650	425	70	355	3	-	3	1,179	110
Non-NHS hospitals - psychiatric														
All ages	945	436	509	767	348	419	162	82	80	16	6	10	606	62
0 - 15	83	57	26	80	55	25	3	2	1	-	-	-	10	-
16 - 17	10	2	8	10	2	8	-	-	-	-	-	-	7	-
18 - 29	150	54	96	122	40	82	16	10	6	12	4	8	76	14
30 - 44	159	66	93	128	47	81	29	18	11	2	1	1	88	8
45 - 59	163	94	69	125	70	55	36	23	13	2	1	1	108	17
60 - 64	62	33	29	45	25	20	17	8	9	-	-	-	48	7
65 - 74	140	67	73	106	54	52	34	13	21	-	-	-	115	10
75 - 84	118	47	71	98	41	57	20	6	14	-	-	-	99	2
85 and over	60	16	44	53	14	39	7	2	5	-	-	-	55	4

Table 3 Type of establishment, migrants and long-term illness – **continued**

Great Britain, England & Wales, England, regions, metropolitan counties, Inner London, Outer London, regional remainders, Wales, Scotland

Persons present in communal establishments

Type of establishment and age	PERSONS PRESENT			Visitors/guests			Residents - non-staff			Residents - staff			With limiting long-term illness	Migrants
	TOTAL	Males	Females	Total	Males	Females	Total	Males	Females	Total	Males	Females		
a	b	c	d	e	f	g	h	i	j	k	l	m	n	o

Inner London – *continued*

Non-NHS hospitals - other

All ages	**2,237**	**857**	**1,380**	**1,204**	**482**	**722**	**819**	**314**	**505**	**214**	**61**	**153**	**1,182**	**380**
0 - 15	78	42	36	70	39	31	2	-	2	6	3	3	29	6
16 - 17	14	4	10	11	2	9	2	1	1	1	1	-	7	2
18 - 29	534	147	387	204	51	153	216	68	148	114	28	86	102	193
30 - 44	413	155	258	219	72	147	139	62	77	55	21	34	160	63
45 - 59	431	198	233	251	120	131	153	73	80	27	5	22	257	27
60 - 64	127	62	65	87	51	36	34	11	23	6	-	6	83	3
65 - 74	205	105	100	141	75	66	60	28	32	4	2	2	160	8
75 - 84	261	106	155	159	60	99	101	45	56	1	1	-	218	36
85 and over	174	38	136	62	12	50	112	26	86	-	-	-	166	42

Local authority homes

All ages	**5,693**	**2,083**	**3,610**	**303**	**139**	**164**	**5,299**	**1,901**	**3,398**	**91**	**43**	**48**	**4,669**	**1,241**
0 - 15	76	56	20	21	15	6	52	39	13	3	2	1	25	28
16 - 17	37	23	14	4	2	2	33	21	12	-	-	-	10	26
18 - 29	646	330	316	99	58	41	516	256	260	31	16	15	248	261
30 - 44	443	291	152	43	22	21	377	255	122	23	14	9	283	150
45 - 59	321	199	122	19	7	12	275	185	90	27	7	20	235	93
60 - 64	164	97	67	9	3	6	152	93	59	3	1	2	145	41
65 - 74	693	313	380	22	16	6	669	295	374	2	2	-	634	124
75 - 84	1,551	480	1,071	46	12	34	1,504	467	1,037	1	1	-	1,418	261
85 and over	1,762	294	1,468	40	4	36	1,721	290	1,431	1	-	1	1,671	257

Table 3 Type of establishment, migrants and long-term illness – **continued**

Persons present in communal establishments

Type of establishment and age	PERSONS PRESENT			Visitors/guests			Residents - non-staff			Residents - staff			With limiting long-term illness	Migrants
	TOTAL	Males	Females	Total	Males	Females	Total	Males	Females	Total	Males	Females		
a	b	c	d	e	f	g	h	i	j	k	l	m	n	o
Inner London – *continued*														
Housing association homes and hostels														
All ages	**4,242**	**2,377**	**1,865**	**447**	**202**	**245**	**3,684**	**2,123**	**1,561**	**111**	**52**	**59**	**1,609**	**1,640**
0 - 15	35	19	16	3	-	3	20	15	5	12	4	8	4	14
16 - 17	76	21	55	42	8	34	34	13	21	-	-	-	3	27
18 - 29	1,665	715	950	255	89	166	1,379	607	772	31	19	12	199	823
30 - 44	733	511	222	75	55	20	628	445	183	30	11	19	304	335
45 - 59	600	495	105	49	42	7	523	442	81	28	11	17	324	209
60 - 64	174	140	34	5	2	3	163	134	29	6	4	2	109	44
65 - 74	373	264	109	4	3	1	365	258	107	4	3	1	226	80
75 - 84	356	168	188	7	2	5	349	166	183	-	-	-	255	71
85 and over	230	44	186	7	1	6	223	43	180	-	-	-	185	37
Nursing homes (non-NHS/ LA/HA)														
All ages	**2,590**	**757**	**1,833**	**188**	**94**	**94**	**2,326**	**648**	**1,678**	**76**	**15**	**61**	**2,358**	**769**
0 - 15	3	2	1	2	2	-	1	-	1	-	-	-	-	-
16 - 17	2	-	2	-	-	-	1	-	1	1	-	1	1	1
18 - 29	128	60	68	23	14	9	74	40	34	31	6	25	75	48
30 - 44	122	76	46	37	24	13	71	48	23	14	4	10	90	28
45 - 59	120	47	73	26	8	18	77	35	42	17	4	13	82	24
60 - 64	98	47	51	16	10	6	73	36	37	9	1	8	83	27
65 - 74	313	136	177	35	17	18	275	119	156	3	-	3	283	106
75 - 84	801	217	584	38	14	24	763	203	560	-	-	-	765	270
85 and over	1,003	172	831	11	5	6	991	167	824	1	-	1	979	265

Table 3 Type of establishment, migrants and long-term illness – **continued**

Persons present in communal establishments

Type of establishment and age	PERSONS PRESENT			Visitors/guests			Residents - non-staff			Residents - staff			With limiting long-term illness	Migrants
	TOTAL	Males	Females	Total	Males	Females	Total	Males	Females	Total	Males	Females		
a	b	c	d	e	f	g	h	i	j	k	l	m	n	o

Inner London – *continued*

Residential homes (non-NHS/LA/HA)

All ages	3,738	1,342	2,396	146	55	91	3,425	1,226	2,199	167	61	106	2,830	781
0 - 15	32	20	12	10	8	2	15	7	8	7	5	2	3	5
16 - 17	5	1	4	1	1	-	2	-	2	2	-	2	1	4
18 - 29	271	141	130	34	16	18	196	104	92	41	21	20	173	92
30 - 44	292	152	140	30	15	15	225	125	100	37	12	25	217	76
45 - 59	273	113	160	18	4	14	203	92	111	52	17	35	203	56
60 - 64	136	60	76	7	4	3	115	51	64	14	5	9	94	24
65 - 74	532	252	280	18	3	15	504	249	255	10	-	10	344	95
75 - 84	1,115	413	702	18	4	14	1,094	408	686	3	1	2	861	222
85 and over	1,082	190	892	10	-	10	1,071	190	881	1	-	1	934	207

Children's homes

All ages	641	337	304	101	57	44	498	260	238	42	20	22	23	335
0 - 15	573	312	261	68	45	23	498	260	238	7	7	-	22	318
16 - 17	3	-	3	-	-	-	-	-	-	3	-	3	-	2
18 - 29	28	10	18	15	6	9	-	-	-	13	4	9	1	8
30 - 44	22	12	10	9	5	4	-	-	-	13	7	6	-	7
45 - 59	12	3	9	6	1	5	-	-	-	6	2	4	-	-
60 - 64	1	-	1	1	-	1	-	-	-	-	-	-	-	-
65 - 74	1	-	1	1	-	1	-	-	-	-	-	-	-	-
75 - 84	1	-	1	1	-	1	-	-	-	-	-	-	-	-
85 and over	-	-	-	-	-	-	-	-	-	-	-	-	-	-

Table 3 Type of establishment, migrants and long-term illness – **continued**

Great Britain, England & Wales, England, regions, metropolitan counties, Inner London, Outer London, regional remainders, Wales, Scotland

Persons present in communal establishments

Type of establishment and age	PERSONS PRESENT			Visitors/guests			Residents - non-staff			Residents - staff			With limiting long-term illness	Migrants
	TOTAL	Males	Females	Total	Males	Females	Total	Males	Females	Total	Males	Females		
a	b	c	d	e	f	g	h	i	j	k	l	m	n	o
Inner London – *continued*														
Prison service establishments														
All ages	**3,613**	**3,154**	**459**	**2,514**	**2,152**	**362**	**1,077**	**980**	**97**	**22**	**22**	**-**	**643**	**672**
0 - 15	31	27	4	10	6	4	-	-	-	21	21	-	4	18
16 - 17	9	7	2	6	5	1	3	2	1	-	-	-	1	2
18 - 29	1,862	1,615	247	1,350	1,152	198	512	463	49	1	1	-	240	334
30 - 44	1,249	1,080	169	857	724	133	391	355	36	1	1	-	245	228
45 - 59	407	375	32	256	233	23	151	142	9	-	-	-	117	82
60 - 64	38	35	3	22	21	1	16	14	2	-	-	-	26	6
65 - 74	15	13	2	11	9	2	4	4	-	-	-	-	9	2
75 - 84	1	1	-	1	1	-	-	-	-	-	-	-	1	-
85 and over	1	1	-	1	1	-	-	-	-	-	-	-	-	-
Defence establishments														
All ages	**434**	**246**	**188**	**70**	**55**	**15**	**364**	**191**	**173**				**13**	**161**
0 - 15	-	-	-	-	-	-	-	-	-				-	-
16 - 17	13	7	6	1	1	-	12	6	6				-	12
18 - 29	354	186	168	50	38	12	304	148	156				8	135
30 - 44	49	40	9	11	11	-	38	29	9				2	12
45 - 59	10	7	3	4	2	2	6	5	1				2	-
60 - 64	2	2	-	-	-	-	2	2	-				-	1
65 - 74	3	2	1	2	2	-	1	1	-				1	1
75 - 84	3	2	1	2	2	-	1	1	-				-	1
85 and over	-	-	-	-	-	-	-	-	-				-	-

Table 3 Type of establishment, migrants and long-term illness – **continued**

Great Britain, England, England & Wales, England, regions, metropolitan counties, Inner London, Outer London, regional remainders, Wales, Scotland

Persons present in communal establishments

Type of establishment and age	PERSONS PRESENT			Visitors/guests			Residents - non-staff			Residents - staff			With limiting long-term illness	Migrants
	TOTAL	Males	Females	Total	Males	Females	Total	Males	Females	Total	Males	Females		
a	b	c	d	e	f	g	h	i	j	k	l	m	n	o
Inner London – *continued*														
Educational establishments														
All ages	**16,646**	**8,409**	**8,237**	**11,515**	**5,808**	**5,707**	**4,506**	**2,374**	**2,132**	**625**	**227**	**398**	**500**	**2,955**
0 - 15	456	268	188	281	188	93	143	67	76	32	13	19	6	65
16 - 17	200	106	94	165	96	69	32	10	22	3	-	3	5	22
18 - 29	13,765	6,910	6,855	10,395	5,131	5,264	3,124	1,692	1,432	246	87	159	277	2,263
30 - 44	1,529	869	660	495	295	200	859	507	352	175	67	108	70	514
45 - 59	428	197	231	145	83	62	155	63	92	128	51	77	46	68
60 - 64	78	29	49	20	8	12	32	13	19	26	8	18	10	4
65 - 74	91	19	72	10	5	5	70	13	57	11	1	10	21	6
75 - 84	68	8	60	4	2	2	60	6	54	4	-	4	37	8
85 and over	31	3	28	-	-	-	31	3	28	-	-	-	28	5
Hotels, boarding houses etc														
All ages	**39,441**	**22,644**	**16,797**	**26,807**	**15,728**	**11,079**	**10,084**	**5,817**	**4,267**	**2,550**	**1,099**	**1,451**	**2,269**	**7,718**
0 - 15	4,188	2,266	1,922	2,504	1,357	1,147	1,606	869	737	78	40	38	110	1,064
16 - 17	637	277	360	404	169	235	211	96	115	22	12	10	30	185
18 - 29	12,374	6,022	6,352	6,343	3,100	3,243	4,513	2,327	2,186	1,518	595	923	512	4,204
30 - 44	11,371	7,301	4,070	8,631	5,598	3,033	2,278	1,479	799	462	224	238	568	1,580
45 - 59	7,387	4,706	2,681	6,105	3,864	2,241	952	684	268	330	158	172	579	523
60 - 64	1,485	911	574	1,185	718	467	209	149	60	91	44	47	165	78
65 - 74	1,510	899	611	1,262	723	539	206	152	54	42	24	18	213	59
75 - 84	438	242	196	341	188	153	90	52	38	7	2	5	78	20
85 and over	51	20	31	32	11	21	19	9	10	-	-	-	14	5

Table 3 Type of establishment, migrants and long-term illness – **continued**

Great Britain, England & Wales, England, regions, metropolitan counties, Inner London, Outer London, regional remainders, Wales, Scotland

Persons present in communal establishments

Inner London – *continued*

Type of establishment and age	PERSONS PRESENT			Visitors/guests			Residents - non-staff			Residents - staff			With limiting long-term illness	Migrants
	TOTAL	Males	Females	Total	Males	Females	Total	Males	Females	Total	Males	Females		
a	b	c	d	e	f	g	h	i	j	k	l	m	n	o
Hostels and common lodging houses (non-HA)														
All ages	5,168	2,820	2,348	887	402	485	4,064	2,314	1,750	217	104	113	1,262	2,361
0 - 15	458	242	216	43	24	19	407	214	193	8	4	4	14	251
16 - 17	116	35	81	10	5	5	106	30	76	-	-	-	5	91
18 - 29	2,088	794	1,294	442	156	286	1,553	605	948	93	33	60	187	1,099
30 - 44	1,007	638	369	129	92	37	831	514	317	47	32	15	311	524
45 - 59	752	581	171	82	56	26	627	502	125	43	23	20	370	288
60 - 64	199	159	40	19	12	7	169	142	27	11	5	6	91	41
65 - 74	339	271	68	46	25	21	280	240	40	13	6	7	136	54
75 - 84	153	85	68	70	24	46	82	60	22	1	1	-	102	10
85 and over	56	15	41	46	8	38	9	7	2	1	-	1	46	3
Other miscellaneous establishments														
All ages	5,806	2,774	3,032	965	527	438	3,843	1,772	2,071	998	475	523	493	2,220
0 - 15	420	226	194	60	45	15	344	174	170	16	7	9	18	242
16 - 17	82	44	38	9	6	3	68	33	35	5	5	-	5	54
18 - 29	3,045	1,419	1,626	476	202	274	2,125	1,005	1,120	444	212	232	92	1,378
30 - 44	999	546	453	198	133	65	560	287	273	241	126	115	85	365
45 - 59	575	268	307	91	67	24	315	133	182	169	68	101	83	119
60 - 64	189	83	106	46	23	23	97	36	61	46	24	22	34	29
65 - 74	268	119	149	74	49	25	144	47	97	50	23	27	56	20
75 - 84	173	61	112	11	2	9	139	50	89	23	9	14	86	8
85 and over	55	8	47	-	-	-	51	7	44	4	1	3	34	5

Table 3 Type of establishment, migrants and long-term illness – **continued**

Great Britain, England & Wales, England, regions, metropolitan counties, Inner London, Outer London, regional remainders, Wales, Scotland

Persons present in communal establishments

Inner London – *continued*

Type of establishment and age	PERSONS PRESENT			Visitors/guests			Residents - non-staff			Residents - staff			With limiting long-term illness	Migrants
	TOTAL	Males	Females	Total	Males	Females	Total	Males	Females	Total	Males	Females		
a	b	c	d	e	f	g	h	i	j	k	l	m	n	o
Persons sleeping rough														
All ages	**1,072**	**906**	**166**	**79**	**67**	**12**	**992**	**839**	**153**				**98**	**775**
0 - 15	-	-	-	-	-	-	-	-	-				-	-
16 - 17	16	10	6	3	3	-	13	7	6				1	12
18 - 29	420	359	61	31	25	6	389	334	55				30	310
30 - 44	360	307	53	18	15	3	342	292	50				32	259
45 - 59	257	214	43	22	19	3	234	195	39				24	186
60 - 64	11	10	1	2	2	-	9	8	1				7	4
65 - 74	7	5	2	3	3	-	4	2	2				4	3
75 - 84	-	-	-	-	-	-	-	-	-				-	-
85 and over	1	1	-	-	-	-	1	1	-				-	1
Campers														
All ages	**55**	**9**	**46**	**1**	**-**	**1**	**54**	**9**	**45**				**55**	**21**
0 - 15	-	-	-	-	-	-	-	-	-				-	-
16 - 17	-	-	-	-	-	-	-	-	-				-	-
18 - 29	-	-	-	-	-	-	-	-	-				-	-
30 - 44	-	-	-	-	-	-	-	-	-				-	-
45 - 59	-	-	-	-	-	-	-	-	-				-	-
60 - 64	-	-	-	-	-	-	-	-	-				-	-
65 - 74	1	-	1	-	-	-	1	-	1				1	1
75 - 84	21	5	16	1	-	1	20	5	15				21	8
85 and over	33	4	29	-	-	-	33	4	29				33	12

Table 3 Type of establishment, migrants and long-term illness – **continued**

Persons present in communal establishments

Type of establishment and age	PERSONS PRESENT			Visitors/guests			Residents - non-staff			Residents - staff			With limiting long-term illness	Migrants
	TOTAL	Males	Females	Total	Males	Females	Total	Males	Females	Total	Males	Females		
a	b	c	d	e	f	g	h	i	j	k	l	m	n	o
Inner London – *continued*														
Civilian ships, boats and barges														
All ages	**11**	**5**	**6**	**-**	**-**	**-**	**11**	**5**	**6**				**-**	**3**
0 - 15	2	1	1	-	-	-	2	1	1				-	-
16 - 17	2	-	2	-	-	-	2	-	2				-	2
18 - 29	1	1	-	-	-	-	1	1	-				-	1
30 - 44	5	3	2	-	-	-	5	3	2				-	-
45 - 59	1	-	1	-	-	-	1	-	1				-	-
60 - 64	-	-	-	-	-	-	-	-	-				-	-
65 - 74	-	-	-	-	-	-	-	-	-				-	-
75 - 84	-	-	-	-	-	-	-	-	-				-	-
85 and over	-	-	-	-	-	-	-	-	-				-	-
Outer London														
All establishments														
All ages	**72,632**	**30,766**	**41,866**	**26,345**	**13,743**	**12,602**	**39,698**	**14,665**	**25,033**	**6,589**	**2,358**	**4,231**	**34,877**	**16,299**
0 - 15	5,125	2,937	2,188	2,566	1,557	1,009	2,328	1,244	1,084	231	136	95	490	1,425
16 - 17	1,468	934	534	1,027	727	300	386	184	202	55	23	32	134	309
18 - 29	20,526	10,241	10,285	8,521	4,402	4,119	8,080	4,661	3,419	3,925	1,178	2,747	2,175	6,551
30 - 44	9,113	5,379	3,734	3,908	2,391	1,517	3,970	2,391	1,579	1,235	597	638	2,544	2,061
45 - 59	5,620	3,158	2,462	2,553	1,539	1,014	2,258	1,301	957	809	318	491	2,488	697
60 - 64	1,929	991	938	865	484	381	935	457	478	129	50	79	1,247	202
65 - 74	5,189	2,208	2,981	2,031	1,026	1,005	3,039	1,139	1,900	119	43	76	4,133	680
75 - 84	11,439	3,119	8,320	3,034	1,207	1,827	8,348	1,902	6,446	57	10	47	10,248	2,074
85 and over	12,223	1,799	10,424	1,840	410	1,430	10,354	1,386	8,968	29	3	3	11,418	2,300

Table 3 Type of establishment, migrants and long-term illness – **continued**

Great Britain, England & Wales, England, regions, metropolitan counties, Inner London, Outer London, regional remainders, Wales, Scotland

Persons present in communal establishments

Type of establishment and age	PERSONS PRESENT			Visitors/guests			Residents - non-staff			Residents - staff			With limiting long-term illness	Migrants
	TOTAL	Males	Females	Total	Males	Females	Total	Males	Females	Total	Males	Females		
a	b	c	d	e	f	g	h	i	j	k	l	m	n	o

Outer London – *continued*

NHS hospitals/homes - psychiatric

All ages	**1,974**	**889**	**1,085**	**520**	**240**	**280**	**1,220**	**525**	**695**	**234**	**124**	**110**	**1,626**	**258**
0 - 15	18	11	7	15	9	6	3	2	1	-	-	-	3	1
16 - 17	12	6	6	10	5	5	2	1	1	-	-	-	9	-
18 - 29	369	199	170	120	63	57	98	66	32	151	70	81	180	109
30 - 44	305	181	124	112	56	56	137	83	54	56	42	14	230	60
45 - 59	268	150	118	77	41	36	166	98	68	25	11	14	227	23
60 - 64	101	58	43	23	12	11	76	45	31	2	1	1	99	5
65 - 74	264	115	149	53	14	39	211	101	110	-	-	-	256	15
75 - 84	389	128	261	74	34	40	315	94	221	-	-	-	383	34
85 and over	248	41	207	36	6	30	212	35	177	-	-	-	239	11

NHS hospitals/homes - other

All ages	**17,557**	**6,133**	**11,424**	**10,889**	**4,294**	**6,595**	**3,390**	**994**	**2,396**	**3,278**	**845**	**2,433**	**9,311**	**2,430**
0 - 15	984	513	471	908	471	437	54	29	25	22	13	9	188	31
16 - 17	61	20	41	51	16	35	8	3	5	2	1	1	13	7
18 - 29	4,803	1,143	3,660	1,540	395	1,145	742	199	543	2,521	549	1,972	476	1,538
30 - 44	2,159	860	1,299	1,207	443	764	395	192	203	557	225	332	651	336
45 - 59	1,481	725	756	1,052	531	521	273	146	127	156	48	108	900	84
60 - 64	696	357	339	577	313	264	104	37	67	15	7	8	520	24
65 - 74	1,919	923	996	1,588	799	789	326	122	204	5	2	3	1,580	64
75 - 84	3,203	1,161	2,042	2,474	982	1,492	729	179	550	-	-	-	2,876	175
85 and over	2,251	431	1,820	1,492	344	1,148	759	87	672	-	-	-	2,107	171

Table 3 Type of establishment, migrants and long-term illness – **continued**

Persons present in communal establishments

Type of establishment and age	PERSONS PRESENT			Visitors/guests			Residents - non-staff			Residents - staff			With limiting long-term illness	Migrants
	TOTAL	Males	Females	Total	Males	Females	Total	Males	Females	Total	Males	Females		
a	b	c	d	e	f	g	h	i	j	k	l	m	n	o

Outer London – *continued*

Non-NHS hospitals - psychiatric

All ages	118	56	62	55	23	32	62	33	29	1	-	1	78	20
0 - 15	2	1	1	2	1	1	-	-	-	-	-	-	-	-
16 - 17	2	1	1	2	1	1	-	-	-	-	-	-	-	-
18 - 29	22	13	9	12	6	6	9	7	2	1	-	1	11	4
30 - 44	37	16	21	17	7	10	20	9	11	-	-	-	21	7
45 - 59	25	14	11	13	5	8	12	9	3	-	-	-	19	4
60 - 64	8	6	2	2	1	1	6	5	1	-	-	-	7	2
65 - 74	18	4	14	5	1	4	13	3	10	-	-	-	15	3
75 - 84	4	1	3	2	1	1	2	-	2	-	-	-	4	-
85 and over	-	-	-	-	-	-	-	-	-	-	-	-	-	-

Non-NHS hospitals - other

All ages	762	296	466	505	216	289	116	34	82	141	46	95	257	90
0 - 15	24	16	8	14	9	5	9	6	3	1	1	-	5	2
16 - 17	3	1	2	2	1	1	-	-	-	1	-	1	-	1
18 - 29	164	45	119	59	16	43	27	9	18	78	20	58	19	58
30 - 44	171	69	102	112	44	68	15	8	7	44	17	27	30	19
45 - 59	159	59	100	127	46	81	18	7	11	14	6	8	61	2
60 - 64	53	28	25	45	27	18	6	-	6	2	1	1	20	1
65 - 74	95	51	44	84	49	35	11	2	9	-	-	-	60	2
75 - 84	70	23	47	51	21	30	18	1	17	1	1	-	44	5
85 and over	23	4	19	11	3	8	12	1	11	-	-	-	18	-

Table 3 Type of establishment, migrants and long-term illness – **continued**

Great Britain, England & Wales, England, regions, metropolitan counties, Inner London, Outer London, regional remainders, Wales, Scotland

Persons present in communal establishments

Outer London – *continued*

Type of establishment and age	PERSONS PRESENT			Visitors/guests			Residents - non-staff			Residents - staff			With limiting long-term illness	Migrants
	TOTAL	Males	Females	Total	Males	Females	Total	Males	Females	Total	Males	Females		
a	b	c	d	e	f	g	h	i	j	k	l	m	n	o
Local authority homes														
All ages	**8,328**	**2,418**	**5,910**	**663**	**239**	**424**	**7,564**	**2,149**	**5,415**	**101**	**30**	**71**	**7,611**	**1,560**
0 - 15	106	63	43	62	39	23	41	22	19	3	2	1	54	25
16 - 17	69	29	40	28	12	16	40	17	23	1	-	1	27	26
18 - 29	598	327	271	91	36	55	483	285	198	24	6	18	454	140
30 - 44	662	351	311	68	21	47	563	321	242	31	9	22	555	83
45 - 59	472	244	228	58	27	31	382	207	175	32	10	22	399	56
60 - 64	165	80	85	21	12	9	139	66	73	5	2	3	149	22
65 - 74	748	291	457	50	23	27	696	268	428	2	-	2	701	151
75 - 84	2,486	597	1,889	140	40	100	2,344	556	1,788	2	1	1	2,356	514
85 and over	3,022	436	2,586	145	29	116	2,876	407	2,469	1	-	1	2,916	543
Housing association homes and hostels														
All ages	**2,219**	**910**	**1,309**	**234**	**119**	**115**	**1,888**	**753**	**1,135**	**97**	**38**	**59**	**1,299**	**655**
0 - 15	53	27	26	7	4	3	42	21	21	4	2	2	3	19
16 - 17	25	14	11	9	7	2	16	7	9	-	-	-	5	10
18 - 29	571	340	231	143	74	69	399	255	144	29	11	18	117	231
30 - 44	246	141	105	30	16	14	198	119	79	18	6	12	134	57
45 - 59	155	83	72	13	8	5	115	66	49	27	9	18	104	40
60 - 64	51	27	24	2	1	1	42	24	18	7	2	5	37	11
65 - 74	207	88	119	4	2	2	194	79	115	9	7	2	154	52
75 - 84	441	119	322	17	5	12	424	114	310	-	-	-	340	107
85 and over	470	71	399	9	2	7	458	68	390	3	1	2	405	128

Table 3 Type of establishment, migrants and long-term illness – **continued**

Great Britain, England & Wales, England, regions, metropolitan counties, Inner London, Outer London, regional remainders, Wales, Scotland

Persons present in communal establishments

Type of establishment and age	PERSONS PRESENT			Visitors/guests			Residents - non-staff			Residents - staff			With limiting long-term illness	Migrants
	TOTAL	Males	Females	Total	Males	Females	Total	Males	Females	Total	Males	Females		
a	b	c	d	e	f	g	h	i	j	k	l	m	n	o

Outer London – continued

Type of establishment and age	PERSONS PRESENT			Visitors/guests			Residents - non-staff			Residents - staff			With limiting long-term illness	Migrants
Nursing homes (non-NHS/LA/HA)														
All ages	**5,051**	**1,072**	**3,979**	**192**	**67**	**125**	**4,709**	**971**	**3,738**	**150**	**34**	**116**	**4,632**	**1,493**
0 - 15	10	5	5	-	-	-	5	2	3	5	3	2	3	1
16 - 17	17	7	-	-	-	-	-	-	-	-	-	-	-	-
18 - 29	106	42	64	7	2	5	60	32	28	39	8	31	51	41
30 - 44	153	78	75	24	8	16	102	62	40	27	8	19	107	41
45 - 59	154	65	89	24	7	17	91	50	41	39	8	31	102	38
60 - 64	128	49	79	13	5	8	98	40	58	17	4	13	105	30
65 - 74	520	167	353	36	21	15	467	143	324	17	3	14	468	150
75 - 84	1,721	381	1,340	60	19	41	1,656	362	1,294	5	-	5	1,624	542
85 and over	2,259	285	1,974	28	5	23	2,230	280	1,950	1	-	1	2,172	650
Residential homes (non-NHS/LA/HA)														
All ages	**8,480**	**2,027**	**6,453**	**249**	**69**	**180**	**7,927**	**1,871**	**6,056**	**304**	**87**	**217**	**7,418**	**1,860**
0 - 15	15	9	6	-	-	-	1	1	-	14	9	5	1	3
16 - 17	17	7	10	8	4	4	5	2	3	4	1	3	7	4
18 - 29	384	186	198	55	19	36	231	137	94	98	30	68	254	91
30 - 44	458	238	220	48	10	38	350	210	140	60	18	42	352	67
45 - 59	397	179	218	26	5	21	281	153	128	90	21	69	285	60
60 - 64	211	104	107	7	2	5	190	101	89	14	1	13	176	43
65 - 74	755	270	485	15	5	10	727	261	466	13	4	9	671	161
75 - 84	2,545	535	2,010	39	13	26	2,501	519	1,982	5	3	2	2,299	654
85 and over	3,698	499	3,199	51	11	40	3,641	488	3,153	6	-	6	3,373	777

Table 3 Type of establishment, migrants and long-term illness – **continued**

Great Britain, England & Wales, England, regions, metropolitan counties, Inner London, Outer London, regional remainders, Wales, Scotland

Persons present in communal establishments

Type of establishment and age	PERSONS PRESENT			Visitors/guests			Residents - non-staff			Residents - staff			With limiting long-term illness	Migrants
	TOTAL	Males	Females	Total	Males	Females	Total	Males	Females	Total	Males	Females		
a	b	c	d	e	f	g	h	i	j	k	l	m	n	o

Outer London – *continued*

Children's homes

All ages	**909**	**453**	**456**	**168**	**80**	**88**	**653**	**339**	**314**	**88**	**34**	**54**	**111**	**335**
0 - 15	761	397	364	94	50	44	653	339	314	14	8	6	105	319
16 - 17	9	4	5	-	-	-	-	-	-	9	4	5	-	6
18 - 29	56	16	40	38	12	26	-	-	-	18	4	14	4	5
30 - 44	48	25	23	23	15	8	-	-	-	25	10	15	2	5
45 - 59	33	11	22	11	3	8	-	-	-	22	8	14	-	-
60 - 64	2	-	2	2	-	2	-	-	-	-	-	-	-	-
65 - 74	-	-	-	-	-	-	-	-	-	-	-	-	-	-
75 - 84	-	-	-	-	-	-	-	-	-	-	-	-	-	-
85 and over	-	-	-	-	-	-	-	-	-	-	-	-	-	-

Prison service establishments

All ages	**1,133**	**1,080**	**53**	**769**	**755**	**14**	**362**	**324**	**38**	**2**	**1**	**1**	**106**	**240**
0 - 15	21	21	-	18	18	-	3	3	-	-	-	-	6	1
16 - 17	165	160	5	130	128	2	35	32	3	-	-	-	17	21
18 - 29	776	748	28	533	527	6	242	220	22	1	1	1	70	151
30 - 44	136	124	12	75	69	6	61	55	6	1	-	-	7	53
45 - 59	33	26	7	12	12	-	20	14	6	1	1	1	5	14
60 - 64	-	-	-	-	-	-	-	-	-	-	-	-	-	-
65 - 74	-	-	-	-	-	-	-	-	-	-	-	-	-	-
75 - 84	2	1	1	1	1	-	1	1	1	-	-	-	1	1
85 and over	-	-	-	-	-	-	-	-	-	-	-	-	-	-

Table 3 Type of establishment, migrants and long-term illness – **continued**

Great Britain, England, England & Wales, England, regions, metropolitan counties, Inner London, Outer London, regional remainders, Wales, Scotland

Persons present in communal establishments

Type of establishment and age	PERSONS PRESENT			Visitors/guests			Residents - non-staff			Residents - staff			With limiting long-term illness	Migrants
	TOTAL	Males	Females	Total	Males	Females	Total	Males	Females	Total	Males	Females		
a	b	c	d	e	f	g	h	i	j	k	l	m	n	o

Outer London – *continued*

Defence establishments

All ages	**2,285**	**1,667**	**618**	**499**	**417**	**82**	**1,786**	**1,250**	**536**				**127**	**737**
0 - 15	-	-	-	-	-	-	-	-	-				-	-
16 - 17	60	57	3	18	18	-	42	39	3				2	33
18 - 29	1,716	1,208	508	238	201	37	1,478	1,007	471				61	601
30 - 44	371	300	71	157	133	24	214	167	47				24	90
45 - 59	95	77	18	59	48	11	36	29	7				11	9
60 - 64	8	5	3	5	3	2	3	2	1				3	-
65 - 74	23	16	7	18	12	6	5	4	1				14	3
75 - 84	8	4	4	4	2	2	4	2	2				8	1
85 and over	4	-	4	-	-	-	4	-	4				4	-

Educational establishments

All ages	**7,362**	**4,134**	**3,228**	**5,949**	**3,372**	**2,577**	**1,133**	**635**	**498**	**280**	**127**	**153**	**286**	**781**
0 - 15	1,173	774	399	1,099	743	356	61	23	38	13	8	5	53	27
16 - 17	743	510	233	694	502	192	47	7	40	2	1	1	32	30
18 - 29	4,709	2,451	2,258	3,913	1,970	1,943	708	443	265	88	38	50	141	580
30 - 44	380	263	117	150	111	39	163	110	53	67	42	25	15	102
45 - 59	187	86	101	71	36	35	57	29	28	59	21	38	12	25
60 - 64	45	22	23	7	2	5	23	9	14	15	11	4	5	1
65 - 74	64	17	47	8	3	5	34	9	25	22	5	17	8	11
75 - 84	44	10	34	5	4	1	28	5	23	11	1	10	13	3
85 and over	17	1	16	2	1	1	12	-	12	3	-	3	7	2

Table 3 Type of establishment, migrants and long-term illness – **continued**

Great Britain, England & Wales, England, regions, metropolitan counties, Inner London, Outer London, regional remainders, Wales, Scotland

Persons present in communal establishments

Outer London – *continued*

Type of establishment and age	PERSONS PRESENT			Visitors/guests			Residents - non-staff			Residents - staff			With limiting long-term illness	Migrants
	TOTAL	Males	Females	Total	Males	Females	Total	Males	Females	Total	Males	Females		
a	b	c	d	e	f	g	h	i	j	k	l	m	n	o
Hotels, boarding houses etc														
All ages	**10,692**	**6,477**	**4,215**	**4,502**	**3,067**	**1,435**	**4,666**	**2,589**	**2,077**	**1,524**	**821**	**703**	**1,138**	**3,453**
0 - 15	1,241	658	583	222	125	97	872	448	424	147	85	62	47	602
16 - 17	205	94	111	53	21	32	118	57	61	34	16	18	13	104
18 - 29	3,859	2,061	1,798	1,228	733	495	1,871	944	927	760	384	376	213	1,724
30 - 44	2,914	2,035	879	1,583	1,231	352	1,058	635	423	273	169	104	264	742
45 - 59	1,544	1,117	427	892	679	213	416	299	117	236	139	97	203	196
60 - 64	288	193	95	139	97	42	113	81	32	36	15	21	77	29
65 - 74	302	191	111	158	92	66	121	88	33	23	11	12	100	35
75 - 84	242	109	133	162	80	82	70	28	42	10	1	9	152	16
85 and over	97	19	78	65	9	56	27	9	18	5	1	4	69	5
Hostels and common lodging houses (non-HA)														
All ages	**1,310**	**680**	**630**	**79**	**32**	**47**	**1,193**	**630**	**563**	**38**	**18**	**20**	**345**	**746**
0 - 15	188	99	89	8	6	2	174	89	85	6	4	2	2	101
16 - 17	32	7	25	1	-	1	31	7	24	-	-	-	4	27
18 - 29	510	219	291	44	9	35	453	207	246	13	3	10	68	348
30 - 44	270	178	92	12	7	5	250	166	84	8	5	3	82	180
45 - 59	138	113	25	8	7	1	120	101	19	10	5	5	78	63
60 - 64	32	24	8	4	2	2	28	22	6	-	-	-	18	9
65 - 74	45	24	21	-	-	-	44	23	21	1	1	-	26	5
75 - 84	45	10	35	1	1	-	44	9	35	-	-	-	26	5
85 and over	50	6	44	1	-	1	49	6	43	-	-	-	41	8

Table 3 Type of establishment, migrants and long-term illness – **continued**

Great Britain, England & Wales, England, regions, metropolitan counties, Inner London, Outer London, regional remainders, Wales, Scotland

Persons present in communal establishments

Outer London – *continued*

Type of establishment and age	PERSONS PRESENT			Visitors/guests			Residents - non-staff			Residents - staff			With limiting long-term illness	Migrants
	TOTAL	Males	Females	Total	Males	Females	Total	Males	Females	Total	Males	Females		
a	b	c	d	e	f	g	h	i	j	k	l	m	n	o
Other miscellaneous establishments														
All ages	4,296	2,335	1,961	989	674	315	2,956	1,508	1,448	351	153	198	492	1,586
0 - 15	529	343	186	117	82	35	410	260	150	2	1	1	20	293
16 - 17	62	21	41	19	10	9	41	11	30	2	-	2	4	39
18 - 29	1,838	1,208	630	478	319	159	1,256	835	421	104	54	50	46	910
30 - 44	748	469	279	267	197	70	412	226	186	69	46	23	57	198
45 - 59	434	167	267	78	54	24	258	81	177	98	32	66	66	73
60 - 64	134	31	103	15	4	11	103	21	82	16	6	10	31	22
65 - 74	228	50	178	11	4	7	190	36	154	27	10	17	79	28
75 - 84	239	40	199	4	4	-	212	33	179	23	3	20	122	18
85 and over	84	6	78	-	-	-	74	5	69	10	1	9	67	5
Persons sleeping rough														
All ages	125	113	12	62	60	2	63	53	10				39	46
0 - 15	-	-	-	-	-	-	-	-	-				-	-
16 - 17	3	3	-	2	2	-	1	1	-				-	1
18 - 29	33	26	7	16	15	1	17	11	6				9	14
30 - 44	44	41	3	16	16	-	28	25	3				13	18
45 - 59	38	36	2	25	24	1	13	12	1				16	10
60 - 64	6	6	-	2	2	-	4	4	-				-	3
65 - 74	1	1	-	1	1	-	-	-	-				1	-
75 - 84	-	-	-	-	-	-	-	-	-				-	-
85 and over	-	-	-	-	-	-	-	-	-				-	-

Table 3 Type of establishment, migrants and long-term illness – **continued**

Great Britain, England & Wales, England, regions, metropolitan counties, Inner London, Outer London, regional remainders, Wales, Scotland

Persons present in communal establishments

Outer London – *continued*

Type of establishment and age	PERSONS PRESENT			Visitors/guests			Residents - non-staff			Residents - staff			With limiting long-term illness	Migrants
	TOTAL	Males	Females	Total	Males	Females	Total	Males	Females	Total	Males	Females		
a	b	c	d	e	f	g	h	i	j	k	l	m	n	o
Campers														
All ages	**13**	**9**	**4**	**4**	**3**	**1**	**9**	**6**	**3**				**1**	**9**
0 - 15	-	-	-	-	-	-	-	-	-				-	-
16 - 17	-	-	-	-	-	-	-	-	-				-	-
18 - 29	10	7	3	4	3	1	6	4	2				1	6
30 - 44	3	2	1	-	-	-	3	2	1				-	3
45 - 59	-	-	-	-	-	-	-	-	-				-	-
60 - 64	-	-	-	-	-	-	-	-	-				-	-
65 - 74	-	-	-	-	-	-	-	-	-				-	-
75 - 84	-	-	-	-	-	-	-	-	-				-	-
85 and over	-	-	-	-	-	-	-	-	-				-	-
Civilian ships, boats and barges														
All ages	**18**	**17**	**1**	**17**	**16**	**1**	**1**	**1**	**-**				**-**	**-**
0 - 15	-	-	-	-	-	-	-	-	-				-	-
16 - 17	-	-	-	-	-	-	-	-	-				-	-
18 - 29	2	2	-	2	2	-	-	-	-				-	-
30 - 44	8	8	-	7	7	-	1	1	-				-	-
45 - 59	7	6	1	7	6	1	-	-	-				-	-
60 - 64	1	1	-	1	1	-	-	-	-				-	-
65 - 74	-	-	-	-	-	-	-	-	-				-	-
75 - 84	-	-	-	-	-	-	-	-	-				-	-
85 and over	-	-	-	-	-	-	-	-	-				-	-

Table 3 Type of establishment, migrants and long-term illness – **continued**

Persons present in communal establishments

Type of establishment and age	PERSONS PRESENT			Visitors/guests			Residents - non-staff			Residents - staff			With limiting long-term illness	Migrants
	TOTAL	Males	Females	Total	Males	Females	Total	Males	Females	Total	Males	Females		
a	b	c	d	e	f	g	h	i	j	k	l	m	n	o

Outer Metropolitan Area

All establishments

All ages	**142,312**	**69,652**	**72,660**	**61,492**	**35,666**	**25,826**	**67,515**	**28,162**	**39,353**	**13,305**	**5,824**	**7,481**	**59,875**	**25,198**
0 - 15	18,932	11,812	7,120	16,323	10,393	5,930	2,091	1,151	940	518	268	250	1,496	1,080
16 - 17	8,417	5,112	3,305	7,164	4,280	2,884	1,084	760	324	169	72	97	481	921
18 - 29	38,408	22,195	16,213	17,450	10,171	7,279	13,135	9,020	4,115	7,823	3,004	4,819	3,952	10,347
30 - 44	16,773	10,801	5,972	7,014	4,558	2,456	7,131	4,810	2,321	2,628	1,433	1,195	5,416	2,575
45 - 59	10,696	6,154	4,542	4,138	2,438	1,700	4,869	2,883	1,986	1,689	833	856	5,079	968
60 - 64	3,245	1,726	1,519	1,128	601	527	1,845	982	863	272	143	129	2,146	296
65 - 74	8,661	3,765	4,896	2,641	1,290	1,351	5,883	2,417	3,466	137	58	79	7,068	1,179
75 - 84	18,072	4,972	13,100	3,662	1,407	2,255	14,359	3,553	10,806	51	12	39	16,330	3,822
85 and over	19,108	3,115	15,993	1,972	528	1,444	17,118	2,586	14,532	18	1	17	17,907	4,010

NHS hospitals/homes - psychiatric

All ages	**7,972**	**3,888**	**4,084**	**1,275**	**627**	**648**	**5,459**	**2,639**	**2,820**	**1,238**	**622**	**616**	**6,250**	**912**
0 - 15	46	27	19	25	15	10	21	12	9	-	-	-	18	5
16 - 17	12	6	6	9	5	4	2	1	1	1	-	1	5	1
18 - 29	1,463	779	684	341	208	133	346	233	113	776	338	438	442	362
30 - 44	1,247	812	435	244	134	110	697	490	207	306	188	118	852	163
45 - 59	1,180	724	456	212	101	111	835	544	291	133	79	54	983	46
60 - 64	511	313	198	45	20	25	448	280	168	18	13	5	482	30
65 - 74	1,232	585	647	135	54	81	1,093	527	566	4	4	-	1,205	84
75 - 84	1,512	495	1,017	183	66	117	1,329	429	900	-	-	-	1,501	141
85 and over	769	147	622	81	24	57	688	123	565	-	-	-	762	80

Table 3 Type of establishment, migrants and long-term illness – **continued**

Great Britain, England & Wales, England, regions, metropolitan counties, Inner London, Outer London, regional remainders, Wales, Scotland

Persons present in communal establishments

Outer Metropolitan Area – *continued*

Type of establishment and age	PERSONS PRESENT			Visitors/guests			Residents - non-staff			Residents - staff			With limiting long-term illness	Migrants
	TOTAL	Males	Females	Total	Males	Females	Total	Males	Females	Total	Males	Females		
a	b	c	d	e	f	g	h	i	j	k	l	m	n	o
NHS hospitals/homes - other														
All ages	**22,323**	**8,904**	**13,419**	**11,438**	**4,541**	**6,897**	**6,868**	**3,210**	**3,658**	**4,017**	**1,153**	**2,864**	**12,706**	**2,640**
0 - 15	1,240	627	613	1,128	590	538	86	26	60	26	11	15	225	46
16 - 17	100	36	64	73	29	44	9	4	5	18	3	15	26	24
18 - 29	5,866	1,630	4,236	1,777	492	1,285	1,013	435	578	3,076	703	2,373	849	1,591
30 - 44	3,703	1,898	1,805	1,294	468	826	1,722	1,096	626	687	334	353	1,971	398
45 - 59	2,504	1,312	1,192	1,033	493	540	1,287	730	557	184	89	95	1,791	119
60 - 64	809	446	363	526	281	245	263	153	110	20	12	8	643	23
65 - 74	2,483	1,187	1,296	1,639	824	815	842	363	479	2	-	2	2,095	81
75 - 84	3,510	1,300	2,210	2,582	994	1,588	926	305	621	2	1	1	3,134	207
85 and over	2,108	468	1,640	1,386	370	1,016	720	98	622	2	-	2	1,972	151
Non-NHS hospitals - psychiatric														
All ages	**385**	**148**	**237**	**115**	**40**	**75**	**230**	**84**	**146**	**40**	**24**	**16**	**283**	**45**
0 - 15	6	2	4	4	1	3	2	1	1	-	-	-	2	-
16 - 17	3	1	2	3	1	2	-	-	-	-	-	-	-	-
18 - 29	73	34	39	26	12	14	18	7	11	29	15	14	27	24
30 - 44	57	32	25	23	7	16	27	19	8	7	6	1	33	9
45 - 59	71	27	44	28	8	20	39	16	23	4	3	1	51	4
60 - 64	30	16	14	4	3	1	26	13	13	-	-	-	28	2
65 - 74	60	25	35	10	5	5	50	20	30	-	-	-	59	4
75 - 84	52	8	44	14	2	12	38	6	32	-	-	-	51	2
85 and over	33	3	30	3	1	2	30	2	28	-	-	-	32	-

Table 3 Type of establishment, migrants and long-term illness – **continued**

Great Britain, England & Wales, England, regions, metropolitan counties, Inner London, Outer London, regional remainders, Wales, Scotland

Persons present in communal establishments

Outer Metropolitan Area – *continued*

Type of establishment and age	PERSONS PRESENT			Visitors/guests			Residents - non-staff			Residents - staff			With limiting long-term illness	Migrants
	TOTAL	Males	Females	Total	Males	Females	Total	Males	Females	Total	Males	Females		
a	b	c	d	e	f	g	h	i	j	k	l	m	n	o
Non-NHS hospitals - other														
All ages	**2,012**	**847**	**1,165**	**1,000**	**403**	**597**	**833**	**373**	**460**	**179**	**71**	**108**	**1,112**	**139**
0 - 15	24	16	8	24	16	8	-	-	-	-	-	-	3	-
16 - 17	6	5	1	6	5	1	-	-	-	-	-	-	3	-
18 - 29	326	134	192	93	40	53	111	47	64	122	47	75	81	82
30 - 44	421	164	257	204	47	157	187	102	85	30	15	15	208	23
45 - 59	461	195	266	254	90	164	184	97	87	23	8	15	242	10
60 - 64	134	66	68	69	34	35	63	32	31	2	-	2	86	1
65 - 74	251	123	128	140	76	64	109	46	63	2	1	1	174	5
75 - 84	266	107	159	144	69	75	122	38	84	-	-	-	213	12
85 and over	123	37	86	66	26	40	57	11	46	-	-	-	102	6
Local authority homes														
All ages	**11,030**	**3,521**	**7,509**	**1,203**	**601**	**602**	**9,646**	**2,850**	**6,796**	**181**	**70**	**111**	**9,827**	**2,386**
0 - 15	468	356	112	346	284	62	114	68	46	8	4	4	165	39
16 - 17	143	92	51	53	37	16	83	53	30	7	2	5	71	37
18 - 29	777	416	361	123	59	64	587	329	258	67	28	39	569	171
30 - 44	788	425	363	107	36	71	634	370	264	47	19	28	649	120
45 - 59	556	290	266	104	28	76	404	246	158	48	16	32	426	70
60 - 64	167	73	94	21	7	14	144	66	78	2	-	2	155	32
65 - 74	924	379	545	81	37	44	841	341	500	2	1	1	878	227
75 - 84	3,187	844	2,343	181	73	108	3,006	771	2,235	-	-	-	3,051	811
85 and over	4,020	646	3,374	187	40	147	3,833	606	3,227	-	-	-	3,863	879

Table 3 Type of establishment, migrants and long-term illness – **continued**

Great Britain, England & Wales, England, regions, metropolitan counties, Inner London, Outer London, regional remainders, Wales, Scotland

Persons present in communal establishments

Type of establishment and age	PERSONS PRESENT			Visitors/guests			Residents - non-staff			Residents - staff			With limiting long-term illness	Migrants
	TOTAL	Males	Females	Total	Males	Females	Total	Males	Females	Total	Males	Females		
a	b	c	d	e	f	g	h	i	j	k	l	m	n	o
Outer Metropolitan Area – *continued*														
Housing association homes and hostels														
All ages	**2,319**	**912**	**1,407**	**115**	**62**	**53**	**2,106**	**823**	**1,283**	**98**	**27**	**71**	**1,443**	**679**
0 - 15	25	19	6	10	9	1	14	9	5	1	1	-	1	8
16 - 17	21	8	13	1	1	-	18	7	11	2	-	2	3	17
18 - 29	393	252	141	49	27	22	323	221	102	21	4	17	96	219
30 - 44	277	192	85	28	16	12	229	168	61	20	8	12	167	92
45 - 59	244	145	99	12	3	9	192	131	61	40	11	29	162	86
60 - 64	79	40	39	1	-	1	71	39	32	7	1	6	59	19
65 - 74	178	71	107	3	2	1	169	67	102	6	2	4	129	55
75 - 84	513	107	406	7	3	4	505	104	401	1	-	1	354	103
85 and over	589	78	511	4	1	3	585	77	508	-	-	-	472	80
Nursing homes (non-NHS/ LA/HA)														
All ages	**10,667**	**2,549**	**8,118**	**623**	**214**	**409**	**9,724**	**2,220**	**7,504**	**320**	**115**	**205**	**9,880**	**3,316**
0 - 15	76	48	28	38	21	17	29	20	9	9	7	2	57	7
16 - 17	21	7	14	14	5	9	2	-	2	5	2	3	14	3
18 - 29	349	127	222	79	26	53	105	48	57	165	53	112	125	106
30 - 44	248	91	157	67	15	52	122	54	68	59	22	37	145	37
45 - 59	318	121	197	65	21	44	194	79	115	59	21	38	213	60
60 - 64	240	95	145	26	10	16	206	81	125	8	4	4	220	57
65 - 74	1,130	416	714	99	41	58	1,023	370	653	8	5	3	1,070	349
75 - 84	3,617	921	2,696	153	60	93	3,458	860	2,598	6	1	5	3,467	1,252
85 and over	4,668	723	3,945	82	15	67	4,585	708	3,877	1	-	1	4,569	1,445

Table 3 Type of establishment, migrants and long-term illness – **continued**

Great Britain, England & Wales, England, regions, metropolitan counties, Inner London, Outer London, regional remainders, Wales, Scotland

Persons present in communal establishments

Outer Metropolitan Area – *continued*

Type of establishment and age	PERSONS PRESENT			Visitors/guests			Residents - non-staff			Residents - staff			With limiting long-term illness	Migrants
	TOTAL	Males	Females	Total	Males	Females	Total	Males	Females	Total	Males	Females		
a	b	c	d	e	f	g	h	i	j	k	l	m	n	o
Residential homes (non-NHS/LA/HA)														
All ages	**15,928**	**4,039**	**11,889**	**606**	**173**	**433**	**14,442**	**3,538**	**10,904**	**880**	**328**	**552**	**13,559**	**3,488**
0 - 15	150	81	69	38	23	15	31	18	13	81	40	41	66	17
16 - 17	37	16	21	14	3	11	7	3	4	16	10	6	11	4
18 - 29	1,086	512	574	123	43	80	625	366	259	338	103	235	656	295
30 - 44	1,007	546	461	88	26	62	741	447	294	178	73	105	762	134
45 - 59	864	429	435	52	12	40	607	338	269	205	79	126	614	115
60 - 64	365	156	209	19	5	14	308	135	173	38	16	22	288	52
65 - 74	1,278	424	854	40	10	30	1,220	407	813	18	7	11	1,109	293
75 - 84	4,669	951	3,718	141	31	110	4,527	920	3,607	1	-	1	4,161	1,239
85 and over	6,472	924	5,548	91	20	71	6,376	904	5,472	5	-	5	5,892	1,339
Children's homes														
All ages	**943**	**513**	**430**	**153**	**82**	**71**	**688**	**376**	**312**	**102**	**55**	**47**	**152**	**388**
0 - 15	790	443	347	81	51	30	688	376	312	21	16	5	114	365
16 - 17	4	3	1	1	-	1	-	-	-	3	3	-	2	1
18 - 29	83	44	39	44	22	22	-	-	-	39	22	17	29	15
30 - 44	29	13	16	14	8	6	-	-	-	15	5	10	2	3
45 - 59	33	8	25	11	1	10	-	-	-	22	7	15	4	2
60 - 64	1	1	-	-	-	-	-	-	-	1	1	-	-	1
65 - 74	2	1	1	1	-	1	-	-	-	1	1	-	-	1
75 - 84	-	-	-	-	-	-	-	-	-	-	-	-	-	-
85 and over	1	-	1	1	-	1	-	-	-	-	-	-	1	-

Table 3 Type of establishment, migrants and long-term illness – **continued**

Persons present in communal establishments

Type of establishment and age	PERSONS PRESENT TOTAL	Males	Females	Visitors/guests Total	Males	Females	Residents - non-staff Total	Males	Females	Residents - staff Total	Males	Females	With limiting long-term illness	Migrants
a	b	c	d	e	f	g	h	i	j	k	l	m	n	o
Outer Metropolitan Area – *continued*														
Prison service establishments														
All ages	**2,184**	**1,883**	**301**	**1,272**	**1,150**	**122**	**908**	**731**	**177**	**4**	**2**	**2**	**361**	**467**
0 - 15	-	-	-	-	-	-	-	-	-	-	-	-	-	-
16 - 17	60	55	5	52	52	-	8	3	5	-	-	-	4	7
18 - 29	1,122	996	126	739	691	48	383	305	78	1	1	-	128	244
30 - 44	700	579	121	337	289	48	362	289	73	1	1	-	122	160
45 - 59	252	214	38	120	100	20	130	114	16	1	-	1	86	49
60 - 64	27	18	9	14	9	5	12	8	4	1	-	1	8	4
65 - 74	18	16	2	10	9	1	8	7	1	-	-	-	12	2
75 - 84	4	4	-	-	-	-	4	4	-	-	-	-	1	1
85 and over	1	1	-	-	-	-	1	1	-	-	-	-	-	-
Defence establishments														
All ages	**8,459**	**7,166**	**1,293**	**1,845**	**1,570**	**275**	**6,614**	**5,596**	**1,018**				**223**	**3,352**
0 - 15	-	-	-	-	-	-	-	-	-				-	-
16 - 17	670	565	105	153	127	26	517	438	79				5	492
18 - 29	6,475	5,423	1,052	1,258	1,054	204	5,217	4,369	848				134	2,592
30 - 44	1,144	1,035	109	375	337	38	769	698	71				50	245
45 - 59	115	98	17	51	48	3	64	50	14				4	13
60 - 64	10	8	2	3	3	-	7	5	2				3	2
65 - 74	18	16	2	2	1	1	16	15	1				9	6
75 - 84	12	9	3	2	-	2	10	9	1				6	1
85 and over	15	12	3	1	-	1	14	12	2				12	1

Table 3 Type of establishment, migrants and long-term illness – **continued**

Great Britain, England & Wales, England, regions, metropolitan counties, Inner London, Outer London, regional remainders, Wales, Scotland

Persons present in communal establishments

Type of establishment and age	PERSONS PRESENT			Visitors/guests			Residents - non-staff			Residents - staff			With limiting long-term illness	Migrants
	TOTAL	Males	Females	Total	Males	Females	Total	Males	Females	Total	Males	Females		
a	b	c	d	e	f	g	h	i	j	k	l	m	n	o

Outer Metropolitan Area – *continued*

Educational establishments

All ages	**36,103**	**21,533**	**14,570**	**31,333**	**18,982**	**12,351**	**2,711**	**1,536**	**1,175**	**2,059**	**1,015**	**1,044**	**2,144**	**1,951**
0 - 15	14,444	9,269	5,175	14,071	9,063	5,008	245	143	102	128	63	65	782	113
16 - 17	6,729	3,943	2,786	6,528	3,855	2,673	176	82	94	25	6	19	316	62
18 - 29	11,435	6,405	5,030	9,275	5,207	4,068	1,383	857	526	777	341	436	471	1,275
30 - 44	1,851	1,173	678	826	536	290	483	326	157	542	311	231	142	388
45 - 59	970	481	489	355	190	165	161	64	97	454	227	227	135	92
60 - 64	202	93	109	55	24	31	57	21	36	90	48	42	46	8
65 - 74	198	78	120	90	44	46	77	21	56	31	13	18	85	5
75 - 84	202	66	136	93	44	49	99	16	83	10	6	4	110	6
85 and over	72	25	47	40	19	21	30	6	24	2	-	2	57	2

Hotels, boarding houses etc

All ages	**14,506**	**9,250**	**5,256**	**7,628**	**5,053**	**2,575**	**3,619**	**2,274**	**1,345**	**3,259**	**1,923**	**1,336**	**1,026**	**3,544**
0 - 15	1,143	657	486	481	285	196	492	286	206	170	86	84	44	304
16 - 17	357	199	158	143	77	66	132	80	52	82	42	40	15	164
18 - 29	5,780	3,467	2,313	2,208	1,339	869	1,635	1,000	635	1,937	1,128	809	185	2,300
30 - 44	3,700	2,688	1,012	2,549	1,915	634	601	413	188	550	360	190	180	520
45 - 59	2,193	1,540	653	1,466	1,039	427	333	260	73	394	241	153	213	169
60 - 64	440	282	158	289	171	118	86	67	19	65	44	21	81	27
65 - 74	512	280	232	325	159	166	149	103	46	38	18	20	118	20
75 - 84	265	103	162	141	58	83	107	42	65	17	3	14	119	21
85 and over	116	34	82	26	10	16	84	23	61	6	1	5	71	19

Table 3 Type of establishment, migrants and long-term illness – **continued**

Great Britain, England & Wales, England, regions, metropolitan counties, Inner London, Outer London, regional remainders, Wales, Scotland

Persons present in communal establishments

Type of establishment and age	PERSONS PRESENT			Visitors/guests			Residents - non-staff			Residents - staff			With limiting long-term illness	Migrants
	TOTAL	Males	Females	Total	Males	Females	Total	Males	Females	Total	Males	Females		
a	b	c	d	e	f	g	h	i	j	k	l	m	n	o
Outer Metropolitan Area – *continued*														
Hostels and common lodging houses (non-HA)														
All ages	**1,164**	**755**	**409**	**83**	**52**	**31**	**979**	**640**	**339**	**102**	**63**	**39**	**259**	**589**
0 - 15	174	94	80	5	3	2	164	89	75	5	2	3	6	94
16 - 17	55	31	24	1	1	-	52	29	23	2	1	1	3	43
18 - 29	427	206	221	41	18	23	347	163	184	39	25	14	57	299
30 - 44	190	143	47	25	21	4	147	111	36	18	11	7	54	100
45 - 59	157	131	26	7	6	1	121	104	17	29	21	8	63	42
60 - 64	55	49	6	2	1	1	47	46	1	6	2	4	25	8
65 - 74	76	73	3	1	1	-	73	71	2	2	1	1	37	3
75 - 84	25	23	2	1	1	-	23	22	1	1	-	1	10	-
85 and over	5	5	-	-	-	-	5	5	-	-	-	-	4	-
Other miscellaneous establishments														
All ages	**5,181**	**2,823**	**2,358**	**1,954**	**1,371**	**583**	**2,401**	**1,096**	**1,305**	**826**	**356**	**470**	**590**	**1,119**
0 - 15	344	171	173	71	31	40	204	102	102	69	38	31	13	81
16 - 17	189	139	50	107	78	29	74	58	16	8	3	5	3	64
18 - 29	2,290	1,474	816	1,014	740	274	839	537	302	437	197	240	83	647
30 - 44	1,014	636	378	490	377	113	356	179	177	168	80	88	64	144
45 - 59	543	220	323	156	100	56	295	89	206	92	31	61	72	75
60 - 64	156	53	103	36	17	19	106	35	71	14	1	13	21	30
65 - 74	292	85	207	57	21	36	212	59	153	23	5	18	84	44
75 - 84	237	33	204	19	5	14	205	27	178	13	1	12	152	26
85 and over	116	12	104	4	2	2	110	10	100	2	-	2	98	8

Table 3 Type of establishment, migrants and long-term illness – **continued**

Great Britain, England & Wales, England, regions, metropolitan counties, Inner London, Outer London, regional remainders, Wales, Scotland

Persons present in communal establishments

Type of establishment and age	PERSONS PRESENT			Visitors/guests			Residents - non-staff			Residents - staff			With limiting long-term illness	Migrants
	TOTAL	Males	Females	Total	Males	Females	Total	Males	Females	Total	Males	Females		
a	b	c	d	e	f	g	h	i	j	k	l	m	n	o

Outer Metropolitan Area – *continued*

Persons sleeping rough

All ages	219	185	34	150	126	24	69	59	10				48	50
0 - 15	-	-	-	-	-	-	-	-	-				-	-
16 - 17	4	2	2	2	1	1	2	1	1				-	-
18 - 29	99	83	16	65	52	13	34	31	3				14	24
30 - 44	57	50	7	36	32	4	21	18	3				14	19
45 - 59	49	42	7	38	33	5	11	9	2				17	7
60 - 64	5	4	1	5	4	1	-	-	-				1	-
65 - 74	4	3	1	3	3	-	1	-	1				2	-
75 - 84	1	1	-	1	1	-	-	-	-				-	-
85 and over	-	-	-	-	-	-	-	-	-				-	-

Campers

All ages	61	41	20	53	36	17	8	5	3				4	2
0 - 15	-	-	-	-	-	-	-	-	-				-	-
16 - 17	1	1	-	-	-	-	1	1	-				-	-
18 - 29	25	16	9	19	12	7	6	4	2				1	1
30 - 44	15	10	5	14	10	4	1	-	1				-	1
45 - 59	12	9	3	12	9	3	-	-	-				2	-
60 - 64	3	2	1	3	2	1	-	-	-				-	-
65 - 74	5	3	2	5	3	2	-	-	-				2	-
75 - 84	-	-	-	-	-	-	-	-	-				-	-
85 and over	-	-	-	-	-	-	-	-	-				-	-

Table 3 Type of establishment, migrants and long-term illness – **continued**

Great Britain, England & Wales, England, regions, metropolitan counties, Inner London, Outer London, regional remainders, Wales, Scotland

Persons present in communal establishments

Type of establishment and age	PERSONS PRESENT			Visitors/guests			Residents - non-staff			Residents - staff			With limiting long-term illness	Migrants
	TOTAL	Males	Females	Total	Males	Females	Total	Males	Females	Total	Males	Females		
a	b	c	d	e	f	g	h	i	j	k	l	m	n	o
Outer Metropolitan Area – *continued*														
Civilian ships, boats and barges														
All ages	856	695	161	646	583	63	210	112	98				8	131
0 - 15	2	2	-	1	1	-	1	1	-				-	1
16 - 17	5	3	2	4	3	1	1	-	1				-	1
18 - 29	339	197	142	176	129	47	163	68	95				6	100
30 - 44	325	314	11	293	284	9	32	30	2				1	20
45 - 59	174	168	6	162	156	6	12	12	-				1	9
60 - 64	11	11	-	10	10	-	1	1	-				-	-
65 - 74	-	-	-	-	-	-	-	-	-				-	-
75 - 84	-	-	-	-	-	-	-	-	-				-	-
85 and over	-	-	-	-	-	-	-	-	-				-	-
Outer South East														
All establishments														
All ages	188,716	94,143	94,573	87,422	49,834	37,588	89,520	38,676	50,844	11,774	5,633	6,141	76,361	33,587
0 - 15	19,439	12,269	7,170	16,306	10,530	5,776	2,375	1,345	1,030	758	394	364	1,717	1,110
16 - 17	8,238	5,331	2,907	6,710	4,185	2,525	1,289	1,035	254	239	111	128	634	1,036
18 - 29	56,045	34,770	21,275	31,229	18,128	13,101	19,142	14,118	5,024	5,674	2,524	3,150	4,622	13,176
30 - 44	19,153	13,163	5,990	9,157	6,233	2,924	7,727	5,681	2,046	2,269	1,249	1,020	4,777	3,392
45 - 59	13,730	8,208	5,522	6,600	3,803	2,797	5,001	3,365	1,636	2,129	1,040	1,089	5,096	1,298
60 - 64	5,204	2,570	2,634	2,492	1,137	1,355	2,361	1,258	1,103	351	175	176	2,852	454
65 - 74	13,692	5,928	7,764	6,309	2,814	3,495	7,159	3,020	4,139	224	94	130	9,234	1,637
75 - 84	26,010	7,312	18,698	6,003	2,311	3,692	19,914	4,967	14,947	93	34	59	22,301	5,637
85 and over	27,205	4,592	22,613	2,616	693	1,923	24,552	3,887	20,665	37	12	25	25,128	5,847

Table 3 Type of establishment, migrants and long-term illness – **continued**

Persons present in communal establishments

Type of establishment and age	PERSONS PRESENT			Visitors/guests			Residents - non-staff			Residents - staff			With limiting long-term illness	Migrants
	TOTAL	Males	Females	Total	Males	Females	Total	Males	Females	Total	Males	Females		
a	b	c	d	e	f	g	h	i	j	k	l	m	n	o

Outer South East – *continued*

NHS hospitals/homes - psychiatric

All ages	**3,228**	**1,483**	**1,745**	**1,216**	**514**	**702**	**1,713**	**864**	**849**	**299**	**105**	**194**	**2,626**	**400**
0 - 15	27	12	15	24	11	13	3	1	2	-	-	-	8	-
16 - 17	9	3	6	9	3	6	-	-	-	-	-	-	8	-
18 - 29	605	266	339	187	99	88	170	91	79	248	76	172	231	188
30 - 44	515	306	209	226	112	114	251	174	77	38	20	18	406	60
45 - 59	486	284	202	154	70	84	319	205	114	13	9	4	442	34
60 - 64	178	98	80	51	21	30	127	77	50	-	-	-	173	8
65 - 74	480	213	267	173	59	114	307	154	153	-	-	-	459	31
75 - 84	619	230	389	271	106	165	348	124	224	-	-	-	598	55
85 and over	309	71	238	121	33	88	188	38	150	-	-	-	301	24

NHS hospitals/homes - other

All ages	**18,351**	**7,041**	**11,310**	**12,265**	**4,790**	**7,475**	**4,202**	**1,703**	**2,499**	**1,884**	**548**	**1,336**	**10,724**	**1,850**
0 - 15	1,162	647	515	1,096	617	479	54	24	30	12	6	6	184	22
16 - 17	90	35	55	78	27	51	9	7	2	3	1	2	32	5
18 - 29	4,211	1,121	3,090	1,729	406	1,323	945	341	604	1,537	374	1,163	657	1,064
30 - 44	2,227	973	1,254	1,221	404	817	743	430	313	263	139	124	1,003	214
45 - 59	1,603	810	793	1,060	494	566	487	296	191	56	20	36	1,111	43
60 - 64	703	366	337	535	276	259	162	84	78	6	6	-	551	21
65 - 74	2,299	1,085	1,214	1,900	906	994	397	178	219	2	1	1	1,858	79
75 - 84	3,736	1,465	2,271	3,019	1,221	1,798	713	243	470	4	1	3	3,222	213
85 and over	2,320	539	1,781	1,627	439	1,188	692	100	592	1	-	1	2,106	189

Table 3 Type of establishment, migrants and long-term illness – **continued**

Great Britain, England & Wales, England, regions, metropolitan counties, Inner London, Outer London, regional remainders, Wales, Scotland

Persons present in communal establishments

Type of establishment and age	PERSONS PRESENT			Visitors/guests			Residents - non-staff			Residents - staff			With limiting long-term illness	Migrants
	TOTAL	Males	Females	Total	Males	Females	Total	Males	Females	Total	Males	Females		
a	b	c	d	e	f	g	h	i	j	k	l	m	n	o

Outer South East – *continued*

Non-NHS hospitals - psychiatric

Type of establishment and age	PERSONS PRESENT			Visitors/guests			Residents - non-staff			Residents - staff			With limiting long-term illness	Migrants
All ages	**1,037**	**513**	**524**	**166**	**67**	**99**	**784**	**397**	**387**	**87**	**49**	**38**	**905**	**142**
0 - 15	3	1	2	3	1	2	-	-	-	-	-	-	-	-
16 - 17	2	-	2	1	-	1	1	-	1	-	-	-	1	-
18 - 29	148	81	67	35	16	19	65	44	21	48	21	27	86	36
30 - 44	236	153	83	37	19	18	175	116	59	24	18	6	198	12
45 - 59	163	96	67	33	14	19	115	72	43	15	10	5	142	6
60 - 64	48	25	23	8	3	5	40	22	18	-	-	-	46	-
65 - 74	154	75	79	22	6	16	132	69	63	-	-	-	151	21
75 - 84	180	53	127	21	5	16	159	48	111	-	-	-	178	40
85 and over	103	29	74	6	3	3	97	26	71	-	-	-	103	27

Non-NHS hospitals - other

Type of establishment and age	PERSONS PRESENT			Visitors/guests			Residents - non-staff			Residents - staff			With limiting long-term illness	Migrants
All ages	**678**	**250**	**428**	**479**	**167**	**312**	**122**	**54**	**68**	**77**	**29**	**48**	**304**	**50**
0 - 15	9	5	4	9	5	4	-	-	-	-	-	-	3	-
16 - 17	5	-	5	2	-	2	-	-	-	3	-	3	-	3
18 - 29	92	30	62	37	11	26	3	2	1	52	17	35	9	22
30 - 44	111	35	76	80	17	63	18	12	6	13	6	7	29	5
45 - 59	125	50	75	103	33	70	15	13	2	7	4	3	39	2
60 - 64	40	21	19	34	19	15	6	2	4	-	-	-	27	2
65 - 74	101	43	58	87	36	51	13	6	7	1	1	1	56	2
75 - 84	120	52	68	92	39	53	28	13	15	-	-	-	76	6
85 and over	75	14	61	35	7	28	39	6	33	1	1	-	65	8

Table 3 Type of establishment, migrants and long-term illness – **continued**

Persons present in communal establishments

Outer South East – *continued*

Type of establishment and age	PERSONS PRESENT			Visitors/guests			Residents - non-staff			Residents - staff			With limiting long-term illness	Migrants
	TOTAL	Males	Females	Total	Males	Females	Total	Males	Females	Total	Males	Females		
a	b	c	d	e	f	g	h	i	j	k	l	m	n	o
Local authority homes														
All ages	**10,809**	**3,610**	**7,199**	**1,457**	**689**	**768**	**9,253**	**2,876**	**6,377**	**99**	**45**	**54**	**9,500**	**1,942**
0 - 15	696	500	196	446	326	120	248	173	75	2	1	1	235	81
16 - 17	140	78	62	87	43	44	53	35	18	-	-	-	89	19
18 - 29	713	400	313	163	92	71	525	296	229	25	12	13	568	145
30 - 44	692	372	320	123	45	78	536	308	228	33	19	14	545	72
45 - 59	478	226	252	82	24	58	371	196	175	25	6	19	385	38
60 - 64	222	88	134	19	4	15	197	80	117	6	4	2	197	34
65 - 74	907	363	544	86	37	49	818	324	494	3	2	1	855	166
75 - 84	3,075	856	2,219	233	71	162	2,839	784	2,055	3	1	2	2,922	672
85 and over	3,886	727	3,159	218	47	171	3,666	680	2,986	2	-	2	3,704	715
Housing association homes and hostels														
All ages	**2,326**	**989**	**1,337**	**173**	**58**	**115**	**2,094**	**916**	**1,178**	**59**	**15**	**44**	**1,456**	**684**
0 - 15	56	37	19	9	7	2	43	28	15	4	2	2	15	19
16 - 17	22	9	13	2	1	1	19	8	11	1	-	1	3	16
18 - 29	448	205	243	64	19	45	373	183	190	11	3	8	146	223
30 - 44	340	233	107	23	9	14	302	220	82	15	4	11	205	131
45 - 59	266	187	79	6	1	5	241	181	60	19	5	14	189	67
60 - 64	92	63	29	12	5	7	73	57	16	7	1	6	67	11
65 - 74	179	79	100	22	5	17	155	74	81	2	-	2	128	32
75 - 84	456	106	350	22	8	14	434	98	336	-	-	-	329	99
85 and over	467	70	397	13	3	10	454	67	387	-	-	-	374	86

Table 3 Type of establishment, migrants and long-term illness – **continued**

Persons present in communal establishments

Type of establishment and age	PERSONS PRESENT			Visitors/guests			Residents - non-staff			Residents - staff			With limiting long-term illness	Migrants
	TOTAL	Males	Females	Total	Males	Females	Total	Males	Females	Total	Males	Females		
a	b	c	d	e	f	g	h	i	j	k	l	m	n	o

Outer South East – *continued*

Nursing homes (non-NHS/LA/HA)

All ages	**16,348**	**4,079**	**12,269**	**1,106**	**367**	**739**	**14,901**	**3,583**	**11,318**	**341**	**129**	**212**	**15,114**	**5,023**
0 - 15	70	36	34	19	10	9	22	14	8	29	12	17	28	13
16 - 17	22	8	14	3	-	3	5	3	2	14	5	9	6	4
18 - 29	336	171	165	56	20	36	204	125	79	76	26	50	198	97
30 - 44	397	192	205	116	27	89	214	136	78	67	29	38	217	72
45 - 59	432	201	231	127	41	86	195	120	75	110	40	70	246	58
60 - 64	455	196	259	70	28	42	367	161	206	18	7	11	395	103
65 - 74	1,763	644	1,119	215	76	139	1,528	560	968	20	8	12	1,610	556
75 - 84	5,682	1,477	4,205	315	120	195	5,360	1,355	4,005	7	2	5	5,438	1,942
85 and over	7,191	1,154	6,037	185	45	140	7,006	1,109	5,897	-	-	-	6,976	2,178

Residential homes (non-NHS/LA/HA)

All ages	**30,551**	**8,292**	**22,259**	**949**	**296**	**653**	**28,361**	**7,508**	**20,853**	**1,241**	**488**	**753**	**26,539**	**6,512**
0 - 15	247	154	93	56	51	5	54	40	14	137	63	74	61	16
16 - 17	101	62	39	15	8	7	54	35	19	32	19	13	60	26
18 - 29	1,362	717	645	112	34	78	992	582	410	258	101	157	979	346
30 - 44	1,365	740	625	103	34	69	1,013	610	403	249	96	153	1,028	164
45 - 59	1,648	887	761	73	19	54	1,176	723	453	399	145	254	1,200	141
60 - 64	960	474	486	32	10	22	848	429	419	80	35	45	808	147
65 - 74	3,197	1,298	1,899	115	41	74	3,032	1,241	1,791	50	16	34	2,820	635
75 - 84	9,448	2,121	7,327	245	59	186	9,187	2,055	7,132	16	7	9	8,451	2,489
85 and over	12,223	1,839	10,384	198	40	158	12,005	1,793	10,212	20	6	14	11,132	2,548

Persons present in communal establishments

Table 3 Type of establishment, migrants and long-term illness – **continued**

Great Britain, England & Wales, England, regions, metropolitan counties, Inner London, Outer London, regional remainders, Wales, Scotland

Type of establishment and age	PERSONS PRESENT			Visitors/guests			Residents - non-staff			Residents - staff			With limiting long-term illness	Migrants
	TOTAL	Males	Females	Total	Males	Females	Total	Males	Females	Total	Males	Females		
a	b	c	d	e	f	g	h	i	j	k	l	m	n	o

Outer South East – *continued*

Children's homes

Type of establishment and age	TOTAL	Males	Females	Total	Males	Females	Total	Males	Females	Total	Males	Females	n	o
All ages	**1,393**	**733**	**660**	**190**	**88**	**102**	**959**	**537**	**422**	**244**	**108**	**136**	**143**	**484**
0 - 15	1,098	618	480	112	64	48	959	537	422	27	17	10	103	428
16 - 17	13	6	7	1	1	-	-	-	-	12	5	7	4	4
18 - 29	99	40	59	25	6	19	-	-	-	74	34	40	9	32
30 - 44	85	35	50	31	12	19	-	-	-	54	23	31	10	13
45 - 59	79	25	54	19	3	16	-	-	-	60	22	38	12	6
60 - 64	10	6	4	2	2	-	-	-	-	8	4	4	-	-
65 - 74	6	3	3	-	-	-	-	-	-	6	3	3	2	1
75 - 84	2	-	2	-	-	-	-	-	-	2	-	2	2	-
85 and over	1	-	1	-	-	-	-	-	-	1	-	1	1	-

Prison service establishments

Type of establishment and age	TOTAL	Males	Females	Total	Males	Females	Total	Males	Females	Total	Males	Females	n	o
All ages	**5,304**	**5,280**	**24**	**2,828**	**2,813**	**15**	**2,456**	**2,450**	**6**	**20**	**17**	**3**	**772**	**1,328**
0 - 15	4	4	-	1	1	-	-	-	-	3	3	-	-	3
16 - 17	71	71	-	62	62	-	9	9	-	-	-	-	9	6
18 - 29	2,855	2,842	13	1,775	1,764	11	1,075	1,073	2	5	5	-	296	612
30 - 44	1,690	1,681	9	712	710	2	966	962	4	12	9	3	257	516
45 - 59	573	571	2	248	246	2	325	325	-	-	-	-	164	155
60 - 64	82	82	-	19	19	-	63	63	-	-	-	-	33	30
65 - 74	20	20	-	9	9	-	11	11	-	-	-	-	9	3
75 - 84	6	6	-	1	1	-	5	5	-	-	-	-	3	2
85 and over	3	3	-	1	1	-	2	2	-	-	-	-	1	1

Table 3 Type of establishment, migrants and long-term illness – **continued**

Great Britain, England & Wales, England, regions, metropolitan counties, Inner London, Outer London, regional remainders, Wales, Scotland

Persons present in communal establishments

Type of establishment and age	PERSONS PRESENT			Visitors/guests			Residents - non-staff			Residents - staff			With limiting long-term illness	Migrants
	TOTAL	Males	Females	Total	Males	Females	Total	Males	Females	Total	Males	Females		
a	b	c	d	e	f	g	h	i	j	k	l	m	n	o
Outer South East *– continued*														
Defence establishments														
All ages	**13,696**	**12,095**	**1,601**	**3,816**	**3,479**	**337**	**9,880**	**8,616**	**1,264**				**413**	**4,993**
0 - 15	-	-	-	-	-	-	-	-	-				-	-
16 - 17	965	894	71	291	266	25	674	628	46				10	568
18 - 29	10,564	9,198	1,366	2,339	2,115	224	8,225	7,083	1,142				217	4,007
30 - 44	1,754	1,650	104	913	875	38	841	775	66				69	373
45 - 59	251	232	19	170	158	12	81	74	7				25	34
60 - 64	42	29	13	34	21	13	8	8	-				11	-
65 - 74	71	57	14	44	31	13	27	26	1				42	5
75 - 84	34	24	10	17	9	8	17	15	2				26	6
85 and over	15	11	4	8	4	4	7	7	-				13	-
Educational establishments														
All ages	**45,985**	**27,318**	**18,667**	**40,186**	**23,781**	**16,405**	**4,107**	**2,676**	**1,431**	**1,692**	**861**	**831**	**2,113**	**2,985**
0 - 15	13,240	8,861	4,379	12,880	8,630	4,250	224	152	72	136	79	57	927	93
16 - 17	5,971	3,695	2,276	5,820	3,596	2,224	130	91	39	21	8	13	367	45
18 - 29	23,423	12,762	10,661	19,988	10,582	9,406	2,878	1,912	966	557	268	289	593	2,269
30 - 44	1,994	1,345	649	923	656	267	581	414	167	490	275	215	52	466
45 - 59	915	499	416	420	253	167	117	60	57	378	186	192	58	89
60 - 64	146	64	82	40	18	22	42	17	25	64	29	35	12	12
65 - 74	153	55	98	77	31	46	44	12	32	32	12	20	38	4
75 - 84	115	32	83	33	12	21	69	16	53	13	4	9	51	6
85 and over	28	5	23	5	3	2	22	2	20	1	-	1	15	1

Table 3 Type of establishment, migrants and long-term illness – **continued**

Great Britain, England & Wales, England, regions, metropolitan counties, Inner London, Outer London, regional remainders, Wales, Scotland

Persons present in communal establishments

Type of establishment and age	PERSONS PRESENT			Visitors/guests			Residents - non-staff			Residents - staff			With limiting long-term illness	Migrants
	TOTAL	Males	Females	Total	Males	Females	Total	Males	Females	Total	Males	Females		
a	b	c	d	e	f	g	h	i	j	k	l	m	n	o
Outer South East – *continued*														
Hotels, boarding houses etc														
All ages	**29,882**	**16,392**	**13,490**	**19,155**	**9,915**	**9,240**	**5,541**	**3,592**	**1,949**	**5,186**	**2,885**	**2,301**	**4,056**	**4,395**
0 - 15	2,448	1,225	1,223	1,591	775	816	464	247	217	393	203	190	91	269
16 - 17	477	192	285	227	81	146	120	53	67	130	58	72	22	138
18 - 29	7,513	4,250	3,263	3,294	1,822	1,472	1,730	1,043	687	2,489	1,385	1,104	342	2,585
30 - 44	5,635	3,748	1,887	3,542	2,328	1,214	1,174	875	299	919	545	374	430	811
45 - 59	5,422	3,250	2,172	3,543	1,980	1,563	906	718	188	973	552	421	768	381
60 - 64	1,947	927	1,020	1,573	663	910	232	183	49	142	81	61	433	53
65 - 74	3,971	1,867	2,104	3,502	1,551	1,951	378	271	107	91	45	46	1,052	52
75 - 84	2,105	827	1,278	1,695	649	1,046	370	165	205	40	13	27	751	70
85 and over	364	106	258	188	66	122	167	37	130	9	3	6	167	36
Hostels and common lodging houses (non-HA)														
All ages	**1,879**	**1,397**	**482**	**381**	**285**	**96**	**1,421**	**1,065**	**356**	**77**	**47**	**30**	**666**	**855**
0 - 15	139	72	67	17	7	10	114	59	55	8	6	2	7	70
16 - 17	72	36	36	10	4	6	59	32	27	3	-	3	14	49
18 - 29	733	486	247	209	147	62	506	332	174	18	7	11	187	365
30 - 44	450	378	72	87	77	10	345	289	56	18	12	6	199	209
45 - 59	315	275	40	44	37	7	245	220	25	26	18	8	168	121
60 - 64	68	66	2	8	8	-	56	54	2	4	4	-	38	19
65 - 74	64	60	4	5	4	1	59	56	3	-	-	-	36	16
75 - 84	20	18	2	1	1	-	19	17	2	-	-	-	8	2
85 and over	18	6	12	-	-	-	18	6	12	-	-	-	9	4

Table 3 Type of establishment, migrants and long-term illness – **continued**

Great Britain, England & Wales, England, regions, metropolitan counties, Inner London, Outer London, regional remainders, Wales, Scotland

Persons present in communal establishments

Type of establishment and age	PERSONS PRESENT			Visitors/guests			Residents - non-staff			Residents - staff			With limiting long-term illness	Migrants
	TOTAL	Males	Females	Total	Males	Females	Total	Males	Females	Total	Males	Females		
a	b	c	d	e	f	g	h	i	j	k	l	m	n	o

Outer South East – *continued*

Other miscellaneous establishments

All ages	**6,112**	**3,691**	**2,421**	**2,242**	**1,816**	**426**	**3,402**	**1,568**	**1,834**	**468**	**307**	**161**	**905**	**1,759**
0 - 15	224	87	137	31	18	13	186	67	119	7	2	5	54	95
16 - 17	272	237	35	97	89	8	155	133	22	20	15	5	9	152
18 - 29	2,635	1,946	689	998	817	181	1,361	934	427	276	195	81	82	1,129
30 - 44	1,212	917	295	702	614	88	436	249	187	74	54	20	93	194
45 - 59	685	358	327	311	241	70	326	94	232	48	23	25	105	79
60 - 64	180	39	141	31	20	11	133	15	118	16	4	12	48	13
65 - 74	299	51	248	29	10	19	253	35	218	17	6	11	109	32
75 - 84	404	39	365	33	6	27	363	27	336	8	6	2	244	35
85 and over	201	17	184	10	1	9	189	14	175	2	2	-	161	30

Persons sleeping rough

All ages	**371**	**307**	**64**	**174**	**143**	**31**	**197**	**164**	**33**				**91**	**130**
0 - 15	-	-	-	-	-	-	-	-	-				-	-
16 - 17	1	1	-	-	-	-	1	1	-				-	1
18 - 29	126	98	28	62	44	18	64	54	10				21	41
30 - 44	131	111	20	55	49	6	76	62	14				32	50
45 - 59	93	80	13	45	40	5	48	40	8				31	35
60 - 64	9	8	1	4	4	-	5	4	1				4	1
65 - 74	11	9	2	8	6	2	3	3	-				3	2
75 - 84	-	-	-	-	-	-	-	-	-				-	-
85 and over	-	-	-	-	-	-	-	-	-				-	-

Table 3 Type of establishment, migrants and long-term illness – **continued**

Great Britain, England & Wales, England, regions, metropolitan counties, Inner London, Outer London, regional remainders, Wales, Scotland

Persons present in communal establishments

Type of establishment and age	PERSONS PRESENT			Visitors/guests			Residents - non-staff			Residents - staff			With limiting long-term illness	Migrants
	TOTAL	Males	Females	Total	Males	Females	Total	Males	Females	Total	Males	Females		
a	b	c	d	e	f	g	h	i	j	k	l	m	n	o

Outer South East – *continued*

Campers

Type of establishment and age	TOTAL	Males	Females	Total	Males	Females	Total	Males	Females	Total	Males	Females	illness	Migrants
All ages	**73**	**42**	**31**	**64**	**37**	**27**	**9**	**5**	**4**				**17**	**2**
0 - 15	6	4	2	3	2	1	3	2	1				1	1
16 - 17	1	1	-	1	1	-	-	-	-				-	-
18 - 29	7	3	4	7	3	4	-	-	-				-	-
30 - 44	12	6	6	11	6	5	1	-	1				1	1
45 - 59	15	9	6	11	7	4	4	2	2				3	-
60 - 64	12	8	4	12	8	4	-	-	-				6	-
65 - 74	14	6	8	14	6	8	-	-	-				5	-
75 - 84	6	5	1	5	4	1	1	1	-				1	-
85 and over	-	-	-	-	-	-	-	-	-				-	-

Civilian ships, boats and barges

Type of establishment and age	TOTAL	Males	Females	Total	Males	Females	Total	Males	Females	Total	Males	Females	illness	Migrants
All ages	**693**	**631**	**62**	**575**	**529**	**46**	**118**	**102**	**16**				**17**	**53**
0 - 15	10	6	4	9	5	4	1	1	-				-	-
16 - 17	4	3	1	4	3	1	-	-	-				-	-
18 - 29	175	154	21	149	131	18	26	23	3				1	15
30 - 44	307	288	19	252	239	13	55	49	6				3	29
45 - 59	181	168	13	151	142	9	30	26	4				8	9
60 - 64	10	10	-	8	8	-	2	2	-				3	-
65 - 74	3	-	3	1	-	1	2	-	2				1	-
75 - 84	2	1	1	-	-	-	2	1	1				1	-
85 and over	1	1	-	1	1	-	-	-	-				-	-

Table 3 Type of establishment, migrants and long-term illness – **continued**

Great Britain, England & Wales, England, regions, metropolitan counties, Inner London, Outer London, regional remainders, Wales, Scotland

Persons present in communal establishments

Type of establishment and age	PERSONS PRESENT			Visitors/guests			Residents - non-staff			Residents - staff			With limiting long-term illness	Migrants
	TOTAL	Males	Females	Total	Males	Females	Total	Males	Females	Total	Males	Females		
a	b	c	d	e	f	g	h	i	j	k	l	m	n	o
SOUTH WEST REGION														
All establishments *														
All ages	187,250	89,974	97,276	89,956	48,142	41,814	82,621	34,542	48,079	14,673	7,290	7,383	76,316	30,537
0 - 15	18,966	10,856	8,110	15,466	8,943	6,523	1,779	1,049	730	1,721	864	857	1,061	1,019
16 - 17	8,387	5,263	3,124	6,915	4,206	2,709	1,036	822	214	436	235	201	502	893
18 - 29	43,985	28,005	15,980	23,078	13,410	9,668	15,688	12,106	3,582	5,219	2,489	2,730	4,051	10,737
30 - 44	19,057	12,388	6,669	9,564	6,081	3,483	6,478	4,739	1,739	3,015	1,568	1,447	4,456	3,021
45 - 59	16,445	9,103	7,342	8,967	4,722	4,245	4,107	2,700	1,407	3,371	1,681	1,690	4,889	1,395
60 - 64	6,964	3,377	3,587	4,480	2,008	2,472	1,993	1,080	913	491	289	202	2,976	439
65 - 74	17,755	7,713	10,042	10,830	4,827	6,003	6,669	2,770	3,899	256	116	140	9,936	1,645
75 - 84	28,412	8,425	19,987	7,832	3,143	4,689	20,457	5,242	15,215	123	40	83	23,379	5,693
85 and over	27,279	4,844	22,435	2,824	802	2,022	24,414	4,034	20,380	41	8	33	25,066	5,695
NHS hospitals/homes - psychiatric														
All ages	3,027	1,362	1,665	1,256	505	751	1,527	774	753	244	83	161	2,442	371
0 - 15	34	11	23	27	8	19	5	2	3	2	1	1	14	-
16 - 17	18	4	14	15	3	12	3	1	2	-	-	-	13	2
18 - 29	494	211	283	198	95	103	91	60	31	205	56	149	167	126
30 - 44	443	254	189	232	104	128	183	129	54	28	21	7	321	64
45 - 59	400	220	180	169	76	93	223	139	84	8	5	3	346	43
60 - 64	187	90	97	72	21	51	115	69	46	-	-	-	172	12
65 - 74	462	231	231	157	55	102	304	176	128	1	-	1	438	50
75 - 84	644	253	391	252	100	152	392	153	239	-	-	-	632	49
85 and over	345	88	257	134	43	91	211	45	166	-	-	-	339	25

Note: * Includes a female member of staff incorrectly enumerated as a resident.

Table 3 Type of establishment, migrants and long-term illness – **continued**

Great Britain, England & Wales, England, regions, metropolitan counties, Inner London, Outer London, regional remainders, Wales, Scotland

Persons present in communal establishments

Type of establishment and age	PERSONS PRESENT			Visitors/guests			Residents - non-staff			Residents - staff			With limiting long-term illness	Migrants
	TOTAL	Males	Females	Total	Males	Females	Total	Males	Females	Total	Males	Females		
a	b	c	d	e	f	g	h	i	j	k	l	m	n	o

SOUTH WEST REGION – *continued*

NHS hospitals/homes - other

All ages	**15,556**	**6,069**	**9,487**	**11,890**	**4,788**	**7,102**	**2,756**	**1,038**	**1,718**	**910**	**243**	**667**	**9,837**	**1,401**
0 - 15	1,010	547	463	924	501	423	57	32	25	29	14	15	170	21
16 - 17	96	33	63	78	23	55	15	9	6	3	1	2	33	7
18 - 29	2,728	703	2,025	1,399	351	1,048	612	204	408	717	148	569	485	713
30 - 44	1,623	660	963	1,077	358	719	413	230	183	133	72	61	717	179
45 - 59	1,325	637	688	1,021	483	538	278	146	132	26	8	18	884	70
60 - 64	692	350	342	605	311	294	86	39	47	1	-	1	513	18
65 - 74	2,314	1,106	1,208	2,063	991	1,072	251	115	136	-	-	-	1,853	81
75 - 84	3,627	1,475	2,152	3,069	1,298	1,771	558	177	381	-	-	-	3,194	161
85 and over	2,141	558	1,583	1,654	472	1,182	486	86	400	1	-	1	1,988	151

Non-NHS hospitals - psychiatric

All ages	**93**	**43**	**50**	**41**	**14**	**27**	**46**	**27**	**19**	**6**	**2**	**4**	**53**	**9**
0 - 15	12	8	4	-	-	-	11	8	3	1	-	1	6	7
16 - 17	4	3	1	2	2	-	2	1	1	-	-	-	1	-
18 - 29	5	2	3	2	-	2	2	2	-	1	-	1	1	1
30 - 44	21	8	13	8	3	5	12	5	7	1	-	1	12	1
45 - 59	20	8	12	10	1	9	7	5	2	3	2	1	11	1
60 - 64	3	1	2	2	-	2	1	1	-	-	-	-	2	-
65 - 74	16	8	8	9	5	4	7	3	4	-	-	-	12	-
75 - 84	12	5	7	8	3	5	4	2	2	-	-	-	8	-
85 and over	-	-	-	-	-	-	-	-	-	-	-	-	-	-

Table 3 Type of establishment, migrants and long-term illness – **continued**

Great Britain, England & Wales, England, regions, metropolitan counties, Inner London, Outer London, regional remainders, Wales, Scotland

Persons present in communal establishments

Type of establishment and age	PERSONS PRESENT			Visitors/guests			Residents - non-staff			Residents - staff			With limiting long-term illness	Migrants
	TOTAL	Males	Females	Total	Males	Females	Total	Males	Females	Total	Males	Females		
a	b	c	d	e	f	g	h	i	j	k	l	m	n	o
SOUTH WEST REGION – continued														
Non-NHS hospitals - other														
All ages	**1,591**	**654**	**937**	**1,072**	**412**	**660**	**505**	**235**	**270**	**14**	**7**	**7**	**1,061**	**88**
0 - 15	145	81	64	141	79	62	3	2	1	1	-	1	45	-
16 - 17	7	3	4	7	3	4	-	-	-	1	-	1	1	-
18 - 29	164	68	96	103	23	80	57	43	14	4	2	2	64	20
30 - 44	232	92	140	148	35	113	80	54	26	4	3	1	107	6
45 - 59	196	96	100	107	39	68	86	56	30	3	1	2	132	3
60 - 64	87	36	51	62	25	37	25	11	14	-	-	-	65	4
65 - 74	233	101	132	167	76	91	65	24	41	1	1	-	177	8
75 - 84	343	136	207	241	103	138	101	33	68	1	1	-	298	30
85 and over	184	41	143	96	29	67	88	12	76	-	-	-	172	17
Local authority homes														
All ages	**11,712**	**4,393**	**7,319**	**1,766**	**1,015**	**751**	**9,731**	**3,266**	**6,465**	**215**	**112**	**103**	**9,780**	**2,225**
0 - 15	832	677	155	679	562	117	115	96	19	38	19	19	187	45
16 - 17	214	167	47	155	134	21	53	29	24	6	4	2	68	27
18 - 29	858	471	387	196	83	113	608	363	245	54	25	29	625	212
30 - 44	826	478	348	112	48	64	672	408	264	42	22	20	687	189
45 - 59	677	343	334	72	21	51	546	290	256	59	32	27	549	131
60 - 64	295	165	130	21	12	9	265	147	118	9	6	3	274	63
65 - 74	1,084	474	610	85	42	43	995	429	566	4	3	1	968	217
75 - 84	3,159	912	2,247	227	63	164	2,930	848	2,082	2	1	1	2,890	666
85 and over	3,767	706	3,061	219	50	169	3,547	656	2,891	1	-	1	3,532	675

Table 3 Type of establishment, migrants and long-term illness – **continued**

Great Britain, England & Wales, England, regions, metropolitan counties, Inner London, Outer London, regional remainders, Wales, Scotland

Persons present in communal establishments

Type of establishment and age	PERSONS PRESENT			Visitors/guests			Residents - non-staff			Residents - staff			With limiting long-term illness	Migrants
	TOTAL	Males	Females	Total	Males	Females	Total	Males	Females	Total	Males	Females		
a	b	c	d	e	f	g	h	i	j	k	l	m	n	o
SOUTH WEST REGION – *continued*														
Housing association homes and hostels														
All ages	**2,549**	**982**	**1,567**	**135**	**60**	**75**	**2,279**	**866**	**1,413**	**135**	**56**	**79**	**1,545**	**700**
0 - 15	56	34	22	3	-	3	30	21	9	23	13	10	8	22
16 - 17	36	14	22	12	4	8	23	10	13	1	-	1	9	19
18 - 29	357	200	157	44	20	24	302	174	128	11	6	5	135	179
30 - 44	288	188	100	23	16	7	246	161	85	19	11	8	169	103
45 - 59	281	185	96	22	13	9	206	157	49	53	15	38	167	80
60 - 64	82	50	32	4	2	2	59	39	20	19	9	10	46	13
65 - 74	192	83	109	4	1	3	180	80	100	8	2	6	131	46
75 - 84	565	125	440	13	3	10	551	122	429	1	-	1	372	118
85 and over	692	103	589	10	1	9	682	102	580	-	-	-	508	120
Nursing homes (non-NHS/ LA/HA)														
All ages	**18,252**	**4,357**	**13,895**	**1,035**	**390**	**645**	**16,861**	**3,831**	**13,030**	**356**	**136**	**220**	**17,104**	**5,549**
0 - 15	71	34	37	4	2	2	19	7	12	48	25	23	6	7
16 - 17	18	11	7	5	4	1	2	1	1	11	6	5	5	2
18 - 29	251	110	141	78	27	51	119	66	53	54	17	37	142	65
30 - 44	376	180	196	136	48	88	164	103	61	76	29	47	198	62
45 - 59	420	183	237	124	42	82	170	94	76	126	47	79	230	53
60 - 64	407	168	239	60	26	34	327	133	194	20	9	11	343	103
65 - 74	1,913	692	1,221	252	118	134	1,649	572	1,077	12	2	10	1,764	575
75 - 84	6,607	1,650	4,957	229	82	147	6,374	1,568	4,806	4	-	4	6,397	2,287
85 and over	8,189	1,329	6,860	147	41	106	8,037	1,287	6,750	5	1	4	8,019	2,395

267

Table 3 Type of establishment, migrants and long-term illness – **continued**

Great Britain, England & Wales, England, regions, metropolitan counties, Inner London, Outer London, regional remainders, Wales, Scotland

Persons present in communal establishments

Type of establishment and age	PERSONS PRESENT			Visitors/guests			Residents - non-staff			Residents - staff			With limiting long-term illness	Migrants
	TOTAL	Males	Females	Total	Males	Females	Total	Males	Females	Total	Males	Females		
a	b	c	d	e	f	g	h	i	j	k	l	m	n	o
SOUTH WEST REGION – *continued*														
Residential homes (non-NHS/LA/HA)														
All ages	**29,702**	**8,459**	**21,243**	**1,108**	**432**	**676**	**26,501**	**7,116**	**19,385**	**2,093**	**911**	**1,182**	**24,472**	**6,060**
0 - 15	418	208	210	37	26	11	26	11	15	355	171	184	31	44
16 - 17	135	87	48	27	20	7	43	31	12	65	36	29	54	36
18 - 29	1,533	852	681	191	88	103	1,002	622	380	340	142	198	1,063	280
30 - 44	1,762	939	823	154	64	90	1,136	684	452	472	191	281	1,172	219
45 - 59	1,637	826	811	93	32	61	875	506	369	669	288	381	925	185
60 - 64	824	405	419	44	23	21	683	333	350	97	49	48	623	133
65 - 74	2,780	1,084	1,696	121	44	77	2,599	1,016	1,583	60	24	36	2,325	573
75 - 84	9,310	2,212	7,098	256	85	171	9,028	2,120	6,908	26	7	19	8,114	2,314
85 and over	11,303	1,846	9,457	185	50	135	11,109	1,793	9,316	9	3	6	10,165	2,276
Children's homes														
All ages	**716**	**390**	**326**	**139**	**61**	**78**	**514**	**301**	**213**	**63**	**28**	**35**	**50**	**295**
0 - 15	608	348	260	84	42	42	514	301	213	10	5	5	45	283
16 - 17	2	1	1	-	-	-	-	-	-	2	1	1	-	-
18 - 29	33	15	18	13	6	7	-	-	-	20	9	11	-	9
30 - 44	40	11	29	26	7	19	-	-	-	14	4	10	1	3
45 - 59	30	13	17	14	5	9	-	-	-	16	8	8	4	-
60 - 64	2	1	1	2	1	1	-	-	-	-	-	-	-	-
65 - 74	-	-	-	-	-	-	-	-	-	-	-	-	-	-
75 - 84	1	1	-	-	-	-	-	-	-	1	1	-	-	-
85 and over	-	-	-	-	-	-	-	-	-	-	-	-	-	-

Table 3 Type of establishment, migrants and long-term illness – **continued**

Great Britain, England & Wales, England, regions, metropolitan counties, Inner London, Outer London, regional remainders, Wales, Scotland

Persons present in communal establishments

Type of establishment and age	PERSONS PRESENT			Visitors/guests			Residents - non-staff			Residents - staff			With limiting long-term illness	Migrants
	TOTAL	Males	Females	Total	Males	Females	Total	Males	Females	Total	Males	Females		
a	b	c	d	e	f	g	h	i	j	k	l	m	n	o
SOUTH WEST REGION – *continued*														
Prison service establishments														
All ages	**3,669**	**3,596**	**73**	**2,051**	**1,993**	**58**	**1,608**	**1,594**	**14**	**10**	**9**	**1**	**537**	**791**
0 - 15	1	1	-	-	-	-	-	-	-	1	1	-	-	-
16 - 17	74	71	3	47	44	3	27	27	-	1	1	-	9	20
18 - 29	2,004	1,965	39	1,271	1,236	35	732	728	4	1	-	1	185	414
30 - 44	1,121	1,103	18	540	525	15	579	576	3	2	2	-	195	252
45 - 59	380	369	11	156	151	5	222	217	5	2	1	1	111	92
60 - 64	45	44	1	25	25	-	19	18	1	1	1	-	19	8
65 - 74	33	32	1	10	10	-	21	20	1	2	2	-	16	3
75 - 84	8	8	-	2	2	-	5	5	-	1	1	-	2	2
85 and over	3	3	-	-	-	-	3	3	-	-	-	-	-	-
Defence establishments														
All ages	**13,333**	**12,265**	**1,068**	**3,481**	**3,298**	**183**	**9,852**	**8,967**	**885**				**282**	**5,092**
0 - 15	-	-	-	-	-	-	-	-	-				-	-
16 - 17	799	772	27	257	248	9	542	524	18				16	468
18 - 29	10,278	9,366	912	2,061	1,937	124	8,217	7,429	788				175	4,118
30 - 44	1,954	1,858	96	942	915	27	1,012	943	69				53	482
45 - 59	250	235	15	177	169	8	73	66	7				18	22
60 - 64	17	16	1	12	11	1	5	5	-				3	1
65 - 74	16	9	7	16	9	7	-	-	-				7	-
75 - 84	19	9	10	16	9	7	3	-	3				10	1
85 and over	-	-	-	-	-	-	-	-	-				-	-

Table 3 Type of establishment, migrants and long-term illness – **continued**

Great Britain, England & Wales, England, regions, metropolitan counties, Inner London, Outer London, regional remainders, Wales, Scotland

Persons present in communal establishments

Type of establishment and age	PERSONS PRESENT			Visitors/guests			Residents - non-staff			Residents - staff			With limiting long-term illness	Migrants
	TOTAL	Males	Females	Total	Males	Females	Total	Males	Females	Total	Males	Females		
a	b	c	d	e	f	g	h	i	j	k	l	m	n	o
SOUTH WEST REGION – *continued*														
Educational establishments														
All ages	**31,690**	**18,005**	**13,685**	**28,933**	**16,324**	**12,609**	**1,783**	**1,178**	**605**	**974**	**503**	**471**	**1,267**	**1,346**
0 - 15	11,376	6,654	4,722	11,098	6,469	4,629	160	117	43	118	68	50	427	57
16 - 17	5,860	3,477	2,383	5,729	3,384	2,345	105	81	24	26	12	14	255	46
18 - 29	12,808	6,958	5,850	11,410	6,086	5,324	1,083	722	361	315	150	165	400	924
30 - 44	1,032	654	378	450	283	167	298	212	86	284	159	125	87	262
45 - 59	446	200	246	196	84	112	58	26	32	192	90	102	60	51
60 - 64	68	32	36	26	7	19	15	6	9	27	19	8	10	5
65 - 74	53	15	38	12	5	7	29	5	24	12	5	7	12	-
75 - 84	39	12	27	10	5	5	29	7	22	-	-	-	12	1
85 and over	8	3	5	2	1	1	6	2	4	-	-	-	4	-
Hotels, boarding houses etc														
All ages	**48,877**	**25,127**	**23,750**	**34,569**	**17,052**	**17,517**	**5,456**	**3,430**	**2,026**	**8,852**	**4,645**	**4,207**	**6,617**	**4,728**
0 - 15	3,873	1,970	1,903	2,301	1,178	1,123	528	271	257	1,044	521	523	103	349
16 - 17	952	528	424	527	316	211	141	66	75	284	146	138	30	181
18 - 29	10,177	5,520	4,657	5,320	2,848	2,472	1,845	1,099	746	3,012	1,573	1,439	408	2,726
30 - 44	7,982	4,864	3,118	5,064	3,107	1,957	1,100	797	303	1,818	960	858	487	836
45 - 59	9,423	5,102	4,321	6,427	3,317	3,110	869	637	232	2,127	1,148	979	1,165	458
60 - 64	3,949	1,834	2,115	3,404	1,469	1,935	240	176	64	305	189	116	794	51
65 - 74	8,187	3,628	4,559	7,700	3,342	4,358	334	210	124	153	76	77	2,086	65
75 - 84	3,799	1,528	2,271	3,457	1,362	2,095	258	138	120	84	28	56	1,292	39
85 and over	535	153	382	369	113	256	141	36	105	25	4	21	252	23

Table 3 Type of establishment, migrants and long-term illness – **continued**

Great Britain, England & Wales, England, regions, metropolitan counties, Inner London, Outer London, regional remainders, Wales, Scotland

Persons present in communal establishments

Type of establishment and age	PERSONS PRESENT			Visitors/guests			Residents - non-staff			Residents - staff			With limiting long-term illness	Migrants
	TOTAL	Males	Females	Total	Males	Females	Total	Males	Females	Total	Males	Females		
a	b	c	d	e	f	g	h	i	j	k	l	m	n	o
SOUTH WEST REGION – *continued*														
Hostels and common lodging houses (non-HA)														
All ages	**1,691**	**1,238**	**453**	**156**	**110**	**46**	**1,442**	**1,071**	**371**	**93**	**57**	**36**	**679**	**810**
0 - 15	179	114	65	7	5	2	157	100	57	15	9	6	5	93
16 - 17	37	17	20	1	1	-	35	15	20	1	1	-	3	33
18 - 29	495	317	178	52	37	15	419	265	154	24	15	9	115	320
30 - 44	356	290	66	48	34	14	292	242	50	16	14	2	164	184
45 - 59	353	288	65	39	28	11	282	246	36	32	14	18	209	132
60 - 64	97	84	13	5	3	2	88	77	11	4	4	-	63	16
65 - 74	102	91	11	4	2	2	97	89	8	1	1	-	61	16
75 - 84	49	32	17	-	-	-	49	32	17	-	-	-	37	9
85 and over	23	5	18	-	-	-	23	5	18	-	-	-	22	7
Other miscellaneous establishments														
All ages	**3,115**	**1,767**	**1,348**	**1,057**	**740**	**317**	**1,351**	**529**	**822**	**707**	**498**	**209**	**373**	**834**
0 - 15	280	125	155	111	38	73	133	70	63	36	17	19	10	84
16 - 17	126	68	58	47	16	31	42	24	18	37	28	9	4	50
18 - 29	1,400	935	465	509	389	120	431	201	230	460	345	115	47	518
30 - 44	539	391	148	259	216	43	174	95	79	106	80	26	48	113
45 - 59	276	138	138	82	62	20	139	54	85	55	22	33	50	31
60 - 64	78	29	49	15	8	7	55	18	37	8	3	5	22	8
65 - 74	148	34	114	14	6	8	132	27	105	2	1	1	33	10
75 - 84	183	38	145	14	3	11	166	33	133	3	2	1	97	14
85 and over	85	9	76	6	2	4	79	7	72	-	-	-	62	6

Table 3 Type of establishment, migrants and long-term illness – **continued**

Great Britain, England & Wales, England, regions, metropolitan counties, Inner London, Outer London, regional remainders, Wales, Scotland

Persons present in communal establishments

Type of establishment and age	PERSONS PRESENT			Visitors/guests			Residents - non-staff			Residents - staff			With limiting long-term illness	Migrants
	TOTAL	Males	Females	Total	Males	Females	Total	Males	Females	Total	Males	Females		
a	b	c	d	e	f	g	h	i	j	k	l	m	n	o

SOUTH WEST REGION – *continued*

Persons sleeping rough

All ages	**325**	**265**	**60**	**79**	**68**	**11**	**245**	**197**	**48**				**82**	**181**
0 - 15	-	-	-	-	-	-	-	-	-				-	-
16 - 17	2	-	2	-	-	2	-	-	-				1	-
18 - 29	146	117	29	37	31	6	108	86	22				31	86
30 - 44	96	82	14	19	17	2	77	65	12				22	54
45 - 59	63	55	8	18	17	1	45	38	7				16	36
60 - 64	5	5	-	1	1	-	4	4	-				2	3
65 - 74	4	4	-	2	2	-	2	2	-				2	1
75 - 84	7	2	5	-	-	-	7	2	5				6	1
85 and over	2	-	2	-	-	-	2	-	2				2	-

Campers

All ages	**642**	**338**	**304**	**574**	**301**	**273**	**68**	**37**	**31**				**119**	**22**
0 - 15	40	23	17	19	12	7	21	11	10				2	7
16 - 17	2	2	-	1	1	-	1	1	-				-	1
18 - 29	90	48	42	62	33	29	28	15	13				5	8
30 - 44	48	28	20	45	26	19	3	2	1				8	1
45 - 59	103	47	56	94	42	52	9	5	4				10	3
60 - 64	106	48	58	104	48	56	2	-	2				24	1
65 - 74	211	115	96	209	114	95	2	1	1				51	-
75 - 84	40	27	13	38	25	13	2	2	-				18	1
85 and over	2	-	2	2	-	2	-	-	-				1	-

Table 3 Type of establishment, migrants and long-term illness – **continued**

Great Britain, England & Wales, England, regions, metropolitan counties, Inner London, Outer London, regional remainders, Wales, Scotland

Persons present in communal establishments

Type of establishment and age	PERSONS PRESENT			Visitors/guests			Residents - non-staff			Residents - staff			With limiting long-term illness	Migrants
	TOTAL	Males	Females	Total	Males	Females	Total	Males	Females	Total	Males	Females		
a	b	c	d	e	f	g	h	i	j	k	l	m	n	o
SOUTH WEST REGION – *continued*														
Civilian ships, boats and barges														
All ages	**710**	**664**	**46**	**614**	**579**	**35**	**96**	**85**	**11**				**16**	**35**
0 - 15	31	21	10	31	21	10	-	-	-				2	-
16 - 17	5	5	-	3	3	-	2	2	-				-	1
18 - 29	164	147	17	132	120	12	32	27	5				3	18
30 - 44	318	308	10	281	275	6	37	33	4				8	12
45 - 59	165	158	7	146	140	6	19	18	1				2	4
60 - 64	20	19	1	16	15	1	4	4	-				1	-
65 - 74	7	6	1	5	5	-	2	1	1				-	-
75 - 84	-	-	-	-	-	-	-	-	-				-	-
85 and over	-	-	-	-	-	-	-	-	-				-	-
WEST MIDLANDS REGION														
*All establishments**														
All ages	**105,681**	**49,177**	**56,504**	**46,168**	**25,482**	**20,686**	**54,252**	**21,492**	**32,760**	**5,261**	**2,203**	**3,058**	**54,565**	**19,098**
0 - 15	8,780	5,484	3,296	6,812	4,374	2,438	1,641	932	709	327	178	149	863	891
16 - 17	3,505	2,212	1,293	2,786	1,780	1,006	627	390	237	92	42	50	457	474
18 - 29	26,857	15,083	11,774	16,056	8,818	7,238	7,907	5,294	2,613	2,894	971	1,923	3,225	5,640
30 - 44	11,186	7,218	3,968	5,779	3,649	2,130	4,485	3,050	1,435	922	519	403	3,694	1,737
45 - 59	8,186	4,960	3,226	3,996	2,311	1,685	3,404	2,274	1,130	786	375	411	3,978	728
60 - 64	3,286	1,899	1,387	1,462	807	655	1,707	1,027	680	117	65	52	2,289	352
65 - 74	9,086	4,290	4,796	3,330	1,668	1,662	5,682	2,585	3,097	74	37	37	7,449	1,453
75 - 84	17,881	5,178	12,703	3,970	1,560	2,410	13,875	3,603	10,272	36	15	21	16,505	4,172
85 and over	16,914	2,853	14,061	1,977	515	1,462	14,924	2,337	12,587	13	1	12	16,105	3,651

Note: * Includes a female member of staff incorrectly enumerated as a resident.

273

Table 3 Type of establishment, migrants and long-term illness – **continued**

Great Britain, England & Wales, England, regions, metropolitan counties, Inner London, Outer London, regional remainders, Wales, Scotland

Persons present in communal establishments

Type of establishment and age	PERSONS PRESENT			Visitors/guests			Residents - non-staff			Residents - staff			With limiting long-term illness	Migrants
	TOTAL	Males	Females	Total	Males	Females	Total	Males	Females	Total	Males	Females		
a	b	c	d	e	f	g	h	i	j	k	l	m	n	o
NHS hospitals/homes - psychiatric														
All ages	**2,697**	**1,241**	**1,456**	**1,137**	**502**	**635**	**1,454**	**682**	**772**	**106**	**57**	**49**	**2,369**	**258**
0 - 15	17	8	9	8	2	6	9	6	3	-	-	-	7	5
16 - 17	14	5	9	12	4	8	2	1	1	-	-	-	9	1
18 - 29	303	175	128	157	86	71	67	51	16	79	38	41	162	66
30 - 44	381	230	151	207	109	98	152	107	45	22	14	8	293	40
45 - 59	375	212	163	168	74	94	203	134	69	4	4	-	331	28
60 - 64	188	98	90	65	29	36	122	68	54	1	1	-	180	7
65 - 74	484	219	265	177	68	109	307	151	156	-	-	-	465	34
75 - 84	618	210	408	228	92	136	390	118	272	-	-	-	608	58
85 and over	317	84	233	115	38	77	202	46	156	-	-	-	314	19
NHS hospitals/homes - other														
All ages	**19,962**	**7,997**	**11,965**	**14,155**	**5,779**	**8,376**	**4,089**	**1,810**	**2,279**	**1,718**	**408**	**1,310**	**12,069**	**1,715**
0 - 15	1,405	776	629	1,337	742	595	44	22	22	24	12	12	235	29
16 - 17	145	52	93	127	44	83	12	8	4	6	-	6	51	8
18 - 29	4,438	1,133	3,305	2,196	539	1,657	798	337	461	1,444	257	1,187	763	1,029
30 - 44	2,489	1,151	1,338	1,424	532	892	856	497	359	209	122	87	1,268	234
45 - 59	2,040	1,018	1,022	1,436	684	752	578	324	254	26	10	16	1,514	53
60 - 64	998	556	442	824	457	367	170	96	74	4	3	1	804	17
65 - 74	2,825	1,454	1,371	2,319	1,197	1,122	503	254	249	3	3	-	2,354	88
75 - 84	3,660	1,410	2,250	3,039	1,209	1,830	619	200	419	2	1	1	3,234	148
85 and over	1,962	447	1,515	1,453	375	1,078	509	72	437	-	-	-	1,846	109

WEST MIDLANDS REGION – *continued*

Table 3 Type of establishment, migrants and long-term illness – **continued**

Persons present in communal establishments

WEST MIDLANDS REGION – *continued*

Type of establishment and age	PERSONS PRESENT			Visitors/guests			Residents - non-staff			Residents - staff			With limiting long-term illness	Migrants
	TOTAL	Males	Females	Total	Males	Females	Total	Males	Females	Total	Males	Females		
a	b	c	d	e	f	g	h	i	j	k	l	m	n	o
Non-NHS hospitals - psychiatric														
All ages	**409**	**192**	**217**	**165**	**72**	**93**	**231**	**116**	**115**	**13**	**4**	**9**	**328**	**30**
0 - 15	4	2	2	4	2	2	-	-	-	-	-	-	-	-
16 - 17	3	2	1	3	2	1	-	-	-	-	-	-	-	-
18 - 29	53	23	30	31	14	17	11	6	5	11	3	8	14	10
30 - 44	47	26	21	34	18	16	11	7	4	2	1	1	33	5
45 - 59	79	41	38	31	12	19	48	29	19	-	-	-	69	5
60 - 64	35	14	21	13	4	9	22	10	12	-	-	-	31	-
65 - 74	86	46	40	23	9	14	63	37	26	-	-	-	82	2
75 - 84	75	31	44	23	9	14	52	22	30	-	-	-	73	7
85 and over	27	7	20	3	2	1	24	5	19	-	-	-	26	1
Non-NHS hospitals - other														
All ages	**569**	**201**	**368**	**338**	**135**	**203**	**230**	**66**	**164**	**1**	**-**	**1**	**352**	**61**
0 - 15	5	1	4	5	1	4	-	-	-	-	-	-	1	-
16 - 17	1	-	1	1	-	1	-	-	-	-	-	-	-	-
18 - 29	36	19	17	26	12	14	10	7	3	-	-	-	15	4
30 - 44	85	27	58	59	16	43	26	11	15	-	-	-	25	4
45 - 59	129	61	68	99	45	54	29	16	13	1	-	1	61	5
60 - 64	45	20	25	35	19	16	10	1	9	-	-	-	27	3
65 - 74	76	33	43	51	22	29	25	11	14	-	-	-	51	9
75 - 84	96	23	73	50	15	35	46	8	38	-	-	-	78	12
85 and over	96	17	79	12	5	7	84	12	72	-	-	-	94	28

Table 3 Type of establishment, migrants and long-term illness – **continued**

Great Britain, England & Wales, England, regions, metropolitan counties, Inner London, Outer London, regional remainders, Wales, Scotland

Persons present in communal establishments

Type of establishment and age	PERSONS PRESENT			Visitors/guests			Residents - non-staff			Residents - staff			With limiting long-term illness	Migrants
	TOTAL	Males	Females	Total	Males	Females	Total	Males	Females	Total	Males	Females		
a	b	c	d	e	f	g	h	i	j	k	l	m	n	o
WEST MIDLANDS REGION – *continued*														
Local authority homes														
All ages	11,479	3,814	7,665	1,070	493	577	10,294	3,276	7,018	115	45	70	10,334	1,990
0 - 15	410	290	120	217	164	53	186	120	66	7	6	1	216	68
16 - 17	162	112	50	61	48	13	97	62	35	4	2	2	86	31
18 - 29	679	422	257	118	75	43	510	335	175	51	12	39	500	153
30 - 44	668	366	302	77	26	51	571	329	242	20	11	9	584	102
45 - 59	620	284	336	66	8	58	527	264	263	27	12	15	532	52
60 - 64	302	177	125	22	11	11	277	165	112	3	1	2	285	54
65 - 74	1,311	565	746	97	40	57	1,212	524	688	2	1	1	1,215	240
75 - 84	3,496	991	2,505	231	84	147	3,265	907	2,358	-	-	-	3,274	702
85 and over	3,831	607	3,224	181	37	144	3,649	570	3,079	1	1	1	3,642	588
Housing association homes and hostels														
All ages	1,824	946	878	66	25	41	1,718	906	812	40	15	25	1,137	663
0 - 15	19	9	10	-	-	-	15	5	10	4	4	-	-	6
16 - 17	50	23	27	3	3	-	46	20	26	1	1	-	6	43
18 - 29	362	236	126	20	10	10	338	226	112	4	-	4	106	231
30 - 44	233	162	71	18	7	11	208	152	56	7	3	4	125	90
45 - 59	222	180	42	8	1	7	193	171	22	21	8	13	143	67
60 - 64	95	72	23	-	-	-	94	72	22	1	-	1	68	21
65 - 74	205	128	77	1	-	1	202	128	74	2	-	2	143	52
75 - 84	341	99	242	11	3	8	330	96	234	-	-	-	285	92
85 and over	297	37	260	5	1	4	292	36	256	-	-	-	261	61

Table 3 Type of establishment, migrants and long-term illness – **continued**

Great Britain, England & Wales, England, regions, metropolitan counties, Inner London, Outer London, regional remainders, Wales, Scotland

Persons present in communal establishments

WEST MIDLANDS REGION – continued

Type of establishment and age	PERSONS PRESENT			Visitors/guests			Residents - non-staff			Residents - staff			With limiting long-term illness	Migrants
	TOTAL	Males	Females	Total	Males	Females	Total	Males	Females	Total	Males	Females		
a	b	c	d	e	f	g	h	i	j	k	l	m	n	o
Nursing homes (non-NHS/LA/HA)														
All ages	**11,097**	**3,002**	**8,095**	**402**	**112**	**290**	**10,565**	**2,837**	**7,728**	**130**	**53**	**77**	**10,693**	**4,070**
0 - 15	22	11	11	1	1	-	3	-	3	18	10	8	3	3
16 - 17	6	3	3	1	1	-	-	-	-	5	2	3	3	-
18 - 29	122	62	60	37	9	28	62	41	21	23	12	11	75	34
30 - 44	221	110	111	48	8	40	148	90	58	25	12	13	156	45
45 - 59	280	144	136	37	5	32	208	126	82	35	13	22	234	56
60 - 64	364	188	176	27	11	16	330	175	155	7	2	5	343	122
65 - 74	1,522	589	933	77	27	50	1,437	560	877	8	2	6	1,480	569
75 - 84	4,230	1,130	3,100	108	35	73	4,115	1,095	3,020	7	-	7	4,146	1,734
85 and over	4,330	765	3,565	66	15	51	4,262	750	3,512	2	-	2	4,256	1,507
Residential homes (non-NHS/LA/HA)														
All ages	**14,678**	**3,823**	**10,855**	**424**	**123**	**301**	**13,800**	**3,513**	**10,287**	**454**	**187**	**267**	**13,314**	**3,440**
0 - 15	83	51	32	7	6	1	17	12	5	59	33	26	19	11
16 - 17	32	18	14	5	4	1	18	10	8	9	4	5	17	8
18 - 29	629	335	294	66	18	48	483	290	193	80	27	53	497	93
30 - 44	737	391	346	70	21	49	580	337	243	87	33	54	582	93
45 - 59	702	368	334	64	16	48	476	289	187	162	63	99	496	70
60 - 64	399	210	189	12	4	8	358	188	170	29	18	11	344	74
65 - 74	1,414	546	868	31	7	24	1,368	532	836	15	7	8	1,296	378
75 - 84	4,811	1,063	3,748	90	28	62	4,714	1,033	3,681	7	2	5	4,533	1,387
85 and over	5,871	841	5,030	79	19	60	5,786	822	4,964	6	-	6	5,530	1,326

Table 3 Type of establishment, migrants and long-term illness – **continued**

Great Britain, England & Wales, England, regions, metropolitan counties, Inner London, Outer London, regional remainders, Wales, Scotland

Persons present in communal establishments

WEST MIDLANDS REGION – *continued*

Type of establishment and age	PERSONS PRESENT			Visitors/guests			Residents - non-staff			Residents - staff			With limiting long-term illness	Migrants
	TOTAL	Males	Females	Total	Males	Females	Total	Males	Females	Total	Males	Females		
a	b	c	d	e	f	g	h	i	j	k	l	m	n	o
Children's homes														
All ages	**936**	**519**	**417**	**225**	**114**	**111**	**612**	**363**	**249**	**99**	**42**	**57**	**73**	**333**
0 - 15	792	460	332	168	92	76	612	363	249	12	5	7	57	322
16 - 17	2	1	1	-	-	-	-	-	-	2	1	1	-	-
18 - 29	51	20	31	20	9	11	-	-	-	31	11	20	6	8
30 - 44	49	20	29	23	9	14	-	-	-	26	11	15	4	3
45 - 59	35	13	22	12	2	10	-	-	-	23	11	12	4	-
60 - 64	5	4	1	2	2	-	-	-	-	3	2	1	1	-
65 - 74	-	-	-	-	-	-	-	-	-	-	-	-	-	-
75 - 84	2	1	1	-	-	-	-	-	-	2	1	1	1	-
85 and over	-	-	-	-	-	-	-	-	-	-	-	-	-	-
Prison service establishments														
All ages	**3,616**	**3,444**	**172**	**2,460**	**2,318**	**142**	**1,150**	**1,120**	**30**	**6**	**6**	**-**	**506**	**599**
0 - 15	15	15	-	10	10	-	5	5	-	5	5	-	1	3
16 - 17	177	177	-	157	157	-	20	20	-	-	-	-	14	12
18 - 29	2,361	2,269	92	1,616	1,543	73	744	725	19	1	1	-	273	422
30 - 44	813	751	62	537	483	54	276	268	8	-	-	-	146	110
45 - 59	220	203	17	119	105	14	101	98	3	-	-	-	62	47
60 - 64	18	17	1	13	12	1	5	5	-	-	-	-	3	2
65 - 74	8	8	-	5	5	-	3	3	-	-	-	-	5	3
75 - 84	2	2	-	2	2	-	-	-	-	-	-	-	1	-
85 and over	2	2	-	1	1	-	1	1	-	-	-	-	1	-

Table 3 Type of establishment, migrants and long-term illness – **continued**

Great Britain, England & Wales, England, regions, metropolitan counties, Inner London, Outer London, regional remainders, Wales, Scotland

Persons present in communal establishments

WEST MIDLANDS REGION – *continued*

Type of establishment and age	PERSONS PRESENT			Visitors/guests			Residents - non-staff			Residents - staff			With limiting long-term illness	Migrants
	TOTAL	Males	Females	Total	Males	Females	Total	Males	Females	Total	Males	Females		
a	b	c	d	e	f	g	h	i	j	k	l	m	n	o
Defence establishments														
All ages	**2,890**	**2,441**	**449**	**711**	**644**	**67**	**2,179**	**1,797**	**382**				**85**	**1,228**
0 - 15	35	29	6	35	29	6	-	-	-				2	-
16 - 17	195	156	39	42	38	4	153	118	35				8	141
18 - 29	2,232	1,855	377	459	407	52	1,773	1,448	325				34	970
30 - 44	340	318	22	154	149	5	186	169	17				22	78
45 - 59	66	61	5	19	19	-	47	42	5				12	25
60 - 64	7	7	-	2	2	-	5	5	-				1	3
65 - 74	13	13	-	-	-	-	13	13	-				6	10
75 - 84	2	2	-	-	-	-	2	2	-				-	1
85 and over	-	-	-	-	-	-	-	-	-				-	-
Educational establishments														
All ages	**18,818**	**11,061**	**7,757**	**16,209**	**9,467**	**6,742**	**2,096**	**1,321**	**775**	**513**	**273**	**240**	**1,165**	**1,394**
0 - 15	4,591	3,098	1,493	4,309	2,937	1,372	228	133	95	54	28	26	261	102
16 - 17	2,400	1,492	908	2,274	1,410	864	115	77	38	11	5	6	243	68
18 - 29	10,110	5,417	4,693	8,734	4,555	4,179	1,222	779	443	154	83	71	450	870
30 - 44	1,163	783	380	614	427	187	395	273	122	154	83	71	72	302
45 - 59	358	191	167	167	88	79	70	40	30	121	63	58	24	40
60 - 64	34	14	20	15	7	8	9	4	5	10	7	3	4	2
65 - 74	53	21	32	25	11	14	21	4	17	7	6	1	21	1
75 - 84	61	27	34	42	20	22	17	5	12	2	2	-	48	3
85 and over	48	18	30	29	12	17	19	6	13	-	-	-	42	6

Table 3 Type of establishment, migrants and long-term illness – **continued**

Great Britain, England & Wales, England, regions, metropolitan counties, Inner London, Outer London, regional remainders, Wales, Scotland

Persons present in communal establishments

Type of establishment and age	PERSONS PRESENT			Visitors/guests			Residents - non-staff			Residents - staff			With limiting long-term illness	Migrants
	TOTAL	Males	Females	Total	Males	Females	Total	Males	Females	Total	Males	Females		
a	b	c	d	e	f	g	h	i	j	k	l	m	n	o
WEST MIDLANDS REGION – *continued*														
Hotels, boarding houses etc														
All ages	**11,480**	**7,316**	**4,164**	**7,472**	**4,781**	**2,691**	**2,200**	**1,550**	**650**	**1,808**	**985**	**823**	**992**	**1,628**
0 - 15	967	508	459	630	339	291	205	100	105	132	69	63	34	135
16 - 17	149	79	70	42	24	18	56	29	27	51	26	25	6	65
18 - 29	3,658	2,163	1,495	1,946	1,177	769	799	502	297	913	484	429	170	962
30 - 44	2,999	2,166	833	2,156	1,549	607	522	417	105	321	200	121	192	317
45 - 59	2,283	1,586	697	1,615	1,122	493	357	304	53	311	160	151	230	114
60 - 64	533	332	201	408	232	176	82	75	7	43	25	18	82	9
65 - 74	621	366	255	504	269	235	97	84	13	20	13	7	150	9
75 - 84	209	97	112	139	60	79	57	30	27	13	7	6	91	13
85 and over	61	19	42	32	9	23	25	9	16	4	1	3	37	4
Hostels and common lodging houses (non-HA)														
All ages	**2,030**	**1,484**	**546**	**116**	**62**	**54**	**1,865**	**1,390**	**475**	**49**	**32**	**17**	**655**	**1,001**
0 - 15	181	100	81	7	3	4	173	96	77	1	1	-	16	125
16 - 17	84	37	47	2	-	2	81	36	45	1	1	-	12	74
18 - 29	615	371	244	62	27	35	545	338	207	8	6	2	96	434
30 - 44	340	268	72	23	17	6	308	246	62	9	5	4	123	185
45 - 59	385	343	42	14	9	5	348	320	28	23	14	9	187	113
60 - 64	136	123	13	1	1	-	129	117	12	6	5	1	76	26
65 - 74	222	191	31	6	4	2	215	187	28	1	-	1	110	36
75 - 84	61	48	13	1	1	-	60	47	13	-	-	-	31	7
85 and over	6	3	3	-	-	-	6	3	3	-	-	-	4	1

Great Britain, England & Wales, England, regions, metropolitan counties, Inner London, Outer London, regional remainders, Wales, Scotland

Table 3 Type of establishment, migrants and long-term illness – **continued**

Persons present in communal establishments

WEST MIDLANDS REGION – *continued*

Type of establishment and age	PERSONS PRESENT			Visitors/guests			Residents - non-staff			Residents - staff			With limiting long-term illness	Migrants
	TOTAL	Males	Females	Total	Males	Females	Total	Males	Females	Total	Males	Females		
a	b	c	d	e	f	g	h	i	j	k	l	m	n	o
Other miscellaneous establishments														
All ages	**3,102**	**1,624**	**1,478**	**1,172**	**824**	**348**	**1,722**	**704**	**1,018**	**208**	**96**	**112**	**469**	**653**
0 - 15	230	125	105	72	46	26	147	74	73	11	5	6	10	80
16 - 17	84	54	30	56	45	11	26	8	18	2	1	1	4	23
18 - 29	1,182	562	620	559	331	228	528	194	334	95	37	58	61	343
30 - 44	603	433	170	330	273	57	233	136	97	40	24	16	65	119
45 - 59	371	239	132	131	115	16	208	107	101	32	17	15	69	45
60 - 64	114	57	57	12	8	4	92	44	48	10	5	5	37	12
65 - 74	239	106	133	9	5	4	215	96	119	15	5	10	69	22
75 - 84	213	42	171	2	-	2	208	40	168	3	2	1	102	8
85 and over	66	6	60	1	1	-	65	5	60	-	-	-	52	1
Persons sleeping rough														
All ages	**63**	**56**	**7**	**19**	**17**	**2**	**43**	**39**	**4**				**18**	**31**
0 - 15	-	-	-	-	-	-	-	-	-				-	-
16 - 17	1	1	-	-	-	-	1	1	-				1	-
18 - 29	24	21	3	7	6	1	17	15	2				3	15
30 - 44	16	14	2	4	4	-	12	10	2				4	9
45 - 59	15	14	1	5	4	1	10	10	-				7	7
60 - 64	4	4	-	2	2	-	2	2	-				2	-
65 - 74	3	2	1	1	1	-	1	1	-				1	-
75 - 84	-	-	-	-	-	-	-	-	-				-	-
85 and over	-	-	-	-	-	-	-	-	-				-	-

Table 3 Type of establishment, migrants and long-term illness – **continued**

Great Britain, England & Wales, England, regions, metropolitan counties, Inner London, Outer London, regional remainders, Wales, Scotland

Persons present in communal establishments

WEST MIDLANDS REGION – *continued*

Type of establishment and age	PERSONS PRESENT			Visitors/guests			Residents - non-staff			Residents - staff			With limiting long-term illness	Migrants
	TOTAL	Males	Females	Total	Males	Females	Total	Males	Females	Total	Males	Females		
a	b	c	d	e	f	g	h	i	j	k	l	m	n	o
Campers														
All ages	**31**	**16**	**15**	**27**	**14**	**13**	**4**	**2**	**2**				**6**	**4**
0 - 15	4	1	3	2	-	2	2	1	1				1	2
16 - 17	-	-	-	-	-	-	-	-	-				-	-
18 - 29	2	-	2	2	-	2	-	-	-				-	1
30 - 44	2	2	-	1	1	-	1	1	-				-	1
45 - 59	6	2	4	5	2	3	1	-	1				3	-
60 - 64	9	6	3	9	6	3	-	-	-				1	-
65 - 74	4	3	1	4	3	1	-	-	-				1	-
75 - 84	4	2	2	4	2	2	-	-	-				-	-
85 and over	-	-	-	-	-	-	-	-	-				-	-
Civilian ships, boats and barges														
All ages	-	-	-	-	-	-	-	-	-				-	-
0 - 15	-	-	-	-	-	-	-	-	-				-	-
16 - 17	-	-	-	-	-	-	-	-	-				-	-
18 - 29	-	-	-	-	-	-	-	-	-				-	-
30 - 44	-	-	-	-	-	-	-	-	-				-	-
45 - 59	-	-	-	-	-	-	-	-	-				-	-
60 - 64	-	-	-	-	-	-	-	-	-				-	-
65 - 74	-	-	-	-	-	-	-	-	-				-	-
75 - 84	-	-	-	-	-	-	-	-	-				-	-
85 and over	-	-	-	-	-	-	-	-	-				-	-

Table 3 Type of establishment, migrants and long-term illness – **continued**

Great Britain, England & Wales, England, regions, metropolitan counties, Inner London, Outer London, regional remainders, Wales, Scotland

Persons present in communal establishments

Type of establishment and age	PERSONS PRESENT			Visitors/guests			Residents - non-staff			Residents - staff			With limiting long-term illness	Migrants
	TOTAL	Males	Females	Total	Males	Females	Total	Males	Females	Total	Males	Females		
a	b	c	d	e	f	g	h	i	j	k	l	m	n	o
West Midlands Metropolitan County														
All establishments *														
All ages	**46,973**	**21,129**	**25,844**	**20,169**	**10,276**	**9,893**	**24,707**	**10,150**	**14,557**	**2,097**	**703**	**1,394**	**25,101**	**8,926**
0 - 15	2,147	1,212	935	1,232	696	536	823	470	353	92	46	46	303	479
16 - 17	444	208	236	248	116	132	177	86	91	19	6	13	99	151
18 - 29	13,898	7,041	6,857	9,158	4,661	4,497	3,460	2,095	1,365	1,280	285	995	1,672	2,573
30 - 44	5,473	3,547	1,926	2,624	1,620	1,004	2,507	1,729	778	342	198	144	1,989	1,065
45 - 59	3,905	2,448	1,457	1,699	970	729	1,937	1,350	587	269	128	141	2,192	436
60 - 64	1,593	994	599	657	385	272	895	586	309	41	23	18	1,188	171
65 - 74	4,433	2,205	2,228	1,623	829	794	2,779	1,365	1,414	31	11	20	3,643	673
75 - 84	7,932	2,342	5,590	1,964	760	1,204	5,952	1,576	4,376	16	6	10	7,275	1,803
85 and over	7,148	1,132	6,016	964	239	725	6,177	893	5,284	7	-	7	6,740	1,575
NHS hospitals/homes - psychiatric														
All ages	**1,179**	**582**	**597**	**535**	**243**	**292**	**616**	**325**	**291**	**28**	**14**	**14**	**1,048**	**125**
0 - 15	12	5	7	8	2	6	4	3	1	-	-	-	5	1
16 - 17	7	3	4	7	3	4	-	-	-	-	-	-	6	-
18 - 29	143	82	61	87	49	38	35	23	12	21	10	11	98	24
30 - 44	197	132	65	102	62	40	89	67	22	6	3	3	162	24
45 - 59	171	103	68	67	31	36	103	71	32	1	1	-	152	23
60 - 64	88	43	45	35	15	20	53	28	25	-	-	-	83	4
65 - 74	208	93	115	94	34	60	114	59	55	-	-	-	196	18
75 - 84	241	85	156	94	33	61	147	52	95	-	-	-	237	25
85 and over	112	36	76	41	14	27	71	22	49	-	-	-	109	6

Note: * Includes a female member of staff incorrectly enumerated as a resident.

Table 3 Type of establishment, migrants and long-term illness – **continued**

Great Britain, England & Wales, England, regions, metropolitan counties, Inner London, Outer London, regional remainders, Wales, Scotland

Persons present in communal establishments

Type of establishment and age	PERSONS PRESENT			Visitors/guests			Residents - non-staff			Residents - staff			With limiting long-term illness	Migrants
	TOTAL	Males	Females	Total	Males	Females	Total	Males	Females	Total	Males	Females		
a	b	c	d	e	f	g	h	i	j	k	l	m	n	o
West Midlands Metropolitan County – *continued*														
NHS hospitals/homes - other														
All ages	**11,833**	**4,813**	**7,020**	**8,262**	**3,436**	**4,826**	**2,375**	**1,112**	**1,263**	**1,196**	**265**	**931**	**6,785**	**1,153**
0 - 15	851	475	376	799	448	351	33	16	17	19	11	8	167	26
16 - 17	81	24	57	73	20	53	5	4	1	3	-	3	25	5
18 - 29	3,012	732	2,280	1,409	348	1,061	590	225	365	1,013	159	854	479	750
30 - 44	1,488	727	761	864	348	516	487	294	193	137	85	52	728	158
45 - 59	1,239	641	598	857	429	428	364	207	157	18	5	13	942	37
60 - 64	582	340	242	476	275	201	102	62	40	4	3	1	472	9
65 - 74	1,622	864	758	1,347	711	636	273	151	122	2	2	-	1,340	46
75 - 84	1,971	782	1,189	1,662	664	998	309	118	191	-	-	-	1,718	70
85 and over	987	228	759	775	193	582	212	35	177	-	-	-	914	52
Non-NHS hospitals - psychiatric														
All ages	**32**	**11**	**21**	**32**	**11**	**21**	-	-	-	-	-	-	**15**	-
0 - 15	-	-	-	-	-	-	-	-	-	-	-	-	-	-
16 - 17	-	-	-	-	-	-	-	-	-	-	-	-	-	-
18 - 29	5	3	2	5	3	2	-	-	-	-	-	-	3	-
30 - 44	15	7	8	15	7	8	-	-	-	-	-	-	6	-
45 - 59	7	1	6	7	1	6	-	-	-	-	-	-	2	-
60 - 64	2	-	2	2	-	2	-	-	-	-	-	-	1	-
65 - 74	2	-	2	2	-	2	-	-	-	-	-	-	2	-
75 - 84	1	-	1	1	-	1	-	-	-	-	-	-	1	-
85 and over	-	-	-	-	-	-	-	-	-	-	-	-	-	-

Table 3 Type of establishment, migrants and long-term illness – **continued**

Persons present in communal establishments

Type of establishment and age	PERSONS PRESENT			Visitors/guests			Residents - non-staff			Residents - staff			With limiting long-term illness	Migrants
	TOTAL	Males	Females	Total	Males	Females	Total	Males	Females	Total	Males	Females		
a	b	c	d	e	f	g	h	i	j	k	l	m	n	o
West Midlands Metropolitan County – *continued*														
Non-NHS hospitals - other														
All ages	**262**	**89**	**173**	**170**	**61**	**109**	**92**	**28**	**64**	**-**	**-**	**-**	**148**	**32**
0 - 15	3	1	2	3	1	2	-	-	-				1	-
16 - 17	1	-	1	1	-	1	-	-	-				-	-
18 - 29	22	9	13	17	6	11	5	3	2				7	-
30 - 44	47	8	39	38	5	33	9	3	6				11	3
45 - 59	59	30	29	45	24	21	14	6	8				29	4
60 - 64	21	8	13	17	8	9	4	-	4				12	3
65 - 74	35	19	16	26	13	13	9	6	3				21	5
75 - 84	30	6	24	19	3	16	11	3	8				24	4
85 and over	44	8	36	4	1	3	40	7	33				43	13
Local authority homes														
All ages	**5,684**	**1,766**	**3,918**	**427**	**174**	**253**	**5,228**	**1,578**	**3,650**	**29**	**14**	**15**	**5,134**	**1,063**
0 - 15	118	80	38	59	44	15	56	33	23	3	3	-	47	29
16 - 17	39	24	15	10	7	3	29	17	12	-	-	-	15	17
18 - 29	337	210	127	49	30	19	282	178	104	6	2	4	254	82
30 - 44	349	189	160	39	14	25	303	172	131	7	3	4	309	59
45 - 59	314	145	169	35	2	33	268	138	130	11	5	6	270	27
60 - 64	152	88	64	11	8	3	140	79	61	1	1	-	142	24
65 - 74	689	286	403	46	21	25	643	265	378	-	-	-	640	130
75 - 84	1,764	461	1,303	94	30	64	1,670	431	1,239	-	-	-	1,642	392
85 and over	1,922	283	1,639	84	18	66	1,837	265	1,572	1	-	1	1,815	303

Table 3 Type of establishment, migrants and long-term illness – **continued**

Great Britain, England & Wales, England, regions, metropolitan counties, Inner London, Outer London, regional remainders, Wales, Scotland

Persons present in communal establishments

Type of establishment and age	PERSONS PRESENT			Visitors/guests			Residents - non-staff			Residents - staff			With limiting long-term illness	Migrants
	TOTAL	Males	Females	Total	Males	Females	Total	Males	Females	Total	Males	Females		
a	b	c	d	e	f	g	h	i	j	k	l	m	n	o
West Midlands Metropolitan County – *continued*														
Housing association homes and hostels														
All ages	1,152	634	518	42	18	24	1,095	609	486	15	7	8	773	395
0 - 15	5	3	2	-	-	-	3	1	2	2	2	-	-	1
16 - 17	17	9	8	3	3	-	14	6	8	-	-	-	-	14
18 - 29	177	115	62	14	8	6	161	107	54	2	-	2	58	104
30 - 44	157	118	39	10	5	5	143	111	32	4	2	2	88	66
45 - 59	163	138	25	5	1	4	151	134	17	7	3	4	114	50
60 - 64	74	59	15	-	-	-	74	59	15	-	-	-	54	18
65 - 74	157	103	54	1	-	1	156	103	53	-	-	-	107	38
75 - 84	208	68	140	6	1	5	202	67	135	-	-	-	182	61
85 and over	194	21	173	3	-	3	191	21	170	-	-	-	170	43
Nursing homes (non-NHS/ LA/HA)														
All ages	4,493	1,259	3,234	147	39	108	4,295	1,203	3,092	51	17	34	4,321	1,657
0 - 15	3	1	2	-	-	-	2	-	2	1	1	-	2	1
16 - 17	3	2	1	-	-	-	-	-	-	3	2	1	-	-
18 - 29	67	41	26	14	4	10	46	34	12	7	3	4	48	21
30 - 44	136	74	62	17	6	11	111	63	48	8	5	3	116	30
45 - 59	170	92	78	15	1	14	139	87	52	16	4	12	148	36
60 - 64	162	91	71	10	4	6	147	86	61	5	1	4	154	49
65 - 74	667	261	406	32	11	21	628	249	379	7	1	6	643	238
75 - 84	1,654	448	1,206	36	10	26	1,615	438	1,177	3	-	3	1,619	680
85 and over	1,631	249	1,382	23	3	20	1,607	246	1,361	1	-	1	1,591	602

Table 3 Type of establishment, migrants and long-term illness – **continued**

Great Britain, England & Wales, England, regions, metropolitan counties, Inner London, Outer London, regional remainders, Wales, Scotland

Persons present in communal establishments

Type of establishment and age	PERSONS PRESENT			Visitors/guests			Residents - non-staff			Residents - staff			With limiting long-term illness	Migrants
	TOTAL	Males	Females	Total	Males	Females	Total	Males	Females	Total	Males	Females		
a	b	c	d	e	f	g	h	i	j	k	l	m	n	o
West Midlands Metropolitan County – *continued*														
Residential homes (non-NHS/LA/HA)														
All ages	**5,763**	**1,504**	**4,259**	**162**	**45**	**117**	**5,459**	**1,406**	**4,053**	**142**	**53**	**89**	**5,228**	**1,428**
0 - 15	29	18	11	3	3	-	13	9	4	13	6	7	17	2
16 - 17	9	4	5	-	-	-	7	3	4	2	1	1	6	2
18 - 29	275	131	144	23	4	19	223	116	107	29	11	18	218	47
30 - 44	308	167	141	28	11	17	254	146	108	26	10	16	248	50
45 - 59	309	162	147	26	5	21	235	138	97	48	19	29	230	38
60 - 64	179	94	85	4	2	2	168	89	79	7	3	4	165	34
65 - 74	577	229	348	11	2	9	560	225	335	6	2	4	524	143
75 - 84	1,870	399	1,471	36	9	27	1,828	389	1,439	6	1	5	1,763	557
85 and over	2,207	300	1,907	31	9	22	2,171	291	1,880	5	-	5	2,057	555
Children's homes														
All ages	**523**	**295**	**228**	**80**	**42**	**38**	**387**	**232**	**155**	**56**	**21**	**35**	**36**	**221**
0 - 15	438	264	174	45	31	14	387	232	155	6	1	5	27	214
16 - 17	1	-	1	-	-	-	-	-	-	1	-	1	-	-
18 - 29	24	7	17	8	3	5	-	-	-	16	4	12	4	4
30 - 44	35	13	22	16	5	11	-	-	-	19	8	11	4	3
45 - 59	22	8	14	9	1	8	-	-	-	13	7	6	1	-
60 - 64	3	3	-	2	2	-	-	-	-	1	1	-	-	-
65 - 74	-	-	-	-	-	-	-	-	-	-	-	-	-	-
75 - 84	-	-	-	-	-	-	-	-	-	-	-	-	-	-
85 and over	-	-	-	-	-	-	-	-	-	-	-	-	-	-

Table 3 Type of establishment, migrants and long-term illness – **continued**

Persons present in communal establishments

Type of establishment and age	PERSONS PRESENT			Visitors/guests			Residents - non-staff			Residents - staff			With limiting long-term illness	Migrants
	TOTAL	Males	Females	Total	Males	Females	Total	Males	Females	Total	Males	Females		
a	b	c	d	e	f	g	h	i	j	k	l	m	n	o
Prison service establishments														
All ages	**1,005**	**997**	**8**	**612**	**611**	**1**	**393**	**386**	**7**	**-**	**-**	**-**	**181**	**225**
0 - 15	-	-	-	-	-	-	-	-	-	-	-	-	-	-
16 - 17	-	-	-	-	-	-	-	-	-	-	-	-	-	-
18 - 29	621	615	6	376	375	1	245	240	5	-	-	-	83	155
30 - 44	303	301	2	187	187	-	116	114	2	-	-	-	76	51
45 - 59	67	67	-	38	38	-	29	29	-	-	-	-	17	17
60 - 64	9	9	-	8	8	-	1	1	-	-	-	-	2	-
65 - 74	5	5	-	3	3	-	2	2	-	-	-	-	3	2
75 - 84	-	-	-	-	-	-	-	-	-	-	-	-	-	-
85 and over	-	-	-	-	-	-	-	-	-	-	-	-	-	-
Defence establishments														
All ages	**229**	**220**	**9**	**146**	**141**	**5**	**83**	**79**	**4**				**31**	**62**
0 - 15	-	-	-	-	-	-	-	-	-				-	-
16 - 17	8	6	2	5	5	-	3	1	2				3	3
18 - 29	109	102	7	94	89	5	15	13	2				7	13
30 - 44	65	65	-	42	42	-	23	23	-				5	14
45 - 59	28	28	-	4	4	-	24	24	-				9	20
60 - 64	6	6	-	1	1	-	5	5	-				1	3
65 - 74	12	12	-	-	-	-	12	12	-				6	9
75 - 84	1	1	-	-	-	-	1	1	-				-	-
85 and over	-	-	-	-	-	-	-	-	-				-	-

West Midlands Metropolitan County – *continued*

Table 3 Type of establishment, migrants and long-term illness – **continued**

Great Britain, England & Wales, England, regions, metropolitan counties, Inner London, Outer London, regional remainders, Wales, Scotland

Persons present in communal establishments

Type of establishment and age	PERSONS PRESENT			Visitors/guests			Residents - non-staff			Residents - staff			With limiting long-term illness	Migrants
	TOTAL	Males	Females	Total	Males	Females	Total	Males	Females	Total	Males	Females		
a	b	c	d	e	f	g	h	i	j	k	l	m	n	o
West Midlands Metropolitan County – *continued*														
Educational establishments														
All ages	**8,104**	**4,350**	**3,754**	**6,681**	**3,456**	**3,225**	**1,295**	**823**	**472**	**128**	**71**	**57**	**327**	**944**
0 - 15	333	179	154	256	133	123	68	42	26	9	4	5	14	30
16 - 17	129	67	62	121	62	59	7	4	3	1	1	-	28	7
18 - 29	6,816	3,581	3,235	5,962	3,043	2,919	824	523	301	30	15	15	246	615
30 - 44	655	440	215	275	185	90	333	229	104	47	26	21	23	263
45 - 59	130	73	57	55	28	27	40	23	17	35	22	13	5	28
60 - 64	10	2	8	5	2	3	2	-	2	3	-	3	1	1
65 - 74	21	5	16	6	2	4	14	2	12	1	1	-	6	-
75 - 84	8	3	5	1	1	-	5	-	5	2	2	-	3	-
85 and over	2	-	2	-	-	-	2	-	2	-	-	-	1	-
Hotels, boarding houses etc														
All ages	**3,945**	**2,763**	**1,182**	**2,532**	**1,774**	**758**	**1,088**	**813**	**275**	**325**	**176**	**149**	**291**	**542**
0 - 15	127	70	57	41	25	16	51	29	22	35	16	19	5	34
16 - 17	40	23	17	12	8	4	20	14	6	8	1	7	2	17
18 - 29	1,480	943	537	913	582	331	437	289	148	130	72	58	60	311
30 - 44	1,252	949	303	912	682	230	276	227	49	64	40	24	76	134
45 - 59	762	577	185	506	382	124	179	155	24	77	40	37	78	36
60 - 64	133	103	30	84	58	26	41	39	2	8	6	2	20	2
65 - 74	100	75	25	48	28	20	51	47	4	1	-	1	21	2
75 - 84	37	20	17	13	8	5	22	11	11	2	1	1	18	6
85 and over	14	3	11	3	1	2	11	2	9	-	-	-	11	-

Table 3 Type of establishment, migrants and long-term illness – **continued**

Great Britain, England & Wales, England, regions, metropolitan counties, Inner London, Outer London, regional remainders, Wales, Scotland

Persons present in communal establishments

Type of establishment and age	PERSONS PRESENT			Visitors/guests			Residents - non-staff			Residents - staff			With limiting long-term illness	Migrants
	TOTAL	Males	Females	Total	Males	Females	Total	Males	Females	Total	Males	Females		
a	b	c	d	e	f	g	h	i	j	k	l	m	n	o
West Midlands Metropolitan County – *continued*														
Hostels and common lodging houses (non-HA)														
All ages	**1,582**	**1,183**	**399**	**101**	**51**	**50**	**1,442**	**1,105**	**337**	**39**	**27**	**12**	**515**	**778**
0 - 15	121	66	55	6	3	3	115	63	52	-	-	-	14	90
16 - 17	75	33	42	2	-	2	72	32	40	1	1	-	11	67
18 - 29	474	288	186	57	24	33	410	259	151	7	5	2	73	322
30 - 44	282	224	58	20	14	6	256	206	50	6	4	2	106	156
45 - 59	297	266	31	8	4	4	269	250	19	20	12	8	144	92
60 - 64	111	107	4	1	1	-	105	101	4	5	5	-	59	21
65 - 74	175	160	15	6	4	2	169	156	13	-	-	-	84	25
75 - 84	42	36	6	1	1	-	41	35	6	-	-	-	21	4
85 and over	5	3	2	-	-	-	5	3	2	-	-	-	3	1
Other miscellaneous establishments														
All ages	**1,174**	**652**	**522**	**235**	**170**	**65**	**852**	**444**	**408**	**87**	**38**	**49**	**261**	**300**
0 - 15	107	50	57	12	6	6	91	42	49	4	2	2	4	51
16 - 17	34	13	21	14	8	6	20	5	15	-	-	-	3	19
18 - 29	332	178	154	128	91	37	185	83	102	19	4	15	32	124
30 - 44	182	131	51	58	46	12	106	73	33	18	12	6	30	54
45 - 59	165	116	49	21	19	2	121	87	34	23	10	13	50	28
60 - 64	58	38	20	-	-	-	51	35	16	7	3	4	20	3
65 - 74	161	92	69	1	-	1	147	87	60	13	5	8	49	17
75 - 84	105	33	72	1	-	1	101	31	70	3	2	1	47	4
85 and over	30	1	29	-	-	-	30	1	29	-	-	-	26	-

Table 3 Type of establishment, migrants and long-term illness – **continued**

Great Britain, England & Wales, England, regions, metropolitan counties, Inner London, Outer London, regional remainders, Wales, Scotland

Persons present in communal establishments

Type of establishment and age	PERSONS PRESENT			Visitors/guests			Residents - non-staff			Residents - staff			With limiting long-term illness	Migrants
	TOTAL	Males	Females	Total	Males	Females	Total	Males	Females	Total	Males	Females		
a	b	c	d	e	f	g	h	i	j	k	l	m	n	o
West Midlands Metropolitan County – *continued*														
Persons sleeping rough														
All ages	**13**	**11**	**2**	**5**	**4**	**1**	**7**	**7**	**-**				**7**	**1**
0 - 15	-	-	-	-	-	-	-	-	-				-	-
16 - 17	-	-	-	-	-	-	-	-	-				-	-
18 - 29	4	4	-	2	2	-	2	2	-				2	1
30 - 44	2	2	-	1	1	-	1	1	-				1	-
45 - 59	2	1	1	1	-	1	1	1	-				1	-
60 - 64	3	3	-	1	1	-	2	2	-				2	-
65 - 74	2	1	1	-	-	-	1	1	-				1	-
75 - 84	-	-	-	-	-	-	-	-	-				-	-
85 and over	-	-	-	-	-	-	-	-	-				-	-
Campers														
All ages	**-**	**-**	**-**	**-**	**-**	**-**	**-**	**-**	**-**				**-**	**-**
0 - 15	-	-	-	-	-	-	-	-	-				-	-
16 - 17	-	-	-	-	-	-	-	-	-				-	-
18 - 29	-	-	-	-	-	-	-	-	-				-	-
30 - 44	-	-	-	-	-	-	-	-	-				-	-
45 - 59	-	-	-	-	-	-	-	-	-				-	-
60 - 64	-	-	-	-	-	-	-	-	-				-	-
65 - 74	-	-	-	-	-	-	-	-	-				-	-
75 - 84	-	-	-	-	-	-	-	-	-				-	-
85 and over	-	-	-	-	-	-	-	-	-				-	-

Table 3 Type of establishment, migrants and long-term illness – **continued**

Great Britain, England & Wales, England, regions, metropolitan counties, Inner London, Outer London, regional remainders, Wales, Scotland

Persons present in communal establishments

Type of establishment and age	PERSONS PRESENT			Visitors/guests			Residents - non-staff			Residents - staff			With limiting long-term illness	Migrants
	TOTAL	Males	Females	Total	Males	Females	Total	Males	Females	Total	Males	Females		
a	b	c	d	e	f	g	h	i	j	k	l	m	n	o

West Midlands Metropolitan County – *continued*

Civilian ships, boats and barges														
All ages	-	-	-	-	-	-	-	-	-					-
0 - 15	-	-	-	-	-	-	-	-	-					-
16 - 17	-	-	-	-	-	-	-	-	-					-
18 - 29	-	-	-	-	-	-	-	-	-					-
30 - 44	-	-	-	-	-	-	-	-	-					-
45 - 59	-	-	-	-	-	-	-	-	-					-
60 - 64	-	-	-	-	-	-	-	-	-					-
65 - 74	-	-	-	-	-	-	-	-	-					-
75 - 84	-	-	-	-	-	-	-	-	-					-
85 and over	-	-	-	-	-	-	-	-	-					-

Remainder of West Midlands Region

All establishments														
All ages	58,708	28,048	30,660	25,999	15,206	10,793	29,545	11,342	18,203	3,164	1,500	1,664	29,464	10,172
0 - 15	6,633	4,272	2,361	5,580	3,678	1,902	818	462	356	235	132	103	560	412
16 - 17	3,061	2,004	1,057	2,538	1,664	874	450	304	146	73	36	37	358	323
18 - 29	12,959	8,042	4,917	6,898	4,157	2,741	4,447	3,199	1,248	1,614	686	928	1,553	3,067
30 - 44	5,713	3,671	2,042	3,155	2,029	1,126	1,978	1,321	657	580	321	259	1,705	672
45 - 59	4,281	2,512	1,769	2,297	1,341	956	1,467	924	543	517	247	270	1,786	292
60 - 64	1,693	905	788	805	422	383	812	441	371	76	42	34	1,101	181
65 - 74	4,653	2,085	2,568	1,707	839	868	2,903	1,220	1,683	43	26	17	3,806	780
75 - 84	9,949	2,836	7,113	2,006	800	1,206	7,923	2,027	5,896	20	9	11	9,230	2,369
85 and over	9,766	1,721	8,045	1,013	276	737	8,747	1,444	7,303	6	1	5	9,365	2,076

Table 3 Type of establishment, migrants and long-term illness – **continued**

Great Britain, England & Wales, England, regions, metropolitan counties, Inner London, Outer London, regional remainders, Wales, Scotland

Persons present in communal establishments

Type of establishment and age	PERSONS PRESENT			Visitors/guests			Residents - non-staff			Residents - staff			With limiting long-term illness	Migrants
	TOTAL	Males	Females	Total	Males	Females	Total	Males	Females	Total	Males	Females		
a	b	c	d	e	f	g	h	i	j	k	l	m	n	o

Remainder of West Midlands Region – continued

NHS hospitals/homes - psychiatric

All ages	**1,518**	**659**	**859**	**602**	**259**	**343**	**838**	**357**	**481**	**78**	**43**	**35**	**1,321**	**133**
0 - 15	5	3	2	-	-	-	5	3	2	-	-	-	2	4
16 - 17	7	2	5	5	1	4	2	1	1	-	-	-	3	1
18 - 29	160	93	67	70	37	33	32	28	4	58	28	30	64	42
30 - 44	184	98	86	105	47	58	63	40	23	16	11	5	131	16
45 - 59	204	109	95	101	43	58	100	63	37	3	3	-	179	5
60 - 64	100	55	45	30	14	16	69	40	29	1	1	-	97	3
65 - 74	276	126	150	83	34	49	193	92	101	-	-	-	269	16
75 - 84	377	125	252	134	59	75	243	66	177	-	-	-	371	33
85 and over	205	48	157	74	24	50	131	24	107	-	-	-	205	13

NHS hospitals/homes - other

All ages	**8,129**	**3,184**	**4,945**	**5,893**	**2,343**	**3,550**	**1,714**	**698**	**1,016**	**522**	**143**	**379**	**5,284**	**562**
0 - 15	554	301	253	538	294	244	11	6	5	5	1	4	68	3
16 - 17	64	28	36	54	24	30	7	4	3	3	-	3	26	3
18 - 29	1,426	401	1,025	787	191	596	208	112	96	431	98	333	284	279
30 - 44	1,001	424	577	560	184	376	369	203	166	72	37	35	540	76
45 - 59	801	377	424	579	255	324	214	117	97	8	5	3	572	16
60 - 64	416	216	200	348	182	166	68	34	34	-	-	-	332	8
65 - 74	1,203	590	613	972	486	486	230	103	127	1	1	-	1,014	42
75 - 84	1,689	628	1,061	1,377	545	832	310	82	228	2	1	1	1,516	78
85 and over	975	219	756	678	182	496	297	37	260	-	-	-	932	57

Table 3 Type of establishment, migrants and long-term illness – **continued**

Great Britain, England & Wales, England, regions, metropolitan counties, Inner London, Outer London, regional remainders, Wales, Scotland

Persons present in communal establishments

Type of establishment and age	PERSONS PRESENT			Visitors/guests			Residents - non-staff			Residents - staff			With limiting long-term illness	Migrants
	TOTAL	Males	Females	Total	Males	Females	Total	Males	Females	Total	Males	Females		
a	b	c	d	e	f	g	h	i	j	k	l	m	n	o

Remainder of West Midlands Region – *continued*

Non-NHS hospitals - psychiatric

All ages	**377**	**181**	**196**	**133**	**61**	**72**	**231**	**116**	**115**	**13**	**4**	**9**	**313**	**30**
0 - 15	4	2	2	4	2	2	-	-	-	-	-	-	-	-
16 - 17	3	2	1	3	2	1	-	-	-	-	-	-	-	-
18 - 29	48	20	28	26	11	15	11	6	5	11	3	8	11	10
30 - 44	32	19	13	19	11	8	11	7	4	2	1	1	27	5
45 - 59	72	40	32	24	11	13	48	29	19	-	-	-	67	5
60 - 64	33	14	19	11	4	7	22	10	12	-	-	-	30	-
65 - 74	84	46	38	21	9	12	63	37	26	-	-	-	80	2
75 - 84	74	31	43	22	9	13	52	22	30	-	-	-	72	7
85 and over	27	7	20	3	2	1	24	5	19	-	-	-	26	1

Non-NHS hospitals - other

All ages	**307**	**112**	**195**	**168**	**74**	**94**	**138**	**38**	**100**	**1**	**-**	**1**	**204**	**29**
0 - 15	2	-	2	2	2	-	-	-	-	-	-	-	-	-
16 - 17	-	-	-	-	-	-	-	-	-	-	-	-	-	-
18 - 29	14	10	4	9	6	3	5	4	1	-	-	-	8	-
30 - 44	38	19	19	21	11	10	17	8	9	-	-	-	14	1
45 - 59	70	31	39	54	21	33	15	10	5	1	-	1	32	1
60 - 64	24	12	12	18	11	7	6	1	5	-	-	-	15	-
65 - 74	41	14	27	25	9	16	16	5	11	-	-	-	30	4
75 - 84	66	17	49	31	12	19	35	5	30	-	-	-	54	8
85 and over	52	9	43	8	4	4	44	5	39	-	-	-	51	15

Table 3 Type of establishment, migrants and long-term illness – **continued**

Great Britain, England & Wales, England, regions, metropolitan counties, Inner London, Outer London, regional remainders, Wales, Scotland

Persons present in communal establishments

Type of establishment and age	PERSONS PRESENT			Visitors/guests			Residents - non-staff			Residents - staff			With limiting long-term illness	Migrants
	TOTAL	Males	Females	Total	Males	Females	Total	Males	Females	Total	Males	Females		
a	b	c	d	e	f	g	h	i	j	k	l	m	n	o
Remainder of West Midlands Region – *continued*														
Local authority homes														
All ages	**5,795**	**2,048**	**3,747**	**643**	**319**	**324**	**5,066**	**1,698**	**3,368**	**86**	**31**	**55**	**5,200**	**927**
0 - 15	292	210	82	158	120	38	130	87	43	4	3	1	169	39
16 - 17	123	88	35	51	41	10	68	45	23	4	2	2	71	14
18 - 29	342	212	130	69	45	24	228	157	71	45	10	35	246	71
30 - 44	319	177	142	38	12	26	268	157	111	13	8	5	275	43
45 - 59	306	139	167	31	6	25	259	126	133	16	7	9	262	25
60 - 64	150	89	61	11	3	8	137	86	51	2	-	2	143	30
65 - 74	622	279	343	51	19	32	569	259	310	2	1	1	575	110
75 - 84	1,732	530	1,202	137	54	83	1,595	476	1,119	-	-	-	1,632	310
85 and over	1,909	324	1,585	97	19	78	1,812	305	1,507	-	-	-	1,827	285
Housing association homes and hostels														
All ages	**672**	**312**	**360**	**24**	**7**	**17**	**623**	**297**	**326**	**25**	**8**	**17**	**364**	**268**
0 - 15	14	6	8	-	-	-	12	4	8	2	2	-	-	5
16 - 17	33	14	19	-	-	-	32	14	18	1	-	1	6	29
18 - 29	185	121	64	6	2	4	177	119	58	2	1	2	48	127
30 - 44	76	44	32	8	2	6	65	41	24	3	1	2	37	24
45 - 59	59	42	17	3	-	3	42	37	5	14	5	9	29	17
60 - 64	21	13	8	-	-	-	20	13	7	1	-	1	14	3
65 - 74	48	25	23	-	-	-	46	25	21	2	-	2	36	14
75 - 84	133	31	102	5	2	3	128	29	99	-	-	-	103	31
85 and over	103	16	87	2	1	1	101	15	86	-	-	-	91	18

Table 3 Type of establishment, migrants and long-term illness – continued

Persons present in communal establishments

Type of establishment and age	PERSONS PRESENT			Visitors/guests			Residents - non-staff			Residents - staff			With limiting long-term illness	Migrants
	TOTAL	Males	Females	Total	Males	Females	Total	Males	Females	Total	Males	Females		
a	b	c	d	e	f	g	h	i	j	k	l	m	n	o

Remainder of West Midlands Region – continued

Nursing homes (non-NHS/LA/HA)

All ages	6,604	1,743	4,861	255	73	182	6,270	1,634	4,636	79	36	43	6,372	2,413
0 - 15	19	10	9	1	1	-	1	-	1	17	9	8	1	2
16 - 17	3	1	2	1	1	-	-	-	-	2	-	2	-	-
18 - 29	55	21	34	23	5	18	16	7	9	16	9	7	27	13
30 - 44	85	36	49	31	2	29	37	27	10	17	7	10	40	15
45 - 59	110	52	58	22	4	18	69	39	30	19	9	10	86	20
60 - 64	202	97	105	17	7	10	183	89	94	2	1	1	189	73
65 - 74	855	328	527	45	16	29	809	311	498	1	1	-	837	331
75 - 84	2,576	682	1,894	72	25	47	2,500	657	1,843	4	-	4	2,527	1,054
85 and over	2,699	516	2,183	43	12	31	2,655	504	2,151	1	1	-	2,665	905

Residential homes (non-NHS/LA/HA)

All ages	8,915	2,319	6,596	262	78	184	8,341	2,107	6,234	312	134	178	8,086	2,012
0 - 15	54	33	21	4	3	1	4	3	1	46	27	19	2	9
16 - 17	23	14	9	5	4	1	11	7	4	7	3	4	11	6
18 - 29	354	204	150	43	14	29	260	174	86	51	16	35	279	46
30 - 44	429	224	205	42	10	32	326	191	135	61	23	38	334	43
45 - 59	393	206	187	38	11	27	241	151	90	114	44	70	266	32
60 - 64	220	116	104	8	2	6	190	99	91	22	15	7	179	40
65 - 74	837	317	520	20	5	15	808	307	501	9	5	4	772	235
75 - 84	2,941	664	2,277	54	19	35	2,886	644	2,242	1	1	-	2,770	830
85 and over	3,664	541	3,123	48	10	38	3,615	531	3,084	1	-	1	3,473	771

Table 3 Type of establishment, migrants and long-term illness – **continued**

Persons present in communal establishments

Remainder of West Midlands Region – *continued*

Type of establishment and age	PERSONS PRESENT			Visitors/guests			Residents - non-staff			Residents - staff			With limiting long-term illness	Migrants
	TOTAL	Males	Females	Total	Males	Females	Total	Males	Females	Total	Males	Females		
a	b	c	d	e	f	g	h	i	j	k	l	m	n	o
Children's homes														
All ages	413	224	189	145	72	73	225	131	94	43	21	22	37	112
0 - 15	354	196	158	123	61	62	225	131	94	6	4	2	30	108
16 - 17	1	1	-	-	-	-	-	-	-	1	1	-	-	-
18 - 29	27	13	14	12	6	6	-	-	-	15	7	8	2	4
30 - 44	14	7	7	7	4	3	-	-	-	7	3	4	2	-
45 - 59	13	5	8	3	1	2	-	-	-	10	4	6	3	-
60 - 64	2	1	1	-	-	-	-	-	-	2	1	1	1	-
65 - 74	-	-	-	-	-	-	-	-	-	-	-	-	-	-
75 - 84	2	1	1	-	-	-	-	-	-	2	1	1	1	-
85 and over	-	-	-	-	-	-	-	-	-	-	-	-	-	-
Prison service establishments														
All ages	2,611	2,447	164	1,848	1,707	141	757	734	23	6	6	-	325	374
0 - 15	15	15	-	10	10	-	-	-	-	5	5	-	1	3
16 - 17	177	177	-	157	157	-	20	20	-	-	-	-	14	12
18 - 29	1,740	1,654	86	1,240	1,168	72	499	485	14	1	1	-	190	267
30 - 44	510	450	60	350	296	54	160	154	6	-	-	-	70	59
45 - 59	153	136	17	81	67	14	72	69	3	-	-	-	45	30
60 - 64	9	8	1	5	4	1	4	4	-	-	-	-	1	2
65 - 74	3	3	-	2	2	-	1	1	-	-	-	-	2	1
75 - 84	2	2	-	2	2	-	-	-	-	-	-	-	1	-
85 and over	2	2	-	1	1	-	1	1	-	-	-	-	1	-

Table 3 Type of establishment, migrants and long-term illness – **continued**

Great Britain, England & Wales, England, regions, metropolitan counties, Inner London, Outer London, regional remainders, Wales, Scotland

Persons present in communal establishments

Type of establishment and age	PERSONS PRESENT			Visitors/guests			Residents - non-staff			Residents - staff			With limiting long-term illness	Migrants
	TOTAL	Males	Females	Total	Males	Females	Total	Males	Females	Total	Males	Females		
a	b	c	d	e	f	g	h	i	j	k	l	m	n	o

Remainder of West Midlands Region – *continued*

Defence establishments

All ages	**2,661**	**2,221**	**440**	**565**	**503**	**62**	**2,096**	**1,718**	**378**				**54**	**1,166**
0 - 15	35	29	6	35	29	6	-	-	-				2	-
16 - 17	187	150	37	37	33	4	150	117	33				5	138
18 - 29	2,123	1,753	370	365	318	47	1,758	1,435	323				27	957
30 - 44	275	253	22	112	107	5	163	146	17				17	64
45 - 59	38	33	5	15	15	-	23	18	5				3	5
60 - 64	1	1	-	1	1	-	-	-	-				-	-
65 - 74	1	1	-	-	-	-	1	1	-				-	1
75 - 84	1	1	-	-	-	-	1	1	-				-	1
85 and over	-	-	-	-	-	-	-	-	-				-	-

Educational establishments

All ages	**10,714**	**6,711**	**4,003**	**9,528**	**6,011**	**3,517**	**801**	**498**	**303**	**385**	**202**	**183**	**838**	**450**
0 - 15	4,258	2,919	1,339	4,053	2,804	1,249	160	91	69	45	24	21	247	72
16 - 17	2,271	1,425	846	2,153	1,348	805	108	73	35	10	4	6	215	61
18 - 29	3,294	1,836	1,458	2,772	1,512	1,260	398	256	142	124	68	56	204	255
30 - 44	508	343	165	339	242	97	62	44	18	107	57	50	49	39
45 - 59	228	118	110	112	60	52	30	17	13	86	41	45	19	12
60 - 64	24	12	12	10	5	5	7	4	3	7	3	4	3	1
65 - 74	32	16	16	19	9	10	7	2	5	6	5	1	15	1
75 - 84	53	24	29	41	19	22	12	5	7	-	-	-	45	3
85 and over	46	18	28	29	12	17	17	6	11	-	-	-	41	6

Table 3 Type of establishment, migrants and long-term illness – **continued**

Great Britain, England & Wales, England, regions, metropolitan counties, Inner London, Outer London, regional remainders, Wales, Scotland

Persons present in communal establishments

Type of establishment and age	PERSONS PRESENT			Visitors/guests			Residents - non-staff			Residents - staff			With limiting long-term illness	Migrants
	TOTAL	Males	Females	Total	Males	Females	Total	Males	Females	Total	Males	Females		
a	b	c	d	e	f	g	h	i	j	k	l	m	n	o
Remainder of West Midlands Region – *continued*														
Hotels, boarding houses etc														
All ages	7,535	4,553	2,982	4,940	3,007	1,933	1,112	737	375	1,483	809	674	701	1,086
0 - 15	840	438	402	589	314	275	154	71	83	97	53	44	29	101
16 - 17	109	56	53	30	16	14	36	15	21	43	25	18	4	48
18 - 29	2,178	1,220	958	1,033	595	438	362	213	149	783	412	371	110	651
30 - 44	1,747	1,217	530	1,244	867	377	246	190	56	257	160	97	116	183
45 - 59	1,521	1,009	512	1,109	740	369	178	149	29	234	120	114	152	78
60 - 64	400	229	171	324	174	150	41	36	5	35	19	16	62	7
65 - 74	521	291	230	456	241	215	46	37	9	19	13	6	129	7
75 - 84	172	77	95	126	52	74	35	19	16	11	6	5	73	7
85 and over	47	16	31	29	8	21	14	7	7	4	1	3	26	4
Hostels and common lodging houses (non-HA)														
All ages	448	301	147	15	11	4	423	285	138	10	5	5	140	223
0 - 15	60	34	26	1	1	-	58	33	25	1	1	-	2	35
16 - 17	9	4	5	-	-	-	9	4	5	-	-	-	1	7
18 - 29	141	83	58	5	3	2	135	79	56	1	1	-	23	112
30 - 44	58	44	14	3	3	-	52	40	12	3	1	2	17	29
45 - 59	88	77	11	6	5	1	79	70	9	3	2	1	43	21
60 - 64	25	16	9	-	-	-	24	16	8	1	-	1	17	5
65 - 74	47	31	16	-	-	-	46	31	15	1	-	1	26	11
75 - 84	19	12	7	-	-	-	19	12	7	-	-	-	10	3
85 and over	1	-	1	-	-	-	1	-	1	-	-	-	1	-

Table 3 Type of establishment, migrants and long-term illness – **continued**

Great Britain, England & Wales, England, regions, metropolitan counties, Inner London, Outer London, regional remainders, Wales, Scotland

Persons present in communal establishments

Type of establishment and age	PERSONS PRESENT			Visitors/guests			Residents - non-staff			Residents - staff			With limiting long-term illness	Migrants
	TOTAL	Males	Females	Total	Males	Females	Total	Males	Females	Total	Males	Females		
a	b	c	d	e	f	g	h	i	j	k	l	m	n	o

Remainder of West Midlands Region – *continued*

Other miscellaneous establishments

Type of establishment and age	b	c	d	e	f	g	h	i	j	k	l	m	n	o
All ages	**1,928**	**972**	**956**	**937**	**654**	**283**	**870**	**260**	**610**	**121**	**58**	**63**	**208**	**353**
0 - 15	123	75	48	60	40	20	56	32	24	7	3	4	6	29
16 - 17	50	41	9	42	37	5	6	3	3	2	1	1	1	4
18 - 29	850	384	466	431	240	191	343	111	232	76	33	43	29	219
30 - 44	421	302	119	272	227	45	127	63	64	22	12	10	35	65
45 - 59	206	123	83	110	96	14	87	20	67	9	7	2	19	17
60 - 64	56	19	37	12	8	4	41	9	32	3	2	1	17	9
65 - 74	78	14	64	8	5	3	68	9	59	2	-	2	20	5
75 - 84	108	9	99	1	-	1	107	9	98	-	-	-	55	4
85 and over	36	5	31	1	1	-	35	4	31	-	-	-	26	1

Persons sleeping rough

Type of establishment and age	b	c	d	e	f	g	h	i	j	k	l	m	n	o
All ages	**50**	**45**	**5**	**14**	**13**	**1**	**36**	**32**	**4**				**11**	**30**
0 - 15	-	-	-	-	-	-	-	-	-				-	-
16 - 17	1	1	-	-	-	-	1	1	-				-	-
18 - 29	20	17	3	5	4	1	15	13	2				1	14
30 - 44	14	12	2	3	3	-	11	9	2				1	9
45 - 59	13	13	-	4	4	-	9	9	-				3	7
60 - 64	1	1	-	1	1	-	-	-	-				-	-
65 - 74	1	1	-	1	1	-	-	-	-				-	-
75 - 84	-	-	-	-	-	-	-	-	-				-	-
85 and over	-	-	-	-	-	-	-	-	-				-	-

Table 3 Type of establishment, migrants and long-term illness – **continued**

Great Britain, England & Wales, England, regions, metropolitan counties, Inner London, Outer London, regional remainders, Wales, Scotland

Persons present in communal establishments

Type of establishment and age	PERSONS PRESENT			Visitors/guests			Residents - non-staff			Residents - staff			With limiting long-term illness	Migrants
	TOTAL	Males	Females	Total	Males	Females	Total	Males	Females	Total	Males	Females		
a	b	c	d	e	f	g	h	i	j	k	l	m	n	o

Remainder of West Midlands Region – *continued*

Type of establishment and age	PERSONS PRESENT			Visitors/guests			Residents - non-staff			Residents - staff			With limiting long-term illness	Migrants
Campers														
All ages	**31**	**16**	**15**	**27**	**14**	**13**	**4**	**2**	**2**				**6**	**4**
0 - 15	4	1	3	2	-	2	2	1	1				1	2
16 - 17	-	-	-	-	-	-	-	-	-				-	-
18 - 29	2	-	2	2	-	2	-	-	-				-	-
30 - 44	2	2	-	1	1	-	1	1	-				-	1
45 - 59	6	2	4	5	2	3	1	-	1				3	1
60 - 64	9	6	3	9	6	3	-	-	-				1	-
65 - 74	4	3	1	4	3	1	-	-	-				1	-
75 - 84	4	2	2	4	2	2	-	-	-				-	-
85 and over	-	-	-	-	-	-	-	-	-				-	-
Civilian ships, boats and barges														
All ages	**-**	**-**	**-**	**-**	**-**	**-**	**-**	**-**	**-**				**-**	**-**
0 - 15	-	-	-	-	-	-	-	-	-				-	-
16 - 17	-	-	-	-	-	-	-	-	-				-	-
18 - 29	-	-	-	-	-	-	-	-	-				-	-
30 - 44	-	-	-	-	-	-	-	-	-				-	-
45 - 59	-	-	-	-	-	-	-	-	-				-	-
60 - 64	-	-	-	-	-	-	-	-	-				-	-
65 - 74	-	-	-	-	-	-	-	-	-				-	-
75 - 84	-	-	-	-	-	-	-	-	-				-	-
85 and over	-	-	-	-	-	-	-	-	-				-	-

Table 3 Type of establishment, migrants and long-term illness – **continued**

Great Britain, England & Wales, England, regions, metropolitan counties, Inner London, Outer London, regional remainders, Wales, Scotland

Persons present in communal establishments

Type of establishment and age	PERSONS PRESENT			Visitors/guests			Residents - non-staff			Residents - staff			With limiting long-term illness	Migrants
	TOTAL	Males	Females	Total	Males	Females	Total	Males	Females	Total	Males	Females		
a	b	c	d	e	f	g	h	i	j	k	l	m	n	o
NORTH WEST REGION														
All establishments *														
All ages	**143,476**	**59,818**	**83,658**	**54,741**	**27,863**	**26,878**	**80,155**	**28,162**	**51,993**	**8,580**	**3,793**	**4,787**	**84,345**	**27,179**
0 - 15	7,747	4,548	3,199	4,360	2,716	1,644	2,521	1,376	1,145	866	456	410	891	1,463
16 - 17	1,784	1,023	761	1,187	723	464	405	207	198	192	93	99	262	336
18 - 29	31,881	16,812	15,069	21,119	10,950	10,169	7,402	4,710	2,692	3,360	1,152	2,208	3,937	5,549
30 - 44	14,316	9,158	5,158	6,986	4,269	2,717	5,542	3,906	1,636	1,788	983	805	5,157	2,189
45 - 59	11,771	6,866	4,905	5,258	2,929	2,329	4,676	3,051	1,625	1,837	886	951	5,992	1,115
60 - 64	5,016	2,655	2,361	2,122	1,076	1,046	2,631	1,439	1,192	263	140	123	3,597	650
65 - 74	14,345	6,301	8,044	5,149	2,392	2,757	9,028	3,850	5,178	168	59	109	11,758	2,545
75 - 84	29,955	8,315	21,640	5,953	2,178	3,775	23,918	6,121	17,797	84	16	68	27,480	7,292
85 and over	26,661	4,140	22,521	2,607	630	1,977	24,032	3,502	20,530	22	8	14	25,271	6,040
NHS hospitals/homes - psychiatric														
All ages	**3,966**	**2,103**	**1,863**	**1,192**	**557**	**635**	**2,625**	**1,464**	**1,161**	**149**	**82**	**67**	**3,509**	**397**
0 - 15	20	15	5	18	13	5	2	2	-	-	-	-	6	-
16 - 17	15	8	7	14	7	7	1	1	-	-	-	-	2	1
18 - 29	533	326	207	158	82	76	280	205	75	95	39	56	339	103
30 - 44	649	493	156	169	94	75	441	367	74	39	32	7	548	65
45 - 59	561	358	203	176	88	88	374	263	111	11	7	4	512	32
60 - 64	253	136	117	82	44	38	167	88	79	4	4	-	235	10
65 - 74	681	342	339	209	96	113	472	246	226	-	-	-	645	48
75 - 84	821	332	489	254	107	147	567	225	342	-	-	-	800	94
85 and over	433	93	340	112	26	86	321	67	254	-	-	-	422	44

Note: * Includes a male member of staff incorrectly enumerated as a resident.

Table 3 Type of establishment, migrants and long-term illness – **continued**

Great Britain, England & Wales, England, regions, metropolitan counties, Inner London, Outer London, regional remainders, Wales, Scotland

Persons present in communal establishments

Type of establishment and age	PERSONS PRESENT			Visitors/guests			Residents - non-staff			Residents - staff			With limiting long-term illness	Migrants
	TOTAL	Males	Females	Total	Males	Females	Total	Males	Females	Total	Males	Females		
a	b	c	d	e	f	g	h	i	j	k	l	m	n	o
NORTH WEST REGION – *continued*														
NHS hospitals/homes - other														
All ages	**27,532**	**11,068**	**16,464**	**19,597**	**7,828**	**11,769**	**5,518**	**2,444**	**3,074**	**2,417**	**796**	**1,621**	**16,373**	**2,291**
0 - 15	1,957	1,051	906	1,865	1,005	860	43	22	21	49	24	25	233	30
16 - 17	165	55	110	151	52	99	10	3	7	4	-	4	52	10
18 - 29	5,996	1,746	4,250	3,132	900	2,232	960	385	575	1,904	461	1,443	962	1,350
30 - 44	3,502	1,689	1,813	2,154	826	1,328	953	583	370	395	280	115	1,686	368
45 - 59	3,146	1,567	1,579	2,204	1,048	1,156	886	491	395	56	28	28	2,333	110
60 - 64	1,428	736	692	1,151	583	568	272	151	121	5	2	3	1,155	21
65 - 74	3,877	1,838	2,039	3,202	1,516	1,686	674	322	352	1	-	1	3,242	93
75 - 84	5,019	1,850	3,169	4,033	1,489	2,544	985	361	624	1	-	1	4,459	183
85 and over	2,442	536	1,906	1,705	409	1,296	735	126	609	2	1	1	2,251	126
Non-NHS hospitals - psychiatric														
All ages	**329**	**169**	**160**	**139**	**54**	**85**	**187**	**114**	**73**	**3**	**1**	**2**	**276**	**57**
0 - 15	3	1	2	2	-	2	1	1	-	-	-	-	2	-
16 - 17	3	1	2	3	1	2	-	-	-	-	-	-	2	-
18 - 29	56	28	28	36	16	20	17	11	6	3	1	2	34	10
30 - 44	62	35	27	35	14	21	27	21	6	-	-	-	49	11
45 - 59	55	32	23	30	12	18	25	20	5	-	-	-	43	5
60 - 64	23	11	12	13	6	7	10	5	5	-	-	-	20	5
65 - 74	44	26	18	8	4	4	36	22	14	-	-	-	44	7
75 - 84	60	30	30	8	-	8	52	30	22	-	-	-	59	15
85 and over	23	5	18	4	1	3	19	4	15	-	-	-	23	4

Great Britain, England & Wales, England, regions, metropolitan counties, Inner London, Outer London, regional remainders, Wales, Scotland

Table 3 Type of establishment, migrants and long-term illness – **continued**

Persons present in communal establishments

Type of establishment and age	PERSONS PRESENT			Visitors/guests			Residents - non-staff			Residents - staff			With limiting long-term illness	Migrants
	TOTAL	Males	Females	Total	Males	Females	Total	Males	Females	Total	Males	Females		
a	b	c	d	e	f	g	h	i	j	k	l	m	n	o

NORTH WEST REGION – *continued*

Non-NHS hospitals - other

All ages	**1,690**	**635**	**1,055**	**1,296**	**481**	**815**	**330**	**129**	**201**	**64**	**25**	**39**	**1,005**	**112**
0 - 15	85	48	37	84	47	37	1	1	-	-	-	-	7	1
16 - 17	12	3	9	10	2	8	2	1	1	-	-	-	3	2
18 - 29	243	53	190	174	28	146	24	12	12	45	13	32	37	31
30 - 44	268	102	166	222	70	152	31	20	11	15	12	3	96	15
45 - 59	229	101	128	195	80	115	30	21	9	4	-	4	122	4
60 - 64	103	59	44	83	44	39	20	15	5	-	-	-	77	1
65 - 74	233	116	117	176	89	87	57	27	30	-	-	-	189	11
75 - 84	337	120	217	248	95	153	89	25	64	-	-	-	306	28
85 and over	180	33	147	104	26	78	76	7	69	-	-	-	168	19

Local authority homes

All ages	**15,705**	**5,095**	**10,610**	**1,640**	**731**	**909**	**13,963**	**4,330**	**9,633**	**102**	**34**	**68**	**14,220**	**2,801**
0 - 15	474	353	121	333	251	82	131	96	35	10	6	4	201	56
16 - 17	136	94	42	73	54	19	62	39	23	1	1	-	66	34
18 - 29	952	528	424	246	131	115	657	384	273	49	13	36	647	212
30 - 44	920	491	429	152	55	97	748	428	320	20	8	12	781	101
45 - 59	793	412	381	88	20	68	687	388	299	18	4	14	710	54
60 - 64	435	219	216	36	11	25	397	207	190	2	1	1	408	84
65 - 74	1,944	818	1,126	141	54	87	1,802	764	1,038	1	-	1	1,811	404
75 - 84	5,059	1,407	3,652	330	109	221	4,729	1,298	3,431	1	-	-	4,808	1,033
85 and over	4,992	773	4,219	241	46	195	4,750	726	4,024	1	1	-	4,788	823

Table 3 Type of establishment, migrants and long-term illness – **continued**

Persons present in communal establishments

Type of establishment and age	PERSONS PRESENT			Visitors/guests			Residents - non-staff			Residents - staff			With limiting long-term illness	Migrants
	TOTAL	Males	Females	Total	Males	Females	Total	Males	Females	Total	Males	Females		
a	b	c	d	e	f	g	h	i	j	k	l	m	n	o
NORTH WEST REGION – *continued*														
Housing association homes and hostels														
All ages	**1,346**	**581**	**765**	**134**	**71**	**63**	**1,157**	**496**	**661**	**55**	**14**	**41**	**792**	**480**
0 - 15	29	19	10	5	4	1	22	14	8	2	1	1	10	11
16 - 17	30	17	13	9	7	2	20	10	10	1	-	1	11	19
18 - 29	277	164	113	53	24	29	217	137	80	7	3	4	80	155
30 - 44	175	117	58	46	28	18	120	88	32	9	1	8	64	71
45 - 59	136	95	41	11	7	4	100	81	19	25	7	18	74	41
60 - 64	49	29	20	-	-	-	43	28	15	6	1	5	35	18
65 - 74	94	46	48	4	1	3	86	45	41	4	-	4	73	17
75 - 84	289	57	232	4	-	4	284	56	228	1	1	-	220	81
85 and over	267	37	230	2	-	2	265	37	228	-	-	-	225	67
Nursing homes (non-NHS/ LA/HA)														
All ages	**22,307**	**5,788**	**16,519**	**1,022**	**371**	**651**	**21,009**	**5,331**	**15,678**	**276**	**86**	**190**	**21,281**	**8,080**
0 - 15	42	22	20	1	-	1	9	4	5	32	18	14	5	6
16 - 17	9	2	7	2	-	2	3	1	2	4	1	3	3	2
18 - 29	193	87	106	49	7	42	100	66	34	44	14	30	102	43
30 - 44	352	161	191	101	21	80	202	127	75	49	13	36	230	61
45 - 59	469	232	237	81	22	59	295	180	115	93	30	63	345	100
60 - 64	797	408	389	77	37	40	695	365	330	25	6	19	729	267
65 - 74	3,008	1,251	1,757	218	115	103	2,771	1,132	1,639	19	4	15	2,862	1,194
75 - 84	8,916	2,303	6,613	316	111	205	8,592	2,192	6,400	8	-	8	8,660	3,552
85 and over	8,521	1,322	7,199	177	58	119	8,342	1,264	7,078	2	-	2	8,345	2,855

Table 3 Type of establishment, migrants and long-term illness – **continued**

Great Britain, England & Wales, England, regions, metropolitan counties, Inner London, Outer London, regional remainders, Wales, Scotland

Persons present in communal establishments

NORTH WEST REGION – *continued*

Type of establishment and age	PERSONS PRESENT			Visitors/guests			Residents - non-staff			Residents - staff			With limiting long-term illness	Migrants
	TOTAL	Males	Females	Total	Males	Females	Total	Males	Females	Total	Males	Females		
a	b	c	d	e	f	g	h	i	j	k	l	m	n	o
Residential homes (non-NHS/LA/HA)														
All ages	**23,996**	**5,896**	**18,100**	**794**	**220**	**574**	**22,404**	**5,355**	**17,049**	**798**	**321**	**477**	**21,380**	**5,642**
0 - 15	166	96	70	44	28	16	13	10	3	109	58	51	56	16
16 - 17	50	28	22	25	14	11	7	3	4	18	11	7	32	5
18 - 29	742	406	336	85	27	58	523	337	186	134	42	92	528	178
30 - 44	1,013	566	447	85	20	65	739	466	273	189	80	109	769	160
45 - 59	991	489	502	77	11	66	656	378	278	258	100	158	673	120
60 - 64	665	310	355	25	9	16	595	284	311	45	17	28	564	153
65 - 74	2,560	919	1,641	92	28	64	2,435	879	1,556	33	12	21	2,278	673
75 - 84	8,290	1,805	6,485	193	50	143	8,089	1,755	6,334	8	-	8	7,617	2,248
85 and over	9,519	1,277	8,242	168	33	135	9,347	1,243	8,104	4	1	3	8,863	2,089
Children's homes														
All ages	**2,080**	**1,109**	**971**	**401**	**214**	**187**	**1,562**	**850**	**712**	**117**	**45**	**72**	**239**	**797**
0 - 15	1,879	1,045	834	305	189	116	1,562	850	712	12	6	6	203	776
16 - 17	11	-	11	-	-	-	-	-	-	11	-	11	-	9
18 - 29	68	33	35	30	11	19	-	-	-	38	22	16	24	7
30 - 44	54	17	37	36	7	29	-	-	-	18	10	8	2	7
45 - 59	45	9	36	27	5	22	-	-	-	18	4	14	3	1
60 - 64	10	4	6	2	2	-	-	-	-	8	2	6	1	1
65 - 74	5	-	5	1	-	1	-	-	-	4	-	4	2	1
75 - 84	6	-	6	-	-	-	-	-	-	6	-	6	3	1
85 and over	2	1	1	-	-	-	-	-	-	2	1	1	1	1

Persons present in communal establishments

Table 3 Type of establishment, migrants and long-term illness – **continued**

Great Britain, England & Wales, England, regions, metropolitan counties, Inner London, Outer London, regional remainders, Wales, Scotland

Type of establishment and age	PERSONS PRESENT			Visitors/guests			Residents - non-staff			Residents - staff			With limiting long-term illness	Migrants
	TOTAL	Males	Females	Total	Males	Females	Total	Males	Females	Total	Males	Females		
a	b	c	d	e	f	g	h	i	j	k	l	m	n	o

NORTH WEST REGION – *continued*

Prison service establishments

All ages	**4,568**	**4,306**	**262**	**3,274**	**3,076**	**198**	**1,292**	**1,228**	**64**	**2**	**2**	**-**	**657**	**709**
0 - 15	8	5	3	7	4	3	-	-	-	-	-	-	-	1
16 - 17	92	86	6	88	82	6	4	4	-	1	1	-	7	1
18 - 29	2,859	2,702	157	2,133	2,013	120	726	689	37	-	-	-	339	433
30 - 44	1,232	1,153	79	801	741	60	431	412	19	-	-	-	199	220
45 - 59	336	323	13	217	211	6	119	112	7	-	-	-	95	49
60 - 64	18	17	1	10	9	1	8	8	-	-	-	-	9	4
65 - 74	15	15	-	13	13	-	1	1	-	1	1	-	8	-
75 - 84	6	4	2	3	2	1	3	2	1	-	-	-	-	1
85 and over	2	1	1	2	1	1	-	-	-	-	-	-	-	-

Defence establishments

All ages	**239**	**228**	**11**	**38**	**37**	**1**	**201**	**191**	**10**				**10**	**49**
0 - 15	-	-	-	-	-	-	-	-	-				-	-
16 - 17	9	9	-	1	1	-	8	8	-				-	1
18 - 29	176	171	5	21	20	1	155	151	4				6	34
30 - 44	46	43	3	13	13	-	33	30	3				4	13
45 - 59	8	5	3	3	3	-	5	2	3				-	1
60 - 64	-	-	-	-	-	-	-	-	-				-	-
65 - 74	-	-	-	-	-	-	-	-	-				-	-
75 - 84	-	-	-	-	-	-	-	-	-				-	-
85 and over	-	-	-	-	-	-	-	-	-				-	-

Table 3 Type of establishment, migrants and long-term illness – **continued**

Great Britain, England & Wales, England, regions, metropolitan counties, Inner London, Outer London, regional remainders, Wales, Scotland

Persons present in communal establishments

Type of establishment and age	PERSONS PRESENT			Visitors/guests			Residents - non-staff			Residents - staff			With limiting long-term illness	Migrants
	TOTAL	Males	Females	Total	Males	Females	Total	Males	Females	Total	Males	Females		
a	b	c	d	e	f	g	h	i	j	k	l	m	n	o

NORTH WEST REGION – *continued*

Educational establishments

All ages	**16,143**	**8,345**	**7,798**	**13,882**	**7,029**	**6,853**	**1,993**	**1,182**	**811**	**268**	**134**	**134**	**595**	**1,313**
0 - 15	1,273	869	404	1,172	822	350	79	36	43	22	11	11	81	62
16 - 17	685	402	283	642	381	261	39	18	21	4	3	1	50	25
18 - 29	12,922	6,335	6,587	11,436	5,412	6,024	1,390	880	510	96	43	53	344	998
30 - 44	854	591	263	482	333	149	293	215	78	79	43	36	37	192
45 - 59	219	103	116	125	67	58	54	16	38	40	20	20	14	26
60 - 64	33	10	23	5	2	3	20	3	17	8	5	3	8	2
65 - 74	66	20	46	11	6	5	40	8	32	15	6	9	15	4
75 - 84	66	11	55	6	3	3	56	5	51	4	3	1	31	2
85 and over	25	4	21	3	3	-	22	1	21	-	-	-	15	2

Hotels, boarding houses etc

All ages	**17,505**	**10,794**	**6,711**	**9,637**	**5,901**	**3,736**	**3,910**	**2,843**	**1,067**	**3,958**	**2,050**	**1,908**	**2,456**	**2,446**
0 - 15	1,337	785	552	430	305	125	303	161	142	604	319	285	59	256
16 - 17	360	200	160	114	70	44	98	53	45	148	77	71	15	100
18 - 29	5,005	3,021	1,984	2,825	1,702	1,123	1,303	858	445	877	461	416	263	1,144
30 - 44	4,042	2,842	1,200	2,242	1,669	573	900	718	182	900	455	445	404	534
45 - 59	3,804	2,475	1,329	1,813	1,182	631	792	667	125	1,199	626	573	747	323
60 - 64	898	520	378	605	304	301	164	134	30	129	82	47	241	36
65 - 74	1,285	643	642	1,014	447	567	210	173	37	61	23	38	383	29
75 - 84	647	271	376	518	199	319	98	67	31	31	5	26	276	21
85 and over	127	37	90	76	23	53	42	12	30	9	2	7	68	3

Table 3 Type of establishment, migrants and long-term illness – **continued**

Great Britain, England & Wales, England, regions, metropolitan counties, Inner London, Outer London, regional remainders, Wales, Scotland

Persons present in communal establishments

NORTH WEST REGION – *continued*

Type of establishment and age	PERSONS PRESENT			Visitors/guests			Residents - non-staff			Residents - staff			With limiting long-term illness	Migrants
	TOTAL	Males	Females	Total	Males	Females	Total	Males	Females	Total	Males	Females		
a	b	c	d	e	f	g	h	i	j	k	l	m	n	o
Hostels and common lodging houses (non-HA)														
All ages	**2,244**	**1,703**	**541**	**254**	**132**	**122**	**1,886**	**1,502**	**384**	**104**	**69**	**35**	**801**	**1,076**
0 - 15	65	26	39	5	2	3	43	18	25	17	6	11	3	33
16 - 17	96	51	45	2	-	2	93	51	42	1	-	1	8	81
18 - 29	738	494	244	118	62	56	592	413	179	28	19	9	132	493
30 - 44	448	355	93	32	21	11	396	321	75	20	13	7	218	234
45 - 59	434	385	49	19	13	6	386	349	37	29	23	6	213	158
60 - 64	149	135	14	11	6	5	131	122	9	7	7	-	80	31
65 - 74	223	189	34	38	16	22	183	172	11	2	1	1	104	32
75 - 84	78	59	19	22	9	13	56	50	6	-	-	-	35	13
85 and over	13	9	4	7	3	4	6	6	-	-	-	-	8	1
Other miscellaneous establishments														
All ages	**3,197**	**1,454**	**1,743**	**988**	**760**	**228**	**1,943**	**561**	**1,382**	**266**	**133**	**133**	**660**	**807**
0 - 15	392	202	190	83	42	41	301	154	147	8	6	2	24	208
16 - 17	102	62	40	51	50	1	51	12	39	-	-	-	11	41
18 - 29	972	590	382	533	436	97	399	133	266	40	21	19	81	322
30 - 44	456	282	174	223	179	44	178	67	111	55	36	19	43	107
45 - 59	360	122	238	50	37	13	225	49	176	85	36	49	74	59
60 - 64	140	48	92	10	9	1	106	26	80	24	13	11	30	15
65 - 74	302	72	230	17	4	13	258	56	202	27	12	15	98	29
75 - 84	358	64	294	15	2	13	318	55	263	25	7	18	205	20
85 and over	115	12	103	6	1	5	107	9	98	2	2	-	94	6

Table 3 Type of establishment, migrants and long-term illness – **continued**

Great Britain, England & Wales, England, regions, metropolitan counties, Inner London, Outer London, regional remainders, Wales, Scotland

Persons present in communal establishments

NORTH WEST REGION – *continued*

Type of establishment and age	PERSONS PRESENT			Visitors/guests			Residents - non-staff			Residents - staff			With limiting long-term illness	Migrants
	TOTAL	Males	Females	Total	Males	Females	Total	Males	Females	Total	Males	Females		
a	b	c	d	e	f	g	h	i	j	k	l	m	n	o
Persons sleeping rough														
All ages	**200**	**163**	**37**	**86**	**68**	**18**	**113**	**94**	**19**				**74**	**93**
0 - 15	-	-	-	-	-	-	-	-	-				-	-
16 - 17	1	1	-	-	-	-	1	1	-				-	1
18 - 29	71	57	14	31	25	6	40	32	8				17	29
30 - 44	61	48	13	25	18	7	36	30	6				23	30
45 - 59	59	49	10	28	23	5	30	25	5				27	28
60 - 64	5	5	-	2	2	-	3	3	-				4	2
65 - 74	3	3	-	-	-	-	3	3	-				3	3
75 - 84	-	-	-	-	-	-	-	-	-				-	-
85 and over	-	-	-	-	-	-	-	-	-				-	-
Campers														
All ages	**52**	**28**	**24**	**49**	**26**	**23**	**3**	**2**	**1**				**7**	**1**
0 - 15	4	2	2	4	2	2	-	-	-				-	-
16 - 17	-	-	-	-	-	-	-	-	-				-	-
18 - 29	2	1	1	1	-	1	1	1	-				-	1
30 - 44	9	5	4	9	5	4	-	-	-				-	-
45 - 59	25	13	12	23	12	11	2	1	1				4	-
60 - 64	4	2	2	4	2	2	-	-	-				1	-
65 - 74	5	3	2	5	3	2	-	-	-				1	-
75 - 84	3	2	1	3	2	1	-	-	-				1	-
85 and over	-	-	-	-	-	-	-	-	-				-	-

Table 3 Type of establishment, migrants and long-term illness – **continued**

Great Britain, England & Wales, England, regions, metropolitan counties, Inner London, Outer London, regional remainders, Wales, Scotland

Persons present in communal establishments

Type of establishment and age	PERSONS PRESENT			Visitors/guests			Residents - non-staff			Residents - staff			With limiting long-term illness	Migrants
	TOTAL	Males	Females	Total	Males	Females	Total	Males	Females	Total	Males	Females		
a	b	c	d	e	f	g	h	i	j	k	l	m	n	o

NORTH WEST REGION – *continued*

Civilian ships, boats and barges

All ages	**377**	**353**	**24**	**318**	**307**	**11**	**59**	**46**	**13**				**10**	**28**
0 - 15	13	9	4	2	2	-	11	7	4				1	7
16 - 17	8	4	4	2	2	-	6	2	4				-	4
18 - 29	76	70	6	58	54	4	18	16	2				2	6
30 - 44	173	168	5	159	155	4	14	13	1				4	6
45 - 59	101	96	5	91	88	3	10	8	2				3	5
60 - 64	6	6	-	6	6	-	-	-	-				-	-
65 - 74	-	-	-	-	-	-	-	-	-				-	-
75 - 84	-	-	-	-	-	-	-	-	-				-	-
85 and over	-	-	-	-	-	-	-	-	-				-	-

Greater Manchester Metropolitan County

All establishments

All ages	**46,085**	**18,478**	**27,607**	**18,795**	**9,206**	**9,589**	**25,385**	**8,576**	**16,809**	**1,905**	**696**	**1,209**	**27,594**	**9,470**
0 - 15	2,230	1,226	1,004	1,261	709	552	871	469	402	98	48	50	331	551
16 - 17	559	271	288	387	193	194	152	74	78	20	4	16	88	130
18 - 29	10,919	5,674	5,245	7,316	3,808	3,508	2,482	1,553	929	1,121	313	808	1,159	2,104
30 - 44	4,153	2,529	1,624	2,365	1,318	1,047	1,425	995	430	363	216	147	1,360	763
45 - 59	3,235	1,858	1,377	1,785	944	841	1,220	821	399	230	93	137	1,757	370
60 - 64	1,534	844	690	714	367	347	785	464	321	35	13	22	1,147	206
65 - 74	4,516	2,030	2,486	1,760	849	911	2,728	1,175	1,553	28	6	22	3,841	810
75 - 84	10,012	2,758	7,254	2,223	783	1,440	7,779	1,972	5,807	10	3	7	9,328	2,485
85 and over	8,927	1,288	7,639	984	235	749	7,943	1,053	6,890	-	-	-	8,583	2,051

Table 3 Type of establishment, migrants and long-term illness – continued

Persons present in communal establishments

Type of establishment and age	PERSONS PRESENT			Visitors/guests			Residents - non-staff			Residents - staff			With limiting long-term illness	Migrants
	TOTAL	Males	Females	Total	Males	Females	Total	Males	Females	Total	Males	Females		
a	b	c	d	e	f	g	h	i	j	k	l	m	n	o

Greater Manchester Metropolitan County – *continued*

NHS hospitals/homes - psychiatric

a	b	c	d	e	f	g	h	i	j	k	l	m	n	o
All ages	**781**	**369**	**412**	**185**	**97**	**88**	**589**	**269**	**320**	**7**	**3**	**4**	**736**	**135**
0 - 15	14	11	3	13	10	3	1	1	-	-	-	-	4	-
16 - 17	11	8	3	10	7	3	1	1	-	-	-	-	1	1
18 - 29	45	31	14	18	15	3	26	16	10	1	-	1	37	15
30 - 44	77	54	23	18	13	5	55	38	17	4	3	1	67	13
45 - 59	90	54	36	12	10	2	76	44	32	2	-	2	86	9
60 - 64	55	24	31	3	3	-	52	21	31	-	-	-	55	4
65 - 74	154	70	84	30	12	18	124	58	66	-	-	-	152	25
75 - 84	219	89	130	52	18	34	167	71	96	-	-	-	219	48
85 and over	116	28	88	29	9	20	87	19	68	-	-	-	115	20

NHS hospitals/homes - other

a	b	c	d	e	f	g	h	i	j	k	l	m	n	o
All ages	**11,117**	**4,331**	**6,786**	**8,574**	**3,405**	**5,169**	**1,439**	**573**	**866**	**1,104**	**353**	**751**	**6,152**	**960**
0 - 15	813	426	387	765	402	363	22	11	11	26	13	13	124	21
16 - 17	81	27	54	76	25	51	4	2	2	1	-	1	25	2
18 - 29	2,697	774	1,923	1,529	452	1,077	288	114	174	880	208	672	323	579
30 - 44	1,265	593	672	947	377	570	148	95	53	170	121	49	480	144
45 - 59	1,146	558	588	997	480	517	125	68	57	24	10	14	780	36
60 - 64	547	281	266	492	246	246	53	34	19	2	1	1	434	6
65 - 74	1,516	735	781	1,344	647	697	172	88	84	-	-	-	1,258	37
75 - 84	2,048	715	1,333	1,704	605	1,099	343	110	233	1	-	1	1,806	85
85 and over	1,004	222	782	720	171	549	284	51	233	-	-	-	922	50

Table 3 Type of establishment, migrants and long-term illness – **continued**

Great Britain, England & Wales, England, regions, metropolitan counties, Inner London, Outer London, regional remainders, Wales, Scotland

Persons present in communal establishments

Type of establishment and age	PERSONS PRESENT			Visitors/guests			Residents - non-staff			Residents - staff			With limiting long-term illness	Migrants
	TOTAL	Males	Females	Total	Males	Females	Total	Males	Females	Total	Males	Females		
a	b	c	d	e	f	g	h	i	j	k	l	m	n	o
Greater Manchester Metropolitan County – *continued*														
Non-NHS hospitals - psychiatric														
All ages	**237**	**110**	**127**	**108**	**38**	**70**	**126**	**71**	**55**	**3**	**1**	**2**	**188**	**29**
0 - 15	3	1	2	2	-	2	1	1	-	-	-	-	2	-
16 - 17	2	1	1	2	1	1	-	-	-	-	-	-	1	-
18 - 29	45	20	25	31	11	20	11	8	3	3	1	2	24	7
30 - 44	40	22	18	27	11	16	13	11	2	-	-	-	28	8
45 - 59	33	16	17	24	9	15	9	7	2	-	-	-	22	-
60 - 64	17	6	11	9	3	6	8	3	5	-	-	-	15	4
65 - 74	33	19	14	6	3	3	27	16	11	-	-	-	33	2
75 - 84	45	21	24	5	-	5	40	21	19	-	-	-	44	6
85 and over	19	4	15	2	-	2	17	4	13	-	-	-	19	2
Non-NHS hospitals - other														
All ages	**1,060**	**395**	**665**	**878**	**327**	**551**	**140**	**46**	**94**	**42**	**22**	**20**	**578**	**63**
0 - 15	67	37	30	67	37	30	-	-	-	-	-	-	6	-
16 - 17	10	2	8	9	2	7	1	-	1	-	-	-	2	1
18 - 29	172	30	142	135	18	117	8	1	7	29	11	18	13	21
30 - 44	173	64	109	155	49	106	5	4	1	13	11	2	54	9
45 - 59	140	62	78	134	59	75	6	3	3	-	-	-	77	2
60 - 64	66	35	31	53	27	26	13	8	5	-	-	-	51	1
65 - 74	149	76	73	117	64	53	32	12	20	-	-	-	119	8
75 - 84	201	69	132	154	56	98	47	13	34	-	-	-	183	16
85 and over	82	20	62	54	15	39	28	5	23	-	-	-	73	5

Table 3 Type of establishment, migrants and long-term illness – **continued**

Persons present in communal establishments

Type of establishment and age	PERSONS PRESENT			Visitors/guests			Residents - non-staff			Residents - staff			With limiting long-term illness	Migrants
	TOTAL	Males	Females	Total	Males	Females	Total	Males	Females	Total	Males	Females		
a	b	c	d	e	f	g	h	i	j	k	l	m	n	o

Greater Manchester Metropolitan County – *continued*

Local authority homes

All ages	**5,826**	**1,699**	**4,127**	**472**	**194**	**278**	**5,348**	**1,505**	**3,843**	**6**	**-**	**-**	**5,556**	**1,104**
0 - 15	82	53	29	58	40	18	24	13	11	-	-	-	62	8
16 - 17	33	21	12	23	16	7	10	5	5	-	-	-	28	4
18 - 29	318	209	109	89	54	35	228	155	73	1	-	-	270	68
30 - 44	282	137	145	49	18	31	233	119	114	-	-	-	248	34
45 - 59	252	113	139	32	8	24	215	105	110	5	-	5	226	22
60 - 64	149	73	76	9	1	8	140	72	68	-	-	-	142	30
65 - 74	688	269	419	41	15	26	647	254	393	-	-	-	664	143
75 - 84	2,022	531	1,491	106	31	75	1,916	500	1,416	-	-	-	1,955	447
85 and over	2,000	293	1,707	65	11	54	1,935	282	1,653	-	-	-	1,961	348

Housing association homes and hostels

All ages	**488**	**251**	**237**	**60**	**41**	**19**	**410**	**207**	**203**	**18**	**3**	**3**	**273**	**174**
0 - 15	-	-	-	-	-	-	-	-	-	-	-	-	-	-
16 - 17	7	1	6	-	-	-	7	1	6	-	-	-	1	7
18 - 29	78	57	21	13	9	4	63	47	16	2	1	1	15	54
30 - 44	85	64	21	38	26	12	44	38	6	3	-	3	24	37
45 - 59	55	47	8	5	5	-	40	40	-	10	2	8	34	25
60 - 64	13	11	2	-	-	-	12	11	1	1	-	1	8	6
65 - 74	39	21	18	2	1	1	35	20	15	2	-	2	24	4
75 - 84	104	34	70	1	-	1	103	34	69	-	-	-	83	22
85 and over	107	16	91	1	-	1	106	16	90	-	-	-	84	19

Table 3 Type of establishment, migrants and long-term illness – **continued**

Great Britain, England & Wales, England, regions, metropolitan counties, Inner London, Outer London, regional remainders, Wales, Scotland

Persons present in communal establishments

Type of establishment and age	PERSONS PRESENT			Visitors/guests			Residents - non-staff			Residents - staff			With limiting long-term illness	Migrants
	TOTAL	Males	Females	Total	Males	Females	Total	Males	Females	Total	Males	Females		
a	b	c	d	e	f	g	h	i	j	k	l	m	n	o
Greater Manchester Metropolitan County – *continued*														
Nursing homes (non-NHS/LA/HA)														
All ages	**6,340**	**1,642**	**4,698**	**228**	**70**	**158**	**6,059**	**1,562**	**4,497**	**53**	**10**	**43**	**6,130**	**2,449**
0 - 15	11	5	6	-	-	-	7	4	3	4	1	3	3	5
16 - 17	6	1	5	1	-	1	3	1	2	2	-	2	3	2
18 - 29	26	8	18	7	-	7	7	5	2	12	3	9	7	9
30 - 44	62	23	39	25	2	23	26	18	8	11	3	8	30	11
45 - 59	85	44	41	25	9	16	49	33	16	11	2	9	64	19
60 - 64	225	125	100	14	7	7	205	118	87	6	-	6	206	82
65 - 74	817	352	465	33	15	18	778	336	442	6	1	5	792	356
75 - 84	2,649	703	1,946	79	22	57	2,569	681	1,888	1	-	1	2,591	1,090
85 and over	2,459	381	2,078	44	15	29	2,415	366	2,049	-	-	-	2,434	875
Residential homes (non-NHS/LA/HA)														
All ages	**7,187**	**1,524**	**5,663**	**221**	**53**	**168**	**6,799**	**1,423**	**5,376**	**167**	**48**	**119**	**6,606**	**1,871**
0 - 15	15	9	6	2	1	1	7	6	1	6	2	4	5	4
16 - 17	7	3	4	-	-	-	3	2	1	4	1	3	3	2
18 - 29	164	87	77	25	7	18	107	73	34	32	7	25	106	50
30 - 44	233	121	112	32	5	27	160	102	58	41	14	27	175	38
45 - 59	262	121	141	31	4	27	167	95	72	64	22	42	169	40
60 - 64	185	102	83	8	3	5	167	97	70	10	2	8	159	44
65 - 74	729	257	472	24	10	14	698	247	451	7	-	7	682	209
75 - 84	2,503	510	1,993	43	14	29	2,457	496	1,961	3	-	3	2,364	755
85 and over	3,089	314	2,775	56	9	47	3,033	305	2,728	-	-	-	2,943	729

Table 3 Type of establishment, migrants and long-term illness – **continued**

Great Britain, England & Wales, England, regions, metropolitan counties, Inner London, Outer London, regional remainders, Wales, Scotland

Persons present in communal establishments

Type of establishment and age	PERSONS PRESENT			Visitors/guests			Residents - non-staff			Residents - staff			With limiting long-term illness	Migrants
	TOTAL	Males	Females	Total	Males	Females	Total	Males	Females	Total	Males	Females		
a	b	c	d	e	f	g	h	i	j	k	l	m	n	o
Greater Manchester Metropolitan County – *continued*														
Children's homes														
All ages	**764**	**409**	**355**	**159**	**79**	**80**	**560**	**312**	**248**	**45**	**18**	**27**	**113**	**341**
0 - 15	683	382	301	116	67	49	560	312	248	7	3	4	98	334
16 - 17	4	-	4	-	-	-	-	-	-	4	-	4	-	3
18 - 29	37	16	21	20	7	13	-	-	-	17	9	8	12	4
30 - 44	20	5	15	13	2	11	-	-	-	7	3	4	2	-
45 - 59	19	5	14	9	2	7	-	-	-	10	3	7	1	-
60 - 64	1	1	-	1	1	-	-	-	-	-	-	-	-	-
65 - 74	-	-	-	-	-	-	-	-	-	-	-	-	-	-
75 - 84	-	-	-	-	-	-	-	-	-	-	-	-	-	-
85 and over	-	-	-	-	-	-	-	-	-	-	-	-	-	-
Prison service establishments														
All ages	**567**	**566**	**1**	**503**	**502**	**1**	**64**	**64**	**-**	**-**	**-**	**-**	**77**	**28**
0 - 15	2	2	-	2	2	-	-	-	-	-	-	-	-	-
16 - 17	62	62	-	58	58	-	4	4	-	-	-	-	6	1
18 - 29	429	429	-	376	376	-	53	53	-	-	-	-	57	24
30 - 44	54	53	1	48	47	1	6	6	-	-	-	-	9	3
45 - 59	17	17	-	16	16	-	1	1	-	-	-	-	3	-
60 - 64	1	1	-	1	1	-	-	-	-	-	-	-	1	-
65 - 74	1	1	-	1	1	-	-	-	-	-	-	-	1	-
75 - 84	1	1	-	1	1	-	-	-	-	-	-	-	-	-
85 and over	-	-	-	-	-	-	-	-	-	-	-	-	-	-

Table 3 Type of establishment, migrants and long-term illness – **continued**

Great Britain, England & Wales, England, regions, metropolitan counties, Inner London, Outer London, regional remainders, Wales, Scotland

Persons present in communal establishments

Type of establishment and age	PERSONS PRESENT			Visitors/guests			Residents - non-staff			Residents - staff			With limiting long-term illness	Migrants
	TOTAL	Males	Females	Total	Males	Females	Total	Males	Females	Total	Males	Females		
a	b	c	d	e	f	g	h	i	j	k	l	m	n	o

Greater Manchester Metropolitan County – *continued*

Defence establishments

Type of establishment and age	b	c	d	e	f	g	h	i	j	k	l	m	n	o
All ages	**13**	**12**	**1**	**3**	**3**	**-**	**10**	**9**	**1**				**1**	**7**
0 - 15	-	-	-	-	-	-	-	-	-				-	-
16 - 17	-	-	-	-	-	-	-	-	-				-	-
18 - 29	4	4	-	-	-	-	4	4	-				-	4
30 - 44	8	7	1	2	2	-	6	5	1				1	3
45 - 59	1	1	-	1	1	-	-	-	-				-	-
60 - 64	-	-	-	-	-	-	-	-	-				-	-
65 - 74	-	-	-	-	-	-	-	-	-				-	-
75 - 84	-	-	-	-	-	-	-	-	-				-	-
85 and over	-	-	-	-	-	-	-	-	-				-	-

Educational establishments

Type of establishment and age	b	c	d	e	f	g	h	i	j	k	l	m	n	o
All ages	**5,226**	**2,849**	**2,377**	**4,253**	**2,259**	**1,994**	**876**	**549**	**327**	**97**	**41**	**56**	**124**	**596**
0 - 15	153	88	65	130	74	56	15	9	6	8	5	3	5	9
16 - 17	176	52	124	166	47	119	9	5	4	1	-	1	1	8
18 - 29	4,320	2,374	1,946	3,640	1,935	1,705	643	427	216	37	12	25	75	466
30 - 44	398	265	133	238	159	79	136	94	42	24	12	12	11	90
45 - 59	111	55	56	67	38	29	28	9	19	16	8	8	4	16
60 - 64	13	5	8	2	1	1	7	2	5	4	2	2	3	1
65 - 74	22	5	17	6	3	3	11	1	10	5	1	4	5	3
75 - 84	25	4	21	4	2	2	19	1	18	2	1	1	14	1
85 and over	8	1	7	-	-	-	8	1	7	-	-	-	6	2

Table 3 Type of establishment, migrants and long-term illness – **continued**

Great Britain, England & Wales, England, regions, metropolitan counties, Inner London, Outer London, regional remainders, Wales, Scotland

Persons present in communal establishments

Type of establishment and age	PERSONS PRESENT			Visitors/guests			Residents - non-staff			Residents - staff			With limiting long-term illness	Migrants
	TOTAL	Males	Females	Total	Males	Females	Total	Males	Females	Total	Males	Females		
a	b	c	d	e	f	g	h	i	j	k	l	m	n	o
Greater Manchester Metropolitan County – continued														
Hotels, boarding houses etc														
All ages	**4,194**	**2,872**	**1,322**	**2,700**	**1,765**	**935**	**1,237**	**971**	**266**	**257**	**136**	**121**	**482**	**706**
0 - 15	161	101	60	70	57	13	55	24	31	36	20	16	12	43
16 - 17	51	33	18	13	10	3	31	20	11	7	3	4	4	29
18 - 29	1,815	1,149	666	1,186	711	475	537	385	152	92	53	39	96	371
30 - 44	1,037	812	225	679	526	153	296	254	42	62	32	30	109	174
45 - 59	677	510	167	406	284	122	220	203	17	51	23	28	155	75
60 - 64	153	98	55	113	65	48	36	31	5	4	2	2	35	7
65 - 74	200	116	84	148	73	75	47	40	7	5	3	2	50	4
75 - 84	84	44	40	73	34	39	11	10	1	-	-	-	19	2
85 and over	16	9	7	12	5	7	4	4	-	-	-	-	2	1
Hostels and common lodging houses (non-HA)														
All ages	**1,028**	**841**	**187**	**58**	**48**	**10**	**926**	**768**	**158**	**44**	**25**	**19**	**363**	**560**
0 - 15	14	3	11	1	1	-	5	-	5	8	2	6	1	8
16 - 17	55	27	28	2	-	2	52	27	25	1	-	1	3	47
18 - 29	326	237	89	26	23	3	291	210	81	9	4	5	66	254
30 - 44	220	185	35	16	13	3	194	167	27	10	5	5	102	124
45 - 59	221	202	19	8	6	2	200	185	15	13	11	2	108	89
60 - 64	70	68	2	2	2	-	65	63	2	3	3	-	33	17
65 - 74	96	93	3	3	3	-	93	90	3	-	-	-	43	14
75 - 84	26	26	-	-	-	-	26	26	-	-	-	-	7	7
85 and over	-	-	-	-	-	-	-	-	-	-	-	-	-	-

Table 3 Type of establishment, migrants and long-term illness – **continued**

Persons present in communal establishments

Type of establishment and age	PERSONS PRESENT			Visitors/guests			Residents - non-staff			Residents - staff			With limiting long-term illness	Migrants
	TOTAL	Males	Females	Total	Males	Females	Total	Males	Females	Total	Males	Females		
a	b	c	d	e	f	g	h	i	j	k	l	m	n	o
Greater Manchester Metropolitan County – *continued*														
Other miscellaneous establishments														
All ages	**1,218**	**575**	**643**	**379**	**314**	**65**	**777**	**225**	**552**	**62**	**36**	**26**	**206**	**427**
0 - 15	212	108	104	35	18	17	174	88	86	3	2	1	9	119
16 - 17	54	33	21	27	27	-	27	6	21	-	-	-	10	23
18 - 29	426	235	191	213	183	30	207	48	159	6	4	2	55	171
30 - 44	189	115	74	76	67	9	95	36	59	18	12	6	17	69
45 - 59	115	44	71	15	11	4	76	21	55	24	12	12	25	30
60 - 64	38	13	25	6	6	-	27	4	23	5	3	2	5	4
65 - 74	72	16	56	5	2	3	64	13	51	3	1	2	18	5
75 - 84	85	11	74	1	-	1	81	9	72	3	2	1	43	6
85 and over	27	-	27	1	-	1	26	-	26	-	-	-	24	-
Persons sleeping rough														
All ages	**39**	**33**	**6**	**14**	**11**	**3**	**25**	**22**	**3**				**9**	**20**
0 - 15	-	-	-	-	-	-	-	-	-				-	-
16 - 17	-	-	-	-	-	-	-	-	-				-	-
18 - 29	17	14	3	8	7	1	9	7	2				3	7
30 - 44	10	9	1	2	1	1	8	8	-				3	6
45 - 59	11	9	2	3	2	1	8	7	1				3	7
60 - 64	1	1	-	1	1	-	-	-	-				-	-
65 - 74	-	-	-	-	-	-	-	-	-				-	-
75 - 84	-	-	-	-	-	-	-	-	-				-	-
85 and over	-	-	-	-	-	-	-	-	-				-	-

Table 3 Type of establishment, migrants and long-term illness – **continued**

Great Britain, England & Wales, England, regions, metropolitan counties, Inner London, Outer London, regional remainders, Wales, Scotland

Persons present in communal establishments

Greater Manchester Metropolitan County – *continued*

Type of establishment and age	PERSONS PRESENT			Visitors/guests			Residents - non-staff			Residents - staff			With limiting long-term illness	Migrants
	TOTAL	Males	Females	Total	Males	Females	Total	Males	Females	Total	Males	Females		
a	b	c	d	e	f	g	h	i	j	k	l	m	n	o
Campers														
All ages	-	-	-	-	-	-	-	-	-				-	-
0 - 15	-	-	-	-	-	-	-	-	-				-	-
16 - 17	-	-	-	-	-	-	-	-	-				-	-
18 - 29	-	-	-	-	-	-	-	-	-				-	-
30 - 44	-	-	-	-	-	-	-	-	-				-	-
45 - 59	-	-	-	-	-	-	-	-	-				-	-
60 - 64	-	-	-	-	-	-	-	-	-				-	-
65 - 74	-	-	-	-	-	-	-	-	-				-	-
75 - 84	-	-	-	-	-	-	-	-	-				-	-
85 and over	-	-	-	-	-	-	-	-	-				-	-
Civilian ships, boats and barges														
All ages	-	-	-	-	-	-	-	-	-				-	-
0 - 15	-	-	-	-	-	-	-	-	-				-	-
16 - 17	-	-	-	-	-	-	-	-	-				-	-
18 - 29	-	-	-	-	-	-	-	-	-				-	-
30 - 44	-	-	-	-	-	-	-	-	-				-	-
45 - 59	-	-	-	-	-	-	-	-	-				-	-
60 - 64	-	-	-	-	-	-	-	-	-				-	-
65 - 74	-	-	-	-	-	-	-	-	-				-	-
75 - 84	-	-	-	-	-	-	-	-	-				-	-
85 and over	-	-	-	-	-	-	-	-	-				-	-

Table 3 Type of establishment, migrants and long-term illness – **continued**

Great Britain, England & Wales, England, regions, metropolitan counties, Inner London, Outer London, regional remainders, Wales, Scotland

Persons present in communal establishments

Type of establishment and age	PERSONS PRESENT			Visitors/guests			Residents - non-staff			Residents - staff			With limiting long-term illness	Migrants
	TOTAL	Males	Females	Total	Males	Females	Total	Males	Females	Total	Males	Females		
a	b	c	d	e	f	g	h	i	j	k	l	m	n	o
All establishments														
All ages	**34,344**	**14,229**	**20,115**	**12,562**	**6,419**	**6,143**	**20,291**	**7,218**	**13,073**	**1,491**	**592**	**899**	**21,120**	**6,363**
0 - 15	1,502	820	682	796	439	357	620	331	289	86	50	36	128	290
16 - 17	176	97	79	69	36	33	92	54	38	15	7	8	41	66
18 - 29	7,768	4,067	3,701	5,408	2,799	2,609	1,651	1,054	597	709	214	495	1,100	1,157
30 - 44	3,364	2,259	1,105	1,584	998	586	1,499	1,091	408	281	170	111	1,486	536
45 - 59	2,625	1,612	1,013	1,169	688	481	1,203	823	380	253	101	152	1,498	251
60 - 64	1,228	649	579	456	252	204	720	375	345	52	22	30	921	181
65 - 74	3,648	1,621	2,027	1,154	560	594	2,440	1,044	1,396	54	17	37	3,036	680
75 - 84	7,425	2,055	5,370	1,336	507	829	6,055	1,542	4,513	34	6	28	6,732	1,777
85 and over	6,608	1,049	5,559	590	140	450	6,011	904	5,107	7	5	2	6,178	1,425
NHS hospitals/homes - psychiatric														
All ages	**1,510**	**995**	**515**	**583**	**297**	**286**	**868**	**658**	**210**	**59**	**40**	**19**	**1,295**	**108**
0 - 15	5	4	1	4	3	1	1	1	-	-	-	-	2	-
16 - 17	2	-	2	2	-	2	-	-	-	-	-	-	-	-
18 - 29	296	205	91	60	27	33	204	161	43	32	17	15	232	44
30 - 44	400	334	66	69	43	26	311	273	38	20	18	2	350	35
45 - 59	261	186	75	101	52	49	155	131	24	5	3	2	229	9
60 - 64	85	55	30	52	29	23	31	24	7	2	2	-	72	1
65 - 74	181	104	77	121	69	52	60	35	25	-	-	-	154	7
75 - 84	199	86	113	131	63	68	68	23	45	-	-	-	182	8
85 and over	81	21	60	43	11	32	38	10	28	-	-	-	74	4

Merseyside Metropolitan County

Table 3 Type of establishment, migrants and long-term illness – **continued**

Great Britain, England & Wales, England, regions, metropolitan counties, Inner London, Outer London, regional remainders, Wales, Scotland

Persons present in communal establishments

Type of establishment and age	PERSONS PRESENT			Visitors/guests			Residents - non-staff			Residents - staff			With limiting long-term illness	Migrants
	TOTAL	Males	Females	Total	Males	Females	Total	Males	Females	Total	Males	Females		
a	b	c	d	e	f	g	h	i	j	k	l	m	n	o

Merseyside Metropolitan County – *continued*

NHS hospitals/homes - other

All ages	5,615	2,226	3,389	4,536	1,860	2,676	475	175	300	604	191	413	3,159	470
0 - 15	544	294	250	531	285	246	9	7	2	4	2	2	40	1
16 - 17	30	12	18	26	12	14	3	-	3	1	-	1	14	3
18 - 29	1,206	341	865	631	192	439	88	32	56	487	117	370	191	288
30 - 44	671	296	375	511	197	314	62	31	31	98	68	30	267	88
45 - 59	548	262	286	489	236	253	46	22	24	13	4	9	402	18
60 - 64	275	152	123	265	147	118	10	5	5	-	-	-	218	4
65 - 74	838	399	439	765	367	398	73	32	41	-	-	-	699	22
75 - 84	1,010	370	640	925	336	589	85	34	51	-	-	-	885	27
85 and over	493	100	393	393	88	305	99	12	87	1	-	1	443	19

Non-NHS hospitals - psychiatric

All ages	83	51	32	30	15	15	53	36	17	-	-	-	82	24
0 - 15	-	-	-	-	-	-	-	-	-	-	-	-	-	-
16 - 17	1	-	1	1	-	1	-	-	-	-	-	-	1	-
18 - 29	8	6	2	5	5	-	3	1	2	-	-	-	8	1
30 - 44	19	10	9	8	3	5	11	7	4	-	-	-	19	2
45 - 59	19	13	6	5	2	3	14	11	3	-	-	-	19	4
60 - 64	6	5	1	4	3	1	2	2	-	-	-	-	5	1
65 - 74	11	7	4	2	1	1	9	6	3	-	-	-	11	5
75 - 84	15	9	6	3	-	3	12	9	3	-	-	-	15	9
85 and over	4	1	3	2	1	1	2	-	2	-	-	-	4	2

Table 3 Type of establishment, migrants and long-term illness – **continued**

Great Britain, England & Wales, England, regions, metropolitan counties, Inner London, Outer London, regional remainders, Wales, Scotland

Persons present in communal establishments

Type of establishment and age	PERSONS PRESENT			Visitors/guests			Residents - non-staff			Residents - staff			With limiting long-term illness	Migrants
	TOTAL	Males	Females	Total	Males	Females	Total	Males	Females	Total	Males	Females		
a	b	c	d	e	f	g	h	i	j	k	l	m	n	o
Merseyside Metropolitan County – *continued*														
Non-NHS hospitals - other														
All ages	**407**	**132**	**275**	**268**	**94**	**174**	**120**	**35**	**85**	**19**	**3**	**16**	**294**	**47**
0 - 15	15	10	5	14	9	5	1	1	-	-	-	-	1	1
16 - 17	2	1	1	1	-	1	1	1	-	-	-	-	1	1
18 - 29	51	12	39	29	7	22	6	3	3	16	2	14	12	9
30 - 44	43	14	29	36	10	26	6	3	3	1	1	-	15	6
45 - 59	31	10	21	27	9	18	2	1	1	2	-	2	15	1
60 - 64	18	10	8	16	8	8	2	2	-	-	-	-	12	-
65 - 74	54	24	30	36	14	22	18	10	8	-	-	-	51	3
75 - 84	107	41	66	69	29	40	38	12	26	-	-	-	101	12
85 and over	86	10	76	40	8	32	46	2	44	-	-	-	86	14
Local authority homes														
All ages	**3,935**	**1,374**	**2,561**	**315**	**135**	**180**	**3,563**	**1,222**	**2,341**	**57**	**17**	**40**	**3,377**	**667**
0 - 15	119	83	36	62	38	24	53	43	10	4	2	2	40	20
16 - 17	42	30	12	10	7	3	32	23	9	-	-	-	12	20
18 - 29	313	127	186	79	31	48	198	87	111	36	9	27	149	82
30 - 44	249	144	105	42	16	26	198	124	74	9	4	5	202	34
45 - 59	255	155	100	18	4	14	232	150	82	5	1	4	236	12
60 - 64	143	82	61	8	3	5	134	79	55	1	-	1	133	26
65 - 74	552	249	303	26	11	15	525	238	287	1	-	1	506	114
75 - 84	1,185	332	853	33	16	17	1,152	316	836	-	-	-	1,099	214
85 and over	1,077	172	905	37	9	28	1,039	162	877	1	1	-	1,000	145

Table 3　Type of establishment, migrants and long-term illness – **continued**

Great Britain, England & Wales, England, regions, metropolitan counties, Inner London, Outer London, regional remainders, Wales, Scotland

Persons present in communal establishments

Type of establishment and age	PERSONS PRESENT			Visitors/guests			Residents - non-staff			Residents - staff			With limiting long-term illness	Migrants
	TOTAL	Males	Females	Total	Males	Females	Total	Males	Females	Total	Males	Females		
a	b	c	d	e	f	g	h	i	j	k	l	m	n	o

Merseyside Metropolitan County – *continued*

Housing association homes and hostels

All ages	**310**	**63**	**247**	**6**	**-**	**6**	**294**	**61**	**233**	**10**	**2**	**8**	**279**	**114**
0 - 15	2	1	1	-	-	-	-	-	-	2	1	1	-	-
16 - 17	1	1	-	-	-	-	1	1	-	-	-	-	1	-
18 - 29	17	6	11	1	-	1	16	6	10	-	-	-	16	6
30 - 44	18	7	11	2	-	2	12	7	5	4	-	4	12	2
45 - 59	13	2	11	1	-	1	10	1	9	2	1	1	9	1
60 - 64	7	2	5	-	-	-	6	2	4	1	-	1	6	3
65 - 74	30	14	16	-	-	-	29	14	15	1	-	1	29	11
75 - 84	98	12	86	1	-	1	97	12	85	-	-	-	88	46
85 and over	124	18	106	1	-	1	123	18	105	-	-	-	118	45

Nursing homes (non-NHS/ LA/HA)

All ages	**7,154**	**1,795**	**5,359**	**298**	**95**	**203**	**6,766**	**1,675**	**5,091**	**90**	**25**	**65**	**6,728**	**2,353**
0 - 15	12	4	8	1	-	1	2	2	-	9	4	5	1	1
16 - 17	3	1	2	1	-	1	-	-	-	2	1	1	-	-
18 - 29	90	35	55	32	4	28	47	27	20	11	4	7	51	21
30 - 44	159	71	88	43	9	34	102	60	42	14	2	12	113	38
45 - 59	150	71	79	28	6	22	87	55	32	35	10	25	98	40
60 - 64	245	114	131	28	8	20	208	103	105	9	3	6	218	70
65 - 74	967	389	578	69	32	37	893	356	537	5	1	4	907	329
75 - 84	2,730	686	2,044	61	23	38	2,664	663	2,001	5	-	5	2,618	1,010
85 and over	2,798	424	2,374	35	13	22	2,763	411	2,352	-	-	-	2,722	845

Table 3 Type of establishment, migrants and long-term illness – **continued**

Great Britain, England & Wales, England, regions, metropolitan counties, Inner London, Outer London, regional remainders, Wales, Scotland

Persons present in communal establishments

Type of establishment and age	PERSONS PRESENT			Visitors/guests			Residents - non-staff			Residents - staff			With limiting long-term illness	Migrants
	TOTAL	Males	Females	Total	Males	Females	Total	Males	Females	Total	Males	Females		
a	b	c	d	e	f	g	h	i	j	k	l	m	n	o

Merseyside Metropolitan County – *continued*

Residential homes (non-NHS/LA/HA)

	TOTAL	Males	Females	Total	Males	Females	Total	Males	Females	Total	Males	Females	n	o
All ages	5,239	1,475	3,764	134	30	104	4,942	1,373	3,569	163	72	91	4,592	1,137
0 - 15	24	18	6	-	-	-	2	2	-	22	16	6	1	3
16 - 17	6	4	2	-	-	-	2	1	1	4	3	1	2	1
18 - 29	200	109	91	21	4	17	148	93	55	31	12	19	149	52
30 - 44	318	185	133	20	6	14	262	164	98	36	15	21	268	64
45 - 59	313	173	140	17	2	15	241	149	92	55	22	33	243	39
60 - 64	195	72	123	2	-	2	185	70	115	8	2	6	167	53
65 - 74	617	232	385	14	4	10	597	227	370	6	1	5	548	151
75 - 84	1,746	409	1,337	36	11	25	1,710	398	1,312	-	-	-	1,571	430
85 and over	1,820	273	1,547	24	3	21	1,795	269	1,526	1	1	-	1,643	344

Children's homes

	TOTAL	Males	Females	Total	Males	Females	Total	Males	Females	Total	Males	Females	n	o
All ages	514	247	267	95	49	46	387	191	196	32	7	25	24	150
0 - 15	459	236	223	70	44	26	387	191	196	2	1	1	16	143
16 - 17	1	-	1	-	-	-	-	-	-	1	-	1	-	1
18 - 29	8	5	3	5	3	2	-	-	-	3	2	1	-	1
30 - 44	14	4	10	10	2	8	-	-	-	4	2	2	-	1
45 - 59	14	-	14	9	-	9	-	-	-	5	-	5	-	-
60 - 64	5	1	4	-	-	-	-	-	-	5	1	4	1	1
65 - 74	5	-	5	1	-	1	-	-	-	4	-	4	2	1
75 - 84	6	-	6	-	-	-	-	-	-	6	-	6	3	1
85 and over	2	1	1	-	-	-	-	-	-	2	1	1	1	1

Table 3 Type of establishment, migrants and long-term illness – **continued**

Great Britain, England & Wales, England, regions, metropolitan counties, Inner London, Outer London, regional remainders, Wales, Scotland

Persons present in communal establishments

Merseyside Metropolitan County – *continued*

Type of establishment and age	PERSONS PRESENT			Visitors/guests			Residents - non-staff			Residents - staff			With limiting long-term illness	Migrants
	TOTAL	Males	Females	Total	Males	Females	Total	Males	Females	Total	Males	Females		
a	b	c	d	e	f	g	h	i	j	k	l	m	n	o
Prison service establishments														
All ages	**1,164**	**1,164**	**-**	**888**	**888**	**-**	**275**	**275**	**-**	**1**	**1**	**1**	**207**	**143**
0 - 15	1	1	-	-	-	-	-	-	-	1	1	-	-	1
16 - 17	-	-	-	-	-	-	-	-	-	-	-	-	-	-
18 - 29	696	696	-	552	552	-	144	144	-	-	-	-	91	84
30 - 44	337	337	-	252	252	-	85	85	-	-	-	-	66	41
45 - 59	112	112	-	74	74	-	38	38	-	-	-	-	42	14
60 - 64	10	10	-	4	4	-	6	6	-	-	-	-	4	3
65 - 74	6	6	-	6	6	-	-	-	-	-	-	-	4	-
75 - 84	2	2	-	-	-	-	2	2	-	-	-	-	-	-
85 and over	-	-	-	-	-	-	-	-	-	-	-	-	-	-
Defence establishments														
All ages	**31**	**29**	**2**	**9**	**9**	**-**	**22**	**20**	**2**				**2**	**10**
0 - 15	-	-	-	-	-	-	-	-	-				-	-
16 - 17	-	-	-	-	-	-	-	-	-				-	-
18 - 29	6	6	-	-	-	-	6	6	-				1	4
30 - 44	20	19	1	7	7	-	13	12	1				1	5
45 - 59	5	4	1	2	2	-	3	3	1				-	1
60 - 64	-	-	-	-	-	-	-	-	-				-	-
65 - 74	-	-	-	-	-	-	-	-	-				-	-
75 - 84	-	-	-	-	-	-	-	-	-				-	-
85 and over	-	-	-	-	-	-	-	-	-				-	-

Table 3 Type of establishment, migrants and long-term illness – **continued**

Great Britain, England & Wales, England, regions, metropolitan counties, Inner London, Outer London, regional remainders, Wales, Scotland

Persons present in communal establishments

Type of establishment and age	PERSONS PRESENT			Visitors/guests			Residents - non-staff			Residents - staff			With limiting long-term illness	Migrants
	TOTAL	Males	Females	Total	Males	Females	Total	Males	Females	Total	Males	Females		
a	b	c	d	e	f	g	h	i	j	k	l	m	n	o
Educational establishments														
All ages	**4,068**	**1,996**	**2,072**	**3,502**	**1,650**	**1,852**	**483**	**302**	**181**	**83**	**44**	**39**	**142**	**320**
0 - 15	99	43	56	55	31	24	36	8	28	8	4	4	12	29
16 - 17	30	14	16	12	5	7	17	8	9	1	1	-	5	7
18 - 29	3,725	1,801	1,924	3,369	1,574	1,795	330	212	118	26	15	11	110	226
30 - 44	157	115	42	53	37	16	78	64	14	26	14	12	10	53
45 - 59	31	11	20	11	1	10	9	6	3	11	4	7	3	5
60 - 64	3	2	1	-	-	-	1	-	1	2	2	-	1	-
65 - 74	12	6	6	1	1	-	4	3	1	7	2	5	1	-
75 - 84	7	3	4	-	-	-	5	1	4	2	2	-	-	-
85 and over	4	1	3	1	1	-	3	-	3	-	-	-	-	-

Merseyside Metropolitan County – *continued*

Type of establishment and age	PERSONS PRESENT			Visitors/guests			Residents - non-staff			Residents - staff			With limiting long-term illness	Migrants
	TOTAL	Males	Females	Total	Males	Females	Total	Males	Females	Total	Males	Females		
b	c	d	e	f	g	h	i	j	k	l	m	n	o	
Hotels, boarding houses etc														
All ages	**2,319**	**1,563**	**756**	**1,319**	**872**	**447**	**810**	**589**	**221**	**190**	**102**	**88**	**372**	**350**
0 - 15	123	76	47	25	14	11	72	48	24	26	14	12	6	49
16 - 17	26	10	16	5	1	4	15	7	8	6	2	4	1	16
18 - 29	652	400	252	382	241	141	221	132	89	49	27	22	33	161
30 - 44	561	442	119	353	272	81	172	146	26	36	24	12	65	66
45 - 59	505	385	120	290	214	76	158	142	16	57	29	28	103	39
60 - 64	123	81	42	71	44	27	45	34	11	7	3	4	40	4
65 - 74	178	108	70	110	54	56	61	51	10	7	3	4	49	8
75 - 84	110	51	59	71	27	44	37	24	13	2	-	2	49	7
85 and over	41	10	31	12	5	7	29	5	24	-	-	-	26	-

Table 3 Type of establishment, migrants and long-term illness – **continued**

Persons present in communal establishments

Type of establishment and age	PERSONS PRESENT			Visitors/guests			Residents - non-staff			Residents - staff			With limiting long-term illness	Migrants
	TOTAL	Males	Females	Total	Males	Females	Total	Males	Females	Total	Males	Females		
a	b	c	d	e	f	g	h	i	j	k	l	m	n	o
Merseyside Metropolitan County – *continued*														
Hostels and common lodging houses (non-HA)														
All ages	**653**	**445**	**208**	**64**	**24**	**40**	**562**	**405**	**157**	**27**	**16**	**11**	**254**	**301**
0 - 15	42	18	24	4	1	3	32	14	18	6	3	3	2	23
16 - 17	19	12	7	-	-	-	19	12	7	-	-	-	3	15
18 - 29	216	122	94	38	10	28	174	110	64	4	2	2	40	131
30 - 44	137	93	44	13	6	7	121	85	36	3	2	1	74	70
45 - 59	125	104	21	7	5	2	106	91	15	12	8	4	64	38
60 - 64	38	33	5	1	1	-	36	31	5	1	1	-	25	8
65 - 74	47	39	8	-	-	-	46	39	7	1	1	1	27	11
75 - 84	23	18	5	1	1	-	22	17	5	-	-	-	15	4
85 and over	6	6	-	-	-	-	6	6	-	-	-	-	4	1
Other miscellaneous establishments														
All ages	**1,029**	**387**	**642**	**259**	**162**	**97**	**614**	**153**	**461**	**156**	**72**	**84**	**279**	**135**
0 - 15	55	30	25	29	13	16	24	15	9	2	2	-	7	20
16 - 17	11	10	1	9	9	-	2	1	1	-	-	-	1	2
18 - 29	196	120	76	140	93	47	42	20	22	14	7	7	8	34
30 - 44	135	70	65	58	36	22	47	14	33	30	20	10	10	20
45 - 59	153	40	113	11	6	5	91	15	76	51	19	32	26	21
60 - 64	71	26	45	2	2	-	53	16	37	16	8	8	17	7
65 - 74	149	43	106	3	1	2	124	32	92	22	10	12	47	17
75 - 84	187	36	151	5	1	4	163	31	132	19	4	15	106	9
85 and over	72	12	60	2	1	1	68	9	59	2	2	-	57	5

Great Britain, England & Wales, England, regions, metropolitan counties, Inner London, Outer London, regional remainders, Wales, Scotland

Persons present in communal establishments

Type of establishment and age	PERSONS PRESENT			Visitors/guests			Residents - non-staff			Residents - staff			With limiting long-term illness	Migrants
	TOTAL	Males	Females	Total	Males	Females	Total	Males	Females	Total	Males	Females		
a	b	c	d	e	f	g	h	i	j	k	l	m	n	o

Merseyside Metropolitan County – *continued*

Persons sleeping rough

All ages	**67**	**50**	**17**	**42**	**32**	**10**	**25**	**18**	**7**				**28**	**19**
0 - 15	-	-	-	-	-	-	-	-	-				-	-
16 - 17	-	-	-	-	-	-	-	-	-				-	-
18 - 29	25	16	9	14	9	5	11	7	4				6	7
30 - 44	22	17	5	15	12	3	7	5	2				10	6
45 - 59	17	14	3	12	10	2	5	4	1				9	5
60 - 64	2	2	-	1	1	-	1	1	-				2	-
65 - 74	1	1	-	-	-	-	1	1	-				1	1
75 - 84	-	-	-	-	-	-	-	-	-				-	-
85 and over	-	-	-	-	-	-	-	-	-				-	-

Campers

All ages	-	-	-	-	-	-	-	-	-				-	-
0 - 15	-	-	-	-	-	-	-	-	-				-	-
16 - 17	-	-	-	-	-	-	-	-	-				-	-
18 - 29	-	-	-	-	-	-	-	-	-				-	-
30 - 44	-	-	-	-	-	-	-	-	-				-	-
45 - 59	-	-	-	-	-	-	-	-	-				-	-
60 - 64	-	-	-	-	-	-	-	-	-				-	-
65 - 74	-	-	-	-	-	-	-	-	-				-	-
75 - 84	-	-	-	-	-	-	-	-	-				-	-
85 and over	-	-	-	-	-	-	-	-	-				-	-

Table 3 Type of establishment, migrants and long-term illness – **continued**

Great Britain, England & Wales, England, regions, metropolitan counties, Inner London, Outer London, regional remainders, Wales, Scotland

Persons present in communal establishments

Type of establishment and age	PERSONS PRESENT			Visitors/guests			Residents - non-staff			Residents - staff			With limiting long-term illness	Migrants
	TOTAL	Males	Females	Total	Males	Females	Total	Males	Females	Total	Males	Females		
a	b	c	d	e	f	g	h	i	j	k	l	m	n	o
Merseyside Metropolitan County – *continued*														
Civilian ships, boats and barges														
All ages	246	237	9	214	207	7	32	30	2				6	15
0 - 15	2	2	-	1	1	-	1	1	-				-	-
16 - 17	2	2	-	2	2	-	-	-	-				-	-
18 - 29	63	60	3	50	47	3	13	13	-				2	6
30 - 44	104	101	3	92	90	2	12	11	1				4	5
45 - 59	73	70	3	67	65	2	6	5	1				-	4
60 - 64	2	2	-	2	2	-	-	-	-				-	-
65 - 74	-	-	-	-	-	-	-	-	-				-	-
75 - 84	-	-	-	-	-	-	-	-	-				-	-
85 and over	-	-	-	-	-	-	-	-	-				-	-
Remainder of North West Region														
All establishments *														
All ages	63,047	27,111	35,936	23,384	12,238	11,146	34,479	12,368	22,111	5,184	2,505	2,679	35,631	11,346
0 - 15	4,015	2,502	1,513	2,303	1,568	735	1,030	576	454	682	358	324	432	622
16 - 17	1,049	655	394	731	494	237	161	79	82	157	82	75	133	140
18 - 29	13,194	7,071	6,123	8,395	4,343	4,052	3,269	2,103	1,166	1,530	625	905	1,678	2,288
30 - 44	6,799	4,370	2,429	3,037	1,953	1,084	2,618	1,820	798	1,144	597	547	2,311	890
45 - 59	5,911	3,396	2,515	2,304	1,297	1,007	2,253	1,407	846	1,354	692	662	2,737	494
60 - 64	2,254	1,162	1,092	952	457	495	1,126	600	526	176	105	71	1,529	263
65 - 74	6,181	2,650	3,531	2,235	983	1,252	3,860	1,631	2,229	86	36	50	4,881	1,055
75 - 84	12,518	3,502	9,016	2,394	888	1,506	10,084	2,607	7,477	40	7	33	11,420	3,030
85 and over	11,126	1,803	9,323	1,033	255	778	10,078	1,545	8,533	15	3	12	10,510	2,564

Note: * Includes a male member of staff incorrectly enumerated as a resident.

Table 3 Type of establishment, migrants and long-term illness – **continued**

Persons present in communal establishments

Type of establishment and age	PERSONS PRESENT			Visitors/guests			Residents - non-staff			Residents - staff			With limiting long-term illness	Migrants
	TOTAL	Males	Females	Total	Males	Females	Total	Males	Females	Total	Males	Females		
a	b	c	d	e	f	g	h	i	j	k	l	m	n	o

Remainder of North West Region – *continued*

NHS hospitals/homes - psychiatric

All ages	1,675	739	936	424	163	261	1,168	537	631	83	39	44	1,478	154
0 - 15	1	-	1	1	-	1	-	-	-	-	-	-	-	-
16 - 17	2	-	2	2	-	2	-	-	-	-	-	-	1	-
18 - 29	192	90	102	80	40	40	50	28	22	62	22	40	70	44
30 - 44	172	105	67	82	38	44	75	56	19	15	11	4	131	17
45 - 59	210	118	92	63	26	37	143	88	55	4	4	-	197	14
60 - 64	113	57	56	27	12	15	84	43	41	2	2	-	108	5
65 - 74	346	168	178	58	15	43	288	153	135	-	-	-	339	16
75 - 84	403	157	246	71	26	45	332	131	201	-	-	-	399	38
85 and over	236	44	192	40	6	34	196	38	158	-	-	-	233	20

NHS hospitals/homes - other

All ages	10,800	4,511	6,289	6,487	2,563	3,924	3,604	1,696	1,908	709	252	457	7,062	861
0 - 15	600	331	269	569	318	251	12	4	8	19	9	10	69	8
16 - 17	54	16	38	49	15	34	3	1	2	2	-	2	13	5
18 - 29	2,093	631	1,462	972	256	716	584	239	345	537	136	401	448	483
30 - 44	1,566	800	766	696	252	444	743	457	286	127	91	36	939	136
45 - 59	1,452	747	705	718	332	386	715	401	314	19	14	5	1,151	56
60 - 64	606	303	303	394	190	204	209	112	97	3	1	2	503	11
65 - 74	1,523	704	819	1,093	502	591	429	202	227	1	-	1	1,285	34
75 - 84	1,961	765	1,196	1,404	548	856	557	217	340	-	-	-	1,768	71
85 and over	945	214	731	592	150	442	352	63	289	1	1	-	886	57

Table 3 Type of establishment, migrants and long-term illness – **continued**

Great Britain, England & Wales, England, regions, metropolitan counties, Inner London, Outer London, regional remainders, Wales, Scotland

Persons present in communal establishments

Type of establishment and age	PERSONS PRESENT			Visitors/guests			Residents - non-staff			Residents - staff			With limiting long-term illness	Migrants
	TOTAL	Males	Females	Total	Males	Females	Total	Males	Females	Total	Males	Females		
a	b	c	d	e	f	g	h	i	j	k	l	m	n	o
Remainder of North West Region – *continued*														
Non-NHS hospitals - psychiatric														
All ages	**9**	**8**	**1**	**1**	**1**	**-**	**8**	**7**	**1**	**-**	**-**	**-**	**6**	**4**
0 - 15	-	-	-	-	-	-	-	-	-	-	-	-		-
16 - 17	-	-	-	-	-	-	-	-	-	-	-	-	-	-
18 - 29	3	2	1	-	-	-	3	2	1	-	-	-	2	2
30 - 44	3	3	-	-	-	-	3	3	-	-	-	-	2	1
45 - 59	3	3	-	1	1	-	2	2	-	-	-	-	2	1
60 - 64	-	-	-	-	-	-	-	-	-	-	-	-	-	-
65 - 74	-	-	-	-	-	-	-	-	-	-	-	-	-	-
75 - 84	-	-	-	-	-	-	-	-	-	-	-	-	-	-
85 and over	-	-	-	-	-	-	-	-	-	-	-	-	-	-
Non-NHS hospitals - other														
All ages	**223**	**108**	**115**	**150**	**60**	**90**	**70**	**48**	**22**	**3**	**-**	**3**	**133**	**2**
0 - 15	3	1	2	3	1	2	-	-	-	-	-	-	-	-
16 - 17	-	-	-	-	-	-	-	-	-	-	-	-	-	-
18 - 29	20	11	9	10	3	7	10	8	2	-	-	-	12	1
30 - 44	52	24	28	31	11	20	20	13	7	1	-	1	27	-
45 - 59	58	29	29	34	12	22	22	17	5	2	-	2	30	1
60 - 64	19	14	5	14	9	5	5	5	-	-	-	-	14	-
65 - 74	30	16	14	23	11	12	7	5	2	-	-	-	19	-
75 - 84	29	10	19	25	10	15	4	-	4	-	-	-	22	-
85 and over	12	3	9	10	3	7	2	-	2	-	-	-	9	-

Table 3 Type of establishment, migrants and long-term illness – **continued**

Great Britain, England & Wales, England, regions, metropolitan counties, Inner London, Outer London, regional remainders, Wales, Scotland

Persons present in communal establishments

Type of establishment and age	PERSONS PRESENT			Visitors/guests			Residents - non-staff			Residents - staff			With limiting long-term illness	Migrants
	TOTAL	Males	Females	Total	Males	Females	Total	Males	Females	Total	Males	Females		
a	b	c	d	e	f	g	h	i	j	k	l	m	n	o

Remainder of North West Region – *continued*

Local authority homes

All ages	**5,944**	**2,022**	**3,922**	**853**	**402**	**451**	**5,052**	**1,603**	**3,449**	**39**	**17**	**22**	**5,287**	**1,030**
0 - 15	273	217	56	213	173	40	54	40	14	6	4	2	99	28
16 - 17	61	43	18	40	31	9	20	11	9	1	1	-	26	10
18 - 29	321	192	129	78	46	32	231	142	89	12	4	8	228	62
30 - 44	389	210	179	61	21	40	317	185	132	11	4	7	331	33
45 - 59	286	144	142	38	8	30	240	133	107	8	3	5	248	20
60 - 64	143	64	79	19	7	12	123	56	67	1	1	-	133	28
65 - 74	704	300	404	74	28	46	630	272	358	-	-	-	641	147
75 - 84	1,852	544	1,308	191	62	129	1,661	482	1,179	-	-	-	1,754	372
85 and over	1,915	308	1,607	139	26	113	1,776	282	1,494	-	-	-	1,827	330

Housing association homes and hostels

All ages	**548**	**267**	**281**	**68**	**30**	**38**	**453**	**228**	**225**	**27**	**9**	**18**	**240**	**192**
0 - 15	27	18	9	5	4	1	22	14	8	-	-	-	10	11
16 - 17	22	15	7	9	7	2	12	8	4	1	-	1	9	12
18 - 29	182	101	81	39	15	24	138	84	54	5	2	3	49	95
30 - 44	72	46	26	6	2	4	64	43	21	2	1	1	28	32
45 - 59	68	46	22	5	2	3	50	40	10	13	4	9	31	15
60 - 64	29	16	13	-	-	-	25	15	10	4	1	3	21	9
65 - 74	25	11	14	2	-	2	22	11	11	1	1	1	20	2
75 - 84	87	11	76	2	-	2	84	10	74	1	1	-	49	13
85 and over	36	3	33	-	-	-	36	3	33	-	-	-	23	3

Table 3 Type of establishment, migrants and long-term illness – **continued**

Great Britain, England & Wales, England, regions, metropolitan counties, Inner London, Outer London, regional remainders, Wales, Scotland

Persons present in communal establishments

Remainder of North West Region – *continued*

Type of establishment and age	PERSONS PRESENT TOTAL	Males	Females	Visitors/guests Total	Males	Females	Residents - non-staff Total	Males	Females	Residents - staff Total	Males	Females	With limiting long-term illness	Migrants
a	b	c	d	e	f	g	h	i	j	k	l	m	n	o
Nursing homes *(non-NHS/LA/HA)*														
All ages	8,813	2,351	6,462	496	206	290	8,184	2,094	6,090	133	51	82	8,423	3,278
0 - 15	19	13	6	-	-	-	-	-	-	19	13	6	1	1
16 - 17	-	-	-	-	-	-	-	-	-	-	-	-	-	-
18 - 29	77	44	33	10	3	7	46	34	12	21	7	14	44	13
30 - 44	131	67	64	33	10	23	74	49	25	24	8	16	87	12
45 - 59	234	117	117	28	7	21	159	92	67	47	18	29	183	41
60 - 64	327	169	158	35	22	13	282	144	138	10	3	7	305	115
65 - 74	1,224	510	714	116	68	48	1,100	440	660	8	2	6	1,163	509
75 - 84	3,537	914	2,623	176	66	110	3,359	848	2,511	2	-	2	3,451	1,452
85 and over	3,264	517	2,747	98	30	68	3,164	487	2,677	2	-	2	3,189	1,135
Residential homes *(non-NHS/LA/HA)*														
All ages	11,570	2,897	8,673	439	137	302	10,663	2,559	8,104	468	201	267	10,182	2,634
0 - 15	127	69	58	42	27	15	4	2	2	81	40	41	50	9
16 - 17	37	21	16	25	14	11	2	-	2	10	7	3	27	2
18 - 29	378	210	168	39	16	23	268	171	97	71	23	48	273	76
30 - 44	462	260	202	33	9	24	317	200	117	112	51	61	326	58
45 - 59	416	195	221	29	5	24	248	134	114	139	56	83	261	41
60 - 64	285	136	149	15	6	9	243	117	126	27	13	14	238	56
65 - 74	1,214	430	784	54	14	40	1,140	405	735	20	11	9	1,048	313
75 - 84	4,041	886	3,155	114	25	89	3,922	861	3,061	5	-	5	3,682	1,063
85 and over	4,610	690	3,920	88	21	67	4,519	669	3,850	3	-	3	4,277	1,016

Table 3 Type of establishment, migrants and long-term illness – **continued**

Persons present in communal establishments

Type of establishment and age	PERSONS PRESENT			Visitors/guests			Residents - non-staff			Residents - staff			With limiting long-term illness	Migrants
	TOTAL	Males	Females	Total	Males	Females	Total	Males	Females	Total	Males	Females		
a	b	c	d	e	f	g	h	i	j	k	l	m	n	o

Remainder of North West Region – *continued*

Children's homes

All ages	**802**	**453**	**349**	**147**	**86**	**61**	**615**	**347**	**268**	**40**	**20**	**20**	**102**	**306**
0 - 15	737	427	310	119	78	41	615	347	268	3	2	1	89	299
16 - 17	6	-	6	-	-	-	-	-	-	6	-	6	-	5
18 - 29	23	12	11	5	1	4	-	-	-	18	11	7	11	2
30 - 44	20	8	12	13	3	10	-	-	-	7	5	2	-	-
45 - 59	12	4	8	9	3	6	-	-	-	3	1	2	2	-
60 - 64	4	2	2	1	1	-	-	-	-	3	1	2	-	-
65 - 74	-	-	-	-	-	-	-	-	-	-	-	-	-	-
75 - 84	-	-	-	-	-	-	-	-	-	-	-	-	-	-
85 and over	-	-	-	-	-	-	-	-	-	-	-	-	-	-

Prison service establishments

All ages	**2,837**	**2,576**	**261**	**1,883**	**1,686**	**197**	**953**	**889**	**64**	**1**	**1**	**-**	**373**	**538**
0 - 15	5	2	3	5	2	3	-	-	-	-	-	-	-	-
16 - 17	30	24	6	30	24	6	-	-	-	-	-	-	1	-
18 - 29	1,734	1,577	157	1,205	1,085	120	529	492	37	-	-	-	191	325
30 - 44	841	763	78	501	442	59	340	321	19	-	-	-	124	176
45 - 59	207	194	13	127	121	6	80	73	7	-	-	-	50	35
60 - 64	7	6	1	5	4	1	2	2	-	-	-	-	4	1
65 - 74	8	8	-	6	6	-	1	-	1	1	1	-	3	-
75 - 84	3	1	2	2	1	1	1	-	1	-	-	-	-	1
85 and over	2	1	1	2	1	1	-	-	-	-	-	-	-	-

Table 3 Type of establishment, migrants and long-term illness – **continued**

Great Britain, England & Wales, England, regions, metropolitan counties, Inner London, Outer London, regional remainders, Wales, Scotland

Persons present in communal establishments

Type of establishment and age	PERSONS PRESENT			Visitors/guests			Residents - non-staff			Residents - staff			With limiting long-term illness	Migrants
	TOTAL	Males	Females	Total	Males	Females	Total	Males	Females	Total	Males	Females		
a	b	c	d	e	f	g	h	i	j	k	l	m	n	o

Remainder of North West Region – *continued*

Defence establishments

All ages	195	187	8	26	25	1	169	162	7				7	32
0 - 15	-	-	-	-	-	-	-	-	-				-	-
16 - 17	9	9	-	1	1	-	8	8	-				-	1
18 - 29	166	161	5	21	20	1	145	141	4				5	26
30 - 44	18	17	1	4	4	-	14	13	1				2	5
45 - 59	2	-	2	-	-	-	2	-	2				-	-
60 - 64	-	-	-	-	-	-	-	-	-				-	-
65 - 74	-	-	-	-	-	-	-	-	-				-	-
75 - 84	-	-	-	-	-	-	-	-	-				-	-
85 and over	-	-	-	-	-	-	-	-	-				-	-

Educational establishments

All ages	6,849	3,500	3,349	6,127	3,120	3,007	634	331	303	88	49	39	329	397
0 - 15	1,021	738	283	987	717	270	28	19	9	6	2	4	64	24
16 - 17	479	336	143	464	329	135	13	5	8	2	2	-	44	10
18 - 29	4,877	2,160	2,717	4,427	1,903	2,524	417	241	176	33	16	17	159	306
30 - 44	299	211	88	191	137	54	79	57	22	29	17	12	16	49
45 - 59	77	37	40	47	28	19	17	1	16	13	8	5	7	5
60 - 64	17	3	14	3	1	2	12	1	11	2	1	1	4	1
65 - 74	32	9	23	4	2	2	25	4	21	3	3	-	9	1
75 - 84	34	4	30	2	1	1	32	3	29	-	-	-	17	1
85 and over	13	2	11	2	2	-	11	-	11	-	-	-	9	-

Table 3 Type of establishment, migrants and long-term illness – **continued**

Great Britain, England & Wales, England, regions, metropolitan counties, Inner London, Outer London, regional remainders, Wales, Scotland

Persons present in communal establishments

Type of establishment and age	PERSONS PRESENT			Visitors/guests			Residents - non-staff			Residents - staff			With limiting long-term illness	Migrants
	TOTAL	Males	Females	Total	Males	Females	Total	Males	Females	Total	Males	Females		
a	b	c	d	e	f	g	h	i	j	k	l	m	n	o

Remainder of North West Region – *continued*

Hotels, boarding houses etc

All ages	**10,992**	**6,359**	**4,633**	**5,618**	**3,264**	**2,354**	**1,863**	**1,283**	**580**	**3,511**	**1,812**	**1,699**	**1,602**	**1,390**
0 - 15	1,053	608	445	335	234	101	176	89	87	542	285	257	41	164
16 - 17	283	157	126	96	59	37	52	26	26	135	72	63	10	55
18 - 29	2,538	1,472	1,066	1,257	750	507	545	341	204	736	381	355	134	612
30 - 44	2,444	1,588	856	1,210	871	339	432	318	114	802	399	403	230	294
45 - 59	2,622	1,580	1,042	1,117	684	433	414	322	92	1,091	574	517	489	209
60 - 64	622	341	281	421	195	226	83	69	14	118	77	41	166	25
65 - 74	907	419	488	756	320	436	102	82	20	49	17	32	284	17
75 - 84	453	176	277	374	138	236	50	33	17	29	5	24	208	12
85 and over	70	18	52	52	13	39	9	3	6	9	2	7	40	2

Hostels and common lodging houses (non-HA)

All ages	**563**	**417**	**146**	**132**	**60**	**72**	**398**	**329**	**69**	**33**	**28**	**5**	**184**	**215**
0 - 15	9	5	4	-	-	-	6	4	2	3	1	2	-	2
16 - 17	22	12	10	-	-	-	22	12	10	3	-	-	2	19
18 - 29	196	135	61	54	29	25	127	93	34	15	13	2	26	108
30 - 44	91	77	14	3	2	1	81	69	12	7	6	1	42	40
45 - 59	88	79	9	4	2	2	80	73	7	4	4	-	41	31
60 - 64	41	34	7	8	3	5	30	28	2	3	3	-	22	6
65 - 74	80	57	23	35	13	22	44	43	1	1	1	-	34	7
75 - 84	29	15	14	21	8	13	8	7	1	-	-	-	13	2
85 and over	7	3	4	7	3	4	-	-	-	-	-	-	4	-

Table 3 Type of establishment, migrants and long-term illness – **continued**

Great Britain, England & Wales, England, regions, metropolitan counties, Inner London, Outer London, regional remainders, Wales, Scotland

Persons present in communal establishments

Type of establishment and age	PERSONS PRESENT			Visitors/guests			Residents - non-staff			Residents - staff			With limiting long-term illness	Migrants
	TOTAL	Males	Females	Total	Males	Females	Total	Males	Females	Total	Males	Females		
a	b	c	d	e	f	g	h	i	j	k	l	m	n	o
Other miscellaneous establishments														
All ages	950	492	458	350	284	66	552	183	369	48	25	23	175	245
0 - 15	125	64	61	19	11	8	103	51	52	3	2	1	8	69
16 - 17	37	19	18	15	14	1	22	5	17	-	-	-	-	16
18 - 29	350	235	115	180	160	20	150	65	85	20	10	10	18	117
30 - 44	132	97	35	89	76	13	36	17	19	7	4	3	16	18
45 - 59	92	38	54	24	20	4	58	13	45	10	5	5	23	8
60 - 64	31	9	22	2	1	1	26	6	20	3	2	1	8	4
65 - 74	81	13	68	9	1	8	70	11	59	2	1	1	33	7
75 - 84	86	17	69	9	1	8	74	15	59	3	1	2	56	5
85 and over	16	-	16	3	-	3	13	-	13	-	-	-	13	1
Persons sleeping rough														
All ages	94	80	14	30	25	5	63	54	9				37	54
0 - 15	-	-	-	-	-	-	-	-	-				-	-
16 - 17	1	1	-	-	-	-	1	1	-				-	1
18 - 29	29	27	2	9	9	-	20	18	2				8	15
30 - 44	29	22	7	8	5	3	21	17	4				10	18
45 - 59	31	26	5	13	11	2	17	14	3				15	16
60 - 64	2	2	-	-	-	-	2	2	-				2	2
65 - 74	2	2	-	-	-	-	2	2	-				2	2
75 - 84	-	-	-	-	-	-	-	-	-				-	-
85 and over	-	-	-	-	-	-	-	-	-				-	-

Remainder of North West Region – *continued*

Table 3   Type of establishment, migrants and long-term illness – **continued**

Persons present in communal establishments

Type of establishment and age	PERSONS PRESENT			Visitors/guests			Residents - non-staff			Residents - staff			With limiting long-term illness	Migrants
	TOTAL	Males	Females	Total	Males	Females	Total	Males	Females	Total	Males	Females		
a	b	c	d	e	f	g	h	i	j	k	l	m	n	o
Remainder of North West Region – *continued*														
Campers														
All ages	**52**	**28**	**24**	**49**	**26**	**23**	**3**	**2**	**1**				**7**	**1**
0 - 15	4	2	2	4	2	2	-	-	-				-	-
16 - 17	-	-	-	-	-	-	-	-	-				-	-
18 - 29	2	1	1	1	-	1	1	1	-				-	1
30 - 44	9	5	4	9	5	4	-	-	-				-	-
45 - 59	25	13	12	23	12	11	2	1	1				4	-
60 - 64	4	2	2	4	2	2	-	-	-				1	-
65 - 74	5	3	2	5	3	2	-	-	-				1	-
75 - 84	3	2	1	3	2	1	-	-	-				1	-
85 and over	-	-	-	-	-	-	-	-	-				-	-
Civilian ships, boats and barges														
All ages	**131**	**116**	**15**	**104**	**100**	**4**	**27**	**16**	**11**				**4**	**13**
0 - 15	11	7	4	1	1	-	10	6	4				1	7
16 - 17	6	2	4	-	-	-	6	2	4				-	4
18 - 29	13	10	3	8	7	1	5	3	2				-	-
30 - 44	69	67	2	67	65	2	2	2	-				-	1
45 - 59	28	26	2	24	23	1	4	3	1				3	1
60 - 64	4	4	-	4	4	-	-	-	-				-	-
65 - 74	-	-	-	-	-	-	-	-	-				-	-
75 - 84	-	-	-	-	-	-	-	-	-				-	-
85 and over	-	-	-	-	-	-	-	-	-				-	-

Table 3 Type of establishment, migrants and long-term illness – **continued**

Great Britain, England & Wales, England, regions, metropolitan counties, Inner London, Outer London, regional remainders, Wales, Scotland

Persons present in communal establishments

WALES

Type of establishment and age	PERSONS PRESENT			Visitors/guests			Residents - non-staff			Residents - staff			With limiting long-term illness	Migrants
	TOTAL	Males	Females	Total	Males	Females	Total	Males	Females	Total	Males	Females		
a	b	c	d	e	f	g	h	i	j	k	l	m	n	o
All establishments														
All ages	**71,892**	**30,950**	**40,942**	**33,993**	**17,090**	**16,903**	**33,960**	**11,988**	**21,972**	**3,939**	**1,872**	**2,067**	**37,538**	**11,367**
0 - 15	6,507	3,577	2,930	5,164	2,835	2,329	1,007	560	447	336	182	154	461	534
16 - 17	1,796	1,028	768	1,482	845	637	229	137	92	85	46	39	148	164
18 - 29	16,837	9,091	7,746	11,626	6,038	5,588	3,356	2,264	1,092	1,855	789	1,066	1,652	2,758
30 - 44	6,048	3,750	2,298	3,153	1,908	1,245	2,166	1,433	733	729	409	320	1,928	881
45 - 59	5,565	3,103	2,462	3,016	1,640	1,376	1,827	1,106	721	722	357	365	2,476	411
60 - 64	2,422	1,187	1,235	1,238	573	665	1,062	558	504	122	56	66	1,547	229
65 - 74	7,245	3,263	3,982	3,299	1,567	1,732	3,898	1,673	2,225	48	23	25	5,617	1,042
75 - 84	13,603	3,954	9,649	3,555	1,342	2,213	10,016	2,604	7,412	32	8	24	12,364	2,884
85 and over	11,869	1,997	9,872	1,460	342	1,118	10,399	1,653	8,746	10	2	8	11,345	2,464
NHS hospitals/homes - psychiatric														
All ages	**2,118**	**938**	**1,180**	**662**	**278**	**384**	**1,422**	**637**	**785**	**34**	**23**	**11**	**1,903**	**217**
0 - 15	8	2	6	8	2	6	-	-	-	-	-	-	-	-
16 - 17	9	2	7	8	2	6	1	-	1	-	-	-	2	-
18 - 29	186	94	92	100	44	56	61	33	28	25	17	8	95	31
30 - 44	248	135	113	124	66	58	116	64	52	8	5	3	190	21
45 - 59	350	193	157	157	72	85	192	120	72	1	1	-	316	20
60 - 64	133	74	59	31	15	16	102	59	43	-	-	-	131	9
65 - 74	406	188	218	90	29	61	316	159	157	-	-	-	395	42
75 - 84	511	190	321	108	36	72	403	154	249	-	-	-	507	62
85 and over	267	60	207	36	12	24	231	48	183	-	-	-	267	32

Table 3 Type of establishment, migrants and long-term illness – **continued**

Persons present in communal establishments

WALES – *continued*

Type of establishment and age	PERSONS PRESENT			Visitors/guests			Residents - non-staff			Residents - staff			With limiting long-term illness	Migrants
	TOTAL	Males	Females	Total	Males	Females	Total	Males	Females	Total	Males	Females		
a	b	c	d	e	f	g	h	i	j	k	l	m	n	o
NHS hospitals/homes - other														
All ages	**13,743**	**5,423**	**8,320**	**9,903**	**3,985**	**5,918**	**2,863**	**1,149**	**1,714**	**977**	**289**	**688**	**9,046**	**1,021**
0 - 15	871	478	393	843	462	381	27	16	11	1	1	1	115	6
16 - 17	78	26	52	70	24	46	3	2	1	5	-	5	20	6
18 - 29	2,442	655	1,787	1,357	329	1,028	246	122	124	839	204	635	397	509
30 - 44	1,482	673	809	855	308	547	517	292	225	110	73	37	809	122
45 - 59	1,395	709	686	981	482	499	394	216	178	20	11	9	1,019	24
60 - 64	632	316	316	506	256	250	126	60	66	-	-	-	529	11
65 - 74	2,134	1,080	1,054	1,767	901	866	367	179	188	-	-	-	1,801	66
75 - 84	3,090	1,159	1,931	2,433	970	1,463	655	188	467	2	1	1	2,814	155
85 and over	1,619	327	1,292	1,091	253	838	528	74	454	-	-	-	1,542	122
Non-NHS hospitals - psychiatric														
All ages	-	-	-	-	-	-	-	-	-	-	-	-	-	-
0 - 15	-	-	-	-	-	-	-	-	-	-	-	-	-	-
16 - 17	-	-	-	-	-	-	-	-	-	-	-	-	-	-
18 - 29	-	-	-	-	-	-	-	-	-	-	-	-	-	-
30 - 44	-	-	-	-	-	-	-	-	-	-	-	-	-	-
45 - 59	-	-	-	-	-	-	-	-	-	-	-	-	-	-
60 - 64	-	-	-	-	-	-	-	-	-	-	-	-	-	-
65 - 74	-	-	-	-	-	-	-	-	-	-	-	-	-	-
75 - 84	-	-	-	-	-	-	-	-	-	-	-	-	-	-
85 and over	-	-	-	-	-	-	-	-	-	-	-	-	-	-

Table 3 Type of establishment, migrants and long-term illness – **continued**

Great Britain, England & Wales, England, regions, metropolitan counties, Inner London, Outer London, regional remainders, Wales, Scotland

Persons present in communal establishments

Type of establishment and age	PERSONS PRESENT			Visitors/guests			Residents - non-staff			Residents - staff			With limiting long-term illness	Migrants
	TOTAL	Males	Females	Total	Males	Females	Total	Males	Females	Total	Males	Females		
a	b	c	d	e	f	g	h	i	j	k	l	m	n	o
WALES – *continued*														
Non-NHS hospitals - other														
All ages	**324**	**111**	**213**	**205**	**79**	**126**	**117**	**30**	**87**	**2**	**2**	**-**	**230**	**30**
0 - 15	8	5	3	7	5	2	1	-	1	-	-	-	1	-
16 - 17	2	-	2	2	-	2	-	-	-	-	-	-	2	-
18 - 29	27	15	12	18	10	8	8	4	4	1	1	-	14	2
30 - 44	52	13	39	35	6	29	16	6	10	1	1	-	17	-
45 - 59	43	17	26	37	15	22	6	2	4	-	-	-	20	1
60 - 64	10	5	5	9	5	4	1	-	1	-	-	-	4	-
65 - 74	41	20	21	28	16	12	13	4	9	-	-	-	40	6
75 - 84	80	28	52	43	18	25	37	10	27	-	-	-	72	9
85 and over	61	8	53	26	4	22	35	4	31	-	-	-	60	12
Local authority homes														
All ages	**7,031**	**2,221**	**4,810**	**615**	**252**	**363**	**6,383**	**1,955**	**4,428**	**33**	**14**	**19**	**6,500**	**1,298**
0 - 15	147	97	50	58	45	13	82	48	34	7	4	3	34	36
16 - 17	55	35	20	16	14	2	39	21	18	-	-	-	29	21
18 - 29	269	156	113	78	46	32	186	108	78	5	2	3	204	65
30 - 44	274	132	142	75	31	44	193	99	94	6	2	4	226	40
45 - 59	231	114	117	61	21	40	161	90	71	9	3	6	185	29
60 - 64	169	84	85	20	4	16	145	78	67	4	2	2	159	23
65 - 74	872	402	470	51	21	30	819	380	439	2	1	1	830	178
75 - 84	2,518	737	1,781	136	46	90	2,382	691	1,691	-	-	-	2,410	517
85 and over	2,496	464	2,032	120	24	96	2,376	440	1,936	-	-	-	2,423	389

Table 3 Type of establishment, migrants and long-term illness – **continued**

Great Britain, England & Wales, England, regions, metropolitan counties, Inner London, Outer London, regional remainders, Wales, Scotland

Persons present in communal establishments

WALES – *continued*

Type of establishment and age	PERSONS PRESENT			Visitors/guests			Residents - non-staff			Residents - staff			With limiting long-term illness	Migrants
	TOTAL	Males	Females	Total	Males	Females	Total	Males	Females	Total	Males	Females		
a	b	c	d	e	f	g	h	i	j	k	l	m	n	o
Housing association homes and hostels														
All ages	**748**	**335**	**413**	**51**	**20**	**31**	**677**	**305**	**372**	**20**	**10**	**10**	**497**	**287**
0 - 15	42	18	24	2	-	2	38	17	21	2	1	1	2	16
16 - 17	20	11	9	-	-	-	19	10	9	1	1	-	2	16
18 - 29	120	64	56	12	6	6	106	56	50	2	2	-	47	69
30 - 44	81	49	32	4	2	2	70	43	27	7	4	3	50	36
45 - 59	81	45	36	13	4	9	62	40	22	6	1	5	65	29
60 - 64	34	14	20	3	1	2	29	12	17	2	1	1	31	17
65 - 74	82	46	36	7	3	4	75	43	32	-	-	-	70	24
75 - 84	195	66	129	9	3	6	186	63	123	-	-	-	152	50
85 and over	93	22	71	1	1	-	92	21	71	-	-	-	78	30
Nursing homes (non-NHS/ LA/HA)														
All ages	**9,180**	**2,363**	**6,817**	**511**	**151**	**360**	**8,550**	**2,162**	**6,388**	**119**	**50**	**69**	**8,723**	**3,010**
0 - 15	11	9	2	1	1	-	-	-	-	10	8	2	-	2
16 - 17	4	1	3	2	-	2	1	-	1	1	-	1	1	1
18 - 29	123	66	57	30	7	23	58	43	15	35	16	19	57	43
30 - 44	129	62	67	40	11	29	64	40	24	25	11	14	71	28
45 - 59	170	70	100	48	20	28	88	39	49	34	11	23	110	20
60 - 64	286	139	147	41	14	27	241	123	118	4	2	2	263	84
65 - 74	1,303	513	790	128	50	78	1,169	461	708	6	2	4	1,242	452
75 - 84	3,462	898	2,564	161	38	123	3,299	860	2,439	2	-	2	3,363	1,240
85 and over	3,692	605	3,087	60	10	50	3,630	595	3,035	2	-	2	3,616	1,140

Table 3 Type of establishment, migrants and long-term illness – **continued**

Persons present in communal establishments

Type of establishment and age	PERSONS PRESENT			Visitors/guests			Residents - non-staff			Residents - staff			With limiting long-term illness	Migrants
	TOTAL	Males	Females	Total	Males	Females	Total	Males	Females	Total	Males	Females		
a	b	c	d	e	f	g	h	i	j	k	l	m	n	o
WALES – *continued*														
Residential homes (non-NHS/LA/HA)														
All ages	**8,906**	**2,226**	**6,680**	**303**	**90**	**213**	**8,235**	**1,987**	**6,248**	**368**	**149**	**219**	**7,940**	**2,003**
0 - 15	57	31	26	-	-	-	7	5	2	50	26	24	2	7
16 - 17	30	17	13	11	6	5	10	8	2	9	3	6	17	5
18 - 29	402	237	165	73	31	42	263	179	84	66	27	39	294	68
30 - 44	348	185	163	44	11	33	234	144	90	70	30	40	241	45
45 - 59	443	213	230	33	12	21	277	151	126	133	50	83	287	42
60 - 64	279	135	144	5	-	5	248	126	122	26	9	17	237	46
65 - 74	925	324	601	29	9	20	889	313	576	7	2	5	862	236
75 - 84	2,936	611	2,325	60	12	48	2,870	598	2,272	6	1	5	2,733	823
85 and over	3,486	473	3,013	48	9	39	3,437	463	2,974	1	1	-	3,267	731
Children's homes														
All ages	**597**	**320**	**277**	**121**	**65**	**56**	**416**	**225**	**191**	**60**	**30**	**30**	**66**	**216**
0 - 15	523	292	231	94	57	37	416	225	191	13	10	3	58	209
16 - 17	4	1	3	-	-	-	-	-	-	4	1	3	-	-
18 - 29	21	11	10	7	2	5	-	-	-	14	9	5	2	2
30 - 44	27	9	18	13	4	9	-	-	-	14	5	9	-	2
45 - 59	15	6	9	6	2	4	-	-	-	9	4	5	3	1
60 - 64	4	-	4	-	-	-	-	-	-	4	-	4	1	1
65 - 74	2	1	1	1	-	1	-	-	-	1	1	-	1	-
75 - 84	1	-	1	-	-	-	-	-	-	1	-	1	1	-
85 and over	-	-	-	-	-	-	-	-	-	-	-	-	-	-

Table 3 Type of establishment, migrants and long-term illness – continued

Great Britain, England & Wales, England, regions, metropolitan counties, Inner London, Outer London, regional remainders, Wales, Scotland

Persons present in communal establishments

WALES – continued

Type of establishment and age	PERSONS PRESENT			Visitors/guests			Residents - non-staff			Residents - staff			With limiting long-term illness	Migrants
	TOTAL	Males	Females	Total	Males	Females	Total	Males	Females	Total	Males	Females		
a	b	c	d	e	f	g	h	i	j	k	l	m	n	o
Prison service establishments														
All ages	876	865	11	618	615	3	256	248	8	2	2	-	165	152
0 - 15	-	-	-	-	-	-	-	-	-	-	-	-	-	-
16 - 17	53	53	-	48	48	-	5	5	-	-	-	-	8	2
18 - 29	555	552	3	423	420	3	131	131	-	1	1	-	76	80
30 - 44	187	186	1	108	108	-	79	78	1	-	-	-	46	50
45 - 59	64	64	-	38	38	-	25	25	-	1	1	-	29	13
60 - 64	2	2	-	1	1	-	1	1	-	-	-	-	-	-
65 - 74	5	5	-	-	-	-	5	5	-	-	-	-	3	2
75 - 84	8	3	5	-	-	-	8	3	5	-	-	-	2	4
85 and over	2	-	2	-	-	-	2	-	2	-	-	-	1	1
Defence establishments														
All ages	1,881	1,698	183	839	786	53	1,042	912	130				30	617
0 - 15	-	-	-	-	-	-	-	-	-				-	-
16 - 17	87	79	8	77	73	4	10	6	4				-	10
18 - 29	1,497	1,330	167	650	601	49	847	729	118				15	507
30 - 44	245	239	6	89	89	-	156	150	6				10	88
45 - 59	52	50	2	23	23	-	29	27	2				5	12
60 - 64	-	-	-	-	-	-	-	-	-				-	-
65 - 74	-	-	-	-	-	-	-	-	-				-	-
75 - 84	-	-	-	-	-	-	-	-	-				-	-
85 and over	-	-	-	-	-	-	-	-	-				-	-

Table 3 Type of establishment, migrants and long-term illness – **continued**

Great Britain, England & Wales, England, regions, metropolitan counties, Inner London, Outer London, regional remainders, Wales, Scotland

Persons present in communal establishments

WALES – *continued*

Type of establishment and age	PERSONS PRESENT			Visitors/guests			Residents - non-staff			Residents - staff			With limiting long-term illness	Migrants
	TOTAL	Males	Females	Total	Males	Females	Total	Males	Females	Total	Males	Females		
a	b	c	d	e	f	g	h	i	j	k	l	m	n	o
Educational establishments														
All ages	**12,011**	**6,279**	**5,732**	**10,697**	**5,495**	**5,202**	**979**	**602**	**377**	**335**	**182**	**153**	**523**	**583**
0 - 15	2,248	1,304	944	2,123	1,218	905	79	60	19	46	26	20	150	35
16 - 17	1,123	602	521	1,069	564	505	50	37	13	4	1	3	53	15
18 - 29	7,785	3,910	3,875	7,056	3,454	3,602	609	383	226	120	73	47	244	413
30 - 44	464	300	164	259	165	94	125	93	32	80	42	38	24	94
45 - 59	223	107	116	135	66	69	33	13	20	55	28	27	11	20
60 - 64	50	18	32	25	10	15	8	-	8	17	8	9	4	2
65 - 74	57	31	26	21	15	6	31	14	17	5	2	3	12	1
75 - 84	54	6	48	8	2	6	38	2	36	8	2	6	20	3
85 and over	7	1	6	1	1	-	6	-	6	-	-	-	5	-
Hotels, boarding houses etc														
All ages	**11,933**	**6,649**	**5,284**	**8,375**	**4,465**	**3,910**	**1,627**	**1,092**	**535**	**1,931**	**1,092**	**839**	**1,451**	**1,290**
0 - 15	2,292	1,190	1,102	1,915	992	923	179	93	86	198	105	93	85	103
16 - 17	241	145	96	118	71	47	62	34	28	61	40	21	9	63
18 - 29	2,723	1,582	1,141	1,461	819	642	533	336	197	729	427	302	131	745
30 - 44	1,865	1,283	582	1,153	813	340	322	245	77	390	225	165	154	214
45 - 59	2,081	1,241	840	1,343	765	578	297	235	62	441	241	200	318	121
60 - 64	710	344	366	572	254	318	73	56	17	65	34	31	154	12
65 - 74	1,269	588	681	1,146	508	638	96	65	31	27	15	12	314	18
75 - 84	646	240	406	591	215	376	42	21	21	13	4	9	238	8
85 and over	106	36	70	76	28	48	23	7	16	7	1	6	48	6

Table 3 Type of establishment, migrants and long-term illness – **continued**

Persons present in communal establishments

WALES – *continued*

Type of establishment and age	PERSONS PRESENT			Visitors/guests			Residents - non-staff			Residents - staff			With limiting long-term illness	Migrants
	TOTAL	Males	Females	Total	Males	Females	Total	Males	Females	Total	Males	Females		
a	b	c	d	e	f	g	h	i	j	k	l	m	n	o
Hostels and common lodging houses (non-HA)														
All ages	**681**	**456**	**225**	**66**	**43**	**23**	**594**	**398**	**196**	**21**	**15**	**6**	**272**	**359**
0 - 15	115	60	55	14	6	8	100	53	47	1	1	-	3	62
16 - 17	23	13	10	5	2	3	18	11	7	-	-	-	2	13
18 - 29	182	95	87	15	10	5	163	83	80	4	2	2	55	143
30 - 44	153	118	35	27	21	6	116	89	27	10	8	2	69	76
45 - 59	117	98	19	4	3	1	107	91	16	6	4	2	81	46
60 - 64	34	30	4	-	-	-	34	30	4	-	-	-	25	11
65 - 74	39	35	4	1	1	-	38	34	4	-	-	-	23	6
75 - 84	14	7	7	-	-	-	14	7	7	-	-	-	10	2
85 and over	4	-	4	-	-	-	4	-	4	-	-	-	4	-
Other miscellaneous establishments														
All ages	**1,228**	**482**	**746**	**568**	**345**	**223**	**623**	**123**	**500**	**37**	**14**	**23**	**178**	**236**
0 - 15	177	84	93	93	42	51	76	41	35	8	1	7	10	57
16 - 17	65	41	24	56	41	15	9	-	9	-	-	-	3	9
18 - 29	356	198	158	241	171	70	101	19	82	14	8	6	17	69
30 - 44	202	86	116	108	62	46	86	21	65	8	3	5	20	47
45 - 59	148	32	116	36	20	16	105	10	95	7	2	5	21	19
60 - 64	65	14	51	12	2	10	53	12	41	-	-	-	8	13
65 - 74	93	19	74	17	7	10	76	12	64	-	-	-	23	10
75 - 84	86	7	79	4	-	-	82	7	75	-	-	-	42	11
85 and over	36	1	35	1	-	1	35	1	34	-	-	-	34	1

Table 3 Type of establishment, migrants and long-term illness – **continued**

Persons present in communal establishments

WALES – *continued*

Type of establishment and age	PERSONS PRESENT			Visitors/guests			Residents - non-staff			Residents - staff			With limiting long-term illness	Migrants
	TOTAL	Males	Females	Total	Males	Females	Total	Males	Females	Total	Males	Females		
a	b	c	d	e	f	g	h	i	j	k	l	m	n	o
Persons sleeping rough														
All ages	**32**	**30**	**2**	**15**	**14**	**1**	**17**	**16**	**1**				**5**	**13**
0 - 15	2	2	-	2	2	-	-	-	-				-	-
16 - 17	-	-	-	-	-	-	-	-	-				-	-
18 - 29	13	11	2	5	4	1	8	7	1				2	6
30 - 44	9	9	-	5	5	-	4	4	-				-	4
45 - 59	5	5	-	2	2	-	3	3	-				1	2
60 - 64	1	1	-	1	1	-	-	-	-				1	-
65 - 74	2	2	-	-	-	-	2	2	-				1	1
75 - 84	-	-	-	-	-	-	-	-	-				-	-
85 and over	-	-	-	-	-	-	-	-	-				-	-
Campers														
All ages	**33**	**15**	**18**	**32**	**14**	**18**	**1**	**1**	**-**				**-**	**-**
0 - 15	-	-	-	-	-	-	-	-	-				-	-
16 - 17	-	-	-	-	-	-	-	-	-				-	-
18 - 29	14	4	10	14	4	10	-	-	-				-	-
30 - 44	1	1	-	1	1	-	-	-	-				-	-
45 - 59	-	-	-	-	-	-	-	-	-				-	-
60 - 64	5	3	2	5	3	2	-	-	-				-	-
65 - 74	12	6	6	11	5	6	1	1	-				-	-
75 - 84	1	1	-	1	1	-	-	-	-				-	-
85 and over	-	-	-	-	-	-	-	-	-				-	-

Table 3 Type of establishment, migrants and long-term illness – **continued**

Great Britain, England & Wales, England, regions, metropolitan counties, Inner London, Outer London, regional remainders, Wales, Scotland

Persons present in communal establishments

Type of establishment and age	PERSONS PRESENT			Visitors/guests			Residents - non-staff			Residents - staff			With limiting long-term illness	Migrants
	TOTAL	Males	Females	Total	Males	Females	Total	Males	Females	Total	Males	Females		
a	b	c	d	e	f	g	h	i	j	k	l	m	n	o

WALES – continued

Civilian ships, boats and barges

All ages	**570**	**539**	**31**	**412**	**393**	**19**	**158**	**146**	**12**				**9**	**35**
0 - 15	6	5	1	4	3	1	2	2	-				1	1
16 - 17	2	2	-	-	-	-	2	2	-				-	1
18 - 29	122	111	11	86	80	6	36	31	5				2	6
30 - 44	281	270	11	213	205	8	68	65	3				2	15
45 - 59	147	139	8	99	95	4	48	44	4				5	12
60 - 64	8	8	-	7	7	-	1	1	-				-	-
65 - 74	3	3	-	2	2	-	1	1	-				-	-
75 - 84	1	1	-	1	1	-	-	-	-				-	-
85 and over	-	-	-	-	-	-	-	-	-				-	-

SCOTLAND

All establishments *

All ages	**154,841**	**74,519**	**80,322**	**77,425**	**42,015**	**35,410**	**68,519**	**28,471**	**40,048**	**8,897**	**4,033**	**4,864**	**70,741**	**23,026**
0 - 15	10,044	5,787	4,257	7,335	4,300	3,035	1,866	1,043	823	843	444	399	813	1,105
16 - 17	3,887	2,348	1,539	3,091	1,899	1,192	571	351	220	225	98	127	275	510
18 - 29	40,869	23,541	17,328	26,876	15,093	11,783	9,788	6,773	3,015	4,205	1,675	2,530	3,666	7,026
30 - 44	19,037	12,727	6,310	10,977	7,396	3,581	6,320	4,398	1,922	1,740	933	807	5,076	2,281
45 - 59	15,403	9,265	6,138	8,891	5,163	3,728	5,089	3,404	1,685	1,423	698	725	6,226	1,015
60 - 64	5,930	3,055	2,875	3,473	1,673	1,800	2,247	1,270	977	210	112	98	3,412	357
65 - 74	15,089	7,042	8,047	7,526	3,440	4,086	7,424	3,552	3,872	139	50	89	10,540	1,587
75 - 84	24,543	7,361	17,182	6,566	2,380	4,186	17,912	4,966	12,946	65	15	50	21,829	4,926
85 and over	20,039	3,393	16,646	2,690	671	2,019	17,302	2,714	14,588	47	8	39	18,904	4,219

Note: * Includes a male member of staff incorrectly enumerated as a resident.

Table 3 Type of establishment, migrants and long-term illness – **continued**

Great Britain, England & Wales, England, regions, metropolitan counties, Inner London, Outer London, regional remainders, Wales, Scotland

Persons present in communal establishments

SCOTLAND – *continued*

Type of establishment and age	PERSONS PRESENT			Visitors/guests			Residents - non-staff			Residents - staff			With limiting long-term illness	Migrants
	TOTAL	Males	Females	Total	Males	Females	Total	Males	Females	Total	Males	Females		
a	b	c	d	e	f	g	h	i	j	k	l	m	n	o
NHS hospitals/homes - psychiatric														
All ages	11,440	4,906	6,534	2,157	920	1,237	9,009	3,860	5,149	274	126	148	10,529	1,181
0 - 15	119	74	45	45	23	22	72	51	21	2	-	2	28	11
16 - 17	36	15	21	26	10	16	7	5	2	3	-	3	16	4
18 - 29	927	501	426	415	215	200	305	199	106	207	87	120	494	153
30 - 44	1,219	720	499	423	231	192	748	458	290	48	31	17	1,052	77
45 - 59	1,481	865	616	298	122	176	1,173	737	436	10	6	4	1,406	66
60 - 64	801	416	385	123	51	72	675	363	312	3	2	1	772	40
65 - 74	2,154	1,053	1,101	295	115	180	1,859	938	921	-	-	-	2,111	197
75 - 84	3,022	968	2,054	372	107	265	2,650	861	1,789	-	-	-	2,980	436
85 and over	1,681	294	1,387	160	46	114	1,520	248	1,272	1	1	1	1,670	197
NHS hospitals/homes - other														
All ages	32,514	11,775	20,739	18,804	7,298	11,506	12,314	4,120	8,194	1,396	357	1,039	22,663	3,789
0 - 15	1,844	979	865	1,766	942	824	73	33	40	5	4	1	383	11
16 - 17	168	56	112	131	44	87	28	12	16	9	-	9	54	17
18 - 29	5,616	1,516	4,100	2,931	663	2,268	1,521	602	919	1,164	251	913	1,076	1,174
30 - 44	3,196	1,481	1,715	1,770	659	1,111	1,245	731	514	181	91	90	1,769	222
45 - 59	2,791	1,385	1,406	1,875	923	952	890	455	435	26	7	19	2,113	67
60 - 64	1,432	701	731	1,077	554	523	346	144	202	9	3	6	1,171	43
65 - 74	4,432	2,057	2,375	3,060	1,460	1,600	1,371	596	775	1	1	-	3,811	337
75 - 84	7,622	2,570	5,052	4,166	1,552	2,614	3,455	1,018	2,437	1	-	1	7,068	1,002
85 and over	5,413	1,030	4,383	2,028	501	1,527	3,385	529	2,856	-	-	-	5,218	916

Table 3 Type of establishment, migrants and long-term illness – **continued**

Persons present in communal establishments

Type of establishment and age	PERSONS PRESENT			Visitors/guests			Residents - non-staff			Residents - staff			With limiting long-term illness	Migrants
	TOTAL	Males	Females	Total	Males	Females	Total	Males	Females	Total	Males	Females		
a	b	c	d	e	f	g	h	i	j	k	l	m	n	o
Non-NHS hospitals - psychiatric						SCOTLAND – *continued*								
All ages	**314**	**142**	**172**	**77**	**36**	**41**	**220**	**99**	**121**	**17**	**7**	**10**	**267**	**40**
0 - 15	3	1	2	3	1	2	-	-	-	-	-	-	1	-
16 - 17	-	-	-	-	-	-	-	-	-	-	-	-	-	-
18 - 29	29	15	14	11	7	4	5	3	2	13	5	8	8	4
30 - 44	21	13	8	11	5	6	8	6	2	2	2	-	11	1
45 - 59	37	22	15	8	4	4	27	18	9	2	-	2	32	-
60 - 64	21	15	6	5	3	2	16	12	4	-	-	-	19	-
65 - 74	63	33	30	17	9	8	46	24	22	-	-	-	59	5
75 - 84	86	27	59	12	3	9	74	24	50	-	-	-	84	16
85 and over	54	16	38	10	4	6	44	12	32	-	-	-	53	14
Non-NHS hospitals - other														
All ages	**1,213**	**363**	**850**	**349**	**124**	**225**	**835**	**236**	**599**	**29**	**3**	**26**	**997**	**173**
0 - 15	19	9	10	11	4	7	8	5	3	-	-	-	3	2
16 - 17	2	1	1	-	-	-	2	1	1	-	-	-	2	-
18 - 29	98	44	54	37	17	20	47	25	22	14	2	12	55	12
30 - 44	142	59	83	74	27	47	63	32	31	5	-	5	92	4
45 - 59	177	77	100	63	26	37	109	50	59	5	1	4	135	9
60 - 64	68	30	38	28	13	15	39	17	22	1	-	1	57	7
65 - 74	137	50	87	47	22	25	88	28	60	2	-	2	118	22
75 - 84	304	63	241	63	14	49	240	49	191	1	-	1	282	68
85 and over	266	30	236	26	1	25	239	29	210	1	-	1	253	49

Table 3 Type of establishment, migrants and long-term illness – **continued**

Great Britain, England & Wales, England, regions, metropolitan counties, Inner London, Outer London, regional remainders, Wales, Scotland

Persons present in communal establishments

SCOTLAND – *continued*

Type of establishment and age	PERSONS PRESENT			Visitors/guests			Residents - non-staff			Residents - staff			With limiting long-term illness	Migrants
	TOTAL	Males	Females	Total	Males	Females	Total	Males	Females	Total	Males	Females		
a	b	c	d	e	f	g	h	i	j	k	l	m	n	o
Local authority homes														
All ages	**10,657**	**3,429**	**7,228**	**1,099**	**502**	**597**	**9,334**	**2,834**	**6,500**	**224**	**93**	**131**	**9,196**	**2,111**
0 - 15	488	335	153	342	246	96	78	53	25	68	36	32	85	34
16 - 17	90	57	33	53	38	15	37	19	18	-	-	-	45	21
18 - 29	443	236	207	95	43	52	307	176	131	41	17	24	279	82
30 - 44	521	230	291	91	32	59	366	175	191	64	23	41	344	55
45 - 59	395	182	213	77	11	66	282	157	125	36	14	22	282	28
60 - 64	188	86	102	26	6	20	156	78	78	6	2	4	156	41
65 - 74	1,142	508	634	78	36	42	1,058	471	587	6	1	5	1,047	239
75 - 84	3,565	1,076	2,489	169	55	114	3,394	1,021	2,373	2	-	2	3,361	832
85 and over	3,825	719	3,106	168	35	133	3,656	684	2,972	1	-	1	3,597	779
Housing association homes and hostels														
All ages	**1,842**	**741**	**1,101**	**80**	**54**	**26**	**1,664**	**661**	**1,003**	**98**	**26**	**72**	**1,150**	**491**
0 - 15	30	23	7	2	2	-	16	13	3	12	8	4	5	16
16 - 17	32	14	18	1	1	-	30	13	17	1	-	1	5	26
18 - 29	269	152	117	33	21	12	228	128	100	8	3	5	105	122
30 - 44	263	159	104	16	12	4	230	143	87	17	4	13	176	90
45 - 59	241	139	102	17	13	4	176	116	60	48	10	38	154	47
60 - 64	55	38	17	4	3	1	44	34	10	7	1	6	41	9
65 - 74	151	77	74	4	2	2	142	75	67	5	-	5	97	33
75 - 84	366	79	287	1	-	1	365	79	286	-	-	-	246	81
85 and over	435	60	375	2	-	2	433	60	373	-	-	-	321	67

Table 3 Type of establishment, migrants and long-term illness – **continued**

Great Britain, England & Wales, England, regions, metropolitan counties, Inner London, Outer London, regional remainders, Wales, Scotland

Persons present in communal establishments

SCOTLAND – continued

Type of establishment and age	PERSONS PRESENT			Visitors/guests			Residents - non-staff			Residents - staff			With limiting long-term illness	Migrants
	TOTAL	Males	Females	Total	Males	Females	Total	Males	Females	Total	Males	Females		
a	b	c	d	e	f	g	h	i	j	k	l	m	n	o
Nursing homes *(non-NHS/LA/HA)*														
All ages	**12,056**	**2,635**	**9,421**	**665**	**227**	**438**	**11,179**	**2,357**	**8,822**	**212**	**51**	**161**	**11,254**	**3,903**
0 - 15	32	13	19	7	1	6	5	3	2	20	9	11	3	4
16 - 17	10	4	6	1	-	1	8	4	4	1	-	1	3	8
18 - 29	156	72	84	36	7	29	94	57	37	26	8	18	65	50
30 - 44	272	130	142	78	24	54	166	100	66	28	6	22	169	45
45 - 59	248	105	143	71	29	42	123	62	61	54	14	40	158	29
60 - 64	338	152	186	59	28	31	266	118	148	13	6	7	297	97
65 - 74	1,372	459	913	165	69	96	1,195	390	805	12	-	12	1,277	437
75 - 84	4,678	1,025	3,653	154	51	103	4,497	970	3,527	27	4	23	4,492	1,699
85 and over	4,950	675	4,275	94	18	76	4,825	653	4,172	31	4	27	4,790	1,534
Residential homes *(non-NHS/LA/HA)*														
All ages	**8,467**	**2,404**	**6,063**	**263**	**72**	**191**	**7,931**	**2,221**	**5,710**	**273**	**111**	**162**	**7,250**	**1,845**
0 - 15	55	27	28	5	2	3	5	1	4	45	24	21	5	10
16 - 17	29	16	13	3	1	2	22	13	9	4	2	2	16	18
18 - 29	353	181	172	48	21	27	264	147	117	41	13	28	257	109
30 - 44	537	278	259	57	16	41	423	237	186	57	25	32	420	59
45 - 59	555	268	287	45	9	36	411	227	184	99	32	67	412	63
60 - 64	248	141	107	7	3	4	227	128	99	14	10	4	197	38
65 - 74	846	381	465	17	4	13	819	373	446	10	4	6	692	203
75 - 84	2,816	676	2,140	44	10	34	2,770	665	2,105	2	1	1	2,494	726
85 and over	3,028	436	2,592	37	6	31	2,990	430	2,560	1	-	1	2,757	619

Table 3 Type of establishment, migrants and long-term illness – **continued**

Great Britain, England & Wales, England, regions, metropolitan counties, Inner London, Outer London, regional remainders, Wales, Scotland

Persons present in communal establishments

SCOTLAND – *continued*

Type of establishment and age	PERSONS PRESENT			Visitors/guests			Residents - non-staff			Residents - staff			With limiting long-term illness	Migrants
	TOTAL	Males	Females	Total	Males	Females	Total	Males	Females	Total	Males	Females		
a	b	c	d	e	f	g	h	i	j	k	l	m	n	o
Children's homes														
All ages	**1,395**	**698**	**697**	**329**	**167**	**162**	**996**	**504**	**492**	**70**	**27**	**43**	**144**	**556**
0 - 15	1,278	652	626	269	145	124	996	504	492	13	3	10	125	543
16 - 17	8	4	4	-	-	-	-	-	-	8	4	4	-	1
18 - 29	30	11	19	13	4	9	-	-	-	17	7	10	7	5
30 - 44	50	21	29	35	16	19	-	-	-	15	5	10	7	5
45 - 59	26	9	17	11	2	9	-	-	-	15	7	8	5	1
60 - 64	2	-	2	1	-	1	-	-	-	1	-	1	-	-
65 - 74	1	1	-	-	-	-	-	-	-	1	1	-	-	1
75 - 84	-	-	-	-	-	-	-	-	-	-	-	-	-	-
85 and over	-	-	-	-	-	-	-	-	-	-	-	-	-	-
Prison service establishments														
All ages	**4,590**	**4,431**	**159**	**2,979**	**2,866**	**113**	**1,611**	**1,565**	**46**	**-**	**-**	**-**	**653**	**584**
0 - 15	1	1	-	1	1	-	-	-	-	-	-	-	-	-
16 - 17	193	189	4	165	163	2	28	26	2	-	-	-	17	20
18 - 29	2,818	2,721	97	2,012	1,936	76	806	785	21	-	-	-	292	309
30 - 44	1,223	1,180	43	619	593	26	604	587	17	-	-	-	222	212
45 - 59	322	308	14	164	156	8	158	152	6	-	-	-	104	39
60 - 64	19	18	1	9	8	1	10	10	-	-	-	-	11	2
65 - 74	10	10	-	7	7	-	3	3	-	-	-	-	7	-
75 - 84	3	3	-	2	2	-	1	1	-	-	-	-	-	1
85 and over	1	1	-	-	-	-	1	1	-	-	-	-	-	1

Table 3 Type of establishment, migrants and long-term illness – **continued**

Great Britain, England & Wales, England, regions, metropolitan counties, Inner London, Outer London, regional remainders, Wales, Scotland

Persons present in communal establishments

Type of establishment and age	PERSONS PRESENT			Visitors/guests			Residents - non-staff			Residents - staff			With limiting long-term illness	Migrants
	TOTAL	Males	Females	Total	Males	Females	Total	Males	Females	Total	Males	Females		
a	b	c	d	e	f	g	h	i	j	k	l	m	n	o
SCOTLAND – *continued*														
Defence establishments														
All ages	**5,962**	**5,412**	**550**	**2,084**	**1,949**	**135**	**3,878**	**3,463**	**415**				**393**	**1,818**
0 - 15	-	-	-	-	-	-	-	-	-				-	-
16 - 17	178	157	21	66	60	6	112	97	15				1	96
18 - 29	4,092	3,651	441	1,152	1,064	88	2,940	2,587	353				58	1,457
30 - 44	1,165	1,100	65	670	640	30	495	460	35				38	214
45 - 59	257	242	15	158	151	7	99	91	8				58	28
60 - 64	38	38	-	14	14	-	24	24	-				26	3
65 - 74	111	107	4	12	9	3	99	98	1				99	8
75 - 84	92	89	3	10	9	1	82	80	2				85	9
85 and over	29	28	1	2	2	-	27	26	1				28	3
Educational establishments														
All ages	**23,271**	**12,982**	**10,289**	**20,392**	**11,259**	**9,133**	**2,195**	**1,421**	**774**	**684**	**302**	**382**	**686**	**1,500**
0 - 15	3,462	2,140	1,322	3,260	2,024	1,236	126	83	43	76	33	43	80	86
16 - 17	2,288	1,355	933	2,200	1,303	897	76	47	29	12	5	7	62	39
18 - 29	15,930	8,540	7,390	14,173	7,489	6,684	1,516	963	553	241	88	153	448	1,062
30 - 44	1,143	735	408	560	355	205	387	274	113	196	106	90	54	276
45 - 59	341	161	180	153	69	84	48	30	18	140	62	78	25	33
60 - 64	51	23	28	24	8	16	15	10	5	12	5	7	9	1
65 - 74	32	16	16	14	7	7	15	7	8	3	2	1	4	1
75 - 84	19	10	9	8	4	4	9	5	4	2	1	1	2	1
85 and over	5	2	3	-	-	-	3	2	1	2	-	2	2	1

Table 3 Type of establishment, migrants and long-term illness – **continued**

Great Britain, England & Wales, England, regions, metropolitan counties, Inner London, Outer London, regional remainders, Wales, Scotland

Persons present in communal establishments

SCOTLAND – *continued*

Type of establishment and age	PERSONS PRESENT			Visitors/guests			Residents - non-staff			Residents - staff			With limiting long-term illness	Migrants
	TOTAL	Males	Females	Total	Males	Females	Total	Males	Females	Total	Males	Females		
a	b	c	d	e	f	g	h	i	j	k	l	m	n	o
Hotels, boarding houses etc														
All ages	**34,026**	**19,213**	**14,813**	**25,254**	**14,108**	**11,146**	**3,411**	**2,288**	**1,123**	**5,361**	**2,817**	**2,544**	**3,805**	**3,573**
0 - 15	2,379	1,329	1,050	1,522	850	672	284	167	117	573	312	261	70	282
16 - 17	603	304	299	295	151	144	125	66	59	183	87	96	32	178
18 - 29	8,484	4,713	3,771	5,057	2,902	2,155	1,072	645	427	2,355	1,166	1,189	328	2,019
30 - 44	7,379	5,060	2,319	5,598	3,902	1,696	717	545	172	1,064	613	451	378	644
45 - 59	6,879	4,128	2,751	5,350	3,126	2,224	600	491	109	929	511	418	797	304
60 - 64	2,268	1,097	1,171	2,006	915	1,091	126	102	24	136	80	56	473	28
65 - 74	4,035	1,859	2,176	3,742	1,658	2,084	207	163	44	86	38	48	961	44
75 - 84	1,718	633	1,085	1,530	550	980	163	77	86	25	6	19	602	38
85 and over	281	90	191	154	54	100	117	32	85	10	4	6	164	36
Hostels and common lodging houses (non-HA)														
All ages	**2,751**	**2,181**	**570**	**216**	**136**	**80**	**2,477**	**2,009**	**468**	**58**	**36**	**22**	**1,261**	**936**
0 - 15	118	79	39	21	8	13	92	68	24	5	3	2	20	47
16 - 17	75	38	37	13	7	6	60	31	29	2	-	2	17	51
18 - 29	521	350	171	101	60	41	405	283	122	15	7	8	122	299
30 - 44	483	371	112	41	30	11	427	331	96	15	10	5	240	227
45 - 59	791	687	104	25	20	5	746	652	94	20	15	5	446	224
60 - 64	245	211	34	7	5	2	237	205	32	1	1	-	151	38
65 - 74	392	346	46	5	5	-	387	341	46	-	-	-	198	41
75 - 84	113	94	19	1	1	-	112	93	19	-	-	-	58	9
85 and over	13	5	8	2	-	2	11	5	6	-	-	-	9	-

Table 3 Type of establishment, migrants and long-term illness – **continued**

Great Britain, England & Wales, England, regions, metropolitan counties, Inner London, Outer London, regional remainders, Wales, Scotland

Persons present in communal establishments

Type of establishment and age	PERSONS PRESENT			Visitors/guests			Residents - non-staff			Residents - staff			With limiting long-term illness	Migrants
	TOTAL	Males	Females	Total	Males	Females	Total	Males	Females	Total	Males	Females		
a	b	c	d	e	f	g	h	i	j	k	l	m	n	o

SCOTLAND – *continued*

Other miscellaneous establishments

Type of establishment and age	PERSONS PRESENT			Visitors/guests			Residents - non-staff			Residents - staff			With limiting long-term illness	Migrants
All ages	**1,968**	**1,120**	**848**	**847**	**697**	**150**	**921**	**347**	**574**	**200**	**76**	**124**	**346**	**322**
0 - 15	141	83	58	39	31	8	79	41	38	23	11	12	1	50
16 - 17	139	113	26	109	101	8	28	12	16	2	-	2	5	28
18 - 29	589	394	195	366	300	66	160	73	87	63	21	42	51	115
30 - 44	429	267	162	184	157	27	197	93	104	48	17	31	68	62
45 - 59	267	148	119	104	82	22	124	47	77	39	19	20	46	32
60 - 64	76	27	49	13	8	5	56	17	39	7	2	5	21	8
65 - 74	163	54	109	21	10	11	129	41	88	13	3	10	46	17
75 - 84	112	31	81	10	8	2	97	20	77	5	3	2	67	7
85 and over	52	3	49	1	-	1	51	3	48	-	-	-	41	3

Persons sleeping rough

Type of establishment and age	PERSONS PRESENT			Visitors/guests			Residents - non-staff			Residents - staff			With limiting long-term illness	Migrants
All ages	**145**	**124**	**21**	**80**	**69**	**11**	**64**	**54**	**10**				**70**	**46**
0 - 15	1	1	-	-	-	-	-	-	-				-	-
16 - 17	1	-	1	1	-	1	-	-	-				-	-
18 - 29	26	22	4	17	16	1	9	6	3				9	8
30 - 44	54	41	13	28	21	7	26	20	6				27	17
45 - 59	52	50	2	30	28	2	22	22	-				26	17
60 - 64	5	5	-	2	2	-	3	3	-				3	2
65 - 74	5	4	1	2	2	-	3	2	1				4	1
75 - 84	1	1	-	-	-	-	1	1	-				1	1
85 and over	-	-	-	-	-	-	-	-	-				-	-

Table 3 Type of establishment, migrants and long-term illness – **continued**

Great Britain, England & Wales, England, regions, metropolitan counties, Inner London, Outer London, regional remainders, Wales, Scotland

Persons present in communal establishments

SCOTLAND – *continued*

Type of establishment and age	PERSONS PRESENT			Visitors/guests			Residents - non-staff			Residents - staff			With limiting long-term illness	Migrants
	TOTAL	Males	Females	Total	Males	Females	Total	Males	Females	Total	Males	Females		
a	b	c	d	e	f	g	h	i	j	k	l	m	n	o
Campers														
All ages	**415**	**238**	**177**	**316**	**180**	**136**	**99**	**58**	**41**				**47**	**34**
0 - 15	63	31	32	31	10	21	32	21	11				1	9
16 - 17	11	6	5	5	3	2	6	3	3				-	2
18 - 29	83	49	34	58	35	23	25	14	11				4	10
30 - 44	95	57	38	72	45	27	23	12	11				5	9
45 - 59	106	63	43	97	57	40	9	6	3				23	3
60 - 64	24	9	15	23	9	14	1	-	1				5	-
65 - 74	26	18	8	24	17	7	2	1	1				7	1
75 - 84	7	5	2	6	4	2	1	1	-				2	-
85 and over	-	-	-	-	-	-	-	-	-				-	-
Civilian ships, boats and barges														
All ages	**1,815**	**1,725**	**90**	**1,434**	**1,351**	**83**	**381**	**374**	**7**				**30**	**124**
0 - 15	11	10	1	11	10	1	-	-	-				3	-
16 - 17	24	19	5	22	17	5	2	2	-				-	1
18 - 29	405	373	32	321	293	28	84	80	4				8	36
30 - 44	845	825	20	650	631	19	195	194	1				4	62
45 - 59	437	426	11	345	335	10	92	91	1				4	25
60 - 64	51	48	3	45	43	2	6	5	1				3	-
65 - 74	17	9	8	16	8	8	1	1	-				2	-
75 - 84	19	11	8	18	10	8	1	1	-				5	-
85 and over	6	4	2	6	4	2	-	-	-				1	-

The products described in this Annex become available in the period May 1992 until mid-1994. Dates of availability are not given, to avoid any confusion as this Report continues to be used during and after the period 1992-94. All products are described as if available, but, in any case of doubt, a check should be made with OPCS Census Customer Services at the address given at the end of this Annex.

The form of results

The statistical results of the Census are made available in two ways:

(a)   in printed *reports* sold by HMSO bookshops (or, in a few cases, directly from the Census Offices); or

(b)   in *statistical abstracts* available, on request and for a charge, from the Census Offices.

The *reports* take three general forms:

* volumes - such as this Report - containing substantial and detailed tables;

* *key statistics*, which give around 150 summary statistics for particular types of areas throughout the country, with national and regional figures, laid out for easy comparison between areas; and

* *Monitors*, pamphlets which either give between 20 and 60 summary statistics for particular types of area in parts of the country, sometimes issued before main reports to give early results, or provide summaries for the country as a whole.

Statistical abstracts are supplied mainly in machine-readable form, although small quantities can be supplied as hard copies, and are generally either:

* in a standard form, commissioned by a number of customers sharing costs, particularly to provide results for areas and populations smaller than those covered in reports; or

* specially designed output commissioned by individual customers.

The Census Offices also supply supplementary products, for example to provide information on the geographical base of the Census, and documentation in a series of OPCS/GRO(S) *1991 Census User Guides*.

There are two broad types of results:

(a)   *local statistics*, which cover the full range of census topics; and

(b)   *topic statistics* - such as this Report, which focus on particular census topics in more detail, mainly at national and regional level.

All the main statistical results and products are described in *Prospectuses* in the *User Guides* series, available from the addresses given in section 12. Prospectuses for reports and abstracts contain complete outlines of the tables which will become available.

All areas for which results are provided in reports and abstracts are as at the time of the 1991 Census (unless otherwise indicated).

Local statistics

Local authorities and smaller areas

Results for local authorities and smaller areas are available, with full comparability, as:

County Reports (England and Wales) and *Region Reports* (Scotland): issued separately in two parts for each County in England and Wales and for each Region in Scotland. Results are presented for the county (Region in Scotland) and its constituent districts.

Key Statistics (Great Britain): a single report giving around 170 summary statistics, with some 1981/91 comparisons, for each local authority (see *User Guide* 29).

County Monitors (England and Wales) and *Region Monitors* (Scotland): pamphlets issued separately for each County or Region in advance of the main *Reports*. Welsh County Monitors are published in bi-lingual format (Welsh and English).

Ward and Civil Parish Monitors (England and Scotland) or *Ward and Community Monitors* (Wales): pamphlets for each county in England and Wales and each Region in Scotland which give some 30 statistics for each ward and civil parish/community, with figures for counties/Regions and districts/boroughs for comparison (see *User Guide* 32).

Local and Small Area Statistics are standard abstracts available from a variety of areas (including local authorities) throughout Great Britain from the smallest - the Census Enumeration District (Output Area in Scotland) - upwards. Further information is available in *User Guide* 49. Further *User Guides* give: the file specification (number 21); the cell numbering system (24 and 25); and explanatory notes (38).

Results for other types of area, in forms comparable with those for local authorities listed above, are available for:

Health authority areas

Health Regions Report: a single report, in a similar form to the County Report, for Regional Health Authorities in England (elsewhere in Great Britain health authority boundaries coincided with those of local authorities at the time of the 1991 Census).

Key Statistics: a single report giving about 150 summary statistics for each Regional and District Health Authority in England and Health Board in Scotland (see *User Guide* 31).

Health Authority Monitors: pamphlets, similar to of County Monitors, for Regional and District Health Authorities.

Local and Small Area Statistics are also available as abstracts at health authority level.

Urban and Rural Areas

Key Statistics: a single report for the larger urban areas and the rural areas in Great Britain, giving about 150 summary statistics for each area, with six 'regional' reports covering urban areas of all sizes and the rural areas in various parts of England and Wales and, separately, for Scotland (see *User Guide* 30).

Urban and rural areas have been specially defined for both the 1981 and 1991 Censuses, and a further report will give figures on change over the decade. 'Urban areas' cover conurbations, cities and towns of all sizes defined on a land use ('bricks and mortar') basis, so, for example, Census results are available for smaller towns *within* the larger local authority areas.

Small Area Statistics are also available as abstracts for each urban and rural area.

Parliamentary and European Constituencies

Parliamentary Constituency Monitors: pamphlets, in a similar form to the County Monitors, but with some additional '10 per cent' statistics, with results for each Parliamentary Constituency (and with figures for Great Britain for comparison). There are separate Monitors for each standard statistical region in England, and for Wales and Scotland (see *User Guide* 34). A single Monitor in the same form is available for the European Parliamentary Constituencies in Great Britain.

Postcode areas

Postcode Sector Monitors: pamphlets for postcode towns or groups of postcode towns in Great Britain, giving summary statistics at postcode sector level (see *User Guide* 33).

Small Area Statistics are also available as abstracts for postcode sectors. For postcode sectors in Scotland, *Local Base Statistics* are also available.

The 1991 Census records for England and Wales are re-sorted to give exact counts for postcode sectors. Results for a wide range of postcode-based areas are available in Scotland.

National versions of local results

Results for Great Britain, regions in England, and Wales and Scotland, for these areas as a whole in forms comparable with those for local authorities and other types of area listed above, are available as:

Report for Great Britain: issued in two parts, in a similar form to the County Reports, for Great Britain as a whole, including results for standard statistical regions in England and for Wales and Scotland; there is also a separate *Report for Wales*, and a *Report for Scotland*.

National Monitor: pamphlet for Great Britain, including summary results for standard statistical regions in England and for Wales and Scotland. Similar summary Monitors are available for Wales (bi-lingual in Welsh and English) and Scotland, including results at County/Region level.

Topic statistics

Results for particular census topics are available in a series of reports, such as this Report, and are summarised in the table on the following page. The reports present results mainly at the national level, but the table shows those which have results at regional level, or at a county or district (or equivalent) level. Prospectuses should be checked for detailed information.

Topic Monitors: pamphlets for selected topics providing summary information and analyses.

Workplace and migration statistics

The analysis of the Census questions on 'address of workplace' and 'usual address one year before the Census' gives results on journeys from residences to workplaces and on migration moves, together with figures on people with workplaces in an area and out-migrants from an area, not only for the larger areas covered by Topic Reports, but also for smaller local areas. The latter are available as:

Regional Migration Statistics: *User Guide* 22 proposed the publication of separate volumes on migration for each standard statistical region of England, for Wales, and for Scotland. The tables proposed for these Reports are now only available in machine-readable form.

Special Migration Statistics: which provide information (in machine-readable form only) on migrants within and between local areas (see *User Guide* 35).

Special Workplace Statistics: which provide information (in machine-readable form only) on workforces in areas of workplace and residence for customer defined zones, and on journeys from residence to workplace between the zones (see *User Guide* 36).

Other products
Commissioned tables

In addition to the standard tables prepared for the local and topic statistics, the Census Offices also supply tables, on

Topic	Processing level (per cent)	Prospectus (number)	With some results for:		
			Standard Statistical Regions*	Counties/ Scottish regions	Districts
Sex, Age and Marital Status (GB)	100	2	yes	yes	no
Historical Tables (GB)	100	4	yes	yes	no
Usual Residence (GB)	100	7	yes	yes	yes
Persons Aged 60 and Over (GB)	100	6	yes	no	no
Housing and Availability of Cars (GB and S)	100	12	yes	yes	yes
Communal Establishments (GB)	100	15	yes	no	no
Household Composition (GB)	100	11	yes	no	no
Limiting Long-term Illness (GB)	100	5	yes	no	no
Ethnic Group and Country of Birth (GB)	100/10	9	yes	yes	yes
Welsh Language	100/10	10	n/a	yes	yes
Gaelic Language	100/10	18	n/a	yes	yes
National Migration (Part 1) (GB)	100	17	yes**	no	no
National Migration (Part 2) (GB)	10	17	yes**	no	no
Regional Migration (Part 1)†	100	22	yes**	yes	yes
Regional Migration (Part 2)†	10	22	yes**	yes	no
Topic Report for Health Areas (GB)	100	39	n/a	n/a	n/a
Economic Activity (GB and S)	10	16	yes	no	no
Workplace and Transport to Work (GB and S)	10	20	yes	yes	yes***
Household and Family Composition (GB)	10	23	no	no	no
Qualified Manpower (GB)	10	8	yes	no	no
Children and Young Adults (GB)	100/10	13	yes	no	no

GB   Volumes for Great Britain
GB and S   Volumes for Great Britain together with additional volumes for Scotland

*   includes Metropolitan Counties in England
**   includes main urban areas
***   includes city centres
†   in machine-readable form only

request, to a customer's own specification, at a charge which meets the marginal cost of production (see section 11). *User Guide* 14 explains how customers may specify and order commissioned tables, and provides guidance on estimation of costs.

Enumeration District/Postcode Directory for England and Wales

This Directory provides a means of associating enumeration districts to postcodes to enable users to undertake their own linkage between census and other datasets. It is available, on magnetic media only, separately for each county. Alternatively, customers may purchase a National Directory. Further details of the file specification, information on availability, cost and ordering are provided in *User Guide* 26.

Scottish Boundary products

Various products based on the digitised boundaries of Scottish postcode units are available from GRO(S). These products include the digital boundaries of output areas (OAs) and index files linking postcodes to OAs, and OAs to 'higher areas' such as district, ward and civil parish. Full details are available in a prospectus from Census Customer Services, GRO(S).

Census Newsletter

News on all aspects of the Census, including the availability of results, is provided by the *Census Newsletter* issued several times a year by the Census Offices and distributed without charge. Names may be added to the mailing list by contacting Census Customer Services. It is also possible to register with Census Customer Services as a user of the Census in order to obtain details of relevant products automatically and to ensure inclusion in consultation over future developments.

User Guide Catalogue

This catalogue is available from the Census Customer Services at the address given below. The catalogue is regularly revised to provide up-to-date information on all User Guides.

Enquiries about products described in this Annex may be addressed, in England and Wales, to:

Census Customer Services
OPCS
Segensworth Road
Titchfield
Fareham
Hampshire
PO15 5RR

telephone 0329 813800

and, in Scotland, to:

Census Customer Services
GRO(S)
Ladywell House
Ladywell Road
Edinburgh
EH12 7TF

telephone 031 314 4254

Please mention this Report when making an enquiry.

1991 Census England/Wales

L Form for Communal Establishments, HM Ships or other vessels

For Enumerator/Census Office use

CD No.	ED No.	Form No.

Instructions

Listing of names

List the names of all people present, as instructed overleaf.

You may start drawing up the list in advance of Census day, but before collection or despatch you must bring it up to date.

Distribution

An Individual form (I form) must be completed for each person listed. Where a person is incapable of making a return, you must arrange for a form to be completed on his or her behalf.

Before you issue each form, enter the name of the establishment or vessel in the panel at top right hand corner on the front of the Individual form (a rubber stamp may be used).

Please issue an envelope to any person who wishes to make a return under sealed cover.

For communal establishments, please give the type of establishment below.

When you have completed this form please fill in and sign the declaration overleaf.

Collection of forms

Communal Establishments

Please have all the completed forms ready for collection by the Enumerator, who will call on Monday 22nd April or soon afterwards.

Vessels other than HM Ships

Please have all of the completed forms ready for collection by the Enumerator who will call on Monday 22 April, or return them to the Enumerator in accordance with the instructions issued at delivery.

HM Ships

Please despatch the completed forms as soon as possible after 21st April to:

Office of Population Censuses and Surveys, PO Box 100 Fareham PO16 OAL

To the Manager, Chief Resident Officer, Commanding Officer or other person in charge of a communal establishment:

To the Captain, Master, Commanding Officer or other person in charge of a vessel or HM Ship:

I am seeking your help in conducting the Census. Under the Census Act 1920 you have a legal obligation to list the names of the people in your establishment or on your vessel, to distribute forms to them and to collect the forms on completion. In a communal establishment you must also complete the 'type of establishment' panel. If you refuse to complete this form, or give false information, you may have to pay a fine of up to 40 0. The instructions opposite tell you what to do and should be followed carefully.

The Individual forms with which you have been supplied are for the returns to be made by or for each person who spends the night of **21-22 April** at this establishment or on board this vessel. To assist you in issuing and collecting the individual forms, spaces have been provided overleaf for listing those people.

The answers given will be treated in strict confidence and used only to produce statistics. Names and addresses will not be put in the computer; only the postcode will be entered. The forms will be kept securely within my Office and treated as confidential for 100 years.

Anyone using or disclosing census information improperly will be liable to prosecution. For example, it would be improper for you to pass on to someone else, information which you have been given in confidence on, or for completion of, an individual form.

Thank you for your co-operation.

P J Wormald
Registrar General

Office of Population Censuses and Surveys
PO Box 100 Fareham PO16 0AL

Telephone 0329 844444

To be completed by the Enumerator or Customs Officer

Name of Establishment/Vessel/HM Ship

For communal establishments: address of establishment

Postcode ☐☐☐☐☐■☐☐

For vessels other than HM Ships: port of registry

Place at which the form is delivered, that is: name of town or port and of harbour, dock, wharf, mooring etc.

Name of master or person in charge of vessel

Communal establishments : type of establishment

Please give a **full description of the type of establishment** and if the establishment caters for a specific group or groups, please describe; *for example mentally ill or handicapped, physically disabled, elderly, children, students, nurses.*

Hospitals, homes and hostels only

- **Please specify type of management:** *private, voluntary (charitable), central government, local authority, housing association, health authority etc.*

- **Please indicate if the establishment is registered** with a local authority or health authority

Hotels or boarding houses only

Please enter the number of rooms in the establishment, including any annexes in which meals are not provided. Do not count kitchens, bathrooms, WCs, rooms used as offices or stores.

List the names of all people present, that is:

everyone who spends Census night **21-22 April 1991** in this establishment or on board this vessel; and everyone who arrives in this establishment or on board on **Monday 22 April** before the forms are collected by the Enumerator (or despatched in the case of HM Ships) and who was in Great Britain on Sunday but has not been included as present on another Census form.

In communal establishments do not list the names of any non-resident personnel who happen to be on duty on the premises on Census night.

Please put a tick in the appropriate column when you issue each form and when you collect it.

Name	Individual form		Name	Individual form	
	Issued	Collected		Issued	Collected
1			31		
2			32		
3			33		
4			34		
5			35		
6			36		
7			37		
8			38		
9			39		
10			40		
11			41		
12			42		
13			43		
14			44		
15			45		
16			46		
17			47		
18			48		
19			49		
20			50		
21			51		
22			52		
23			53		
24			54		
25			55		
26			56		
27			57		
28			58		
29			59		
30			60		

Enter the number of **Individual** forms collected on this L form. ☐

Declaration - If more than one 'L' form is used, only complete this panel on the first form

Enter the total number of 'L' forms completed for this establishment/vessel. ☐	Signature	
Enter the total number of **Individual** forms collected (sum of all L forms). ☐	Date	April 1991

Printed in the United Kingdom for HMSO
Dd.0297580, 12/93, C7, 3397/5, 5673, 268858